FRANK WOOD'S
Business Accounting 2

We work with leading authors to develop the
strongest educational materials in business and finance,
bringing cutting-edge thinking and best learning
practice to a global market.

Under a range of well-known imprints, including
Financial Times Prentice Hall, we craft high quality print
and electronic publications which help readers to
understand and apply their content, whether studying
or at work.

To find out more about the complete range of our
publishing, please visit us on the World Wide Web at:
www.pearsoneduc.com

FRANK WOOD'S

Business Accounting 2
NINTH EDITION

Frank Wood BSc (Econ), FCA

and

Alan Sangster BA, MSc, Cert TESOL, CA

FINANCIAL TIMES
Prentice Hall

An imprint of Pearson Education

Harlow, England · London · New York · Reading, Massachusetts · San Francisco · Toronto · Don Mills, Ontario · Sydney
Tokyo · Singapore · Hong Kong · Seoul · Taipei · Cape Town · Madrid · Mexico City · Amsterdam · Munich · Paris · Milan

Pearson Education Limited

Edinburgh Gate
Harlow
Essex CM20 2JE

and Associated Companies throughout the world.

Visit us on the World Wide Web at:
www.pearsoneduc.com

First edition published in 1967
Second edition published under the
Longman imprint in 1972
Third edition published in 1979
Fourth edition published in 1984
Fifth edition published under the
Pitman Publishing imprint in 1989
Sixth edition published in 1993
Seventh edition published in 1996
Eighth edition published under the Financial Times
Pitman Publishing imprint in 1999
Ninth edition published in 2002

© Frank Wood 1967
© Longman Group UK Limited 1972, 1979, 1984, 1989, 1993
© Pearson Professional Limited 1996
© Financial Times Professional Limited 1999
© Pearson Education Limited 2002

ISBN 0 273 65557 4

British Library Cataloguing-in-Publication Data
A catalogue record for this book is available from the British Library

Library of Congress Cataloging-in-Publication Data
A catalog record for this book is available from the Library of Congress

10 9 8 7 6 5 4 3 2 1
06   05   04   03

Typeset in 10/11.5 pt Sabon by 35.
Printed and bound in China.
EPC/01

Contents

Notes for teachers and lecturers

This textbook has been written so that a very thorough introduction to accounting is covered in two volumes. The split into two volumes is a recognition of the fact that many students new to accounting will find all that they require in Volume 1. This second volume takes students who have completed their first accounting course to a more advanced stage.

It completes the coverage of the financial accounting part of quite a few examinations in accounting. As examination syllabuses are constantly being revised, it would not make sense to be too specific as to which chapters would be needed by students taking each of the various examinations. In particular, it can be said to be very suitable for students who are studying the subject for A-level, Scottish Higher Grade, or General Certificate of Secondary Education examinations, the Open University Certificate in Accounting, and for those studying with the Association of Accounting Technicians, the Institute of Secretaries and Administrators, or any of the six UK and Irish Chartered Accountancy bodies.

This volume examines all the current accounting standards (both *Statements of Standard Accounting Practice* – SSAPs – and *Financial Reporting Standards* – FRSs) in as much detail as is needed by most students at this level. However, where an entire examination paper is devoted to this topic, students may need a much more detailed knowledge of accounting standards than a textbook of this kind can provide. In this case, students would be well advised to refer to a specialist textbook on the topic, or to the standards themselves.

Some improvements have been made to the pedagogical devices used in this book:

1 Each chapter:
   (a) starts with Learning Objectives (these have been completely revised for this edition);
   (b) contains Activities designed to broaden and reinforce students' understanding of the concepts being covered and, in some cases, to introduce new concepts in such a way that they do not come as a surprise when introduced formally later in the book;
   (c) ends with Learning Outcomes that can be mapped back to the Learning Objectives, so reinforcing the major topics and concepts covered in the chapter;
   (d) contains answers to all the Activities immediately after the Learning Outcomes.
2 The book now has an alphabetical Glossary (in Appendix 3) of all the significant terms introduced. Each entry is referenced back to the chapter in which it appeared.
3 A set of Notes for Students has been added at the front of the book. This covers how to use this book, how to tackle the end-of-chapter Review Questions, and how to study for and sit examinations. It should be read by students before they start working through the main text.
4 Use of a second colour has been introduced to enhance readability and bring out key points in the text.

The 43 chapters that remain from the eighth edition cover the same topics as before. Some changes have been made to the content of the book in order to make it more relevant in today's accounting environment:

● Three new chapters have been added: Chapter 45, *The Balanced Scorecard*, Chapter 46, *The Supply Chain and Enterprise Resource Planning Systems*, and Chapter 47, *E-commerce and Accounting*.
● Three chapters from the eighth edition (3, *Container Accounts*, 17, *Value Added Statements*, and 18, *Investment Accounts*) have been removed from the book and will be available on the *Frank Wood website*.

- Chapter 46 of the eighth edition, *Discounting Techniques*, has been split into two chapters in order that the techniques of capital investment appraisal can be taught without needing to cover the material on annuities and interest rates that occupied the first part of that chapter. The new chapter titles are, Chapter 43, *Interest, Annuities and Leasing*, and Chapter 44, *Capital Expenditure Appraisal*.
- Throughout the book, the term 'financial statements' has replaced 'final accounts', as many reviewers felt it was more appropriate.
- All chapters have been updated. Where a specific update has been done, this is mentioned below.
- The material on deferred tax in Chapter 7, *Taxation in Company Financial Statements*, includes reference to FRS 19.
- Chapter 10, *Accounting Standards and Related Documents* has been updated to incorporate all standards in issue in December 2001, including the replacement of SSAP 2 by FRS 18.
- Chapter 14, *FRS 1: Cash Flow Statements*, has been updated for the changes in FRS 1.
- Chapter 15, *Contract Accounts*, has been revised to bring in material relating to the treatment of long-term contracts under SSAP 9.
- Chapters 17 and 18, *Consolidation of Balance Sheets*, I and II, have been amended to replace capital reserves with negative goodwill in accordance with the rules of FRS 10.
- Chapters 25 and 26 – the final question in Chapter 25 has been moved to Chapter 26 as the question deals with associated undertakings and investments which are not covered until Chapter 26.
- Chapter 27, *Accounting Ratios*, has been revised and the sequence altered to be more in line with how the reviewers felt the material should be covered.
- Chapter 29, *Accounting Theory*, has been slightly rewritten so as to improve the readability and enhance the understanding of students reading it unguided.
- Chapter 30, *Current Cost Accounting*, now has a title that better reflects its content. (It was previously entitled, *Alternatives to Historic Cost Accounting*.)
- Chapter 32, *Accounting for Management Control*, now has a title that better reflects its content. (It was previously entitled, *Accounting as an Information System*.)
- Chapter 34, *Absorption and Marginal Costing*, has had material added concerning Pricing Policy and Activity Based Costing. Also, the term, 'indirect manufacturing costs' has replaced 'factory indirect expenses' and 'fixed manufacturing costs' has replaced 'fixed factory overheads'. Plus, one question added on full cost versus marginal cost.
- Chapter 41, *Overhead and Sales Variances*, has been extensively revised. Plus, the final question in the eighth edition chapter has been moved to Chapter 40.

We hope that you find these changes helpful and appropriate and would welcome comments on these and any other changes you feel ought to be made in future editions. You can contact Alan Sangster by email at **alan@sangster.co.uk** or by letter via the publishers.

We would like to thank all those teachers and lecturers who gave us their advice as to the changes they would like to see incorporated in this edition. We are especially grateful to Mary Bishop, Mike Brookes, John Dunn, Chris McMahon, Mak Yeun Teen, Stuart Mansen, John Morely, Roger Newman, Gideon Nyatuame, Steve Selijko, Rob Triggs, Wan Fadzilah Wan Yusoff and, of course, Michael Siaw Jun Choi and Muhammad Hanif Ghanghi for their insightful suggestions. There are many others too numerous to mention to whom we are indebted, and we trust that they will not be offended by our inability to list them all here.

We wish to acknowledge the permission to use past examination papers granted by the Institute of Chartered Accountants in England and Wales; the Association of Chartered Certified Accountants; the Chartered Institute of Management Accountants; the Association of Accounting Technicians; the Institute of Chartered Secretaries and Administrators; Oxford, Cambridge and RSA Examinations (OCR); the Assessment and Qualifications

Alliance (AQA) (Northern Examinations and Assessment Board and Associated Examining Board questions); Edexcel; and the Welsh Joint Education Committee.

As in previous editions, all answers to questions are the product of our own work and have not been supplied by any of the examining bodies. The examining bodies bear no responsibility for the example answers to questions taken from their past examination papers which are contained in this publication.

A *Solutions Manual* giving suggested solutions to those questions with the suffix A in the book (e.g. 5.8A) is available from the publishers free of charge to teachers and lecturers adopting this book on their course, or can be downloaded from the lecturers' section of the website for *Business Accounting 1* and *Business Accounting 2* at **www.booksites.net/wood**

Frank Wood and Alan Sangster

Notes for students

This textbook is organised so as to provide you with what has been found to be the most appropriate sequencing of topics as you build upon the foundations of your accounting knowledge that you developed when you studied *Business Accounting 1*. You will find that a number of features of the book, properly used, will enhance your understanding and extend your ability to cope with what will possibly appear, at first, to be a mystifying array of rules and procedures.

While a lot, but by no means all, of what follows was written in *Business Accounting 1*, all of the advice given to you in that book will apply to you throughout your studies of accounting, whatever the level. We therefore offer no apologies for repeating some of it here along with new advice appropriate to the level of *Business Accounting 2*.

In order to make best use of this resource, you should consider the following as being a proven path to success:

- At the start of each chapter, **read the Learning Objectives**. Then, while you work through the material, try to detect when you have achieved each of these objectives.
- At the end of each chapter **check what you have learnt against the Learning Outcomes** that follow the main text.
- If you find that you cannot say 'yes, I have achieved this' to any of the Learning Outcomes, look back through the chapter and reread the topic you have not yet learnt.
- **Learn the meaning of each new term as it appears.** Do not leave learning what terms mean until you are revising for an exam. Accounting is best learnt as a series of building blocks. If you don't remember what terms mean, your knowledge and ability to 'do' accounting will be very seriously undermined, in much the same way as a wall built without mortar is likely to collapse the first time someone leans against it.
- **Attempt each of the Activities in the book at the point** *at which they appear.* This is *very* important. The Activities will reinforce your learning and help set in context some of the material that may otherwise appear very artificial and distant from the world you live in. The answers are at the end of each chapter. **Do not look at the answers before you attempt the questions; you'll just be cheating yourself.** Once you have answered one, check your answer against the one in the book and be sure you understand it before moving on.
- Above all, remember that accounting is a vehicle for providing financial information in a form that assists decision-making. Work hard at presenting your work as neatly as possible and remember that pictures (in this case, financial figures) only carry half the message. When you are asked for them, words of explanation and insight are essential in order to make an examiner appreciate what you know and that you actually understand what the figures mean.

There are two subjects we would like you to consider very carefully: making best use of the end-of-chapter Review Questions and your examination technique.

Review Questions: the best approach

As we did in *Business Accounting 1*, we have set Review Questions at the end of most chapters for you to gauge how well you understand and can apply what you have learnt. **If you simply read the text without attempting the questions, then we can tell you now that you**

will not pass your examinations. You should first of all attempt the question, and then check it fully against the answers at the back of the book.

What you should not do is perform a 'ticking' exercise. By this we mean that you should not simply compare the question with the answer and tick off the bits of the answer which relate to each part of the question. No one ever learnt to do accounting properly that way. It is tempting to save time in so doing but, believe us, you will regret it eventually. We have deliberately had the answers printed using a different page layout to try to stop you indulging in a 'ticking' exercise.

Need for practice

You should also try to find the time to answer as many Review Questions as possible. Our reasons for saying this are as follows:

1 Even though you may think you understand the text, when you come to answer the questions you may often find your understanding incomplete. The true test of understanding is whether or not you can tackle the questions competently.

2 It is often said that practice makes perfect, a sentiment we don't fully agree with. There is enough sense in it, however, in that if you don't do quite a lot of accounting questions you will almost certainly not become good at accounting.

3 You simply have got to get up to a good speed in answering questions: you will always fail accounting examinations if you are a very slow worker. The history of accountancy examinations so far has always been that a ridiculously large amount of work has been expected from a student during a short time. However, examining boards maintain that the examination could be completed in the time by an adequately prepared student. You can take it for granted that *adequately prepared students* are those who not only have the knowledge, but have also been trained to work quickly and at the same time maintain accuracy and neatness.

4 Speed itself is not enough; **you also have to be neat and tidy,** and follow all the proper practices and procedures while working at speed. Fast but really scruffy work can also mean failing the exam. Why is this so? At this level the examiner is very much concerned with your practical ability in the subject. Accounting is a practical subject, and your practical competence is about to be tested. The examiner will therefore expect the answers to be neat and well set out. Untidy work with figures spread over the page in a haphazard way, badly written figures, and columns of figures in which the vertical columns are not set down in straight lines, will incur the examiner's displeasure.

5 Appropriate presentation of information is important. Learn how to present the various financial statements you may need to produce in an examination. Examiners expect to see the items in trading and profit and loss accounts, balance sheets and cash flow statements in the correct order and will probably deduct marks if you don't do so. Practise by writing down examples of these statements without any numbers until you always get the layout correct. One exam trick most students overlook is that the layout of a financial statement is often included in an examination paper as part of one question while another question asks you to produce the same financial statement. The one you need to produce will contain different numbers but the general layout should be very similar.

Need for headings

The next thing is that work should not only be neat and well laid out. **Headings should always be given, and any dates needed should be inserted.** The test you should apply is to imagine that you are a partner in a firm of professional accountants and you are away on

holiday for a few weeks. During that time your assistants have completed all sorts of work including reports, drafting final accounts, various forms of other computations and so on. All of this work is deposited on your desk while you are away. When you return you look at each item in the pile awaiting your attention.

Suppose the first item looks like a balance sheet as at 31 December in respect of one of your clients. When you looked at it you could see that it was a balance sheet, but you didn't know for which client, neither did you know which year it was for. Would you be annoyed with your staff? Of course you would. So therefore in an examination why should the examiner accept as a piece of your work a balance sheet answer without either the date or the name of the business or the fact that it is a balance sheet written clearly across the top? If proper headings are not given you may lose a lot of marks. **Don't wait until your examination to start this correct practice.** Always put in the headings properly. Similar attention should be paid to sub-totals which need showing, e.g. for Fixed assets, Current assets.

We will be looking at examination technique in the next section.

The examiner

Really, what you should say to yourself is: 'Suppose I were in charge of an office, doing this type of accounting work, what would I say if one of my assistants put on my desk a sheet of paper with accounting entries on it written in the same manner as my own efforts in attempting this question?' Just look at some of the work you have done in the past. Would you have told your assistant to go back and do the work again because it is untidy? If you say that about your own work, why should the examiner think any differently?

Anyone who works in accounting knows well that untidy work leads to completely unnecessary errors. Therefore the examiner's insistence on clear, tidy, well laid out work is not an outdated approach; they want to ensure that you are not going to mess up the work of an accounting department. Imagine going to the savings bank and the manager says to you: 'We don't know whether you've got £5 in the account or £5,000. You see, the work of our clerks is so untidy that we can never sort out exactly how much is in anybody's account.' We would guess that you would not want to put a lot of money into an account at that bank. How would you feel if someone took you to court for not paying a debt of £100 when in fact you owed them nothing? This sort of thing would happen all the time if we simply allowed people to keep untidy accounts. The examiner is there to ensure that the person to whom they give a certificate will be worthy of it, and will not continually mess up the work of any firm at which they may work in the future.

We can imagine quite a few of you groaning at all this, and if you do not want to pass the examination please give up reading here. If you do want to pass, and your work is untidy, what can you do about it? The answer is simple enough: **start right now to be neat and orderly in your work.**

Quite a lot of students have said to us over the years: 'I may be giving you untidy work now, but when I actually get in the exam room I will then do my work neatly enough.' This is as near impossible as anything can be. You cannot suddenly become able to do accounting work neatly, and certainly not when you are under the stress and strain of an examination. Even the neatest worker may well find in an examination that their work may not be of its usual standard as nervousness will cause them to make mistakes. If this is true, then if you are an untidy worker now, your work in an examination is likely to be even more untidy. Have we convinced you yet? Present your work neatly.

The structure of the questions

We have tried to build up the Review Questions in a structured way, starting with the easiest and then going on to more difficult ones. We would have liked to omit all the

difficult questions, on the basis that you may well spend a lot of time doing them without adding very much to your knowledge about accounting. However, if all the questions were straightforward, the shock of meeting more complicated questions for the first time in an examination could lead you to fail it. We have therefore tried to include a mixture of straightforward and complicated questions to give you the maximum benefit.

The answers

At the back of the book, you will find answers to approximately half of the Review Questions. The answers to the other Review Questions (indicated by the letter 'A' after the question number) are only available to you from your teacher or lecture. Don't worry if you are studying this subject on your own. There are still more than sufficient Review Questions with answers in this book to ensure you know and can confirm that you understand the material.

Examination technique

If you were completely devoid of examination technique you would probably not have advanced to this stage of your accounting studies. A lot of what follows was written in *Business Accounting 1*. Don't avoid reading it just because you read it when you were studying the material in that book.

In your first accounting examination you were competing with people who had probably never sat an accounting examination before. A lot of them will not get past Stage 1. In Stage 2 you are competing against people who have already proved they have a certain degree of competence in the subject. You might have got away with a certain amount of poor examination technique at Stage 1, but that will not be as easy at Stage 2.

Here we want to concentrate on the main deficiencies noted by examiners. These have never changed during the past 50 years. Students really should read examiners' reports – they will learn a lot from them.

Students do not read the questions properly

A large number of students do not answer the questions as set by the examiner, because they have not read the question properly. They answer what they think the examiner wants, not what the examiner is asking for.

Let us take a simple example. Suppose the examiner sets the following question: 'Describe the use of accounting ratios in assessing the performance of businesses.'

A lot of students will immediately start to describe how to calculate various accounting ratios. Marks which will be obtained – nil. The question asked for the *use* of accounting ratios, not *how to calculate* them.

Many other students will have concentrated on the word *use*. They will then write their answer based on comparing this year's accounting ratios in a business with those of last year. They may well even mention trend ratios which will earn them some extra marks. If they keep their discussion to comparing ratios in a business in the year with other years, however, they cannot get top marks, no matter how well they have written their answers.

Why not? Well, they picked up the word *use*, but from then on they stopped reading properly. The question does not in any way limit itself to the ratios of one business only. First of all you can compare the performance of a business with its own performance in the past. Secondly, you may be able to compare one business with another business of a similar kind. In addition, if you miss out mentioning interfirm comparisons you will lose marks.

Therefore, (a) *read* the question carefully, (b) *underline* the *key* words to get to the meaning of the question, (c) *think carefully* about how widespread your answer should be.

On the other hand, there is no point in widening the question more than is needed. It is for the *use* of *accounting* ratios, *not* the use of *all types* of ratios. Besides accounting ratios there are marketing ratios – e.g. size of share of market, how long it takes to supply orders, ratios of defective goods etc. The question does not ask for all of these. If you give them, you will not get any extra marks.

Poor time management

Using time well to gain the highest possible marks is essential. Examiners constantly report that examinees are very poor in this aspect of tackling an examination. How, then, can you avoid the usual pitfalls?

First of all, **read the *rubric* carefully**. These are the instructions at the top of the paper, e.g. 'Attempt four questions only: the three questions in Section A and one from Section B. Begin each answer on a separate page.'

You would be surprised to know that a lot of students would try to answer more than one question from Section B. If you tackle two questions from Section B, you will get marks for only one of your answers. Few examiners will mark both and then give you the marks for your highest marked answer. Many will simply mark the first of the optional questions answered and ignore the next, unnecessary answer.

Secondly, **start each answer on a new page**. You'll only annoy the examiner if you don't. It is your job to make the examiner's work as easy as possible. Examiners are only human, and it would not be surprising if their annoyance did not result in its influencing the marking of your paper.

You really must attempt each and every question you are required to answer according to the rubric of the examination. If you have to answer five questions then you must avoid attempting only four questions.

Students often feel that they would be better off by handing in the complete answers to only four questions, instead of five incomplete answers. In accounting examinations this is not true. Why is this so?

1 Examiners use positive marking in accounting examinations. If you have done 80 per cent of an answer worth 20 marks in total, and you have got it absolutely correct, then you get 80% of 20 = 16 marks.
2 The first marks in a question are the easiest to obtain. Thus it is easier to get the first 10 marks out of 20 than it is to get the second lot of marks to get full marks. By ensuring that you get the easiest marks on every question it therefore makes your task easier.

To ensure that you tackle (not necessarily finish) each question you should **mark the number of minutes to be allowed by *yourself* for each question**. Thus a 20-mark question, in a 100-mark examination, should be given 20 per cent of the time, i.e. 20% of 3 hours = 36 minutes. When 36 minutes have passed, *stop answering the question* unless it is the last question to be attempted, and go on to the next question.

If you don't know the answer, or part of an answer, you should guess. You don't lose marks for guessing, and if you guess correctly you get the marks. Intuition will often give the correct answer. Very often if you don't guess on part of a computational question you will be unable to go on to the remainder of the question which you can answer.

Workings

You may wonder why we have put this under a separate heading. We cannot emphasise enough how important it is that you should:

(*a*) submit all your workings, and
(*b*) ensure that the workings are set out so that the examiner can follow them.

A very high percentage of candidates in an examination are near the pass mark, within either a few percentage points above it or below it. If you are one of these candidates, and, as we have said, there are a lot of them, handing in workings which can be understood by the examiner will often ensure you a pass mark. Conversely, no workings, or completely unintelligible workings may well ensure your failing the examination.

This last point is important. Some students think that putting down a set of random jottings and calling them 'workings' will gain marks. It won't. **Examiners won't waste time searching through random jottings for something relevant.** Treat your workings as if they, themselves, are part of your answer. **Insert titles and headings to indicate what a particular working is about.**

Tackle the easiest questions first

Never start off your examination by tackling a difficult question. You must be able to settle down properly and not let your nerves get out of control. Starting off on the easiest question is the best way to enable you to get off to a good start. Much more about this was written in *Business Accounting 1*.

State your assumptions

It does happen that sometimes a question can contain ambiguities. Examination bodies try to prevent it happening, but it does occur occasionally. Unfortunately, questions do sometimes contain errors.

In both of these cases you must point out the ambiguity/error. You should then make an assumption, based on what you thought the examiner meant, and carry on with your answer. **You must, however, state what your assumption is.** Try to make your assumption as sensible as possible. The examiner will then mark your answer accordingly. If you make a ridiculous assumption, it is unlikely that you will be given any marks for that part of your answer. Don't be sarcastic in your comments or complain about inefficiency – there are other times and places for that.

Answering essay questions

The problem

Unlike computational-type answers, you will not know whether your written answers are up to the mark until you receive your examination result. Likewise, written questions lack the certainty and precision of accounting problems and it is often difficult to fathom out exactly what the examiners require of you. For this reason, sound examination technique is absolutely essential together with precise knowledge of relevant law and regulations.

There are several major aspects to success in written papers. *Plan* your answer, answer the question *as set*, pay attention to good *layout*, and explain in clear and simple terms what you are doing. Remember you can only be marked on what you write down. You have no opportunity to explain some ambiguity or other and if what you write is unclear you will *not* get the benefit of the doubt.

Plan

First read the question and jot down the key *verb*, i.e. your instructions; this may be to discuss, explain, advise, set out, list, draft an audit programme, write a letter, etc.

If the question requires a discussion or an explanation it should be written in proper paragraph form. Each paragraph should be self-contained and explain the point it makes. Sentences should be short and to the point. The ideal length for a paragraph is three sentences

with four as a maximum. Over four and you are probably making more than one point and should have gone into two paragraphs.

Plan how many points you are going to make and what the answer is. This is essential as otherwise your answer will 'drift' as you struggle to come to some conclusion. The plan should consist of arrows connecting points to each other so that the answer will flow and be logical. The plan need not be too extensive; it is silly to waste time on a 'mini-answer'. It should consist of the *headings* you are going to use.

Layout

Whenever examiners meet to discuss results, or write down their commentary on students' performance, they all agree on the importance of good layout; yet students generally tend to take no notice. The range of marks between good papers and poor papers tends to be quite small. Anything you can do to put the examiner on your side will pay off in those few extra marks.

The main areas for good layout are:

1 *Tabulate* in numbered points, unless you are writing an essay-type question (as explained above).
2 Leave at least a clear line between each point or paragraph.
3 Use headings whenever possible to indicate what major point or series of points you are about to make. Make it easy for the examiner to read your work and follow what you are doing. A solid mass of material is difficult to read, provides no respite for the eye and shows a lack of discipline. Remember that you are taking a *professional* examination and there is no room for academic licence.
4 Take care with your *language*. Be objective and avoid the use of the words 'I' or 'we' at too frequent intervals. Be direct and concise, say what you mean, do not use pompous terminology, and use technical words with their correct meaning.

   Short sentences are far more effective and punchy than long ones. An accounting programme or evaluation of an internal control system could well start with a series of *verbs*. Good ones are: test, examine, inspect, calculate, reconcile, compare, summarise, inquire, investigate. These key words will help you to construct answers to these types of questions much more direct and to the point. If you start with them you are bound to avoid falling into the trap of being long-winded, or of padding out your answer. You only have a limited time and everything you write down must earn you marks.
5 *Think* while you are writing out your answer to make sure you are answering the question *as set*. Keep on reading the instructions and make sure you are following them. Use the question to help you to get the answer and, while this should be tackled at the planning stage, it is always possible that inspiration will strike while you are writing out your answer. In which case jot the point down on your plan, otherwise you might forget it and that can cause frustration. What you say should be relevant, but if you are in doubt about the relevance but sure about the accuracy – include it in your answer. You cannot lose and it may be one of the key points the examiner was looking for.

Key points

Do try to find a couple of key points to each question. These are points which you feel are vital to answer the question. You may well be right, and anyway, jotting them down after you have read the question carefully can help to give your answer much needed direction.

Practice

You will need to practise the above routine. Written answers in fact need more practice than computational ones. Have a go at the question. Write out the answer as you would in the examination. Compare with the suggested answers.

Write out at the foot of your answer what you left out and what you got wrong. Learn from the answers and from the work you do, so that when you see a similar question you will produce a better answer.

Time pressure

You will experience a lot of pressure of time as you progress with written questions. Do not worry; this is a good sign.

In the examination, spread your time sensibly. Start with the questions you like the look of most and, if you have to go slightly over the time you allotted for those, do so. End with the question you think you cannot answer or will be hardest to answer, but do give yourself time to have a reasonable go at it.

If a written question is included in a computational paper do not go over the time on it but *do spend the allocated time*. Examiners pay great attention to the written parts of computational papers, so do not skimp this part.

All this sounds formidable and, of course, it is. It requires skill, application and, above all, confidence. Practice makes perfect and once the skill is acquired then, like riding a bicycle, it will not be forgotten. Take pride in your work and be critical of your own efforts, but do not imagine your answers will have to be perfect to pass the examination. Suggested answers tend to be too long because tutors are afraid to reveal any signs of weakness or ignorance.

Go for the main points and make them well. That is the secret of success.

Summary

Remember:

1 Read the rubric, i.e. the instructions.
2 Plan your time before you start.
3 Tackle the easiest questions first.
4 Finish off answering each question when your time allocation for the question is up.
5 Hand in all your workings.
6 Do remember to be neat, also include all proper headings, dates, sub-totals, etc. A lot of marks can be lost here.
7 Only answer as many questions as you are asked to tackle by the examiner. Extra answers will not normally be marked.
8 Underline the *key* words in each question to ensure that you answer the question set, and not the question you wrongly take it to be.
9 Never write out the text of essay questions.

Best of luck with your examination. We hope you get the rewards you deserve!

Frank Wood and Alan Sangster

A Companion Website accompanies
BUSINESS ACCOUNTING VOLUME 2, 9th edition
by Frank Wood and Alan Sangster

Visit the *Business Accounting* Companion Website at
www.booksites.net/wood to find valuable teaching and
learning material including:

For Students:
- Study material designed to help you improve your results
- Multiple-choice questions to test your knowledge
- Weblinks to sites of interest
- Accounting standards updates
- Extra material from the eighth edition of the textbook
- A fully searchable glossary

For Lecturers:
- A secure, password-protected site with material designed to help you teach
- *Solutions Manual*
- Downloadable OHP PowerPoints of learning objectives and selected diagrams from the book
- Direct email feedback to the author

PART 1

Special accounts

1 Branch accounts

2 Hire purchase accounts

Introduction

This part is concerned with two items that are treated in a similar way, irrespective of the form of business involved.

CHAPTER 1

Branch accounts

Learning objectives

After you have studied this chapter, you should be able to:
- explain two methods of recording the entries relating to branch accounts
- describe how double column trading and profit and loss accounts can be used in order to monitor any unexpected losses
- explain the difference between using a memoranda columns approach and an integrated stock monitoring system for stock control
- explain the issues relating to foreign branch accounts

Introduction

In this chapter you'll learn about two methods of recording branch transactions and of the issues that arise when items are in transit between branches. You'll also learn about how to record the entries in the books when branches are located in different countries.

1.1 Accounting records and branches

When we look at accounting records to show transactions at the branches of an organisation, we have a choice of two main methods. These are:

(a) the head office keeps all the accounting records, or
(b) each branch has its own full accounting system.

It is easier to understand branch accounts if these two main methods are dealt with separately.

1.2 If the head office maintains all the accounts

The accounts are used for three main purposes:

(a) to record transactions showing changes in assets, liabilities and capital;
(b) to ascertain the profitability of each branch; and, if possible,
(c) to check whether anyone at the branches is stealing goods or cash.

This third purpose is very important for firms that have many branches. The people who manage or work in these branches are receiving and paying out large sums of money. In addition they may be handling large amounts of stocks of goods. The branch or branches may be a considerable distance away from the head office. This may mean that the manager, or any of the staff, may think that they can steal things without being caught.

1.3 Methods for checking stock and cash

If a firm with only a few branches sells only very expensive cars, it would be easy to check on purchases and sales of the cars. The number of cars sold would not be very great. Checking that cars or money have not been stolen would be easy. However, a firm such as a store with branches selling many thousands of cheap items could not be checked so easily. To keep a check on each carton of salt or bag of flour sold would be almost impossible. Even if it could be done, such checking would cost too much.

The accounting answer to this problem is to record all transactions at the branch in terms of selling prices. Then for each accounting period, it should be possible to check whether the closing stock is as it should be. For a small branch, for example, you may be given the following figures:

	£
Stock on hand at 1 January – at selling price	500
January – Goods sent to the branch by the head office – at selling price	4,000
January – Sales by the branch – obviously at selling price	3,800

The calculation of the closing stock becomes:

	£
Opening Stock 1 January (selling price)	500
Add Goods sent to the branch (selling price)	4,000
Goods which the branch had available for sale (selling price)	4,500
Less Goods sold (selling price)	3,800
Closing stock at 31 January should therefore be (selling price)	700

1.4 Allowances for deficiencies

In every business there will be:

(a) wastage of goods for some reason – goods may be damaged or broken, or they may be kept too long or somehow waste away;
(b) stealing by customers, especially in the retail business;
(c) thefts by employees.

No one can be certain how much stock is wasted or stolen during a period. Only experience will enable a firm to make a good estimate of these losses.

1.5 The double column system

At regular intervals, obviously at least once a year but usually more frequently, the head office may draft a trading and profit and loss account for each branch. The trading account can be shown with two columns, one in which goods sent to the branch or in stock are shown at cost price, i.e. the normal basis for any business. This column is therefore part of a normal trading account for the branch.

The other column will show all trading account items at selling price. This column allows deficiencies in trading to be compared with the normal deficiency allowed for wastages, etc. It is not a part of the double entry recording; it is a memorandum column for control purposes only.

Exhibit 1.1

Branch Trading and Profit and Loss Account for the year ended 31.12.20X8						
		At selling price			*At selling price*	
	£	£		£	£	
Stock 1 Jan 20X8	1,600	1,200	Sales	7,428	7,428	
Goods from head office	8,000	6,000	Deficiency (difference)	172		
	9,600	7,200				
Less Stock 31 Dec 20X8	2,000	1,500				
	7,600	5,700				
Gross profit c/d		1,728				
	7,600	7,428		7,600	7,428	
Expenses		1,000	Gross profit b/d		1,728	
Net profit		728				
		1,728			1,728	

Exhibit 1.1 is drafted from the following details for a firm which sells goods at a uniform mark-up of $33^{1}/_{3}$ per cent on cost price:

	£
Stock 1 Jan 20X8 (at cost)	1,200
Goods sent to the branch during the year (at cost)	6,000
Sales (selling price)	7,428
Stock 31 Dec 20X8 (at cost)	1,500
Expenses	1,000

Allowances for wastage, etc., 1 per cent of sales.

As the actual deficiency of £172 exceeds the amount expected, i.e. 1 per cent of £7,428 = £74, an investigation will be made.

This method is suitable where all the sales are for cash, there being no sales on credit, or when debtors make their payments to the branch where the sale took place.

Activity 1.1

Why should it make any difference if debtors make payment to a branch other than the one where the sale took place?

1.6 The stock and debtors system

Further adjustments are needed when there are credit sales as well as cash sales. There are two ways of making the entries. These are:

(a) using memoranda columns only to keep a check on stock, in a similar way to that shown in Section 1.5;
(b) building the control of stock fully into the double entry system. This is often called an integrated system.

We can now examine both of these methods.

Using the following basic data, Exhibit 1.2 shows the records when the memoranda method is used, while Exhibit 1.3 shows the records when the integrated method is in use.

Data: A branch sells all its goods at a uniform mark-up of 50 per cent on cost price. Credit customers are to pay their accounts directly to the head office.

		£
First day of the period:		
Stock (at cost)	(A)	2,000
Debtors	(B)	400
During the period:		
Goods sent to the branch (at cost)	(C)	7,000
Sales – cash	(D)	6,000
Sales – credit	(E)	4,800
Cash remitted by debtors to head office	(F)	4,500
At the close of the last day of the period:		
Stock (at cost)	(G)	1,800
Debtors	(H)	700

Note: The letters A to H beside the figures have been inserted to identify the entries in Exhibit 1.3. The entries for each of the above items will have the relevant letter shown beside them.

Memoranda columns method

Exhibit 1.2

Branch Stock

	Selling price memo. only			Selling price memo. only	
	£	£		£	£
Stock b/d	3,000	2,000	Sales: Cash	6,000	6,000
Goods sent	10,500	7,000	Credit	4,800	4,800
Gross profit to			Stock c/d	2,700	1,800
profit and loss		3,600			
	13,500	12,600		13,500	12,600
Stock b/d	2,700	1,800			

Branch Debtors

	£		£
Balances b/d	400	Cash	4,500
Branch stock	4,800	Balance c/d	700
	5,200		5,200
Balance b/d	700		

Goods Sent to Branches

	£		£
Transfer to head office			
trading account	7,000	Branch stock	7,000

Cash Book

	£		
Branch stock – cash sales	6,000		
Branch debtors	4,500		

The branch stock account is thus, in effect, a trading account, and is identical to the type used in the double column system. In addition, however, a branch debtors account is in use.

The balance of the goods sent to the branches account is shown as being transferred to the head office trading account. This figure is deducted from the purchases in the head office trading account, so that goods bought for the branch can be disregarded when the gross profit earned by the head office is calculated.

The integrated system

The integrated system introduces the idea that the gross profit earned by a firm can be calculated by reference to profit margins only. A simple example illustrates this point. Assume that a self-employed travelling salesman sells all his goods at cost price plus 25 per cent for profit. At the start of a week he has £4 stock at cost, he buys goods costing £40, he sells goods for £45 (selling price) and he has goods left in stock at the end of the week which have cost him £8. A normal trading account based on this data is shown below.

Trading Account for the week ended . . .

	£		£
Opening stock	4	Sales	45
Add Purchases	40		
	44		
Less Closing stock	(8)		
Cost of goods sold	36		
Gross profit	9		
	45		45

This could, however, also be shown as:

	£
Profit made when opening stock is sold	1
Profit made when purchases are sold	10
Profit made when all goods are sold	11
But he still has left unsold goods (cost £8) on which the profit still has to be realised	(2)
Therefore profit realised	9

This could be expressed in account form as:

Salesman's Adjustment Account

	£		£
Gross profit	9	Unrealised profit b/d	1
Unrealised profit c/d	2	Goods bought	10
	11		11

The integrated system uses an adjustment account which is needed because goods sent to the branch are shown at cost price in a 'goods sent to branches account'. In the branch stock account these goods are shown at selling price. Obviously if one entry is made at cost price and the other at selling price, the accounts would not balance. To correct this, an extra account called a branch adjustment account is opened. The entries in this account are in respect of the profit content only of goods.

The branch stock account acts as a check upon stock deficiencies. The branch adjustment account shows the amount of gross profit earned during the period.

Exhibit 1.3 shows the ledger accounts needed for the integrated system from the same information given at the beginning of Section 1.6 that was used to complete Exhibit 1.2. In this example a stock deficiency does not exist. The letters A to H in Exhibit 1.3 conform to the letters A to H shown against the information.

Exhibit 1.3

Branch Stock (Selling Price)

		£			£
Balance b/d	(A)	3,000	Sales: Cash	(D)	6,000
Goods sent to branch	(C)	10,500	Credit	(E)	4,800
			Balance c/d	(G)	2,700
		13,500			13,500
Balance b/d	(G)	2,700			

Branch Debtors (Selling Price)

		£			£
Balances b/d	(B)	400	Cash	(F)	4,500
Branch stock	(E)	4,800	Balances c/d	(H)	700
		5,200			5,200
Balances b/d	(H)	700			

Goods Sent to Branches (Cost Price)

		£			£
Transfer to head office trading account		7,000	Branch stock	(C)	7,000

Branch Adjustment (Profit Content)

		£			£
Gross profit to profit and loss		3,600	Unrealised profit b/d	(A)	1,000
Unrealised profit c/d	(G)	900	Branch stock – goods sent	(C)	3,500
		4,500			4,500
			Unrealised profit b/d	(G)	900

The opening and closing stocks are shown in the branch stock account at selling price. However, the balance sheet should show the stock at cost price. The previous balance sheet should therefore have shown stock at cost £2,000. This is achieved by having a compensating £1,000 credit balance brought forward in the branch adjustment account so that the debit balance of £3,000 in the branch stock account, when it comes to being shown in the balance sheet, has the £1,000 credit balance deducted to show a net figure of £2,000. Similarly, at the close of the period the balance sheet will show stock at £1,800 (branch stock debit balance £2,700 *less* branch adjustment credit balance £900).

1.7 The stock and debtors integrated system – further points

Returns

Goods may be returned:

(a) from the branch stock to the head office
(b) from the branch debtors to the branch stock
(c) from the branch debtors to the head office.

Exhibit 1.4

To examine the entries needed, suppose a firm sells goods at cost plus 25 per cent profit, and, according to the categories stated, the following goods were returned, all prices shown being selling prices: (a) £45, (b) £75, (c) £15. The entries needed are:

Branch Stock (Selling Price)

		£			£
Returns from debtors	(b)	75	Returns to head office	(a)	45

Branch Adjustment (Profit Loading)

		£	
Returns from branch	(a)	9	
Returns from debtors	(c)	3	

Goods Sent to Branches (Cost Price)

		£	
Returns from branch	(a)	36	
Returns from debtors	(c)	12	

Branch Debtors (Selling Price)

			£
	Returns to branch	(b)	75
	Returns to head office	(c)	15

Entries (b), both being in accounts shown at selling price, were two in number, i.e. £75 Dr and £75 Cr; entries (a) and (c) each needed entries in three accounts, (a) being £45 Cr and £9 Dr and £36 Dr, (c) being £15 Cr and £12 Dr and £3 Dr.

1.8 If each branch maintains full accounting records

This method is rarely used in firms with many branches. It is more common in a firm with just one or two or a few branches, and is particularly relevant if a branch is large enough to warrant employing a separate accounting staff.

A branch cannot operate on its own without resources, and it is the firm that provides these in the first instance. The firm will want to know how much money it has invested in each branch, and from this arises the concept of branch and head office current accounts. The relationship between the branch and the head office is seen as that of a debtor/creditor. The current account shows the branch as a debtor in the head office records, while the head office is shown as a creditor in the branch records.

The current accounts are used for transactions concerned with supplying resources to the branch or in taking back resources. For such transactions full double entry records are needed both in the branch records and in the head office records, i.e. each item will be recorded twice in each set of records. Some transactions will, however, concern the branch only, and these will merely need two entries in the branch records and none in the head office records. Exhibit 1.5 shows several transactions and the records needed.

Exhibit 1.5

A firm with its head office in London opened a branch in Manchester. The following transactions took place in the first month:

(A) Opened a bank account at Manchester by transferring £1,000 from the London bank account.
(B) Bought premises in Manchester, paying by cheque drawn on the London bank account, £5,000.
(C) Manchester bought a motor van, paying by cheque £600 from its own bank account.
(D) Manchester bought fixtures on credit from A B Equipment Ltd, £900.
(E) London supplied a machine valued at £250 from its own machinery.
(F) Manchester bought goods from suppliers, paying by cheque on its own account, £270.
(G) Manchester's cash sales banked immediately in its own bank account, £3,000.

(H) Goods invoiced at cost to Manchester during the month by London (no cash or cheques being paid specifically for these goods by Manchester), £2,800.

(I) A cheque is paid to London by Manchester as general return of funds, £1,800.

(J) Goods returned to London by Manchester – at cost price, £100.

The exact dates have been deliberately omitted. It will be seen later that complications arise because of differences in the timing of transactions. Each transaction has been identified by a capital letter. The relevant letter will be shown against each entry in the accounts.

Head Office Records (in London)
Manchester Branch Current Account

		£			£
Bank	(A)	1,000	Bank	(I)	1,800
Bank – premises	(B)	5,000	Returns from Branch	(J)	100
Machinery	(E)	250			
Goods sent to Branch	(H)	2,800			

Bank

		£			£
Manchester Branch	(I)	1,800	Manchester Branch	(A)	1,000
			Manchester premises	(B)	5,000

Machinery

					£
			Manchester Branch	(E)	250

Goods Sent to Branch

		£			£
Returns from Branch	(J)	100	Manchester Branch	(H)	2,800

Branch Records (in Manchester)
Head Office Current Account

		£			£
Bank	(I)	1,800	Bank	(A)	1,000
Returns	(J)	100	Premises	(B)	5,000
			Machinery	(E)	250
			Goods from Head Office	(H)	2,800

Bank

		£			£
Head Office	(A)	1,000	Motor van	(C)	600
Cash sales	(G)	3,000	Purchases	(F)	270
			Head Office	(I)	1,800

Premises

		£	
Head Office	(B)	5,000	

Motor Van

		£	
Bank	(C)	600	

Fixtures

		£	
A B Equipment Ltd	(D)	900	

A B Equipment Ltd

				£
	Fixtures	(D)		900

Machinery

		£		
Head Office	(E)	250		

Purchases

		£		
Bank	(F)	270		

Sales

				£
	Bank	(G)		3,000

Goods from Head Office

		£			£
Head Office	(H)	2,800	Head Office – returns	(J)	100

Note: It can be seen that items C, D, F and G are entered only in the Manchester records. This is because these items are purely internal transactions and are not concerned with resources flowing between London and Manchester.

1.9 Profit or loss and current accounts

The profit earned by the branch (or loss incurred by it) does not belong to the branch. It belongs to the firm and must therefore be shown as such. The head office represents the central authority of the firm and profit of the branch should be credited to the Head Office Current Account, any loss being debited.

The branch will therefore draw up its own trading and profit and loss account. After agreement with the head office the net profit will then be transferred to the credit of the Head Office Current Account. The head office will then debit the Branch Current Account in its own records and credit its own profit and loss account. Taking the net profit earned in Exhibit 1.5 as £700, the two sets of books would appear thus:

Head Office Records (in London)
London Profit and Loss Account

			£
	Net profit earned by the Manchester Branch		700

Manchester Branch Current Account

	£		£
Bank	1,000	Bank	1,800
Bank: premises	5,000	Returns from Branch	100
Machinery	250		
Goods sent to Branch	2,800		
Net profit to main profit			
and loss account	700	Balance c/d	7,850
	9,750		9,750
Balance b/d	7,850		

Branch Records (in Manchester)
Manchester Profit and Loss Account

	£	
Net profit carried to the Head Office Current Account	700	

Head Office Current Account

	£		£
Returns to Head Office	100	Bank	1,000
Bank	1,800	Premises	5,000
		Machinery	250
		Goods from Head Office	2,800
Balance c/d	7,850	Profit and loss account	700
	9,750		9,750
		Balance b/d	7,850

1.10 The combined balance sheet

After the trading and profit and loss accounts have been drawn up a balance sheet is required for the whole firm. The branch will send its trial balance to the head office which will add the assets in its own trial balance to those in the branch trial balance to give the total for each type of asset to be shown in the balance sheet, and a similar procedure will be carried out for the liabilities.

In the trial balances the Head Office Current Account will be a debit balance while the Branch Current Account will be a credit balance, e.g. the two figures of £7,850 in the London and Manchester books. These therefore cancel out and are not shown in the combined balance sheet. This is in order, as the two balances do not in fact represent assets or liabilities.

> ### Activity 1.2
> If they do not represent assets and liabilities, what do they represent?

1.11 Items in transit

It was stated earlier that the timing of transactions raised complications. Obviously a cheque sent by a Manchester branch one day would probably arrive in London the next day, while goods sent from London to Manchester, or returned from Manchester to London, could well take longer than that. Both the head office and the branch will have entered the transactions at the dates of remittance or receipt, and as the remittance from one place will occur on one day and the receipt occur at the other place on another day, then where items are in transit at the end of a financial period each set of records will not contain identical figures. This will mean that the balances on the current accounts will not be equal to one another.

It is, however, necessary to have identical amounts of balances on the current accounts so that they will cancel out when the combined balance sheet is prepared. As the two sets of records contain some figures which are different from each other they must somehow be reconciled so that the balances carried down are the same. Which set of figures are to be altered? The answer is one of expediency. It would be normal to find the most experienced

accountants at the head office, and therefore the amendments should all be made in the head office books instead of leaving it to junior accountants at the branches who would be more likely to make mistakes. Also if there are several branches the problems of communicating specific instructions to several accountants some distance away make it easier for all amendments to be made at the head office.

Exhibit 1.6 is for a second month of the business shown in Exhibit 1.5. However, whereas there were no items in transit at the end of the first month, this does not hold true at the conclusion of the second month.

Exhibit 1.6

Head Office records (showing current accounts only)	£
Goods sent to Branch	3,700
Cheques received from Branch	2,950
Returns received from Branch	440
Branch records	
Goods received from Head Office	3,500
Cheques sent to Head Office	3,030
Returns sent to Head Office	500

It may be assumed that the net profit as shown by the profit and loss account of the branch is £800.

Branch Records (in Manchester)
Head Office Current Account

	£		£
Bank	3,030	Balance b/d	7,850
Returns to Head Office	500	Goods from Head Office	3,500
Balance c/d	8,620	Net profit	800
	12,150		12,150
		Balance b/d	8,620

Head Office Records (in London)
Manchester Branch Current Account

		£			£
Balance b/d		7,850	Bank	(B)	2,950
Goods sent to Branch	(A)	3,700	Returns received	(C)	440
Net profit		800			

At this point, the following items are observed to be in transit at the end of the period (these should be confirmed to ensure that they are not merely errors in accounting records):

1 Goods sent to the branch amounting to £200 (£3,700 – £3,500).
2 Cheques sent by the branch amounting to £80 (£3,030 – £2,950).
3 Returns from the branch amounting to £60 (£500 – £440).

● (A) needs amending to £3,500. This is done by crediting the account with £200.
● (B) needs amending to £3,030. This is done by crediting the account with £80.
● (C) needs amending to £500. This is done by crediting the account with £60.

As these are items in transit, they need to be taken to the period in which they arrive, i.e. the next month. This is effected by carrying them down as balances into the next period. The branch current account will now be completed.

It may appear at first sight to be rather strange that all the items in transit are shown as debit balances. However, it must be appreciated that goods (including returns) and money in transit are assets of the firm at the end of a financial period. That they are in transit is merely stipulating that the assets are neither at the head office nor at the branch but are

somewhere else. Assets are always shown as debit balances and there is no reason why it should be different just because they have not reached their destination on a certain date.

Manchester Branch Current Account

	£		£
Balance b/d	7,850	Bank	2,950
Goods sent to branch	3,700	Returns received	440
Net profit	800	Goods in transit c/d	200
		Cheques in transit c/d	80
		Returns in transit c/d	60
		Balance c/d	8,620
	12,350		12,350
Balance b/d	8,620		
Goods in transit b/d	200		
Cheques in transit b/d	80		
Returns in transit b/d	60		

All of these four balances are shown in the trial balance. When the combined balance sheet is being prepared the balance of the two current accounts, in this case £8,620, will cancel out as it is a debit balance in one trial balance and a credit balance in the other. The goods in transit £200 and the returns in transit £60, both being goods, are added to the stock in the balance sheet. This is because at the end of the second month, stock is made up of the following items:

	£
Stock at London	
Add Stock at Manchester	
Add Stocks in transit (£200 + £60)	260
Total stock	

Similarly, the balance for cheques or remittances in transit is added to the bank balances at London and Manchester:

	£
Bank balance at London	
Add Bank balance in Manchester	
Add Remittances in transit	80

This is rather like a man who has £14 in one pocket and £3 in another. He takes a £5 note from the pocket containing the larger amount and is transferring it to his other pocket when someone asks him to stay perfectly still and calculate the total cash in his possession. He therefore has:

	£
Pocket 1	9
Pocket 2	3
Cash in transit	5
	17

1.12   Items in transit and the balance sheet

Using the figures already given in Exhibit 1.6 but adding some further information, trial balances for London head office and the Manchester branch are now shown in Exhibit 1.7 after the profit and loss accounts have been drawn up for the second month.

Exhibit 1.7

Trial Balances as at 29 February 20X8				
	London Head Office		Manchester Branch	
	Dr	Cr	Dr	Cr
	£	£	£	£
Premises	10,000		5,000	
Machinery	2,000		400	
Fixtures	3,100		1,400	
Motor vans	1,500		900	
Closing stock	3,800		700	
Debtors	1,100		800	
Bank	12,200		600	
Head Office Current Account				8,620
Branch Current Account	8,620			
Goods in transit	200			
Cheques in transit	80			
Returns in transit	60			
Creditors		1,300		1,180
Capital account as at 1 Jan 20X8		37,860		
Net profit for the two months (Branch £1,500 + Head Office £2,000)		3,500		
	42,660	42,660	9,800	9,800

The combined balance sheet can now be drawn up.

Balance Sheet as at 29 February 20X8

	£	£
Fixed assets		
Premises		15,000
Machinery		2,400
Fixtures		4,500
Motor vans		2,400
		24,300
Current assets		
Stocks	4,760	
Debtors	1,900	
Bank	12,880	
	19,540	
Less Current liabilities		
Creditors	(2,480)	
Working capital		17,060
		41,360
Capital		
Balance at 1 January 20X8		37,860
Add Net profit:		
London		2,000
Manchester		1,500
		41,360

Notes:

	£		£
Stocks: London	3,800	Bank: London	12,200
Manchester	700	Manchester	600
In transit (£200 + £60)	260	In transit	80
	4,760		12,880

1.13   Foreign branch accounts

The treatment of the accounts of foreign branches is subject to only one exception from that of branches in your own country. This is concerned with the fact that when the trial balance is drawn up by the branch then this will be stated in a foreign currency. To amalgamate these figures with your own country's figures will mean that the foreign branch figures will have to be translated into your currency.

There are rules for general guidance as to how this can be done. These are given in SSAP 20: *Foreign currency translation*. These are the ones which will be shown. (Before you read further you should check whether or not this topic is part of your examination requirements.)

The amount of a particular currency which one can obtain for another currency is known as the exchange rate. Taking an imaginary country with a currency called *chips*, there might be a general agreement that the exchange rate should stay about 5 chips to equal £1. At certain times the exchange rate will exactly equal that figure, but due to all sorts of economic reasons it may well be 5.02 chips to £1 on one day and 4.97 chips to £1 several days later. In addition, some years ago there may have been an act of devaluation by one of the countries involved; the exchange rate could then have been 3 chips to £1. To understand more about exchange rates and devaluation the reader is advised to consult a relevant economics textbook.

It is clear, however, that all items in the trial balance should not be converted to your currency on the basis of the exchange rate ruling at the date of the trial balance. The rules in SSAP 20 have been devised in an attempt to bring about conversion into your currency so as not to distort reported trading results.

1.14   Conversion rules per SSAP 20

1 (*a*) Fixed assets at the exchange rate ruling when the assets were bought – the **temporal method**. If fixed assets have been bought on different dates, then different rates will have to be used for each separate purchase.
   (*b*) Depreciation on the fixed assets at the same rate as the fixed assets concerned.
2 Current assets and current liabilities – at the rate ruling at the date of the trial balance. This is known as the **closing method**.
3 Opening stock in the trading account – at the rate ruling at the previous balance sheet date.
4 Goods sent by the head office to the branch, or returns from the branch – at the actual figures shown in the Goods Sent to Branches Account in the head office books.
5 Trading and profit and loss account items, other than depreciation, opening and closing stocks, or goods sent to or returned by the branch – at the average rate for the period covered by the accounts.
6 The Head Office Current Account – at the same figures as shown in the Branch Current Account in the head office books.

1.15   Conversion of trial balance figures

When the conversion of the figures into your currency is completed, the totals of the debit and credit sides of your currency trial balance will not normally be equal to one another. This is due to different exchange rates being taken for conversion purposes. A balancing figure will therefore be needed to bring about the equality of the totals. For this purpose a **difference on exchange account** will be opened and a debit entry made therein if the lesser total is on the debit side of the trial balance. When the head office redrafts the profit and loss account any debit balance on the difference on exchange account should be transferred

to it as an expense. A credit balance on the difference on exchange account should be transferred to the credit of the profit and loss account as a gain.

In consolidated accounts, special rules are applied for foreign exchange conversion.

Exhibit 1.8

An example of the conversion of a trial balance into UK currency is now shown. The branch is in Flavia, and the unit of currency is the Flavian dollar. The exchange rates needed are:

(a) On 1 January 20X3, 10 dollars = £1
(b) On 1 January 20X5, 11 dollars = £1
(c) On 1 January 20X8, 17 dollars = £1
(d) On 31 December 20X8, 15 dollars = £1
(e) If no further information were given the average rate for 20X8 would have to be taken as (c) + (d) ÷ 2, i.e. 16 dollars = £1. This is not an advisable procedure in practice; the fact that the average has been calculated from only two readings could mean that the average calculated might be far different from a more accurate one calculated from a larger number of readings.

Trial Balance as at 31 December 20X8

	Dr (F$)	Cr (F$)	Exchange rates	Dr (£)	Cr (£)
Fixed assets:					
Bought 1 Jan 20X3	10,000		10 = £1	1,000	
Bought 1 Jan 20X5	8,800		11 = £1	800	
Stock 1 Jan 20X8	6,800		17 = £1	400	
Expense accounts	8,000		16 = £1	500	
Sales		32,000	16 = £1		2,000
Goods from Head Office	21,900		£ per account in Head Office books	1,490	
Head Office current account		43,000	£ per account in Head Office books		3,380
Debtors	9,000		15 = £1	600	
Creditors		4,500	15 = £1		300
Bank	15,000		15 = £1	1,000	
	79,500	79,500		5,790	5,680
Difference on exchange account					110
				5,790	5,790

The stock at 31 December 20X8 is 12,000 dollars. When the trading account is drawn up this will be converted at 15 dollars = £1, i.e. £800.

Learning outcomes

You should now have learnt:

1 There are two main methods used to record transactions of the branches of an organisation:
   (a) all accounting records are kept by the head office
   (b) each branch has its own full accounting system.

2 When all sales are for cash a double column trading and profit and loss account can be used in order to monitor any unexpected losses.

3 When some sales are on credit, either memoranda columns can be used in the branch stock account in order to monitor stock or stock control can be integrated into the double entry system.

4 Foreign branch figures need to be translated using the principles set down in SSAP 20: *Foreign currency translation.*

Answers to activities

1.1 When a second branch or head office is also involved in receiving payments from debtors of another branch, the focus of control shifts from being purely connected with one branch. More sophisticated methods of recording the transaction data are therefore required.

1.2 They are merely a measure of the resources at the branch.

REVIEW QUESTIONS

1.1 Octopus Ltd, whose head office is at Cardiff, operates a branch at Swansea. All goods are purchased by head office and invoiced to and sold by the branch at cost plus 33$\frac{1}{3}$ per cent.

Other than a sales ledger kept at Swansea, all transactions are recorded in the books at Cardiff.

The following particulars are given of the transactions at the branch during the year ended 28 February 20X7.

	£
Stock on hand, 1 March 20X6, at invoice price	4,400
Debtors on 1 March 20X6	3,946
Stock on hand, 28 February 20X7, at invoice price	3,948
Goods sent from Cardiff during the year at invoice price	24,800
Credit sales	21,000
Cash sales	2,400
Returns to head office at invoice price	1,000
Invoice value of goods stolen	600
Bad debts written off	148
Cash from debtors	22,400
Normal loss at invoice price due to wastage	100
Cash discount allowed to debtors	428

You are required to write up the branch stock account and branch total debtors account for the year ended 28 February 20X7, as they would appear in the head office books.

(Institute of Chartered Accountants)

1.2 A Co Ltd has a branch in Everton at which a full set of books is kept. At the end of the year the following summary is compiled of the transactions between the branch and the head office as recorded in the latter's books:

	£
Balance due from branch 1 January	20,160
Cash received from branch	30,000
Goods supplied to branch	23,160
Goods returned by branch	400
Expenses paid on behalf of branch	6,000

At 30 June the branch profit and loss account showed a net profit of £3,500.

(a) Show the above items as they would appear in the ledger of the head office.

(b) How can any resulting balance from these figures be proved, and what does it indicate?

1.3 RST Limited is a family-controlled company which operates a chain of retail outlets specialising in motor spares and accessories.

Branch stocks are purchased by a centralised purchasing function in order to obtain the best terms from suppliers.

A 10 per cent handling charge is applied by head office to the cost of the purchases, and branches are expected to add 25 per cent to the resulting figure to arrive at normal selling prices, although branch managers are authorised to reduce normal prices in special situations. The effect of such reductions must be notified to head office.

On 1 April 20X6, a new branch was established at Derham. The following details have been recorded for the year ended 31 March 20X7:

	£
Purchase cost to head office of stock transferred to Derham	82,400
Derham branch sales: cash	89,940
credit	1,870
Stocks transferred from Derham to other branches, at normal selling prices	3,300
Authorised reductions from normal selling prices during the year	2,250

All records in respect of branch activities are maintained at head office, and the branch profit margin is dealt with through a branch stock adjustment account.

Required:
(a) Prepare:
    (i) the branch stock account (maintained at branch selling prices);
    (ii) the branch stock adjustment account.
    The *book stock* should be taken for this part of the question.
(b) List four of the possible reasons for the stock difference revealed when a physical stocktaking at the Derham branch on 31 March 20X7 showed stock valued at selling prices amounting to £14,850.
(c) State which of the following is the figure to be included in RST Limited's balance sheet at 31 March 20X7, for Derham branch stock:
    (i) £11,138
    (ii) £11,880
    (iii) £10,800
    (iv) None of these

    Justify your choice with appropriate calculations.

(*Chartered Institute of Management Accountants*)

1.4A   Paper Products has a head office in London and a branch in Bristol. The following information has been extracted from the head office books of account as at 31 March 20X6:

Information relating to the branch

Balances	Opening £000		Closing £000
Branch bank account (positive balance)	3		12
Branch debtors	66		81
Branch stock (at transfer price)	75		90
Transactions during the year		£000	
Bad debts written off		15	
Branch general expenses (paid from bank branch account)		42	
Cash received from credit customers and banked		390	
Cash sales banked		120	
Cash transferred from branch to head office bank account		459	
Credit sales		437	
Discounts allowed to credit customers		9	
Goods returned by credit customers		8	
Goods returned from branch (at transfer price from head office)			30
Goods sent to branch (at transfer price from head office)			600

Information relating to head office

Balances	Opening £000		Closing £000
Stock	180		220
Transactions during the year		£000	
Bad debts written off		24	
Cash sales		1,500	
Credit sales		2,000	
Discounts allowed to credit customers		29	
General expenses		410	
Goods returned by credit customers		40	
Purchases		2,780	

Additional information:

1 Most of the accounting records relating to the branch are kept by the head office in its own books of account.

2 All purchases are made by the head office, and goods are invoiced to the branch at selling price, that is, at cost price plus 50 per cent.

Required:

(a) Write up the following ledger accounts for the year to 31 March 20X6, being careful to bring down any balances as at that date:

  (i)   branch stock account;

  (ii) goods sent to branch account;

  (iii) branch stock adjustment account;

  (iv) branch debtors account; and

  (v)   branch bank account.

(b) Compile Paper Products' trading, and profit and loss account for the year to 31 March 20X6.

(c) Examine briefly the merits and demerits of Paper Products' method of branch bookkeeping including comments on the significance of the 'balancing figure' in the branch stock account.

(Association of Accounting Technicians)

1.5 Packer and Stringer were in partnership as retail traders sharing profits and losses: Packer three-quarters, Stringer one-quarter. The partners were credited annually with interest at the rate of 6 per cent per annum on their fixed capitals; no interest was charged on their drawings.

Stringer was responsible for the buying department of the business. Packer managed the head office and Paper was employed as the branch manager. Packer and Paper were each entitled to a commission of 10 per cent of the net profits (after charging such commission) of the shop managed by him.

All goods were purchased by head office and goods sent to the branch were invoiced at cost.

The following was the trial balance as on 31 December 20X4.

	Head Office Books		Branch Books	
	Dr	Cr	Dr	Cr
	£	£	£	£
Drawings accounts and fixed capital accounts: Packer	2,500	14,000		
Stringer	1,200	4,000		
Furniture and fittings, at cost	1,500		1,100	
Furniture and fittings, provision for depreciation as at 31 December 20X3		500		350
Stock on 31 December 20X3	13,000		4,400	
Purchases	37,000			
Goods sent to branches		18,000	17,200	
Sales		39,000		26,000
Provision for doubtful debts		600		200
Branch and head office current accounts	6,800			3,600
Salaries and wages	4,500		3,200	
Paper, on account of commission			240	
Carriage and travelling expenses	2,200		960	
Administrative expenses	2,400			
Trade and general expenses	3,200		1,800	
Sundry debtors	7,000		3,000	
Sundry creditors		5,800		400
Bank balances	600			1,350
	81,900	81,900	31,900	31,900

You are given the following additional information:

(a) Stocks on 31 December 20X4, amounted to: head office £14,440, branch £6,570.

(b) Administrative expenses are to be apportioned between head office and the branch in proportion to sales.

(c) Depreciation is to be provided on furniture and fittings at 10 per cent of cost.

(d) The provision for doubtful debts is to be increased by £50 in respect of head office debtors and decreased by £20 in the case of those of the branch.

(e) On 31 December 20X4 cash amounting to £2,400, in transit from the branch to head office, has been recorded in the branch books but not in those of head office; and on that date goods invoiced at £800, in transit from head office to the branch, had been recorded in the head office books but not in the branch books.

Any adjustments necessary are to be made in the head office books.

You are required to:

(a) prepare trading and profit and loss accounts and the appropriation account for the year ended 31 December 20X4, showing the net profit of the head office and branch respectively;

(b) prepare the balance sheet as on that date; and

(c) show the closing entries in the branch current accounts giving the make-up of the closing balance.

Income tax is to be ignored.

(*Institute of Chartered Accountants*)

1.6A   LR, a trader, commenced business on 1 January 20X9, with a head office and one branch.

All goods were purchased by the head office and goods sent to the branch were invoiced at a fixed selling price of 25 per cent above cost. All sales, both by the head office and the branch, were made at the fixed selling price.

The following trial balance was extracted from the books at the head office at 31 December 20X9.

Trial Balance

	£	£
Capital		52,000
Drawings	1,740	
Purchases	123,380	
Sales		83,550
Goods sent to branch (at selling price)		56,250
Branch current account	24,550	
Fixed assets	33,000	
Debtors and creditors	7,980	11,060
General expenses	8,470	
Balance at bank	3,740	
	202,860	202,860

No entries had been made in the head office books for cash in transit from the branch to head office at 31 December 20X9, £1,000.

When the balances shown below were extracted from the branch books at 31 December 20X9, no entries had been made in the books of the branch for goods in transit on that date from head office to branch, £920 (selling price).

In addition to the balances which can be deduced from the information given above, the following balances appeared in the branch books on 31 December 20X9.

	£
Fixed assets	6,000
General expenses	6,070
Debtors	7,040
Creditors (excluding head office)	1,630
Sales	51,700
Balance at bank	1,520

When stock was taken on 31 December 20X9, it was found that there was no shortage at the head office, but at the branch there were shortages amounting to £300, at selling price.

You are required to prepare trading and profit and loss accounts (*a*) for head office and (*b*) for the branch, as they would have appeared if goods sent to the branch had been invoiced at cost, and a balance sheet of the whole business as on 31 December 20X9.

   Head office and branch stocks are to be valued at cost.

   Ignore depreciation of fixed assets.

(*Institute of Chartered Secretaries and Administrators*)

1.7   Nion is a retail stock outlet operating from a head office in London and a branch in Brighton. The following trial balances have been extracted from the books of account as at 31 October 20X1.

	Head Office Books		Branch Books	
	Dr	Cr	Dr	Cr
	£	£	£	£
Drawings	40,000			
Fixed assets: at cost	350,000		100,000	
accumulated depreciation				
(at 1 November 20X0)		140,000		30,000
Stock (at 1 November 20X0)	8,000		20,000	
Provision for unrealised profit		4,000		
Purchases	914,000			
Goods sent to branch at invoiced value		380,000	375,000	
Sales		850,000		437,000
Provision for doubtful debts		9,000		2,500
Head office/branch current accounts	175,000			120,000
Distribution expenses	80,500		5,000	
Administrative expenses	200,000		16,500	
Trade debtors	60,000		60,000	
Trade creditors		50,000		
Cash and bank balances	15,500		13,000	
Capital		410,000		
	£1,843,000	£1,843,000	£589,500	£589,500

Additional information:

1 All goods are purchased by the head office. Those goods sent to the branch are invoiced at cost plus 25 per cent.

2 Stocks were valued at 31 October 20X1 as being at head office, £12,000; and at the branch, £15,000 at their invoiced price.

3 Depreciation is to be provided for the year on the fixed assets at a rate of 10 per cent on the historic cost.

4 The provision for doubtful debts is to be maintained at a rate of 5 per cent of outstanding trade debtors as at the end of the financial year.

5 As at 31 October 20X1, there was £50,000 cash in transit from the branch to the head office; this cash was received in London on 3 November 20X1. There was also £5,000 of goods in transit at invoice price from the head office to the branch; the branch received these goods on 10 November 20X1.

Required:
Prepare in adjacent columns: (*a*) the head office, and (*b*) the branch trading and profit and loss accounts for the year to 31 October 20X1; and a **combined** balance sheet for Nion as at that date.

Notes:
(*i*) a combined trading and profit and loss account is NOT required; and
(*ii*) separate balance sheets for the head office and the branch are also NOT required.

(*Association of Accounting Technicians*)

1.8A Star Stores has its head office and main store in Crewe, and a branch store in Leek. All goods are purchased by the head office. Goods are invoiced to the branch at cost price plus a profit loading of 20 per cent. The following trial balances have been extracted from the books of account of both the head office and the branch as at 31 December 20X9:

	Head Office Books		Branch Books	
	Dr	Cr	Dr	Cr
	£000	£000	£000	£000
Administrative expenses	380		30	
Distribution costs	157		172	
Capital (at 1 January 20X9)		550		
Cash and bank	25		2	
Creditors and accruals		176		20
Current accounts	255			180
Debtors and prepayments	130		76	
Motor vehicles:				
at cost	470		230	
accumulated depreciation at 31 December 20X9		280		120
Plant and equipment:				
at cost	250		80	
accumulated depreciation at 31 December 20X9		120		30
Proprietor's drawings during the year	64			
Provision for unrealised profit on branch stocks				
at 1 January 20X9		5		
Purchases	880			
Sales		1,200		570
Stocks at cost/invoiced amount at 1 January 20X9	80		30	
Transfer of goods to the branch/from				
the head office		360	300	
	£2,691	£2,691	£920	£920

Additional information:

1 The stocks in hand at 31 December 20X9 were estimated to be as follows:

	£000
At head office (at cost)	100
At the branch (at invoiced price)	48

In addition, £60,000 of stocks at invoiced price had been despatched to the branch on 28 December 20X9. These goods had not been received by the branch until 5 January 20X0 and so they had not been included in the branch books of account.

2 On 31 December 20X9, the branch had transferred £15,000 of cash to the head office bank, but this was not received in Crewe until 2 January 20X0.

Required:
(a) Prepare in adjacent columns and using the vertical format: (*i*) the head office, and (*ii*) the branch trading and profit and loss accounts for the year to 31 December 20X9 (*note*: a combined profit and loss account is NOT required); and
(b) Prepare in the vertical format, Star Stores' balance sheet as at 31 December 20X9 (*note*: separate balance sheets for the head office and the branch are NOT required).

(*Association of Accounting Technicians*)

1.9 EG Company Limited, a manufacturing business, exports some of its products through an overseas branch whose currency is 'florins', which carries out the final assembly operations before selling the goods.

The trial balances of the head office and branch at 30 June 20X8 were:

	Head Office £	Head Office £	Branch 'Fl.'	Branch 'Fl.'
Freehold buildings at cost	14,000		63,000	
Debtors/creditors	8,900	9,500	36,000	1,560
Sales		104,000		432,000
Authorised and issued capital		40,000		
Components sent to branch		35,000		
Head office/branch accounts	60,100			504,260
Branch cost of sales			360,000	
Depreciation provision, machinery		1,500		56,700
Head office cost of sales (including goods to branch)	59,000			
Administration costs	15,200		18,000	
Stock at 30 June 20X8	28,900		11,520	
Profit and loss account		2,000		
Machinery at cost	6,000		126,000	
Remittances		28,000	272,000	
Balance at bank	4,600		79,200	
Selling and distribution costs	23,300		28,800	
	220,000	220,000	994,520	994,520

The following adjustments are to be made:

1 The cost of sales figures include a depreciation charge of 10 per cent per annum on cost for machinery.
2 A provision of £300 for unrealised profit in branch stock is to be made.
3 On 26 June 20X8 the branch remitted 16,000 'Fl.'; these were received by the head office on 4 July and realised £1,990.
4 During May a branch customer in error paid the head office for goods supplied. The amount due was 320 'Fl.' which realised £36. It has been correctly dealt with by head office but not yet entered in the branch books.
5 A provision has to be made for a commission of 5 per cent of the net profit of the branch after charging such commission, which is due to the branch manager.

The rates of exchange were:

At 1 July 20X7	10 'Fl.' = £1
At 30 June 20X8	8 'Fl.' = £1
Average for the year	9 'Fl.' = £1
On purchase of buildings and machinery	7 'Fl.' = £1

You are required to prepare, for internal use:
(a) detailed operating accounts for the year ended 30 June 20X8;
(b) combined head office and branch balance sheet as at 30 June 20X8;
(c) the branch account in the head office books, in both sterling and currency, the opening balance on 1 July 20X7 being £25,136 (189,260 'Fl.').
Taxation is to be ignored.

(*Chartered Institute of Management Accountants*)

1.10   OTL Ltd commenced business on 1 January 20X0. The head office is in London and there is a branch in Highland. The currency unit of Highland is the crown.

The following are the trial balances of the head office and the Highland branch as at 31 December 20X0:

	Head Office £	£	Highland Branch Crowns	Crowns
Branch account	65,280			
Balances at bank	10,560		66,000	
Creditors		21,120		92,400
Debtors	18,480		158,400	
Fixed assets (purchased 1 January 20X0)	39,600		145,200	
Head office account				316,800
Profit and loss account				
(net profit for year)		52,800		79,200
Issued share capital		86,400		
Stocks	26,400		118,800	
	160,320	160,320	488,400	488,400

The trial balance of the head office was prepared before any entries had been made in respect of any profits or losses of the branch.

Remittances from head office to branch and from branch to head office were recorded in the books at the actual amounts paid and received.

The rates of exchange were:

On 1 January 20X0	5 crowns = £1
Average rate for year 20X0	4.4 crowns = £1
On 31 December 20X0	4 crowns = £1

Required:
(a) The trial balance of the Highland branch as at 31 December 20X0, in sterling.
(b) The closing entries, as at 31 December 20X0, in the branch account in the books of the head office.
(c) A summary of the balance sheet of OTL Ltd as at 31 December 20X0.
Ignore depreciation of fixed assets.
Ignore taxation.

(*Institute of Chartered Secretaries and Administrators*)

1.11A Home Ltd is incorporated in the UK and rents mobile homes to holidaymakers in this country and in Carea. The company has a head office in London and a branch in Carea where the local currency is 'Mics'. The following balances are extracted from the books of the head office and its 'self-accounting' branch at 31 December 20X4.

	Head Office £	Branch Mics
Debit balances		
Fixed assets at cost	450,000	900,000
Debtors and cash	17,600	36,000
Operating costs	103,700	225,000
Branch current account	42,600	
	613,900	1,161,000
Credit balances		
Share capital	200,000	–
Retained profit, 1 January 20X4	110,800	–
Sales revenue	186,300	480,000
Creditors	9,700	25,000
Head office current account	–	420,000
Accumulated depreciation	107,100	236,000
	613,900	1,161,000

The following information is provided regarding exchange rates, some of which is relevant.

The fixed assets of the branch were acquired when there were 8 Mics to the £. Exchange rates ruling during 20X4 were:

	Mics to the £
1 January	6
Average	5
31 December	4

There are no cash or goods in transit between head office and branch at the year end.

Required:

The final accounts of Home Ltd for 20X4. The accounts should be expressed in £s sterling and, for this purpose, the conversion of Mics should be made in accordance with the temporal method of translation as specified in SSAP 20: *Foreign currency translation*.

(*Institute of Chartered Secretaries and Administrators*)

Hire purchase accounts

After you have studied this chapter, you should be able to:

- explain the term 'hire purchase'
- explain what distinguishes hire purchase from outright purchase
- explain what distinguishes hire purchase from a lease
- record the entries relating to hire purchase transactions

Introduction

In this chapter you'll learn about the nature of hire purchase; of the difference to the cost to the buyer of paying the same amount each period as compared with paying a variable amount linked to the outstanding amount owed; and the accounting treatment and entries required when hire purchase transactions occur. You will also be introduced to leases and to the differences between leases and hire purchase agreements.

2.1 Nature of hire purchase

Hire purchase is a means of buying assets that avoids the need to pay in full either at the time of purchase or very soon thereafter. The essential differences between a hire purchase and a 'normal' purchase are:

1 The asset does not belong to the purchaser when it is received from the supplier. Instead it belongs to the supplier providing the hire purchase.
2 The purchaser will pay for the item by instalments over a period of time. This may be for as long as two or three years, or even longer.
3 The cost to the buyer will be higher than it would have been had the item been paid for at the time of purchase. The extra money paid is for interest.
4 The asset does not legally belong to the purchaser until two things happen:
   (a) the final instalment is paid, and
   (b) the purchaser agrees to a legal option to buy the asset.

If the purchasers want to, they could stop paying the instalments. They would then have to give the asset back to the seller. They would not be able to get a refund of instalments already paid.

If the purchaser is unable to continue paying the instalments, the seller could normally repossess the asset. The seller would keep all the instalments already paid.

Activity 2.1
Why do you think organisations purchase assets on hire purchase?

2.2   Law of hire purchase

The Hire Purchase Act 1964 governs all hire purchase transactions.

2.3   Interest payable on hire purchase

Each payment made on a hire purchase contract consists of two things:

1 **Capital.** Part of the instalment will be paying off part of the amount owing for the cash price of the asset;
2 **Interest.** The other part of the instalment will be for the interest that has accrued for the period of time.

The total payment (1) + (2) made for each instalment may be the same, or may differ. Normally, however, the same amount in total is paid each time an instalment is due.

Exhibit 2.1 Unequal instalments

1 A machine is bought from A King at the start of year 1. Cash price is £2,000.
2 Hire purchase price is £2,300.
3 Payable in two annual instalments at the end of each year. Each instalment to be £1,000 plus interest accrued for that year.
4 Rate of interest is 10 per cent per annum.

			£
Year 1:	Cash price	(A)	2,000
	Add Interest 10% of (A) £2,000		200
			2,200
	Less Instalment paid		(1,200)
	Owing at end of year 1	(B)	1,000
Year 2:	*Add* Interest 10% of (B) £1,000		100
			1,100
	Less Instalment paid		(1,100)
	Owing at end of year 2		–

Exhibit 2.2 Equal instalments

The facts are the same as in Exhibit 2.1, except that each instalment is £1,152. (Each figure of interest is rounded down to the nearest £.)

			£
Year 1:	Cash price	(A)	2,000
	Add Interest 10% of (A) £2,000		200
			2,200
	Less Instalment paid		(1,152)
	Owing at end of year 1	(B)	1,048
Year 2:	*Add* Interest 10% of (B) £1,048		104
			1,152
	Less Instalment paid		(1,152)
	Owing at end of year 2		–

Note: The interest for year 1 is the same for both equal or unequal instalments, as the whole of the cash price is owed in both cases for a full year.

Activity 2.2

Why is the amount paid in Year 2 in Exhibit 2.2 different from the amount paid in Year 2 in Exhibit 2.1?

2.4   Accounting for hire purchase

Accounting treats assets bought on hire purchase as though they belonged immediately to the purchaser.

This is because businesses normally buy assets on hire purchase with the intention of paying all the instalments, so that the asset finally will belong to them. As they mean to keep the asset and legally own it on the final payment, accounting enters it as though legal ownership occurred on purchase.

This is an illustration of the use of the 'substance over form' concept. Legally the firm does not yet own the asset (form) yet it does own it from an economic perspective (substance).

The total purchase price is split into two parts for the financial statements:

1 **Cash price.** This is the amount to be debited to the fixed asset account.
2 **Interest.** This is an expense of borrowing money and needs charging to an expense account, i.e. hire purchase interest account.

As interest accrues over time, each period should be charged only with the interest accrued for that period. This is shown in Exhibit 2.3.

Exhibit 2.3

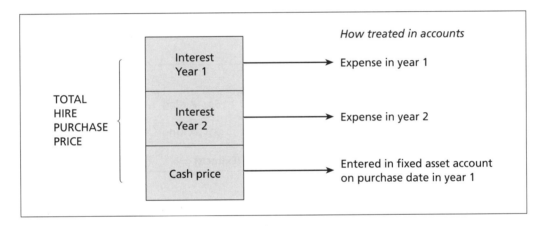

2.5   Illustrations of purchaser's accounts

The double entry needed is:

(A) Cash price: Debit fixed asset
                                                 Credit supplier

(B) Hire purchase interest: Debit hire purchase interest
        (for each period's interest)   Credit supplier
(C) Hire purchase instalments: Debit supplier
                                                 Credit cash book
(D) Charge interest to profit and loss: Debit profit and loss
                                                 Credit hire purchase interest

We can now look at the ledger accounts which would have been used to enter the facts as in Exhibit 2.1. (For simplicity, depreciation has been omitted from the example.) Letters entered against the entries refer to the double entries given above.

Machinery

			£	
Year 1				
Jan 1	A King	(A)	2,000	

Hire Purchase Interest

			£					£
Year 1				Year 1				
Dec 31	A King	(B)	200	Dec 31	Profit and loss	(D)	200
Year 2				Year 2				
Dec 31	A King	(B)	100	Dec 31	Profit and loss	(D)	100

A King

			£					£
Year 1				Year 1				
Dec 31	Bank	(C)	1,200	Jan 1	Machinery	(A)	2,000
Dec 31	Balance c/d		1,000	Dec 31	HP interest	(B)	200
			2,200				2,200
Year 2				Year 2				
Dec 31	Bank	(C)	1,100	Jan 1	Balance b/d		1,000
				Dec 31	HP interest	(B)	100
			1,100				1,100

Cash Book

						£
		Year 1				
		Dec 31	A King	(C)	1,200
		Year 2				
		Dec 31	A King	(C)	1,100

Profit and Loss Account (Extracts)

		£	
Year 1 Hire purchase interest	(D)	200	
Year 2 Hire purchase interest	(D)	100	

2.6 Depreciation and assets bought on hire purchase

Depreciation is based on the cash price. The interest does not enter depreciation calculations.

2.7 Balance sheets and assets bought on hire purchase

In the balance sheet for a sole trader or partnership, fixed assets being bought on hire purchase can be shown as follows:

Fixed assets		£	£
Machinery at cost			20,000
Less Owing on hire purchase		6,000	
Depreciation to date		10,000	
			(16,000)
			4,000

In Exhibit 2.1 above, if the machinery had been depreciated using the straight line method at 20 per cent, the balance sheet entries would have been:

Balance Sheet (end of year 1)

	£	£
Fixed assets		
Machinery at cost		2,000
Less Owing on hire purchase[Note]	1,000	
Depreciation to date	400	
		(1,400)
		600

Note: This is the balance of A King's account.

Balance Sheet (end of year 2)

	£	£
Fixed assets		
Machinery at cost		2,000
Less Depreciation to date		(800)
		1,200

Note: At the end of year 2 there was nothing owing to A King for hire purchase.

However, in company balance sheets this is *not* allowed. The Companies Acts do not permit an amount owing on a hire purchase contract to be deducted from the value of the asset in the balance sheet.

In a company's balance sheet, the entries would be:

Balance Sheet (end of year 1)

	£	£
Fixed assets		
Machinery at cost		2,000
Less Depreciation to date		(400)
		1,600
Liabilities		
Creditors (Owing on hire purchase)[Note]		1,000

Note: This is the balance of A King's account.

Balance Sheet (end of year 2)

	£	£
Fixed assets		
Machinery at cost	2,000	
Less Depreciation to date	(800)	
		1,200

2.8   A fully worked example

Exhibit 2.4 illustrates hire purchase more fully. It covers three years of hire purchase and shows the balance sheet figures that would appear if sole traders and partnerships adopted the first approach shown in section 2.7.

Exhibit 2.4

1 A machine is bought by K Thomas for £3,618, hire purchase price, from Suppliers Ltd on 1 January 20X3.
2 It is paid by 3 instalments of £1,206 on 31 December of 20X3, 20X4 and 20X5.
3 The cash price is £3,000.
4 Rate of interest is 10 per cent.
5 Straight line depreciation of 20 per cent per annum is to be provided.

Note: The letters (A) to (F) refer to the description of entries following the account.

Machinery

20X3				£						
Jan	1	Suppliers Ltd	(A)	3,000						

Suppliers Ltd

20X3				£	20X3					£
Dec	31	Bank	(B)	1,206	Jan	1	Machinery	(A)		3,000
Dec	31	Balance c/d	(D)	2,094	Dec	31	HP interest	(C)		300
				3,300						3,300
20X4					20X4					
Dec	31	Bank	(B)	1,206	Jan	1	Balance b/d	(D)		2,094
Dec	31	Balance c/d	(D)	1,097	Dec	31	HP interest	(C)		209
				2,303						2,303
20X5					20X5					
Dec	31	Bank	(B)	1,206	Jan	1	Balance b/d	(D)		1,097
					Dec	31	HP interest	(C)		109
				1,206						1,206

Hire Purchase Interest

20X3				£	20X3					£
Dec	31	Suppliers Ltd	(C)	300	Dec	31	Profit and loss	(E)		300
20X4					20X4					
Dec	31	Suppliers Ltd	(C)	209	Dec	31	Profit and loss	(E)		209
20X5					20X5					
Dec	31	Suppliers Ltd	(C)	109	Dec	31	Profit and loss	(E)		109

Provision for Depreciation: Machinery

					20X3					£
					Dec	31	Profit and loss	(F)		600
					20X4					
					Dec	31	Profit and loss	(F)		600
					20X5					
					Dec	31	Profit and loss	(F)		600

Balance Sheets as at 31 December

			£	£	£
			£	£	£
20X3	Machinery (at cost)			3,000	
	Less Depreciation		600		
	Owing on hire purchase agreement		2,094		
				(2,694)	
					306
20X4	Machinery (at cost)			3,000	
	Less Depreciation to date		1,200		
	Owing on hire purchase agreement		1,097		
				(2,297)	
					703
20X5	Machinery (at cost)			3,000	
	Less Depreciation to date			(1,800)	
					1,200

Description of entries:

(A) When the asset is acquired the cash price is debited to the asset account and the credit is in the supplier's account.

(B) The instalments paid are credited to the bank account and debited to the supplier's account.

(C) The interest is credited to the supplier's account for each period as it accrues, and it is debited to the expense account, later to be transferred to the profit and loss account for the period (E).

(D) The balance carried down each year is the amount of the cash price still owing.

(F) Depreciation provisions are calculated on the full cash price, as the depreciation of an asset is in no way affected by whether or not it has been fully paid for.

The balance sheet consists of balance (A), the cash price, *less* balance (F), the amount of the cash price apportioned as depreciation. Balance (D), the amount of the cash price still owing at each balance sheet date, is shown separately under creditors.

2.9   The seller's books: apportionment of profits

There are many ways of drawing up the final accounts of a business which sells goods on hire purchase. The method used should be the one most suitable for the business.

The total profit for the seller of goods on hire purchase breaks down as follows:

	£
Profit on item sold: Cash price *less* cost	xxx
Profit made because of interest charged	xxx
	xxx

In Exhibit 2.4, Suppliers Ltd sold a machine to K Thomas. Assume that the machine had cost Suppliers Ltd £2,100. The total profit upon the final instalment being paid is:

		£	£
Profit on sale of machine:	Cash price	3,000	
	Cost	(2,100)	
			900
Profit earned by charging interest:	20X3	300	
	20X4	209	
	20X5	109	
			618
Total profit over 3 years			1,518

Apportionment of profit on sale

There are two main methods of dealing with the problem of how to split the £900 profit on sale of the machine:

1 It is considered profit in the period in which it was first sold to the purchaser. In this case the £900 would all be shown as profit for 20X3.

2 The profit is divided among the three years.

The ratio is calculated as follows:

$$\frac{\text{Cash received in period}}{\text{Total cash to be received}} \times \text{Profit}$$

In this case the profits will be shown as:

$$20X3 \quad \frac{£1,206}{£1,206 \times 3} \times £900 = \frac{1}{3} \times £900 = £300$$

$$20X4 \quad \frac{£1,206}{£1,206 \times 3} \times £900 = \frac{1}{3} \times £900 = £300$$

$$20X5 \quad \frac{£1,206}{£1,206 \times 3} \times £900 = \frac{1}{3} \times £900 = £300$$

Total profit on sale for three years   £900

This case shows equal profits because equal instalments were paid each year. Unequal payments would result in unequal profits.

Apportionment of interest to profit and loss account

The interest accrued for each period should be taken into profit calculations. As the amount owed reduces, so does the interest:

	£
Year 20X3	300
Year 20X4	209
Year 20X5	109
Total interest for the three years	618

2.10 The seller's books: accounts needed

We can now look at Exhibit 2.5 taking the details from Exhibit 2.4 as it would appear in the seller's books. Items (A) to (C) have already been shown in Exhibit 2.4.

Exhibit 2.5

(A) The machine was sold on 1 January 20X3 to K Thomas on hire purchase terms. Cash price was £3,000 plus hire purchase interest.

(B) Hire purchase interest was at a rate of 10 per cent.

(C) There are to be three instalments of £1,206 each, receivable on 31 December of 20X3, 20X4 and 20X5. These were paid by K Thomas on the correct dates.

(D) This was the only hire purchase sale during the three years.

(E) The profit on the cash price is to be shown as profits for 20X3, the year in which the sale was made.

(F) The cost of the machine to Suppliers Ltd was £2,100.

Hire Purchase Sales

20X3			£	20X3				£
Dec 31	Trading		3,000	Jan 1	K Thomas		(A)	3,000

K Thomas

20X3			£	20X3			£
Jan 1	Sales (A)		3,000	Dec 31	Bank (C)		1,206
Dec 31	HP interest (B)		300	Dec 31	Balance c/d		2,094
			3,300				3,300
20X4				20X4			
Jan 1	Balance b/d		2,094	Dec 31	Bank (C)		1,206
Dec 31	HP interest (B)		209	Dec 31	Balance c/d		1,097
			2,303				2,303
20X5				20X5			
Jan 1	Balance b/d		1,097	Dec 31	Bank (C)		1,206
Dec 31	HP interest (B)		109				
			1,206				1,206

Hire Purchase Interest

20X3		£	20X3			£
Dec 31	Trading	300	Dec 31	K Thomas (B)		300
20X4			20X4			
Dec 31	Trading	209	Dec 31	K Thomas (B)		209
20X5			20X5			
Dec 31	Trading	109	Dec 31	K Thomas (B)		109

Cost of Hire Purchase Goods

20X3			£	20X3			£
Jan	1	Bank	(F)	2,100	Dec	31	Trading	2,100

Cash Book

20X3				£	20X3			£
Dec	31	K Thomas	(C)	1,206	Jan	1	Hire purchase goods (F)	2,100
20X4								
Dec	31	K Thomas	(C)	1,206				
20X5								
Dec	31	K Thomas	(C)	1,206				

Trading Accounts
Year ended 31 December 20X3

	£		£
Cost of goods sold	2,100	Hire purchase sales	3,000
		Hire purchase interest	300

Year ended 31 December 20X4

		£
	Hire purchase interest	209

Year ended 31 December 20X5

		£
	Hire purchase interest	109

In Exhibit 2.5 all the profit was taken as being earned in 20X3. If we decided to take the profit as being earned when the instalments are received, then the only account which would be altered would be the trading account. All the other accounts would be exactly the same as in Exhibit 2.5.

The amendments needed are shown as Exhibit 2.6.

Exhibit 2.6

Trading Accounts
Year ended 31 December 20X3

		£			£
Cost of goods sold		2,100	Hire purchase sales		3,000
Hire purchase profit suspense			Hire purchase interest		300
profit not yet earned	(G)	600			

Year ended 31 December 20X4

		£
Hire purchase profit suspense		
profit for 20X4	(H)	300
Hire purchase interest		209

Year ended 31 December 20X5

		£
Hire purchase profit suspense		
profit for 20X5	(H)	300
Hire purchase interest		109

Hire Purchase Profit Suspense

20X3			£	20X3			£
Dec 31	Trading	(H)	300	Dec 31	Trading	(G)	600
Dec 31	Balance c/d		300				
			600				600
20X5				20X5			
Dec 31	Trading	(H)	300	Jan 1	Balance b/d		300

The double entry needed was:

(G) In year of sale: Debit trading account with profits carried to future years
                         Credit hire purchase profit suspense

(H) In following years: Debit hire purchase profit suspense with profits earned in each year
                         Credit trading account

The entries for hire purchase interest have not changed.

2.11   Repossessions

When customers stop paying their instalments before they should do, the goods can be taken away from them. This is called **repossession**. The amounts already paid by the customers will be kept by the seller.

The repossessed items should be entered in the books of the seller, as they are now part of his stock, but they will not be valued as new stock. The items must be valued as used goods. Exhibit 2.7 shows how the accounts must be changed.

1 On 1 January 20X4 we buy 15 calculators for £300 each.
2 On 1 January 20X4 we sell 12 of them for a cash price of £480 plus £120 interest to be paid = £600 total.
3 24 monthly instalments are to be paid of £25 each = £600.
4 Because of the difficulties of apportioning interest, each instalment is taken to include £5 interest, i.e. 24 × £5 = £120 interest.
5 On 1 November 20X4, after 10 instalments have been received, a customer who bought 2 calculators cannot pay any more instalments. Both calculators are returned by him. We do not have to repay the instalments paid by him.
6 The 2 calculators returned are valued at £140 each. Also in stock on 31 December 20X4 are 3 of the calculators bought on 1 January 20X4 for £300 each and still valued at that.
7 Profit is to be calculated based on the number of instalments paid.

Exhibit 2.7

Trading Account for the year ended 31 December 20X4

		£			£
Purchases	(a)	4,500	Sales at cash price	(b)	4,800
Less Stock	(e)	(1,180)	Hire purchase interest	(c)	600
Cost of goods sold		3,320	Instalments received		
			on repossessions	(d)	500
Provision for unrealised					
profit	(f)	900			
Gross profit	(g)	1,680			
		5,900			5,900

Notes
Calculations are made as follows:
(a) 15 × £300 each = £4,500.
(b) 10 were sold (and not returned) at cash price of £480 each.

(c) Interest on 10 sold (and not returned) × £5 × 12 months = £600.

(d) 10 instalments paid (including interest) on 2 calculators = 10 × £25 × 2 = £500.

(e) Stock =   new items 3 × £300   =   £900
              repossessed items 2 × £140 =   £280
                                               £1,180

(f) Profit per calculator = cash price £480 – cost £300   =   £180
    To be paid: 12 instalments out of 24 = ½ profit   =   £90
    Number sold and not returned, 10 × £90   =   £900

(g) Gross profit can be checked:
    Earned to date 10 × £90   =   £900
    Interest earned to date £5 × 10 × 12 months   =   £600
    Profit on repossessions:
    Instalments received   £500
    Loss of value on repossessions
        Cost 2 × £300   £600
        Value taken back   £280   =   £320
                                                                                £180
                                                                                £1,680

2.12 SSAP 21: Accounting for leases and hire purchase contracts

In August 1984, when SSAP 21 was issued, the background was stated in the following terms.

Leasing and hire purchase contracts are means by which companies acquire the right to use (lease) or purchase (hire purchase) fixed assets. In the UK there is normally no provision in a lease contract for legal title to the leased asset to pass to the lessee during the term of a lease. In contrast, under a hire purchase contract the hirer may acquire legal title by exercising an option to purchase the asset upon fulfilment of certain conditions (normally the payment of an agreed number of instalments).

Lessors fall into three broad categories. They may be companies, including banks and finance houses, which provide finance under lease contracts to enable a single customer to acquire the use of an asset for the greater part of its useful life; they may operate a business which involves the renting out of assets for varying periods of time probably to more than one customer; or they may be manufacturer or dealer lessors who use leasing as a means of marketing their products, which may involve leasing a product to one customer or to several customers. As a lessor and lessee are both parties to the same transaction it is appropriate that the same definitions should be used and the accounting treatment recommended should ideally be complementary. However, this will not mean that the recorded balances in both financial statements will be the same, because the pattern of cash flows and the taxation consequences will be different.

Leases can appropriately be classified into **finance leases** and **operating leases**. The distinction between a finance lease and an operating lease will usually be evident from the substance of the contract between the lessor and the lessee. A finance lease usually involves repayment to a lessor by a lessee of the full cost of the asset together with a return on the finance provided by the lessor. As such, a lease of this type is normally non-cancellable or cancellable only under certain conditions, and the lessee enjoys substantially all the risks and rewards associated with the ownership of an asset, other than the legal title.

An operating lease involves the lessee paying a rental for the hire of an asset for a period of time which is normally substantially less than its useful economic life. The lessor retains the risks and rewards of ownership of an asset in an operating lease and normally assumes responsibility for repairs, maintenance and insurance.

Briefly, this standard requires that a finance lease should be accounted for by the lessee as if it were the purchase of the property rights in an asset with simultaneous recognition of the obligation to make future payments, in the same way that a hire purchase is normally accounted for. Under an operating lease, only the rental will be taken into account by the lessee. The standard recognises that the substance of a transaction rather than its legal form should govern the accounting treatment.

Learning outcomes

You should now have learnt:

1 Hire purchase is a means of buying assets where:
   (a) the asset does not belong to the purchaser until the final instalment is paid *and* the purchaser agrees to a legal option to buy the asset; *but*
   (b) for accounting purposes, the asset is treated immediately as if it belonged to the purchaser.

2 Each payment made on a hire purchase contract is part interest and part payment of the cash price of the asset.

3 How to record the various entries relating to hire purchase.

4 How to treat hire purchase transactions in the trading and profit and loss account and balance sheet.

5 The difference between hire purchase and leasing.

6 The difference between a finance lease and an operating lease.

Answers to activities

2.1 An organisation may have a shortage of cash, or may prefer to use its cash for other purposes; it may not wish to keep the asset permanently and may buy it on hire purchase so that after a couple of years it can stop paying the instalments; sometimes, hire purchase is offered at zero interest so it is actually cheaper to purchase an item on hire purchase (because interest can be earned by the buyer on the amount not yet paid).

2.2 Because £48 less was paid in Exhibit 2.2 at the end of Year 1. Interest was charged at 10% on that £48, resulting in an additional £4 having to be paid in Year 2 as well as the £48 that was not paid in Year 1. Overall, this meant that the Year 2 payment in Exhibit 2.2 was £52 greater than in Exhibit 2.1. However, over the two years, the difference in cost to the buyer was the £4 interest that arose as a result of the first-year payment having been slightly lower in Exhibit 2.2.

REVIEW QUESTIONS

2.1   An engineering concern purchased machines on the HP system over a period of three years, paying £846 on 1 January 20X3, and further annual payments of £2,000 due on 31 December 20X3, 20X4 and 20X5.

The cash price of the machine was £6,000, the vendor company charging interest at 8 per cent per annum on outstanding balances.

Show the appropriate ledger accounts in the purchaser's books for the three years and how the items would appear in the balance sheet at 31 December 20X5; depreciation at 10 per cent per annum on the written-down value is to be charged and interest calculated to the nearest £.

2.2A   On 1 January 20X3 J Donkins bought a machine (cash price £2,092) from CD & Co. Ltd on the following hire purchase terms. Donkins was to make an immediate payment of £600 and three

annual payments of £600 on 31 December in each year. The rate of interest chargeable is 10 per cent per annum.

Donkins depreciates this machinery by 10 per cent on the diminishing balance each year.

(a) Make the entries relating to this machine in Donkins' ledger for the years 20X3, 20X4 and 20X5. (All calculations are to be made to the nearest £.)

(b) Show how the item 'machinery' would appear in the balance sheet as at 31 December 20X3.

2.3 Bulwell Aggregates Ltd wish to expand their transport fleet and have purchased three heavy lorries with a list price of £18,000 each. Robert Bulwell has negotiated hire purchase finance to fund this expansion, and the company has entered into a hire purchase agreement with Granby Garages plc on 1 January 20X1. The agreement states that Bulwell Aggregates will pay a deposit of £9,000 on 1 January 20X1, and two annual instalments of £24,000 on 31 December 20X1, 20X2 and a final instalment of £20,391 on 31 December 20X3.

Interest is to be calculated at 25 per cent on the balance outstanding on 1 January each year and paid on 31 December each year.

The depreciation policy of Bulwell Aggregates Ltd is to write off the vehicles over a four-year period using the straight line method and assuming a scrap value of £1,333 for each vehicle at the end of its useful life.

The cost of the vehicles to Granby Garages is £14,400 each.

Required:

(a) Account for the above transactions in the books of Bulwell Aggregates Ltd, showing the entries in the profit and loss account and balance sheet for the years 20X1, 20X2, 20X3 and 20X4.

(b) Account for the above transactions in the books of Granby Garages plc, showing the entries in the hire purchase trading account for the years 20X1, 20X2, 20X3. This is the only hire purchase transaction undertaken by this company.

Calculations to the nearest £.

(*Association of Accounting Technicians*)

2.4A J York was acquiring two cars under hire purchase agreements, details of which are as follows:

Registration number	JY 1	JY 2
Date of purchase	31 May 20X6	31 October 20X6
Cash price	£18,000	£24,000
Deposit	£3,120	£4,800
Interest (deemed to accrue evenly over the period of the agreement)	£1,920	£2,400

Both agreements provided for payment to be made in 24 monthly instalments commencing on the last day of the month following purchase.

On 1 September 20X7, vehicle JY 1 became a total loss. In full settlement on 20 September 20X7:

(a) an insurance company paid £12,500 under a comprehensive policy, and

(b) the hire purchase company accepted £6,000 for the termination of the agreement.

The firm prepared accounts annually to 31 December and provided depreciation on a straight line basis at a rate of 20 per cent per annum for motor vehicles, apportioned as from the date of purchase and up to the date of disposal.

All instalments were paid on due dates.

The balance on the hire purchase company account in respect of vehicle JY 1 is to be written off.

You are required to record these transactions in the following accounts, carrying down the balances as on 31 December 20X6 and 31 December 20X7:

(a) Motor vehicles

(b) Depreciation

(c) Hire purchase company

(d) Assets disposal.

2.5   On 30 September 20X7, B Wright, who prepares final accounts annually to 30 September, bought a motor lorry on hire purchase from the Vehicles and Finance Co. Ltd. The cash price of the lorry was £3,081. Under the terms of the hire purchase agreement, Wright paid a deposit of £1,000 on 30 September 20X7, and two instalments of £1,199 on 30 September, 20X8 and 20X9. The hire vendor charged interest at 10 per cent per annum on the balance outstanding on 1 October each year. All payments were made on the due dates.

Wright maintained the motor lorry account at cost and accumulated the annual provision for depreciation, at 25 per cent on the diminishing balance method, in a separate account.

Required:
(a) Prepare the following accounts as they would appear in the ledger of B Wright for the period of the contract:
  (i)   Vehicles and Finance Co Ltd
  (ii) Motor lorry on hire purchase
  (iii) Provision for depreciation of motor lorry
  (iv) Hire purchase interest payable
(b) Show how the above matters would appear in the balance sheet of B Wright at 30 September 20X8.

The Vehicles and Finance Co. Ltd prepares final accounts annually to 30 September, on which date it charges B Wright with the interest due.
Make calculations to the nearest £.

2.6   S Craven started business on 1 October 20X5 selling machines of one standard type on hire purchase terms. During the year to 30 September 20X6 he purchased machines at a uniform price of £60 and sold 1,900 machines at a total price under hire purchase agreements of £100 per machine, payable by an initial deposit of £30 and 10 quarterly instalments of £7.

The following trial balance was extracted from Craven's books as at 30 September 20X6.

	£	£
Capital		76,000
Drawings	4,000	
Fixed assets	10,000	
Purchases	120,000	
Cash collected from customers		83,600
Rent, rates and insurance	4,500	
Wages	8,600	
General expenses	10,270	
Balance at bank	10,630	
Sundry trade creditors		8,400
	168,000	168,000

The personal accounts of customers are memorandum records (i.e. they are not part of the double entry system).

Craven prepares his annual accounts on the basis of taking credit for profit (including interest) in proportion to cash collected from customers.

Prepare Craven's hire purchase trading account and a profit and loss account for the year ended 30 September 20X6 and a balance sheet as at that date.

Ignore depreciation of fixed assets.

2.7   RJ commenced business on 1 January 20X8. He sells refrigerators, all of one standard type, on hire purchase terms. The total amount, including interest, payable for each refrigerator, is £300. Customers are required to pay an initial deposit of £60, followed by eight quarterly instalments of £30 each. The cost of each refrigerator to RJ is £200.

The following trial balance was extracted from RJ's books as on 31 December 20X8.

Trial Balance

	£	£
Capital		100,000
Fixed assets	10,000	
Drawings	4,000	
Bank overdraft		19,600
Creditors		16,600
Purchases	180,000	
Cash collected from customers		76,500
Bank interest	400	
Wages and salaries	12,800	
General expenses	5,500	
	£212,700	£212,700

850 machines were sold on hire purchase terms during 20X8.

The annual accounts are prepared on the basis of taking credit for profit (including interest) in proportion to the cash collected from customers.

You are required to prepare the hire purchase trading account, and the profit and loss account for the year 20X8 and balance sheet as on 31 December 20X8.

Ignore depreciation of fixed assets.

Show your calculations.

(*Institute of Chartered Secretaries and Administrators*)

2.8A Object Limited is a retail outlet selling word processing equipment both for cash and on hire purchase terms. The following information has been extracted from the books of account as at 31 August 20X6:

	Dr £	Cr £
Authorised, issued and fully paid share capital		
(ordinary shares of £1 each)		75,000
Administration and shop expenses	130,000	
Cash at bank and in hand	6,208	
Cash received from hire purchase customers		315,468
Cash sales		71,000
Depreciation of premises and equipment (at 1 September 20X5)		45,000
Hire purchase debtors (at 1 September 20X5)	2,268	
Premises and equipment at cost	100,000	
Profit and loss account (at 1 September 20X5)		8,000
Provision for unrealised profit (at 1 September 20X5)		1,008
Purchases	342,000	
Stock (at 1 September 20X5)	15,000	
Trade creditors		80,000
	£595,476	£595,476

Additional information:

1 The company's policy is to take credit for gross profit (including interest) for hire purchase sales in proportion to the instalments collected. It does this by raising a provision against the profit included in hire purchase debtors not yet due.

2 The cash selling price is fixed at 50 per cent and the hire purchase selling price at 80 per cent respectively above the cost of goods purchased.

3 The hire purchase contract requires an initial deposit of 20 per cent of the hire purchase selling price, the balance to be paid in four equal instalments at quarterly intervals. The first instalment is due three months after the agreement is signed.

4 Hire purchase sales for the year amounted to £540,000 (including interest).

5 In February 20X6 the company repossessed some goods which had been sold earlier in the year. These goods had been purchased for £3,000, and the unpaid instalments on them amounted to £3,240. They were then taken back into stock at a value of £2,500. Later on in the year they were sold on cash terms for £3,500.

6 Depreciation is charged on premises and equipment at a rate of 15 per cent per annum on cost.

Required:

Prepare Object Limited's trading, and profit and loss account for the year to 31 August 20X6, and a balance sheet as at that date.

Your workings should be submitted.

(Association of Accounting Technicians)

2.9A On 1 January 20X6, F Limited commenced business selling goods on hire purchase. Under the terms of the agreements, an initial deposit of 20 per cent is payable on delivery, followed by four equal quarterly instalments, the first being due three months after the date of sale. During the year sales were made as follows:

	Cost price	HP sales price
	£	£
10 January	150	225
8 March	350	525
12 May	90	135
6 July	200	300
20 September	70	105
15 October	190	285
21 November	160	240

The goods sold in July were returned in September and eventually sold in November for £187 cash. All other instalments are paid on the due dates.

It may be assumed that:

(a) gross profit and interest are credited to profit and loss account in the proportion that deposits and instalments received bear to hire purchase price, or

(b) the cost is deemed to be paid in full before any credit is taken for gross profit and interest.

You are to prepare for the first year of trading, a hire purchase trading account compiled firstly on assumption (a) and secondly on assumption (b) and give the relevant balance sheet entries under each assumption.

Workings should be clearly shown.

(Chartered Institute of Management Accountants)

2.10A On 1 January 20X7, Carver bought a machine costing £20,000 on hire purchase. He paid a deposit of £6,000 on 1 January 20X7 and he also agreed to pay two annual instalments of £5,828 on 31 December in each year, and a final instalment of £5,831 on 31 December 20X9.

The implied rate of interest in the agreement was 12 per cent. This rate of interest is to be applied to the amount outstanding in the hire purchase loan account as at the beginning of the year.

The machine is to be depreciated on a straight line basis over five years on the assumption that the machine will have no residual value at the end of that time.

Required:

(a) Write up the following accounts for each of the three years to 31 December 20X7, 20X8 and 20X9 respectively:

(i) machine account;

(ii) accumulated depreciation on machine account; and

(iii) hire purchase loan account; and

(b) Show the balance sheet extracts for the year as at 31 December 20X7, 20X8 and 20X9 respectively for the following items:
  (i)   machine at cost;
  (ii) accumulated depreciation on the machine;
  (iii) long-term liabilities: obligations under hire purchase contract; and
  (iv) current liabilities: obligations under hire purchase contract.

(Association of Accounting Technicians)

2.11   Dundas Limited purchased a machine under a hire purchase agreement on 1 January 20X8. The agreement provided for an immediate payment of £2,000, followed by five equal instalments of £3,056, each instalment to be paid on 30 June and 31 December respectively.

The cash price of the machine was £10,000. Dundas estimated that it would have a useful economic life of five years, and its residual value would then be £1,000.

In apportioning interest to respective accounting periods, the company uses the 'sum of digits'[Note] method.

Required:
(a) Write up the following ledger accounts for each of the three years to 31 December 20X8, 20X9 and 20X0 respectively:
  (i)   machine hire purchase loan account; and
  (ii) machine hire purchase interest account; and
(b) Show the following balance sheet extracts relating to the machine as at 31 December 20X8, 20X9 and 20X0 respectively:
  (i)   fixed assets: machine at net book value;
  (ii) creditors: amounts payable within one year – obligation under hire purchase contract; and
  (iii) creditors: amounts falling due after more than one year – obligation under hire purchase contract.

Authors' note – Sum of digits
This is very similar to the 'rule of 78', explained on pp. 627–8. It is explained in detail on p. 425 in the ninth edition of *Business Accounting 1*. In brief, if a machine is expected to last 4 years, you write off the cost by weighting year 1 as 4, year 2 as 3, year 3 as 2 and year 4 as 1. The total of these weights is used as the denominator. Thus, year 1 depreciation would be 4/10 of the amount to be written off; year 2 would be 3/10, year 3 would be 2/10 and year 4 would be 1/10.

(Association of Accounting Technicians)

PART 2

Companies

Introduction

This part is concerned with the accounts and financial statements of limited
companies. It considers how various accounting transactions should be
entered in the books and how the financial statements should be presented,
including the requirements of the Companies Acts and of accounting standards.

CHAPTER 3

Limited companies: general background

Learning objectives

After you have studied this chapter, you should be able to:

- explain the legal nature of limited companies
- explain the importance of the concept of limited liability
- describe the statutory framework governing limited companies
- describe some of the major characteristics of limited companies
- explain the difference between the Memorandum of Association and the Articles of Association

Introduction

In this chapter you'll learn about the legislation that governs how companies are formed and lays out the rules within which companies operate. You'll learn about the importance of limited liability and of the relationship between companies, their shares and the stock exchange.

3.1 Preliminary study

An introduction was made to the financial statements of limited companies in *Business Accounting 1*. It was intended to show some of the basic outlines of the financial statements of limited companies to those people who would be finishing their studies of accounting with the completion of *Business Accounting 1*. This volume now carries the study of limited companies accounting to a more advanced stage.

3.2 The Companies Acts

The Acts of Parliament now governing limited companies are the Companies Acts 1985 and 1989. The 1989 Act both adds to and amends the 1985 Act, so that both Acts have to be read together. In this volume we cannot deal with many of the complicated issues arising from the Companies Acts. These are better left until readers have reached a more advanced stage in their studies.

The Companies Acts are the descendants of modern limited liability company legislation which can be traced back to the passing of the Companies Act 1862. This Act was a triumph for the development of the limited liability principle which had been severely restricted since the 'Bubble Act' of 1720, this latter Act being the remedy for a multitude of spectacular frauds perpetrated behind the cloak of limited liability. Not until 1862 was general prejudice overcome, and the way paved for the general use of the limited liability principle which is

now commonplace. Company law therefore consists of the Companies Acts 1985 and 1989, together with a considerable body of case law which has been built up over the years. It must be borne in mind that there are still a number of chartered companies in existence which were incorporated by Royal Charter, such as the Hudson's Bay Company, or else which were formed by special Acts of Parliament.

3.3   Changes in company law

Company law has changed considerably since the mid-1960s. This has been brought about because of the obligation to observe the company law directives issued by the Council of the European Community. Such changes do not eliminate completely the differences in company law throughout the European Union, but they have considerably reduced such differences and have provided minimum standards to be observed.

The 1985 and 1989 Companies Acts lay down detailed rules of the format of the final accounts of limited companies. These will be considered later.

Banks and insurance companies do not come under the same legislation as that for other companies. A separate part of the 1989 Act deals with banks, while insurance companies are the subject of a special directive.

3.4   Other forms of company

The Companies Acts also cover companies with unlimited liability. These are now rarely met in practice. Also covered are companies limited by guarantee, which may or may not have a share capital, but the Companies Act 1985 forbids the future formation of such companies, if they have a share capital. Both of these types of limited company are relatively unimportant, and therefore any future reference to a limited company or merely a company will be concerned with limited liability companies of the normal type.

3.5   Separate legal entity

The outstanding feature of a **limited company** is that, no matter how many individuals have bought shares in it, it is treated in its dealings with the outside world as if it were a person in its own right: it is said to be a separate 'legal entity'. Just as the law can create this separate legal person, then so also can it eliminate it, but its existence can only be terminated by using the proper legal procedures. Thus the identity of the shareholders in a large concern may be changing daily as shares are bought and sold by different people.

On the other hand, a small private company may have the same shareholders from when it is incorporated (the day it legally came into being), until the date when liquidation is completed (the cessation of the company, often known also as 'winding up' or being 'wound up'). A prime example of its identity as a separate legal entity is that it may sue other business entities, people – even its own shareholders – or, in turn, be sued by them.

> *Activity 3.1*
> Why would it be advantageous for a company to be able to sue other business entities, rather than for the directors or an employee to do so?

The legal formalities by which the company comes into existence can be gleaned from any textbook on company law. It is not the purpose of this book to discuss company law in

any great detail; this is far better left to a later stage of one's studies. As companies must, however, comply with the law, the essential company law concerning accounting matters will be dealt with in this book as far as is necessary.

What is important is that the basic principles connected with company accounts can be seen in operation. In order that the student may not be unduly confused, points which rarely occur, or on which the legal arguments are extremely involved and may not yet have been finally settled, will be left out completely or merely mentioned in passing. This means that some generalisations will bear closer scrutiny when your accounting studies reach a more advanced stage.

3.6 Memorandum and Articles of Association

Each company is governed by two documents, known as the **Memorandum of Association** and the **Articles of Association**, generally referred to as the *memorandum* and the *articles*. The memorandum consists of five clauses for private companies, and six for public companies, which contain the following details:

1 The name of the company.
2 The part of the UK where the registered office will be situated.
3 The objects of the company.
4 A statement (if a limited liability company) that the liability of its members is limited.
5 Details of the share capital which the company is authorised to issue.
6 A public limited company will also have a clause stating that the company is a public limited company.

The memorandum is said to be the document which discloses the conditions which govern the company's relationship with the outside world.

3.7 Limited liability

The principle of limited liability underlying clause 4 has been of the utmost importance in industry and commerce. It is inconceivable that large business units, such as Imperial Chemical Industries Ltd or Great Universal Stores Ltd, could have existed except for a very few instances. The investor in a limited company, who therefore buys shares in it, is a shareholder. The most he can lose is the money he has paid for the shares, or, where he has only partly paid for them, then he is also liable for the unpaid part in addition. With public companies, whose shares are traded on a stock exchange, he can easily sell them whenever he so wishes. The sale of a share in a private company is not so easily effected.

Activity 3.2
Why is it unlikely that many large companies could have existed if limited liability did not exist?

3.8 Classes of shares

The main classes of shares are **ordinary shares** and **preference shares**. Unless clearly stated in the Memorandum or Articles of Association, preference shares are assumed to be of the cumulative variety already described in Volume 1.

There are also a variety of other shares. The rights attaching to these shares are purely dependent on the skill and ingenuity of the draftsperson of the Memorandum and Articles of Association. An entirely new type of share may be created provided it does not contravene the law.

The shares which carry the right to the whole of the profits remaining after the preference shares (and any other fixed dividend shares) have been paid a dividend are often known as the equity share capital or as **equities**.

Until 1981 the only type of share which could be bought back from the shareholders by the company itself were redeemable preference shares. This has changed completely, and is considered in detail in Chapter 5.

3.9 Distributable profits

In *Business Accounting 1*, the calculation of dividends from profits available for distribution was described. This means that there should be some way of knowing what **distributable profits** are.

In the Companies Acts there is a definition of **realised profits** and **realised losses**. This definition also applies for the purpose of calculating a company's distributable profits. A company's realised profits and losses are defined as 'those profits and losses which are treated as realised in the financial statements, in accordance with principles generally accepted with respect to the determination of realised profits and losses for accounting purposes at the time when those accounts are prepared'. In accounting, the realisation concept recognises profit or loss at the point when a contract is made in the market to buy or sell assets.

3.10 Table A

Besides the Memorandum of Association, every company must also have Articles of Association. Just as the memorandum governs the company's dealings with the outside world, the articles govern the relationships which exist between the members and the company, between one member and the other members, and other necessary regulations. The Companies Act has a model set of articles known as Table A. A company may, if it so wishes, have its articles exactly the same as Table A, commonly known as 'adopting Table A', or else adopt part of it and have some sections altered. The adoption of the major part of Table A is normal for most private companies. In accounting textbooks, unless stated to the contrary, the accounting examples shown are usually on the basis that Table A has been adopted.

Table A lays down regulations concerning the powers of the directors of the company. On the other hand, the company may draft its own regulations for the powers of directors. Any such regulations are of the utmost importance when it is realised that the legal owners of the business, the shareholders, have entrusted the running of the company to the directors. The shareholders' own rights are largely limited to attending annual general meetings and having voting rights thereat, although some shares do not carry voting rights. The Companies Acts make the keeping of proper sets of accounting records and the preparation of Final Accounts (financial statements) compulsory for every company. In addition the financial statements must be audited, this being quite different from the situation in a partnership or a sole trader's business where an audit is not compulsory at all.

Companies having limited liability, whether they are private or public companies, have to send a copy of their Final Accounts, drawn up in a prescribed manner, to the Registrar of Companies. Public companies must submit accounts within seven months of their financial year end; private companies within ten months of their year end. Chapters 12–14 are concerned with stating the accounting requirements of the Companies Acts.

3.11   Public companies and the stock exchange

The shares of most of the public companies are dealt in on one or other of the recognised stock exchanges. The shares of private companies cannot be bought and sold on any stock exchange, as this would contravene the requirements for the company being recognised as a 'private' company. The sales and purchases of shares on the stock exchanges have no effect on the accounting entries made in the company's books. The only entry made in the company's books when a shareholder sells all, or some, of his shares to someone else, is to record the change of identity of the shareholders. The price at which the shares were sold on the stock exchange is not entered into the company's books.

Although no accounting entries are made, the price of the shares on the stock exchange does have repercussions upon the financial policy of the company.

> ### Activity 3.3
> Why?

It must be recognised that the stock exchanges are the 'second-hand market' for a company's shares. The company does not actually sell (normally called **issue**) its shares by using the stock exchange as a selling place. The company issues new shares directly to the people who make application to it for the shares at the time when the company has shares available for issue. The company does not sell to, or buy from, the stock exchanges. This means that the shares of a public company sold and bought on stock exchanges are passing from one shareholder to another person who will then become a shareholder. Apart from the effect upon the financial policies of the firm, the double entry accounts of the company are not affected.

3.12   Stocks and shares

Later in this book you are shown the procedure whereby the shares of a company may be made into **stock**. Thus 500 ordinary shares of £1 each may be made into £500 stock. The dividends paid on the shares or the stock would be the same, and the voting powers would also be the same. Apart from administrative convenience there is really no difference between shares and stock.

Learning outcomes

You should now have learnt:

1 Limited companies are governed by the Companies Acts.

2 Limited companies are each a separate legal entity.

3 Each company is governed by two documents:
   (a) the Memorandum of Association, and
   (b) the Articles of Association.

4 What is meant by 'limited liability'.

5 Investors in limited companies can only lose the amount they paid (plus any amount still unpaid if the shares are only part-paid) when they acquired their investment in the company, i.e. they have 'limited liability'.

Answers to activities

3.1 If a director sued another business entity on behalf of a company, the director would be liable for any legal costs incurred were the case unsuccessful. Perhaps more meaningfully, if companies could not be sued, directors and employees could be exposed to the risk of being sued for actions taken by the company, even when they were not personally involved in what had occurred. In effect, granting companies a legal identity separate from their owners makes it possible to operate limited liability effectively.

3.2 Without limited liability, investors would be very unwilling to buy shares in companies. They would fear that they may lose everything they owned if the company failed. Companies would, therefore, find it very difficult to raise funds other than from banks and other financial institutions. Such finds would carry interest costs that would have to be paid irrespective of how well the companies were doing. In the early years of a new business, it can take quite a long time to become profitable and the reliance upon loan funding would increase the possibility that the company will fail. As a result, in an economic environment where there was no limited liability, the investors in the failed company could lose everything they own. It is unlikely that many would be willing to take this risk. Hence, it is unlikely that many large companies would exist were it not for limited liability.

3.3 If some new shares are to be issued, the price they are to be issued at will be largely dependent on the stock exchange valuation. If another firm is to be taken over by the company, part of the purchase price being paid using some of the company's shares, then the stock exchange value will also affect the value placed upon the shares being given. A takeover bid from another firm may well be caused because the stock exchange value of the shares has made a takeover seem worthwhile.

CHAPTER 4

The issue of shares and debentures

Learning objectives

After you have studied this chapter, you should be able to:
- explain the terminology relating to the issue of shares and debentures
- describe the steps in the process of issuing of shares and debentures
- record the accounting entries relating to the issue of shares and debentures
- make the necessary entries in the ledger accounts when shares are forfeited

Introduction

In this chapter you'll learn about the alternatives available to companies when they wish to issue shares and of the various entries to be made in the ledger accounts. You'll learn about how to issue shares at a premium and how to issue shares to existing holders of shares, rather than to non-shareholders wishing to purchase them. You will also learn about the difference in accounting entries made when debentures, rather than shares, are issued.

4.1 The issue of shares

In the case of public companies, a new issue of shares can be very costly indeed, and the number of shares issued must be sufficient to make the cost worthwhile. However, for simplicity, so that the principles are not obscured by the difficulties of grappling with large amounts, the numbers of shares shown as issued in the illustrations that follow will be quite small.

Shares can be issued being payable for (*a*) immediately on application, or (*b*) by instalments. The first instances will be of shares being paid for immediately. Issues of shares may take place on the following terms connected with the price of the shares:

1 Shares issued at par. This would mean that a share of £1 nominal value would be issued for £1 each.
2 Shares issued at a premium. In this case a share of £1 nominal value would be issued for more than £1 each, say for £3 each.
3 At one time, shares could be issued at a discount. Thus, shares each of £5 nominal value might have been issued for £3 each. However, this is no longer permitted, having been expressly forbidden in the Companies Act 1980.

Activity 4.1
Why do you think companies may wish to issue shares at a discount and how do you think companies avoid being in this position?

4.2   Share premiums and discounts

This will all seem rather strange at first. How can a £1 share, which states that value on the face of it, be issued for £3 each, and who would be foolish enough to buy it? The reasons for this apparently strange state of affairs stem from the Companies Act requirement that the share capital accounts always show shares at their nominal value, irrespective of how much the shares are worth or how much they are issued for. To illustrate this, the progress of two firms, firm A and firm B, can be looked at. Both firms started in business on 1 January 20X1 and issued 1,000 ordinary shares each of £4 nominal value at par. Ignoring any issue expenses, the balance sheets on that date would appear:

Firms A Ltd and B Ltd
Balance Sheet as at 1 January 20X1

	£
Bank	4,000
Capital	4,000

Five years later, on 31 December 20X5, the balance sheets show that the companies have fared quite differently. It is to be assumed here, for purposes of illustration, that the balance sheet values and any other interpretation of values happen to be identical.

A Ltd needs £4,000 capital, and this is to be met by issuing more ordinary shares. Suppose that another 1,000 ordinary shares of £4 nominal value each are issued at par. Column (*a*) below shows the balance sheet before the issue, and column (*b*) shows the balance sheet after the issue has taken place.

A Ltd Balance Sheets (Solution 1) as at 31 December 20X5

	(a) £	(b) £
Fixed and current assets (other than bank)	9,000	9,000
Bank	1,000	5,000
	10,000	14,000
Financed by:		
Ordinary share capital	4,000	8,000
Profit and loss	6,000	6,000
	10,000	14,000

Now the effect of what has happened can be appreciated. Before the new issue there were 1,000 shares. As there were £10,000 of assets and no liabilities, then each share was worth £10. After the issue there are 2,000 shares and £14,000 of assets, so that now each share is worth £7. This would be extremely disconcerting to the original shareholders who see the value of each of their shares fall immediately by £3.

On the other hand, the new shareholder who has just bought shares for £4 each sees them rise immediately to be worth £7 each. Only in one specific case would this be just, and that is where each original shareholder buys an equivalent number of new shares. Otherwise this obviously cannot be the correct solution. What is required is a price which is equitable as far as the interests of the old shareholders are concerned, and yet will attract sufficient applications to provide the capital required. As in this case the balance sheet value and the real value are the same, the answer is that each old share was worth £10 and therefore each new share should be issued for £10 each. The balance sheets will now appear:

A Ltd Balance Sheets (Solution 2) as at 31 December 20X5

	(a) £	(b) £
Fixed and current assets (other than bank)	9,000	9,000
Bank	1,000	11,000
	10,000	20,000
Financed by:		
Ordinary share capital (at nominal value)	4,000	8,000
Share premium (*see* note below)		6,000
Profit and loss	6,000	6,000
	10,000	20,000

Thus in (*a*) above, 1,000 shares own between them £10,000 of assets = £10 each, while in (*b*) 2,000 shares are shown as owning £20,000 of assets = £10 each. Both the old and new shareholders are therefore satisfied with the bargain that has been made.

Note: The share premium shown on the capital side of the balance sheet is needed (ignoring for a moment the legal requirements to be complied with in company balance sheets) simply because the balance sheet would not balance without it. If shares are stated at nominal value but issued at another price, the actual amount received increases the bank balance, but the share capital shown is increased by a different figure. The share premium therefore represents the excess of the cash received over the nominal value of the shares issued.

The other, B Ltd, has not fared so well. It has, in fact, lost money. The accumulated losses are reflected in a debit balance on the profit and loss appropriation account as shown in the following balance sheet at (*c*). It can be seen that there are £3,000 of assets to represent the shareholders' stake in the firm of 1,000 shares, i.e. each share is worth £3 each. If more capital was needed, 1,000 more shares could be issued. From the action taken in the previous case it will now be obvious that each new share of £4 nominal value would be issued for its real value of £3 each, were it permitted to do so. The balance sheets would appear:

B Ltd Balance Sheets (correct solution) as at 31 December 20X5

	(c)	(d)
Fixed and current assets (other than bank)	2,000	2,000
Bank	1,000	4,000
	3,000	6,000
Ordinary share capital	4,000	8,000
Discounts on shares (*see* below)		(1,000)
Profit and loss – debit balance	(1,000)	(1,000)
	3,000	6,000

Once again, as the share capital is shown at nominal value, but the shares are issued at a different figure, the difference being discounts on shares must be shown in order that the balance sheet may balance. It is, of course, a balancing figure needed because the entries already made for an increase in the ordinary share capital and the increase in the bank balance have been at different figures. The figure for discounts on shares therefore rectifies the double entry 'error'.

Although shares cannot now be issued at a discount, there will very occasionally still be items in company balance sheets for discounts on shares issued before 1980. Although not listed as an item in the balance sheet formats per the Companies Act 1985, a separate heading will have to be inserted to accommodate the item.

For the purpose of making the foregoing explanations easier it was assumed that balance sheet values and other values were the same. This is rarely true for all the assets, and in fact

there is more than one other 'value'. A balance sheet is a historical view of the past based on records made according to the firm's interpretation and use of accounting concepts and conventions. When shares are being issued it is not the view of the past that is important, but the view of the future. Therefore the actual premiums and discounts on shares being issued are a matter not merely of balance sheet values, but of the issuing company's view of the future and its estimate of how the investing public will react to the price at which the shares are being offered.

It is to be noted that there are no restrictions on issuing shares at par or at a premium. The actual double entry accounts can be seen in the next section.

4.3 Shares payable in full on application

The issue of shares in illustrations (1), (2) and (3) which follow are based on the balance sheets that have just been considered.

1 Shares issued at par

One thousand ordinary shares with a nominal value of £4 each are to be issued. Applications, together with the necessary money, are received for exactly 1,000 shares. The shares are then allotted to the applicants.

Bank

		£	
Ordinary share applicants	(A)	4,000	

Ordinary Share Applicants

		£			£
Ordinary share capital	(B)	4,000	Bank	(A)	4,000

Ordinary Share Capital

			£
	Ordinary share applicants	(B)	4,000

It may appear that the ordinary share applicants account is unnecessary, and that the only entries needed are a debit in the bank account and a credit in the ordinary share capital account. However, applicants do not always become shareholders; this is shown later. The applicant must make an offer for the shares being issued, accompanied by the necessary money: this is the application. After the applications have been vetted the allotments of shares are made by the company. This represents the acceptance of the offer by the company and it is at this point that the applicant becomes a shareholder. Therefore (A) represents the offer by the applicant, while (B) is the acceptance by the company. No entry must therefore be made in the share capital account until (B) happens, for it is not until that point that the share capital is in existence. The share applicants account is therefore an intermediary account pending allotments being made.

2 Shares issued at a premium

One thousand ordinary shares with a nominal value of £4 each are to be issued for £10 each (*see* A Ltd previously). Thus a premium of £6 per share has been charged. Applications and the money are received for exactly 1,000 shares.

Bank

	£		
Balance b/d	1,000		
Ordinary share applicants	10,000		

Ordinary Share Applicants

		£			£
Ordinary share capital	(A)	4,000	Bank		10,000
Share premium	(B)	6,000			
		10,000			10,000

Share Premium

			£
	Ordinary share applicants	(B)	6,000

Ordinary Share Capital (A Ltd)

			£
	Balance b/d		4,000
	Ordinary share applicants	(A)	4,000

Note: (A) is shown as £4,000 because the share capital is shown at nominal value and not as total issued value. The £6,000 share premiums (B) must therefore be credited to a share premium account to preserve double entry balancing.

3 Shares issued at a discount (prior to 1980)

One thousand ordinary shares with a nominal value of £4 each are to be issued for £3 each (*see* B Ltd previously). Thus a discount of £1 per share is being allowed. Applications and the money are received for exactly 1,000 shares.

Bank

	£		
Balance b/d	1,000		
Ordinary share applicants	3,000		

Ordinary Share Applicants

	£		£
Ordinary share capital	4,000	Bank	3,000
		Discounts on shares	1,000
	4,000		4,000

Ordinary Share Capital

		£
	Balance b/d	4,000
	Ordinary share capital	4,000

Discounts on Shares

	£		
Ordinary share applications	1,000		

4 Oversubscription and undersubscription for shares

When a public company invites investors to apply for its shares it is obviously rare indeed if applications for shares equal exactly the number of shares to be issued. Where more shares

are applied for than are available for issue, then the issue is said to be **oversubscribed**. Where fewer shares are applied for than are available for issue, then the issue has been **undersubscribed**.

With a new company, a minimum amount is fixed as being necessary to carry on any further with the running of the company. If the applications are less than the minimum stated, then the application monies must be returned to the senders. This does not apply to an established company. If, therefore, 1,000 shares of £1 each are available for issue, but only 875 shares are applied for, then only 875 will be issued, assuming that this is above the fixed minimum figure. The accounting entries will be in respect of 875 shares, no entries being needed for the 125 shares not applied for, as this part does not represent a transaction.

The opposite of this is where the shares are oversubscribed. In this case, some sort of rationing is applied so that the issue is restricted to the shares available for issue. The process of selecting who will get how many shares depends on the policy of the firm. Some firms favour large shareholders because this leads to lower administrative costs.

Why the costs will be lower will be obvious if the cost of calling a meeting of two companies each with 20,000 shares is considered. H Ltd has 20 shareholders with an average holding of 1,000 shares each. J Ltd has 1,000 shareholders with an average holding of 20 shares each. They all have to be notified by post and given various documents including a set of the final accounts. The cost of printing and sending these is less for H Ltd with 20 shareholders than for J Ltd with 1,000 shareholders. This is only one example of the costs involved, but it will also apply with equal force to many items connected with the shares. Conversely, the directors may prefer to have more shareholders with smaller holdings, one reason being that it decreases the amount of voting power in any one individual's hands.

The actual process of rationing the shares is then a simple matter once a policy has been agreed. It may consist of scaling down applications, of drawing lots or some other chance selection, but it will eventually bring the number of shares to be issued down to the number of shares available. Excess application monies will then be refunded by the company.

An issue of shares where 1,000 ordinary shares of £1 nominal value each are to be issued at par payable in full, but 1,550 shares are applied for, will appear as follows:

Bank

	£		£
Ordinary share applicants	1,550	Ordinary share applicants (refunds)	550

Ordinary Share Applicants

	£		£
Bank	550	Bank	1,550
Ordinary share capital	1,000		
	1,550		1,550

Ordinary Share Capital

		£
	Ordinary share applicants	1,000

4.4 Issue of shares payable by instalments

The shares considered so far have all been issued as paid in full on application. Conversely, many issues are made which require payment by instalments. These are probably more common with public companies than with private companies. It should be noted that a public company is now not allowed to allot a share unless there has been paid on it a sum equal to at least one-quarter of its nominal value plus the whole of any premium.

The various stages, after the initial invitation has been made to the public to buy shares by means of advertisements (if it is a public company) etc. are as follows:

(A) Applications are received together with the application monies.
(B) The applications are vetted and the shares allotted, letters of allotment being sent out.
(C) The excess application monies from wholly unsuccessful applicants, or, where the application monies received exceed both the application and allotment monies required, from wholly and partly unsuccessful applicants, are returned to them. Usually, if a person has been partly unsuccessful, his excess application monies are held by the company and will reduce the amount needed to be paid by him on allotment.
(D) Allotment monies are received.
(E) The next instalment, known as the first call, is requested.
(F) The monies are received from the first call.
(G) The next instalment, known as the second call, is requested.
(H) The monies are received from the second call.

This carries on until the full number of calls have been made, although there is not usually a large number of calls to be made in an issue.

The reasons for the payments by instalments become obvious if it is realised that a company will not necessarily require the immediate use of all the money to be raised by the issue. Suppose a new company is to be formed: it is to buy land, erect a factory, equip it with machinery and then go into production. This might take two years altogether. If the total sum needed was £1,000,000 the allocation of this money could be:

Ordinary Share Capital

	£
Cost of land, payable within 1 month	300,000
Cost of buildings, payable in 1 year's time	200,000
Cost of machinery, payable in 18 months' time	200,000
Working capital required in 2 years' time	300,000
	1,000,000

The issue may therefore well be on the following terms:

	Per cent
Application money per share, payable immediately	10
Allotment money per share, payable within 1 month	20
First call, money payable in 12 months' time	20
Second call, money payable in 18 months' time	20
Third call, money payable in 24 months' time	30
	100

The entries made in the share capital account should equal the amount of money requested to that point in time. However, instead of one share applicants account, this is usually split into several accounts to represent the different instalments. For this purpose application and allotment are usually joined together in one account, the *application and allotment account*, as this cuts out the need for transfers where excess *application monies* are held over and set off against allotment monies needed. When allotment is made, and not until then, an entry of £300,000 (10 per cent + 20 per cent) would be made in the share capital account. On the first call an entry of £200,000 would be made in the share capital account; likewise £200,000 on the second call and £300,000 on the third call. The share capital account will therefore contain not the monies received, but the amount of money requested. Exhibit 4.1 now shows an instance of a share issue.

Exhibit 4.1

A company is issuing 1,000 7 per cent preference shares of £1 each, payable 10 per cent on application, 20 per cent on allotment, 40 per cent on the first call and 30 per cent on the second call. Applications are received for 1,550 shares. A refund of the money is made in respect of 50 shares, while for the remaining 1,500 applied for, an allotment is to be made on the basis of 2 shares for every 3 applied for (assume that this will not involve any fractions of shares). The excess application monies are set off against the allotment monies asked for. The remaining requested instalments are all paid in full. The letters by the side of each entry refer to the various stages outlined earlier.

Bank

		£			£
Application and allotment:			Application and allotment refund	(C)	5
Application monies	(A)	155			
Allotment monies					
(£1,000 × 20% *less* excess					
application monies £50)	(D)	150			
First call	(F)	400			
Second call	(H)	300			

Application and Allotment

		£			£
Bank – refund of application monies	(C)	5	Bank	(A)	155
Preference share capital	(B)	300	Bank	(D)	150
		305			305

First Call

		£			£
Preference share capital	(E)	400	Bank	(F)	400

Second Call

		£			£
Preference share capital	(G)	300	Bank	(H)	300

7 per cent Preference Share Capital

	£			£
		Application and allotment	(B)	300
		First call	(E)	400
Balance c/d	1,000	Second call	(G)	300
	1,000			1,000
		Balance b/d		1,000

If more than one type of share is being issued at the same time, e.g. preference shares and ordinary shares, then separate share capital accounts and separate application and allotment accounts and call accounts should be opened.

4.5 Forfeited shares

Sometimes, although it is probably fairly rare in recent times, a shareholder fails to pay the calls requested from him. The Articles of Association of the company will probably provide that the shareholder will have his shares forfeited, provided that certain safeguards for his protection are fully observed. In this case the shares will be cancelled, and the instalments already paid by the shareholder will be lost to him.

After the forfeiture, the company may reissue the shares, unless there is a provision in the Articles of Association to prevent it. There are certain conditions as to the prices at which the shares can be reissued. These are that the amount received on reissue plus the amount received from the original shareholder should at least equal (*a*) the called-up value where the shares are not fully called up, or (*b*) the nominal value where the full amount has been called up. Any premium previously paid is disregarded in determining the minimum reissue price.

Exhibit 4.2

Take the same information as that contained in Exhibit 4.1, but instead of all the calls being paid, Allen, the holder of 100 shares, fails to pay the first and second calls. He had already paid the application and allotment monies on the required dates. The directors conform to the provisions of the Articles of Association and (A) Allen is forced to suffer the forfeiture of his shares. (B) The amount still outstanding from Allen will be written off. (C) The directors then reissue the shares at 75 per cent of nominal value to J. Dougan. (D) Dougan pays for the shares.

First Call

		£				£
Preference share capital		400	Bank			360
			Forfeited shares	(B)		40
		400				400

Second Call

		£				£
Preference share capital		300	Bank			270
			Forfeited shares	(B)		30
		300				300

7 per cent Preference Share Capital

		£			£
Forfeited shares	(A)	100	Application and allotment		300
Balance c/d		900	First call		400
			Second call		300
		1,000			1,000
			Balance b/d		900
Balance c/d		1,000	J. Dougan	(C)	100
		1,000			1,000
			Balance b/d		1,000

Forfeited Shares

		£			£
First call	(B)	40	Preference share capital	(A)	100
Second call	(B)	30			
Balance c/d		30			
		100			100
J. Dougan[Note]		25	Balance b/d		30
Balance c/d		5			
		30			30

Bank

		£	
First call (£900 × 40%)		360	
Second call (£900 × 30%)		270	
J. Dougan	(D)	75	

J. Dougan

	£			£
Preference share capital	100	Bank	(D)	75
		Forfeited shares (discount on reissue)[Note]		25
	100			100

Note: The transfer of £25 from the forfeited shares account to J. Dougan's account is needed because the reissue was entered in the preference share capital account and Dougan's account at nominal value, i.e. following standard practice by which a share capital account is concerned with nominal values. But Dougan was not to pay the full nominal price. Therefore the transfer of £25 is needed to close his account.

Activity 4.2

Why do you think companies make new share issues?
[Note: these are not the same as the shares issued when a company is first formed.]

The balance of £5 on the forfeited shares account can be seen to be: cash received from original shareholder on application and allotment £30 + from Dougan £75 = £105. This is £5 over the nominal value so that the £5 appears as a credit balance. This may be stated to be transferred to a profit on reissue of forfeited shares account, but it really cannot be thought that this is followed in practice for small amounts. More normally it would be transferred to the credit of a share premium account.

4.6 Calls in advance and in arrear and the balance sheet

At the balance sheet date some shareholders will not have paid all the calls made. These are collectively known as **calls in arrear**. On the other hand, some shareholders may have paid amounts in respect of calls not made by the balance sheet date. These are **calls in advance**.

Calls in arrear, i.e. **called-up share capital not paid**, is to be shown in the balance sheet in one of the positions shown in the format per the Companies Act 1985 (*see* Chapter 12). There is no specified place for calls in advance, so this will be inserted in the balance sheet as an extra heading.

4.7 Rights issues

The costs of making a new issue of shares can be quite high. A way to reduce the costs of raising new long-term capital in the form of issuing shares may be by way of a **rights issue**. To do this the company contacts the existing shareholders, and informs them of the new issue to be made and the number of shares which each one of them is entitled to buy of the new issue. In most cases the shareholder is allowed to renounce his rights to the new shares in favour of someone else. The issue is usually pitched at a price which will make the rights capable of being sold, i.e. if the existing shareholder does not want the shares he can renounce them to A who will give him £x for the right to apply for the shares in his place, a right that A could not otherwise obtain. If any shareholder does not either buy the shares or transfer his rights, then the directors will usually have the power to dispose of such shares not taken up by issuing them in some other way.

4.8 Debentures

A **debenture** is a bond acknowledging a loan to a company. It is usually under the company's seal and bears a fixed rate of interest. Unlike shares, which normally depend on profits out of which to appropriate dividends, debenture interest is payable whether profits are made or not.

A debenture may be redeemable, i.e. repayable at or by a specified date. Conversely it may be irredeemable, redemption taking place only when the company is eventually liquidated, or in a case such as when the debenture interest is not paid within a given time limit.

People lending money to companies in the form of debentures will obviously be interested in how safe their investment will be. In the case of some debentures, the debenture holders are given the legal right that on certain happenings they will be able to take control of specific assets, or of the whole of the assets. They can then sell the assets and recoup the amount due under their debentures, or deal with the assets in ways specified in the deed under which the debentures were issued. Such debentures are known as being secured against the assets, the term **mortgage debenture** often being used. Other debentures carry no prior right to control the assets under any circumstances. These are known as **simple** or **naked debentures**.

Activity 4.3

Why do you think companies issue debentures rather than making a new share issue?

4.9 The issue of debentures

The entries for the issue of debentures are similar to those for shares. It would, however, certainly not be the normal modern practice to issue debentures at a premium. If the word 'debentures' appears instead of 'share capital', then the entries in the ledger accounts would be identical.

4.10 Shares of no par value

It can be seen that the idea of a fixed par value for a share can be very misleading. For anyone who has not studied accounting, it may well come as a shock to find that a share with a par value of £1 might in fact be issued for £5. If the share is dealt in on the stock exchange they might find a £1 share selling at £10 or even £20, or equally well it may sell for only 10p.

Another disadvantage of a par value is that it can give people entirely the wrong impression of the activities of a business. If a par value is kept to, and the dividend based on that, then with a certain degree of inflation the dividend figure can look excessive. Many trade union leaders would howl with disapproval if a dividend of 100 per cent were declared by a company. But is this so excessive? Exhibit 4.3 gives a rather different picture.

Exhibit 4.3

Allen bought a share 40 years ago for £1. At the time, he was satisfied with a return of 5 per cent on his money. With a 5 per cent dividend he could buy a certain amount of goods which will be called x. Forty years later to buy that same amount of goods, x, he would need, say, 20 times as much money. Previously £5 would have bought x, now it would take £100. To keep his dividend at

the same level of purchasing power he would need a dividend now of 100 per cent, as compared with the 5 per cent he was receiving 40 years ago.

In the USA, Canada, and Belgium, as well as other countries, no par value is attached to shares being issued. A share is issued at whatever price is suitable at the time, and the money received is credited to a share capital account.

Activity 4.4
Why do you think companies are not allowed to issue shares at no par value in the UK?

Learning outcomes

You should now have learnt:

1 Shares may be issued either:
  (*a*) at par, or nominal value – i.e. a £1 ordinary share would be issued in exchange for payment of £1, or
  (*b*) at a premium, i.e. if a £1 ordinary share were issued at a premium of 25p, it would cost the buyer £1.25 (and the 25p would be put into the issuing company's *share premium* account).

2 How to make the accounting entries when shares are issued.

3 How to make the accounting entries when shares are forfeited.

4 How to make the accounting entries when debentures are issued.

5 The accounting entries made on the issue of debentures are identical to the accounting entries made on the issue of shares though, obviously, debenture ledger accounts are used rather than share capital ledger accounts.

Answers to activities

4.1 If a company is not performing very well and its share price had fallen below its nominal value, it would find it very difficult to issue shares at par or above. Hence, it may wish to issue shares at a discount. As they are prohibited from doing so, it is common nowadays for shares to be issued in the first instance at a price considerably in excess of their nominal value. This makes the likelihood of companies ever being in a position where they would wish to issue shares at a discount extremely rare. In effect, by adopting very low nominal values for the shares, companies overcome the restriction on their being able to issue shares at a discount.

4.2 Companies normally make new share issues in order to obtain funds or in order to use the new shares to purchase another business entity.

4.3 Issuing shares may not be appropriate because the current share price is low and it is felt that issuing new shares at this time will enable investors to buy into the company too cheaply. That is, when the share price rises, the new investors will make substantial profits on their investment. A company may prefer to wait until the share price is higher before selling new shares. It may also be the case that the share price is low because investors do not feel that the company is a good buy at present. Selling new shares may be difficult. Debentures do not involve transference of rights of ownership. Buyers of debentures receive interest, rather than a share of profit. If the company feels its profits are going to grow, it may prefer to issue debentures so that existing shareholders receive the maximum long-term benefit of their investment in the company. That is, their share of future profits is not diluted by the issue of new shares.

4.4 When shares are issued at a premium, the excess above the nominal value is put into a reserve (the share premium account). Such a reserve can, in certain circumstances, be distributed or

utilised. Doing so has no effect upon the share capital account. If shares are issued with no nominal value, share capital in the balance sheet would represent the total amount received by a company when it issued shares. The share premium account would no longer be readily identifiable. In fact, it would not and could not exist (as no notion of par value would exist). By requiring shares to have a nominal value, additional flexibility is granted to the company in how it uses the funds received when it issued shares.

REVIEW QUESTIONS

4.1 A limited company has a nominal capital of £120,000 divided into 120,000 ordinary shares of £1 each. The whole of the capital was issued at par on the following terms:

	Per share
Payable on application	£0.125
Payable on allotment	£0.25
First call	£0.25
Second call	£0.375

Applications were received for 160,000 shares and it was decided to allot the shares on the basis of three for every four for which applications had been made. The balance of application monies were applied to the allotment, no cash being refunded. The balance of allotment monies were paid by the members.

The calls were made and paid in full by the members, with the exception of a member who failed to pay the first and second calls on the 800 shares allotted to him. A resolution was passed by the directors to forfeit the shares. The forfeited shares were later issued to D. Regan at £0.90 each.

Show the ledger accounts recording all the above transactions, and the relevant extracts from a balance sheet after all the transactions had been completed.

4.2 Badger Ltd has an authorised capital of £100,000 divided into 20,000 ordinary shares of £5 each. The whole of the shares were issued at par, payments being made as follows:

	£
Payable on application	0.5
Payable on allotment	1.5
First call	2.0
Second call	1.0

Applications were received for 32,600 shares. It was decided to refund application monies on 2,600 shares and to allot the shares on the basis of two for every three applied for. The excess application monies sent by the successful applicants is not to be refunded but is to be held and so reduce the amount payable on allotment.

The calls were made and paid in full with the exception of one member holding 100 shares who paid neither the first nor the second call and another member who did not pay the second call on 20 shares. After requisite action by the directors the shares were forfeited. They were later reissued to B. Mills at a price of £4 per share.

You are to draft the ledger accounts to record the transactions.

4.3 The authorised and issued share capital of Cosy Fires Ltd was £75,000 divided into 75,000 ordinary shares of £1 each, fully paid. On 2 January 20X7, the authorised capital was increased by a further 85,000 ordinary shares of £1 each to £160,000. On the same date 40,000 ordinary shares of £1 each were offered to the public at £1.25 per share payable as to £0.60 on application (including the premium), £0.35 on allotment and £0.30 on 6 April 20X7.

The lists were closed on 10 January 20X7, and by that date applications for 65,000 shares had been received. Applications for 5,000 shares received no allotment and the cash paid in respect of such shares was returned. All shares were then allocated to the remaining applicants pro rata to their original applications, the balance of the monies received on applications being applied to the amounts due on allotment.

The balances due on allotment were received on 31 January 20X7, with the exception of one allottee of 500 shares and these were declared forfeited on 4 April 20X7. These shares were reissued as fully paid on 2 May 20X7, at £1.10 per share. The call due on 6 April 20X7 was duly paid by the other shareholders.

You are required:

(a) To record the above-mentioned transactions in the appropriate ledger accounts; and
(b) To show how the balances on such accounts should appear in the company's balance sheet as on 31 May 20X7.

(*Association of Chartered Certified Accountants*)

4.4A   During the year to 30 September 20X7, Kammer plc made a new offer of shares. The details of the offer were as follows:

1 100,000 ordinary shares of £1 each were issued payable in instalments as follows:

	Per share £
On application at 1 November 20X6	0.65
On allotment (including the share premium of £0.50 per share) on	
1 December 20X6	0.55
On first and final call on 1 June 20X7	0.30
	£1.50

2 Applications for 200,000 shares were received, and it was decided to deal with them as follows:
(a) to return cheques for 75,000 shares;
(b) to accept in full applications for 25,000 shares; and
(c) to allot the remaining shares on the basis of three shares for every four shares applied for.
3 On the first and final call, one applicant who had been allotted 5,000 shares failed to pay the due amount, and his shares were duly declared forfeited. They were then reissued to Amber Ltd on 1 September 20X7 at a price of £0.80 per share fully paid.

Note: Kammer's issued share capital on 1 October 20X6 consisted of 500,000 ordinary shares of £1 each.

Required:
Record the above transactions in the following ledger accounts:

(a) ordinary share capital;
(b) share premium;
(c) application and allotment;
(d) first and final call;
(e) forfeited shares; and
(f) Amber Ltd's account.

(*Association of Accounting Technicians*)

4.5   M Limited has an authorised share capital of £1,500,000 divided into 1,500,000 ordinary shares of £1 each. The issued share capital at 31 March 20X7 was £500,000 which was fully paid, and had been issued at par. On 1 April 20X7, the directors, in accordance with the company's Articles, decided to increase the share capital of the company by offering a further 500,000 ordinary shares of £1 each at a price of £1.60 per share, payable as follows:

On application, including the premium	£0.85 per share
On allotment	£0.25 per share
On first and final call on 3 August 20X7	£0.50 per share

On 13 April 20X7, applications had been received for 750,000 shares and it was decided to allot the shares to applicants for 625,000 shares, on the basis of four shares for every five shares for which applications had been received. The balance of the money received on application was to be

applied to the amounts due on allotment. The shares were allotted on 1 May 20X7, the unsuccessful applicants being repaid their cash on this date. The balance of the allotment money was received in full by 15 May 20X7.

With the exception of one member who failed to pay the call on the 5,000 shares allotted to him, the remainder of the call was paid in full within two weeks of the call being made.

The directors resolved to forfeit these shares on 1 September 20X7, after giving the required notice. The forfeited shares were reissued on 30 September 20X7 to another member at £0.90 per share.

You are required to write up the ledger accounts necessary to record these transactions in the books of M Limited.

(*Chartered Institute of Management Accountants*)

4.6A Applications were invited by the directors of Grobigg Ltd for 150,000 of its £1 ordinary shares at £1.15 per share payable as follows:

	Per share
On application on 1 April 20X8	£0.75
On allotment on 30 April 20X8 (including the premium of £0.15 per share)	£0.20
On first and final call on 31 May 20X8	£0.20

Applications were received for 180,000 shares and it was decided to deal with these as follows:

1 To refuse allotment to applicants for 8,000 shares.
2 To give full allotment to applicants for 22,000 shares.
3 To allot the remainder of the available shares pro rata among the other applicants.
4 To utilise the surplus received on applications in part payment of amounts due on allotment.

An applicant, to whom 400 shares had been allotted, failed to pay the amount due on the first and final call and his shares were declared forfeit on 31 July 20X8. These shares were reissued on 3 September 20X8 as fully paid at £0.90 per share.

Show how the transactions would be recorded in the company's books.

(*Association of Chartered Certified Accountants*)

CHAPTER 5

Companies purchasing and redeeming their own shares and debentures

Introduction

In this chapter you'll learn the difference between the terms 'redemption' and 'purchase' of a company's own shares and debentures and the rules relating to companies that do either of these things. You will learn how to record such activities in the ledger accounts and of the effects of such activities upon the balance sheet.

5.1 Purchasing and redeeming own shares

In the context of shares and debentures, to all intents and purposes, the words 'purchasing' and 'redeeming' may appear to be identical and interchangeable. They both involve an outflow of cash incurred by a company in getting back its own shares in order that it may then cancel them. However, from a rather more legal and precise point of view, 'redeeming' means the buying back of shares which were originally issued as being 'redeemable' in that the company stated when they were issued that they would be, or could be, redeemed (i.e. bought back by the company). The terms of the redemption (buying back) would be stated at the time when the shares were issued. However, when shares are issued and are not stated to be redeemable, then, when they are bought back by the company, the company is said to be 'purchasing' its own shares, usually in the open market.

Until 1981 a company in the UK could not, in normal circumstances, 'purchase' its own shares. In addition 'redemption' was limited to one type of share, **redeemable preference shares**. This had not been the case in the USA and much of Europe where, for many years, companies had, with certain restrictions, been allowed to buy back their own shares. The basic reason why this was not allowed in the UK was the fear that the interests of creditors could be adversely affected if the company used its available cash to buy its own shares,

thus leaving less to satisfy the claims of the creditors. The possibilities of abuse with preference shares was considered to be less than with ordinary shares, thus it was possible to have redeemable preference shares.

Since 1981, under the Companies Acts, if it is authorised to do so by its Articles of Association, a company may:

(a) issue redeemable shares of any class (preference, ordinary, etc.). Redeemable shares include those that are to be redeemed on a particular date as well as those that are merely liable to be redeemed at the discretion of the shareholder or of the company. There is an important proviso that a company can only issue redeemable shares if it has in issue shares that are *not* redeemable. Without this restriction a company could issue only redeemable shares, then later redeem all of its shares, and thus finish up without any shareholders;

(b) 'purchase' its own shares (i.e. shares that were not issued as being redeemable shares). Again there is a proviso that the company must, *after* the purchase, have other shares in issue at least some of which are not redeemable. This again is to stop the company redeeming its whole share capital and thus ceasing to have members. The company must have, after the purchase, at least one member.

Activity 5.1

Why do you think the rules concerning purchase and redemption were changed in 1981?

5.2 Advantages of purchase and redemption of shares

There are many possible advantages to a company arising from its being able to buy back its own shares. These are strongest in the case of private companies. For public companies, the main advantage is that those with surplus cash resources could find it useful to be able to return some of this surplus cash back to its shareholders by buying back some of its own shares, rather than have pressure put on them to use such cash in uneconomic ways.

For private companies the main possible advantages would appear to be overcoming snags which occur when a shareholder cannot sell his shares on the 'open market', i.e. a stock exchange. This means that:

1 It will help shareholders who have difficulties in selling their shares to another individual to realise their value when needed, for any reason.
2 People will be more willing to buy shares from private companies. The fear of not being able to dispose of them previously led to finance being relatively difficult for private companies to obtain from people other than the original main proprietors of the company.
3 In many 'family' companies cash is needed to pay for taxes on the death of the shareholder.
4 Shareholders with grievances against the company can be bought out, thus contributing to the more efficient management of the company.
5 Family-owned companies will be helped in their desire to keep control of the company when a family shareholder with a large number of shares dies or retires.
6 In a similar way to public companies, as described above, the company could return unwanted cash resources to its shareholders.
7 For both private companies, and for public companies whose shares are not listed on a stock exchange, it may help boost share schemes for employees, as the employees would know that they could fairly easily dispose of the shares instead of being stuck with them.

5.3   Accounting entries

The accounting entries for either purchase or redemption of shares are exactly the same, except that the word 'redeemable' will appear as the first word in the title of the accounts for shares that are redeemable. The figures to be entered will naturally be affected by the **terms** under which shares are redeemed or purchased, but the **location** of the debits and credits to be made will be the same.

Readers will more easily understand the rather complicated entries needed if they understand the reasoning behind the Companies Acts. The protection of the creditor was uppermost in the minds of Parliament. The general idea is that **capital** should not be returned to the shareholders, except under certain circumstances. If capital is returned to the shareholders, thus reducing the cash and bank balances, then the creditors could lose out badly if there was not then sufficient cash/bank balances to pay their claims. Thus the shareholders, seeing that things were not progressing too well in the company, could get their money out possibly at the expense of the creditors.

There are dividends which can quite legitimately be paid to the shareholders out of distributable profits, but the idea is to stop the shareholders withdrawing their capital while leaving nothing to meet the amounts owing to creditors. Included under the general heading of 'capital' for this purpose are those particular reserves which cannot be used up for the payment of cash dividends.

There are exceptions to this, namely the reduction of capital by public companies (*see* Chapter 9) and the special powers of a private company to purchase or redeem its own shares out of capital (*see* later in this chapter). However, apart from these special cases, the company law regulations are intended to ensure that capital does not fall when shares are redeemed or purchased. This general objective lies behind the accounting entries which we will now consider.

5.4   Rules for redemption or purchase

It is important to note that in *all* cases shares can only be redeemed or purchased when they are fully paid.

> ### Activity 5.2
> Why do you think shares need to be fully paid before they can be redeemed or purchased?

The safeguards for the protection of capital contained in the Companies Acts are summarised in Sections 5.5–5.9.

5.5   Nominal value

In respect of the **nominal value** of shares redeemed or purchased, either (*a*) there must be a new issue of shares to provide the funds for redemption or purchase or (*b*) sufficient distributable profits must be available (i.e. a large enough credit balance on the appropriation account) which could be diverted from being used up as dividends to being treated as used up for the purpose of redeeming or purchasing the shares.

Therefore, when shares are redeemed or purchased other than out of the proceeds of a new issue, then, and only then, the amount of distributable profits treated as being used up by the nominal value of shares redeemed or purchased is debited to the appropriation

account and credited to a **capital redemption reserve**. (At one time, this was called a 'capital redemption reserve fund'. However, use of the word 'fund' has now been dropped.)

Thus the old share capital will equal the total of the new share capital *plus* the capital redemption reserve. The capital redemption reserve is a 'non-distributable' reserve. This means that it cannot be transferred back to the credit of the appropriation account, and so increase the profits available for distribution as cash dividends. The process of diverting profits from being usable for dividends means that the non-payment of the dividends leaves more cash in the company against which creditors could claim if necessary.

Note: In all the examples which follow, the shares being redeemed/purchased could be either redeemable shares or those not specifically stated to be redeemable. In a real company, the titles of the accounts would state which shares were redeemable.

To get you used to journal entries, and then seeing the effect on the face of the balance sheet, journal-style entries will be shown first, followed by the balances for the balance sheet.

Exhibit 5.1

£2,000 preference shares are redeemed/purchased at par, a new issue of £2,000 ordinary shares at par being made for the purpose.

		Dr £	Cr £
(A1)	Bank	2,000	
(A2)	Ordinary share applicants		2,000
	Cash received from applicants		
(B1)	Ordinary share applicants	2,000	
(B2)	Ordinary share capital		2,000
	Ordinary shares allotted		
(C1)	Preference share capital	2,000	
(C2)	Preference share purchase Note		2,000
	Shares to be redeemed/purchased		
(D1)	Preference share purchase Note	2,000	
(D2)	Bank		2,000
	Payment made to redeem/purchase shares		

Note: To make it easier to follow, all these examples refer only to redemption of preference shares. However, the process is identical whatever the type of shares being redeemed or purchased, only the names of the accounts to be used are different. When shares are being redeemed, they are transferred to a 'share redemption account'. If they were being purchased, a 'share purchase account' is used instead.

	Balances before £		Effect Dr £		Cr £	Balances after £
Net assets (except bank)	7,500					7,500
Bank	2,500	(A1)	2,000	(D2)	2,000	2,500
	10,000					10,000
Ordinary share capital	5,000			(B2)	2,000	7,000
Ordinary share applicants	–	(B1)	2,000	(A2)	2,000	–
Preference share capital	2,000	(C1)	2,000			–
Preference share purchase	–	(D1)	2,000	(C2)	2,000	–
	7,000 Note					Note 7,000
Profit and loss	3,000					3,000
	10,000					10,000

Note: Total 'capitals' remain the same.

Exhibit 5.2

£2,000 preference shares are redeemed/purchased at par, with no new issue of shares to provide funds for the purpose. Therefore an amount equal to the nominal value of the shares redeemed *must* be transferred from the profit and loss appropriation account to the credit of a capital redemption reserve.

		Dr £	Cr £
(A1)	Preference share capital	2,000	
(A2)	Preference share purchase		2,000
	Shares to be redeemed/purchased		
(B1)	Preference share purchase	2,000	
(B2)	Bank		2,000
	Cash paid as purchase/redemption		
(C1)	Profit and loss appropriation	2,000	
(C2)	Capital redemption reserve		2,000
	Transfer per Companies Act 1985 section 45		

	Balances before £		Effect Dr £		Effect Cr £	Balances after £
Net assets (except bank)	7,500					7,500
Bank	2,500			(B2)	2,000	500
	10,000					8,000
Ordinary share capital	5,000					5,000
Preference share capital	2,000	(A1)	2,000			–
Preference share purchase	–	(B1)	2,000	(A2)	2,000	–
Capital redemption reserve	–			(C2)	2,000	2,000
	7,000 Note					Note 7,000
Profit and loss	3,000	(C1)	2,000			1,000
	10,000					8,000

Note: Total 'capitals' (share capital + non-distributable reserves) remain the same at £7,000.

Exhibit 5.3

£2,000 preference shares are redeemed/purchased at par, being £1,200 from issue of ordinary shares at par and partly by using appropriation account balance.

		Dr £	Cr £
(A1)	Bank	1,200	
(A2)	Ordinary share applicants		1,200
	Cash received from applicants		
(B1)	Ordinary share applicants	1,200	
(B2)	Ordinary share capital		1,200
	Ordinary shares allotted		
(C1)	Profit and loss appropriation	800	
(C2)	Capital redemption reserve		800
	Part of redemption/purchase not covered by new issue, to comply with Companies Act 1985		
(D1)	Preference share capital	2,000	
(D2)	Preference share purchase		2,000
	Shares being redeemed/purchased		
(E1)	Preference share purchase	2,000	
(E2)	Bank		2,000
	Payment made for redemption/purchase		

	Balances before £		Effect Dr £		Cr £	Balances after £
Net assets (except bank)	7,500					7,500
Bank	2,500	(A1)	1,200	(E2)	2,000	1,700
	10,000					9,200
Ordinary share capital	5,000			(B2)	1,200	6,200
Ordinary share applicants	–	(B1)	1,200	(A2)	1,200	–
Preference share capital	2,000	(D1)	2,000			–
Preference share purchase	–	(E1)	2,000	(D2)	2,000	–
Capital redemption reserve	–			(C2)	800	800
	7,000Note					Note7,000
Profit and loss	3,000	(C1)	800			2,200
	10,000					9,200

Note: Total 'capitals' remain the same.

5.6 Premiums

The next requirement under the Companies Acts is that when shares are being redeemed/purchased at a premium, but they were *not* originally issued at a premium, then an amount equal to the premium *must* be transferred from the appropriation account to the credit of the share purchase/redemption account. This again is to divert profits away from being distributable to being part of 'capital'.

Exhibit 5.4

£2,000 preference shares which were originally issued at par are redeemed/purchased at a premium of 20 per cent. There is no new issue of shares for the purpose. In this example the ordinary shares had been originally issued at a premium, thus the reason for the share premium account being in existence. However, it is *not* the ordinary shares which are being redeemed and therefore the share premium *cannot* be used for the premium on redemption/purchase of the preference shares.

		Dr £	Cr £
(A1)	Preference share capital	2,000	
(A2)	Preference share purchase		2,000
	Shares being redeemed/purchased		
(B1)	Profit and loss appropriation	400	
(B2)	Preference share purchase		400
	Premium on purchase/redemption of shares *not* previously issued at premium		
(C1)	Profit and loss appropriation	2,000	
(C2)	Capital redemption reserve		2,000
	Transfer because shares redeemed/purchased out of distributable profits		
(D1)	Preference share purchase	2,400	
(D2)	Bank		2,400
	Payment on purchase/redemption		

	Balances before		Effect			Balances after
			Dr		*Cr*	
	£		£		£	£
Net assets (except bank)	7,500					7,500
Bank	2,500			(D2)	2,400	100
	10,000					7,600
Ordinary share capital	4,500					4,500
Preference share capital	2,000	(A1)	2,000			–
Preference share purchase	–	(D1)	2,400	(A2)	2,000	
				(B2)	400	–
Capital redemption reserve	–			(C2)	2,000	2,000
Share premium	500					500
	7,000 Note					Note 7,000
Profit and loss	3,000	(C1)	2,000			
		(B1)	400			600
	10,000					7,600

Note: Total 'capitals' remain the same.

Under the Companies Acts, when shares are being redeemed or purchased at a premium, *and* they were originally issued at a premium, *and* a new issue of shares is being made for the purpose, then the share premium account *can* have an amount calculated as follows transferred to the credit of the share purchase/redemption account. This is shown as (E) below.

Share Premium Account

		£
Balance before new issue	(A)	xxx
Add Premium on new issue	(B)	xxx
Balance after new issue	(C)	xxx
Amount that *may* be transferred is lesser of:	(E)	
Premiums that were received when it first issued the shares now being redeemed/purchased (D)	xxx	
or		
Balance after new issue (C) above	xxx	
Transfer to share purchase/redemption	(E)	xxx
New balance for balance sheet (could be nil)		xxx

Where the amount being deducted (E) is *less* than the premium paid on the *current* redemption or purchase, then an amount equivalent to the difference must be transferred from the debit of the appropriation account to the credit of the share purchase/redemption account. (An instance of this is shown in Exhibit 5.5.) This again diverts profits away from being distributable.

Exhibit 5.5

£2,000 preference shares originally issued at a premium of 20 per cent are now purchased/redeemed at a premium of 25 per cent. The position can be shown in three different companies for the purpose of purchase/redemption:

- Company 1 issues 2,400 ordinary £1 shares at par.
- Company 2 issues 2,000 ordinary £1 shares at 20 per cent premium.
- Company 3 issues 1,600 ordinary £1 shares at 50 per cent premium.

Share Premium Account

		Company 1 £	Company 2 £	Company 3 £
Balance before new issue	(A)	150[Note (a)]	400	400
Premium on new issue		____	400	800 (B)
Balance after new issue	(C)	150	800	1,200
Amount transferable to share purchase/ redemption is therefore lower of (C) or original premium on issue (£400)		150[Note (b)]	400[Note (b)]	400[Note (b)]
New balance for balance sheet		–	400	800

Note (a): In Company 1 it is assumed that of the original £400 premium the sum of £250 had been used up to issue bonus shares (*see* Chapter 9 later).

Note (b): As these figures are less than the premium of £500 *now* being paid, the differences (Company 1 £350; Companies 2 and 3 £100 each) must be transferred from the debit of the appropriation account to the credit of the preference share/purchase redemption account.

Journal entries:

	Company 1 Dr £	Company 1 Cr £	Company 2 Dr £	Company 2 Cr £	Company 3 Dr £	Company 3 Cr £
(A1) Bank	2,400		2,400		2,400	
(A2) Ordinary share applicants		2,400		2,400		2,400
Cash received from applicants						
(B1) Ordinary share applicants	2,400		2,400		2,400	
(B2) Ordinary share capital		2,400		2,000		1,600
(B3) Share premium		–		400		800
Ordinary shares allotted						
(C1) Preference share capital	2,000		2,000		2,000	
(C2) Preference share purchase		2,000		2,000		2,000
Shares being redeemed/purchased						
(D1) Share premium account	150		400		400	
(D2) Preference share purchase		150		400		400
Amount of share premium account used for redemption/purchase						
(E1) Profit and loss appropriation	350		100		100	
(E2) Preference share purchase		350		100		100
Excess of premium payable over amount of share premium account usable for the purpose						
(F1) Preference share purchase	2,500		2,500		2,500	
(F2) Bank		2,500		2,500		2,500
Amount paid on redemption/purchase						

Exhibit 5.6

The following balance sheets for the three companies of Exhibit 5.5 are given *before* the purchase/redemption. The balance sheets are then shown *after* purchase/redemption.

Balance Sheets (*before* redemption/purchase)

	Company 1	Company 2	Company 3
	£	£	£
Net assets (except bank)	7,500	7,500	7,500
Bank	2,500	2,500	2,500
	10,000	10,000	10,000
Ordinary share capital	4,850	4,600	4,600
Preference share capital	2,000	2,000	2,000
Share premium	150	400	400
	7,000	7,000	7,000
Profit and loss account	3,000	3,000	3,000
	10,000	10,000	10,000

Balance Sheets (*after* redemption/purchase)

	Company 1	Company 2	Company 3
	£	£	£
Net assets (except bank)	7,500	7,500	7,500
Bank	2,400	2,400	2,400
	9,900	9,900	9,900
Ordinary share capital	7,250	6,600	6,200
Share premium	–	400	800
	7,250	7,000	7,000
Profit and loss account	2,650	2,900	2,900
	9,900	9,900	9,900

5.7 Private companies: redemption or purchase of shares out of capital

The Companies Act 1981 introduced a new power for a *private* company to redeem/purchase its own shares where *either* it has insufficient distributable profits for the purpose *or* it cannot raise the amount required by a new issue. Previously it would have had to apply to the court for **capital reduction** as per Chapter 9. The 1981 legislation made it far easier to achieve the same objectives, in terms of both time and expense. This is carried on in the current Companies Acts.

The detail of the various matters which must be dealt with are beyond the scope of this textbook and you would need to consult a book on company law if you wish to go into this topic to that level of detail. For our purposes, a very brief outline may be given as follows:

1 The company must be authorised to do so by its Articles of Association.
2 **Permissible capital payment** is the amount by which the price of redemption or purchase exceeds the aggregate of (*a*) the company's distributable profits and (*b*) the proceeds of any new issue. This means that a private company should use its available profits and any share proceeds before making a payment out of capital.
3 Directors must certify that, after the permissible capital payment, the company will be able to carry on as a going concern during the next twelve months, and be able to pay its debts immediately after the payment and also during the next twelve months.
4 Auditors to make a satisfactory report.

Activity 5.3
Why do you think the rules are less restrictive for private companies?

5.8   Permissible capital payments

1 Where the permissible capital payment is *less* than the nominal value of shares redeemed/purchased, the amount of the difference *shall* be transferred to the capital redemption reserve from the appropriation account (or undistributed profits).
2 Where the permissible capital payment is *greater* than the nominal value of shares redeemed/purchased, *any* non-distributable reserves (e.g. share premium account, capital redemption reserve, revaluation reserve, etc.) or fully paid share capital can be reduced by the excess.

This can best be illustrated by taking two companies, R and S, with similar account balances *before* the purchase/redemption, but redeeming on different terms:

Exhibit 5.7

	Before £		Dr £		Cr £	After £
Company R						
Net assets (except bank)	2,500					2,500
Bank	7,500			(B2)	4,000	3,500
	10,000					6,000
Ordinary shares	1,000					1,000
Preference shares	4,000	(A1)	4,000			–
Non-distributable reserves	2,000					2,000
Capital redemption reserve				(C2)	3,000	3,000
Preference share purchase	–	(B1)	4,000	(A2)	4,000	
	7,000					
Profit and loss	3,000	(C1)	3,000			
	10,000					6,000

Preference shares redeemed at par £4,000. No new issue.

Therefore pay	£4,000
Less Profit and loss account	(3,000)
Permissible capital payment	1,000
Nominal amount shares redeemed/purchased	£4,000
Less Permissible capital payment	(1,000)
Deficiency to transfer to capital redemption reserve (C1 and C2)	3,000

(A1) and (A2) represents transfer of shares redeemed/purchased.
(B1) and (B2) represents payment to shareholders.

	Before £		Dr £		Cr £	After £
Company S						
Net assets (except bank)	2,500					2,500
Bank	7,500			(D2)	7,200	300
	10,000					2,800
Ordinary share capital	1,000					1,000
Preference shares	4,000	(A1)	4,000			–
Non-distributable reserves	2,000	(C1)	200			1,800
Capital redemption reserve	–					–
Preference share purchase		(D1)	7,200	(A2)	4,000	
				(B2)	3,000	
				(C2)	200	
	7,000					2,800
Profit and loss	3,000	(B1)	3,000			–
	10,000					2,800

Preference shares redeemed/purchased at premium 80%. No new issue.

Therefore pay	£7,200
Less Profit and loss account	(3,000)
Permissible capital payment	4,200
Permissible capital payment	£4,200
Less Nominal amount redeemed/purchased	(4,000)
Excess from *any* of non-distributable reserves (or capital) (C1 and C2)	200

- (A1) and (A2) represent shares redeemed/purchased.
- (B1) and (B2) are transfer to redemption/purchase account of part of source of funds.
- (D1) and (D2) are payment to shareholders.

5.9 Cancellation of shares purchased/redeemed

All shares purchased/redeemed must be cancelled immediately. They cannot be kept in hand by the company and traded in like any other commodity.

5.10 Redemption of debentures

Unless they are stated to be irredeemable, debentures are redeemed according to the terms of the issue. The necessary funds to finance the redemption may be from:

(*a*) an issue of shares or debentures for the purpose;
(*b*) the liquid resources of the company.

As it resembles the redemption of redeemable preference shares, when the redemption is financed as in (*a*), no transfer of profits from the profit and loss appropriation account to a reserve account is needed. However, when financed as in (*b*), it is good accounting practice, although not legally necessary, to divert profits from being used as dividends by transferring an amount equal to the nominal value redeemed from the debit of the profit and loss appropriation account to the credit of a reserve account.

Redemption may be effected:

1 by annual drawings out of profits;
2 by purchase in the open market when the price is favourable, i.e. less than the price which will have to be paid if the company waited until the last date by which redemption has to be carried out;
3 in a lump sum to be provided by the accumulation of a sinking fund.

These can now be examined in more detail.

Regular annual drawings out of profits

(a) When redeemed at a premium

In this case the source of the bank funds with which the premium is paid should be taken to be (*a*) the share premium account, or if this does not exist, or the premium is in excess of the balance on the account, then any part not covered by a share premium account is deemed to come from (*b*) the profit and loss appropriation account. Exhibit 5.8 shows the effect on a balance sheet where there is no share premium account, while Exhibit 5.9 illustrates the case when a share premium account is in existence.

Exhibit 5.8

Starting with the *before* balance sheet, £400 of the debentures are redeemed at a premium of 20 per cent.

Balance Sheets

	Before	+ or −	After
	£	£	£
Other assets	12,900		12,900
Bank	3,400	−480 (A)	2,920
	16,300		15,820
Share capital	10,000		10,000
Debenture redemption reserve	−	+400 (B)	400
Debentures	2,000	−400 (A)	1,600
Profit and loss	4,300	−400 (B)	
		−80 (A)	3,820
	16,300		15,820

Exhibit 5.9

Starting with the *before* balance sheet, £400 of the debentures are redeemed at a premium of 20 per cent.

Balance Sheets

	Before	+ or −	After
	£	£	£
Other assets	13,500		13,500
Bank	3,400	−480 (A)	2,920
	16,900		16,420
Share capital	10,000		10,000
Share premium	600	−80 (A)	520
Debenture redemption reserve	−	+400 (B)	400
Debentures	2,000	−400 (A)	1,600
Profit and loss	4,300	−400 (B)	3,900
	16,900		16,420

In both Exhibits 5.8 and 5.9 the debenture redemption reserve account is built up each year by the nominal value of the debentures redeemed each year. When the whole issue of debentures has been redeemed, then the balance on the debenture redemption reserve account should be transferred to the credit of a general reserve account. It is, after all, an accumulation of undistributed profits.

(b) Redeemed – originally issued at a discount

The discount originally given was in fact to attract investors to buy the debentures, and is therefore as much a cost of borrowing as is debenture interest. The discount therefore needs to be written off during the life of the debentures. It might be more rational to write it off to the profit and loss account, but in fact accounting custom, as permitted by law, would first of all write it off against any share premium account or, secondly, against the profit and loss appropriation account.

The amounts written off over the life of the debentures are:

(a) equal annual amounts over the life of the debentures, or
(b) in proportion to the debenture debt outstanding at the start of each year. Exhibit 5.10 shows such a situation.

Exhibit 5.10

£30,000 debentures are issued at a discount of 5 per cent. They are repayable at par over five years at the rate of £6,000 per annum.

Year	Outstanding at start of each year	Proportion written off		Amount
	£			£
1	30,000	$^{30}/_{90} \times £1,500$	=	500
2	24,000	$^{24}/_{90} \times £1,500$	=	400
3	18,000	$^{18}/_{90} \times £1,500$	=	300
4	12,000	$^{12}/_{90} \times £1,500$	=	200
5	6,000	$^{6}/_{90} \times £1,500$	=	100
	90,000			1,500

Redeemed by purchase in the open market

A sum equal to the cash actually paid on redemption should be transferred from the debit of the profit and loss appropriation account to the credit of the debenture redemption reserve account. The sum actually paid will have been credited to the Cash Book and debited to the debentures account.

Any discount (or profit) on purchase will be transferred to a reserve account. Any premium (or loss) on purchase will be deemed to come out of such a reserve account, or if no such account exists or if it is insufficient, then it will be deemed to come out of the share premium account. Failing the existence of these accounts any loss must come out of the profit and loss appropriation account. It may seem that purchase would not be opportune if the debentures had to be redeemed at a premium. However, it would still be opportune if the premium paid was not as high as the premium to be paid if the final date for redemption was awaited.

Redemption of debentures by a sinking fund

Where debentures are issued which are redeemable (and most are redeemable) consideration should be given to the availability of cash funds at the time.

This method involves the investment of cash outside the business. The aim is to make a regular investment of money which, together with the accumulated interest or dividends, is sufficient to finance the redemption of the debentures at the requisite time.

Before calculations become too involved a simple proposition can be examined. As each period's interest (or dividend) is received, then that amount is immediately reinvested. Apart from the reinvestment of interest the other money taken for investment is to be an equal amount each period. This being so, if the money is to be invested at 5 per cent per annum, and the debenture is £500 to be redeemed in five years' time, then how much should be taken for investment each year? If £100 were taken each year for five years, then this would amount to more than £500 because of the interest and of the interest on the reinvested interest. Most readers will recognise this as money being invested at compound interest. Therefore something less than £100 per annum is needed. The exact amount can be calculated by the use of the compound interest formula. Chapter 44 illustrates how the amount needed can be calculated. As these calculations are left until later in the book, a summarised set of tables is now shown to help the student at this stage.

Annual sinking fund instalments to provide £1

Years	3%	3½%	4%	4½%	5%
3	0.323530	0.321933	0.320348	0.318773	0.317208
4	0.239028	0.237251	0.235490	0.233744	0.232012
5	0.188354	0.186481	0.184627	0.182792	0.180975
6	0.154597	0.152668	0.150761	0.148878	0.147017
7	0.130506	0.128544	0.126609	0.124701	0.122819
8	0.112456	0.110476	0.108527	0.106609	0.104721
9	0.098433	0.096446	0.094493	0.092574	0.090690
10	0.087230	0.085241	0.083291	0.081378	0.079504

The table gives the amount required to provide £1 at the end of the relevant number of years. To provide £1,000 multiply by 1,000; to provide for £4,986 multiply by 4,986.

5.11   Double entry records for sinking fund

When the annual instalment has been found, the double entry needed each year is:

1 Annual instalment:
    Dr Profit and loss appropriation
        Cr Debenture redemption reserve
2 Investment of 1st instalment:
    Dr Debenture sinking fund investment
        Cr Bank
3 Interest/dividends on sinking fund investment:
    Dr Bank
        Cr Debenture redemption reserve
4 Investment of second and later instalments (these consist of equal annual instalment plus interest/dividend just received):
    Dr Debenture sinking fund investment
        Cr Bank

Exhibit 5.11

Debentures of £10,000 are issued on 1 January 20X1. They are redeemable five years later on 31 December 20X5 on identical terms. The company therefore decides to set aside an equal annual amount, which at an interest rate of 5 per cent will provide £10,000 on 31 December 20X5. According to the table, £0.180975 invested annually will provide £1 in five years' time. Therefore £0.180975 × 10,000 will be needed annually = £1,809.75.

Profit and Loss Appropriation for years ended 31 December

(20X1) Debenture redemption reserve 1,809.75	
(20X2) Debenture redemption reserve 1,809.75	
(20X3) Debenture redemption reserve 1,809.75	
(20X4) Debenture redemption reserve 1,809.75	
(20X5) Debenture redemption reserve 1,809.75	

Debenture Redemption Reserve

		£				£
			20X1			
			Dec 31	Profit and loss		1,809.75
			20X2			
			Dec 31	Bank interest		
20X2				(5% of £1,809.75)		90.49
Dec 31	Balance c/d	3,709.99	Dec 31	Profit and loss		1,809.75
		3,709.99				3,709.99
			20X3			
			Jan 1	Balance b/d		3,709.99
			Dec 31	Bank interest		
20X3				(5% of £3,709.99)		185.49
Dec 31	Balance c/d	5,705.23	Dec 31	Profit and loss		1,809.75
		5,705.23				5,705.23
			20X4			
			Jan 1	Balance b/d		5,705.23
			Dec 31	Bank interest		
20X4				(5% of £5,705.23)		285.26
Dec 31	Balance c/d	7,800.24	Dec 31	Profit and loss		1,809.75
		7,800.24				7,800.24
			20X5			
			Jan 1	Balance b/d		7,800.24
			Dec 31	Bank interest		
20X5				(5% of £7,800.24)		390.01
Dec 31	Debentures now redeemed	10,000.00	Dec 31	Profit and loss		1,809.75
		10,000.00				10,000.00

Debenture Sinking Fund Investment

20X1		£					£
Dec 31	Bank	1,809.75					
20X2							
Dec 31	Bank[Note (a)]	1,900.24					
20X3							
Dec 31	Bank[Note (b)]	1,995.24		20X5			
20X4							
Dec 31	Bank[Note (c)]	2,095.01		Dec 31	Cash: Sale of investment	7,800.24	
		7,800.24				7,800.24	

Notes:

Cash invested	(a)	(b)	(c)
	£	£	£
The yearly instalment	1,809.75	1,809.75	1,809.75
Add interest received reinvested immediately	90.49	185.49	285.26
	1,900.24	1,995.24	2,095.01

Bank (extracts)

20X1		£	20X1		£
Jan 1	Debentures (issued)	10,000.00	Dec 31	Debenture sinking fund investment	1,809.75
20X2			20X2		
Dec 31	Debenture redemption reserve (interest on investment)	90.49	Dec 31	Debenture sinking fund investment	1,900.24
20X3			20X3		
Dec 31	Debenture redemption reserve (interest on investment)	185.49	Dec 31	Debenture sinking fund investment	1,995.24
20X4			20X4		
Dec 31	Debenture redemption reserve (interest on investment)	285.26	Dec 31	Debenture sinking fund investment	2,095.01
20X5			20X5		
Dec 31	Debenture redemption reserve (interest on investment)	309.01	Jan 1	Debentures (redemption)	10,000.00

Debentures

20X6		£	20X1		£
Jan 1	Bank (redemption)	10,000.00	Jan 1	Bank	10,000.00

The instalment for 20X5 is not in fact invested, nor is the interest received on 31 December 20X5 reinvested. The money to redeem the debentures is required on 1 January 20X6, and there is not much point (even if it were possible, which would very rarely hold true) in investing money one day only to withdraw it the day afterwards. The amount required is £10,000 and is available from the following sources:

		£
Dec 31	20X5 Sale of investment	7,800.24
Dec 31	20X5 Interest received but not reinvested	390.01
Dec 31	20X5 The fifth year's instalment not invested	1,809.75
		10,000.00

Sometimes debentures bought in the open market are not cancelled, but are kept 'alive' and are treated as investments of the sinking fund. The annual appropriation of profits is credited to the sinking fund account, while the amount expended on the purchase of the debentures is debited to the sinking fund investment account. Interest on such debentures is debited to the profit and loss account and credited to the sinking fund account, thus the interest, as far as the sinking fund account is concerned, is treated in the same fashion as if it was cash actually received by the firm from an outside investment. The sum expended on investments will then be equal to the annual appropriation + the interest on investments actually received + the interest on debentures kept in hand.

5.12 Convertible loan stock

Particularly in periods of high inflation the attraction to lenders to provide funds at reasonable rates of interest is much reduced as they stand to lose significantly on the real value of the funds lent, since the repayment of the loan is normally fixed at its original cash value. One way of attracting lenders has been to give them the right to convert their loan into shares. The right can usually be exercised once a year over a stated number of years at a given rate of conversion from loan to shares. The value of the conversion right will depend on the performance of the shares in the market. If the shares increase in value significantly, the conversion value will increase and attract the lender to opt into shares. If the shares do badly, the lender can retain the loan stock with its higher levels of security.

The accounting entries are as previously described for the redemption of the loan. The value of the shares issued to meet the redemption will be fixed under the terms of the original agreement by reference to the market prices at specified dates.

Learning outcomes

You should now have learnt:

1 The difference between the terms 'redemption' and 'purchase' in the context of shares and debentures.

2 How to make the accounting entries relating to the redemption or purchase by a company of its own shares.

3 That the accounting entries made on the redemption by a company of its own shares are the same as when it purchases its own shares, except that the word 'redeemable' will appear as the first word in the title of the accounts for shares that are redeemed.

4 That in order to protect creditors, companies *must* still have irredeemable shares in issue after undertaking any purchase or redemption of its own shares.

5 That a company cannot redeem or purchase its own shares unless they are fully paid.

6 That the rules on reserves to use when purchasing or issuing their own shares at a premium are less strict for private companies.

7 How to make the accounting entries relating to the redemption or purchase by a company of its own debentures.

8 That debentures are redeemed according to the terms of their issue.

Answers to activities

5.1 Apart from moving into line with the rest of Europe, the restriction that remained (of having one member, i.e. shareholder) minimised the risk of abuse of creditors, which was the main reason for having the rule preventing purchase and redemption in the first place.

5.2 It would be very sharp practice to issue shares and then redeem them before they were fully paid. This would suggest that the company issued them only in order to have free use of the funds they realised for a short time. In effect, they would have represented an interest-free loan. By requiring that shares be fully paid before being redeemed or purchased back by the company, the possibility that companies would engage in this form of sharp practice is minimised.

5.3 Private companies are much smaller than public ones. Their shares are often held by a far smaller group of shareholders, often all known to each other. There is not, therefore, the same need to protect shareholders, but there is often a greater need to assist shareholders wishing to reduce their shareholdings. Private companies also tend to have far smaller and less extensive groups of creditors in need of protection. If you refer back to the advantages listed in Section 5.2, you can see why it is important that private companies have greater flexibility in this respect than public ones.

REVIEW QUESTIONS

5.1 Exercises (a) to (e) are based on the following balance sheet.

RSV Ltd
Balance Sheet

	£
Net assets (except bank)	20,000
Bank	13,000
	33,000
Preference share capital	5,000
Ordinary share capital	15,000
Share premium	2,000
	22,000
Profit and loss	11,000
	33,000

Note also that each of exercises (a) to (e) is independent of any other. The exercises are not cumulative.

Required:
(a) RSV Ltd redeems £5,000 preference shares at par, a new issue of £5,000 ordinary shares at par being made for the purpose. Show the balance sheet after completion of these transactions. Workings are to be shown as journal entries.
(b) RSV Ltd redeems £5,000 preference shares at par, with no new issue of shares to provide funds. Show the balance sheet after completing the transaction. Workings: show journal entries.
(c) RSV Ltd redeems £5,000 preference shares at par. To help finance this an issue of £1,500 ordinary shares at par is effected. Show the balance sheet after these transactions have been completed; also show the necessary journal entries.
(d) RSV Ltd redeems £5,000 preference shares at a premium of 25 per cent. There is no new issue of shares for the purpose. In this question the share premium account is taken as being from the issue of ordinary shares some years ago. Show the balance sheet after these transactions have been completed, and the supporting journal entries.
(e) RSV Ltd redeems £5,000 preference shares at a premium of 40 per cent. There is an issue of £7,000 ordinary shares at par for the purpose. The preference shares had originally been issued at a premium of 30 per cent. Show the balance sheet after these transactions have been completed, and also the supporting journal entries.

5.2A   Exercises (a) to (e) are based on the following balance sheet.

BAR Ltd
Balance Sheet

	£
Net assets (except bank)	31,000
Bank	16,000
	47,000
Preference share capital	8,000
Ordinary share capital	20,000
Share premium	4,000
	32,000
Profit and loss	15,000
	47,000

Note also that exercises (a) to (e) are independent of each other. They are not cumulative.

Required:
(a) BAR Ltd purchases £10,000 of its own ordinary share capital at par. To help finance this £7,000 preference shares are issued at par. Show the necessary journal entries and the balance sheet after the transactions have been completed.
(b) BAR Ltd purchases £12,000 of its own ordinary shares at a premium of 20 per cent. No new issue of shares is made for the purpose. It is assumed that the share premium account is in respect of the issue of preference shares some years before. Show the balance sheet after the transactions have been completed, and also the supporting journal entries.
(c) BAR Ltd purchases all the preference share capital at par. These shares were not originally redeemable preference shares. There is no new issue of shares to provide funds. Show the requisite journal entries, and the closing balance sheet when the transaction has been completed.
(d) BAR Ltd purchases £12,000 of its own ordinary shares at par, a new issue of £12,000 preference shares at par being made for the purpose. Show the journal entries needed and the balance sheet after completing these transactions.
(e) BAR Ltd purchases £6,000 ordinary shares at a premium of 50 per cent. They had originally been issued at a premium of 20 per cent. There is an issue of £10,000 preference shares at par for the purpose. Show the amended balance sheet, together with the journal entries.

5.3   A company's balance sheet appears as follows:

	£
Net assets (except bank)	12,500
Bank	13,000
	25,500
Preference share capital	5,000
Ordinary share capital	10,000
Non-distributable reserves	6,000
	21,000
Profit and loss	4,500
	25,500

Required:
(a) If £6,000 of the ordinary shares were purchased at par, there being no new issue of shares for the purpose, show the journal entries to record the transactions and the amended balance sheet.
(b) If, instead of (a), £6,000 ordinary shares were purchased at a premium of 100 per cent, there being no new issue of shares for the purpose, show the journal entries to record the transactions and the amended balance sheet.

5.4A Debentures of £30,000 are issued on 1 January 20X3. Redemption is to take place, on equal terms, four years later. The company decides to put aside an equal amount to be invested at 5 per cent which will provide £30,000 on maturity. Tables show that £0.232012 invested annually will produce £1 in four years' time.

You are required to show:
(a) debenture redemption reserve account
(b) debenture sinking fund investment account
(c) debentures account
(d) profit and loss account extracts.

5.5 Some years ago M plc had issued £375,000 of 10 per cent debentures 20X6/20X0 at par. The terms of the issue allow the company the right to repurchase these debentures for cancellation at or below par, with an option to redeem, at a premium of 1 per cent, on 30 September 20X6. To exercise this option the company must give three months' notice, which it duly did on 30 June 20X6 indicating its intention to redeem all the debentures outstanding at 30 September 20X6.

M plc had established a sinking fund designed to accumulate the sum of £378,750 by 30 September 20X6 and had appropriated profits annually and invested these, together with the interest from such investments and the profits made on any realisations from time to time. A special No. 2 bank account was established specifically to deal with the receipts and payments relating to the debentures and the sinking fund.

By 30 June 20X6 annual contributions amounting to £334,485, together with the interest on the sinking fund investments of £39,480, had all been invested except for £2,475 which remained in the No. 2 bank account at that date.

The only investments sold, prior to 30 June 20X6, had cost £144,915 and realised £147,243. This was used to repurchase debentures with a par value of £150,000.

Transactions occurring between 1 July and 30 September 20X6 were:

(i) interest received on the sinking fund investments:
   7 July   £1,756
   13 September   £1,455
(ii) proceeds from the sale of investments:
   2 August   £73,215 (book value was £69,322)
   25 September   £160,238 (remaining investments)
(iii) redemption of all the debentures, on 30 September, with the exception of £15,000 held by B Limited. The company had received notice of a garnishee order.*
(iv) M plc deposited with the W Bank plc the sum of £15,150 on 30 September 20X6.

You are to ignore debenture interest and income tax.

You are required, from the information given above, to prepare the ledger accounts (including the No. 2 bank account) in the books of M plc for the period 30 June to 30 September 20X6, showing the transfer of the final balances to the appropriate accounts.

*Note – Garnishee order
This order, issued by the court, instructs M plc not to release the money owing to B Limited until directed by the court to do so.

(*Chartered Institute of Management Accountants*)

5.6A **The following information relates to White Rabbit Trading plc:**

Summarised Balance Sheet as at 31 January 20X7

	£000
Fixed assets	2,400
Investments	120
Net current assets	1,880
	4,400

	£000
Financed by:	
Capital and reserves	
Ordinary shares of 50p each fully paid	2,000
Redeemable shares of £1 each (20X7/20X1)	500
Share premium	200
Revaluation surplus	400
Profit and loss account	900
	4,000
Long-term liabilities	
8% debentures (20X7/20X0)	400
	4,400

On 1 February 20X7 the company closed the list of applications for 400,000 ordinary shares at a premium of 50p. The shares were to be paid for as follows: 60p on application, 25p on allotment and 15p on the first and final call, which was to be made on 1 May 20X7. A total of £1,320,000 was received, the shares were allotted and £1,032,000 was returned to unsuccessful applicants. The call money was received by 31 May from all shareholders, with the exception of two shareholders, one of whom had been allotted 500 shares. The other subscriber for 100 shares still owed £25 for allotment in addition to the call money. Eventually both lots of shares were forfeited and reissued to an existing shareholder for a payment of £500 which was duly received.

At a board meeting on 15 February 20X7 the directors decided to make a fresh issue of 500,000 £1 redeemable shares at a premium of 60p, and to redeem all of the existing redeemable shares at a premium of 40p. The shares had originally been issued for £1.20 each. All moneys due on application were duly received by 31 March 20X7, and the redemption took place on 6 April 20X7.

In January 20X5 White Rabbit Trading plc had purchased, for cash, 80,000 25p ordinary shares in March Hares Ltd for £25,000, and this is included in investments on the balance sheet at 31 January 20X7. On 1 April 20X7 the company purchased 400,000 out of a total issue of 500,000 25p ordinary shares in March Hares Ltd, by exchanging 200,000 of its own ordinary shares.

The 8 per cent debentures were redeemed on 15 May 20X7 at a 10 per cent premium, and on the same date £500,000 7 per cent debentures (20X0/20X3) were issued at a discount of 5 per cent.

Required:
Show the full journal entries to record the above events, including cash/bank transactions, in the books of White Rabbit Trading plc.

(*Association of Chartered Certified Accountants*)

5.7 During the year to 30 September 20X9, Popham plc issued 100,000 £1 ordinary shares. The terms of the offer were as follows:

20X9		£
31 March	on application	0.30 (including the premium)
30 April	on allotment	0.70
30 June	first and final call	0.20

Applications were received for 200,000 shares. The directors decided to allot the shares on the basis of 1 for every 2 shares applied for and apply the excess application money received against the amount due on allotment.

All amounts due on application and allotment were received on the due dates, with the exception of one shareholder who had been allotted 10,000 shares, and who defaulted on the first and final call. These shares were forfeited on 31 July 20X9, and reissued on 31 August 20X9 at a price of £1.10 per share.

Required:
Write up the above details in the books of account of Popham plc using the following ledger accounts:
(*i*)   application and allotment
(*ii*) first and final call
(*iii*) investment – own shares.

(*Association of Accounting Technicians*)

5.8A   Alas plc has an authorised share capital of 150,000 ordinary shares of £10 each. Upon incorporation, 50,000 shares were issued and fully paid. The company has decided to issue another 50,000 shares, the details of which are as follows:

	Per share £
Upon:	
Application	3
Allotment (including a premium of £5)	8
First call	2
Final call	2
	15

Additional information:

1 Applications were received for 85,000 shares out of which 10,000 shares were rejected, the cash being returned immediately to the applicants. The remaining applicants were allotted two shares for every three shares applied for, and the surplus application money was carried forward to the allotment stage.

2 The total amount due on allotment was duly received.

3 All cash due at the first call was received, but the final call resulted in 5,000 shares being forfeited. These shares were subsequently reissued at a price of £13 per share.

Required:

Compile the following ledger accounts:

(a) ordinary share capital
(b) ordinary share applications
(c) ordinary share allotment
(d) share premium
(e) ordinary share first call
(f) ordinary share final call
(g) investments – own shares (originally known as the forfeited shares account).

5.9   The following information relates to Grigg plc:

1 On 1 April 20X8 the company had £100,000 10 per cent debentures in issue. The interest on these debentures is paid on 30 September and 31 March.

2 The debenture redemption fund balance (relating to the redemption of these debentures) at 1 April 20X8 was £20,000. This fund is being built up by annual appropriations of £2,000. The annual appropriation (along with any dividends or interest on the investments) is invested on 31 March.

3 Debenture redemption fund investments can be realised at any time in order to purchase debentures in the open market either at or below par value. Such debentures are then cancelled.

4 On 31 December 20X8 £10,000 of investments were sold for £11,400, and the proceeds were used to purchase debentures with a par value of £12,000.

5 Dividends and interest on redemption fund investments during the year to 31 March 20X9 amounted to £1,600.

6 The cost of dealing with the above matters and any taxation effects may be ignored.

Required:

Write up the following ledger accounts for the year to 31 March 20X9:

(a) 10 per cent debentures
(b) debenture redemption fund
(c) debenture redemption fund investments
(d) debenture redemption
(e) debenture interest.

Note: The debenture redemption fund is sometimes known as a **sinking fund**.

CHAPTER 6

Limited companies taking over other businesses

Learning objectives

After you have studied this chapter, you should be able to:
- explain how goodwill may arise on the purchase of a business
- explain the difference between goodwill and negative goodwill
- record the accounting entries relating to a limited company taking over another business
- describe the difference in the accounting treatment of takeovers by limited companies of sole traders, partnerships and limited companies
- describe the two methods whereby a limited company may take over another limited company
- deal with pre-incorporation profits and losses

Introduction

In this chapter you'll learn about goodwill and negative goodwill and you will learn how to record the purchase of a business in the books of the purchaser using a variety of methods of paying for the purchase. You will also learn about how to deal with pre-incorporation losses and profits.

6.1 Background

Limited companies will often take over other businesses which are in existence as going concerns. The purchase considerations may either be in cash, by giving the company's shares to the owners, by giving the company's debentures, or by any combination of these three factors.

It must not be thought that because the assets bought are shown in the selling firm's books at one value the purchasing company must record the assets taken over in its own books at the same value. The values shown in the purchasing company's books are those values at which the company is buying the assets, such values being frequently quite different than those shown in the selling firm's books. As an instance of this, the selling firm may have bought premises many years ago for £10,000 but they may now be worth £50,000. The company buying the premises will obviously have to pay £50,000 and it is therefore this value that is recorded in the buying company's books.

Alternatively, the value at which it is recorded in the buying company's books may be less than that shown in the selling firm's books. Where the total purchase consideration exceeds the total value of the identifiable assets then such excess is the **goodwill**, and will need entering in a goodwill account in the purchasing company's books.

Should the total purchase consideration be less than the values of the identifiable assets, the difference is known as **negative goodwill**. (Previously, such negative goodwill was entered in a capital reserve account. Nowadays, it is entered as a credit figure in the goodwill account.)

Before looking at the accounting entries necessary to record the purchase of an ongoing business, it must be pointed out that the recording of the transactions is the simple part. The negotiations that take place before agreement is reached, and the various strategies undertaken by the various parties, are a study in themselves. The accounting entries are, in effect, the tip of the iceberg, i.e. that part of the whole affair which is seen by the eventual reader of the financial statements.

Activity 6.1

Why do you think the amount paid for a business may be different from the total value of its net assets as shown in its financial statements?

6.2 Taking over a sole trader's business

It is easiest to start with the takeover of the simplest sort of business unit, that of a sole trader. Some of the balance sheets shown will be deliberately simplified so that the principles involved are not hidden behind a mass of complicated calculations.

Exhibit 6.1

Earl Ltd is to buy the business of M Kearney. The purchase consideration is to be £6,000 cash, the company placing the following values on the assets taken over – machinery £3,000, stock £1,000. The goodwill must therefore be £2,000, because the total price of £6,000 exceeds the values of machinery £3,000 and stock £1,000 by the sum of £2,000. The company's balance sheets will be shown before and after the takeover, it being assumed that the transactions are all concluded immediately.

M Kearney
Balance Sheet

	£
Machinery	3,000
Stock	1,000
	4,000
Capital	4,000

Earl Ltd
Balance Sheets

	Before £	+ or – £	After £
Goodwill		+2,000	2,000
Machinery	11,000	+3,000	14,000
Stock	5,000	+1,000	6,000
Bank	9,000	−6,000	3,000
	25,000		25,000
Share capital	20,000		20,000
Profit and loss	5,000		5,000
	25,000		25,000

Exhibit 6.2

Suppose the purchase had been made instead by issuing 7,000 shares of £1 each at par to Kearney. The goodwill would then be £7,000 – assets taken over £4,000 = £3,000. The balance sheets of Earl Ltd would be:

Earl Ltd
Balance Sheets

	Before £	+ or – £	After £
Goodwill		+3,000	3,000
Machinery	11,000	+3,000	14,000
Stock	5,000	+1,000	6,000
Bank	9,000		9,000
	25,000		32,000
Share capital	20,000	+7,000	27,000
Profit and loss	5,000		5,000
	25,000		32,000

Exhibit 6.3

If the purchase had been made by issuing 5,000 shares of £1 each at a premium of 50 per cent, then the total consideration would have been worth £7,500 which, if the assets of £4,000 are deducted, leaves goodwill of £3,500. The balance sheets would then be:

Earl Ltd
Balance Sheets

	Before £	+ or – £	After £
Goodwill		+3,500	3,500
Machinery	11,000	+3,000	14,000
Stocks	5,000	+1,000	6,000
Bank	9,000		9,000
	25,000		32,500
Share capital	20,000	+5,000	25,000
Share premium		+2,500	2,500
Profit and loss	5,000		5,000
	25,000		32,500

Exhibit 6.4

If the purchase had been made by the issue of 1,000 shares of £1 each at a premium of 40 per cent, £3,000 worth of 7 per cent debentures at par and £4,000 in cash, then the total purchase consideration would be shares valued at £1,400, debentures valued at £3,000 and cash £4,000, making in all £8,400. The assets are valued at £4,000, the goodwill must be £4,400. The balance sheets would be:

Earl Ltd
Balance Sheets

	Before £	+ or – £	After £
Goodwill		+4,400	4,400
Machinery	11,000	+3,000	14,000
Stocks	5,000	+1,000	6,000
Bank	9,000	–4,000	5,000
	25,000		29,400
Less Debentures		+3,000	(3,000)
	25,000		26,400
Share capital	20,000	+1,000	21,000
Share premium		+400	400
Profit and loss	5,000		5,000
	25,000		26,400

In each of Exhibits 6.1 to 6.4 it has been assumed that all transactions were started and completed within a few moments. The fact is that an intermediary account would be created but then closed almost immediately when the purchase consideration was handed over.

Taking Exhibit 6.3 as an example, there will be a credit in the share capital account and in the share premium account, and debits in the goodwill, machinery and stock accounts. Nevertheless, shares cannot be issued to goodwill, machinery or stocks. They have, in fact, been issued to M Kearney. This means that there should have been an account for M Kearney, but that the balance on it was cancelled on the passing of the purchase consideration. The actual accounts for Exhibit 6.3 were as follows in the books of Earl Ltd:

Share Premium

			£
	M Kearney		2,500

Share Capital

	£		£
Balance c/d	25,000	Balance b/d	20,000
		M Kearney	5,000
	25,000		25,000
		Balance b/d	25,000

Profit and Loss

			£
	Balance b/d		5,000

Goodwill

	£	
M Kearney	3,500	

Machinery

	£		£
Balance b/d	11,000	Balance c/d	14,000
M Kearney	3,000		
	14,000		14,000
Balance b/d	14,000		

Stock

	£		£
Balance b/d	5,000	Balance c/d	6,000
M Kearney	1,000		
	6,000		6,000
Balance b/d	6,000		

(In fact, the £1,000 would probably be entered in the purchases account. It does, however, obviously increase the actual amount of stock.)

Bank

	£	
Balance b/d	9,000	

M Kearney

	£		£
Consideration passing:		Assets taken over:	
Share capital	5,000	Goodwill	3,500
Share premium	2,500	Machinery	3,000
		Stock	1,000
	7,500		7,500

Some accountants would have preferred to use a business purchase account instead of a personal account such as that of M Kearney.

Sometimes the company taking over the business of a sole trader not only pays a certain amount for the assets but also assumes responsibility for paying the creditors in addition. Take the case of a sole trader with assets valued at premises £5,000 and stock £4,000. To gain control of these assets the company is to pay the sole trader £11,000 in cash, and in addition the company will pay off creditors £1,000. This means that the goodwill is £3,000, calculated as follows:

	£
Paid by the company to gain control of the sole trader's assets:	
Cash to the sole trader	11,000
Cash to the sole trader's creditors	1,000
	12,000

	£	
The company receives assets:		
Premises	5,000	
Stock	4,000	
		(9,000)
Excess paid for goodwill		3,000

6.3 Partnership business taken over by a limited company

The entries are basically the same as for those of taking over a sole trader. The main difference is the distribution of the purchase consideration. In the case of a sole trader, the sole trader gets all of it. In a partnership it has to be divided between the partners.

This means that in a partnership a realisation account will have to be drawn up to calculate the profit or loss on sale of the partnership business. The profit or loss on sale will then be shared between the partners in their profit/loss-sharing ratios.

The double entry needed in the partnership books is:

(A) Transfer assets being disposed of to realisation account:
    Dr Realisation
        Cr Assets (various)

(B) Enter purchase price:
    Dr Limited company (purchaser)
        Cr Realisation

(C) If profit on sale:
    Dr Realisation
        Cr Partners' capitals (profit-sharing ratio)

(D) If loss on sale:
    Dr Partners' capitals (profit-sharing ratio)
        Cr Realisation

(E) Receipt purchase price:
    Dr Cash
    Dr Shares (if any) in limited company
    Dr Debentures (if any) in limited company
        Cr Limited company (purchaser)

(F) Final settlement with partners:

        Dr Partners' capital and current accounts

           Cr Cash

           Cr Shares (if any) in limited company

           Cr Debentures (if any) in limited company

Entries for these are illustrated in Exhibit 6.5.

Exhibit 6.5

Kay and Lee were in partnership, sharing profits and losses in the ratio 2:1 respectively. The following was their balance sheet as at 31 December 20X4.

Kay and Lee
Balance Sheet as at 31 December 20X4

		£
Fixed assets		
Buildings		30,000
Motor vehicles		15,000
		45,000
Current assets		
Stock	8,000	
Debtors	6,000	
Bank	1,000	
	15,000	
Current liabilities		
Creditors	(5,000)	
		10,000
		55,000
Capitals: Kay	32,000	
Lee	16,000	
		48,000
Current accounts: Kay	3,000	
Lee	4,000	
		7,000
		55,000

On 1 January 20X5 Cayley Ltd was to take over the assets, other than bank. The purchase price is £80,000, payable by £60,000 in £1 shares in Cayley Ltd at par, plus £20,000 cash. Kay and Lee will pay off their own creditors. Shares are to be divided between the partners in their profit-sharing ratio.

First we will see the closing entries in the accounts of Kay and Lee. The only asset account shown will be that of the bank account. The creditors' accounts are also not shown. The letters in brackets refer to the description of the double entry already given.

Books of Kay and Lee
Realisation

		£				£
Assets taken over:				Cayley Ltd	(B)	80,000
Buildings	(A)	30,000				
Motor vehicles	(A)	15,000				
Stock	(A)	8,000				
Debtors	(A)	6,000				
Profit on realisation:						
Kay $^2/_3$	(C)	14,000				
Lee $^1/_3$	(C)	7,000	21,000			
			80,000			80,000

Cayley Ltd

		£			£
Realisation: sale price	(B)	80,000	Bank	(E)	20,000
			Shares in Cayley Ltd	(E)	60,000
		80,000			80,000

Shares in Cayley Ltd

		£			£
Cayley Ltd	(E)	60,000	Capitals: Kay	(F)	40,000
			Lee	(F)	20,000
		60,000			60,000

Capitals

		Kay £	Lee £			Kay £	Lee £
Shares in Cayley	(F)	40,000	20,000	Balances b/d		32,000	16,000
Bank	(F)	6,000	3,000	Profit on realisation	(C)	14,000	7,000
		46,000	23,000			46,000	23,000

Current Accounts

		Kay £	Lee £			Kay £	Lee £
Bank	(F)	3,000	4,000	Balances b/d		3,000	4,000

Bank

		£		£
Bank b/d		1,000	Creditors	5,000
Cayley Ltd	(E)	20,000	Capitals: Kay	6,000
			Lee	3,000
			Current accounts: Kay	3,000
			Lee	4,000
		21,000		21,000

Note: **It would have been possible to transfer the balances of the current accounts to the capital accounts before settlement.**

Assuming that Cayley values the buildings at £41,000 and stock at £7,000, its balance sheet at 1 January 20X5 would appear as (B) under. The items shown under (A) were the balances before the takeover.

Balance Sheet(s)

	(A) Before £	+ £	– £	(B) After £
Goodwill		11,000		11,000
Buildings	50,000	41,000		91,000
Motor vehicles	25,000	15,000		40,000
Stock	28,000	7,000		35,000
Debtors	17,000	6,000		23,000
Bank	30,000		20,000	10,000
	150,000	80,000	20,000	210,000
Share capital (£1 shares)	100,000	60,000		160,000
Profit and loss	40,000			40,000
Creditors	10,000			10,000
	150,000	60,000		210,000

6.4 The takeover of a limited company by another limited company

One company may take over another company by one of two methods:

1 By buying all the assets of the other company, the purchase consideration being by cash, shares or debentures. The selling company may afterwards be wound up: either the liquidators may distribute the purchasing company's shares and debentures among the shareholders of the selling company, or else the shares and debentures of the buying company may be sold and the cash distributed instead.
2 By giving its own shares and debentures in exchange for the shares and debentures of the selling company's share and debenture holders.

Exhibit 6.6 is an illustration of each of these methods.

Exhibit 6.6

The following are the balance sheets of three companies as at the same date.

Balance Sheets

	R Ltd £	S Ltd £	T Ltd £
Buildings	13,000	–	1,000
Machinery	4,000	2,000	1,000
Stock	3,000	1,000	2,000
Debtors	2,000	1,000	3,000
Bank	1,000	2,000	3,000
	23,000	6,000	10,000
Share capital (£1 shares)	18,000	3,000	5,000
Profit and loss	2,000	1,000	4,000
Current liabilities	3,000	2,000	1,000
	23,000	6,000	10,000

R takes over S by exchanging with the shareholders of S two shares in R at a premium of 10 per cent for every share they hold in S.

R takes over T by buying all the assets of T, the purchase consideration being 12,000 £1 shares in R at a premium of 10 per cent, and R will pay off T's creditors. R values T's assets at buildings £2,000, machinery £600, stock £1,400, debtors £2,500, and the bank is £3,000, a total of £9,500.

R's deal with the shareholders of S means that R now has complete control of S Ltd, so that S Ltd becomes what is known as a subsidiary undertaking of R Ltd, and will be shown as an investment in R's balance sheet.

On the other hand, the deal with T has resulted in the ownership of the assets resting with R. These must therefore be added to R's assets in its own balance sheet. As R has given 12,000 £1 shares at a premium of 10 per cent plus taking over the responsibility for creditors £1,000, the total purchase consideration for the assets taken over is £12,000 + £1,200 (10 per cent of £12,000) + £1,000 = £14,200. Identifiable assets as already stated are valued at £9,500, therefore the goodwill is £14,200 − £9,500 = £4,700.

The distinction between the acquisition of the two going concerns can be seen to be a rather fine one. With S, the shares are taken over, the possession of these in turn giving rise to the ownership of the assets. In the books of R this is regarded as an investment. With T, the actual assets and liabilities are taken over so that the assets now directly belong to R. In the books of R this is therefore regarded as the acquisition of additional assets and liabilities and not as an investment (using the meaning of 'investment' which is used in the balance sheets of companies). The balance sheet of R Ltd therefore becomes:

R Ltd
Balance Sheet

	Before £	+ or -	£	After £
Goodwill		+(T)	4,700	4,700
Buildings	13,000	+(T)	2,000	15,000
Machinery	4,000	+(T)	600	4,600
Investment in S at cost		+(S)	6,600	6,600
Stock	3,000	+(T)	1,400	4,400
Debtors	2,000	+(T)	2,500	4,500
Bank	1,000	+(T)	3,000	4,000
	23,000			43,800
Less Current liabilities	(3,000)	+(T)	1,000	(4,000)
	20,000			39,800
Share capital	18,000	+(S)	6,000	
		+(T)	12,000	= 36,000
Share premium		+(S)	600	
		+(T)	1,200	= 1,800
Profit and loss	2,000			2,000
	20,000			39,800

No entry is necessary in the books of S Ltd, as it is merely the identity of the shareholders that has changed. This would be duly recorded in the register of members, but this is not really an integral part of the double entry accounting system.

If, however, T Ltd is now liquidated, then a realisation account must be drawn up and the distribution of the shares (or cash if the shares are sold) to the shareholders of T Ltd must be shown. Such accounts would appear as follows:

Books of T Ltd
Realisation

	£		£
Book values of assets disposed of:		R Ltd: Total purchase	
Buildings	1,000	consideration	14,200
Machinery	1,000		
Stock	2,000		
Debtors	3,000		
Bank	3,000		
Profit on realisation transferred			
to sundry shareholders	4,200		
	14,200		14,200

Share Capital

	£		£
Sundry shareholders	5,000	Balance b/d	5,000

Profit and Loss

	£		£
Sundry shareholders	4,000	Balance b/d	4,000

Creditors

	£		£
R Ltd – taken over	1,000	Balance b/d	1,000

R Ltd

	£		£
Realisation:		Creditors	1,000
Total consideration	14,200	Sundry shareholders: 12,000	
		£1 shares received at premium	
		of 10 per cent	13,200
	14,200		14,200

Sundry Shareholders

	£		£
R Ltd: 12,000 £1 shares at premium		Share capital	5,000
of 10 per cent	13,200	Profit and loss	4,000
		Profit on realisation	4,200
	13,200		13,200

It can be seen that the items possessed by the sundry shareholders have been transferred to an account in their name. These are (*a*) the share capital which obviously belongs to them, (*b*) the credit balance on the profit and loss account built up by withholding cash dividends from the shareholders, and (*c*) the profit on realisation which they, as owners of the business, are entitled to take. As there were 5,000 shares in T Ltd, and 12,000 shares have been given by R Ltd, then each holder of 5 shares in T Ltd will now be given 12 shares in R Ltd to complete the liquidation of the company.

6.5 The exchange of debentures

Sometimes the debentures in the company taking over are to be given in exchange for the debentures of the company being taken over. This may be straightforward on the basis of £100 debentures in company A in exchange for £100 debentures in company B. However, the problem often arises where the exchange is in terms of one or both sets of debentures being at a discount or at a premium. The need for such an exchange may be twofold:

1 To persuade the debenture holders in company B to give up their debentures some form of inducement may be needed, such as letting them have A's debentures at a discount even though they may well be worth the par value.

2 There may be a difference in the debenture interest rates. For instance, a person with a £100 7 per cent debenture would not normally gladly part with it in exchange for a £100 6 per cent debenture in another company. The first debenture gives the investor £7 a year interest, the second one only £6 per year. Thus the debenture in the second company may be issued at a discount to redeem the debenture in the first company at a premium. As the amount of interest is only one factor – there are also others such as the certainty of the debenture holder regaining his/her money if the firm had to close down – the precise terms of the exchange cannot be based merely on arithmetical calculations of interest rates, but it is one of the measures taken when negotiating the exchange of debentures.

Exhibit 6.7

1 D Ltd is to give the necessary debentures at a discount of 10 per cent required to redeem £9,000 debentures in J Ltd at a premium of 5 per cent. The problem here is to find exactly what amount of debentures must be given by D Ltd.

$$\frac{\text{Total nominal value of debentures}}{\text{to be redeemed (exchanged)}} \times \frac{\text{Redeemable value of each £100 debenture of J Ltd}}{\text{Issue value of each £100 debenture of D Ltd}}$$

= Total nominal value of D Ltd to be issued

$$= £9,000 \times \frac{105}{90}$$

$$= £10,500$$

Thus, to satisfy the agreement, debentures of D Ltd of a total nominal value of £10,500 are issued at a discount of 10 per cent to the debenture holder of J Ltd.

2 H Ltd is to give the necessary debentures at par to redeem £5,000 debentures in M Ltd at a premium of 4 per cent.

$$£5,000 \times \frac{104}{100} = \text{Debentures of £5,200 nominal value are given by H Ltd at par}$$

6.6 Profit (or loss) prior to incorporation

Quite frequently, companies take over businesses from a date which is actually before the company was itself incorporated. It could be that two persons enter into business and start trading with the intention of running the business as a limited company. However, it takes more than a few days to attend to all the necessary formalities before the company can be incorporated. Obviously the time taken depends on the speed with which the formation is pushed through and the solution of any snags which crop up.

When the company is incorporated it may enter into a contract whereby it adopts all the transactions retrospectively to the date that the firm (i.e. with two persons it was a partnership) had started trading. This means that the company accepts all the benefits and disadvantages which have flowed from the transactions which have occurred. The example used was that of a new business; it could well have been an old, established business that was taken over from a date previous to incorporation.

Legally a company cannot earn profits before it comes into existence, i.e. is incorporated, and therefore to decide what action will have to be taken, such profits will first of all have to be calculated. Any such profits are of a capital nature and must be transferred to a capital reserve account, normally titled *Pre-incorporation Profit Account* or *Profit Prior to Incorporation Account*. That this should be so is apparent if it is realised that, though the actual date from which the transactions have been adopted falls before the date of incorporation, the price at which the business is being taken over is influenced by the values of the assets etc. at the date when the company actually takes over, i.e. the date of incorporation.

Suppose that Doolin and Kershaw start a business on 1 January 20X5 with £1,000 capital, and very shortly afterwards Davie and Parker become interested as well, and the four of them start to form a company in which they will all become directors, Davie and Parker to start active work when the company is incorporated. The company is incorporated on 1 May 20X5 and the original owners of the business, Doolin and Kershaw, are to be given shares in the new company to compensate them for handing over the business. If they know, not necessarily with precision, that the original £1,000 assets will have grown to net assets of £6,000, then they most certainly would not part with the business to the company for £1,000. Ignoring goodwill they would want £6,000 of shares. Conversely, if the net assets have shrunk to £400, would Davie and Parker be happy to see £1,000 of shares handed over? This means that the price at which the business is taken over is dependent on the expected value at the date of the company incorporation, and not on the value at the date on which the company is supposed to take over.

Taking the case of the increase in net assets to £6,000, the £5,000 difference is made up of profits. If these profits could be distributed as dividends then, in effect, the capital payment of £6,000 in shares is being part used up for dividend purposes. This is in direct contradiction to the normal accounting practice of retaining capital intact (the accountant's meaning of 'capital' and not the meaning given to 'capital' by the economist). The £5,000 profits must therefore be regarded as not being available for dividends. They are thus a capital reserve.

Although the profit cannot be regarded as free for use as dividends, any such loss can be taken to restrict the dividends which could be paid out of the profits made after incorporation. This is the concept of prudence once again coming into play, and if the price paid on

takeover was misjudged and a high figure was paid, and it was discovered later that a loss had been made, then the restriction of dividends leads to the capital lost being replaced by assets held back within the firm. Alternatively the amount of the pre-incorporation loss could be charged to a goodwill account, as this is also another way of stating that a higher price has been paid for the assets of the firm than is represented by the value of the tangible assets taken over.

It is possible for the profits up to the date of incorporation to be calculated quite separately from those after incorporation. However, the cost of stocktaking etc. may be felt to be not worthwhile merely to produce financial statements when, in fact, the financial statements could be left until the normal financial year end. This is invariably the case in examination questions. Therefore when the financial statements for the full financial year are being made up, they will consist of profits before and after incorporation. The financial statements must therefore be split to throw up the two sets of profit (or loss), so that distinction can be made between those profits usable, and those not usable, for dividend purposes. There is no hard-and-fast rule as to how this shall be done. Known facts must prevail, and where an arbitrary apportionment must be made, it should meet the test of common sense in the particular case. Exhibit 6.8 shows an attempt to calculate such profits.

Exhibit 6.8

Slack and King, partners in a firm, are to have their business taken over as from 1 January 20X4 by Monk Ltd which is incorporated on 1 April 20X4. It was agreed that all profits made from 1 January 20X4 should belong to the company, and that the vendors be entitled to interest on the purchase price from 1 January to date of payment. The purchase price was paid on 30 April 20X4, including £1,600 interest. A profit and loss account is drawn up for the year ended 31 December 20X4. This is shown as column (X). This is then split into before incorporation, shown as column (Y), and after incorporation as column (Z). The methods used to apportion the particular items are shown after the profit and loss account, the letters (A) to (I) against the items being the references to the notes.

These particular methods must definitely not be used in all cases for similar expenses; they are only an indication of different methods of apportionment. The facts and the peculiarities of each firm must be taken into account, and no method should be slavishly followed.

Assume for this example that all calendar months are of equal length.

Monk Ltd
Profit and Loss Account for the year ended 31 December 20X4

		(X) Full year £	(X) Full year £	(Y) Pre-incorporation £	(Y) Pre-incorporation £	(Z) After £	(Z) After £
Gross profit	(A)		38,000		8,000		30,000
Less							
Partnership salaries	(B)	1,000		1,000			
Employees' remuneration	(C)	12,000		3,000		9,000	
General expenses	(C)	800		200		600	
Commission on sales	(D)	1,700		200		1,500	
Distribution expenses	(E)	1,900		400		1,500	
Bad debts	(F)	100		20		80	
Bank overdraft interest	(G)	200				200	
Directors' remuneration	(H)	5,000				5,000	
Directors' expenses	(H)	400				400	
Debenture interest	(H)	500				500	
Depreciation	(C)	1,000		250		750	
Interest paid to vendors	(I)	1,600		1,200		400	
			(26,200)		(6,270)		(19,930)
Net profit			11,800				
Transferred to capital reserves					1,730		
Carried down to the appropriation account							10,070

Notes:

(A) For the three months to 31 March sales amounted to £40,000, and for the remaining nine months they were £150,000. Gross profit is at a uniform rate of 20 per cent of selling price throughout the year. Therefore the gross profit is apportioned (Y) 20 per cent of £40,000 = £8,000, and (Z) 20 per cent of £150,000 = £30,000.

(B) The partnership salaries of the vendors, Slack and King, obviously belong to (Y), because that is the period of the partnership.

(C) These expenses, in this particular case, have accrued evenly throughout the year and are therefore split on the time basis of (Y) three-twelfths, (Z) nine-twelfths.

(D) Commission to the salespeople was paid at the rate of $\frac{1}{2}$ per cent on sales up to 31 March, and 1 per cent thereafter. The commission figure is split:

(Y) $\frac{1}{2}$ per cent of £40,000 =   200
(Z) 1 per cent of £150,000 = <u>1,500</u>
<u>1,700</u>

(E) In this particular case (but not always true in every case) the distribution expenses have varied directly with the value of sales. They are therefore split:

(Y) $\dfrac{\text{Y sales}}{\text{Total sales}} \times \text{Expenses} = \dfrac{40,000}{190,000} \times £1,900 = \dfrac{4}{19} \times £1,900 = £400$

(Z) $\dfrac{\text{Z sales}}{\text{Total sales}} \times \text{Expenses} = \dfrac{150,000}{190,000} \times £1,900 = \dfrac{15}{19} \times £1,900 = £1,500$

(F) The bad debts were two in number:
   (i) in respect of a sale in January, the debtor dying penniless in March, £20;
   (ii) in respect of a sale in June, the debtor being declared bankrupt in December, £80.

(G) The bank account was never overdrawn until June, so that the interest charged must be for period (Z).

(H) Only in companies are such expenses as directors' salaries, directors' expenses and debenture interest to be found. These must naturally be shown in period (Z).

(I) The interest paid to the vendors was due to the fact that the company was receiving all the benefits from 1 January but did not in fact pay any cash for the business until 30 April. This is therefore in effect loan interest which should be spread over the period it was borrowed, i.e. three months to (Y) and 1 month to (Z).

Learning outcomes

You should now have learnt:

1 Why goodwill may arise when a business is taken over.

2 The difference between goodwill and negative goodwill.

3 The basic accounting entries are the same whether a limited company takes over a sole trader or a partnership.

4 Limited companies may take over other limited companies either:
   (a) by buying all the assets of the other company, or
   (b) by giving its own shares and debentures in exchange for the shares and debentures of the company being taken over.

5 How to record pre-incorporation losses and profits.

6 That pre-incorporation profits are not available for distribution.

Answers to activities

6.1 Apart from the obvious difference that may arise between the net book value of an individual asset and its true worth, such as the example of the property given in the text, when a business is sold the purchaser may have to pay extra to cover the value of intangible assets that do not

appear in the balance sheet. Examples would include the reputation and customer base of the business being purchased, neither of which can appear in a balance sheet.

It is also possible that less may be paid than the net worth of a business because some assets may be considered as not being worth the amounts shown in the financial statements – it may be considered, for example, that debtors are likely to be overvalued or that individual assets are worth less to the purchaser than the values shown in the financial statements.

Of course, buyers generally try to pay as little as possible for a business. If a seller is very keen to sell, a price may be agreed that is below the net worth as shown in the balance sheet, even though that value is correct. It all depends on how the transaction is negotiated by the purchaser and the seller.

REVIEW QUESTIONS

6.1   Checkers Ltd was incorporated on 1 April 20X5 and took over the business of Black and White, partners, as from 1 January 20X5. It was agreed that all profits made from 1 January should belong to the company and that the vendors should be entitled to interest on the purchase price from 1 January to date of payment. The purchase price was paid on 31 May 20X5 including £1,650 interest.
   The following is the profit and loss account for the year to 31 December 20X5:

	£		£
Salaries of vendors	1,695	Gross profit	28,000
Wages and general expenses	8,640		
Rent and rates	860		
Distribution expenses	1,680		
Commission on sales	700		
Bad debts	314		
Interest paid to vendors	1,650		
Directors' remuneration	4,000		
Directors' expenses	515		
Depreciation	£		
Motors	1,900		
Machinery	575		
	2,475		
Bank interest	168		
Net profit	5,303		
	28,000		28,000

You are given the following information:

1 Sales amounted to £20,000 for the three months to 31 March 20X5 and £50,000 for the nine months to 31 December 20X5. Gross profit is at a uniform rate of 40 per cent of selling price throughout the year, and commission at a rate of 1 per cent is paid on all sales.
2 Salaries of £1,695 were paid to the vendors for their assistance in running the business up to 31 March 20X5.
3 The bad debts written off are:
   (a) a debt of £104 taken over from the vendors;
   (b) a debt of £210 in respect of goods sold in August 20X5.
4 On 1 January 20X5, motors were bought for £7,000 and machinery for £5,000. On 1 March 20X5 another motor van was bought for £3,000 and on 1 October 20X5 another machine was added for £3,000. Depreciation has been written off motors at 20 per cent per annum, and machinery 10 per cent per annum.
5 Wages and general expenses and rent and rates accrued at an even rate throughout the year.
6 The bank granted an overdraft in June 20X5.

Assuming all calendar months are of equal length:

(a) set out the profit and loss account in columnar form, so as to distinguish between the period prior to the company's incorporation and the period after incorporation;
(b) state how you would deal with the profit prior to incorporation;
(c) state how you would deal with the results prior to incorporation if they turned out to be a net loss.

6.2 On 31 December 20X6 Breeze Ltd acquired all the assets, except the investments, of Blow Ltd. The following are the summaries of the profit and loss account of Blow Ltd for the years 20X4, 20X5 and 20X6:

	20X4	20X5	20X6		20X4	20X5	20X6
Motor expenses	1,860	1,980	2,100	Trading profits	22,050	25,780	25,590
Depreciation of plant				Investment income	290	340	480
and machinery	4,000	3,200	2,560	Rents received	940	420	–
Bank overdraft interest	180	590	740	Profit on sale of			
Wrapping expenses	840	960	1,020	property		4,800	
Preliminary expenses							
written off	–	690	–				
Net profit	16,400	23,920	19,650				
	23,280	31,340	26,070		23,280	31,340	26,070

The purchase price is to be the amount on which an estimated maintainable profit would represent a return of 25 per cent per annum.

The maintainable profit is to be taken as the average of the profits of the three years 20X4, 20X5 and 20X6, after making any necessary adjustments.

You are given the following information:

(a) The cost of the plant and machinery was £20,000. It is agreed that depreciation should have been written off at the rate of $12\frac{1}{2}$ per cent per annum using the straight line method.

(b) A form of new plastic wrapping material introduced on to the market means that wrapping expenses will be halved in future.

(c) By a form of long-term rental of motor vehicles, it is estimated that motor expenses will be cut by one-third in future.

(d) Stock treated as valueless at 31 December 20X3 was sold for £1,900 in 20X5.

(e) The working capital of the new company is such that an overdraft is not contemplated.

(f) Management remuneration has been inadequate and will have to be increased by £1,500 a year in future.

You are required to set out your calculation of the purchase price. All workings must be shown. In fact, your managing director, who is not an accountant, should be able to decipher how the price was calculated.

6.3 CJK Ltd was incorporated on 15 December 20X9 with an authorised capital of 200,000 ordinary shares of £0.20 each to acquire as at 31 December 20X9 the business of CK, a sole trader, and RP Ltd, a company.

From the following information you are required to prepare:

(a) the realisation and capital accounts in the books of CK and RP Ltd showing the winding up of these two concerns;

(b) the journal entries to open the books of CJK Ltd, including cash transactions and the raising of finance;

(c) the balance sheet of CJK Ltd after the transactions have been completed.

The balance sheet of CK as at 31 December 20X9 is as follows:

Balance Sheet

	£
Freehold premises	8,000
Plant	4,000
Stock	2,000
Debtors	5,000
Cash	200
	19,200
Capital	16,000
Creditors	3,200
	19,200

The assets (excluding cash) and the liabilities were taken over at the following values: freehold premises £10,000, plant £3,500, stock £2,000, debtors £5,000 less a bad debts provision of £300, goodwill £7,000, creditors £3,200 less a discount provision of £150. The purchase consideration, based on these values, was settled by the issue of shares at par.

The balance sheet of RP Ltd as at 31 December 20X9 is as follows:

Balance Sheet

	£
Freehold premises	4,500
Plant	2,000
Stock	1,600
Debtors	3,400
	11,500
Share capital: 10,000 shares at £0.40 each	4,000
Revenue surplus	2,500
Creditors	1,500
Bank overdraft	3,500
	11,500

The assets and liabilities were taken over at book value with the exception of the freehold premises which were revalued at £5,500. The purchase consideration was a cash payment of £1 and three shares in CJK Ltd at par in exchange for every two shares in RP Ltd.

Additional working capital and the funds required to complete the purchase of RP Ltd were provided by the issue for cash of:

(*i*) 10,000 shares at a premium of £0.30 per share;
(*ii*) £8,000 7 per cent debenture stock at 98.

The expenses of incorporating CJK Ltd were paid, amounting to £1,200.

(*Chartered Institute of Management Accountants*)

6.4A The balance sheet of Hubble Ltd as at 31 May 20X0 is shown below.

Hubble Ltd

	£	£
Fixed assets		
Freehold premises at cost		375,000
Plant and machinery at cost		
Less Depreciation £48,765		101,235
Motor vehicles at cost		
Less Depreciation £1,695		6,775
Current assets		483,010
Stock-in-trade	102,550	
Debtors	96,340	
Cash in hand	105	
		198,995
		682,005
Authorised share capital		
650,000 ordinary shares of £1 each		650,000
Issued share capital		
400,000 ordinary shares of £1 each fully paid		400,000
Profit and loss account		180,630
Current liabilities		580,630
Trade creditors	63,200	
Bank overdraft	38,175	
		101,375
		682,005

Hubble Ltd agreed to purchase at this date the freehold premises, plant and machinery and stock of A Bubble at agreed valuations of £100,000, £10,000 and £55,000, respectively. The purchase price was to be fully settled by the issue to Bubble of 120,000 ordinary shares of £1 each in Hubble Ltd, and a cash payment to Bubble of £25,000. Bubble was to collect his debts and to pay his creditors.

Hubble Ltd sold one of its own premises prior to taking over Bubble for £75,000 (cost £55,000) and revalued the remainder at £400,000 (excluding those acquired from Bubble).

You are required to:
(a) show the journal entries, including cash items, in the books of Hubble Ltd to give effect to the above transactions; and
(b) show the balance sheet of Hubble Ltd after completing them.

(*Association of Chartered Certified Accountants*)

6.5A From the following information you are required to prepare a statement apportioning the unappropriated profit between the pre-incorporation and post-incorporation periods, showing the basis of apportionment:

VU Limited was incorporated on 1 July 20X9 with an authorised share capital of 60,000 ordinary shares of £1 each, to take over the business of L and Sons as from 1 April 20X9.

The purchase consideration was agreed at £50,000 for the net tangible assets taken over, plus a further £6,000 for goodwill.

Payment was satisfied by the issue of £30,000 8 per cent debentures and 26,000 ordinary shares both at par, on 1 August 20X9. Interest at 10 per cent per annum on the purchase consideration was paid up to this date.

The company raised a further £20,000 on 1 August 20X9 by the issue of ordinary shares at a premium of £0.25 per share.

The abridged profit and loss account for the year to 31 March 20X0 was as follows:

	£	£
Sales:		
1 April 20X9 to 30 June 20X9	30,000	
1 July 20X9 to 31 March 19Y0	95,000	
		125,000
Cost of sales for the year	80,000	
Depreciation	2,220	
Directors' fees	500	
Administration salaries and expenses	8,840	
Sales commission	4,375	
Goodwill written off	1,000	
Interest on purchase consideration, gross	1,867	
Distribution costs (60 per cent variable)	6,250	
Preliminary expenses written off	1,650	
Debenture interest, gross	1,600	
Proposed dividend on ordinary shares	7,560	
		115,862
Unappropriated profit carried forward		9,138

The company sells one product only, of which the unit selling price has remained constant during the year, but due to improved buying the unit cost of sales was reduced by 10 per cent in the post-incorporation period as compared with the pre-incorporation period.

Taxation is to be ignored.

(*Chartered Institute of Management Accountants (part (a) of question only)*)

6.6A Rowlock Ltd was incorporated on 1 October 20X8 to acquire Rowlock's mail order business, with effect from 1 June 20X8.

The purchase consideration was agreed at £35,000 to be satisfied by the issue on 1 December 20X8 to Rowlock or his nominee of 20,000 ordinary shares of £1 each, fully paid, and £15,000 7 per cent debentures.

The entries relating to the transfer were not made in the books which were carried on without a break until 31 May 20X9.

On 31 May 20X9 the trial balance extracted from the books is:

	£	£
Sales		52,185
Purchases	38,829	
Wrapping	840	
Postage	441	
Warehouse rent and rates	921	
Packing expenses	1,890	
Office expenses	627	
Stock on 31 May 20X8	5,261	
Director's salary	1,000	
Debenture interest (gross)	525	
Fixed assets	25,000	
Current assets (other than stock)	9,745	
Current liabilities		4,162
Formation expenses	218	
Capital account – Wysocka, 31 May 20X8		29,450
Drawings account – Wysocka, 31 May 20X8	500	
	85,797	85,797

You also ascertain the following:

1 Stock on 31 May 20X9 amounted to £4,946.
2 The average monthly sales for June, July and August were one-half of those for the remaining months of the year. The gross profit margin was constant throughout the year.
3 Wrapping, postage and packing expenses varied in direct proportion to sales, whilst office expenses were constant each month.
4 Formation expenses are to be written off.

You are required to prepare the trading and profit and loss account for the year ended 31 May 20X9 apportioned between the periods before and after incorporation, and the balance sheet as at that date.

(*Chartered Institute of Management Accountants*)

CHAPTER 7

Taxation in company financial statements

Learning objectives

After you have studied this chapter, you should be able to:

- explain why profit per the profit and loss account is normally different from assessable profit for corporation tax calculations
- explain how income tax on interest affects companies and individuals
- describe how the 'imputation system' operates
- describe how and why deferred tax is relevant to capital allowances

Introduction

In this chapter you'll learn that depreciation is not allowed as an expense for tax purposes and that capital allowances are granted instead. You'll also learn that the result of replacing depreciation with capital allowances when calculating tax is that taxable profit is very rarely the same as net profit as shown in the financial statements. You'll learn how to apportion taxable profit across two tax periods, about when corporation tax is payable and of the differences between the tax system for companies compared with the one that operates for sole traders and partnerships. Finally, you will learn about deferred tax and how it is calculated and applied in order to avoid financial statements being misleading in how they present future tax liabilities in the balance sheet.

7.1 Background

This chapter is concerned with the entries made in the financial statements of companies in respect of taxation. It is not concerned with the actual calculation of the taxes. Taxation legislation is now extremely complex and contains many exceptions to the general rules applicable to companies. It is impossible in a book at this level to delve into too many of the complications. It should, therefore, be appreciated that so far as companies are concerned, though the facts in this chapter apply to the great majority of limited companies, there are some other complications in a small minority of cases.

Taxation that affects companies can be split between:

1 Direct taxes, payable to the Inland Revenue, this being the government department responsible for the calculation and collection of the taxes. For a company these taxes are corporation tax and income tax. FRS 16: *Current tax* deals with the treatment of taxation in company financial statements, and will be adhered to in this chapter.
2 Value added tax, abbreviated as VAT. This has been dealt with in *Business Accounting 1*.

7.2 Limited companies: corporation tax and income tax

The tax suffered by limited companies is known as corporation tax. Legally, it is an appropriation of profits, it is not an expense, and it should therefore be shown in the profit and loss appropriation account. Many years ago, two law cases settled the argument as to whether it was an expense or an appropriation. Both cases were decided in favour of the view that it was an appropriation of profits.

When a company makes profits, those profits are assessable to corporation tax. It does not mean that corporation tax is payable on the net profits as shown in the financial statements. What it does mean is that the corporation tax is assessable on the profit calculated after certain adjustments have been made to the net profit shown according to the profit and loss account. These adjustments are not made in the financial statements, they are made in calculations performed quite separately from the drafting of financial statements.

Suppose that K Ltd has the following profit and loss account:

K Ltd Profit and Loss Account for the year ended 31 March 20X8

	£	£
Gross profit		100,000
Less: General expenses	25,000	
Depreciation of machinery	20,000	
		(45,000)
Net profit		55,000

The depreciation provision for machinery is the accounting figure used for the financial statements. It is not usually the same figure as that allowed by the Inland Revenue for the depreciation of the machinery. The allowances made for depreciation by the Inland Revenue are known as **capital allowances**. These are calculated by rules which usually vary at one point or another from the methods applied by companies in determining their depreciation provisions.

Activity 7.1
Why do you think the rules for capital allowances are different from the rules for depreciation?

A detailed study of a textbook on taxation would be necessary to see exactly how capital allowances are calculated. In some fairly rare cases, hardly ever found in large or medium-sized concerns but probably more common in very small firms, the capital allowances are calculated and the financial provision for depreciation is taken at the same figure. In the case of K Ltd, assume that the capital allowances amount to £27,000 and that the rate of corporation tax is 40 per cent on assessable profits. The calculation of the corporation tax liability would be:

	£
Net profit per the financial statements	55,000
Add Depreciation provision not allowed as a deduction for corporation tax purposes	20,000
	75,000
Less Capital allowances	(27,000)
Adjusted profits assessable to corporation tax	48,000

As the corporation tax is assumed to be at the rate of 40 per cent of assessable profits, the corporation tax liability will be £48,000 × 40 per cent = £19,200. Sometimes the adjusted profits are greater than the net profits shown in the financial statements, but may equally well be less.

This illustrates the fact that it is relatively rare for the external observer to be able to calculate the corporation tax payable merely by knowing the net profit made by the company. In fact, there are other items besides depreciation provisions that need adjusting to find the correct assessable profits for corporation tax purposes. All that is needed here is the understanding that profit per the profit and loss account is normally different from assessable profit for corporation tax calculations.

7.3 The rate of corporation tax

The rate of corporation tax is fixed by the Chancellor of the Exchequer in the Budget, presented to Parliament each year. In the Budget, the corporation tax rates are fixed covering the period from 1 April until 31 March of the year following. This rate is to be applied to the assessable profits of companies earned during this period. A company whose financial year end is not 31 March will, therefore, span two governmental financial years, and will need to apportion its taxable profits across the two periods.

Exhibit 7.1

Company T Ltd: adjusted profits for the year ended 31 December 20X8 = £160,000.

Rates of corporation tax:
For the government financial year ended 31.3.20X8, 45 per cent.
For the government financial year ended 31.3.20X9, 40 per cent.

	£
3 months' profit 1.1.20X8 to 31.3.20X8	
3/12 months × £160,000 = £40,000 × 45 per cent	18,000
9 months' profit 1.4.20X8 to 31.12.20X8	
9/12 months × £160,000 = £120,000 × 40 per cent	48,000
	66,000

7.4 Corporation tax – when payable

All companies have a payment date of 9 months after the end of each accounting period. For the rest of this chapter, although companies with relatively small profits can pay tax at a lower rate than companies with greater profits, unless mentioned otherwise, for the purposes of illustration, corporation tax will be assumed to be at the rate of 40 per cent.

7.5 Advance corporation tax (ACT)

In the past, when a company paid a dividend, a sum equal to a fraction of that figure had to be paid to the Inland Revenue as *advance corporation tax* (ACT). When a company was due to pay its corporation tax bill, it adjusted the amount it sent to the Inland Revenue by the amount of ACT it had paid or reclaimed during the relevant period. FRS 16: *Current tax* changed the rules relating to inclusion of dividends received to require them to be shown net of any associated tax credit. ACT was repealed with effect from 1999 and is not included in any of the examples or questions in this book.

7.6 Income tax

As already stated, companies do not pay income tax, instead they suffer corporation tax. In the case of a sole trader, income tax is not directly connected with the business, as its

calculation depends on many factors including, for example, whether the sole trader is married or not and on the amount and type of other income received by him/her. It should therefore be charged to the drawings account.

The income tax charged upon a partnership is also subject to the personal situation of the partners. The actual apportionment of the tax between the partners must be performed by someone who has access to the personal tax computations; it most certainly is not apportioned in the partners' profit-sharing ratios. When the apportionment has been made, each partner should have the relevant amount debited to his drawings account. Sole traders and partnerships are not liable to corporation tax.

Income tax does, however, come into the financial statements of limited companies in that the company, when paying charges such as debenture interest or some types of royalty, will deduct income tax from the amount to be paid to the debenture holder or royalty owner. This figure of income tax is then payable by the company to the Inland Revenue. This means simply that the company is acting as a tax collector on behalf of the Inland Revenue.

Suppose, for example, that the company has a thousand different debenture holders. It is far easier for the Inland Revenue if the company pays only the net amount (i.e. the amount of debenture interest less income tax) due to each debenture holder and then pays the income tax deducted, in one figure, to the Inland Revenue. This saves the Inland Revenue having to trace a thousand debenture holders and then collect the money from them. It obviously cuts down on the bad debts that the Inland Revenue might suffer, it makes it more difficult to evade the payment of income tax, plus it makes it cheaper for the Inland Revenue to administer the system. This system is based on the same principles as PAYE on wages or salaries.

For clarity, throughout the rest of this chapter it will be assumed that the basic rate of income tax is 25 per cent. The real rate will obviously differ from time to time. In addition, where an individual has a high or low income he/she will pay rates of income tax which may differ from 25 per cent. However, even though individual debenture holders may have to pay income tax at higher rates, or indeed pay lower rates or no income tax at all, a company will generally deduct income tax at the basic rate.

This means that if a company had 8 per cent debentures amounting to £100,000 then, assuming that the debenture interest was payable in one amount, cheques amounting to a total of £6,000 (8 per cent of £100,000 = £8,000 less 25 per cent income tax, £2,000 = £6,000) will be paid to the debenture holders. A cheque for £2,000 will then be paid to the Inland Revenue by the company. Assume that debenture holder AB is liable on his income to income tax at the rate of 25 per cent, and that he receives interest of £75 net (i.e. £100 gross less income tax £25), on his debenture of £1,250, then he has already suffered his rightful income tax by deduction at source. He will not get a further bill from the Inland Revenue for £25 tax: he has already suffered the full amount due by him, and the company will have paid the £25 income tax as part of the total income tax cheque of £2,000.

On the other hand, debenture holder CD may not be liable to income tax because his income is low, or he may have sufficient factors qualifying for tax relief that he is not liable to pay any income tax. If he has a debenture of £1,000 he will receive a cheque for interest amounting to £60 (i.e. £80 gross, less income tax £20). As he is not liable to income tax, but £20 of his money has been included in the total cheque paid by the company to the Inland Revenue of £2,000, then he will be able to claim a refund of £20 from the Inland Revenue. Such a claim is made direct to the Inland Revenue, the company having nothing to do with the refund.

Another debenture holder, EF, is liable to a higher rate of income tax of 40 per cent on his income. If he has a debenture of £25,000, then the company will pay a cheque to him of £1,500 (£2,000 gross less income tax £500). In fact, he is really liable for £800 income tax (£2,000 at 40 per cent) on this income. As £500 income tax has been taken from him and

handed over by the company in the total cheque of £2,000 income tax paid to the Inland Revenue, eventually the Inland Revenue will send an extra demand for income tax of £300 to EF (£800 liable less £500 already paid). The company will have nothing to do with this extra demand.

7.7 Income tax on interest

Of course, a company may well have bought debentures or may own royalties etc. in another company. This may mean that the company not only pays charges, such as debenture interest, but also receives similar items from other companies. The company will receive such items net after income tax has been deducted. When the company both receives and pays such items, it may set off the tax already suffered by it from such interest etc. received against the tax collected by it from its own charges, and pay the resultant net figure of income tax to the Inland Revenue.

The figures of charges to be shown as being paid or received by the company in the company's own profit and loss account are the gross charges, i.e. the same as they would have been if income tax had never been invented. Exhibit 7.2 will illustrate this more clearly.

Exhibit 7.2

RST Ltd has 7 per cent debentures amounting to £10,000 and has bought a £4,000 debenture of 10 per cent in a private company, XYZ Ltd. During the year, cheques amounting to £525 (£700 less 25 per cent) have been paid to debenture holders, and a cheque of £300 (£400 less 25 per cent) has been received from XYZ Ltd. Instead of paying over the £175 income tax deducted on payment of debenture interest, RST Ltd waits until the cheque is received from XYZ Ltd and then pays a cheque for £75 (£175 collected by it less £100 already suffered by deduction by XYZ Ltd) to the Inland Revenue in settlement.

Debenture Interest Payable

	£		£
Cash	525	Profit and loss	700
Income tax	175		
	700		700

Debenture Interest Receivable

	£		£
Profit and loss	400	Cash	300
		Income tax	100
	400		400

Income Tax

	£		£
Unquoted investment income	100	Debenture interest	175
Cash	75		
	175		175

It may well have been the case that although the income tax had been deducted at source from both the payment out of the company and the amount received, no cash has been paid specifically to the Inland Revenue by the company by the balance sheet date. This means that the balance of £75 owing to the Inland Revenue will be carried down as a credit balance and will be shown under current liabilities in the balance sheet.

7.8 Franked payments and franked investment income

When a dividend is paid by a company, this is done without any specific deduction of tax of any kind from the dividend payment. Previously, when a company paid a dividend, it also incurred a liability to pay ACT – *see* Section 7.5. The recipient received the dividend plus a tax credit, equal to the ACT, which could then be set against the recipient's income tax liability. When the dividend was paid to another company, the total of the dividend paid plus the tax credit was known as the *franked payment*. The total of the dividend received plus the tax credit was called *franked investment income*. With the repeal of ACT in 1999, these two terms appear unlikely to continue to be used.

7.9 Deferred taxation

It was pointed out earlier in the chapter that *profits per the financial statements* and *profits on which tax is payable* are often quite different from each other. The main reasons for this are as follows:

1 The figure of depreciation shown in the profit and loss account may be far different from the Inland Revenue's figure for 'capital allowances', which is *their* way of calculating allowances for depreciation.
2 Some items of expense charged in the profit and loss account will not be allowed by the Inland Revenue as expenses. Examples are political donations, fines for illegal acts, and expenses of entertaining UK customers.

Timing differences

In the case of capital allowances under (1) above, the amount of 'depreciation' charged for an asset over the years will eventually equal the amount allowed by the Inland Revenue as 'capital allowances'. Where the difference lies is in the periods when these items will be taken into account.

For instance, let us take an asset which will be used for three years and then put out of use. It costs £4,800 and will be sold three years later for £2,025. The depreciation rate is to be $33^{1}/_{3}$ per cent straight line. Inland Revenue capital allowances are 25 per cent reducing balance.

Years ended 5 April	20X2	20X3	20X4	Total
	£	£	£	£
Depreciation in accounts	925	925	925	2,775
Capital allowances in tax calculations	1,200	900	675	2,775
Timing differences	+275	−25	−250	nil

Activity 7.2
Why do you think the depreciation is £925 per year?

Let us suppose that profits for each year, after charging depreciation, amounted to £1,000. A comparison of profits per financial statements and profits for tax purposes becomes as follows:

Years ended 5 April	20X2	20X3	20X4	Total
	£	£	£	£
Profits per accounts after depreciation	1,000	1,000	1,000	3,000
Profits for tax purposes	725	1,025	1,250	3,000
Differences	−275	+25	+250	nil

As you can see, profits have in fact remained the same at £1,000; it is the timing difference of capital allowances which gives different figures for tax purposes. Taking the point of view that profits of £1,000 per year give a more sensible picture than the £725, £1,025 and £1,250 per the Inland Revenue calculations, the company's way of depreciating is probably more suitable than the Inland Revenue's method which does not vary between different companies.

You may well be asking if it matters at all. Analysts and potential investors and shareholders themselves place a great reliance on *earnings per share after tax*. Suppose that corporation tax was 40 per cent for each of the three years and that there were 10,000 shares. This would give the following figures:

Tax based on 'real profits', i.e. company's calculations:

	20X2	20X3	20X4
	£	£	£
Profit per financial statements before taxation	1,000	1,000	1,000
Less Corporation tax (40%)	(400)	(400)	(400)
Profit after tax	600	600	600
Earnings per share = Profit after tax ÷ 10,000 =	6.0p	6.0p	6.0p

Tax based on Inland Revenue calculations:

	20X2	20X3	20X4
	£	£	£
Profit per financial statements before tax	1,000	1,000	1,000
Less Corporation tax:			
40% of £725	(290)		
40% of £1,025		(410)	
40% of £1,250			(500)
Profit after tax	710	590	500
Earnings per share = Profit after tax ÷ 10,000 =	7.1p	5.9p	5.0p

In truth, each of the years has been equally as profitable as any other – this is shown by the company's calculation of 6.0p earnings per share each year. On the other hand, if no adjustment is made, the financial statements when based on actual tax paid would show 7.1p, 5.9p and 5.0p. This could confuse shareholders and would-be shareholders.

In order not to distort the picture given by financial statements, the concept of deferred taxation was brought in by accountants. There have been three accounting standards on this topic. The latest, FRS 19: *Deferred tax*, was issued in December 2000.

FRS 19 requires that deferred tax is provided on timing differences relating to:

- accelerated capital allowances and depreciation;
- accruals for and pension costs and other post-retirement benefits;
- the elimination of unrealised intragroup profits;
- unrelieved tax losses;
- annual revaluations of assets where changes in fair value are taken to the profit and loss account;
- other short-term timing differences.

The double entry is as follows:

1 In the years when taxation is lower than it would be on comparable accounting profits:
    Dr Profit and loss appropriation account
        Cr Deferred taxation account
  with the amount of taxation understated.

2 In the years when taxation is higher than it would be on comparable accounting profits:
    Dr Deferred taxation account
        Cr Profit and loss appropriation account
  with the amount of taxation overstated.

Let's now look at Exhibit 7.3 to see how the profit and loss appropriation account and deferred taxation account would have been drawn up for the example given above. To make the exhibit follow the wording for published company financial statements, instead of 'Profit per financial statements before taxation' we will call it instead 'Profit on ordinary activities before taxation'.

Exhibit 7.3

Profit and Loss Appropriation Account for the years ended 5 April

	20X2		20X3		20X4	
	£	£	£	£	£	£
Profit on ordinary activities before taxation		1,000		1,000		1,000
Tax on profit on ordinary activities:						
Corporation tax	290		410		500	
Deferred taxation	110	(400)	(10)	(400)	(100)	(400)
Profit on ordinary activities after taxation		600		600		600

For purposes of shareholders, stock exchange analysts, would-be shareholders, etc., the profit after taxation figures on which earnings per share (EPS) would be calculated is the figure of £600 for each of the three years. The distortion has thus been removed.

Assuming that corporation tax is payable on 1 January following each accounting year end, the ledger accounts for corporation tax and deferred tax would be as follows:

Corporation Tax

20X2		£	20X2		£
Apr 5	Balance c/d	290	Apr 5	Profit and loss appropriation	290
		290			290
20X3			20X2		
Jan 1	Bank	290	Apr 6	Balance b/d	290
			20X3		
Apr 5	Balance c/d	410	Apr 5	Profit and loss appropriation	410
		700			700
20X4			20X3		
Jan 1	Bank	410	Apr 6	Balance b/d	410
			20X4		
Apr 5	Balance c/d	500	Apr 5	Profit and loss appropriation	500
		910			910
			20X4		
			Apr 6	Balance b/d	500

Deferred Taxation

20X2		£	20X2		£
Apr 5	Balance c/d	110	Apr 5	Profit and loss appropriation	110
		110			110
20X3			20X2		
Apr 5	Profit and loss appropriation	10	Apr 6	Balance b/d	110
Apr 5	Balance c/d	100			
		110			110
20X4			20X3		
Apr 5	Profit and loss appropriation	100	Apr 6	Balance b/d	100
		100			100

The balance sheets would appear:

	20X2	20X3	20X4
	£	£	£
Creditors: amounts falling due within one year			
Corporation tax	290	410	500
Provisions for liabilities and charges			
Deferred taxation	110	100	–

Permanent differences

Differences in profits for accounting purposes and those for tax purposes because of non-allowable items such as political donations, entertaining expenses etc. are not adjusted for.

A fully worked example

Exhibit 7.4 shows the ledger accounts in which tax will be involved for the first year of a new company, Harlow Ltd. Exhibit 7.5 follows with the second year of that company. This should make your understanding easier – to consider one year alone very often leaves students with many unanswered questions in their minds.

Exhibit 7.4

Harlow Ltd has just finished its first year of trading on 31 December 20X4. Corporation tax throughout was 35 per cent, and income tax was 25 per cent. You are given the following information:

(A) Net trading profit for the year was £165,000, before adjustment for debenture interest.
(B) Debenture interest (net) of £12,000 was paid on 31 December 20X4 and (C) the income tax deducted was paid on the same date.
(D) An ordinary interim dividend of 10 per cent on the 210,000 £1 ordinary shares was paid on 1 July 20X4.
(E) A proposed final ordinary dividend of 25 per cent for the year is to be accrued.
(F) Depreciation of £12,000 has been charged before arriving at net trading profit. Capital allowances of £37,000 have been approved by the Inland Revenue. Account for timing differences.
(G) Corporation tax on the first year's trading is expected to be £38,500.

You are required to:
(a) show double entry accounts (other than bank) to record the above;
(b) prepare extracts from the profit and loss account and balance sheet.

Exhibit 7.5 will carry on to Harlow Ltd's second year in trading.

Debenture Interest

20X4			£	20X4			£
Dec 31	Bank	(B)	12,000	Dec 31	Profit and loss		16,000
Dec 31	Income tax	(C)	4,000				
			16,000				16,000

Income Tax

20X4			£	20X4				£
Dec 31	Bank	(C)	4,000	Dec 31	Debenture interest	(C)		4,000

Ordinary Dividends

20X4			£	20X4			£
Jul 1	Bank	(D)	21,000	Dec 31	Profit and loss		73,500
Dec 31	Accrued c/d		52,500				
			73,500				73,500

Deferred Taxation

20X4		£	20X4			£
Dec 31 Balance c/d		8,750	Dec 31 Profit and loss*	(F)		8,750

*(F) allowed £37,000 but only charged £12,000 = £25,000 × 35% corporation tax deferred = £8,750.

Corporation Tax

20X4		£	20X4			£
Dec 31 Balance c/d		38,500	Dec 31 Profit and loss	(G)		38,500

Profit and Loss Account (extracts) for the year ended 31 December 20X4

		£	£
Net trading profit	(A)		165,000
Less Debenture interest	(B)		16,000
Profit on ordinary activities before taxation			149,000
Corporation tax	(G)	38,500	
Deferred taxation	(F)	8,750	
			(47,250)
Profit on ordinary activities after taxation			101,750
Less Dividends on ordinary shares:			
Interim paid 10 per cent	(D)	21,000	
Proposed final dividend 25 per cent		52,500	
			(73,500)

Balance Sheet (extracts) as at 31 December 20X4

Creditors: amounts falling due within one year	£
Proposed ordinary dividend	52,500
Corporation tax	38,500
Deferred tax	8,750

Exhibit 7.5

Harlow Ltd, as per Exhibit 7.4, has now finished its second year of trading. From 20X4 there will be three balances (concerned with the exhibit) to be brought forward. These accounts are:

Proposed ordinary dividend	(A)	Cr	£52,500
Corporation tax	(B)	Cr	£38,500
Deferred taxation	(C)	Cr	£8,750

The following information is given to you:

(D) The proposed ordinary dividend £52,500 was paid on 1 March 20X5.

(E) Corporation tax remains at 35 per cent and income tax remains at 25 per cent.

(F) Shares had been bought in STU Ltd and a dividend of £1,500 was received on 31 August 20X5.

(G) An interim dividend of 15 per cent on the 210,000 £1 ordinary shares was paid on 1 July 20X5.

(H) Debentures had been bought in RRR Ltd and interest (net) of £4,500 was received on 30 December 20X5.

(I)   Harlow Ltd paid its own debenture interest (net) of £12,000 on 31 December 20X5, and (J) the income tax account (net) was paid on the same date.

(K) The corporation tax due for 20X4 was paid on 30 September 20X5.

(L) A final ordinary dividend for the year of 30 per cent was proposed. This will be paid in March 20X6.

(M) Corporation tax for the year ended 31 December 20X5 is expected to be £41,300.

(N) Depreciation of £28,000 has been charged in the accounts, while capital allowances amounted to £22,000.

(O) Net trading profit after deducting depreciation but before adjusting for the above was £178,000.

It would have been quite possible to open a tax on profit on ordinary activities account and transfer tax items to there, prior to closing to the profit and loss account. We will now use this method.

Ordinary Dividends

20X5				£	20X5				£
Mar	1	Bank	(D)	52,500	Jan	1	Balance b/d	(M)	52,500
Jul	1	Bank interim	(G)	31,500	Dec	31	Profit and loss		94,500
Dec	31	Accrued c/d	(L)	63,000					
				147,000					147,000

Investment Income

20X5			£	20X5				£
Dec	31	Profit and loss	1,500	Aug	31	Bank	(F)	1,500
			1,500					1,500

Debenture Interest Payable

20X5				£	20X5			£
Dec	31	Bank	(I)	12,000	Dec	31	Profit and loss	16,000
Dec	31	Income tax		4,000				
				16,000				16,000

Debenture Interest Receivable

20X5			£	20X5				£
Dec	31	Profit and loss	6,000	Dec	30	Bank	(H)	4,500
				Dec	30	Income tax		1,500
			6,000					6,000

Income Tax

20X5				£	20X5			£
Dec	30	Debenture interest			Dec	31	Debenture interest	
		receivable		1,500			payable	4,000
Dec	31	Bank	(J)	2,500				
				4,000				4,000

Deferred Taxation

20X5				£	20X5				£
Dec	31	Tax on profit on			Jan	1	Balance b/d	(C)	8,750
		ordinary activities							
		(6,000 x 35%)	(N)	2,100					
Dec	31	Balance c/d		6,650					
				8,750					8,750

Corporation Tax

20X5				£	20X5				£
Sep	30	Bank	(K)	38,500	Jan	1	Balance b/d	(B)	38,500
Dec	31	Accrued c/d		41,300	Dec	31	Tax on profit on		
							ordinary activities	(M)	41,300
				79,800					79,800

Tax on Profit on Ordinary Activities

20X5				£	20X5				£
Dec	31	Corporation tax	(M)	41,300	Dec	31	Deferred taxation	(N)	2,100
					Dec	31	Profit and loss		39,200
				41,300					41,300

Profit and Loss account (extracts) for the year ended 31 December 20X5

		£	£
Net trading profit	(O)		178,000
Add Debenture interest received		6,000	
Investment income		1,500	
			7,500
			185,500
Less Debenture interest payable			(16,000)
Profit on ordinary activities before taxation			169,500
Tax on profit on ordinary activities			(39,200)
Profit on ordinary activities after taxation			129,700
Less Dividends on ordinary shares			
Interim paid 15 per cent		31,500	
Proposed final dividend		63,000	
			(94,500)

Balance Sheet (extracts) as at 31 December 20X5

	£
Creditors: amounts falling due within one year	
Proposed ordinary dividend	63,000
Corporation tax	41,300
Deferred tax	6,650

Learning outcomes

You should now have learnt:

1 Depreciation is not allowed as an expense when calculating tax liability.

2 Capital allowances are the equivalent of depreciation that the government allows to be deducted when calculating tax liability.

3 The profit shown in the financial statements is normally different from assessable profit for corporation tax calculations.

4 Deferred tax eliminates the differences that arise as a result of depreciation being replaced by capital allowances when calculating corporation tax payable.

5 FRS 19: *Deferred tax* regulates the calculation of the figure for deferred tax that appears in the balance sheet.

Answers to activities

7.1 To answer this question, you need to consider why each of these rules is in place. Depreciation is governed by FRS 15: *Tangible fixed assets*. It is calculated so as to reflect the reduction in economic value of an asset over an accounting period. In other words, it is intended to give a true and fair view of the true remaining value of an asset, subject to the effect of the basis upon which the base value of the asset has been derived. For example, if historical cost is the base, the remaining amount after depreciation has been deducted represents that proportion of the original value of the asset that remains at the balance sheet date.

Capital allowances are the government's assessment of how much of the historical cost of an asset can legitimately be treated as an expense in a given year. In most cases, the rate and method of calculation selected bear little relation to either the actual expected economic life of an individual asset or to the extent to which use of an asset has reduced its future economic life.

In some cases, capital allowances are intended to encourage successful business by enabling taxable profits to be reduced significantly in one year so that tax is lower than it would otherwise be. For examples, capital allowances of 100% may be permitted for any company operating in economically depressed parts of the UK. The motivation for capital allowances is, therefore, very different from the princples underlying depreciation provisions.

7.2 You will either have found this question simple, straightforward and obvious, or you will have struggled to find the answer. Whichever position you were in, it is important that you remember this question whenever you are thinking about depreciation and/or about deferred tax. The answer is that depreciation is based on the difference bewteen cost and the estimated disposal value of the asset. This asset cost £4,800. It is to be used for three years and its disposal value is estimated at £2,025. The amount to be depreciated over the three years is, therefore, £2,775. At $33^1/_3$ per cent per annum straight line, the annual depreciation charge is £925.

REVIEW QUESTIONS

Note: Questions 7.5 and 7.6 will be sufficient for those taking examinations with little tax content.

7.1 Long Acre Ltd has just finished its first year of trading to 31 December 20X3. Corporation tax throughout was 35 per cent and income tax 25 per cent. You are given the following information:

(*i*)   Net trading profit, after adjustment for (*ii*) but before other adjustments, was £220,000.
(*ii*)   Depreciation of £50,000 was charged in the accounts. Capital allowances amounted to £90,000.
(*iii*) An interim dividend of 5 per cent on 400,000 £1 ordinary shares was paid on 1 July 20X3.
(*iv*)   Debenture interest of £9,600 (net) was paid on 31 December 20X3.
(*v*)   Income tax deducted from debenture interest was paid on 31 January 20X4.
(*vi*)   A final dividend of $7^1/_2$ per cent was proposed for the year.
(*vii*) Corporation tax for the year was estimated to be £90,000.

You are required to:
(*a*) draw up the double entry accounts recording the above (except bank);
(*b*) show the relevant extracts from the profit and loss account and the balance sheet.

Note that question 7.2A is concerned with the second year of trading for Long Acre Ltd.

7.2A Long Acre Ltd has just finished its second year of trading to 31 December 20X4. Balances from question 7.1 need to be brought forward into this question. Tax rates are the same as for 20X3.
    The following information is available:

(*i*)   The proposed final dividend for 20X3 (*see* 7.1) was paid on 31 January 20X4.
(*ii*)   Shares in Covent Ltd were bought on 1 January 20X4. A dividend of £2,400 was received on 30 September 20X4.
(*iii*)   Debentures in Covent Ltd were bought 1 July 20X4. Debenture interest of £7,200 (net) was paid to us on 31 December 20X4.
(*iv*)   Debenture interest of £9,600 (net) was paid by us on 31 December 20X4.
(*v*)   Income tax owing to the Inland Revenue for 20X4 was not paid by us until 20X5. The 20X3 income tax had been paid on 30 January 20X4.
(*vi*)   An interim dividend of $7^1/_2$ per cent on 400,000 £1 ordinary shares was paid by us on 10 July 20X4.
(*vii*)   A final dividend of $17^1/_2$ per cent was proposed for the year.
(*viii*) Depreciation of £70,000 was charged in the accounts. Capital allowances amounted to £96,000.
(*ix*)   Net trading profit (before taking into account (*ii*), (*iii*), and (*iv*)) was £360,000.
(*x*)   The corporation tax due for 20X3 was paid on 1 October 20X4. Corporation tax for the year to 31 December 20X4 is expected to be £95,000.

You are required to:
(*a*) Draw up the double entry accounts recording the above (except bank).
(*b*) Show the relevant extracts from the profit and loss account for the year and balance sheet at the year end.

Note: Question 7.3 is a typical professional accounting body's examination question. It is not easy. Remember to bring forward the balances from the previous year which will often have to be deduced. The letters (A) to (L) against the information will make it easier for you to check your answer against that given at the back of the book.

7.3 Corporation tax for financial years 20X1, 20X2, and 20X3 was 35 per cent and income tax for each year was 25 per cent.

(A) Barnet Ltd's draft profit and loss account for the year ended 31 December 20X2 shows net trading profit of £560,000. This figure is before taking into account (B) and (C1) and (C2).
(B) Debenture interest paid on 30 November 20X2 (gross) was £80,000. Ignore accruals.
(C1) Fixed rate interest received is £24,000 (net). Date received 31 October 20X2. Ignore accruals.
(C2) A dividend of £900 was received from CD Ltd on 1 September.
(D) Depreciation, already charged before calculating net trading profit, was £50,000. This compares with £90,000 capital allowances given by the Inland Revenue. There is to be full provision for all timing differences for 20X2.
(E) The income tax bill (net) in respect of (B) and (C1) was paid on 15 December 20X2.
(F) Preference dividend paid on 30 June 20X2 £18,000.
(G) Ordinary interim dividend paid 15 July 20X2 £75,000.
(H) Proposed final ordinary dividend for 20X2 (paid in 20X3) was £120,000.
(I) Proposed final ordinary dividend for 20X1 (paid 31 March 20X2) was £90,000.
(J) There was a credit balance on deferred taxation account on 31 December 20X1 of £67,000.
(K) Tax for 20X1 had been provided for at £115,000 but was finally agreed at £112,000 (paid on 30 September 20X2).
(L) Corporation tax for 20X2 is estimated to be £154,000.

You are required to enter up the following accounts for the year ended 31 December 20X2 for Barnet Ltd: Deferred tax; Income tax; Interest receivable; Debenture interest; Investment income; Corporation tax; Tax on profit on ordinary activities; Preference dividends; Ordinary dividends; Profit and loss account extract. Also balance sheet extracts as at 31 December 20X2.

7.4A   KK Ltd has a trading profit, before dealing with any of the undermentioned items, for the year ended 31 December 20X9 of £200,000. You are to complete the profit and loss account for the year.

(a) The standard rate of income tax is taken as being 30 per cent.
(b) KK Ltd has bought £80,000 of 10 per cent debentures in another company. KK Ltd receives its interest, less income tax, for the year on 15 December 20X9.
(c) KK has issued £150,000 of 8 per cent debentures, and pays interest, less income tax for the year on 20 December 20X9.
(d) No cheque has been paid to the Inland Revenue for income tax.
(e) KK Ltd has a liability for corporation tax, based on the year's profits for 20X9, of £97,000.
(f) KK Ltd owns 60,000 ordinary shares of £1 each in GHH Ltd, and receives a cheque for the dividend of 20 per cent in November 20X9. GHH Ltd is neither a subsidiary company nor a related company.
(g) KK Ltd proposed a dividend of 15 per cent on the 100,000 ordinary shares of £1 each, payable out of the profits for 20X9.
(h) Transfer £20,000 to general reserve.
(i) Unappropriated profits brought forward from last year amounted to £19,830.

7.5   BG Ltd has a trading profit for the year ended 31 December 20X7, before dealing with the following items, of £50,000. You are to complete the profit and loss account.

(a) The standard rate of income tax is taken as being 30 per cent.
(b) BG Ltd had £40,000 of 9 per cent debentures. It sent them cheques for debenture interest for the year less income tax, on 31 December 20X7.
(c) BG Ltd had bought £10,000 of 11 per cent debentures in another company. It received a year's interest, less income tax, on 30 December 20X7.
(d) No cheque has been paid to the Inland Revenue for income tax.
(e) BG Ltd had bought 15,000 ordinary shares of £1 each in MM Ltd. MM Ltd paid a dividend to BG Ltd of 20 per cent on 30 November 20X7. MM Ltd is a 'related company'.
(f) BG Ltd had a liability for corporation tax, based on profits for 20X7, of £24,000.
(g) BG proposed a dividend of 30 per cent on its 70,000 ordinary shares of £1 each, out of the profits for 20X7.
(h) Transfer £5,000 to general reserve.
(i) Unappropriated profits brought forward from last year amounted to £9,870.

7.6   The following information relates to Kemp plc for the year to 31 March 20X9:

	£m
1 Dividends	
Proposed final ordinary dividend for the year to 31 March 20X8	
paid on 31 August 20X8	28
Interim ordinary dividend paid on 31 December 20X8	12
Proposed final ordinary dividend for the year 31 March 20X9 to be	
paid on 31 July 20X9	36
2 Deferred taxation account	
Credit balance at 1 April 20X8	3
During the year to 31 March 20X9 a transfer of £5 million was made from the profit and loss account to the deferred taxation account.	
3 Tax rates	
Corporation tax 35 per cent	
Income tax 25 per cent	

Required:
Write up the following accounts for the year to 31 March 20X9, being careful to insert the appropriate date for each entry, and to bring down the balances as at 31 March 20X9:

(*i*) ordinary dividends
(*ii*) deferred taxation.

(*Association of Accounting Technicians*)

7.7A   The following figures appeared in W Ltd's balance sheet at 31 March 20X2:

Current liability – corporation tax	<u>£600,000</u>
Deferred taxation	<u>£300,000</u>

During the year ended 31 March 20X3, W Ltd made a payment of £520,000 to the Collector of Taxes in settlement of the company's corporation tax for the year ended 31 March 20X2. Dividend payments totalling £60,000 were made during the year ended 31 March 20X2 and a further dividend of £200,000 had been proposed at the year end.

Two dividend payments were made during the year ended 31 March 20X3. A payment of £200,000 was made in respect of the final dividend for the year ended 31 March 20X2. An interim dividend of £40,000 was paid in respect of the year ended 31 March 20X3. These payments were made in May 20X2 and September 20X2 respectively. The directors have provided a final dividend of £240,000 for the year ended 31 March 20X3.

W Ltd received a dividend of £12,000 from a UK quoted company. This was received in August 20X2.

W Ltd's tax advisers believe that corporation tax of £740,000 will be charged on the company's profits for the year ended 31 March 20X3. This amount is net of the tax relief of £104,000 which should be granted in respect of the exceptional loss which the company incurred during the year. It has been assumed that corporation tax will be charged at a rate of 35%. The basic rate of income tax was 25%.

It has been decided that the provision for deferred tax should be increased by £20,000. No provision is to be made in respect of timing differences of £400,000.

You are required:
(*a*) to prepare the note which will support the figure for the provision for corporation tax in W Ltd's published profit and loss account for the year ended 31 March 20X3;
(*b*) to calculate the liability for corporation tax which will appear in W Ltd's published balance sheet at 31 March 20X3;
(*c*) to prepare the deferred tax note which will support the figure for the liability which will appear in W Ltd's published balance sheet at 31 March 20X3.

(*Chartered Institute of Management Accountants*)

CHAPTER 8

Provisions, reserves and liabilities

Learning objectives

After you have studied this chapter, you should be able to:
- explain the difference between a provision and a liability
- explain the difference between revenue reserves and capital reserves
- describe how capital reserves may be used
- describe what normally comprises distributable profits

Introduction

In this chapter you'll learn about the difference between provisions and liabilities and the difference between revenue reserves and capital reserves. You will also learn about some of the restrictions on the use of reserves and about what is meant by 'distributable profit'.

8.1 Provisions

A **provision** is an amount written off or retained by way of providing for renewals or diminution in value of assets, or retained by way of providing for any known liability of which the amount cannot be determined with 'substantial' accuracy. This therefore covers such items as **provisions for depreciation** and **provisions for doubtful debts**. A **liability** is an amount owing which can be determined with substantial accuracy.

Sometimes, therefore, the difference between a provision and a liability hinges around what is meant by 'substantial' accuracy. Rent owing at the end of a financial year would normally be known with precision; this would obviously be a liability. Legal charges for a court case which has been heard, but for which the lawyers have not yet submitted their bill, would be a provision. The need for the distinction between liabilities and provisions will not become obvious until Chapter 11, where the requirements of the Companies Acts regarding disclosures in the financial statements are examined.

8.2 Revenue reserves

A **revenue reserve** is where an amount has been voluntarily transferred from the profit and loss appropriation account by debiting it, thus reducing the amount of profits left available for cash dividend purposes, and crediting a named **reserve account**. The reserve may be for some particular purpose, such as a **foreign exchange reserve account** created just in case the firm should ever meet a situation where it would suffer loss because of devaluation of a foreign currency; or it could be a **general reserve account** that could be used for any purpose. (We will look further at general reserves in Section 8.3.)

Such transfers are, in fact, an indication to the shareholders that it would be unwise at that particular time to pay out all the available profits as dividends. The resources represented by part of the profits should more wisely and profitably be kept in the firm, at least for the time being. Revenue reserves can be called upon in future years to help swell the profits shown in the profit and loss appropriation account as being available for dividend purposes. This is effected quite simply by debiting the particular reserve account and crediting the profit and loss appropriation account.

Activity 8.1

Why do you think special revenue reserves are used, rather than simply leaving everything in the profit and loss account (which is, itself, a revenue reserve)?

8.3 General reserve

A general reserve is one that can be used for any purpose. For example, it may be needed because of the effect of inflation: assume a company needs £4,000 working capital in 20X3 and that the volume of trade remains the same for the next three years but that the price level increases by 25 per cent, then the working capital requirements will now be £5,000. If all the profits are distributed, the company will still have only £4,000 working capital which cannot possibly finance the same volume of trade as it did in 20X3. Transferring annual amounts of profits to a general reserve instead of paying them out as dividends is one way to help overcome this problem.

Activity 8.2

In terms of the amount of working capital, what is the difference between doing this and leaving the amount transferred in profit and loss?

On the other hand, it may just be the convention of conservatism asserting itself, with a philosophy of 'it's better to be safe than sorry' in this case to restrict dividends because the funds they would withdraw from the business may be needed in a moment of crisis. This is sometimes overdone, with the result that a business has excessive amounts of liquid funds being inefficiently used whereas, if they were paid out to the shareholders, who are, after all, the owners of the business, the shareholders could put the funds to better use themselves.

This then leaves the question of the balance on the profit and loss appropriation account. If it is a credit balance, is it a revenue reserve? Yes. If profits are not distributed by way of dividend, they are revenue reserves until such time as they are transferred to share capital or to other reserves.

8.4 Capital reserves

A **capital reserve** is normally quite different from a revenue reserve. It is a reserve which is not available for transfer to the profit and loss appropriation account to swell the profits shown as available for cash dividend purposes. Most capital reserves can never be utilised for cash dividend purposes – notice the use of the word 'cash', as it will be seen later that bonus shares may be issued as a 'non-cash' dividend.

Let us look at the ways in which capital reserves are created.

Capital reserves created in accordance with the Companies Acts

The Companies Acts state that the following are capital reserves and can never be utilised for the declaration of dividends payable in cash:

1 Capital redemption reserve – *see* Chapter 5.
2 Share premium account – *see* Chapter 4.
3 Revaluation reserve – where an asset has been revalued, an increase is shown by a debit in the requisite asset account and a credit in the revaluation account. The recording of a reduction in value is shown by a credit in the asset account and a debit in the revaluation account.

Capital reserves created by case law

Distributable profits per the Companies Acts have been described earlier in this volume. The definition includes the words 'in accordance with principles generally accepted'. As accounting develops and changes there will obviously be changes made in the 'principles generally accepted'.

Quite a few law cases have been decided to establish exactly whether an item represents a distributable profit and, therefore, available for cash dividend purposes. Where it is not, the item that is not distributable should be transferred to a capital reserve account. These cases will have to be studied at the more advanced stages of accounting, and so will not be dealt with here.

8.5   Capital reserves put to use

These can only be used in accordance with the Companies Acts. The following description of the actions which can be taken assumes that the Articles of Association are the same as Table A for this purpose, and that therefore there are no provisions in the articles to prohibit such actions.

Capital redemption reserve (for creation *see* Chapter 5)

1 To be applied in paying up unissued shares of the company as fully paid shares. These are commonly called bonus shares, and are dealt with in Chapter 9.
2 Can be reduced only in the manner as to reduction of share capital (*see* Chapter 9).
3 Can be reduced, in the case of a private company, where the permissible capital payment is greater than the nominal value of shares redeemed/purchased (*see* Chapter 5).

Share premium account (for creation *see* Chapter 4)

1 The same provision referring to bonus shares as exists with the capital redemption reserve.
2 Writing off preliminary expenses.
3 Writing off expenses and commission paid on the issue of shares or debentures.
4 In writing off discounts on shares or debentures issued (for creation of these accounts, *see* Chapter 4).
5 Providing any premium payable on redemption or purchases of shares or debentures.

Revaluation reserve

Where the directors are of the opinion that any amount standing to the credit of the revaluation reserve is no longer necessary then the reserve must be reduced accordingly. An instance

of this would be where an increase in the value of an asset had been credited to the revaluation account, and there had subsequently been a fall in the value of that asset.

The revaluation reserve may also be reduced where the permissible capital payment exceeds the nominal value of the shares redeemed/purchased.

Profits prior to incorporation (for creation *see* Chapter 6)

These can be used for the issuing of bonus shares, in paying up partly paid shares, or alternatively they may be used to write down goodwill or some such similar fixed asset.

Created by case law

These can be used in the issue of bonus shares or in the paying up of partly paid shares.

8.6 Distributable profits

Distributable profits have already been defined. Accounting standards will apply unless they come into conflict with the Companies Acts themselves.

Normally the revenue reserves, including any credit balance on the profit and loss account, would equal distributable profit.

Development costs

Under section 269 of the Companies Act 1985, any development costs which have been capitalised have to be deducted from distributable profits, *unless* there are special circumstances justifying the capitalisation. Normally this means that SSAP 13: *Research and development* will apply.

Depreciation on revalued assets

There is a conflict here between FRS 15: *Tangible fixed assets* and the Companies Acts. The Companies Acts require depreciation on revalued assets to be based on the revalued amounts. However, the Companies Acts allow the extra depreciation because of the revaluation to be *added back* when calculating distributable profit.

Distributions in kind

Where a company makes a non-cash distribution, for example by giving an investment, and that item (i.e. in this case the investment) has been revalued, it could generally be said that part of the distribution was unrealised profit locked into investment. However, the Companies Acts allow this because the 'unrealised' profit is 'realised' by the distribution (from the company's viewpoint, anyway).

8.7 Distributions and auditors' reports

The Companies Acts prohibit any particular distribution if the auditor's report is qualified, with one exception. The exception is that if the amount involved is *not* material and the auditor agrees to this fact, then distribution of an item can take place.

If a distribution is unlawfully made, any member knowing it to be so could be made to repay it. If the company could not recover such distributions then legal proceedings could be taken against the directors.

Answers to activities

8.1 There is no simple answer to this question. Reserves of this type were fairly common some years ago, mainly because they signalled that the business was being prudent and preparing to meet some future expense. Some people might suggest that some transfers of this type were made so as to retain cash in the business and thus avoid the interest costs of borrowing funds. (Funds already held by a business are the cheapest form of finance available to a business.) It could be argued that transferring reserves from the profit and loss account to a repairs reserve, for example, stops shareholders complaining that they have not received a high enough dividend, thus enabling the company to use its cash resources for other purposes.

However, nowadays, investors are more sophisticated than in the past and they are unlikely to be confused by such a transfer between reserves. That is, the fact that reserves had been transferred into a repairs reserve would not prevent investors from complaining that they had not received a high enough dividend. Also, nowadays, they would both wish to know why the transfer had taken place *and* expect it to be used for the purpose indicated.

In reality, it matters not a bit whether businesses make reserve transfers of this type. They may feel it is more informative to do so, but there is no need for such transfers to occur.

8.2 There is no difference. The cash has not been paid out so, in both cases, working capital increases accordingly. Transferring the amount from profit and loss to a general reserve simply indicates that some funds are being retained for an undefined purpose.

REVIEW QUESTION

8.1 An extract from the draft accounts of Either Ltd at 30 November 20X5 shows the following figures before allowing for any dividend which might be proposed:

	£000
Ordinary shares of £1 each	400
6% preference shares of £1 each	150
Capital redemption reserve	300
Revaluation reserve	125
General reserve	80
Profit and loss account	13
	1,068
Operating profit before taxation for the year	302
Taxation	145
	157

Additional information includes:

(*i*)   The revaluation reserve consists of an increase in the value of freehold property following a valuation in 20X3. The property concerned was one of three freehold properties owned by the company and was subsequently sold at the revalued amount.

(*ii*) It has been found that a number of stock items have been included at cost price, but were being sold after the balance sheet date at prices well below cost. To allow for this, stock at 30 November 20X5 would need to be reduced by £35,000.

(*iii*) Provision for directors' remuneration should be made in the sum of £43,000.

(*iv*) Included on the balance sheet is £250,000 of research and development expenditure carried forward.

(*v*)   No dividends have yet been paid on either ordinary or preference shares for the year to 30 November 20X5, but the directors wish to pay the maximum permissible dividends for the year.

(*vi*) Since the draft accounts were produced it has been reported that a major customer of Either Ltd has gone into liquidation and is unlikely to be able to pay more than 50p in the £ to its creditors. At 30 November 20X5 this customer owed £60,000 and this has since risen to £180,000.

(*vii*) It has been decided that the depreciation rates for plant and machinery are too low but the effect of the new rates has not been taken into account in constructing the draft accounts. The following information is available:

	£
Plant and machinery	
Purchases at the commencement of the business on 1 December 20X1 at cost	100,000
Later purchases were: 1 June 20X3	25,000
29 February 20X4	28,000
31 May 20X4	45,000
1 December 20X4	50,000

In the draft financial statements depreciation has been charged at the rate of 25 per cent using the reducing balance method and charging a full year's depreciation in the year of purchase. It has been decided to change to the straight line method using the same percentage but charging only an appropriate portion of the depreciation in the year of purchase. There have been no sales of plant and machinery during the period.

Required:

(*a*) Calculate the maximum amount which the directors of Either Ltd may propose as a dividend to be paid to the ordinary shareholders whilst observing the requirements of the Companies Acts. Show all workings and state any assumptions made.

(*b*) Outline and discuss any differences which might have been made to your answer to (*a*) if the company were a public limited company.

For the purposes of this question you may take it that corporation tax is levied at the rate of 50 per cent.

(*Association of Chartered Certified Accountants*)

CHAPTER 9

The increase and reduction of the share capital of limited companies

Learning objectives

After you have studied this chapter, you should be able to:

- explain the various ways in which a limited company may alter its share capital
- describe the difference between a bonus issue and a rights issue of shares
- explain why a company may introduce a scheme for the reduction of its capital
- describe the effect upon the balance sheet of bonus issues, rights issues and schemes for the reduction of capital

Introduction

In this chapter you'll learn about the alternatives available to a company when it wishes to change its share capital. You'll learn about the difference between scrip issues and rights issues and how to record the appropriate ledger account entries when either occurs. You will also learn that share capital can be reduced in nominal value and of how to do so.

9.1 Alteration of capital

A limited company may, if so authorised by its articles, and if the correct legal formalities are observed, alter its share capital in any of the following ways.

1 Increase its share capital by new shares, e.g. increase authorised share capital from £5,000 to £15,000.
2 Consolidate and divide all or any of its share capital into shares of a larger amount than its existing shares, for instance to make 5,000 ordinary shares of £1 each into 1,000 ordinary shares of £5 each.
3 Convert all or any of its paid-up shares into stock, and reconvert that stock into shares of any denomination, e.g. 10,000 ordinary shares of £1 each made into £10,000 ordinary stock.
4 Subdivide all, or any, of its shares into shares of smaller denominations, e.g. 1,000 ordinary shares of £6 each made into 2,000 ordinary shares of £3 each, or 3,000 ordinary shares of £2 each, etc.
5 Cancel shares which have not been taken up. This is 'diminution' of capital, not to be confused with reduction of capital described later in the chapter. Thus a firm with an authorised capital of £10,000 and an issued capital of £8,000 can alter its capital to be authorised capital £8,000 and issued capital £8,000.

Activity 9.1
Why do you think a company would wish to change its share capital?

9.2 Bonus shares

These are shares issued to existing shareholders free of charge. An alternative name is **scrip issue**.

If the articles give the power, and the requisite legal formalities are observed, the following may be applied in the issuing of bonus shares:

1 The balance of the profit and loss appropriation account.
2 Any other revenue reserve.
3 Any capital reserve, e.g. share premium.

This thus comprises all of the reserves.

The reason why this should ever be needed can be illustrated by taking the somewhat exaggerated example shown in Exhibit 9.1.

Exhibit 9.1

A company, Better Price Ltd, started business 50 years ago with 1,000 ordinary shares of £1 each and £1,000 in the bank. The company has constantly had to retain a proportion of its profits to finance its operations, thus diverting them from being used for cash dividend purposes. Such a policy has conserved working capital.

The firm's balance sheet as at 31 December 20X7 is shown as:

Better Price Ltd
Balance Sheet as at 31 December 20X7
(before bonus shares are issued)

	£
Fixed assets	5,000
Current assets *less* current liabilities	5,000
	10,000
Share capital	1,000
Reserves (including profit and loss appropriation balance)	9,000
	10,000

If an annual profit of £1,500 was now being made, this being 15 per cent on capital employed, and £1,000 could be paid annually as cash dividends, then the dividend declared each year would be 100 per cent, i.e. a dividend of £1,000 on shares of £1,000 nominal value. It is obvious that the dividends and the share capital have got out of step with one another. Employees and trade unions may well become quite belligerent, as owing to the lack of accounting knowledge, or even misuse of it, it might be believed that the firm was making unduly excessive profits. Customers, especially if they are members of the general public, may also be deluded into thinking that they are being charged excessive prices, or, even though this could be demonstrated not to be true because of the prices charged by competitors, they may still have the feeling that they are somehow being duped.

In point of fact, an efficient firm in this particular industry or trade may well be only reasonably rewarded for the risks it has taken by making a profit of 15 per cent on capital employed. The figure of 100 per cent for the dividend is due to the very misleading convention in accounting in the UK of calculating dividends in relationship to the nominal amount of the share capital.

If it is considered, in fact, that £7,000 of the reserves could not be used for dividend purposes, due to the fact that the net assets should remain at £8,000, made up of fixed assets £5,000 and working capital £3,000, then besides the £1,000 share capital which cannot be returned to the shareholders there are also £7,000 reserves which cannot be rationally returned to them. Instead of this £7,000 being called reserves, it might as well be called capital, as it is needed by the business on a permanent basis.

To remedy this position, as well as some other less obvious needs, bonus shares were envisaged. The reserves are made non-returnable to the shareholders by being converted into share capital. Each holder of one ordinary share of £1 each will receive seven bonus shares (in the shape of seven ordinary shares) of £1 each. The balance sheet, if the bonus shares had been issued immediately, would then appear:

Better Price Ltd
Balance sheet as at 31 December 20X7
(after bonus shares are issued)

	£
Fixed assets	5,000
Current assets *less* current liabilities	5,000
	10,000
Share capital (£1,000 + £7,000)	8,000
Reserves (£9,000 – £7,000)	2,000
	10,000

When the dividends of £1,000 per annum are declared in the future, they will amount to:

$$\frac{£1,000}{£8,000} \times \frac{100}{1} = 12.5 \text{ per cent}$$

This will cause less disturbance in the minds of employees, trade unions and customers.

Of course the issue of bonus shares may be seen by any of the interested parties to be some form of diabolical liberty. To give seven shares of £1 each free for one previously owned may be seen as a travesty of social justice. In point of fact the shareholders have not gained at all. Before the bonus issue there were 1,000 shareholders who owned between them £10,000 of net assets. Therefore, assuming just for this purpose that the book 'value' is the same as any other 'value', each share was worth £10. After the bonus issue each previous holder now has eight shares for every one share he held before. If he had owned one share only, he now owns eight shares. He is therefore the owner of $^{8}/_{8,000}$ part of the firm, i.e. a one-thousandth part. The 'value' of the net assets are £10,000, so that he owns £10 of them, so his shares are worth £10. This is exactly the same 'value' as that applying before the bonus issue was made.

It would be useful, in addition, to refer to other matters for comparison. Anyone who had owned a £1 share 50 years ago, then worth £1, would now have eight shares worth £8. A new house of a certain type 50 years ago might have cost £x; it may now cost £8x. The cost of a bottle of beer may now be y times greater than it was 50 years ago, a loaf of bread may be z times more and so on. Of course, the firm has brought a lot of trouble on itself by waiting so many years to capitalise reserves. It should have been done by several stages over the years.

This is all a very simplified, and in many ways an exaggerated version. There is, however, no doubt that misunderstanding of accounting and financial matters has caused a great deal of unnecessary friction in the past and will probably still do so in the future. Yet another very common misunderstanding is that the assumption the reader was asked to accept, namely that the balance sheet values equalled 'real values', is often one taken by the reader of a balance sheet. Thus a profit of £10,000 when the net assets' book values are £20,000 may appear to be excessive, yet in fact a more realistic value of the assets may be saleable value – in this case the value may be £100,000.

The accounting entries necessary are to debit the reserve accounts utilised, and to credit a bonus account. The shares are then issued and the entry required to record this is to credit the share capital account and to debit the bonus account. The journal entries would be:

The Journal

	Dr	Cr
	£	£
Reserve account(s) (show each account separately)	7,000	
Bonus account		7,000
Transfer of an amount equal to the bonus payable in fully paid shares		
Bonus account	7,000	
Share capital account		7,000
Allotment and issue of 7,000 shares of £1 each, in satisfaction of the bonus declared		

9.3 Rights issue

A company can increase its share capital by making a **rights issue**. This is the issue of shares to existing shareholders at a price lower than the ruling market price of the shares.

The price at which the shares of a very profitable company are quoted on the stock exchange is usually higher than the nominal value of the shares. For instance, the market price of the shares of a company might be quoted at £2.50 while the nominal value per share is only £1.00. If the company has 8,000 shares of £1 each and declares a rights issue of one for every eight held at a price of £1.50 per share, it is obvious that it will be cheaper for the existing shareholders to buy the rights issue at this price instead of buying the same shares in the open market for £2.50 per share. Assume that all the rights issue were taken up, then the number of shares taken up will be 1,000 (i.e. 8,000 ÷ 8), and the amount paid for them will be £1,500. The journal entries will be:

The Journal

	Dr	Cr
	£	£
Cash	1,500	
Share capital		1,000
Share premium		500
Being the rights issue of 1 for every 8 shares		
held at a price of £1.50 nominal value being £1.00		

It is to be noted that because the nominal value of each share is £1.00 while £1.50 was paid, the extra 50p constitutes a share premium to the company.

Notice also that the market value of the shares will be reduced or 'diluted' by the rights issue, as was the case for bonus shares. Before the rights issue there were 8,000 shares at a price of £2.50, giving a market capitalisation of £20,000. After the issue there are 9,000 shares and the assets have increased by £1,500. The market value may therefore reduce to £2.39 [(20,000 + 1,500)/9,000)], although the precise market price at the end of the issue will have been influenced by the information given surrounding the sale about the future prospects of the company and may not be exactly the amount calculated.

9.4 Reduction of capital

Where capital is not represented by assets

Any scheme for the reduction of capital needs to go through the legal formalities via the shareholders and other interested parties, and must receive the consent of the court. It is assumed that all of this has been carried out correctly.

Capital reduction means that the share capital – all of it if there is only one class such as ordinary shares, or all or part of it if there is more than one class of shares – has been subjected to a lessening of its nominal value, or of the called-up part of the nominal value. Thus:

(a) a £4 share might be made into a £3 share;
(b) a £5 share might be made into a £1 share;
(c) a £3 share, £2 called up, might be made into a £1 share fully paid up;
(d) a £5 share, £3 called up, might be made into a £3 share £1 called up;

plus any other variations.

Why should such a step be necessary? The reasons are rather like the issue of bonus shares in reverse. In this case the share capital has got out of step with the assets, in that the

share capital is not fully represented by assets. Thus Robert Ltd may have a balance sheet as follows:

Robert Ltd
Balance Sheet as at 31 December 20X7

	£
Net assets	30,000
Ordinary share capital	
10,000 ordinary shares of £5 each fully paid	50,000
Less Debit balance – profit and loss account	(20,000)
	30,000

The net assets are shown at £30,000, it being felt in this particular firm that the book value represented a true and fair view of their 'actual value'. The company will almost certainly be precluded from paying dividends until the debit balance on the profit and loss appropriation account has been eradicated and a credit balance brought into existence. Some firms, in certain circumstances, may still pay a dividend even though there is a debit balance, but it is to be assumed that Robert Ltd is not one of them. If profits remaining after taxation are now running at the rate of £3,000 per annum, it will be more than seven years before a dividend can be paid. As the normal basic reason for buying shares is to provide income, although there may well enter another reason such as capital appreciation, the denial of income to the shareholders for this period of time is serious indeed.

A solution would be to cancel, i.e. reduce, the capital which was no longer represented by assets. In this case there is £20,000 of the share capital which can lay no claim to any assets. The share capital should therefore be reduced by £20,000. This is done by making the shares into £3 shares fully paid instead of £5 shares. The balance sheet would become:

Robert Ltd
Balance Sheet as at 31 December 20X7

	£
Net assets	30,000
	30,000
Ordinary share capital	30,000
	30,000

Now that there is no debit balance on the profit and loss appropriation account the £3,000 available profit next year can be distributed as dividends.

Of course, the firm of Robert Ltd is a much simplified version. Often both preference and ordinary shareholders are involved and sometimes debenture holders as well. Even creditors occasionally sacrifice part of the amount owing to them, the idea being that the increase in working capital so generated will help the firm to achieve prosperity, in which case the creditors hope to enjoy the profitable contact that they used to have with the firm. These capital reduction schemes are matters of negotiation between the various interested parties. For instance, preference shareholders may be quite content for the nominal value of their shares to be reduced if the rate of interest they receive is increased. As with any negotiation the various parties will put forward their points of view and discussions will take place, until eventually a compromise solution is arrived at. When the court's sanction has been obtained, the accounting entries are:

1 For amounts written off assets:
    Dr Capital reduction account
        Cr Various asset accounts
2 For reduction in liabilities (e.g. creditors):
    Dr Liability accounts
        Cr Capital reduction account

3 The reduction in the share capital:
   Dr Share capital accounts (each type)
      Cr Capital reduction account
4 If a credit balance now exists on the capital reduction account:
   Dr Capital reduction account (to close)
      Cr Capital reserve

It is unlikely that there would ever be a debit balance on the capital reduction account, as the court would rarely agree to any such scheme which would bring about that result.

Capital reduction schemes for private companies will be used less frequently with the advent of powers to companies to purchase their own shares. The new powers given will normally be more suitable for private companies.

Where some of the assets are no longer needed

Where some of the firm's assets are no longer needed, probably due to a contraction in the firm's activities, a company may find itself with a surplus of liquid assets. Subject to the legal formalities being observed, in this case the reduction of capital is effected by returning cash to the shareholders, i.e.:

1 *Dr* Share capital account (with amount returnable)
      Cr Sundry shareholders
2 *Dr* Sundry shareholders
      Cr Bank (amount actually paid)

Such a scheme could be objected to by the creditors if it affected their interests.

Learning outcomes

You should now have learnt:
1 That a limited company may alter its share capital if it is authorised to do so by its Articles of Association.
2 Alterations to share capital can be made by a limited company:
   (*a*) issuing new shares;
   (*b*) consolidating all or any of its share capital into shares of a higher nominal value;
   (*c*) converting paid-up shares into debentures and then reconverting the debentures back into shares of another denomination;
   (*d*) subdividing all or any of its share capital into shares of a lower nominal value;
   (*e*) cancelling shares that have not been 'taken up' – the difference between the 'authorised share capital' and the 'issued share capital'.
3 Some reasons why companies change their share capital.
4 That where share capital is overvalued in relation to assets, a capital reduction scheme may be adopted in order to bring the share capital into line with the underlying asset value of the business as reported in the balance sheet.

Answers to activities

9.1 As you will see later in this chapter, there are many possible reasons. It may be that the nominal value of the share capital is significantly understated compared with current earnings. An increase in nominal share capital would help redress this imbalance and make things like earnings per share more intuitively meaningful. Alternatively, it may be that large of reserves have been built up and the company wishes to increase the amount of its share capital by converting the

reserves into shares. Another possibility is that the share price has risen significantly since the shares were first quoted on the stock exchange and it now appears unreasonably high relative to comparable shares. By splitting each share into a number of shares of a lower nominal value, the share price can be brought back to an appropriate level. Don't forget, companies can both increase and reduce the nominal value of their share capital.

REVIEW QUESTIONS

9.1 The Merton Manufacturing Co Ltd has been in business for many years making fitted furniture and chairs. During 20X4 and 20X5 substantial losses have been sustained on the manufacture of chairs and the directors have decided to concentrate on the fitted furniture side of the business which is expected to produce a profit of a least £22,500 per annum before interest charges and taxation. A capital reduction scheme has been proposed under which:

(*i*)   a new ordinary share of 50p nominal value will be created;

(*ii*)   the £1 ordinary shares will be written off and the shareholders will be offered one new ordinary share for every six old shares held;

(*iii*) the £1 6 per cent redeemable preference shares will be cancelled and the holders will be offered for every three existing preference shares, one new ordinary share and £1 of a new 8 per cent debenture;

(*iv*)   the existing 11 per cent debenture will be exchanged for a new debenture yielding 8 per cent and in addition existing debenture holders will be offered one new ordinary share for every £4 of the old debenture held;

(*v*)   existing reserves will be written off;

(*vi*)   goodwill is to be written off;

(*vii*) any remaining balance of write-off which is necessary is to be achieved by writing down plant and equipment; and

(*viii*) existing ordinary shareholders will be invited to subscribe for two fully paid new ordinary shares at par for every three old shares held.

The balance sheet of the Merton Manufacturing Co Ltd immediately prior to the capital reduction is as follows:

	£	£
Fixed intangible assets		
Goodwill at cost less amounts written off		50,000
Fixed tangible assets		
Freehold land and buildings at cost		95,000
Plant and equipment at cost	275,000	
Less Depreciation to date	(89,500)	
		185,500
		330,500
Current assets		
Stocks	25,000	
Debtors	50,000	
	75,000	
Current liabilities	£	
Creditors	63,500	
Bank overdraft	15,850	
	(79,350)	
Excess of current liabilities		(4,350)
		326,150
Long-term loan		
11½ per cent debenture, secured on the freehold land and buildings		(100,000)
		226,150

	£
Share capital and reserves	
£1 ordinary shares fully paid	90,000
6 per cent £1 redeemable preference shares fully paid	150,000
Share premium account	25,000
Profit and loss account	(38,850)
	226,150

On a liquidation, freehold land and buildings are expected to produce £120,000, plant and equipment £40,000, stocks £15,000 and debtors £45,000. Goodwill has no value.

There are no termination costs associated with ceasing the manufacture of chairs.

Required:
(a) Assuming that the necessary approval is obtained and that the new share issue is successful, produce a balance sheet of the company showing the position immediately after the scheme has been put into effect.
(b) Show the effect of the scheme on the expected earnings of the old shareholders.
(c) Indicate the points which a preference shareholder should take into account before voting on the scheme.

Corporation tax may be taken at $33\frac{1}{3}$ per cent.

(Association of Chartered Certified Accountants)

9.2   Deflation Ltd, which had experienced trading difficulties, decided to reorganise its finances. On 31 December 20X5 a final trial balance extracted from the books showed the following position:

	£	£
Share capital, authorised and issued:		
150,000 6 per cent cumulative preference shares of £1 each		150,000
200,000 ordinary shares of £1 each		200,000
Share premium account		40,000
Profit and loss account	114,375	
Preliminary expenses	7,250	
Goodwill (at cost)	55,000	
Trade creditors		43,500
Debtors	31,200	
Bank overdraft		51,000
Leasehold property (at cost)	80,000	
(provision for depreciation)		30,000
Plant and machinery (at cost)	210,000	
(provision for depreciation)		62,500
Stock in hand	79,175	
	577,000	577,000

Approval of the Court was obtained for the following scheme for reduction of capital:

1 The preference shares to be reduced to £0.75 per share.
2 The ordinary shares to be reduced to £0.125 per share.
3 One £0.125 ordinary share to be issued for each £1 of gross preference dividend arrears; the preference dividend had not been paid for three years.
4 The balance on share premium account to be utilised.
5 Plant and machinery to be written down to £75,000.
6 The profit and loss account balance, and all intangible assets, to be written off.

At the same time as the resolution to reduce capital was passed, another resolution was approved restoring the total authorised capital to £350,000, consisting of 150,000 6 per cent cumulative preference shares of £0.75 each and the balance in ordinary shares of £0.125 each. As soon as the above resolutions had been passed 500,000 ordinary shares were issued at par, for cash, payable in full upon application.

You are required:

(a) to show the journal entries necessary to record the above transactions in the company's books; and

(b) to prepare a balance sheet of the company, after completion of the scheme.

(Institute of Chartered Accountants)

9.3 On 31 March 20X6 the following was the balance sheet of Finer Textiles.

Balance Sheet

	£	£
Fixed assets		
Goodwill and trade marks as valued	225,000	
Plant and machinery (at cost *less* depreciation)	214,800	
Furniture and fittings (at cost *less* depreciation)	12,600	
		452,400
Current assets		
Stock-in-trade	170,850	
Sundry debtors	65,100	
Cash in hand	150	
		236,100
		688,500
Authorised capital		
150,000 7 per cent preference shares of £1 each	150,000	
2,100,000 ordinary shares of £0.5 each	1,050,000	
		1,200,000
Issued and fully paid capital		
150,000 7 per cent preference shares of £1 each	150,000	
1,200,000 ordinary shares of £0.5 each	600,000	
		750,000
Capital reserve		48,000
		798,000
Deduct profit and loss account (debit balance)		(183,900)
		614,100
Current liabilities		
Sundry creditors		31,800
Bank overdraft		42,600
		688,500

The following scheme of capital reduction was sanctioned by the Court and agreed by the shareholders:

(a) Preference shares were to be reduced to £0.75 each.
(b) Ordinary shares were to be reduced to £0.2 each.
(c) The capital reserve was to be eliminated.
(d) The reduced shares of both classes were to be consolidated into new ordinary shares of £1 each.
(e) An issue of £150,000 8 per cent debentures at par was to be made to provide fresh working capital.
(f) The sum written off the issued capital of the company and the capital reserve to be used to write off the debit balance of the profit and loss account and to reduce fixed assets by the following amounts:

Goodwill and trade marks	£210,000
Plant and machinery	£45,000
Furniture and fittings	£6,600

(g) The bank overdraft was to be paid off out of the proceeds of the debentures which were duly issued and paid in full.

A further resolution was passed to restore the authorised capital of the company to 1,200,000 ordinary shares of £1 each.

Required:
Prepare journal entries (cash transactions to be journalised) to give effect to the above scheme and draw up the balance sheet of the company after completion of the scheme.

9.4A The balance sheet of Planners Ltd on 31 March 20X6 was as follows:

Balance Sheet

	£	£
Goodwill		20,000
Fixed assets		100,000
		120,000
Current assets		
Stock	22,000	
Work in progress	5,500	
Debtors	34,000	
Bank	17,500	
		79,000
Capital expenses		
Formation expenses		1,000
		200,000
Issued share capital		
120,000 ordinary shares of £1 each		120,000
50,000 6 per cent cumulative preference shares of £1 each		50,000
		170,000
Less Profit and loss account debit balance		(40,000)
		130,000
6 per cent debentures		50,000
Current liabilities		
Creditors		20,000
		200,000

The dividend on the preference shares is £9,000 in arrears. A scheme of reconstruction was accepted by all parties and was completed on 1 April 20X6.

A new company was formed, Budgets Ltd, with an authorised share capital of £200,000, consisting of 200,000 ordinary shares of £1 each. This company took over all the assets of Planners Ltd. The purchase consideration was satisfied partly in cash and partly by the issue, at par, of shares and debentures by the new company in accordance with the following arrangements:

1 The creditors of the old company received, in settlement of each £10 due to them, £7 in cash and three fully paid ordinary shares in the new company.
2 The holders of preference shares in the old company received seven fully paid ordinary shares in the new company to every eight preference shares in the old company and three fully paid ordinary shares in the new company for every £5 of arrears of dividend.
3 The ordinary shareholders in the old company received one fully paid share in the new company for every five ordinary shares in the old company.
4 The holders of 6 per cent debentures in the old company received £40 cash and £60 6 per cent debentures issued at par for every £100 debenture held in the old company.
5 The balance of the authorised capital of the new company was issued at par for cash and was fully paid on 1 April 20X6.
6 Goodwill was eliminated, the stock was valued at £20,000 and the other current assets were brought into the new company's books at the amounts at which they appeared in the old company's balance sheet. The balance of the purchase consideration represented the agreed value of the fixed assets.

You are required to show:
(a) the closing entries in the realisation account and the sundry shareholders account in the books of Planners Ltd.

(b) your calculation of:
   (i) the purchase consideration for the assets, and
   (ii) the agreed value of the fixed assets;
(c) the summarised balance sheet of Budgets Ltd as on 1 April 20X6.

9.5A The summarised balance sheet of Owens Ltd at 31 December 20X9 was as follows:

	£
Freehold premises	60,000
Plant	210,000
Stock	64,000
Debtors	70,000
Development expenditure	75,000
Cash at bank	6,000
Profit and loss account	85,000
	570,000
Issued capital:	
150,000 6 per cent preference shares of £1 each	150,000
300,000 ordinary shares of £1 each	300,000
Creditors	120,000
	570,000

A capital reduction scheme has been sanctioned under which the 150,000 preference shares are to be reduced to £0.75 each, fully paid, and the 300,000 ordinary shares are to be reduced to £0.10 each, fully paid.

Development expenditure and the debit balance on profit and loss account are to be written off, the balance remaining being used to reduce the book value of the plant.

Required:
Prepare the journal entries recording the reduction scheme and the balance sheet as it would appear immediately after the reduction. Narrations are not required in connection with journal entries.

CHAPTER 10

Accounting standards and related documents

Learning objectives

After you have studied this chapter, you should be able to:

- explain the measures being taken by the Accounting Standards Board to develop a framework for the preparation and presentation of financial statements
- describe the full range of accounting standards currently in issue, and their aims and objectives

Introduction

In this chapter you'll learn about the background to the formation of the Accounting Standards Board and of the range of accounting standards that have been issued since 1971.

10.1 Background

The external users of accounts need to be sure that reliance can be placed on the methods used by a business in calculating its profits and balance sheet values. In the late 1960s there was a general outcry that the methods used by different businesses were showing vastly different profits on similar data. In the UK, a controversy had arisen following the takeover of AEI Ltd by GEC Ltd. In fighting the takeover bid made by GEC, the AEI directors had produced a forecast, in the tenth month of their financial year, that the profit before tax for the year would be £10 million. After the takeover, the financial statements of AEI for that same year showed a loss of £4.5 million. The difference was attributed to being £5 million as 'matters substantially of fact' and £9.5 million to 'adjustments which remain matters substantially of judgement'.

There was a general outcry in the financial pages of the national press against the failure of the accounting profession to lay down consistent principles for businesses to follow.

In December 1969, the Institute of Chartered Accountants in England and Wales issued a *Statement of Intent on Accounting Standards in the 1970s*. The Institute set up the Accounting Standards Steering Committee in 1970. Over the following six years, they were joined by the five other UK and Irish accountancy bodies and, in 1976, the committee became the Accounting Standards Committee (ASC). The six accountancy bodies formed the Consultative Committee of Accountancy Bodies (CCAB).

Prior to the issue of any accounting standard issued by the ASC, a great deal of preparatory work was done culminating in the publication of an exposure draft (ED). Copies of the exposure draft were then sent to those with a special interest in the topic. The journals of the CCAB also give full details of the exposure drafts. After full and proper consultation,

when it was seen to be desirable, an accounting standard on the topic was issued. The standards issued by the ASC were called statements of standard accounting practice (SSAPs).

Because the ASC had to obtain approval from its six professional accountancy body members, it did not appear to be as decisive and independent as was desired and, in 1990, a new body, the Accounting Standards Board (ASB), took over the functions of the ASC. The ASB is more independent of the accounting bodies and can issue its recommendations, known as financial reporting standards (FRSs), without approval from any other body. The ASB accepted the SSAPs in force and they each remain effective until replaced by an FRS. As with the ASC, the ASB issues exposure drafts – FREDs – developed in a similar fashion to before.

In 1997, the ASB issued a third category of standard – the Financial Reporting Standard for Smaller Entities (FRSSE). SSAPs and FRSs had generally been developed with the larger company in mind. The FRSSE was the ASB's response to the view that smaller companies should not have to apply all the cumbersome rules contained in the SSAPs and FRSs. It is, in effect, a collection of some of the rules from virtually all the other accounting standards. Small companies can choose whether to apply it or, as seems unlikely, continue to apply all the other accounting standards.

In addition to the FRSs and the FRSSE, the ASB also issues Urgent Issues Task Force Abstracts (UITFs). These are issued in response to an urgent need to regulate something pending the issue of a new or amended FRS. They have the same status as an FRS.

While there is no general law compelling observation of the standards, accounting standards have had statutory recognition since the Companies Act 1989 became law. As a result, apart from entities exempted from certain standards or sections within standards – SSAPs 13 (*Research and development*) and 25 (*Segmental reporting*), and FRS 1 (*Cash flow statements*), for example, all contain exemption clauses based on company size – accounting standards must be complied with when preparing financial statements intended to present a true and fair view. The Companies Acts state that failure to comply with the requirements of an accounting standard must be explained in the financial statements.

The main method of ensuring compliance with the standards has always been through the professional bodies' own disciplinary procedures on their members. The ASB, however, set up a Review Panel that has power to prosecute companies under civil law where their financial statements contain a major breach of the standards.

This book deals in outline with all accounting standards issued to December 2001. It does not deal with all the many detailed points contained in the standards and exposure drafts. It would be a far larger book if this was attempted. Students at the later stages of their professional examinations will need to get full copies of all standards and study them thoroughly [see also J Blake, *Accounting Standards* and A Sangster, *Workbook of Accounting Standards* (Financial Times Prentice Hall)].

This chapter deals with all the current accounting standards and related documents which are not covered in detail elsewhere in this book.

10.2 International accounting standards

The Accounting Standards Board deals with the UK. Besides this there is an international organisation concerned with accounting standards. The International Accounting Standards Committee (IASC) was established in 1973. Representatives from each of the founder members, which includes the UK, sit on the committee as well as co-opted members from other countries.

The need for an IASC has been said to be mainly due to the following:

1 The considerable growth in international investment means it is desirable to have similar methods the world over so that investment decisions are more compatible.

2 The growth in multinational firms which have to produce financial statements covering a large number of countries. Standardisation between countries makes the accounting work easier, and reduces costs.

3 As quite a few countries have now their own standard-setting bodies, it is desirable that their efforts should be harmonised.

4 The need for accounting standards in countries that cannot afford a standard-setting body of their own.

In the UK, the FRSs have precedence over International Accounting Standards (IASs). In fact, most of the provisions of IASs are incorporated into existing SSAPs and FRSs. Each FRS indicates the level of compliance with the relevant IAS.

The UK is scheduled to adopt international accounting standards with effect from 2005. There is no doubt that this will lead to many significant changes in the way financial statements are prepared thereafter.

Activity 10.1
Why do you think there is to be a switch in the UK towards international acounting standards?

10.3   Statement of Principles

In 1999, the Accounting Standards Board issued its *Statement of Principles*. The objective of this document is to assist the ASB, and all other users of financial statements, by clarifying the concepts that underlie its work and so, therefore, underpin the rules issued by the ASB relating to the preparation and presentation of financial statements. The *Statement of Principles* is not, however, an accounting standard. It does not contain any requirements on how financial statements should be prepared and does not override any standard.

When the ASB first started developing the *Statement of Principles*, it drew heavily upon the IASC's *Framework for the Preparation and Presentation of Financial Statements*. The *Statement of Principles* is very similar in content to the framework documents issued by the accounting standard-setters in Australia, Canada, New Zealand and the USA, so aiding the move towards internationalisation of accounting standards and harmonisation of accounting practice.

The users identified by the ASB are the same as those shown in Chapter 27, and they are not reproduced here.

Objectives

'The objective of Financial Statements is to provide information about the financial position, performance and financial adaptability of an enterprise, that is useful to a wide range of users in making economic decisions.'

Information

The *Statement of Principles* emphasises that a key characteristic of the information contained in financial statements is that it be useful. In an early draft of the *Statement of Principles*, there was a diagram that shows how these characteristics related to each other. The diagram is shown in Exhibit 10.1.

Exhibit 10.1 **The qualitative characteristics of accounting information**

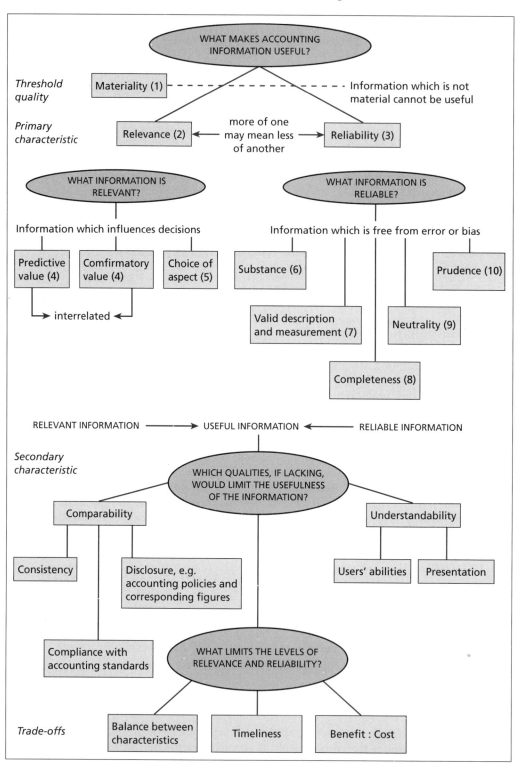

Reproduced with the permission of the Accounting Standards Board from Accounting Standards Board Statement of Principles 1991

Qualitative characteristics of financial information

The aim is to ensure that financial statements contain information that is 'useful'. Information is useful if it is relevant, reliable, comparable and understandable. The four terms are defined by the ASB as follows:

1 **Relevant.** Information is relevant if it has the ability to influence the economic decisions of users and is provided in time to influence those decisions.

2 **Reliable.** Information is reliable if:

  (*a*) it can be depended upon to represent faithfully what it either purports to represent or could reasonably be expected to represent, and therefore reflects the substance of the transactions and other events that have taken place;

  (*b*) it is complete and is free from deliberate or systematic bias and material error; and

  (*c*) in its preparation under conditions of uncertainty, a degree of caution has been applied in exercising the necessary judgements.

3 **Comparable.** Information is comparable if it enables users to discern and evaluate similarities in, and differences between, the nature and effects of transactions and other events over time and across different reporting entities.

4 **Understandable.** Information is understandable if its significance can be perceived by users that have a reasonable knowledge of business and economic activities and accounting and a willingness to study with reasonable diligence the information provided.

Where there is a conflict between these four characteristics, the objectives of financial statements must be met by arriving at a trade-off. For example, relevance is considered to be more important than reliability.

Looking further at Exhibit 10.1, the notes indicated on the exhibit give further insights into these four characteristics.

Note 1

An item of information is material to the financial statements if its omission or mis-statement might influence an economic decision of a user of the financial statements. It follows that information which is not material is not useful and is therefore beyond the threshold for inclusion in the financial statements.

Note 2

To be useful, information must be relevant to the decision-taking needs of users. Relevance relates to the influence of the information on the user's evaluation of events – past, present or future. This evaluation can be influenced by the way items in financial statements are presented.

Note 3

As you saw earlier, reliability means information free from material error and bias and which can be relied on by users to conform with descriptions given.

It is clear that information may be very relevant but unreliable – e.g. a betting tip at a horse race. Reliability may not ensure relevance, e.g. reliable analysis of last year's performance may exclude important indicators of future potential, such as new management in position. *Relevance* and *reliability* are primary characteristics of accounting information. They are broken down into further characteristics as follows.

Notes on relevance

Note 4

Predictive value means using an analysis of current or past performance to predict a future outcome. The same information can be used to confirm whether predictions in past periods have come true. Confirmatory value is this second part, i.e. checking past predictions.

Note 5

The term 'choice of aspect' implies that there may be significant choice for the preparer of accounts as to which aspects of transactions to represent. For example, a business might acquire a new building in a good position for trading and on which it owns the freehold. Another relevant piece of information is that the property is in an area proposed for a new motorway and could well be the subject of a compulsory purchase order. To be relevant to a user who wishes to value the business for future prospects, both aspects of the information are relevant. Note that a simple statement that the property was owned and showing its purchase price would be a valid description and measurement and therefore reliable – so far as it went.

Notes on reliability

Note 6

Substance indicates that information should represent the events it purports to represent. Sometimes complex legal arrangements may be entered into to obscure the ownership of assets. To be reliable, the true operation and ownership of the assets with respect to the substance must be reflected in the financial statements. Artificial legal transactions should not obscure the substance.

Note 7

Although the title indicates the intention, it is important to relate this aspect of reliability to Note 5 'choice of aspect'. 'Valid description and measurement' needs to be applied to the appropriate aspects of events.

Note 8

This indicates that incomplete information may make it false or misleading and thus not relevant.

Note 9

Neutrality implies freedom from bias. This indicates that financial statements should not be prepared with the intention of influencing decisions in any particular way.

Note 10

Prudence implies a degree of caution (anticipating losses) in the valuation of assets. In many cases this is subjective as it relates to the future, e.g. in predicting doubtful debts. This aspect should not be used to overestimate potential losses and thus misrepresent the affairs of an organisation.

In the second part of the chart, secondary characteristics which, if lacking, would limit the usefulness of the information are shown. Comparability and understandability have already been covered above. The other items shown are self-explanatory and are not discussed further in this text.

> ### Activity 10.2
> Why do you think there is such an emphasis on the 'qualitative' aspects of information in the *Statement of Principles*?

We'll now look at each of the accounting standards that have been issued since 1971. We'll look at them in number order. However, because it underpins every other accounting standard, we'll start by looking at FRS 18: *Accounting policies*.

10.4 FRS 18: Accounting policies

Users of financial statements issued by organisations want to analyse and evaluate the figures contained within them. They cannot do this effectively unless they know which accounting policies have been used when preparing such statements. This FRS was issued to help continue the improvement in the quality of financial reporting that had been started in 1971 by the accounting standard it replaced, SSAP 2.

The FRS focuses upon **accounting policies** and considers the **estimation techniques** used in implementing them. It also looks in detail at the various accounting concepts.

Accounting policies

These are defined in FRS 18 as:

> *those principles, bases, conventions, rules and practices applied by an entity that specify how the effects of transactions and other events are to be reflected in its financial statements through:*
> *(i)   recognising,*
> *(ii) selecting measurement basis for, and*
> *(iii) presenting*
> *assets, liabilities, gains, losses and changes to shareholders' funds.*

In other words, accounting policies define the processes whereby transactions and other events are reflected in the financial statements. The accounting policies selected should enable the financial statements to give a true and fair view and should be consistent with accounting standards, UITFs and company legislation.

When selecting an accounting policy, its appropriateness should be considered in the context of the four 'objectives' (or characteristics of information as covered above when you learnt about the *Statement of Principles*):

1 *Relevance* – Does it produce information that is useful for assessing stewardship and for making economic decisions?
2 *Reliability* – Does it reflect the substance of the transaction and other events that have occurred? Is it free of bias, i.e. neutral? Is it free of material error? If produced under uncertainty, has prudence been exercised?
3 *Comparability* – Can it be compared with similar information about the entity for some other period or point in time?
4 *Understandability* – Is it capable of being understood by users who have a reasonable knowledge of business and economic activities and accounting?

Estimation techniques

These are the methods adopted in order to arrive at estimated monetary amounts for items that appear in the financial statements.

Examples of accounting policies

1 The treatment of gains and losses on disposals of fixed assets – they could be applied to adjust the depreciation charge for the period, or they may appear as separate items in the financial statements.
2 The classification of overheads in the financial statements – for example, some indirect costs may be included in the trading account, or they may be included in administration costs in the profit and loss account.

3 The treatment of interest costs incurred in connection with the construction of fixed assets – these could be charged to profit and loss as a finance cost, or they could be capitalised and added to the other costs of creating the fixed assets – this is allowed by FRS 15: *Tangible fixed assets*.

10.5 SSAP 1: Accounting for associated companies

This standard was superseded by FRS 9: *Associates and joint ventures* issued in November 1997. FRS 9 is dealt with in Chapter 26 of this book.

10.6 SSAP 2: Disclosure of accounting policies

This standard was superseded by FRS 18: *Accounting policies* issued in December 2000.

10.7 SSAP 3: Earnings per share

This standard was replaced in 1998 by FRS 14: *Earnings per share* which is discussed in Section 10.44 below.

10.8 SSAP 4: Accounting for government grants

Many different types of grant are or have been obtainable from government departments. Where these relate to revenue expenditure, e.g. subsidies on wages, they should be credited to revenue in the period when the revenue is incurred. The principle is that the grants should be recognised in the profit and loss account so as to match the expenditure to which they are intended to contribute.

Where there are grants relating to capital expenditure, then SSAP 4 states that they should be credited to revenue *over the expected useful economic life of the asset*. This may be achieved by treating the amount of the grant as a deferred income, a portion of which is credited to the profit and loss account annually, over the life of the asset, on a basis consistent with depreciation. The amount of the deferred credit should, if material, be shown separately. It should not be shown as part of shareholders' funds.

The same effect as treating the grant as deferred income would be achieved by crediting the grant to the fixed asset account and depreciating only the net balance of the cost of the asset over its lifetime (depreciation is thus reduced by the grant). However, although this method is acceptable in principle, it is considered to be illegal under the Companies Act 1985 Schedule 4 para. 17, which requires the balance sheet value of a fixed asset to be its purchase price or production cost.

10.9 SSAP 5: Accounting for value added tax

All that needs to be noted here is that *Business Accounting 1* deals with SSAP 5. There is no need here to go into further detail at this stage of your studies.

10.10 SSAP 6: Extraordinary items and prior year adjustments

This standard was replaced by FRS 3: *Reporting financial performance* (*see* Section 11.9).

10.11 SSAP 7: Accounting for changes in the purchasing power of money

This was the original standard on inflation accounting, later replaced by SSAP 16: *Current cost accounting.*

10.12 SSAP 8: The treatment of taxation under the imputation system in the accounts of companies

This standard was replaced by FRS 16: *Current tax* in December 1999 – *see* Section 10.46.

10.13 SSAP 9: Stocks and long-term contracts

Due to the many varying kinds of businesses and conditions in companies, there simply cannot be one system of valuation for stocks and work in progress. All that the standard can do is to narrow down the different methods that could be used.

Stocks should be stated at the total of the lower of cost and net realisable value of the separate items of stock or of groups of similar items. Profit should not, except in the case of long-term contracts, be recognised in advance, but immediate account should be made for anticipated losses.

In the balance sheet (or in the notes), stocks should be sub-classified so as to indicate the amounts held in each of the main categories in the standard balance sheet formats (as adapted where appropriate) of the Companies Act 1985. (These categories are *raw materials and consumables, work in progress, finished goods and goods for resale*, and *payments on account*.)

Net realisable value consists of the expected selling price less any expenses necessary to sell the product. This may be below cost because of obsolescence, deterioration and similar factors. SSAP 9 also defines 'cost' and certainly in the case of a manufacturing business it will also include overhead expenses, so that prime cost could not be used. **Cost** is defined in SSAP 9 in relation to the different categories of stocks and work in progress as being:

> that expenditure which has been incurred in the normal course of business in bringing the product or service to its present location and condition. This expenditure should include, in addition to cost of purchase [as defined later] such costs of conversion [as defined later] as are appropriate to that location and condition.

Cost of purchase comprises purchase price including import duties, transport and handling costs and any other directly attributable costs, less trade discounts, rebates and subsidies.

Cost of conversion comprises:

(a) costs which are specifically attributable to units of production, i.e. direct labour, direct expenses and subcontracted work;
(b) production overheads (as defined later);
(c) other overheads, if any, attributable in the particular circumstances of the business to bringing the product or service to its present location and condition.

Production overheads based on the normal level of activity and including fixed production overheads, taking one year with another, should all be included. Obviously, neither selling nor general administration costs should be included in cost.

Notice that abnormal costs should not be included, as they should not have the effect of increasing stock valuation.

The last in, first out (LIFO) and base stock methods should not be used, as they do not provide an up-to-date valuation. Although LIFO is not accepted by the SSAP, the Companies Act 1985 accepts its use.

The standard does accept that replacement cost may, in certain circumstances, be acceptable. As a result, the lower of replacement cost or net realisation value may be used. Again, this is in accord with the Companies Act 1985.

Long-term contract work

Chapter 15 of this book deals with long-term contracts.

10.14 SSAP 10: Statement of source and application of funds

This was replaced by FRS 1: *Cash flow statements*, covered in Chapter 14 of this book.

10.15 SSAP 11: Deferred tax

This was the original standard on deferred tax. It was replaced in 1978 by SSAP 15 which was itself replaced by FRS 19 (*see* Chapter 7).

10.16 SSAP 12: Accounting for depreciation

This standard was replaced in 1999 by FRS 15, *Tangible fixed assets – see* Section 10.45.

10.17 SSAP 13: Accounting for research and development

SSAP 13 divides research and development expenditure under three headings, except for the location or exploitation of oil, gas or mineral deposits, or where all expenditure will be reimbursed by a third party. The three headings are:

1 **Pure (or basic) research.** Experimental or theoretical work undertaken primarily to acquire new scientific or technical knowledge for its own sake rather than directed towards any specific aim or application.
2 **Applied research.** Original or critical investigation undertaken in order to gain new scientific or technical knowledge and directed towards a specific practical aim or objective.
3 **Development.** Use of scientific or technical knowledge in order to produce new or substantially improved materials, devices, products or services, to install new processes or systems prior to the commencement of commercial production or commercial applications, or to improve substantially those already produced or installed.

Expenditure incurred on pure and applied research can be regarded as part of a continuing operation required to maintain a company's business and its competitive position. In general, one particular period rather than another will not be expected to benefit and therefore it is appropriate that these costs should be written off as they are incurred.

The development of new and improved products is, however, distinguishable from pure and applied research. Expenditure on such development is normally undertaken with a reasonable expectation of specific commercial success and of future benefits arising from the work, either from increased revenue and related profits or from reduced costs. However,

development expenditure should be written off in the year of expenditure, except in the following circumstances when it may be deferred to future periods:

1 there is a clearly defined project; and
2 the related expenditure is separately identifiable; and
3 the outcome of such a project has been assessed with reasonable certainty as to:
   (*a*) its technical feasibility; and
   (*b*) its ultimate commercial viability considered in the light of factors such as:
      (*i*)   likely market conditions (including competing products);
      (*ii*) public opinion;
      (*iii*) consumer and environmental legislation;
4 furthermore, a project will be of value only if:
   (*a*) the aggregate of the deferred development cost and any further development costs to be incurred on the same project together with related production, selling and administration costs is reasonably expected to be exceeded by related future revenues; and
   (*b*) adequate resources exist, or are reasonably expected to be available, to enable the project to be completed and to provide any consequential increases in working capital.

The elements of uncertainty inherent in the considerations set out in points 1 to 4 are considerable. There will be a need for different persons having differing levels of judgement to be involved in assessing the technical, commercial and financial viability of the project. Combinations of the possible different assessments which they might validly make can produce widely differing assessments of the existence and amounts of future benefits.

If these uncertainties are viewed in the context of the concept of prudence, the future benefits of most development projects would be too uncertain to justify carrying the expenditure forward. Nevertheless, in certain industries it is considered that there are numbers of major development projects that satisfy the stringent criteria set out above.

The standard says that if the criteria are satisfied then expenditure may be deferred to the extent that its recovery can reasonably be regarded as assured. It is also required that where this policy is adopted, all projects meeting the criteria should be included.

If development costs are deferred, they should be amortised over the period of sale or use of the product.

At each accounting date the unamortised balance of development expenditure should be examined project by project to ensure that it still fulfils the criteria. Where any doubt exists as to the continuation of those circumstances the balance should be written off.

Fixed assets may be acquired or constructed in order to provide facilities for research and/or development activities. The use of such fixed assets will usually extend over a number of accounting periods and accordingly they should be capitalised and written off over their usual life.

The standard requires that accounting policy on research and development expenditure should be stated and explained. The total amount of research and development expenditure charged in the profit and loss account should be disclosed, analysed between the current year's expenditure and amounts amortised from deferred expenditure. Movement on deferred expenditure and the amount carried forward at the beginning and end of the period should be disclosed. Deferred development expenditure should be disclosed under intangible fixed assets in the balance sheet.

10.18 SSAP 14: Group accounts

This standard was replaced in 1992 by FRS 2: *Accounting for subsidiary undertakings* (*see* Chapter 26).

10.19 SSAP 15: Accounting for deferred taxation

This standard was superseded by FRS 19: *Deferred tax* issued in December 2000 – *see* Chapter 7.

10.20 SSAP 16: Current cost accounting

An outline of this outdated and suspended SSAP is given in Chapter 30 of this book.

10.21 SSAP 17: Accounting for post-balance sheet events

Quite often there will be events occurring after a balance sheet date which will provide evidence of the value of assets, or of the amounts of liabilities, as at the balance sheet date. Obviously any event up to the balance sheet date will have affected the balance sheet. Once the board of directors has formally approved the financial statements it becomes impossible to alter them. However, there is the period between these dates during which events may throw some light upon the valuation of assets or amounts of liabilities. SSAP 17 directs its attention to such events during this period.

SSAP 17 introduced two new terms: 'adjusting events' and 'non-adjusting events'.

Adjusting events

These are events which provide additional evidence relating to conditions existing at the balance sheet date. They require changes in amounts to be included in financial statements. Examples of adjusting events are:

1 **Fixed assets.** The subsequent determination of the purchase price or of the proceeds of sale of assets purchased or sold before the year end.
2 **Property.** A valuation which provides evidence of a permanent diminution in value.
3 **Investments.** The receipt of a copy of the financial statements or other information in respect of an unlisted company which provides evidence of a permanent diminution in the value of a long-term investment.
4 **Stocks and work in progress:**
   (*i*) the receipt of proceeds of sales after the balance sheet date or other evidence concerning the net realisable value of stocks;
   (*ii*) the receipt of evidence that the previous estimate of accrued profit on a long-term contract was materially inaccurate.
5 **Debtors.** The renegotiation of amounts owing by debtors, or the insolvency of a debtor.
6 **Dividends receivable.** The declaration of dividends by subsidiaries and associated companies relating to periods prior to the balance sheet date of the holding company.
7 **Taxation.** The receipt of information regarding rates of taxation.
8 **Claims.** Amounts received or receivable in respect of insurance claims which were in the course of renegotiation at the balance sheet date.
9 **Discoveries.** The discovery of errors or frauds which show that the financial statements were incorrect.

Non-adjusting events

These are events which arise after the balance sheet date and concern conditions which did not exist at that time. Consequently they do not result in changes in amounts in financial

statements. They may, however, be of such materiality that their disclosure is required by way of notes to ensure that the financial statements are not misleading. Examples of non-adjusting events which may require disclosure are:

1 Mergers and acquisitions.
2 Reconstructions and proposed reconstructions.
3 Issues of shares and debentures.
4 Purchases and sales of fixed assets and investments.
5 Loss of fixed assets or stocks as a result of a catastrophe such as fire or flood.
6 Opening new trading activities or extending existing trading activities.
7 Closing a significant part of the trading activities if this was not anticipated at the year end.
8 Decline in the value of property and investments held as fixed assets, if it can be demonstrated that the decline occurred after the year end.
9 Changes in rates of foreign exchange.
10 Government action, such as nationalisation.
11 Strikes and other labour disputes.
12 Augmentation of pension benefits.

10.22 SSAP 18: Accounting for contingencies

This standard was replaced in 1998 by FRS 12: *Provisions, contingent liabilities and contingent assets* which is discussed in Section 10.42 below.

10.23 SSAP 19: Accounting for investment properties

Under the accounting requirements of FRS 15: *Tangible fixed assets*, tangible fixed assets are generally subject to annual depreciation charges to reflect on a systematic basis the wearing out, consumption or other loss of value whether arising from use, effluxion of time or obsolescence through technology and market changes. Under those requirements it is also accepted that an increase in the value of such a fixed asset does not generally remove the necessity to charge depreciation to reflect on a systematic basis the consumption of the asset.

A different treatment is, however, required where a significant proportion of the fixed assets of an enterprise is held not for consumption in the business operations but as investments, the disposal of which would not materially affect any manufacturing or trading operations of the enterprise. In such a case the current value of these investments, and changes in that current value, are of prime importance rather than a calculation of systematic annual depreciation. Consequently, for the proper appreciation of the financial position, a different accounting treatment is considered appropriate for fixed assets held as investments (called in this standard 'investment properties').

Investment properties may be held by a company which holds investments as part of its business such as an investment trust or a property investment company. Investment properties may also be held by a company whose main business is not the holding of investments.

Where an investment property is held on a lease with a relatively short unexpired term, it is necessary to recognise the annual depreciation in the financial statements to avoid the situation whereby a short lease is amortised against the investment revaluation reserve while the rentals are taken to the profit and loss account.

This statement requires investment properties to be included in the balance sheet at open market value. The statement does not require the valuation to be made by qualified or independent valuers, but calls for disclosure of the names or qualifications of the valuers,

the bases used by them and whether the person making the valuation is an employee or officer of the company. However, where investment properties represent a substantial proportion of the total assets of a major enterprise (e.g. a listed company) the valuation thereof would normally be carried out:

(a) annually by persons holding a recognised professional qualification and having recent post-qualification experience in the location and category of the properties concerned, and

(b) at least every five years by an external valuer.

10.24 SSAP 20: Foreign currency translation

The rules of SSAP 20 are already shown in Chapter 1 of this book. There is only need here for a few extra comments.

Hyperinflation

If there is hyperinflation the methods described in Chapter 1 may not give a fair view of the results. In these cases it may first of all be necessary to produce accounts adjusted for inflation. However, no guidance is provided in the standard as to how to define a 'high rate' of inflation or how to perform the adjustment to current price. UITF 9: *Accounting for operations in hyper-inflationary economies* was issued in June 1993 in order to clarify this area.

UITF 9 confirmed that adjustments are required when the hyperinflationary impact will affect the true and fair view. It also states that adjustments are required where the cumulative inflation rate over three years is approaching or exceeds 100 per cent – effectively a rule-of-thumb definition of the term 'hyperinflation'.

It suggested two methods that could be adopted in order to eliminate the distortions caused by hyperinflation. (If neither was deemed suitable, the reasons should be stated and another method should be adopted.) Either the local currency financial statements should be adjusted to reflect current price levels before being translated, or a relatively stable currency (e.g. the US dollar or sterling) should be used as the currency of measurement (the *functional* currency) for the relevant foreign operations. In the latter case, the functional currency would effectively be the *local* currency as defined in SSAP 20; and, if the transactions are not initially recorded in the functional currency, they must be measured in that currency by applying the temporal method based on the functional currency.

Hedging against exchange losses

Losses incurred may be set off against profits made in the computation of exchange dealings.

Disclosure

The method used to translate currencies should be disclosed. Net profits/net losses on translation must be disclosed, irrespective of whether they are shown in the profit and loss account or as a movement of reserves.

10.25 SSAP 21: Accounting for leases and hire purchase contracts

Details of SSAP 21 are given in Chapter 2.

10.26 SSAP 22: Accounting for goodwill

This standard was superseded by FRS 10: *Goodwill and intangible assets* issued in December 1997 – *see* Section 10.40 below.

10.27 SSAP 23: Accounting for acquisitions and mergers

This standard was replaced by FRS 6: *Acquisitions and mergers* in 1994 – *see* Chapter 25.

10.28 SSAP 24: Accounting for pension costs

This standard was replaced by FRS 17: *Retirement benefits* in November 2000.

10.29 SSAP 25: Segmental reporting

This standard was introduced to help interpret the requirement of the Companies Act 1985 that the information in the financial statements should be broken down (segmented) in two principal ways: by class of business and geographically. A **class of business** is a distinguishable component of an entity that provides a separate product or service. A **geographical segment** is an area comprising an individual country or group of countries in which an entity operates.

The main provisions of the standard can be summarised as follows. If an entity has two or more classes of business and operates in two or more geographical segments, then it should report for each class and segment:

(*a*) **turnover** – split between that to external activities and that to other segments;
(*b*) **result**, i.e. profit before taxation, minority interest and extraordinary items;
(*c*) **net assets**.

10.30 Statements of Recommended Practice and UITF Consensus Pronouncements

In 1986 the Accounting Standards Committee (ASC) issued the first statement of recommended practice (SORP). It is important to note that SORPs are different from accounting standards. Provisions in standards must be carried out, unless there is sufficient and adequate evidence to prove otherwise and, in addition, any non-compliance must be clearly stated. A SORP simply sets out what is considered to be the best practice on a particular topic in respect of which it is not considered suitable to issue a standard at that time. Companies are simply encouraged to use the SORP. No action will be taken by the accounting bodies if a SORP is not followed.

A sub-category of SORPs was introduced, called 'franked SORPs'. Generally these refer to topics which are of limited application for a specific industry and they are not included in this text.

The ASB will not issue its own SORPs. In the event that the ASB's own authority is required to standardise practice within a specialised industry, the ASB's preference is to issue an industry standard if the issue cannot be resolved under the existing accounting standards.

In 1991, the ASB set up a committee known as the Urgent Issues Task Force (UITF). This committee assists the ASB in areas where an accounting standard or Companies Act provision

exists but where unsatisfactory or conflicting interpretations have developed or seem likely to do so. In these circumstances, the UITF issues a 'consensus pronouncement' (or 'abstract'). The ASB considers that compliance with consensus pronouncements will form an important element in detecting whether accounts give a true and fair view. Consequently, they have the same status as accounting standards and *must* be observed. As at October 2001, 30 UITF abstracts had been issued, of which 21 were still in force (the others having been withdrawn following the issue of related FRSs). Wherever appropriate, UITFs are included in this book when the topic to which they relate is being discussed.

10.31   FRS 1: Cash flow statements

See Chapter 14.

10.32   FRS 2: Accounting for subsidiary undertakings

See Chapter 26.

10.33   FRS 3: Reporting financial performance

See Chapter 11.

10.34   FRS 4: Capital instruments

FRS 4 is concerned with accounting for capital instruments by the entities that issue them. A capital instrument is anything issued to raise finance. This includes shares, debentures, loans and debt instruments, and options and warrants that give the holder the right to sub-scribe for or obtain capital instruments. The term includes those issued by subsidiaries, except when held by another member of the group. Leases, warrants issued under employee share schemes, and equity shares issued as part of a business combination that is accounted for as a merger are not covered by FRS 4, nor are investments in capital instruments issued by other entities.

   The objective of FRS 4 is to ensure that financial statements provide a clear, coherent and consistent treatment of capital instruments, in particular in relation to:

(a) the classification of capital instruments;
(b) treating the costs associated with capital instruments in a manner consistent with their classification (and allocated to accounting periods on a fair basis over the period the instrument is in issue, in the case of redeemable instruments);
(c) ensuring that financial statements provide relevant information concerning the nature and amount of the entity's sources of finance and the associated costs, commitments and potential commitments.

   All capital instruments should be accounted for in the balance sheet within one of the following categories:

(a) shareholders' funds;
(b) liabilities; or, for consolidated financial statements,
(c) minority interests.

Shareholders' funds

Shares and warrants should be reported as part of shareholders' funds. When issued, the net proceeds should be reported in the reconciliation of movements in shareholders' funds. When repurchased or redeemed, shareholders' funds should be reduced by the value of the consideration given.

The balance sheet should show the total amount of shareholders' funds, analysed between the amount attributable to non-equity interests (i.e. the aggregate of amounts relating to all classes of non-equity shares and warrants for non-equity shares) and the amount attributable to equity interests (i.e. the difference between total shareholders' funds and the total amount attributable to non-equity interests). When the entitlement to dividends in respect of non-equity shares is calculated by reference to time, the dividends should be reported as appropriations of profit and accounted for on an accruals basis except when ultimate payment is remote (for example, when profits are insufficient to justify a dividend and the dividend rights are non-cumulative). Where the finance costs of non-equity shares are not equal to the dividends, the difference should be accounted for in the profit and loss account as an appropriation of profit. The finance costs for non-equity shares should be calculated on the same basis as the finance costs for debt.

Liabilities

All capital instruments other than shares should be classified as liabilities if they contain an obligation to transfer economic benefits. Otherwise, they should be reported within shareholders' funds. Convertible debt should be reported within liabilities separately from non-convertible debt. Debt should be analysed on the basis of its maturity distinguishing between debt with up to one year, one to five years, and five or more years to maturity, maturity being determined on the basis of the earliest date on which the lender can require payment.

The finance cost of convertible debt should be calculated on the basis that the debt will never be converted. When converted, the amount recognised in shareholders' funds in respect of the shares issued should be the amount at which the liability for the debt is stated at the date of conversion, and therefore no gain or loss should be recognised.

When issued, debt should be stated at the amount of the net proceeds and its finance cost should be allocated over the term of the debt at a constant rate on the carrying amount, charged in the profit and loss account (unless the entity is an investment company, in which case it may be included in the statement of total gains and losses to the extent that it relates to capital). The carrying amount of debt should be increased by the finance cost in respect of the reporting period and reduced by payments made in respect of the debt in that period. Accrued finance costs may be included in accruals (rather than in the carrying amount of debt) to the extent that the period costs have accrued in one period and will be paid in cash in the next. However, in the event that the debt is repurchased or settled early, any such accrual should be included in the carrying amount of the debt for the purposes of calculating finance costs and gains and losses on the transaction, and any such gains or losses should be recognised in the profit and loss account in the period during which the transaction occurs.

Minority interests

Where subsidiaries have issued shares outside the group, those shares should be reported as minority interests, unless the group as a whole has an obligation to transfer economic benefit in connection with the shares. In such cases, they should be accounted for as liabilities within the consolidated financial statements. The amount of minority interests in the

balance sheet should be split between the amounts attributable to equity and non-equity interests, the calculation of the amounts attributed to non-equity minority interests (and their associated finance costs) being calculated in the same way as those for non-equity shares. The finance costs associated with such interests should be included in minority interests in the profit and loss account.

10.35 FRS 5: Reporting the substance of transactions

The purpose of FRS 5 is to ensure that the substance of an entity's transactions is reported in its financial statements. The commercial effect of the entity's transactions, and any resulting assets, liabilities, gains or losses, should be faithfully represented in its financial statements.
   The standard does not apply to:

(a) forward contracts and futures;
(b) foreign exchange and interest rate swaps;
(c) contracts where a net amount will be paid or received based on a movement in a price or an index;
(d) expenditure commitments and orders placed, until the earlier of delivery or payment;
(e) employment contracts.

   In determining the substance of a transaction, all its aspects and implications should be identified and greater weight given to those more likely to have a commercial effect in practice. Where a group or series of transactions achieves, or is intended to achieve, an overall commercial effect, the transactions should be viewed as a whole, not as individual transactions.
   The substance of a transaction depends upon whether it has given rise to new assets or liabilities for the reporting entity, and whether it has changed the entity's existing assets and liabilities. An entity has rights or other access to benefits (and therefore has an asset) if the entity is exposed to the risks inherent in the benefits, taking into account the likelihood of those risks having a commercial effect. Evidence that an obligation to transfer benefits (i.e. a liability) exists is shown if there is some circumstance in which the entity cannot avoid, legally or commercially, an outflow of benefits.
   Where an asset or a liability results from a transaction, it should be recognised in the balance sheet if there is sufficient evidence of its existence (including, where relevant, any future inflow or outflow of benefit), and if it can be measured at a monetary amount with sufficient reliability.
   Where transactions have no significant effect upon either the entity's rights or other access to benefits arising from a previously recognised asset, or to the entity's exposure to the risks inherent in those benefits, the entire asset should continue to be recognised. When the transactions transfer *all* the significant rights or other access to benefits *and all* the significant exposure to risk, the entire asset should cease to be recognised. Where a stage between nil and full effect is found, and it is a significant change, the description or monetary amounts relating to an asset should be changed and a liability recognised for any obligations to transfer benefits that are assumed. However, the standard also states that this partial case arises in only three situations:

(a) a transfer of only part of the item;
(b) a transfer of all of the item for only part of its life;
(c) a transfer of all of the item for all of its life but where the entity retains some significant right to benefits or exposure to risk.

   Where a transaction is in substance a financing of a recognised asset (whether previously recognised or not), the finance should be shown deducted from the gross amount of the item it finances on the face of the balance sheet within a single asset caption of 'linked

presentation'. The gross amounts of both the item and the finance should be shown on the face of the balance sheet. Profit on a linked presentation should be recognised on entering into the arrangement only to the extent that the non-returnable proceeds received exceed the previous carrying value of the item. Thereafter, any profit or loss arising should be recognised in the period in which it arises, both in the profit and loss account and in the notes.

Assets and liabilities should not be offset, except where they do not constitute separate assets and liabilities.

Where an entity has a quasi-subsidiary (i.e. a company, trust, partnership or other vehicle that is directly or indirectly controlled by the reporting entity, but that is not a subsidiary, and which gives rise to benefits for the reporting entity that are in substance no different from those that would arise were the vehicle a subsidiary) the substance of the transactions entered into by the quasi-subsidiary should be reported in the consolidated statements. The fact that a quasi-subsidiary has been included in the consolidated financial statements should be disclosed and a summary of the financial statements of the quasi-subsidiary should be provided in the notes.

Disclosure of a transaction in the financial statements should be sufficient to enable the user of those statements to understand its commercial effect. Where a transaction has resulted in the recognition of assets or liabilities whose nature differs from that of items usually included under the relevant balance sheet heading, the differences should be explained.

10.36 FRS 6: Acquisitions and mergers

See Chapter 25.

10.37 FRS 7: Fair values in acquisition accounting

See Chapter 22.

10.38 FRS 8: Related party disclosures

This FRS requires disclosure of all material related party transactions. The FRS extends the disclosure requirements contained in the Companies Acts, thus providing guidance in an area that had previously not been covered adequately by either statute or the Stock Exchange Rules.

10.39 FRS 9: Associates and joint ventures

See Chapter 26.

10.40 FRS 10: Goodwill and intangible assets

FRS 10 was issued in December 1997, repealing SSAP 22. Although written with a focus upon goodwill arising from the acquisition of a subsidiary undertaking by a parent company that prepares consolidated accounts, the standard also applies to reporting entities acquiring a business or an investment that is accounted for using the equity method (*see* Section 29.8).

A brief summary of the FRS is as follows:

1 Positive purchased goodwill should be capitalised as an asset on the balance sheet.
2 Internally generated goodwill should not be capitalised.
3 An intangible asset acquired as part of the acquisition of a business should be capitalised separately from goodwill, initially at its fair value. Unless the asset has a readily ascertainable market value, the fair value should be limited to an amount that does not create or increase any negative goodwill arising on the acquisition.
4 An intangible asset acquired as part of the acquisition of a business whose fair value cannot be measured reliably should be included within the amount of the purchase price attributed to goodwill.
5 An intangible asset purchased separately should be capitalised at cost.
6 An internally developed intangible asset may be capitalised only if it has a readily ascertainable market value.
7 Where goodwill and intangible assets are regarded as having limited useful economic lives, they should be amortised on a systematic basis over those lives.
8 Where goodwill and intangible assets are regarded as having indefinite useful economic lives, they should *not* be amortised. A life of longer than 20 years can only be used if the durability of the acquired business or intangible asset can be demonstrated and the goodwill or intangible asset is capable of continued measurement over the period selected. Companies legislation requires goodwill to be amortised over a finite period. When no amortisation occurs, this departure from the legislation must be justified as being required in order to provide a true and fair view.
9 The useful economic lives of goodwill and intangible assets should be reviewed at the end of each reporting period and revised if necessary.
10 The straight line method of amortisation should be adopted, unless another method can be demonstrated to better reflect the expected pattern of depletion of the goodwill or intangible asset.
11 Intangible assets may be revalued but, if one is, all others of the same class must also be revalued. Any revalued intangible assets must be subject to sufficiently frequent further revaluations to ensure that the carrying value does not differ materially from the market value at the balance sheet date.
12 Goodwill should not be revalued, except when previous adjustments for impairment losses (that arose, for example, when part of an acquired business was held to have a lower value than had been adopted at the time of acquisition) are reversed and it causes the recoverable amount of the goodwill above its current carrying value. (The same impairment-derived adjustment rules apply to intangible assets.)
13 When the fair value of the assets acquired exceed the fair value of the consideration given, the resulting negative goodwill should be recognised and separately disclosed on the face of the balance sheet immediately below the goodwill heading, followed by a subtotal showing the net amount of positive and negative goodwill.

Note: In the chapters dealing with consolidated financial statements, a figure for goodwill will often be calculated. It must be borne in mind that this is subject to the contents of FRS 10 just as much as for a company simply buying the business of a sole trader or partnership.

10.41 FRS 11: Impairment of fixed assets and goodwill

This FRS was issued in July 1998. It applies to all fixed assets and purchased goodwill that is recognised in the balance sheet except:

(a) fixed assets within the scope of any FRS addressing disclosures of derivatives and other financial instruments (this is covered by FRS 13: *Derivatives and other financial instruments: disclosures – see* Section 10.43 below);

(b) investment properties as defined by SSAP 19 (*see* Section 10.23 above);

(c) an entity's own shares held by an ESOP (employee share ownership plan) and shown as a fixed asset in the balance sheet under UITF 13: *Accounting for ESOP trusts*; and

(d) costs capitalised while a field is being appraised under the Oil Industry Accounting Committee's SORP, *Accounting for oil and gas exploration and development activities*.

Investments in subsidiary undertakings, associates, and joint ventures *do* fall within the scope of FRS 11. However, smaller entities applying the FRSSE are exempt from the FRS.

A brief summary of the FRS is as follows:

1 An impairment review should be carried out if events or changes in circumstances indicate that the carrying amount of a fixed asset or of goodwill may not be recoverable.

2 Impairment is measured by comparing the carrying value of an asset with its recoverable amount (the higher of its net realisable value and its value in use).

3 Impairment losses are recognised in the profit and loss account except that impairment losses on revalued fixed assets are shown in the statement of total recognised gains and losses. Impairments on both unrevalued and revalued assets below the depreciated historical cost are recognised in the profit and loss account.

4 If the recoverable amount of a previously impaired asset or investment increases because of a change in economic conditions or in the expected use of the asset, the resulting reversal of the impairment loss should be recognised in the current period to the extent that it increases the carrying amount up to the amount that it would have been had the original impairment not occurred. The reversal should be recognised in the profit and loss account unless it arises on a previously revalued fixed asset, in which case it should be recognised in the profit and loss account to the extent that the previous impairment loss (adjusted for subsequent depreciation) was recognised in the profit and loss account, any remaining impairment reversal balance being recognised in the statement of total recognised gains and losses.

10.42 FRS 12: Provisions, contingent liabilities and contingent assets

This FRS was issued in September 1998, repealing SSAP 18. FRS 12 defines a provision as:

> a liability that is of uncertain timing or amount, to be settled by the transfer of economic benefits.

A provision should be recognised only when it is probable that a transfer of economic benefits will have to occur and a reasonable estimate can be made of the amount involved.

It defines a contingent liability as:

> either a possible obligation arising from past events whose existence will be confirmed only by the occurrence of one or more uncertain future events not wholly within the entity's control; or a present obligation that arises from past events but is not recognised because it is not probable that a transfer of economic benefits will be required to settle the obligation or because the amount of the obligation cannot be measured with sufficient reliability.

It defines a contingent asset as:

> a possible asset arising from past events whose existence will be confirmed only by the occurrence of one or more uncertain events not wholly within the entity's control.

Neither contingent liabilities nor contingent assets should be recognised.

Smaller entities applying the FRSSE are exempt from FRS 12.

10.43 FRS 13: Derivatives and other financial instruments: disclosures

This FRS was issued in September 1998. It defines a derivative as:

> *a financial instrument that derives its value from the price or rate of some underlying item. Underlying items include equities, bonds, commodities, interest rates, exchange rates, and stock market and other indices.*

The disclosures required by the standard focus mainly upon the risks that arise in connection with financial instruments and how they have been managed. It requires a range of information to be presented concerning the risks arising from the entity's financial instruments, and its attitude and response to those risks. In effect, entities are required to publish in summary form details of their loans, investments and hedging transactions.

Smaller entities applying the FRSSE are exempt from FRS 13.

10.44 FRS 14: Earnings per share

This FRS was issued in October 1998, repealing SSAP 3. The figure for earnings per share is calculated by dividing the net profit or loss attributable to ordinary shareholders by the weighted average number of ordinary shares outstanding during the period.

The FRS prescribes how to adjust the average number of shares when events occur to change the number of ordinary shares, such as bonus issues, share splits, and share consolidations. Students taking examinations which cover FRS 14 in detail should read the actual standard. It contains many examples concerning how the adjustment to the denominator should be made.

Earnings per share (EPS) is a widely used stock market measure. The FRS tries to bring about a more consistent method to aid comparability and reduce misunderstandings.

Basically, EPS is the profit per ordinary share calculated as follows:

		£	£
Profit on ordinary activities after taxation			XXXX
Extraordinary activities (less tax)			XXXX
			XXXX
Less	Minority interest (see chapters on group accounts)	XXXX	
	Preference dividends	XXXX	
			(XXXX)
Profit available to equity shareholders			XXXX

$$\text{EPS} = \frac{\text{Profit available to equity shareholders}}{\text{Number of ordinary shares}} = \text{EPS in pence}$$

As you will see later, minority interest exists only where the company controls another undertaking, and outsiders own part of that undertaking.

10.45 FRS 15: Tangible fixed assets

This FRS replaced SSAP 12. It applies to all tangible fixed assets except investment properties, which are dealt with in SSAP 19.

First, some definitions:

- **Depreciation.** The measure of the cost or revalued amount of the economic benefits of the tangible fixed asset that have been consumed during the period. Consumption includes

the wearing out, using up or other reduction in the useful economic life of a tangible fixed asset whether arising from use, effluxion of time or obsolescence through either technology or demand for the goods and services produced by the asset.

- **Useful economic life.** The period over which the entity expects to derive economic benefit from that asset.
- **Residual value.** The net realisable value of an asset at the end of its economic life. Residual values are based on prices prevailing at the date of the acquisition (or revaluation) of the asset and do not take account of expected future price changes.
- **Recoverable amount.** The higher of net realisable value and the amount recoverable from its further use.

Depreciation should be provided in respect of all tangible fixed assets which have a finite useful economic life. It should be provided by allocating the cost (or revalued amount) less net realisable value over the periods expected to benefit from the use of the asset being depreciated. No depreciation method is prescribed, but the method selected should be that which produces the most appropriate allocation of depreciation to each period in relation to the benefit being received in that period through use of the asset. The depreciation should be calculated on the value as shown on the balance sheet and not on any other figure. It *must* be charged against the profit and loss account, *not* against reserves.

When the useful economic life of an asset is longer than 50 years, impairment reviews must be performed so as to ensure that the carrying amount of the asset is not overstated.

Useful economic lives should be reviewed at the end of every reporting period. If it is revised, the carrying amount at the date of the revision should be depreciated over the revised remaining useful economic life of the asset.

The depreciation method may be changed only when to do so will give a fairer presentation of the results and of the financial position. A change in depreciation method does not constitute a change in accounting policy. When the method is changed, the carrying amount should be depreciated over the remaining useful economic life of the asset, commencing with the period when the change occurred. Where a change of method occurs, the effect, if material, should be shown as a note attached to the financial statements.

UITF Abstract 5, issued in July 1992, introduced rules relating to situations where current assets are included in the balance sheet at the lower of cost and net realisable value. Specifically, it addressed the question of an appropriate transfer value when a current asset becomes a fixed asset through its being retained for use on a continuing basis. (This could arise, for example, when a motor dealer removes a second-hand car from sale and provides it as a company car to the company secretary.) To avoid entities being able to effect transfers from current assets to fixed assets at above net realisable value and subsequently to write down the value through a debit to a revaluation reserve, UITF 5 requires that all such transfers are done at the lower of cost and net realisable value, with any diminution in value at that point being charged in the profit and loss account.

Asset revaluation

Asset revaluation is permitted and, if a policy of revaluation is adopted, the valuations should be kept up to date. If one asset is revalued, all the assets of that class (i.e. those with a similar nature, function or use) must be revalued.

Revaluation losses caused by use of the asset should be recognised in the profit and loss account. Other revaluation losses should be recognised in the statement of total recognised gains and losses until the carrying amount of the asset is less than the amount the asset would be carried at had depreciated historical cost been adopted rather than asset revaluation.

For example, imagine an asset is revalued from a carrying amount of £20,000 down to £6,000 because the asset had become obsolete. Had it never been revalued, its carrying amount would have been £11,000. The carrying amount of the asset (£6,000) is, therefore, below £11,000 and so the loss on revaluation of £14,000 would be split with £9,000 being recognised in the statement of total recognised gains and losses and £5,000 being recognised in profit and loss.

Revaluation gains should be recognised in the statement of total recognised gains and losses unless they relate to an asset that had previously had revaluation losses charged to the profit and loss acount. Where that is the case, the revaluation gain should also be charged to profit and loss, after adjusting for depreciation since the revaluation loss was recognised.

Depreciation should be charged irrespective of when the asset was revalued. An increased value arising from a revaluation does not mean that depreciation should not be charged. The new value is the one on which future depreciation should be based. Depreciation charged before revaluation should not be credited back to profit and loss.

According to paragraph 21 of FRS 3: *Reporting financial performance*, the profit or loss on the disposal of an asset should be accounted for in the profit and loss account of the period in which the disposal occurs as the difference between the net sale proceeds and the net carrying amount, whether carried at historical cost (less any provisions made) or at a valuation.

Land and buildings

Freehold land

As this normally lasts for ever there is no need to depreciate, unless subject to depletion or loss of value for reasons which may be applicable in certain circumstances, such as desirability of location, land erosion, extraction of minerals, dumping of toxic waste, etc.

It is rare to encounter circumstances under which freehold land should be subject to depreciation. The problem that most often occurs is the distinction between the cost/value of freehold land and the cost/value of the buildings upon it. FRS 15 states that the distinction should be made as only the buildings have a limited useful economic life and should be depreciated. Land has an unlimited life and should not be depreciated. Failure to separate the two elements of the cost/value will result in non-compliance with the standard.

Buildings

These have finite lives and should be depreciated.

Notes to accounts

The FRS requires that the following should be disclosed:

1 Methods of depreciation used.
2 Useful economic lives or the depreciation rates in use.
3 Total depreciation charged for the period.
4 Where material, the financial effect of a change in either useful economic lives or estimates of residual values.
5 The cost or revalued amount at both the start and end of the accounting period.
6 The cumulative amount of provisions for depreciation or impairment at the beginning and end of the financial period.
7 A reconciliation of the movements, separately disclosing additions, disposals, revaluations, transfers, depreciation, impairment losses, and reversals of past impairment losses written back in the period.
8 The net carrying amount at the beginning and end of the financial period.

10.46 FRS 16: Current tax

This FRS replaced SSAP 8. In brief, the FRS requires that:

1 Current tax for the period is recognised in the profit and loss account. The only exception is tax on gains and losses that have been recognised in the statement of total recognised gains and losses. Any such tax should be recognised in that statement, not in the profit and loss account.
2 Dividends received from UK companies are reported at the net amount received. Dividends received from other countries are reported gross only to the extent that they have suffered a withholding tax.
3 Income and expenses subject to non-standard rates of tax (or exempt from tax) should be included in the pre-tax results on the basis of the income or expenses actually receivable or payable, without any adjustment to reflect a notional amount of tax that would have been paid or relieved in respect of the transaction if it had been taxable, or allowable for tax purposes, on a different basis.
4 Current tax should be measured using tax rates and laws that have been enacted or substantively enacted by the balance sheet date.

10.47 FRS 17: Retirement benefits

This standard was issued in November 2000. It superseded SSAP 24: *Accounting for pension costs*. Basically the objective is that the employer should recognise the expected cost of providing pensions on a 'systematic and rational basis' over the period during which he/she derives benefit from the employees' services. The main requirements are as follows:

1 Pension scheme assets are measured using market values.
2 Pension scheme liabilities are measured using a projected unit method and discounted at an AA corporate bond rate.
3 The pension scheme surplus (to the extent it can be recovered) or deficit is recognised in full on the balance sheet.
4 The movement in the scheme surplus/deficit is analysed into:
    (a) the current service cost and any past service costs; these are recognised in operating profit
    (b) the interest cost and expected return on assets; these are recognised as other finance costs
    (c) actuarial gains and losses; these are recognised in the statement of total recognised gains and losses.

10.48 FRS 18: Accounting policies

This standard was covered in Section 10.4 above.

10.49 FRS 19: Deferred tax

This FRS superseded SSAP 15. It is covered in Chapter 7.

10.50 FRSSE: Financial Reporting Standard for Smaller Entities

The FRSSE was first issued in November 1997 and has been updated regularly thereafter. It may be applied to all financial statements intended to give a true and fair view of the financial

position and profit or loss (or income and expenditure) of all entities that are small companies or groups or entities (other than building societies) that would be classified as such were they incorporated under companies legislation.

Small companies are defined in the FRSSE according to the definition contained in sections 247 and 247A of the Companies Act 1985 as being those that in a year satisfy at least two of the following:

1 Turnover no greater than £2.8 million.
2 A balance sheet total no greater than £1.4 million.
3 An average of no more than 50 employees.

Other than in the case of newly incorporated companies, the condition must have been satisfied in two of the last three years. For small groups, the threshold limits are aggregate turnover not exceeding £2.8 million 'net' (i.e. after set-offs and other adjustments required by Schedule 4A of the Companies Act 1985) or £3.6 million 'gross' (i.e. before the set-offs and adjustments); aggregate balance sheet total not exceeding £1.4 million net, £1.68 million gross; and aggregate number of employees not exceeding 50. (Companies Act 1985 sections 248 and 249.)

Application of the FRSSE is voluntary – reporting entities may choose instead to apply all the other accounting standards and UITFs. Those that do apply it are exempt from complying with the other accounting standards and UITFs.

The FRSSE contains a simplified, but lengthy, set of requirements derived from those included in all the other standards and UITFs. It would not be appropriate to describe these in detail here. For information concerning the precise contents of the FRSSE, reference should be made to the FRSSE itself or to a book specialising in accounting standards.

Learning outcomes

You should now have learnt:

1 That accounting standards have statutory recognition and must, therefore, be complied with when preparing financial statements intended to present a true and fair view.

2 That the *Statement of Principles* provides details of the concepts that underpin accounting standards.

3 That as at October 2001, there were 29 accounting standards (9 SSAPs, 19 FRSs and 1 FRSSE) and 21 UITF abstracts in force.

4 About the main requirements of a range of accounting standards.

Answers to activities

1 International accounting standards are becoming increasingly adopted across the world. At the same time, there is an increasing internationalisation of business and a need for greater international uniformity in the regulations underpinning the preparation of company financial statements, particularly for multinational companies.

2 Most non-accountants assume that the information in financial statements is accurate, correct and free of bias. They believe this to be the case because they assume that all such information is based on firm facts – for example, what something cost is shown in the invoice and confirmed by the amount paid for it as shown in the bank statement. They do not realise that many of the figures shown are based on estimates and subject to the subjective interpretation of a situation by the person preparing the financial statements. They are unaware that accountants have many choices to make, so much so that it is unlikely that two accountants would ever produce identical financial statements for any but the smallest of organisations.

By placing an emphasis on the qualitative aspects of information, the *Statement of Principles* seeks to restrict diversity in the range of options open to the preparers of financial statements and so guide them towards a more uniform interpretation of the options available to them, thereby increasing the level of faith that users of those statements may have in the information they contain.

REVIEW QUESTIONS

10.1 In preparing its accounts for the year to 31 May 20X7, Whiting plc had been faced with a number of accounting problems, the details of which were as follows:

(*i*)   The company had closed down its entire American operations which represented a significant part of Whiting plc's business.

(*ii*) The corporation tax for the year to 31 May 20X6 had been over-provided by £5,000.

(*iii*) Land and buildings had been revalued at an amount well in excess of the historic cost (note: the current value is to be adjusted in the financial statements).

(*iv*) A trade debtor had gone into liquidation owing Whiting plc an amount equivalent to 20 per cent of Whiting's turnover for the year. It is highly unlikely that any of this debt will ever be repaid.

(*v*)   During the year, the company changed its method of valuing stock. If the same method had been adopted in the previous year, the profits for that year would have been considerably less than had previously been reported.

Required:

(*a*) Being careful to give your reasons, explain how each of the above matters should be treated in the financial statements of Whiting plc for the year to 31 May 20X7 if the company follows the requirements of FRS 3.

(*b*) Outline the provisions of FRS 10 (*Goodwill and intangible assets*) for the treatment of both non-purchased and purchased goodwill in the balance sheets of companies and groups of companies.

(*Association of Accounting Technicians*)

10.2 The directors are preparing the published accounts of Dorman plc for the year to 31 October 20X5. The following information is provided for certain of the items which are to be included in the final accounts.

(*i*)   *Stocks of raw material, monolite:*

	£
Cost	26,500
Replacement cost	48,100

(*ii*) *Stocks of finished goods:*

	Paramite £	Paraton £
Direct costs	72,600	10,200
Proportion of fixed factory overhead	15,300	4,600
Proportion of selling expenses	6,870	1,800
Net realisable value	123,500	9,520

(*iii*) *Plant and machinery.* An item of plant was shown in the 20X4 accounts at a net book value of £90,000 (£160,000 cost less accumulated depreciation £70,000). The plant was purchased on 1 November 20X2 and has been depreciated at 25 per cent reducing balance. The directors now consider the straight line basis to be more appropriate: they have estimated that at 1 November 20X4 the plant had a remaining useful life of six years and will possess zero residual value at the end of that period.

(*iv*) *Freehold property.* The company purchased a freehold property for £250,000 11 years ago, and it is estimated that the land element was worth £50,000 at that date.

The company has never charged depreciation on the property but the directors now feel that it should have done so; the building is expected to have a total useful life of 40 years.

(v) *Research expenditure* incurred in an attempt to discover a substitute for raw materials currently purchased from a politically sensitive area of the world amounted to £17,500 during the year.

(vi) *Development expenditure* on Tercil, which is nearly ready for production, amounted to £30,000. Demand for Tercil is expected significantly to exceed supply for at least the next four years.

(vii) *Accident.* On 1 December 20X5 there was a fire in the warehouse which damaged stocks, other than the items referred to in (i) and (ii) above. The book value of these stocks was £92,000. The company has discovered that it was underinsured and only expects to recover £71,000 from the insurers.

(viii) *Investments.* Dorman purchased 30,000 ordinary shares in Lilleshall Ltd on 1 November 20X4 for £96,000, and immediately succeeded in appointing two of its directors to Lilleshall's board. The issued share capital of Lilleshall consists of 100,000 ordinary shares of £1 each. The profits of Lilleshall for the year to 31 October 20X5 amounted to £40,000. (Ignore taxation.)

Required:
Explain how each of the above items should be dealt with in the published financial statements of Dorman plc.

(Institute of Chartered Secretaries and Administrators)

10.3A   In preparing the published financial statements of a company, briefly state the significant accounting/disclosure requirements you would have in mind in ensuring that the financial statements comply with best accounting practice as embodied in accounting standards concerning:

(a) Value added tax.
(b) Earnings per share.
(c) The disclosure requirements of each major class of depreciable assets.
(d) Research expenditure.
(e) Capital-based grants relating to fixed assets.
(f) Goodwill on consolidation.
(g) The disclosure requirements relating to generally accepted fundamental accounting concepts.
(h) The accounts of a subsidiary undertaking having similar activities to that of the parent undertaking.

(Association of Accounting Technicians)

10.4A   Oldfield Enterprises Limited was formed on 1 January 20X5 to manufacture and sell a new type of lawn mower. The bookkeeping staff of the company have produced monthly figures for the first ten months to 31 October 20X5 and from these figures together with estimates for the remaining two months, Barry Lamb, the managing director, has drawn up a forecast profit and loss account for the year to 31 December 20X5 and a balance sheet as at that date.

These statements together with the notes are submitted to the board for comment. During the board meeting discussion centres on the treatment given to the various assets. The various opinions are summarised by Barry Lamb who brings them, with the draft accounts, to you as the company's financial adviser.

Oldfield Enterprises Ltd
Draft Profit and Loss Account for the year to 31 December 20X5

	£000	£000
Sales		3,000
Cost of sales		1,750
Gross profit		1,250
Administration overheads	350	
Selling and distribution overheads	530	
		880
Net profit before taxation		370

Draft Balance Sheet at 31 December 20X5

Fixed assets – tangible	Cost £000	Depreciation and amortisation £000	Net £000
Leasehold land and buildings	375	125	250
Freehold land and buildings	350	–	350
Plant and machinery	1,312	197	1,115
	2,037	322	1,715
Fixed assets – intangible			
Research and development			375
Current assets			
Stock		375	
Debtors		780	
		1,155	
Current liabilities			
Creditors	250		
Bank overdraft	125	375	
			780
			2,870
Share capital			2,500
Net profit for year			370
			2,870

Notes:
(a) Administration overheads include £50,000 written-off research and development.
(b) The lease is for 15 years and cost £75,000. Buildings have been put up on the leasehold land at a cost of £300,000. Plant and machinery has been depreciated at 15 per cent. Both depreciation and amortisation are included in cost of sales.

Opinions put forward
Leasehold land and buildings:
The works director thinks that although the lease provides for a rent review after three years the buildings have a 50-year life. The buildings should therefore be depreciated over 50 years and the cost of the lease should be amortised over the period of the lease.
   The managing director thinks that because of the rent review clause the whole of the cost should be depreciated over three years.
   The sales director thinks it is a good idea to charge as much as the profits will allow in order to reduce the tax bill.

Freehold land and buildings:
The works director thinks that as the value of the property is going up with inflation no depreciation is necessary.
   The sales director's opinion is the same as for leasehold property.
   The managing director states that he has heard that if a property is always kept in good repair no depreciation is necessary. This should apply in the case of his company.

Plant and machinery:
The managing director agrees with the 15 per cent for depreciation and proposes to use the reducing balance method.
   The works director wants to charge 25 per cent straight line.

Research and development:
The total spent in the year will be £425,000. Of this £250,000 is for research into the cutting characteristics of different types of grass, £100,000 is for the development of an improved drive system for lawn mowers and £75,000 is for market research to determine the ideal lawn mower characteristics for the average garden.
   The managing director thinks that a small amount should be charged as an expense each year.

The works director wants to write off all the market research and 'all this nonsense of the cutting characteristics of grass'.

The sales director thinks that, as the company has only just started, all research and development expenditure relates to future sales so all this year's expenditure should be carried forward.

Stock:

Both the managing director and the works director are of the opinion that stock should be shown at prime cost.

The sales director's view is that stocks should be shown at sales price as the stock is virtually all sold within a very short period.

Required:

(a) You are asked to comment on each opinion stating what factors should be taken into account to determine suitable depreciation and write-off amounts.

(b) Indicate what amounts should, in your opinion, be charged to profit and loss and show the adjusted profit produced by your recommendations, stating clearly any assumptions you may make.

(Association of Chartered Certified Accountants)

10.5 The accountant of Hook, Line and Sinker, a partnership of seven people, has asked your advice in dealing with the following items in the partnership accounts for the year to 31 May 20X7.

(a) (i) Included in invoices prepared and dated in June 20X7 were £60,000 of goods despatched during the second half of May 20X7.

(ii) Stocks of components at 31 May 20X7 include parts no longer used in production. These components originally cost £50,000 but have been written down for purposes of the accounts to £25,000. Scrap value of these items is estimated to be £1,000. Another user has expressed interest in buying these parts for £40,000.

(b) After May 20X7 a customer who accounts for 50 per cent of Hook, Line and Sinker sales suffered a serious fire which has disrupted his organisation. Payments for supplies are becoming slow and Hook, Line and Sinker sales for the current year are likely to be substantially lower than previously. This customer owed £80,000 to Hook, Line and Sinker at 31 May 20X7.

(c) During the year to 31 May, Hook, Line and Sinker commenced a new advertising campaign using television and expensive magazine advertising for the first time. Sales during the year were not much higher than previous years as the partners consider that the effects of advertising will be seen in future years.

Expenditure on advertising during the year is made up of:

	£
Television	50,000
Advertisements in magazines	60,000
Advertisements in local papers	25,000

All the expenditure has been treated as expense in the accounts but the partners wish to carry forward three-quarters of the television and magazine costs as it is expected that this cost will benefit future years' profits and because this year's profits will compare unfavourably with previous years if all the expenditure is charged in the accounts.

(d) Three projects for the construction of sinkers have the following cost and revenue characteristics:

	Project A	Project B	Project C
Degree of completion	75%	50%	15%
	£	£	£
Direct costs to date	30,000	25,000	6,000
Sales price of complete project	55,000	50,000	57,500
Overheads allocated to date	4,000	2,000	500
Costs to complete – Direct	10,000	25,000	40,000
– Overheads	2,000	2,000	3,000

No profits or losses have been included in the accounts.

(e) After considerable discussion with management, the sales of a newly developed special purpose hook have been given the following probabilities:

First year of production

Sales	Probability
£	
15,000	0.2
30,000	0.5
40,000	0.3

Second year of production

Increase over first year	Probability
£	
10,000	0.1
20,000	0.5
30,000	0.4

Second year sales may be assumed independent of first year levels.
Cost–volume–profit analysis shows that the breakeven point is £50,000.

Production of the special purpose hook started prior to the end of the accounting year and
stocks of the finished product are included at cost amounting to £20,000. It has been decided
that if there is less than 0.7 probability of breakeven being reached in the second year then
stocks should be written down by 25 per cent.

(f) During the year it was discovered that some stock sheets had been omitted from the calculations at the previous year end. The effect is that opening stock for the current year, shown as
£35,000, should be £42,000. No adjustment has yet been made.

Required:
Discuss the treatment of each item with reference to relevant accounting standards and accounting
concepts and conventions. Recommend the appropriate treatment for each item showing the
profit effect of each recommendation made.

(Association of Chartered Certified Accountants)

10.6   The chief accountant of Uncertain Ltd is not sure of the appropriate accounting treatment
for a number of events occurring during the year 20X5/6.

(i)   A significant number of employees have been made redundant, giving rise to redundancy
payments of £100,000 which have been included in manufacturing cost of sales.
(ii)   One of Uncertain Ltd's three factories has been closed down. Closure costs amounted to
£575,000. This amount has been deducted from reserves in the balance sheet.
(iii)   The directors have changed the basis of charging depreciation on delivery vehicles. The difference between the old and new methods amounts to £258,800. This has been charged as a
prior period adjustment.
(iv)   During October 20X6 a fire occurred in one of the remaining factories belonging to Uncertain
Ltd and caused an estimated £350,000 of additional expenses. This amount has been included
in manufacturing cost of sales.
(v)   It was discovered on 31 October 20X6 that a customer was unable to pay his debt to the company of £125,000. The £125,000 was made up of sales in the period July to September 20X6.
No adjustment has been made in the draft accounts for this item.

Uncertain Ltd
Draft Profit and Loss Account for the year ended 30 September 20X6

	£	£
Sales		5,450,490
Manufacturing cost of sales		3,284,500
Gross profit		2,165,990
Administration expenses	785,420	
Selling expenses	629,800	
		(1,415,220)
		750,770
Corporation tax (50%)		(375,385)
		375,385
Proposed dividend on ordinary shares		(125,000)
		250,385
Prior period adjustment	258,800	
Corporation tax	(129,400)	
		(129,400)
		120,985

Required:

(a) Write a report to the chief accountant of Uncertain Ltd with suggestions for appropriate treatment for each of the items (i) to (iv), with explanations for your proposals.

(b) Amend the draft profit and loss account to take account of your proposals.

(*Association of Chartered Certified Accountants*)

10.7   With reference to SSAP 17: *Accounting for post-balance sheet events* and FRS 12: *Provisions,
contingent liabilities and contingent assets*:

(a) define the following terms:
   (i)   post-balance sheet events
   (ii) adjusting events
   (iii) non-adjusting events
   (iv) contingent asset/liability;

(b) give FOUR examples of adjusting events, and FOUR examples of non-adjusting events; and

(c) state how
   (i)   a material contingent liability, and
   (ii) material contingent assets should be accounted for in financial statements.

CHAPTER 11

The financial statements of limited companies: profit and loss accounts, related statements and notes

After you have studied this chapter, you should be able to:

- state how the Companies Act defines company size
- explain the alternative presentation formats available under the Companies Acts that must be used when preparing profit and loss accounts for external reporting purposes
- explain how to present information under the most commonly used of the Companies Act formats
- describe the differences between the statutory format and formats generally adopted for internal use
- describe the FRS 3 requirements that relate to the profit and loss account concerning:
  - continuing operations
  - acquisitions
  - discontinued operations
  - sale or termination of an operation
  - reorganisation and restructuring costs
  - profits and losses on disposal of fixed assets
  - exceptional and extraordinary items
  - prior period adjustments
- describe the impact of FRS 3 upon the Companies Act format
- describe the format of the statement of total recognised gains and losses
- describe the format of the note of historical cost profits and losses

Introduction

In this chapter you'll learn about the way in which the Companies Acts govern the presentation of information in published company financial statements.

11.1 Background

When a company draws up its own financial statements, purely for internal use by directors and the management, it can draft them in any way it wishes. You should be aware that drawing up a trading and profit and loss account and balance sheet for a company's own use is not necessarily the same as drawing up such financial statements for examination purposes. If an organisation wishes to charge something in the trading account that, in theory, ought to be shown in the profit and loss account, there is nothing to prevent it from doing so. On the other hand, students sitting an exam must base their answers on accounting theory and not on the internal reporting practice of an organisation that they may know.

When it comes to publication, i.e. when the financial statements are sent to the shareholders or to the Registrar of Companies, the Companies Acts lay down the information which must be shown, and also how it should be shown. Prior to 1981, provided the necessary information was shown, it was up to each company to decide how it wanted to present it. The provisions of the 1981 Act brought the UK into line with the Fourth Directive of the EC, and the freedom previously available to companies on how to show the information was removed. There are, however, some advantages to be gained from such standardisation.

> **Activity 11.1**
> What do you think these advantages may be?

11.2 Layout of accounts

The Companies Acts give companies the choice of two alternative formats (layouts) for balance sheets, and four alternative formats for profit and loss accounts. As you will most probably be studying this topic for the first time, it would be inappropriate (and unnecessary) to give you all the details of all the formats. Only those who are at the final stages of sudying accounting need such details.

In this book, therefore, you will be shown a profit and loss account produced for use within the company (an 'internal' profit and loss account) which can easily be adapted to cover publication requirements under the Acts, along with a balance sheet.

All companies, even the smallest, have to produce financial statements for shareholders that adhere to the requirements of the Companies Acts. 'Small' and 'medium-sized' companies can, however, file summarised accounts with the Registrar of Companies, but they must still prepare full accounts for their shareholders. In addition, listed companies may send their shareholders summary financial statements in place of the full version, unless a shareholder specifically requests a full version. We will consider these points later.

Note: A 'small' company is one for which two of the following are true: turnover does not exceed £2.8 million; the balance sheet total does not exceed £1.4m; the average number of employees does not exceed 50. For 'medium-sized' companies, the equivalent limits are £11.2 million, £5.6 million, and 250 employees.

Of the four formats which could be used, the format we will use in this book for the published profit and loss account is called Format 1.

11.3 Format 1

The Companies Acts show Format 1 as in Exhibit 11.1.

Exhibit 11.1

Profit and loss account
Format 1

1 Turnover
2 Cost of sales
3 Gross profit or loss
4 Distribution costs
5 Administrative expenses
6 Other operating income
7 Income from shares in group undertakings
8 Income from participating interests
9 Income from other fixed asset investments
10 Other interest receivable and similar income
11 Amounts written off investments
12 Interest payable and similar charges
13 Tax on profit or loss on ordinary activities
14 Profit or loss on ordinary activities after taxation
15 Extraordinary income
16 Extraordinary charges
17 Extraordinary profit or loss
18 Tax on extraordinary profit or loss
19 Other taxes not shown under the above items
20 Profit or loss for the financial year

This is simply a list and it does not show where subtotals should be placed. The important point is that the items 1 to 20 have to be displayed in that order. If some items do not exist for the company in a given year, then those headings are omitted from the published profit and loss account. Thus, if the company has no investments, items 7, 8, 9, 10 and 11 will not exist, and item 6 will be followed by item 12 in that company's published profit and loss account. The category reference numbers on the left-hand side of items do not have to be shown in the published accounts.

11.4 Accounts for internal use

Exhibit 11.2 shows a trading and profit and loss account drawn up for internal use by a company. As mentioned earlier, there are no statutory rules concerning how financial statements are drawn up for internal use. However, if the internal financial statements were drawn up in a completely different fashion from those needed for publication, then there would be quite a lot of work needed in order to reassemble the figures into a profit and loss account for publication. Unsurprisingly, many companies use the same format but expand some of the detail for the internal version.

In Exhibit 11.2, the internal accounts have been drawn up in a style which makes it much easier to get the figures for the published profit and loss account. Examination questions on this topic often ask for both (*a*) internal and (*b*) published accounts, and it therefore makes it simpler for students if the internal and published accounts follow a similar order of display.

Exhibit 11.2 Accounts for internal use

Block plc

Trading and Profit and Loss Account for the year ended 31 December 20X6

	£000	£000	£000
Turnover			800
Less Cost of sales:			
Stock 1 January 20X6		100	
Add Purchases		525	
		625	
Less Stock 31 December 20X6		(125)	
			(500)
Gross profit			300
Distribution costs			
Salaries and wages	30		
Motor vehicle costs: Distribution	20		
General distribution expenses	5		
Depreciation: Motors	3		
Machinery	2		
		60	
Administrative expenses			
Salaries and wages	25		
Motor vehicle costs: Administration	2		
General administration expenses	7		
Auditors' remuneration	2		
Depreciation: Motors	3		
Machinery	1		
		40	
			(100)
			200
Other operating income			30
			230
Income from shares in group undertakings		20	
Income from participating interests		10	
Income from shares from non-related companies		5	
Other interest receivable		15	
			50
			280
Amounts written off investments		4	
Interest payable			
Loans repayable within five years	10		
Loans repayable in ten years' time	6		
		16	
			(20)
Profit on ordinary activities before taxation			260
Tax on profit on ordinary activities			(95)
Profit on ordinary activities after taxation			165
Retained profits brought forward from last year			60
			225
Transfer to general reserve		40	
Proposed ordinary dividend		100	
			(140)
Retained profits carried forward to next year			85

11.5   Accounts for publication

Note that there are no items in Exhibit 11.2 that would appear under items 15 to 19 in Companies Act Format 1. Exhibit 11.3 redrafts Exhibit 11.2 into a form suitable for publication according to Format 1. However, as before, the category reference numbers to the left-hand side of Exhibit 11.3 are for your benefit only, they do not have to be included.

Exhibit 11.3 Accounts for publication presented according to Format 1

Block plc
Profit and Loss Account for the year ending 31 December 20X6

	£000	£000
1 Turnover		800
2 Cost of sales		(500)
3 Gross profit		300
4 Distribution costs	60	
5 Administrative expenses	40	
		(100)
		200
6 Other operating income		30
		230
7 Income from shares in group undertakings	20	
8 Income from participating interests	10	
9 Income from other fixed asset investments	5	
10 Other interest receivable and similar income	15	
		50
		280
11 Amounts written off investments	4	
12 Interest payable and similar charges	16	
		(20)
Profit or loss on ordinary activities before taxation		260
13 Tax on profit or loss on ordinary activities		(95)
14 Profit or loss on ordinary activities after taxation		165
Transfer to reserves	40	
Dividends paid and proposed	100	
		(140)
Retained profits for the period		25

Note: The retained profit from the previous year is not shown. It would normally appear in a note to the financial statements concerning movements on the reserves.

It would be legally possible for the internal accounts, as shown in Exhibit 11.2, to be published just as they are, because all the items are shown in the correct order. This would not have been possible if the internal accounts were drafted in a different order. The Companies Act does not force companies to publish fully detailed accounts (for example, as detailed as Exhibit 11.2). It states the minimum information which must be disclosed. A company can show more than the minimum should it so wish.

Activity 11.2
Why would companies not want to publish fully detailed accounts?

11.6 Definition of items in Format 1

Format item 1

Turnover is defined as the amounts derived from the provision of goods and services falling within the company's ordinary activities, net after deduction of VAT and trade discounts.

Format items 2, 4 and 5

The figures for cost of sales, distribution costs and administrative expenses must include any depreciation charges connected with these functions. In the case of Block plc, because of the type of business, there are depreciation charges as part of distribution costs and administration expenses, but not cost of sales.

Format item 6

This is operating income which does not fall under item 1. Such items as rents receivable or royalties receivable might be found under this heading.

Format item 7

In Chapter 19 of this book the reader will be introduced to parent and subsidiary undertakings. A parent is able to exert a dominant influence (i.e. control) over the activities of the subsidiary usually, but not necessarily, as a result of its owning a majority of the voting rights in the subsidiary. The parent and all its subsidiaries are a 'group'. Any dividends received by a company from its investments in shares in any member of the group have to be shown separately.

Format item 8

The term 'participating interest' means one where the parent company has a long-term holding of shares or their equivalent in an undertaking for the purpose of securing a contribution to the investor's own activities by the exercise of control or influence arising from or related to that interest. Where the equity stake exceeds 20 per cent, there is a presumption of such influence unless the contrary is shown.

Format item 12

This includes bank interest on loans and overdrafts, debenture interest, etc.

The profit and loss account produced will not appear precisely as presented in Exhibit 11.1. As can be seen in Exhibit 11.3, the published profit and loss account for Block plc contains no items in categories 15, 16, 17, 18, 19 or 20. In addition, after item 14, there are several more lines, those of transfer to reserves, and proposed dividends. Although the format omits them, they are required according to the detailed rules accompanying the format. This also applies to line 20, 'Profit or loss for the financial year' shown in Exhibit 11.1, when that line is included.

It would also have been possible to amalgamate items, for instance 4 and 5 could have been shown together as 'Net operating expenses £100,000'. In this case, included in the notes appended to the financial statements would be an item showing the composition of the figure of £100,000.

In the notes attached to the profit and loss account, the Companies Acts require that the following be shown separately:

1 Interest on bank loans, overdrafts and other loans:
   (a) repayable within 5 years from the end of the accounting period;
   (b) finally repayable after 5 years from the end of the accounting period.
2 Amounts set aside for redemption of share capital and for redemption of loans.
3 Rents from land, if material.
4 Costs of hire of plant and machinery.
5 Auditors' remuneration, including expenses.

Where a company carries on business of two or more classes differing substantially from each other, a note is required of the amount of turnover for each class of business, and the division of the profit and loss before taxation between each class. Information also has to be given of the turnover between geographical markets.

Notes are also required concerning numbers of employees, wages and salaries, social security costs, and pension costs.

Three further disclosure requirements of the Companies Act are expanded by FRS 3:

1 The effect must be stated of any amount relating to any preceding financial year included in any item in the profit and loss account.
2 Particulars must be given of any extraordinary income or charges arising in the financial year.
3 The effect of any transaction of exceptional size or incidence that falls within the ordinary activities of the company must be stated.

11.7 Layout of the profit and loss account

If Block plc had items relevant to the other Format 1 categories, the profit and loss account would have been presented as shown in Exhibit 11.4. Note that the lines added have been included simply to show what the statement would look like. Where a category has no value, it would normally be omitted from the statement, as was the case in Exhibit 11.3. In addition, Exhibit 11.4 shows the extra lines that must be included but were not shown in Format 1 in the Companies Act. It is also worthwhile noting that the four lines in Format 1 that relate to *extraordinary items* are virtually eliminated as a result of the definition of the term that was introduced in FRS 3: *Reporting financial performance*. As a result of its issuing FRS 3, the Accounting Standards Board does not expect any company to identify an item as 'extraordinary' in its financial statements and so items 15 to 18 are unlikely to be seen in any future published profit and loss accounts. (This will be covered in greater detail in Section 11.11.)

Exhibit 11.4

Block plc
Profit and Loss Account for the year ending 31 December 20X6

	£000	£000
1 Turnover		800
2 Cost of sales		(500)
3 Gross profit		300
4 Distribution costs	60	
5 Administrative expenses	40	
		(100)
		200
6 Other operating income		30
		230
7 Income from shares in group undertakings	20	
8 Income from participating interests	10	
9 Income from fixed asset investments	5	
10 Other interest receivable and similar income	15	
		50
		280
11 Amounts written off investments	4	
12 Interest payable and similar charges	16	
		(20)
Profit or loss on ordinary activities before taxation		260
13 Tax on profit or loss on ordinary activities		(95)
14 Profit or loss on ordinary activities after taxation		165
15 Extraordinary income	0	
16 Extraordinary charges	0	
17 Extraordinary profit or loss	0	
18 Tax on extraordinary profit or loss	0	
		0
		165
19 Other taxes not shown under the above items		0
20 Profit or loss for the year		165
Transfer to reserves	40	
Dividends paid and proposed	100	
		(140)
Retained profits for the year		25

11.8 Allocation of expenses

It will be obvious under which heading most expenses will be shown, whether they are

(a) cost of sales
(b) distribution costs, or
(c) administrative expenses.

However, as the Companies Acts do not define these terms, some items are not so easy to allocate with certainty. Some companies may choose one heading for a particular item, while another company will choose another. These items can now be examined.

1 **Discounts received.** These are for prompt payment of amounts owing by us. Where they are for payments to suppliers of goods they could be regarded either as a reduction in the cost of goods or, alternatively, as a financial recompense, i.e. the reward for paying money on time. If regarded in the first way they would be deducted from cost of sales, whereas the alternative approach would be to deduct them from administrative expenses. However, these discounts are also deducted when paying bills in respect of distribution

costs or administrative expenses, and it would also be necessary to deduct from these headings if the cost of sales deduction approach is used. As this raises complications in the original recording of discounts received, it would be more suitable in this book if all cash discounts received are deducted in arriving at the figure of administrative expenses.

2 **Discounts allowed.** To be consistent in dealing with discounts, this should be included in administrative expenses.

3 **Bad debts.** These could be regarded as an expense connected with sales: after all, they are sales which are not paid for. The other point of view is that for a debt to become bad, at least part of the blame must be because the proper administrative procedures in checking on customers' creditworthiness has not been thorough enough. In this book all bad debts will be taken as being part of administrative expenses.

11.9 FRS 3: Reporting financial performance

Accounting is not a static subject. Changes occur over the years as they are seen to be necessary, and also get general agreement as to their usefulness. Since the advent of SSAPs and FRSs the number of changes that practitioners and students have had to learn has increased at a very fast rate. A prime example of this is the introduction of FRS 3, which necessitates changes to the formats of profit and loss accounts when certain events have occurred.

This standard superseded SSAP 6: *Extraordinary items and prior year adjustments*, temporarily amended SSAP 3: *Earnings per share* (FRS 14: *Earnings per share* was issued five years after FRS 3), and also made changes as a consequence of various other accounting standards.

Suppose that you are considering the affairs of a business over the years. The business has not changed significantly, there have been no acquisitions, no discontinued operations, no fundamental reorganisation or restructuring of the business, nor have there been any extraordinary items affecting the financial statements. In these circumstances, when comparing the financial statements over the years, you are comparing like with like, subject to the problem of the effect of inflation or deflation.

On the other hand, suppose that some of the things mentioned have occurred. When trying to see what the future might hold for the company, simply basing your opinions on what has happened in the past can be very confusing.

To help you to distinguish the past and the future, and to give you some idea as to what changes have occurred, FRS 3 requires that the following are highlighted in the profit and loss account if they are material in amount:

1 *What the results of continuing operations are, including the results of acquisitions.* Obviously acquisitions affect future results, and are therefore included in continuing operations.

2 *What the results have been of discontinued operations.* This should help distinguish the past from the future.

3 *The profits or losses on the sale or termination of an operation, the costs of fundamental reorganisation or restructuring* and *the profits and losses on the disposal of fixed assets.* The profits and losses concerning these matters are not going to happen again, and so this also helps us distinguish the past from the future.

We can see how FRS 3 requires these items to be shown on the face of the profit and loss account in Exhibit 11.5. Not only is the turnover split to show the figures relevant to continuing operations, acquisitions and discontinued operations, the operating profit is split in a similar fashion. In addition any profit or loss on the disposal of the discontinued operations would also be shown. Exhibit 11.5 is restricted to the first six categories of Format 1 as this is the part of the statement affected by these FRS 3 requirements. Once again, it uses Block plc for the example.

Exhibit 11.5

Block plc
Profit and Loss Account for the year ending 31 December 20X6 (extract)

	£000	£000
1 Turnover		
Continuing operations	520	
Acquisitions	110	
	630	
Discontinued operations	170	
		800
2 Cost of sales		(500)
3 Gross profit		300
4 Distribution costs	60	
5 Administrative expenses	40	
		(100)
Operating profit		
Continuing operations	160	
Acquisitions	60	
	220	
Discontinued operations (loss)	(20)	
		200
Profit on disposal of discontinued operations (*a*)		10
		210
6 Other operating income		20
Profit or loss on ordinary activities before interest		230

The item marked (*a*) can be described as an exceptional item. It is material in amount, falls within the ordinary activities of the firm, and needs to be shown so that the financial statements will give a 'true and fair view'.

It is exceptional in that it is not the ordinary daily occurrence, but remember that it falls within the ordinary activities of the company. FRS 3 requires that three categories of exceptional items be shown separately on the face of the profit and loss account after operating profit and before interest, and included under the appropriate heading of continued or discontinued operations:

1 Profits or losses on the sale or termination of an operation.
2 Costs of a fundamental reorganisation or restructuring having a material effect on the nature and focus of the reporting entity's operations.
3 Profits or losses on the disposal of fixed assets.

Other exceptional items should be credited or charged in arriving at the profit or loss on ordinary activities by inclusion under the heading to which they relate. The amount of each exceptional item should be disclosed in a note, or on the face of the profit and loss account, if necessary in order to give a true and fair view.

11.10 Other statements and notes required by FRS 3

Statement of total recognised gains and losses

The *statement of total recognised gains and losses* is one of two new primary statements introduced by FRS 3. It shows the extent to which shareholders' funds have increased or decreased from all the various gains and losses recognised in the period, and enables users

to consider all recognised gains and losses of a reporting entity in assessing its overall performance; an example of what would be included in the statement would be unrealised gains on fixed asset revaluations. Exhibit 11.6 presents an example of the statement using the data from Block plc.

Exhibit 11.6

Block plc
Statement of Total Recognised Gains and Losses

	20X6
	£000
Profit for the financial year	165
Unrealised surplus on revaluation of properties	12
Unrealised (loss)/gain on trade investment	(8)
	169
Currency translation differences on foreign currency investments	(5)
Total recognised gains and losses relating to the year	164
Prior period adjustment	(19)
Total gains and losses recognised since last annual report	145

Note: Only the profit figure can be found in the profit and loss account. The others have been inserted to demonstrate what the statement looks like. Also, as with all these statements, including the profit and loss account, comparative figures would also be shown.

Note of historical cost profits and losses

Where assets have been revalued, which obviously affects depreciation, the revalued figures may have a material effect upon the results shown in the financial statements. If this is the case, FRS 3 requires that there should also be shown as a note what the profit and loss account would have been if the account had been shown using historical (i.e. not revalued) figures. The note should also show how the reported profit on ordinary activities (using accounts with revalued assets) can be reconciled with that calculated using historical figures, and should also show the retained profit figure for the financial year reported on the historical cost basis. The note should be presented immediately following the profit and loss account or the statement of total recognised gains and losses. An example of the note is presented in Exhibit 11.7.

Exhibit 11.7

Block plc
Note of Historical Cost Profits and Losses

	20X6
	£000
Reported profit on ordinary activities before taxation	260
Realisation of property revaluation gains of previous years	12
Difference between a historical cost depreciation charge and the actual depreciation charge of the year calculated on the revalued amount	1
Historical cost profit on ordinary activities before taxation	273
Historical cost profit for the year retained after taxation, minority interests, extraordinary items and dividends (273 – 95 – 100)	78

Note: As with the statement of total recognised gains and losses, only the profit figure can be identified in the profit and loss account. Also, comparative figures should be shown.

Reconciliation of movements in shareholders' funds

The profit and loss account and the statement of total recognised gains and losses reflect the performance of a reporting entity in a period, but there are other changes that can occur in shareholders' funds that these two statements do not disclose, and which can be important in understanding the change in the financial position of the entity – for example, a new share issue or goodwill written off. For this reason, FRS 3 also gave the *reconciliation of movements in shareholders' funds* the status of a primary statement, its purpose being to highlight these other changes in the financial position. When shown as a primary statement (there is an option to show it as a note), the reconciliation should be shown separately from the statement of total recognised gains and losses. Exhibit 11.8 presents an example of the statement.

Exhibit 11.8

Block plc
Reconciliation of Movements in Shareholders' Funds

	20X6
	£000
Profit for the financial year	165
Dividends	(100)
	65
Other recognised gains and losses relating to the year (net)	(1)
New share capital subscribed	20
Goodwill written off	(25)
Net addition to shareholders' funds	59
Opening shareholders' funds (originally £321,000 before deducting prior period adjustment of £19,000)	302
Closing shareholders' funds	361

Note: The figures can be found in the other statements except for the new share capital, the goodwill written off and the opening shareholders' funds amounts. As before, comparative figures should also be presented.

11.11 FRS 3 and extraordinary items

You have just seen that in FRS 3 some of the exceptional items have to be highlighted on the face of the profit and loss account, whilst others can be put under appropriate headings with notes giving details being attached to the financial statements.

In Exhibit 11.3 all of these exceptional items will have been dealt with by the time that item 14, 'Profit for the year on ordinary activities after taxation', has been reached. Extraordinary items, as per Format 1, would be shown after that as items 15, 16, 17 and 18.

Before FRS 3, the distinction between what was an exceptional item and what was an extraordinary item was not as well defined as it could have been. This led to directors of companies sometimes manipulating the figures for their own ends while keeping within the necessary legal boundaries.

They did this because the profit per item 14 was a very well used figure for assessing how well, or otherwise, a company was being managed. It was a vital part of calculating the earnings per share (EPS) which is a main indicator to many people of the company's performance. If a favourable item could be called an 'exceptional item' it would increase the size of the profit as shown by item 14. On the other hand, should an item be unfavourable, and therefore lower the figure of profit shown by item 14, then perhaps it could be (and it often was) called an 'extraordinary item' instead. In this way, the profit per item 14 could be shown at a higher figure than was really justified. Such actions could affect the stock exchange values of the company's shares.

FRS 3 is more strict about what is, or is not, an extraordinary item, and thus to be shown after item 14 in the profit and loss account. Extraordinary items:

(a) should be material items possessing a high degree of abnormality which arise from events or transactions that fall outside the ordinary activities of the business, and
(b) are not expected to recur,
(c) do not include exceptional items, and
(d) do not include items relating to a prior period merely because they relate to a prior period.

Extraordinary items fall *outside* the 'ordinary' activities of a company, whereas exceptional items fall *within* them. 'Ordinary activities' are any activities undertaken by a reporting entity as part of its business and such related activities in which the reporting entity engages in furtherance of, incidental to or arising from these activities. Ordinary activities include the effects on the reporting entity of any event in the various environments in which it operates. It is little wonder that the ASB did not believe that anything could ever be described as an extraordinary item after the introduction of FRS 3.

11.12 FRS 3 and prior period adjustments

A prior period adjustment is a material adjustment applicable to prior periods arising from changes in accounting policies or from the correction of fundamental errors. They do not include normal recurring adjustments or corrections of accounting estimates made in prior periods.

Prior period adjustments are accounted for by restating the comparative figures for the preceding period in the primary statements and notes and adjusting the opening balance of reserves for the cumulative effect. The cumulative effect of the adjustments should also be noted at the foot of the statement of total recognised gains and losses of the current period (*see* Exhibit 11.6). The effect of prior period adjustments on the results for the preceding period should be disclosed where practicable.

11.13 FRS 3 and comparative figures

Comparative figures should be shown for all items in the primary statements and the notes to the statements required by FRS 3. The comparative figures in respect of the profit and loss account should include in the continuing category only the results of those operations included in the current period's continuing operations.

Learning outcomes

You should now have learnt:

1 How the Companies Act defines company size.

2 There are set formats for the preparation of published financial statements.

3 Accounts for internal use need not comply with these set formats.

4 FRS 3: *Reporting financial performance* has altered the set format for the profit and loss account by requiring further details to be disclosed concerning:
   (a) continuing and discontinued operations
   (b) restructuring
   (c) disposal of fixed assets.

5 In addition, by defining extraordinary items out of existence, FRS 3 effectively made obsolete a number of the categories contained in the set format profit and loss accounts relating to extraordinary items.

6 FRS 3 introduced two additional primary financial statements:
   (*a*) the statement of total recognised gains and losses
   (*b*) the reconciliation of movements in shareholders' funds (may be shown as a note).

7 It also introduced a new note – the note of historical cost profits and losses.

Answers to activities

11.1 Combined with the regulations enshrined in accounting standards that govern how data will be processed and selected for inclusion as information in the financial statements, the standardisation brought about by the Companies Act 1981 makes meaningful comparison between the financial statements of different companies feasible.

11.2 Because their competitors may thereby be given information which would lead to their being placed in a better competitive position.

Advice: It is important for you to know that the published profit and loss account of a company must show certain items in a given order.

   The contents of FRS 3 are likely to attract quite a lot of exam questions. In particular the definition of extraordinary items per FRS 3 will undoubtedly see quite a crop of questions. Some may come in the form of the directors of a company wanting to classify something as extraordinary, and therefore shown after item 14, 'Profit or loss on ordinary activities after taxation'.

REVIEW QUESTIONS

11.1 From the following selected balances of Rogers plc as at 31 December 20X2 draw up (*i*) a trading and profit and loss account for internal use, and (*ii*) a profit and loss account for publication.

	£
Profit and loss account as at 31 December 20X1	15,300
Stock 1 January 20X2	57,500
Purchases	164,000
Sales	288,000
Returns inwards	11,500
Returns outwards	2,000
Carriage inwards	1,300
Wages and salaries (*see* Note (*b*))	8,400
Rent and rates (*see* Note (*c*))	6,250
General distribution expenses	4,860
General administrative expenses	3,320
Discounts allowed	3,940
Bad debts	570
Debenture interest	2,400
Motor expenses (*see* Note (*d*))	7,200
Interest received on bank deposit	770
Income from shares in undertakings in which the company has a participating interest	660
Motor vehicles at cost: Administrative	14,000
Distribution	26,000
Equipment at cost: Administrative	5,500
Distribution	3,500
Royalties receivable	1,800

Notes:

(a) Stock at 31 December 20X2 £64,000.
(b) Wages and salaries are to be apportioned: Distribution costs $\frac{1}{3}$, Administrative expenses $\frac{2}{3}$.
(c) Rent and rates are to be apportioned: Distribution costs 60 per cent, Administrative expenses 40 per cent.
(d) Apportion motor expenses equally between distribution costs and administrative expenses.
(e) Depreciate motor vehicles 25 per cent and equipment 20 per cent on cost.
(f) Accrue auditors' remuneration of £500.
(g) Accrue corporation tax for the year on ordinary activity profits £30,700.
(h) A sum of £8,000 is to be transferred to general reserve.
(i) An ordinary dividend of £30,000 is to be proposed.

11.2 You are given the following selected balances of Federal plc as at 31 December 20X4. From them draw up (i) a trading and profit and loss account for the year ended 31 December 20X4 for internal use and (ii) a profit and loss account for publication.

	£
Stock 1 January 20X4	64,500
Sales	849,000
Purchases	510,600
Carriage inwards	4,900
Returns inwards	5,800
Returns outwards	3,300
Discounts allowed	5,780
Discounts received	6,800
Wages (putting goods into saleable condition)	11,350
Salaries and wages: Sales and distribution staff	29,110
Salaries and wages: Administrative staff	20,920
Motor expenses (see Note (c))	15,600
Rent and rates (see Note (d))	25,000
Investments in undertakings in which the	
company has a participating interest (market value £66,000)	80,000
Income from shares in undertakings in which the	
company has a participating interest	3,500
General distribution expenses	8,220
General administrative expenses	2,190
Bad debts	840
Interest from government securities	1,600
Haulage costs: Distribution	2,070
Debenture interest payable	3,800
Profit and loss account: 31 December 20X3	37,470
Motor vehicles at cost: Distribution and sales	75,000
Administrative	35,000
Plant and machinery at cost: Distribution and sales	80,000
Administrative	50,000
Production	15,000
Directors' remuneration	5,000

Notes:

(a) The production department puts goods bought into a saleable condition.
(b) Stock at 31 December 20X4 £82,800.
(c) Apportion motor expenses: distribution $\frac{2}{3}$, administrative $\frac{1}{3}$.
(d) Apportion rent and rates: distribution 80 per cent, administrative 20 per cent.
(e) Write £14,000 off the value of investments in undertakings in which the company has a participating interest.
(f) Depreciate motor vehicles 20 per cent on cost, plant and machinery 10 per cent on cost.
(g) Accrue auditors' remuneration £2,000.

(h) Accrue corporation tax on ordinary activity profits £74,000.
(i) A sum of £20,000 is to be transferred to debenture redemption reserve.
(j) An ordinary dividend of £50,000 is to be proposed.

11.3 The following information has been extracted from the books of account of Rufford plc for the year to 31 March 20X6:

	Dr £000	Cr £000
Administration expenses	97	
Deferred taxation		24
Depreciation on office machinery (for the year to 31 March 20X6)	8	
Depreciation on delivery vans (for the year to 31 March 20X6)	19	
Distribution costs	33	
Dividends received (from a UK listed company on 31 July 20X5)		14
Factory closure expenses (closed on 1 April 20X5)	12	
Interest payable on bank overdraft (repayable within five years)	6	
Interim dividend (paid on 30 September 20X5)	21	
Interest receivable		25
Purchases	401	
Retained profit at 31 March 20X5		160
Sales (net of VAT)		642
Stock at 1 April 20X5	60	

Additional information:

1 Administrative expenses include the following items:

	£000
Auditors' remuneration	20
Directors' emoluments	45
Travelling expenses	1
Research expenditure	11
Hire of plant and machinery	12

2 It is assumed that the following tax rates are applicable for the year to 31 March 20X6:

Corporation tax	50%
Income tax	30%

3 There was an overprovision for corporation tax of £3,000 relating to the year to 31 March 20X5.
4 Corporation tax payable for the year to 31 March 20X6 (based on the profits for that year) is estimated to be £38,000. The company, in addition, intends to transfer a further £9,000 to its deferred taxation account.
5 A final dividend of £42,000 for the year to 31 March 20X6 is expected to be paid on 2 June 20X6.
6 Stock at 31 March 20X6 was valued at £71,000.
7 As a result of a change in accounting policy, a prior period charge of £15,000 (net of tax) is to be made.
8 The company's share capital consists of 420,000 ordinary shares of £1 each. There are no preference shares, and no change had been made to the company's issued share capital for some years.

Required:
(a) In so far as the information permits, prepare the company's published profit and loss account for the year to 31 March 20X6 in the vertical format in accordance with the Companies Act and with related accounting standards.
   (NB: A statement of the company's accounting policies is not required.)
(b) Prepare balance sheet extracts in order to illustrate the balances still remaining in the following accounts at 31 March 20X6:
   (i) corporation tax;
   (ii) proposed dividend; and
   (iii) deferred taxation.
   (NB: A detailed balance sheet is not required.)

(Association of Accounting Technicians)

11.4A   The following balance has been extracted from the books of Falconer plc as on 31 August 20X4. From them draw up (i) a trading and profit and loss account, for internal use, for the year ended 31 August 20X4, also (ii) a profit and loss account for publication for the year.

	£
Purchases	540,500
Sales	815,920
Returns inwards	15,380
Returns outwards	24,620
Carriage inwards	5,100
Wages – productive	6,370
Discounts allowed	5,890
Discounts received	7,940
Stock 31 August 20X3	128,750
Wages and salaries: Sales and distribution	19,480
Wages and salaries: Administrative	24,800
Motor expenses: Sales and distribution	8,970
Motor expenses: Administrative	16,220
General distribution expenses	4,780
General administrative expenses	5,110
Rent and rates (see Note (c))	9,600
Directors' remuneration	12,400
Profit and loss account: 31 August 20X3	18,270
Advertising costs	8,380
Bad debts	1,020
Hire of plant and machinery (see Note (b))	8,920
Motor vehicles at cost: Sales and distribution	28,000
Administrative	36,000
Plant and machinery: Distribution	17,500
Debenture interest payable	4,800
Income from shares in group undertakings	12,800
Income from shares in undertakings in which the company has a participating interest	10,500
Preference dividend paid	15,000
Profit on disposal of investments	6,600
Tax on profit on disposal of investments	1,920

Notes:

(a) Stock at 31 August 20X4 £144,510.
(b) The hire of plant and machinery is to be apportioned: productive £5,200, administrative £3,720.
(c) Rent and rates to be apportioned: distribution ²/₃, administrative ¹/₃.
(d) Motors are to be depreciated at 25 per cent on cost; plant and machinery to be depreciated at 20 per cent on cost.
(e) Auditors' remuneration of £1,700 to be accrued.
(f) Corporation tax on profit from ordinary activities for the year is estimated at £59,300, excluding tax on disposal of investments.
(g) Transfer £25,000 to general reserve.
(h) Ordinary dividend of £60,000 is proposed.

11.5A   From the following balance of Danielle plc you are to draw up (i) a trading and profit and loss account for the year ended 31 December 20X6, for internal use, and (ii) a profit and loss account for publication:

	£
Plant and machinery, at cost (*see* Note (*c*))	275,000
Bank interest receivable	1,850
Discounts allowed	5,040
Discounts received	3,890
Hire of motor vehicles: Sales and distribution	9,470
Hire of motor vehicles: Administrative	5,710
Licence fees receivable	5,100
General distribution expenses	11,300
General administrative expenses	15,800
Wages and salaries: Sales and distribution	134,690
Administrative	89,720
Directors' remuneration	42,000
Motor expenses (*see* Note (*e*))	18,600
Stock 31 December 20X5	220,500
Sales	880,000
Purchases	405,600
Returns outwards	15,800
Returns inwards	19,550
Profit and loss account as at 31 December 20X5	29,370

Notes:

(*a*) Stock at 31 December 20X6 £210,840.
(*b*) Accrue auditor's remuneration £3,000.
(*c*) Of the plant and machinery, £150,000 is distributive in nature, while £125,000 is for administration.
(*d*) Depreciate plant and machinery 20 per cent on cost.
(*e*) Of the motor expenses, ²/₃ is for sales and distribution and ¹/₃ for administration.
(*f*) Corporation tax on ordinary profits is estimated at £28,350.
(*g*) Proposed ordinary dividend is £50,000.
(*h*) A sum of £15,000 is to be transferred to general reserve.

11.6A Bunker plc is a trading company; it does not carry out *any* manufacturing operations. The following information has been extracted from the books of account for the year to 31 March 20X0:

	£000
Auditors' remuneration	30
Corporation tax: based on the accounting profit for the year to 31 March 20X0	7,200
overprovision for the year to 31 March 20X9	200
United Kingdom corporation tax relief on	
overseas operations: closure costs	30
Delivery expenses	1,200
Dividends: final (proposed – to be paid 1 August 20X0)	200
interim (paid on 1 October 20X9)	100
Fixed assets at cost:	
Delivery vans	200
Office cars	40
Stores plant and equipment	5,000
Investment income (amount received from listed companies)	1,600
Office expenses	800
Overseas operations: closure costs of entire operations on 1 April 20X9	350
Purchases (net of value added tax)	24,000
Sales (net of value added tax)	35,000
Stocks at cost:	
at 1 April 20X9	5,000
at 31 March 20X0	6,000
Storeroom costs	1,000
Wages and salaries:	
Delivery staff	700
Directors' emoluments	300
Office staff	100
Storeroom staff	400

Additional information:

1 Depreciation policy:
Depreciation is provided at the following annual rates on a straight line basis: delivery vans 20 per cent; office cars 7.5 per cent; stores plant and equipment 10 per cent.

2 The following taxation rates may be assumed:
corporation tax 35 per cent; income tax 25 per cent; value added tax 15 per cent.

3 The investment income arises from investments held in fixed asset investments.

4 It has been decided to transfer an amount of £150,000 to the deferred taxation account.

5 There were 1,000,000 ordinary shares of £1 each in issue during the year to 31 March 20X0. There were no preference shares in issue.

Required:
In so far as the information permits, prepare Bunker plc's published profit and loss account for the year to 31 March 20X0 in accordance with the minimum requirements of the Companies Act 1985 and related accounting standards.

Note: A statement of accounting policies is NOT required, but where appropriate, other formal notes SHOULD be attached to your profit and loss account. Detailed workings should also be submitted with your answer.

(Association of Accounting Technicians)

11.7A Fresno Group plc have prepared their financial statements for the year ended 31 January 20X4. However, the financial accountant of Fresno Group plc had difficulty in preparing the statements required by FRS 3: *Reporting financial performance*, and approached you for help in preparing those statements. The financial accountant furnished you with the following information:

(i)

Fresno Group plc

Profit and Loss Account extract for year ended 31 January 20X4

	£ million
Operating profit – continuing operations	290
Profit on sale of property in continuing operations	10
Profit on ordinary activities before taxation	300
Tax on ordinary activities	(90)
Profit after taxation	210
Dividends	(15)
Retained profit for year	195

The financial accountant did not provide for the loss on any discontinued operations in the profit and loss account. (However, you may assume that the taxation provision incorporated the effects of any provision for discontinued operations.)

(ii) The shareholders' funds at the beginning of the financial year were as follows:

	£ million
Share capital – £1 ordinary shares	350
Merger reserve	55
Revaluation reserve	215
Profit and loss reserve	775
	1,395

(iii) Fresno Group plc regularly revalues its fixed assets and at 31 January 20X4, a revaluation surplus of £375 million had been credited to revaluation reserve. During the financial year, a property had been sold on which a revaluation surplus of £54 million had been credited to reserves. Further, if the company had charged depreciation on a historical cost basis rather than the revalued amounts, the depreciation charge in the profit and loss account for fixed assets would have been £7 million. The current year's charge for depreciation was £16 million.

(iv) The group has a policy of writing off goodwill on the acquisition of subsidiaries directly against a merger reserve. The goodwill for the period amounted to £250 million. In order to facilitate the purchase of subsidiaries, the company had issued £1 ordinary shares of nominal value £150 million and share premium of £450 million. The premium had been taken to the merger reserve. All subsidiaries are currently 100 per cent owned by the group.

(*v*) During the financial year to 31 January 20X4, the company had made a decision to close a 100 per cent owned subsidiary, Reno plc. However, the closure did not take place until May 20X4. Fresno Group plc estimated that as at 31 January 20X4 the operating loss for the period 1 February 20X4 to 31 May 20X4 would be £30 million and that in addition redundancy costs, stock and plant write-downs would amount to £15 million. In the event, the operating loss for the period 1 February 20X4 to 31 May 20X4 was £65 million, but the redundancy costs, stock and plant write-downs only amounted to £12 million.

(*vi*) The following information relates to Reno plc for the period 1 February 20X4 to 31 May 20X4.

Reno plc

	£ million
Turnover	175
Cost of sales	(195)
Gross loss	(20)
Administrative expenses	(15)
Selling expenses	(30)
Operating loss before taxation	(65)

Required:

(*a*) Prepare the following statements in accordance with current statutory requirements and FRS 3: *Reporting financial performance* for Fresno Group plc for the year ending 31 January 20X4:
    (*i*)   statement of total recognised gains and losses;
    (*ii*) reconciliation of movements in shareholders' funds;
    (*iii*) analysis of movements on reserves;
    (*iv*) note of historical cost profits and losses.

(*b*) Explain to the financial accountant:
    (*i*)   how the decision to close the subsidiary, Reno plc, affects the financial statements of Fresno Group plc for the year ended 31 January 20X4;
    (*ii*) how the subsidiary, Reno plc, should be dealt with in the financial statements of Fresno Group plc for the year ended 31 January 20X5.

(*Association of Chartered Certified Accountants*)

CHAPTER 12

The financial statements of limited companies: balance sheets

Learning objectives

After you have studied this chapter, you should be able to:

- describe the most commonly used format available under the Companies Acts that may be used when preparing balance sheets for external reporting purposes
- present information under the most commonly used of the Companies Acts formats
- describe the differences between the statutory format and formats generally adopted for internal use
- describe the exemption of some 'small' companies from having their financial statements audited
- describe the exemptions available to small and medium-sized companies in respect of filing modified financial statements
- describe the option available to public limited companies to send members a summary financial statement

Introduction

In this chapter you'll learn about the format to be adopted for balance sheets prepared for publication. You will be reminded of the fundamental accounting concepts that you covered in *Business Accounting 1* and introduced to the rules relating to the preparation of modified financial statements for small and medium-sized companies.

12.1 Balance sheet formats

The Companies Acts set out two formats for the balance sheet. The method chosen for this book is that of Format 1 because this most resembles previous UK practice.

Format 1 is shown as Exhibit 12.1. Monetary figures have been included to illustrate it more clearly.

Exhibit 12.1

Balance Sheet – Format 1

	£000	£000	£000
A CALLED-UP SHARE CAPITAL NOT PAID*			10
B FIXED ASSETS			
I Intangible assets			
1 Development costs	20		
2 Concessions, patents, licences, trade marks and similar rights and assets	30		
3 Goodwill	80		
4 Payments on account	5		
		135	
II Tangible assets			
1 Land and buildings	300		
2 Plant and machinery	500		
3 Fixtures, fittings, tools and equipment	60		
4 Payments on account and assets in course of construction	20		
		880	
III Investments			
1 Shares in group undertakings	15		
2 Loans to group undertakings	10		
3 Participating interests	20		
4 Loans to undertakings in which the company has a participating interest	5		
5 Other investments other than loans	30		
6 Other loans	16		
7 Own shares	4		
		100	
			1,115
C CURRENT ASSETS			
I Stock			
1 Raw materials and consumables	60		
2 Work in progress	15		
3 Finished goods and goods for resale	120		
4 Payments on account	5		
		200	
II Debtors			
1 Trade debtors	200		
2 Amounts owed by group undertakings	20		
3 Amounts owed by undertakings in which the company has a participating interest	10		
4 Other debtors	4		
5 Called-up share capital not paid*	–		
6 Prepayments and accrued income†	–		
		234	
III Investments			
1 Shares in group undertakings	40		
2 Own shares	5		
3 Other investments	30		
		75	
IV Cash at bank and in hand		26	
		535	
D PREPAYMENTS AND ACCRUED INCOME†		15	
		550	

E CREDITORS: AMOUNTS FALLING DUE WITHIN ONE YEAR
   1 Debenture loans   5
   2 Bank loans and overdrafts   10
   3 Payments received on account   20
   4 Trade creditors   50
   5 Bills of exchange payable   2
   6 Amounts owed to group undertakings   15
   7 Amounts owed to undertakings in which the
        company has a participating interest   6
   8 Other creditors including taxation and social security   54
   9 Accruals and deferred income‡   –
                                                                          (162)
F NET CURRENT ASSETS (LIABILITIES)   388
G TOTAL ASSETS LESS CURRENT LIABILITIES   1,513
H CREDITORS: AMOUNTS FALLING DUE AFTER MORE
     THAN ONE YEAR
   1 Debenture loans   20
   2 Bank loans and overdrafts   15
   3 Payments received on account   5
   4 Trade creditors   25
   5 Bills of exchange payable   4
   6 Amounts owed to group undertakings   10
   7 Amounts owed to undertakings in which the
        company has a participating interest   5
   8 Other creditors including taxation and social security   32
   9 Accruals and deferred income‡   –
                                                                          116

I PROVISIONS FOR LIABILITIES AND CHARGES
   1 Pensions and similar obligations   20
   2 Taxation, including deferred taxation   40
   3 Other provisions   4
                                                                           64
J ACCRUALS AND DEFERRED INCOME‡   20
                                                                              (200)
                                                                            1,313

K CAPITAL AND RESERVES
I   Called-up share capital   1,000
II Share premium account   100
III Revaluation reserve   20
IV Other reserves:
    1 Capital redemption reserve   40
    2 Reserve for own shares   10
    3 Reserves provided for by the articles of association   20
    4 Other reserves   13
                                                                               83
V Profit and loss account   110
                                                                            1,313

*†‡ These items may be shown in any of the positions indicated.

It should be noted that various items can be shown in alternative places, i.e.:

(a) *called-up share capital not paid*, either in position A or position CII 5;
(b) *prepayments and accrued income*, either CII 6 or as D;
(c) *accruals and deferred income*, either E9 or H9, or in total as J.

Items preceded by letters or roman numerals must be disclosed on the face of the balance sheet, e.g. B Fixed assets, KII Share premium account, whereas those shown with arabic

numerals (1, 2, 3, 4, etc.) may be combined where they are not material or the combination facilitates assessment of the company's affairs. Where they are combined, the details of each item should be shown in the notes accompanying the financial statements. The actual letters, roman numerals or arabic numbers do *not* have to be shown on the face of the published balance sheets.

12.2 Further details for Format 1

The following also apply to the balance sheet in Format 1.

BI Intangible assets are assets not having a 'physical' existence compared with tangible assets which do have a physical existence. For instance, you can see and touch the tangible assets of land and buildings, plant and machinery, etc., whereas goodwill does not exist in a physical sense.

For each of the items under fixed assets, whether it is an intangible asset, tangible asset or investment, full details must be given in the notes accompanying the financial statements of (a) cost, at beginning and end of financial year, (b) effect on that item of acquisitions, disposals, revaluations, etc. during the year, and (c) full details of depreciation, i.e. accumulated depreciation at start of year, depreciation for year, effect of disposals on depreciation in the year and any other adjustments.

All fixed assets, including property and goodwill, must be depreciated over the period of the useful economic life of each asset. Prior to this, many companies had not depreciated property because of rising money values of the asset. Costs of research must not be treated as an asset, and development costs may be capitalised only in special cases. Any hire purchase owing must not be deducted from the assets concerned. Only goodwill which has been purchased can be shown as an asset; internally generated goodwill must not be capitalised. (This does not refer to goodwill in consolidated financial statements – *see* Chapter 17.)

Where an asset is revalued, normally this will be fixed assets being shown at market value instead of cost. Any difference on revaluation must be debited or credited to a revaluation reserve – *see* KIII in Format 1.

Investments shown as CIII will be in respect of those not held for the long term.

Two items which could previously be shown as assets – (a) preliminary expenses (these are the legal expenses etc. in forming the company), and (b) expenses of and commission on any issue of shares or debentures – must not now be shown as assets. They can be written off against any share premium account balance; alternatively they should be written off to the profit and loss account.

Full details of each class of share capital, and of authorised capital, will be shown in notes accompanying the balance sheet.

12.3 Choice of formats

The Acts leave the choice of a particular format for the balance sheet and the profit and loss account to the directors. Once adopted, the choice must be adhered to in subsequent years except in the case that there are special reasons for the change. If a change is made, then full reasons for the change must be stated in the notes attached to the financial statements.

12.4 Fundamental accounting principles

The Companies Acts set out the accounting principles (or 'valuation rules' as they are called in the Fourth Directive of the EC) to be followed when preparing company financial statements.

The following principles are stated in the Acts. The reader is referred to Chapter 10 of *Business Accounting 1* for a fuller discussion of some of them.

1 A company is presumed to be a going concern.
2 Accounting policies must be applied consistently from year to year.
3 The prudence concept must be followed.
4 The accruals concept must be observed.
5 Each component item of assets and liabilities must be valued separately. As an instance of this, if a company has five different types of stock, each type must be valued separately at the lower of cost and net realisable value, rather than be valued on an aggregate basis.
6 Amounts in respect of items representing assets or income may *not* be set off against items representing liabilities or expenditure. Thus an amount owing on a hire purchase contract cannot be deducted from the value of the asset in the balance sheet.

12.5 True and fair view

If complying with the requirements of the Companies Acts would cause the financial statements not to be 'true and fair' then the directors must set aside such requirements. This should not be done lightly, and it would not be common to find such instances.

12.6 Small and medium-sized company reporting requirements

Small and medium-sized companies do not have to file a full set of financial statements with the Registrar of Companies. They could, if they wished, send a full set of financial statements, but what they *have* to file is a minimum of 'modified financial statements'. They would still have to send a full set to their own shareholders – the modified financial statements refer only to those filed with the Registrar.

The definition of small and medium-sized companies is that, for the financial year in question and the previous year, the company comes within the limits of at least two of the following three criteria:

	Small	Medium-sized
Turnover not more than	£2.8 million	£11.2 million
Balance sheet total not more than	£1.4 million	£5.6 million
Employees not more than	50	250

In addition, there is no longer an audit requirement for small companies with a turnover of not more than £1 million and a balance sheet total of not more than £1.4 million, unless 10 per cent or more of shareholders sign a formal notice requesting an audit and lodge this at the registered office.

> ### Activity 12.1
> Why do you think these small companies are exempted from having their financial statements audited?

12.7 Modified financial statements of small companies

1 Neither a profit and loss account nor a directors' report has to be filed with the Registrar.
2 A modified balance sheet showing only those items to which a letter or roman numeral are attached (*see* Format 1, Exhibit 12.1) has to be shown. For example, the total for CI Stock has to be shown but not the figures for each of the individual items comprising this total.

12.8 Modified financial statements of medium-sized companies

1 The profit and loss account per Format 1 does not have to show item 1 (Turnover), item 2 (Cost of sales) or item 6 (Other operating income). It will therefore begin with the figure of gross profit or loss.
2 The analyses of turnover and profit normally required as notes to the financial statements need not be given.
3 The balance sheet, however, must be given in full.

Note: Review questions on published company financial statements including notes required by law are shown at the end of Chapter 13.

12.9 Summary financial statements

A public limited company (plc) may send a summary financial statement to members in place of the full statements, but any member who requests the full statements must be sent them. The summary statement must:

(*a*) state that it is only a summary of information in the company's financial statements and the directors' report;
(*b*) contain a statement by the company's auditors of their opinion as to whether the summary financial statement is consistent with those financial statements and that report and complies with the requirements of the section in the Companies Act (CA 85 section 251) that permits the distribution of this summary financial statement and the regulations made under it;
(*c*) state whether the auditors' report on the financial statements was unqualified or qualified, and if it was qualified set out the report in full together with any further material needed to understand the qualification;
(*d*) state whether the auditors' report on the annual accounts contained a statement under either:
  (*i*) CA 85 section 237(2) – accounting records or returns inadequate or financial statements not agreeing with records or returns; or
  (*ii*) CA 85 section 237(3) – failure to obtain necessary information and explanations and, if so, set out the statement in full.

Activity 12.2
Why do you think companies are allowed to send their shareholders summary financial statements rather than the full statements?

Learning outcomes

You should now have learnt:
1 There are set formats for the preparation of published financial statements.
2 Financial statements for internal use need not comply with these set formats.
3 Accounting standards have statutory recognition and must, therefore, be complied with when preparing financial statements intended to present a true and fair view.
4 Some small companies are exempted from having their financial statements audited.
5 Small and medium-sized companies may file modified financial statements with the Registrar if they wish.
6 Public limited companies may send a summary financial statement to members in place of the full statements, but any member who requests the full statements must be sent them.

Answers to activities

12.1 Having financial statements audited is estimated as costing an average of £1,200. While this appears a small amount of money, it can be relatively expensive for small companies, particularly when they are newly formed and are making little or no profit. However, although this is a good reason for such companies not incurring the expense of having an audit, as the sole reason for not having an audit it goes against the principles upon which the need for an audit was based. A far more realistic explanation is that errors and misleading items in the financial statements of small companies have far less of an impact than in the case of larger organisations and, on a purely cost/benefit basis, it is unlikely that the costs of having an audit will be sufficiently offset by any amendments or clarifications that an audit may bring.

12.2 Many shareholders are not accountants and have no understanding of many of the items in full financial statements. Rather than sending them information they will not understand, shareholders may be sent simplified information containing those parts of the financial statements that they are both more likely to understand and more likely to be interested in having. This saves the companies (and their shareholders) money which, in itself, is a good thing. It also increases the possibility that shareholders will look at the financial statements in the first place.

REVIEW QUESTIONS

12.1 The following balances remained in the books of Owen Ltd on 31 December 20X1, *after* the profit and loss account and appropriation account had been drawn up. You are to draft the balance sheet as at 31 December 20X1 in accordance with the Companies Acts.

	Dr £	Cr £
Ordinary share capital: £1 shares		50,000
Preference share capital: 50p shares		25,000
Calls account (ordinary shares)	150	
Development costs	3,070	
Goodwill	21,000	
Land and buildings – at cost	48,000	
Plant and machinery – at cost	12,500	
Provision for depreciation: Buildings		16,000
Provision for depreciation: Plant and machinery		5,400
Shares in undertakings in which the company has a participating interest	35,750	
Stock: Raw materials	3,470	
Stock: Finished goods	18,590	
Debtors: Trade	17,400	
Amounts owed by undertakings in which the company has a participating interest	3,000	
Prepayments	1,250	
Debentures (*see* Note 1)		10,000
Bank overdraft (repayable within 6 months)		4,370
Creditors: Trade (payable within 1 year)		12,410
Bills payable (*see* Note 2)		3,600
Share premium		20,000
Capital redemption reserve		5,000
General reserve		4,000
Profit and loss account		8,400
	164,180	164,180

Notes:

1 Of the debentures £6,000 is repayable in 3 months' time, while the other £4,000 is repayable in 5 years' time.
2 Of the bills payable, £1,600 is in respect of a bill to be paid in 4 months' time and £2,000 for a bill payable in 18 months' time.
3 The depreciation charged for the year was: Building £4,000, Plant and machinery £1,800.

12.2 After the profit and loss appropriation account has been prepared for the year ended 30 September 20X4, the following balances remain in the books of Belle Works plc. You are to draw up a balance sheet in accordance with the Companies Acts.

	£	£
Ordinary share capital		70,000
Share premium		5,000
Revaluation reserve		10,500
General reserve		6,000
Foreign exchange reserve		3,500
Profit and loss		6,297
Patents, trade marks and licences	1,500	
Goodwill	17,500	
Land and buildings	90,000	
Provision for depreciation: Land and buildings		17,500
Plant and machinery	38,600	
Provision for depreciation: Plant and machinery		19,200
Stock of raw materials: 30 September 20X4	14,320	
Work in progress: 30 September 20X4	5,640	
Finished goods: 30 September 20X4	13,290	
Debtors: Trade	11,260	
Debtors: Other	1,050	
Prepayments and accrued income	505	
Debentures (redeemable in 6 months' time)		6,000
Debentures (redeemable in 4½ years' time)		12,000
Bank overdraft (repayable in 3 months)		3,893
Trade creditors (payable in next 12 months)		11,340
Trade creditors (payable after 12 months)		1,260
Bills of exchange (payable within 12 months)		4,000
Corporation tax (payable in 9 months' time)		14,370
National insurance (payable in next month)		305
Pensions contribution owing		1,860
Deferred taxation		640
	193,665	193,665

12.3 The following trial balance has been extracted from the books of Baganza plc as at 30 September 20X7:

	£000	£000
Administrative expenses	400	
Called up share capital (1,200,000 ordinary shares of £1 each)		1,200
Cash at bank and in hand	60	
Corporation tax (overpayment for the year to 30 September 20X6)		20
Deferred taxation (at 1 October 20X6)		460
Distribution costs	600	
Dividends received (on 31 March 20X7)		249
Extraordinary item (net of tax)		1,500
Freehold property:		
at cost	2,700	
accumulated depreciation (at 1 October 20X6)		260
Interim dividend (paid on June 20X7)	36	
Investments in United Kingdom companies	2,000	
Plant and machinery:		
at cost	5,200	
accumulated depreciation (at 1 October 20X6)		3,600
Profit and loss account (at 1 October 20X6)		2,022
Purchases	16,000	
Research expenditure	75	
Stock (at 1 October 20X6)	2,300	
Tax on extraordinary item		360
Trade creditors		2,900
Trade debtors	2,700	
Turnover		19,500
	£32,071	£32,071

Additional information:

1 The stock at 30 September 20X7 was valued at £3,600,000.
2 Depreciation for the year to 30 September 20X7 is to be charged on the historic cost of the fixed assets as follows:
   Freehold property: 5 per cent
   Plant and machinery: 15 per cent
3 The basic rate of income tax is assumed to be 27 per cent.
4 The directors propose a final dividend of 60p per share.
5 The company was incorporated in 20X0.
6 Corporation tax based on the profits for the year at a rate of 35 per cent is estimated to be £850,000.
7 A transfer of £40,000 is to be made to the deferred taxation account.

Required:
In so far as the information permits, prepare Baganza plc's profit and loss account for the year to 30 September 20X7, and a balance sheet as at that date in accordance with the Companies Act 1985 and appropriate accounting standards.

However, formal notes to the accounts are not required, although detailed workings should be submitted with your answer, which should include your calculation of earnings per share.

(Association of Accounting Technicians)

12.4A The trial balance of Payne Peerbrook plc as on 31 December 20X6 is as follows:

	Dr	Cr
	£	£
Preference share capital: £1 shares		50,000
Ordinary share capital: 50p shares		60,000
General reserve		45,000
Exchange reserve		13,600
Profit and loss account as on 31 December 20X5		19,343
Stock 31 December 20X5	107,143	
Sales		449,110
Returns inwards	11,380	
Purchases	218,940	
Carriage inwards	2,475	
Wages (putting goods into a saleable condition)	3,096	
Wages: Warehouse staff	39,722	
Wages and salaries: Sales staff	28,161	
Wages and salaries: Administrative staff	34,778	
Motor expenses (see note (ii))	16,400	
General distribution expenses	8,061	
General administrative expenses	7,914	
Debenture interest	10,000	
Royalties receivable		4,179
Directors' remuneration	18,450	
Bad debts	3,050	
Discounts allowed	5,164	
Discounts received		4,092
Plant and machinery at cost (see note (iii))	175,000	
Provision for depreciation: Plant and machinery		58,400
Motor vehicles at cost (see note (ii))	32,000	
Provision for depreciation: Motors		14,500
Goodwill	29,500	
Development costs	16,320	
Trade debtors	78,105	
Trade creditors		37,106
Bank overdraft (repayable any time)		4,279
Bills of exchange payable (all due within 1 year)		6,050
Debentures (redeemable in 5 years' time)		80,000
	845,659	845,659

Notes:

(*i*) Stock of finished goods on 31 December 20X6 £144,081.

(*ii*) Motor expenses and depreciation on motors to be apportioned: Distribution ¾, Administrative ¼.

(*iii*) Plant and machinery depreciation to be apportioned: Cost of sales ⅕, Distribution ⅗, Administrative ⅕.

(*iv*) Depreciate the following fixed assets on cost: Motor vehicles 25 per cent, Plant and machinery 20 per cent.

(*v*) Accrue corporation tax on profits of the year £14,150. This is payable 1 October 20X7.

(*vi*) A preference dividend of £5,000 is to be paid and an ordinary dividend of £10,000 is to be proposed.

You are to draw up:

(*a*) a trading and profit and loss account for the year ended 31 December 20X6 for internal use, and

(*b*) a profit and loss account for publication, also a balance sheet as at 31 December 20X6.

12.5A You are presented with the following information relating to Plott plc for the year to 31 March 20X1:

	£000
Bank overdraft	500
Called-up share capital (issued and fully paid)	2,100
Corporation tax (based on the profit for the year to 31 March 20X1)	900
Creditors	300
Debtors	200
Deferred taxation (credit)	80
Fixed assets: at cost	3,800
accumulated depreciation (at 31 March 20X1)	1,400
Fixed asset investments: at cost	100
Profit and loss account (at 1 April 20X0: credit)	1,200
Proposed dividend	420
Retained profit (for the year to 31 March 20X1)	585
Share premium account	315
Stocks: at cost (at 31 March 20X1)	400
Trade creditors	2,000
Trade debtors	5,300

Additional information:

1 The above information has been obtained after the compilation of the company's profit and loss account for the year to 31 March 20X1.

2 Details of fixed assets for the year to 31 March 20X1 are as follows:

	£000
(*a*) At cost	
At 1 April 20X0	3,400
Additions	600
Disposals	200
(*b*) Accumulated depreciation	
At 1 April 20X0	1,200
Additions	500
Disposals	300

3 The market value of the fixed asset investments at 31 March 20X1 was £110,000. There were no purchases or sales of fixed asset investments during the year.

4 Stocks comprise finished goods. The replacement cost of these goods is similar to the value indicated in the balance sheet.

5 Assume that the basic rate of income tax is 25 per cent.

6 The authorised share capital of the company consists of 2,500,000 ordinary shares of £1 each.

Required:
In so far as the information permits, prepare Plott plc's balance sheet as at 31 March 20X1 in accordance with the *minimum* requirements of the Companies Act 1985 and related accounting standards.

Notes:

1 Where appropriate, formal notes must be attached to your balance sheet; and
2 Detailed working should be submitted with your answer.

(*Association of Accounting Technicians*)

12.6A The following information has been extracted from the books of Quire plc as at 30 September 20X1.

	£000	£000
Bank overdraft		2,400
Called-up share capital (ordinary shares of £1 each)		4,000
Deferred taxation		200
Delivery expenses	2,800	
Fixed assets: at cost	3,500	
accumulated depreciation (at 1 October 20X0)		1,100
Debentures held	100	
Debenture interest (net)		40
Interest payable	400	
Interim dividend paid	60	
Office expenses	3,000	
Other creditors		180
Other debtors	160	
Profit and loss account (at 1 October 20X0)		820
Purchases	12,000	
Sales		19,000
Stocks (at 1 October 20X0)	500	
Trade creditors		100
Trade debtors	5,320	
	£27,840	£27,840

The following additional information is to be taken into account:

1 Stocks at 30 September 20X1 were valued at £400,000.
2 All items in the above trial balance are shown net of value added tax.
3 At 30 September 20X1, £130,000 was outstanding for office expenses, and £50,000 had been paid in advance for delivery van licences.
4 Depreciation at a rate of 50 per cent is to be charged on the historic cost of the tangible fixed assets using the reducing balance method: it is to be apportioned as follows:

	%
Cost of sales	60
Distribution	30
Administration	10
	100

There were no purchases or sales of fixed assets during the year to 30 September 20X1.
5 The following rates of taxation are to be assumed:

	%
Corporation tax	35
Income tax	25
Value added tax	17.5

The corporation tax payable based on the profits for the year to 30 September 20X1 has been estimated at £80,000.

6 A transfer of £60,000 is to be made from the deferred taxation account.

7 The directors propose to pay a final ordinary dividend of 3p per share.

Required:

In so far as the information permits, prepare Quire plc's profit and loss account for the year to 30 September 20X1, and a balance sheet as at that date in accordance with the MINIMUM requirements of the Companies Act 1985 and related accounting standards.

Note: Formal notes to the accounts are NOT required, but detailed workings should be submitted with your answer.

(Association of Accounting Technicians)

12.7A The following trial balance has been extracted from the books of Patt plc as at 31 March 20X0:

	Dr £000	Cr £000
Bank overdraft		25
Called-up share capital (ordinary shares of £1 each)		1,440
Creditors		55
Debtors	50	
Fixed assets: at cost	300	
accumulated depreciation (at 1 April 20X9)		120
Marketing expenses	100	
Office expenses	200	
Profit and loss account (at 1 April 20X9)		200
Production expenses	2,230	
Purchases (net of VAT)	3,700	
Sales (amounts invoiced, net of VAT)		7,000
Stocks (at 1 April 20X9)	130	
Trade creditors		160
Trade debtors	2,290	
	£9,000	£9,000

Additional information:

1 Following the preparation of the above trial balance, the following additional matters need to be taken into account:

(a) stock at 31 March 20X0 was valued at £170,000;

(b) at 31 March 20X0, £20,000 was owing for office expenses, and £15,000 had been paid in advance for marketing expenses;

(c) a customer had gone into liquidation owing the company £290,000; the company does not expect to recover any of this debt;

(d) the company decides to set up a provision for doubtful debts amounting to 5 per cent of the outstanding trade debtors as at the end of each financial year; and

(e) depreciation is to be charged on the fixed assets at a rate of 20 per cent on cost; it is to be apportioned as follows:

	%
Marketing	20
Office	10
Production	70
	100

Note: There were no acquisitions or disposals of fixed assets during the year to 31 March 20X0.

2 Corporation tax (based on the accounting profit for the year at a rate of 35 per cent) is estimated to be £160,000. The basic rate of income tax is assumed to be 25 per cent.

3 The directors are to recommend the payment of a dividend of 10p per ordinary share.

Required:

In so far as the information permits, prepare Patt plc's profit and loss account for the year to 31 March 20X0, and a balance sheet as at that date in accordance with the Companies Act 1985 and related accounting standards.

Notes:

(*i*) Where appropriate, formal notes should be attached to your profit and loss account and balance sheet. However, a statement of accounting policies is NOT required.

(*ii*) Detailed workings should also be submitted with your solution. They should be clearly designated as such, and they must not form part of your formal notes.

(*Association of Accounting Technicians*)

CHAPTER 13

Published financial statements of limited companies: accompanying notes

Learning objectives

After you have studied this chapter, you should be able to:

- describe the additional notes to published financial statements that are required by the Companies Acts
- describe the requirement to include a directors' report with the published financial statements

Introduction

In this chapter you'll learn about the notes that must be included when company financial statements are published and about the report that must be prepared by the directors to accompany the financial statements.

13.1 Notes to accompany the balance sheet

Companies may include as many notes as they wish with financial statements when they are published. However there are some notes that the Companies Acts require to be included:

1 Particulars of turnover

An analysis of turnover is required into:

(a) each class of business and by
(b) geographical markets. In addition, the amount of profit or loss before taxation, in the opinion of the directors, attributable to each class of business must be shown.

Such disclosure does not have to be made if it would be prejudicial to the business of the company. The fact of non-disclosure would have to be stated. An example of such a note might be as in Exhibit 13.1:

Exhibit 13.1

Analysis of Turnover

	Turnover £	Profit £
Motors	26,550,000	2,310,000
Aircraft	58,915,000	4,116,000
	85,465,000	6,426,000

The geographical division of turnover is:	£
UK	31,150,000
The Americas	43,025,000
Rest of the World	10,290,000
	84,465,000

It should be noted that these requirements were extended by SSAP 25: *Segmental reporting*, but only for:

(*a*) plcs or parent undertakings that have one or more plcs as a subsidiary;
(*b*) banking and insurance companies or groups;
(*c*) private companies and other entities that exceed the criteria, multiplied in each case by ten, for defining a medium-sized company under section 247 of the Companies Act 1985. (*See* Chapter 12, Section 12.6 for a table of these criteria.)

The Acts require that for each segment, turnover (analysed between sales to external customers and sales between segments), results and net assets should be disclosed. Geographical segmental analysis should, in the first instance, be on the basis of source (i.e. the geographical location of the supplying segment). In addition, turnover to third parties should be segmentally reported on the basis of destination (i.e. the geographical location of the receiving segment).

Where associated undertakings account for at least 20 per cent of the total results or net assets of the reporting entity, additional disclosure should be made in aggregate for all associated undertakings. This comprises segmental disclosure of the reporting entity's share of the aggregate profits or losses before tax, minority interests and extraordinary items of the associated undertakings, and the reporting entity's share of the net assets of the associated undertakings (including goodwill to the extent that it has not been written off) after attributing, where possible, fair values to the net assets at the date of acquisition of the interest in each associated undertaking.

2 Particulars of staff

1 Average number employed by the company (or by group in consolidated accounts), divided between categories of workers, e.g. between manufacturing and administration.
2 (*a*) Wages and salaries paid to staff.
  (*b*) Social security costs of staff.
  (*c*) Other pension costs for employees.
3 Number of employees (excluding those working wholly or mainly overseas) earning over £30,000, analysed under successive multiples of £5,000. Exclude pension contributions.

Exhibit 13.2 is an example of a note concerning higher-paid employees.

Exhibit 13.2

The number of employees earning over £30,000 was 28, analysed as follows:

Gross salaries	*Number of employees*
£30,001–35,000	16
£35,001–40,000	8
£40,001–45,000	4
	28

3 Directors' emoluments

1 Aggregate amounts of:
   (a) emoluments, including pension contributions and benefits in kind. Distinction to be made between those emoluments as fees and those for executive duties;
   (b) pensions for past directors;
   (c) compensation for loss of office.
2 The chairman's emoluments and those of the highest-paid director, if paid more than the chairman. In both cases, pension contributions are to be excluded.
3 Number of directors whose emoluments, excluding pension contributions, fall within each bracket of £5,000.
4 Total amounts waived by directors and the number concerned.

The disclosures under 2 and 3 above are not needed for a company being neither a parent nor subsidiary undertaking where its directors' emoluments under 1 do not exceed £60,000. The disclosures under 2 and 3 are also not necessary for directors working wholly or mainly overseas.

An illustration is now given in Exhibit 13.3.

Exhibit 13.3

Name	Fee (as directors)	Remuneration (as executives)	Pension contributions
A (Chairman)	£5,000	£85,000	£20,000
B	£2,500	£95,000	£30,000
C	£2,500	£55,000	£15,000
D	£1,500	£54,000	£12,500
E	£1,500	£30,000	£10,000

Note to accounts:
Directors' remuneration: the amounts paid to directors were as follows:

Fees as directors	£13,000
Other emoluments, including pension contributions	£406,500

Emoluments of the Chairman – excluding pension contributions – amounted to £90,000, and those of the highest paid director to £97,500. Other directors' emoluments were in the following ranges:

£30,001 to £35,000	1
£55,001 to £60,000	2

4 Various charges to be shown as notes

1 Auditors' remuneration, including expenses.
2 Hire of plant and machinery.
3 Interest payable on:
   (a) bank loans, overdrafts and other loans repayable by instalments or otherwise within five years;
   (b) loans of any other kind.
4 Depreciation:
   (a) amounts of provisions for both tangible and intangible assets;
   (b) effect on depreciation of change of depreciation method;
   (c) effect on depreciation of revaluation of assets.

5 Income from listed investments

6 Rents receivable from land, after deducting outgoings

7 Taxation (see also FRS 16: *Current tax*)

1 Tax charges split between:
   (*a*) UK corporation tax, and basis of computation;
   (*b*) UK income tax, and basis of computation;
   (*c*) irrecoverable VAT;
   (*d*) tax attributable to franked investment income.
2 If relevant, split between tax on ordinary and tax on extraordinary activities.
3 Show, as component part, charge for deferred tax.
4 Any other special circumstances affecting tax liability.

8 Extraordinary and exceptional items and prior period adjustments

See FRS 3: *Reporting financial performance*, which is dealt with in Chapter 11.

9 Redemption of shares and loans

Show amounts set aside for these purposes.

10 Earnings per share (listed companies only)

See FRS 14: *Earnings per share*, which is dealt with in Section 10.44.

11 Statement showing movements on reserves

Activity 13.1
Why do you think these notes are required rather than leaving it up to companies to provide the information they believe to be worthwhile including?

13.2 The directors' report

As well as a balance sheet and profit and loss account, the shareholders must also receive a directors' report. The contents of the report are given in the Companies Acts, but no formal layout is given. Such a report is additional to the notes, which have to be attached to the financial statements; the directors' report does not replace such notes.

1 A fair review of the development of the business of the company (and its subsidiaries) during the financial year and of the position at the end of the year. The dividends proposed and transfers to reserves should be given.
2 Principal activities of the company and any changes therein.
3 Post-balance sheet events, i.e. details of important events affecting the company (and its subsidiaries) since the end of the year.
4 Likely future developments in the business.
5 An indication of research and development carried on.
6 Significant changes in fixed assets. In the case of land, the difference between book and market values, if significant.
7 Political and charitable contributions; if, taken together, these exceed £200 there must be shown:

(a) separate totals for each classification;

(b) where political contributions exceeding £200 have been made, the names of recipients and amounts.

8 Details of own shares purchased.

9 Employees:

(a) statement concerning health, safety and welfare at work of company's employees;

(b) for companies with average workforce exceeding 250, details of employment of disabled people.

10 Directors:

(a) names of all persons who had been directors during any part of the financial year;

(b) their interests in contracts;

(c) for each director, the name; also:

(i) the number of shares held at the start of the year;

(ii) the number of shares held at the end of the year;

(iii) for each director elected in the year there shall also be shown shares held when elected;

(iv) all the above to show nil amounts where appropriate.

Note: Under the Companies Acts the directors' report is considered during the external audit. If the external auditors' judgement is that the directors' report is inconsistent with the audited company accounts, then this must be stated in the auditors' report.

Activity 13.2

Why do you think the directors' report is audited?

13.3 Illustrative company accounts: specimen question 1

F Clarke Ltd are specialist wholesalers. This is their trial balance at 31 December 20X4.

	Dr £	Cr £
Ordinary share capital: £1 shares		1,000,000
Share premium		120,000
General reserve		48,000
Profit and loss account as at 31.12.19X3		139,750
Stock: 31.12.19X3	336,720	
Sales		4,715,370
Purchases	2,475,910	
Returns outwards		121,220
Returns inwards	136,200	
Carriage inwards	6,340	
Carriage outwards	43,790	
Warehouse wages (average number of workers 59)	410,240	
Salespeople's salaries (average number of workers 21)	305,110	
Administrative wages and salaries	277,190	
Plant and machinery	610,000	
Motor vehicle hire	84,770	
Provisions for depreciation: plant and machinery		216,290
General distribution expenses	27,130	
General administrative expenses	47,990	
Directors' remuneration	195,140	
Rents receivable		37,150
Trade debtors	1,623,570	
Cash at bank and in hand	179,250	
Trade creditors (payable before 31.3.20X5)		304,570
Bills of exchange payable (payable 28.2.20X5)		57,000
	6,759,350	6,759,350

Notes:

(a) Stock at 31.12.20X4: £412,780, consists of goods for resale.
(b) Plant and machinery is apportioned: distributive 60 per cent; administrative 40 per cent.
(c) Accrue auditors' remuneration: £71,000.
(d) Depreciate plant and machinery: 20 per cent on cost.
(e) Of the motor hire, £55,000 is for distributive purposes.
(f) Corporation tax on profits, at a rate of 35 per cent, is estimated at £238,500, and is payable on 1.10.20X5.
(g) There is a proposed ordinary dividend of 37½ per cent for the year.
(h) All of the sales are of one type of goods. Net sales of £3,620,000 have been made in the UK with the remainder in Europe, and are shown net of VAT.
(i) Pension contributions for staff amounted to £42,550 and social security contributions to £80,120. These figures are included in wages and salaries in the trial balance. No employee earned over £30,000.
(j) Plant of £75,000 had been bought during the year.
(k) Directors' remuneration has been as follows:

	£
Chairman	46,640
Managing Director	51,500
Finance Director	46,000
Marketing Director	43,000
	187,140

In addition each of them drew £2,000 as directors' fees. Pensions are the personal responsibility of directors.

Required:
Subject to the limits of the information given you, draw up a profit and loss account for the year ended 31 December 20X4, and a balance sheet as at that date. They should be in published form and accompanied by the necessary notes prescribed by statute.

Specimen answer 1

Workings	£		£	£
Turnover: Sales	4,715,370	Cost of sales:		
Less Returns in	(136,200)	Opening stock		336,720
	4,579,170	Add Purchases	2,475,910	
		Less Returns out	(121,220)	
			2,354,690	
		Add Carriage in	6,340	2,361,030
				2,697,750
		Less Closing stock		(412,780)
				2,284,970
Distribution costs:		Administrative expenses:		
Warehouse wages	410,240	Wages and salaries		277,190
Salespeople's salaries	305,110	Motor hire		29,770
Carriage out	43,790	General expenses		47,990
General expenses	27,130	Directors' remuneration		150,140
Motor hire	55,000	Auditors' remuneration		71,000
Depreciation: plant	73,200	Depreciation: plant		48,800
				624,890
Marketing Director's remuneration	45,000			
	959,470			

F Clarke Ltd
Profit and Loss Account for the year ended 31 December 20X4

	£	£
Turnover		4,579,170
Cost of sales		(2,284,970)
Gross profit		2,294,200
Distribution costs	959,470	
Administrative expenses	624,890	
		(1,584,360)
		709,840
Other operating income		37,150
Profit on ordinary activities before taxation		746,990
Tax on profit on ordinary activities		(238,500)
Profit on ordinary activities after taxation		508,490
Proposed ordinary dividend		(375,000)
Retained profits for the year		133,490

F Clarke Ltd
Balance Sheet as at 31 December 20X4

	£	£	£
Fixed assets			
Tangible assets: Plant and machinery			271,710
Current assets			
Stock: Finished goods and goods for resale		412,780	
Debtors: Trade debtors		1,623,570	
Cash at bank and in hand		179,250	
		2,215,600	
Creditors: amounts falling due within one year			
Trade creditors	304,570		
Bills of exchange payable	57,000		
Other creditors including taxation and social security	684,500		
		(1,046,070)	
Net current assets			(1,169,530)
Total assets less current liabilities			1,441,240
Capital and reserves			£
Called-up share capital			1,000,000
Share premium account			120,000
Other reserves:			
General reserve			48,000
Profit and loss account			273,240
			1,441,240

Notes to the accounts

1 Turnover

This is the value, net of VAT, of goods of a single class of business. Turnover may be analysed as follows:

	£
UK	3,680,000
Europe	899,170
	4,579,170

2 Employees

Average number of workers was:

Warehousing	59
Sales	21
	80

Remuneration of employees was:

	£
Wages and salaries	869,870
Social security costs	80,120
Pension contributions	42,550
	992,540

3 Directors' remuneration

The amounts paid to directors were as follows:

	£
Fees as directors	8,000
Other emoluments	187,140

Emoluments of the Chairman amounted to £46,640, and those of the highest paid director £51,500. Other directors' emoluments were in the following ranges:

£40,001–45,000	1
£45,001–50,000	1

4 Operating profit is shown after charging

	£
Auditors' remuneration	71,000
Hire of motors	84,770

5 Fixed assets

	£	£
Plant and machinery		
Cost at 1.1.20X4	535,000	
Additions	75,000	
		610,000
Depreciation to 31.12.20X3	216,290	
Charge for the year	122,000	
		(338,290)
		271,710

6 Other creditors including taxation

	£	£
Proposed dividend	375,000	
Auditors' remuneration	71,000	
Corporation tax	238,500	
		684,500

13.4 Illustrative company accounts: specimen question 2

The trial balance of Quartz plc on 31 December 20X3 was as follows:

	Dr £000	Cr £000
Preference share capital: £1 shares		200
Ordinary share capital: £1 shares		1,000
Exchange reserve		75
General reserve		150
Profit and loss account 31.12.20X2		215
Sales		4,575
Purchases	2,196	
Carriage inwards	38	
Stock 31.12.20X2	902	
Wages (adding value to goods)	35	
Wages: warehousing	380	
Wages and salaries: administrative	120	
Wages and salaries: sales	197	
Motor expenses	164	
Bad debts	31	
Debenture interest	40	
Bank overdraft interest	19	
General distribution expenses	81	
General administrative expenses	73	
Directors' remuneration	210	
Investments in undertakings in which the company has a participating interest	340	
Income from shares in undertakings in which the company has a participating interest		36
Discounts allowed and received	55	39
Buildings: at cost	1,200	
Plant and machinery: at cost	330	
Motor vehicles: at cost	480	
Provisions for depreciation:		
Land and buildings		375
Plant and machinery		195
Motors		160
Goodwill	40	
Patents, licences and trade marks	38	
Trade debtors and creditors	864	392
Bank overdraft (repayable any time)		21
Debentures 10 per cent		400
	7,833	7,833

Notes:

(a) Stock at 31.12.20X3: £1,103,000 at cost.

(b) Motor expenses and depreciation on motors to be apportioned: distribution 75 per cent; administrative 25 per cent.

(c) Depreciation on buildings and plant and machinery to be apportioned: distribution 50 per cent; administrative 50 per cent.

(d) Depreciate on cost: motor vehicles 25 per cent; plant and machinery 20 per cent.

(e) Accrue corporation tax on profits of the year £266,000. This is payable 1 October 20X4.

(f) A preference dividend of 10 per cent is to be paid and an ordinary dividend of 50 per cent is to be proposed.

(g) During the year new vehicles were purchased at a cost of £60,000.

(h) During June 20X3 one of the buildings, which had originally cost £130,000, and which had a written-down value at the date of the sale of £80,000, was sold for £180,000. Depreciation on buildings to be charged against the year's profits £60,000. The buildings are revalued by B & Co., Chartered Surveyors, at £1,500,000 at 31.12.20X3 (and this figure is to be included in the financial statements).

(i) Directors' remuneration was as follows:

	£
Marketing	42,000
Chairman	37,000
Managing	61,000
Finance	50,000
	190,000

In addition each director drew £5,000 fees.

(j) Of the goodwill, 50 per cent is to be written off during this year, and 50 per cent in the following year.

(k) The debentures are to be redeemed in five equal annual instalments, starting in the following year 20X4.

(l) The investments are in listed companies with a market value at 31 December 20X3 of £438,000.

(m) Auditors' remuneration, including expenses, was £7,000.

You are required to prepare a balance sheet as at 31 December 20X3. It should:

(a) conform to the requirements of the Companies Act 1985;

(b) conform to the relevant accounting standards;

(c) give the notes necessary to the accounts.

Specimen answer 2

Workings

	£000			Dist. £000	Admin. £000
Cost of sales:		Wages		577	120
Opening stock	902	Motor expenses		123	41
Add Purchases	2,196	General		81	73
Add Carriage in	38	Depreciation: plant		33	33
	3,136		motors	90	30
Less Closing stock	(1,103)		buildings	30	30
	2,033	Directors		47	163
Wages (added value)	35	Discounts (net) 55–39			16
	2,068	Bad debts			31
				981	537

Quartz plc
Profit and Loss Account for the year ended 31 December 20X4

	£000	£000
Turnover		4,575
Cost of sales		(2,068)
Gross profit		2,507
Distribution costs	981	
Administrative expenses	537	
		(1,518)
		989
Income from shares in undertakings in which the company has a participating interest		36
		1,025
Interest payable and similar charges		(59)
Profit on ordinary activities before taxation		966
Tax on profit on ordinary activities		(266)
Profit for the year on ordinary activities after taxation		700
Goodwill written off	20	
Dividends paid and proposed	520	
		(540)
Retained profits for the year		160

Quartz plc
Balance Sheet as at 31 December 20X3

	£000	£000	£000
Fixed assets			
Intangible assets			
Patents, licences and trade marks		38	
Goodwill		20	
		58	
Tangible assets			
Buildings	1,500		
Plant and machinery	69		
Vehicles	200		
		1,769	
Investments			
Shares in undertakings in which the company has a participating interest		340	
			2,167
Current assets			
Stock	1,103		
Trade debtors	864		
		1,967	
Creditors: amounts falling due within one year			
Debenture loans	80		
Bank overdraft	21		
Trade creditors	392		
Other creditors	786		
		(1,279)	
Net current assets			688
			2,855
Creditors: amounts falling due after more than one year			
Debenture loans			(320)
			2,535
Capital and reserves			
Called-up share capital			1,200
Revaluation reserve			735
Profit and loss account			375
Other reserves			225
			2,535

Notes to the accounts

1 Share capital called up

	£
200,000 10 per cent preference shares of £1 each	200,000
1,000,000 ordinary shares of £1 each	1,000,000
	1,200,000

2 Accounting policies

Goodwill has been written off £20,000 against this year. The directors intend to write off the remaining £20,000 against next year's profits.

3 Tangible assets

	Buildings £000	Plant £000	Vehicles £000
Cost at 1.1.20X4	1,330	330	480
Disposals (at cost)	(130)	–	–
Adjustment for revaluation	735		
	1,935	330	480
Depreciation at 1.1.20X4	425	195	160
Provided in year	60	66	120
Disposals	(50)		
	435	261	280
Net book values	1,500	69	200

4 Investments

The market value of investments at 31 December 20X3 was £438,000.

5 Ten per cent debenture loans

These are redeemable in five equal annual instalments, starting next year. Interest of £40,000 is charged in this year's accounts.

6 Other creditors including taxation

	£
Preference dividend proposed	20,000
Ordinary dividend proposed 50 per cent	500,000
Corporation tax based on year's profits	266,000
	786,000

7 Other reserves

	£
Exchange reserve	75,000
General reserve	150,000
	225,000

8 Directors' remuneration

The amounts paid to directors were as follows:

	£	£
Fees as directors	20,000	
Other emoluments	190,000	210,000

Emoluments of the chairman amounted to £42,000 and those of the highest paid director £66,000. Other directors' emoluments were in the following ranges:

£45,001–£50,000	1
£50,001–£55,000	1

9 Operating profit is shown after charging

	£
Auditors' remuneration	7,000
Bank overdraft interest	19,000

Learning outcomes

You should now have learnt:

1 The Companies Acts require that additional notes be prepared and included with the published financial statements.

2 In some cases, the contents of these notes have been extended through the issuing of an accounting standard. For example, SSAP 25: *Segmental reporting* extended the disclosure required of many entities concerning segmental performance.

3 Along with the notes to the financial statements, a directors' report must be presented that summarises the activities and performance of the entity, along with specific details on a number of matters, including directors' shareholdings and information concerning significant changes in fixed assets.

4 The notes to the accounts and the directors' report are both audited and covered by the auditors' report that is attached to companies' published annual reports.

Answers to activities

13.1 These items are all of a type considered to be important and likely to influence the economic decisions of the users of financial statements. They are subject to review by the auditors of the company in the same way as the financial statements.

13.2 The directors' report contains a review of the company's performance, activities and future intentions. It also contains many other qualitative and quantitative items of information considered likely to influence the economic decisions of the users of financial statements. The audit report indicates whether, in the opinion of the auditors, the directors' report presents a true and fair view of the items contained within it. If the directors' report was not audited, unscrupulous directors could paint pictures concerning the company that gave an overly favourable impression of its performance, so biasing the judgement of those taking economic decisions based on its content.

REVIEW QUESTIONS

13.1 The following trial balance of X Limited, a non-listed company, has been extracted from the books after the preparation of the profit and loss and appropriation accounts for the year ended 31 March 20X7.

	£000	£000
Ordinary share capital – authorised, allotted and called-up fully paid shares of £1 each		1,000
12% debentures (repayable in 9 years)		500
Deferred taxation		128
Provisions for depreciation:		
Plant and machinery at 31 March 20X7		650
Freehold properties at 31 March 20X7		52
Vehicles at 31 March 20X7		135
Investments (listed), at cost	200	
Trade debtors and prepayments	825	
Corporation tax		270
Proposed final dividend		280
Tangible fixed assets:		
Freehold properties at 31 March 20X7	1,092	
Plant and machinery at 31 March 20X7	1,500	
Vehicles at 31 March 20X7	420	
Profit and loss account – balance at 31 March 20X7		356
Share premium account		150
Trade creditors and accruals		878
Research and development costs	35	
Stocks:		
Raw materials	200	
Work in progress	50	
Finished goods	250	
Bank balance	439	
Revaluation reserve on freehold properties		612
	5,011	5,011

You are also provided with the following information:

1 Investments

The listed investments consist of shares in W plc quoted on the Stock Exchange at £180,000 on 31 March 20X7. This is not considered to be a permanent fall in the value of this asset.

2 Trade debtors and prepayments

The company received notice, during April 20X7, that one of its major customers, Z Limited, had gone into liquidation. The amount included in trade debtors and prepayments is £225,000 and it is estimated that a dividend of 24p in the £ will be paid to unsecured creditors.

3 Taxation

(a) *Corporation tax*

The figure in the trial balance is made up as follows:

	£000
Based on profits for the year	174
Tax on exceptional item (*see* Note 4)	96
	270

(b) *Deferred taxation*

A transfer of £50,000 was made from the profit and loss account during the year ended 31 March 20X7.

4 Tangible fixed assets

(a) In arriving at the profit for the year, depreciation of £242,000 was charged, made up of freehold properties £12,000, plant and machinery £150,000 and vehicles £80,000.

(b) During the year to 31 March 20X7, new vehicles were purchased at a cost of £200,000.

(c) During March 20X7, the directors sold one of the freehold properties which had originally cost £320,000 and which had a written-down value at the date of the sale of £280,000. A profit of £320,000 on the sale, which was regarded as exceptional, has already been dealt with in arriving at the profit for the year. The estimated corporation tax liability in respect of the capital gain will be £96,000, as shown in Note 3. After this sale, the directors decided to have the remaining freehold properties revalued, for the first time, by Messrs V & Co, Chartered Surveyors and to include the revalued figure of £1,040,000 in the 20X7 accounts.

5 Research and development costs

The company carries out research and development and accounts for it in accordance with the relevant accounting standard. The amount shown in the trial balance relates to development expenditure on a new product scheduled to be launched in April 20X7. Management is confident that this new product will earn substantial profits for the company in the coming years.

6 Stocks

The replacement cost of the finished goods, if valued at 31 March 20X7, would amount to £342,000.

You are required to prepare a balance sheet at 31 March 20X7 to conform to the requirements of the Companies Acts and relevant accounting standards in so far as the information given allows. The vertical format must be used.

The notes necessary to accompany this statement should also be prepared.

Workings should be shown, but comparative figures are not required.

(*Chartered Institute of Management Accountants*)

13.2   The following information has been extracted from the books of account of Billinge plc as at 30 June 20X6:

	Dr £000	Cr £000
Administration expenses	242	
Cash at bank and in hand	157	
Cash received on sale of fittings		3
Corporation tax (over-provision for the previous year)		10
Deferred taxation		60
Depreciation on fixtures, fittings, tools and equipment (1 July 20X5)		132
Distribution costs	55	
Factory closure costs	30	
Fixtures, fittings, tools and equipment at cost	340	
Profit and loss account (at 1 July 20X5)		40
Purchase of equipment	60	
Purchases of goods for resale	855	
Sales (net of VAT)		1,500
Share capital (500,000 authorised, issued and fully paid ordinary shares of £1 each)		500
Stock (at 1 July 20X5)	70	
Trade creditors		64
Trade debtors	500	
	£2,309	£2,309

Additional information:

1 The company was incorporated in 20X0.
2 The stock at 30 June 20X6 (valued at the lower of cost or net realisable value) was estimated to be worth £100,000.
3 Fixtures, fittings, tools and equipment all related to administrative expenses. Depreciation is charged on them at a rate of 20 per cent per annum on cost. A full year's depreciation is charged in the year of acquisition, but no depreciation is charged in the year of disposal.
4 During the year to 30 June 20X6, the company purchased £60,000 of equipment. It also sold some fittings (which had originally cost £20,000) for £3,000 and for which depreciation of £15,000 had been set aside.
5 The corporation tax based on the profits for the year at a rate of 35 per cent is estimated to be £100,000. A transfer of £40,000 is to be made to the deferred taxation account.
6 The company proposes to pay a dividend of 20p per ordinary share.
7 The standard rate of income tax is 30 per cent.

Required:

In so far as the information permits, prepare Billinge plc's profit and loss account for the year to 30 June 20X6, and a balance sheet as at that date in accordance with the Companies Acts and appropriate accounting standards.

(*Association of Accounting Technicians*)

13.3A Cosnett Ltd is a company principally involved in the manufacture of aluminium accessories for camping enthusiasts. Its trial balance at 30 September 20X5 was:

	£	£
Issued ordinary share capital (£1 shares)		600,000
Retained profit at 1 October 20X4		625,700
Debentures redeemable 20X9		150,000
Bank loan		25,000
Plant and machinery at cost	1,475,800	
Accumulated depreciation to 30 September 20X5		291,500
Investments in UK companies at cost	20,000	
Turnover		3,058,000
Dividends from investments		2,800
Loss arising on factory closure	86,100	
Cost of sales	2,083,500	
Political and charitable contributions	750	
Distribution costs	82,190	
Salaries of office staff	42,100	
Directors' emoluments	63,000	
Rent and rates of offices	82,180	
Hire of plant and machinery	6,700	
Travel and entertainment expenses	4,350	
General expenses	221,400	
Trade debtors	396,100	
Trade creditors and accruals		245,820
Stocks	421,440	
Bank	17,950	
Interim dividend paid	21,000	
Interest charged	19,360	
Provision for deferred taxation		45,100
	5,043,920	5,043,920

You are provided with the following additional information:

(*a*) The company's shares are owned, equally, by three brothers: John, Peter and Henry Phillips; they are also the directors.

(*b*) The bank loan is repayable by five annual instalments of £5,000 commencing 31 December 20X5.

(*c*) The investments were acquired with cash, surplus to existing operating requirements, which will be needed to pay for additional plant the directors plan to acquire early in 20X6.

(*d*) On 1 January 20X5 the company closed a factory which had previously contributed approximately 20 per cent of the company's total production requirements.

(*e*) Trade debtors include £80,000 due from a customer who went into liquidation on 1 September 20X5; the directors estimate that a dividend of 20p in the £ will eventually be received.

(*f*) Trade creditors and accruals include:

(*i*) £50,000 due to a supplier of plant, of which £20,000 is payable on 1 January 20X6 and the remainder at the end of the year;

(*ii*) accruals totalling £3,260.

(*g*) The mainstream corporation tax liability for the year is estimated at £120,000.

(*h*) The directors propose to pay a final dividend of 10.5p per share and to transfer £26,500 to the deferred tax account.

Required:

The profit and loss account of Cosnett Ltd for the year to 30 September 20X5 and balance sheet at that date together with relevant notes attached thereto. The accounts should comply with the minimum requirements of the Companies Acts and accounting standards so far as the information permits.

(*Institute of Chartered Secretaries and Administrators*)

13.4A The following trial balance has been extracted from the books of Arran plc as at 31 March 20X7:

	£000	£000
Administrative expenses	95	
Called-up share capital (all ordinary shares of £1 each)		200
Cash at bank and in hand	25	
Debtors	230	
Deferred taxation (at 1 April 20X6)		60
Distribution costs	500	
Fixed asset investments	280	
Income from fixed asset investments		12
Interim dividend paid	21	
Overprovision of last year's corporation tax		5
Land and buildings at cost	200	
Land and buildings: accumulated depreciation at 1 April 20X6		30
Plant and machinery at cost	400	
Plant and machinery: accumulated depreciation at 1 April 20X6		170
Profit and loss account (at 1 April 20X6)		229
Profit on exceptional item		50
Purchases	1,210	
Sales		2,215
Stocks at 1 April 20X6	140	
Trade creditors		130
	£3,101	£3,101

Additional information:

1 Stocks at 31 March 20X7 were valued at £150,000.
2 Depreciation for the year to 31 March 20X7 is to be charged against administrative expenses as follows:

	£000
Land and buildings	5
Plant and machinery	40

3 Assume that the basic rate of income tax is 30 per cent.
4 Corporation tax of £180,000 is to be charged against profits on ordinary activities for the year to 31 March 20X7.
5 £4,000 is to be transferred to the deferred taxation account.
6 The company proposes to pay a final ordinary dividend of 30p per share.

Required:

In so far as the information permits, prepare the company's profit and loss account for the year to 31 March 20X7 and a balance sheet as at that date in accordance with the Companies Acts and related accounting standards. (*Note*: Profit and loss account and balance sheet notes are not required, but you should show the basis and computation of earnings per share at the foot of the profit and loss account, and your workings should be submitted.)

(*Association of Accounting Technicians*)

13.5A The following trial balance has been extracted from the books of account of Greet plc as at 31 March 20X8

	Dr £000	Cr £000
Administrative expenses	210	
Called up share capital (ordinary shares of £1 fully paid)		600
Debtors	470	
Cash at bank and in hand	40	
Corporation tax (overprovision in 20X7)		25
Deferred taxation (at 1 April 20X7)		180
Distribution costs	420	
Exceptional item		60
Fixed asset investments	560	
Investment income		72
Plant and machinery: at cost	750	
accumulated depreciation (at 31 March 20X8)		220
Profit and loss (at 1 April 20X7)		182
Purchases	960	
Stock (at 1 April 20X7)	140	
Trade creditors		261
Turnover		1,950
	£3,550	£3,550

Additional information:

1 Stock at 31 March 20X8 was valued at £150,000.
2 The following items *are already included* in the balances listed in the above trial balance:

	Distribution costs £000	Administrative expenses £000
Depreciation (for the year to 31 March 20X8)	27	5
Hire of plant and machinery	20	15
Auditors' remuneration	–	30
Directors' emoluments	–	45

3 The following rates of taxation are to be assumed:

	%
Corporation tax	35
Income tax	27

4 The corporation tax charge based on the profits for the year is estimated to be £52,000.
5 A transfer of £16,000 is to be made to the credit of the deferred taxation account.
6 The exceptional item relates to the profit made on the disposal of a factory in Belgium following the closure of the company's entire operations in that country.
7 The company's authorised share capital consists of 1,000,000 ordinary shares of £1 each.
8 A final ordinary payment of 50p per share is proposed.
9 There were no purchases or disposals of fixed assets during the year.
10 The market value of the fixed assets investments as at 31 March 20X8 was £580,000. There were no purchases or sales of such investments during the year.

Required:
In so far as the information permits, prepare the company's published profit and loss account for the year to 31 March 20X8 and a balance sheet as at that date in accordance with the Companies Acts and with related accounting standards.
   Relevant notes to the profit and loss account and balance sheet and detailed workings should be submitted with your answer, but a statement of the company's accounting policies is not required.

(Association of Accounting Technicians)

13.6 The accountant of Scampion plc, a retailing company listed on the London Stock Exchange, has produced the following draft financial statements for the company for the year to 31 May 20X7.

Profit and Loss Account for year to 31 May 20X2

	£000	£000
Sales		3,489
Income from investments		15
		3,504
Purchases of goods and services	1,929	
Value added tax paid on sales	257	
Wages and salaries including pension scheme	330	
Depreciation	51	
Interest on loans	18	
General administration expenses		
– Shops	595	
– Head office	25	
		3,205
Net profit for year		299
Corporation tax at 40%		120
Profit after tax for year		179

Balance Sheet at 31 May 20X2

	£000	£000
Fixed assets		
Land and buildings		1,178
Fixtures, fittings, equipment and motor vehicles		194
Investments		167
		1,539
Current assets		
Stock	230	
Debtors	67	
Cash at bank and in hand	84	
	381	
Current liabilities		
Creditors	487	
		(106)
		1,433
Ordinary share capital (£1 shares)		660
Reserves		703
Loans		70
		1,433

You discover the following further information:

(*i*)   Fixed assets details are as follows:

	Cost	Depreciation	Net
	£000	£000	£000
Freehold land and buildings	1,212	34	1,178
Fixtures, fittings and equipment	181	56	125
Motor vehicles	137	68	69

Purchases of fixed assets during the year were freehold land and buildings £50,000, fixtures, fittings and equipment £40,000, motor vehicles £20,000. The only fixed asset disposal during the year is referred to in note (*x*). Depreciation charged during the year was £5,000 for freehold buildings, £18,000 for fixtures, fittings and equipment and £28,000 for motor vehicles. Straight-line depreciation method is used assuming the following lives: Freehold buildings 40 years, fixtures, fittings and equipment 10 years and motor vehicles 5 years.

(*ii*)   A dividend of 10 pence per share is proposed.

(*iii*) A valuation by Bloggs & Co Surveyors shows the freehold land and buildings to have a market value of £1,350,000.

(*iv*) Loans are:

£20,000 bank loan with a variable rate of interest repayable by 30 September 20X2;

£50,000 12 per cent debenture repayable 20X6;

£100,000 11 per cent debenture repaid during the year.

There were no other loans during the year.

(*v*)   The income from investments is derived from fixed asset investments (shares in related companies) £5,000 and current asset investment (government securities) £10,000.

(*vi*) At the balance sheet date the shares in related companies (cost £64,000) are valued by the directors at £60,000. The market value of the government securities is £115,000 (cost £103,000).

(*vii*) After the balance sheet date but before the financial statements are finalised there is a very substantial fall in share and security prices. The market value of the government securities had fallen to £50,000 by the time the directors signed the accounts. No adjustment has been made for this item in the accounts.

(*viii*) Within two weeks of the balance sheet date a notice of liquidation was received by Scampion plc concerning one of the company's debtors. £45,000 is included in the balance sheet for this debtor and enquiries reveal that nothing is likely to be paid to any unsecured creditor. No adjustment has been made for this item in the accounts.

(*ix*) The corporation tax charge is based on the accounts for the year and there are no other amounts of tax owing by the company.

(*x*)   Reserves at 31 May 20X1 were:

	£
Revaluation reserve	150,000
Share premium account	225,000
Profit and loss account	149,000

The revaluation reserve represents the after-tax surplus on a property which was valued in last year's balance sheet at £400,000 and sold during the current year at book value.

Required:

A profit and loss account for the year to 31 May 20X2 and a balance sheet at that date for Scampion plc complying with the Companies Acts in so far as the information given will allow.

Ignore advance corporation tax.

(*Association of Chartered Certified Accountants*)

13.7A The Companies Acts and accounting standards require a great deal of information to be disclosed in a company's annual report and accounts.

Required:

List the disclosure requirements for the following items:

(*i*)   employees;

(*ii*) directors' emoluments; and

(*iii*) fixed assets.

(*Association of Accounting Technicians*)

CHAPTER 14

FRS 1: Cash flow statements

Learning objectives

After you have studied this chapter, you should be able to:
- explain the purpose of cash flow information
- explain the difference between cash flow and profit
- prepare a cash flow statement for a company following the format given in FRS 1

Introduction

In this chapter you'll build on what you learnt in *Business Accounting 1* relating to cash flow statements. You will learn more about the nine standard headings within a cash flow statement and be reminded of the layouts as given in FRS 1 and shown how to use them in practice.

14.1 Background

Business Accounting 1 introduced cash flow statements and this chapter moves on to consider the accounting standard relating to these statements – FRS 1: *Cash flow statements*. The standard requires that a cash flow statement be prepared according to prescribed formats for all companies other than those exempt from doing so, either because they are 'small', as defined by the Companies Act (*see* Chapter 12, Section 12.6), or because they are subsidiary undertakings and the group they belong to is publishing group financial statements in the European Union. The standard requires that the statement be included as a primary statement within the financial statements, i.e. it has the same status as the profit and loss account and the balance sheet.

14.2 Standard headings

The objective of FRS 1 is to ensure that reporting entities report the cash generation and cash absorption for a period by highlighting the significant components of cash flow in a way that facilitates comparison of the cash performance of different businesses; and that they provide information that assists in the assessment of their liquidity, solvency and financial adaptability. For this reason, the statement must show the flows of cash and cash equivalents for the period under the headings:

- operating activities
- dividends from joint ventures and associates
- returns on investments and servicing of finance
- taxation

- capital expenditure and financial investment
- acquisitions and disposals
- equity dividends paid
- management of liquid resources
- financing.

The first seven headings should be in the order shown. The other two can be combined under a single heading provided that each of their cash flows are shown separately and separate subtotals are given. Operating cash flows can be presented by either the *direct* method (showing the relevant constituent cash flows) or the *indirect* method (calculating operating cash flows by adjustment to the operating profit reported in the profit and loss account).

The standard indicates in which section various items are to be located and these are described in Sections 14.4 to 14.11. Further guidance concerning where items appear in the statement can be seen in the examples presented later in this chapter.

The standard requires that either adjoining the statement, or in a separate note, reconciliations are presented between operating profit and net cash flow from operating activities for the period, and between the movement in cash in the period and the movement in net debt. Neither reconciliation forms part of the statement. The reconciliation to net debt should identify the cash flows of the entity, the acquisition or disposal of subsidiary undertakings (excluding cash balances), other non-cash changes, and the recognition of changes in the market value and exchange rate movements.

14.3   Cash flow

The cash flow statement reports cash flow. Cash flow is defined in paragraph 2 of FRS 1 as 'an increase or decrease in an amount of cash'. Anything that falls outside this definition is not a cash flow and should not appear in the statement (though it could appear in the notes).

Cash is defined as 'cash in hand and deposits repayable on demand with any qualifying financial institution, less overdrafts from any qualifying financial institution repayable on demand'.

'Deposits repayable on demand' are deposits that can be withdrawn at any time without notice and without penalty or if a maturity or period of notice of not more than 24 hours or one working day has been agreed.

Cash includes cash in hand and deposits denominated in foreign currencies.

14.4   Operating activities and cash flows

Operating activities are generally the cash effects of transactions and other events relating to operating or trading activities. The net cash flow from operating activities represents the net increase or decrease in cash resulting from the operations shown in the profit and loss account in arriving at operating profit.

The reconciliation between operating profit and net cash flow from operating activities for the period should disclose separately the movements in stocks, debtors, and creditors related to operating activities, and other differences between cash flows and profits. It should also show separately the difference between dividends received and results taken into account for equity accounted entities.

In the cash flow statement, **operating cash flows** may be shown using either the indirect method or the direct method. Using the **indirect method**, it would be laid out in a manner similar to that shown in Exhibit 14.1.

Exhibit 14.1

	£
Operating profit	12,000
Depreciation charges	500
Loss on sale of tangible fixed assets	10
Increase in stocks	(200)
Increase in debtors	(100)
Increase in creditors	300
Net cash inflow from operating activities	12,510

FRS 1 requires that a reconciliation be shown between the net cash flow from operating activities and the operating profit as shown in the profit and loss account, which is precisely what is produced if the *indirect* method is adopted. Consequently, by adopting the indirect method, as the detailed information is to be included in a reconciliation, the main part of the statement may only include a single line 'net cash flow from operating activities'. Thus, instead of being included in the body of the cash flow statement, the details shown in Exhibit 14.1 would be included in the notes to the statement. When the indirect method is adopted, no details of the equivalent *direct* method analysis is required.

On the other hand, when the **direct method** is adopted for preparation of the statement, the reconciliation (i.e. the *indirect* method analysis) must also be prepared and included as a note to the statement. The direct method, would produce an analysis in the cash flow statement similar to that shown in Exhibit 14.2.

Exhibit 14.2

Operating activities	£
Cash received from customers	120,000
Cash payments to suppliers	(40,000)
Cash paid to and on behalf of employees	(60,000)
Other cash payments	(7,490)
Net cash inflow from operating activities	12,510

It is generally easier for an entity to adopt the indirect method – the figures are readily available from the profit and loss account and balance sheet data. The direct method, on the other hand, requires that the Cash Book is analysed. Despite there being much more work involved in preparing it, in Appendix III to FRS 1, the ASB encourages the use of the direct method when the potential benefits to users outweigh the costs of doing so – it does help provide a far clearer view of cash flow than the bookkeeping adjustments to profit that are undertaken under the indirect method.

Note: In an examination, if sufficient information on cash flows is provided for you to adopt the *direct* method, you should assume that is the approach to take – however, you would still require to adopt the *indirect* method when completing the reconciliation if that was also required by the question set.

14.5 Dividends from joint ventures and associates

This category was added following the issue of FRS 9: *Associates and joint ventures* in 1997. It was felt appropriate to show these dividends as a separate item as they were not part of operating income and they have a different nature from that of dividends from a company's returns on investment.

14.6 Returns on investment and servicing of finance

This section concerns receipts resulting from the ownership of an investment and payments to providers of finance, non-equity shareholders, and minority interests.

Generally, the standard endeavours to classify all cash flows according to the substance of the transaction that gave rise to them. As a result, this section of the statement excludes any item that may be classified under one of the other headings. For example, payments to *non-equity* shareholders (e.g. holders of preference shares in the entity) are included in this section, but payments to *equity* shareholders appear in the 'equity dividends paid' section.

Among the cash inflows included in this section are interest and dividends received (other than dividends from equity accounted entities whose results are included as part of operating profit). Cash outflows in this section include interest paid; finance costs, as defined under FRS 4: *Capital instruments – see* Chapter 10; the interest element of finance lease rental payments, as defined under SSAP 21: *Accounting for leases and hire purchase contracts – see* Chapter 2; and dividends paid to minority interests and to non-equity shareholders of the entity.

14.7 Taxation

This section includes cash flows to and from taxation authorities in respect of the reporting entity's revenue and capital profits. Other tax cash flows should be included under the same heading as the cash flow which gave rise to them – Property taxes, such as rates, and VAT, for example, are seen as relating to 'operating activities'. Thus, the net amount of VAT paid to or received from the tax authorities is included under that section. The exception to this arises when VAT is irrecoverable, in which case it is added to the originating transaction value and not distinguished from it within the cash flow statement.

14.8 Capital expenditure and financial investment

Capital expenditure means *buying and selling fixed assets*. **Financial investment** means *buying and selling shares held as investments*. Included in this section are cash flows relating to the acquisition or disposal of any fixed asset other than those required to be classified under the 'acquisitions and disposals' section of the statement, and those relating to any current asset investment not included in the 'management of liquid resources' section.

The heading can be reduced to 'capital expenditure' if there are no cash flows relating to financial investment.

The cash inflows include:

(a) receipts from the sale or disposal of property, plant or equipment, and
(b) receipts from the repayment of the reporting entity's loans to other entities and sales of debt instruments of other entities (other than receipts forming part of an acquisition or disposal or a movement in liquid resources and classified as falling within either of those two sections of the statement).

The cash outflows include:

(a) payments to acquire property, plant or equipment, and
(b) loans made by the reporting entity and payments to acquire debt instruments of other entities (other than payments forming part of an acquisition or disposal or a movement in liquid resources and classified as falling within either of those two sections of the statement).

14.9 Acquisitions and disposals

It is quite normal for businesses to buy and sell other businesses or interests in other businesses. This category of cash flow records the cash-related results of these activities.

Included in this section are therefore those cash flows relating to the acquisition or disposal of any trade or business, or of an investment in an entity that is or, as a result of the transaction, becomes or ceases to be either an associate, a joint venture or a subsidiary undertaking.

14.10 Equity dividends paid

This section includes the dividends paid on the reporting entity's or, in a group, the parent's equity shares.

14.11 Management of liquid resources

The FRS defines liquid resources as 'current asset investments held as readily disposable stores of value'. A 'readily disposable investment' is one that is disposable without curtailing or disrupting the entity's business and is either readily convertible into known amounts of cash or traded in an active market. In other words, this heading is concerned with short-term investments.

Cash inflows in this section include withdrawals from short-term deposits not qualifying as cash and inflows from the disposal or redemption of any other investments held as liquid resources.

Cash outflows in this section include payments into short-term deposits not qualifying as cash and outflows to acquire any other investment held as a liquid resource.

Each entity must explain what it includes in liquid resources and declare any change in its policy.

Activity 14.1

Imagine you are running a business and you have £500,000 that you won't need for three months. How will you invest it?

14.12 Financing

This category reports the cash flow effects of changes to share capital and long-term borrowings. Receipts and repayments of the principal amounts (i.e. the advance, not the interest) from or to external providers of finance are entered in this section. Examples include receipts from issuing and payments towards the redemption of shares and other equity instruments, debentures, loans, notes, bonds, and from long-term and short-term borrowings (other than overdrafts); the capital element of finance lease rental payment; and payments of expenses or commission on any issue of equity shares.

The amount of any financing cash flows received from or paid to an equity accounted entity should be disclosed separately.

14.13 Material transactions not resulting in any cash flows

FRS 1 also requires that details of material transactions that do not result in any cash flows should be included in a note if it is necessary for an understanding of the underlying transactions. A possible example would be an operating lease. It would involve the acquisition of an asset, but the reporting entity is paying rent, not purchasing the asset.

Activity 14.2
Why do you think that such items not affecting cash flows should still be reported in a note?

14.14 Exceptional and extraordinary items

Cash flows relating to items classed as exceptional or extraordinary in the profit and loss account should be shown under the appropriate standard headings, according to their nature. They should be identified in the cash flow statement or a note to it and the relationship between the cash flows and the originating exceptional or extraordinary item should be explained.

Where the cash flows themselves are exceptional because of their size or incidence but the underlying event that gave rise to them is not, sufficient disclosure should be given to explain their cause and effect.

14.15 An example of the FRS 1 layout using the indirect method

The following example was given in *Business Accounting 1*. It is included here to remind you of the format. We will then look at two examples of cash flow statements, one using the indirect method and the other using the direct method.

Exhibit 14.3

X Limited
Cash Flow Statement for the year ended 31 December 20X7

	£000	£000
1 **Net cash inflow/(outflow) from operating activities** (*see* Note 1)		XXX
2 *Dividends from joint ventures and associates*		XXX
3 *Returns on investments and servicing of finance*		
Interest received	XXX	
Interest paid	(XXX)	
Preference dividends paid	(XXX)	
Net cash inflow/(outflow) from returns on investments and servicing of finance		XXX
4 *Taxation*		XXX
5 *Capital expenditure and financial investment*		
Payments to acquire intangible fixed assets	XXX	
Payments to acquire tangible fixed assets	XXX	
Receipts from sales of tangible fixed assets	XXX	
Net cash inflow/(outflow) from capital expenditure and financial investment		XXX
6 *Acquisitions and disposals*		
Purchase of subsidiary undertaking	(XXX)	
Sale of business	XXX	
Net cash inflow/(outflow) from acquisitions and disposals		XXX
7 *Equity dividends paid*		(XXX)
8 *Management of liquid resources*		
Cash withdrawn from 7 day deposit	XXX	
Purchase of government securities	(XXX)	
Sale of corporate bonds	XXX	
Net cash inflow/(outflow) from management of liquid resources		XXX
9 *Financing*		
Issue of ordinary share capital	XXX	
Repurchase of debenture loan	(XXX)	
Expenses paid in connection with share issues	(XXX)	
		XXX
Increase/(decrease) in cash in the period		XXX

Reconciliation of net cash flow to movement in net debt/funds

	£000	£000
Increase/(decrease) in cash in the period	XXX	
Cash inflow/(outflow) from increase/decrease in debt and lease financing	XXX	
Cash inflow/(outflow) from decrease/increase in liquid resources	XXX	
Change in net debt resulting from cash flows		XXX
Loans and finance leases acquired with subsidiary		(XXX)
New finance leases		(XXX)
Exchange rate translation differences		XXX
Movement in net debt in the period		XXX
Net debt at 1 January 20X7		XXX
Net debt at 31 December 20X7		XXX

Note to the cash flow statement:

1 *Reconciliation of operating profit to net cash inflow/(outflow) from operating activities*

	£000
Operating profit	XXX
Depreciation charges	XXX
(Profit)/Loss on sale of tangible fixed assets	XXX
(Increase)/Decrease in stocks	XXX
(Increase)/Decrease in debtors	XXX
Increase/(Decrease) in creditors	XXX
Net cash inflow/(outflow) from operating activities	XXX

Each of the nine headings of the cash flow statement can be shown as one line in the statement and the detail in a note. (The numbers have been shown in Exhibit 14.3 in order to make it clear what the nine headings are. The numbers would not normally be included.)

The reconciliation to net debt does not form part of the statement, nor does the reconciliation of operating profit to net cash flow from operating activities. Either can be shown in a separate note (as the reconciliation of operating profit to net cash flow from operating activities is shown above) or adjoining the statement (as in the case of the reconciliation of the movement of cash to net debt above).

14.16 Two further examples

Exhibits 14.4 and 14.5 further illustrate how a cash flow statement is prepared, this time using numbers to add clarity. Some key points to remember include:

1 It is amounts paid rather than charged or accrued that are included. Thus for both tax and dividends, it is the actual payments and receipts that occurred during the period that are included in the statement, not the amounts provided for that will be paid or received in a future period.
2 Profit on sale of fixed assets is already included in the sale amount and should not be included a second time.
3 Care should be taken to identify and eliminate non-cash adjustments to the original profit before tax figure, for example depreciation and bad debt provisions.
4 If the layout presented in Exhibits 14.4 and 14.5 is followed, the entries in the 'Financing' section will have the opposite signs to the others, i.e. income will be shown with negative values, rather than positive as is the case in the other sections of the statement.

Exhibit 14.4

From the following profit and loss and balance sheet information, prepare a cash flow statement as required by FRS 1 *using the indirect method.*

Profit and Loss Account for the year ending 31 December 20X4

	£000	£000
Sales		10,000
Cost of goods sold		(6,000)
		4,000
Expenses		
Depreciation	600	
Interest	150	
Other expenses	2,100	
		(2,850)
Profit for the year before tax		1,150
Tax		(200)
Profit for the year after tax		950
Proposed dividend		(150)
Retained profit		800

Balance Sheet as at 31 December

	20X4		20X3	
	£000	£000	£000	£000
Fixed assets at cost		6,000		6,000
Less accumulated depreciation		3,000		2,400
Net book value		3,000		3,600
Current assets				
Stock	650		700	
Trade debtors	200		250	
Cash	1,610		150	
		2,460		1,100
Less Current liabilities				
Trade creditors	310		300	
Taxation	200		150	
Proposed dividends	150		250	
		(660)		(700)
		4,800		4,000
Financed by:				
Ordinary share capital		2,000		2,000
Revenue reserves		2,800		2,000
		4,800		4,000

Outline solution

Cash Flow Statement (using the indirect method) for the year ended 31 December 20X4

	£000
Net cash inflow from operating activities	2,010
Dividends from joint ventures and associates	–
Returns on investments and servicing of finance	
Interest paid	(150)
Taxation	(150)
Capital expenditure and financial investment	–
Acquisitions and disposals	–
Equity dividends paid	(250)
Management of liquid resources	–
Financing	–
Increase in cash in the period	1,460

Note to the cash flow statement:

1 Reconciliation of operating profit to net cash inflow from operating activities:

Operating profit	1,300
Depreciation charges	600
Decrease in stocks	50
Decrease in debtors	50
Increase in creditors	10
Net cash inflow from operating activities	2,010

Working:

Operating profit = Retained profit (800) + Interest (150) + Dividend (150) + Tax (200) = 1,300

Exhibit 14.5

From the summarised cash account and the fixed asset schedule of Thistle Ltd for 20X2, prepare a cash flow statement as required by FRS 1 *using the direct method.*

Summarised Cash Account

	£000		£000
Opening balance	500	Wages	1,350
Cash from cash sales	3,500	Other expenses	600
Cash from credit sales	5,750	Cash paid to suppliers	4,320
Cash from issue of shares	1,200	Tax paid	100
Cash from sale of building	970	Cash paid on finance lease	700
		Final dividend for 20X1	100
		Interim dividend 20X2	50
		Closing balance	4,700
	11,920		11,920

Fixed Asset Schedule

	Plant £000	Buildings £000	Total £000
Cost at 1.1.20X2	10,000	15,000	25,000
Acquisitions	4,730	–	4,730
Disposals	–	(5,000)	(5,000)
Cost at 31.12.20X2	14,730	10,000	24,730
Accumulated depreciation at 1.1.20X2	3,500	6,000	9,500
Charge for year	650	1,500	2,150
Disposals	–	(4,500)	(4,500)
Accumulated depreciation at 31.12.20X2	4,150	3,000	7,150

Other information:

(a) The tax charge for the year was £400,000. The opening balance on the tax liability was £100,000.

(b) The proposed final dividend for 20X2 was £120,000.

(c) Other expenses include insurance, which is paid a year in advance, on 30 June. In 20X1, insurance of £300,000 was paid. The amount paid in 20X2 was £400,000.

(d) Accrued wages were £75,000 at 1.1.20X2, and £95,000 at 31.12.20X2.

(e) Stocks were £1,500,000 at 1.1.20X2, and £1,700,000 at 31.12.20X2.

(f) All £700,000 paid on the finance lease in 20X2 represented capital. This was the first year of the lease and interest was not paid until the second payment, which was made in 20X3. Interest of £403,000 was included in the 20X3 payment and was accrued in the 20X2 financial statements.

(g) Opening and closing trade debtors and trade creditors were:

	1.1.20X2	31.12.20X2
Trade debtors	300,000	450,000
Trade creditors	500,000	475,000

(h) 600,000 £1 ordinary shares were issued at a premium on 1.3.20X2.
(i) Retained profits for the year to 31.12.20X2 were £732,000.

Outline solution

Cash Flow Statement (using the direct method)
for Thistle Ltd for the year ended 31 December 20X2

	£000	£000
Operating activities		
Cash received from customers	9,250	
Cash paid to suppliers	(4,320)	
Cash paid to employees	(1,350)	
Other cash payments	(600)	
Net cash inflow from operating activities		2,980
Dividends from joint ventures and associates		–
Returns on investment and servicing of finance		–
Taxation		(100)
Capital expenditure and financial investment		
Sale of buildings		970
Acquisitions and disposals		–
Equity dividend paid		(150)
Management of liquid resources		–
Financing		
Issue of share capital	1,200	
Capital element of finance lease rental payments	(700)	
Net cash inflow from financing		500
Increase in cash in the period		4,200

Note to the cash flow statement:

1 Reconciliation of operating profit to net cash inflow from operating activities:	£000
Operating profit	1,705
Depreciation charges	2,150
Profit on sale of building	(470)
Increase in stocks	(200)
Increase in debtors	(150)
Increase in prepayments	(50)
Decrease in creditors	(25)
Increase in accruals	20
Net cash inflow from operating activities	2,980

Workings:
(W1) Dividends paid in 20X2 are the proposed dividends from the previous year, plus the interim dividend paid during 20X2. The dividend charge in the profit and loss account will be the interim dividend and the proposed dividend for 20X2.
(W2) Assume tax paid during 20X2 is the amount outstanding at the opening balance sheet date. The tax charge for 20X2 in the profit and loss account is £400,000.

(W3)

	£
Retained profit	732,000
Add Dividends	170,000
Add Tax	400,000
Add Interest	403,000
Operating profit	1,705,000

Activity 14.3

When the items needed for the additional information required by the direct method are so easy to identify from the Cash Book, why do you think most companies prefer to use the indirect method?

Learning outcomes

You should now have learnt:

1 The objective of FRS 1 is to require entities to report their cash generation and absorption for a period on a standard basis.

2 This aids comparison between entities.

3 The statement must show the flows of cash for the period under the nine headings:
   - operating activities
   - dividends from joint ventures and associates
   - returns on investments and servicing of finance
   - taxation
   - capital expenditure and financial investment
   - acquisitions and disposals
   - equity dividends paid
   - management of liquid resources
   - financing.

4 The headings should be in that order and the statement should include a total for each heading.

5 Cash flow is an increase or decrease in cash resulting from a transaction.

6 Operating activities are generally the cash effects of transactions and other events relating to operating and trading activities.

7 Operating cash flows can be shown using either the *indirect* method or the *direct* method.

8 Reconciliations are presented between operating profit and net cash flow from operating activities for the period, and between the movement in cash in the period and the movement in net debt.

9 The ASB recommends that the *direct* method be used *if the benefits of doing so outweigh the costs.*

Answers to activities

14.1 Possible short-term investments include term deposits (e.g. 30- or 60-day deposit accounts), government stock (e.g. Treasury stock) and corporate bonds (e.g. loan stock issued by companies).

14.2 As the example of the operating lease given in the text indicates, it is a question of the substance of the transaction. The asset leased generated revenue through its use. Had it been purchased, the cash flow statement would have indicated that an additional asset was purchased. This information could then be used to explain changes in revenues. As it was leased not purchased, no such information is available to the user of the financial statements. By including a note about this, the user of the financial statements is able to draw similar conclusions concerning the asset to those that could be drawn if the asset had been purchased and, at the same time, is made aware that the company has adopted this approach which, in itself, has a direct impact upon cash flows.

14.3 In principle, the direct method is very easy to calculate. You just add up all the cash inflows and outflows relating to trading activities shown in the Cash Book. However, in practice, the volume of cash flows generated by any but the smallest business means that this can be a difficult and time-consuming task. It is not surprising that very few companies adopt this approach.

REVIEW QUESTIONS

14.1 List the nine headings in the cash flow statement, as required by FRS 1.

14.2A Give an example of the information to be included under each of the headings in the cash flow statement and indicate why this information might be useful.

14.3 Prepare a cash flow statement for Lee Ltd for the year ended 31 December 20X4 as required under FRS 1 using the direct method, together with note 1 to the statement. The profit and loss account, balance sheet and cash account for Lee Ltd for the year 20X4 are given below. (Do not attempt to provide the reconciliation of net cash flow to net debt.)

Profit and Loss Account for the year ending 31 December 20X4

	£	£
Sales		6,500
Less Cost of goods sold		(3,000)
		3,500
Less Expenses		
Wages	2,000	
Other costs	600	
Depreciation	500	
Interest	100	
		(3,200)
Profit for the year		300
Proposed dividend		(40)
Retained profit		260

Balance Sheet as at 31 December

	20X4		20X3	
	£	£	£	£
Fixed assets at cost		4,500		3,800
Less Accumulated depreciation		2,300		1,800
Net book value		2,200		2,000
Current assets				
Stock	400		500	
Trade debtors	150		200	
Cash	200		100	
		750		800
Less Current liabilities				
Trade creditors	275		250	
Accrued wages	25		50	
Proposed dividends	40		50	
		(340)		(350)
		2,610		2,450
Financed by:				
Debentures		900		1,000
Ordinary share capital		1,000		1,000
Retained profits		710		450
		2,610		2,450

Cash Account for 20X4

	£		£
Opening balance	100	Wages	2,025
Cash from customers	6,550	Other expenses	600
		Cash paid to suppliers	2,875
		Interest paid	100
		Cash purchase of fixed assets	700
		Cash paid to debenture holders	100
		Dividends paid	50
		Closing balance	200
	6,650		6,650

14.4A The balance sheets and additional information relating to Pennylane Ltd are given below. Prepare a cash flow statement for Pennylane Ltd for the year ended 31 December 20X3 as required under FRS 1 using the indirect method, together with note 1 to the statement. (Do not attempt to provide the reconciliation of net cash flow to net debt.)

Pennylane Ltd
Balance Sheets as at 31 December

	20X3 £000	20X2 £000
Fixed assets		
Tangible assets	400	325
Intangible assets	230	180
Investments	–	25
	630	530
Current assets		
Stocks	120	104
Debtors	400	295
Short-term investments	50	–
Cash in hand	10	4
	580	403
Creditors: amounts falling due within one year		
Trade creditors	122	108
Bank overdraft	88	105
Taxation	120	110
Dividends proposed	100	80
	430	403
Net current assets	150	–
Total assets less current liabilities	780	530
Creditors: amounts falling due after one year		
Long-term loan	(100)	–
Provisions for liabilities and charges: deferred taxation	(80)	(60)
	600	470
Capital and reserves		
Share capital (£1 ordinary shares)	200	150
Share premium account	160	150
Revaluation reserve	100	90
Profit and loss account	140	80
	600	470

Additional information:

(a) During the year interest of £75,000 was paid, and interest of £25,000 was received.

(b) The following information relates to tangible fixed assets.

At 31 December	20X3	20X2
	£000	£000
Cost	740	615
Accumulated depreciation	(340)	(290)
Net book value	400	325

(c) The proceeds of the sale of fixed asset investments were £30,000.
(d) Plant, with an original cost of £90,000 and a net book value of £50,000, was sold for £37,000.
(e) Tax paid to the Inland Revenue during 20X3 amounted to £110,000.

14.5 State the purposes of a cash flow statement.

(*Association of Chartered Certified Accountants*)

14.6 The following information has been extracted from the books of Nimmo Limited for the year to 31 December 20X9:

Profit and Loss Accounts for year to 31 December

	20X8	20X9
	£000	£000
Profit before taxation	9,500	20,400
Taxation	(3,200)	(5,200)
Profit after taxation	6,300	15,200
Dividends:		
Preference (paid)	(100)	(100)
Ordinary: interim (paid)	(1,000)	(2,000)
final (proposed)	(3,000)	(6,000)
Retained profit for the year	2,200	7,100

Balance Sheets at 31 December

	20X8	20X9
	£000	£000
Fixed assets		
Plant, machinery and equipment, at cost	17,600	23,900
Less Accumulated depreciation	9,500	10,750
	8,100	13,150
Current assets		
Stocks	5,000	15,000
Trade debtors	8,600	26,700
Prepayments	300	400
Cash at bank and in hand	600	–
	14,500	42,100
Current liabilities		
Bank overdraft	–	(16,200)
Trade creditors	(6,000)	(10,000)
Accruals	(800)	(1,000)
Taxation	(3,200)	(5,200)
Dividends	(3,000)	(6,000)
	(13,000)	(38,400)
	9,600	16,850
Share capital		
Ordinary shares of £1 each	5,000	5,000
10% preference shares of £1 each	1,000	1,000
Profit and loss account	3,000	10,100
	9,000	16,100
Loans		
15% debenture stock	600	750
	9,600	16,850

Additional information:

1 The directors are extremely concerned about the large bank overdraft as at 31 December 20X9 and they attribute this mainly to the increase in trade debtors as a result of alleged poor credit control.
2 During the year to 31 December 20X9, fixed assets originally costing £5,500,000 were sold for £1,000,000. The accumulated depreciation on these assets as at 31 December 20X8 was £3,800,000.

Required:
Prepare a cash flow statement for the year to 31 December 20X9.

Authors' note: Use the indirect method but do not attempt to provide the reconciliation of net cash flow to net debt.

(*Association of Accounting Technicians*)

14.7 The following summarised balance sheets relate to Track Limited:

Balance Sheets at 30 June

	20X0	20X1
	£000	£000
Fixed assets at cost	500	650
Less Accumulated depreciation	200	300
	300	350
Investments at cost	200	50
Current assets		
Stocks	400	700
Debtors	1,350	1,550
Cash and bank	100	–
	1,850	2,250
Current liabilities		
Bank overdraft	–	(60)
Creditors	(650)	(790)
Taxation	(230)	(190)
Proposed dividend	(150)	(130)
	(1,030)	(1,170)
	1,320	1,480
Capital and reserves		
Called-up share capital (£1 ordinary shares)	500	750
Share premium account	150	200
Profit and loss account	670	530
	1,320	1,480

Additional information:

1 During the year to 30 June 20X1, some fixed assets originally costing £25,000 had been sold for £20,000 in cash. The accumulated depreciation on these fixed assets at 30 June 20X0 amounted to £10,000. Similarly, some of the investments originally costing £150,000 had been sold for cash at their book value.
2 The taxation balances disclosed in the above balance sheets represent the actual amounts agreed with the Inland Revenue. All taxes were paid on their due dates. Advance corporation tax may be ignored.
3 No interim dividend was paid during the year to 30 June 20X1.
4 During the year to 30 June 20X1, the company made a 1-for-2 rights issue of 250 ordinary £1 shares at 120p per share.

Required:
Prepare Track Ltd's cash flow statement for the year to 30 June 20X1 in accordance with the requirements of FRS 1 using the indirect method. (Do not attempt to provide the reconciliation of net cash flow to net debt.)

(*Association of Accounting Technicians*)

14.8A   You are presented with the following summarised information relating to Ward plc:

Profit and Loss Account for the year to 30 June 20X8

	£000
Net profit for the year before taxation	900
Taxation (*see* Note 1)	(636)
Profit for the year after taxation	264
Extraordinary item (after tax relief of £35,000)	(90)
Profit for the year after taxation and extraordinary item	174
Dividends paid and proposed	(119)
Retained profit for the year	£55

Balance Sheet at 30 June 20X8

	20X7	20X8
	£000	£000
Fixed assets (*see* Note 2)	1,515	1,810
Investments	40	40
Current assets		
Stocks	175	200
Debtors	100	60
Cash at bank and in hand	20	–
	295	260
Creditors: amounts falling due within one year		
Bank loans and overdrafts	–	(21)
Trade creditors	(130)	(100)
Other creditors including taxation and social security (*see* Note 3)	(500)	(595)
	(630)	(716)
Creditors: amounts falling due after more than one year		
Debenture loans	(200)	(50)
Provisions for liabilities and charges		
Taxation, including deferred taxation (*see* Note 4)	(120)	(229)
	£900	£1,115
Capital and reserves		
Called-up share capital	750	910
Profit and loss account	150	205
	£900	£1,115

Notes:

1 The taxation charge in the profit and loss account includes the following items:

	£000
Corporation tax based on the profit for the year	542
Overprovision of last year's corporation tax	(15)
Transfer to deferred taxation account	109
	£636

2 During the year to 30 June 20X8, Ward sold an asset originally costing £150,000 for £5,000 in cash. The depreciation charged on this asset was £135,000. The total depreciation charged in the profit and loss account for the year to 30 June 20X8 was £384,000.

3 Other creditors including taxation and social security includes the following items:

	20X7	20X8
	£000	£000
Corporation tax	400	465
Proposed dividend	100	130
	£500	£595

4 The deferred taxation balances include the following items:

	20X7 £000	20X8 £000
Opening balance	70	120
Transfer from the profit and loss account	50	109
	£120	£220

Required:

In so far as the information permits, prepare Ward plc's statement of cash flow for the year to 30 June 20X8 in accordance with FRS 1.

(Association of Accounting Technicians)

14.9A The accountant of a private company has been able to get the use of a computer to produce the spreadsheets shown below but as yet the computer lacks a program to print out final accounts. The accountant nevertheless expects to use the spreadsheet data to reconstruct a summary profit and loss account and a cash flow statement for the year to 30 April 20X6.

Movements of Assets during the year 20X5/X6 (£000)

	Balance sheet value last year	Depreci- ation or amortis- ation for year	Additions during year	Sales during year	Other changes	Balance sheet value this year
Goodwill	–	–	40	–	–	40
Property	760	(36)	–	–	–	724
Plant and vehicles	540	(84)	420	(60)	–	816
Stocks	230	–	–	–	24	254
Debtors	254	–	–	–	76	330
Bank and cash	50	–	–	–	14	64
	1,834	(120)	460	(60)	114	2,228

Movement of Liabilities during the year 20X5/X6 (£000)

	Balance sheet value last year	New capital issued	Payments during year	Transfers to reserves and for provisions	Other changes	Balance sheet value this year
Ordinary shares (£1 each)	1,060	440	–	–	–	1,500
Deferred taxation	36	–	–	176	–	212
General reserve	152	–	–	32	–	184
Creditors	136	–	–	–	24	160
Provision for corporation tax	340	–	(340)	52	–	52
Provision for net dividend	110	–	(110)	120	–	120
	1,834	440	(450)	380	24	2,228

Notes:

(*i*) Proceeds of £40,000 were received from the sale of plant and vehicles.

(*ii*) During the year the company redeemed 10,000 of its £1 ordinary shares for £125,000 wholly out of distributable profits and this transaction has not been included in the spreadsheets.

Required:

(*a*) Reconstruct the profit and loss account for the year to 30 April 20X6.

(*b*) Prepare a cash flow statement for the year to 30 April 20X6.

(Institute of Chartered Secretaries and Administrators)

14.10 You are presented with the following forecast information relating to Baker Limited for the nine months to 30 September 20X7.

Forecast profit and loss accounts (abridged) for the three quarters to 30 September 20X7:

	March 20X7 £000	June 20X7 £000	Sept 20X7 £000
Sales	250	300	350
Cost of goods sold	(200)	(240)	(280)
Gross profit	50	60	70
Depreciation	(3)	(20)	(4)
Administration, selling and distribution expenses	(37)	(40)	(42)
Forecast net profit	£10	–	£24

Forecast balances at	31 Dec 20X6 £000	31 March 20X7 £000	30 June 20X7 £000	30 Sept 20X7 £000
Debit balances				
Tangible fixed assets at cost	360	240	480	480
90 day deposit at cost	15	5	5	10
Stocks at cost	40	30	40	55
Trade debtors	50	65	75	80
Cash at bank and in hand	80	–	–	–
Credit balances				
Debentures (10%)	–	–	–	50
Trade creditors	80	120	140	150
Taxation	8	–	–	–
Proposed dividend	15	–	–	–

Additional information:

1 Sales of tangible fixed assets in March 20X7 were expected to realise £12,000 in cash.
2 Administration, selling and distribution expenses were expected to be settled in cash during the month in which they were incurred.
3 Baker Limited includes as liquid resources term deposits of less than one year.

Required:
(a) calculate Baker Limited's forecast net cash position at 31 March, 30 June and 30 September 20X7 respectively; and
(b) prepare a forecast statement of cash flow for the nine months to 30 September 20X7.

(Association of Accounting Technicians)

14.11A The following information has been extracted from the draft financial information of V Ltd:

Profit and Loss Account for the year ended 31 December 20X3

	£000	£000
Sales		495
Raw materials consumed	(49)	
Staff costs	(37)	
Depreciation	(74)	
Loss on disposal	(4)	
		(164)
Operating profit		331
Interest payable		(23)
Profit before tax		308
Taxation		(87)
		221
Dividend		(52)
Profit retained for year		169
Balance brought forward		389
		558

Balance Sheets

	31 December 20X3		31 December 20X2	
	£000	£000	£000	£000
Fixed assets (see below)		1,145		957
Current assets				
Stock	19		16	
Trade debtors	38		29	
Bank	31		37	
	88		82	
Current liabilities				
Trade creditors	(12)		(17)	
Taxation	(79)		(66)	
Proposed dividend	(21)		(15)	
	(112)		(98)	
Working capital		(24)		(16)
		1,121		941
Long-term liabilities				
Long-term loans		(70)		(320)
		1,051		621
Share capital		182		152
Share premium		141		80
Revaluation reserve		170		
Profit and loss		558		389
		1,051		621

	Land & buildings £000	Machinery £000	Fixtures & fittings £000	Total £000
Fixed assets				
Cost or valuation:				
At 31 December 20X2	830	470	197	1,497
Additions	–	43	55	98
Disposals	–	(18)	–	(18)
Adjustment on revaluation	70	–	–	70
At 31 December 20X3	900	495	252	1,647
Depreciation				
At 31 December 20X2	(90)	(270)	(180)	(540)
Charge for year	(10)	(56)	(8)	(74)
Disposals	–	12	–	12
Adjustment on revaluation	100	–	–	100
At 31 December 20X3	0	(314)	(188)	(502)
Net book value				
At 31 December 20X3	900	181	64	1,145
At 31 December 20X2	740	200	17	957

(a) **You are required to** prepare a cash flow statement for V Ltd for the year ended 31 December 20X3 in accordance with the requirements of Financial Reporting Standard 1 (FRS 1).

(b) It has been suggested that the management of long-term profitability is more important than short-term cash flow. Explain why this might be so.

(*Chartered Institute of Management Accountants*)

Contract accounts

Introduction

In this chapter you'll learn how to record revenues and expenditures arising on contracts in contract accounts and how to estimate profits and losses on long-term contracts so that appropriate entries may be included in the financial statements.

15.1 Financial statements and the business cycle

The span of production differs between businesses, and some fit into the normal pattern of annual financial statements more easily than others. A farmer's financial statements are usually admirably suited to the yearly pattern, as the goods they produce are in accordance with the seasons, and therefore repeat themselves annually. With a firm whose production span is a day or two, the annual financial statements are also quite suitable.

On the other hand, there are businesses whose work does not fit neatly with a financial year's calculation of profits. Assume that a firm of contractors has only one contract being handled, and that is the total construction of a very large oil refinery complex. This might take five years to complete. Not until it is completed can the actual profit or loss on the contract be correctly calculated. However, if the company was formed especially with this contract in mind, the shareholders would not want to wait for five years before the profit could be calculated and dividends paid. Therefore an attempt is made to calculate profits yearly. Obviously, most firms will have more than one contract under way at a time and, of course, it would be rare for a contract to take such a long time to complete.

15.2 Opening contract accounts

An account is opened for each contract. It is, in fact, a form of trading account for each contract. Therefore if the firm has a contract to build a new college building, it may be numbered Contract 71. Thus a Contract 71 Account would be opened. All expenditure traceable to the contract will be charged to the contract account. This is far easier than ascertaining direct expenses in a factory, as any expenditure on the site will be treated as

direct, e.g. wages for the manual workers on the site, telephone rental for telephones on the site, hire of machinery for the contract, wages for the timekeepers, clerks, etc., on the site.

Activity 15.1

As each contract has or will have a unique flow of revenue, it makes sound business sense to know the profit or loss it generates. Hence the use of individual contract accounts. When financial statements are produced that include long-term contracts (those that extend into future accounting periods), which fundamental accounting concept is adhered to by maintaining a separate contract account for each contract?

15.3 Certification of work done

The contractor is paid by agreement on the strength of architects' certificates in the case of buildings, or engineers' certificates for an engineering contract. The architect, or engineer, will visit the site at regular intervals and will issue a certificate stating his or her estimate of the value of the work done, in terms of the total contract price (the sale price of the whole contract). Thus he may issue a certificate for £10,000. Normally the terms governing the contract will contain a clause concerning retention money. This is the amount, usually stated as a percentage, which will be retained, i.e. held back, in case the contract is not completed by a stated date, or against claims for faulty workmanship, etc. A 10 per cent retention in the case already mentioned would lead to £9,000 being payable by the person for whom the contract was being performed.

15.4 Allocation of overheads

The administration overhead expenses not traceable directly to the sites are sometimes split on an arbitrary basis and charged to each contract. Of course, if there were only one contract then all the overhead expenses would quite rightly be chargeable against it. On the other hand, if there are twenty contracts being carried on, any apportionment must be arbitrary. No one can really apportion on a 'scientific' basis the administration overhead expenses of the managing director's salary, the cost of advertising to give the firm the right 'image', or the costs of running accounting machinery for the records of the whole firm, and these are only a few of such expenses.

In a way similar to the departmental accounts principle in Chapter 38 of *Business Accounting 1*, allocation of overheads sometimes gives misleading results, and it is therefore far better left for the administrative overhead expenses which are obviously not chargeable to a contract to be omitted from the contract accounts. The surplus left on each contract account is thus the 'contribution' of each contract to administrative overhead expenses and to profit.

15.5 Example

In many cases, contracts will start and finish in the same financial period. In such cases, there is no need to estimate profits and losses at the period end. However, when a contract extends into one or more periods after it started, it is known as a 'long-term contract' and an appropriate estimate of profits and losses must be made in order that entries can be made in financial statements. In the example which follows, Contract 44 extends into a second accounting period.

Exhibit 15.1

Contract 44 is for a school being built for the Blankshire County Council. By the end of the year the following items have been charged to the contract account:

Contract 44

	£
Wages – labour on site	5,000
Wages – foreman and clerks on the site	600
Materials	4,000
Subcontractors on the site	900
Other site expenses	300
Hire of special machinery	400
Plant bought for the contract	2,000

The entries concerning expenditure traceable direct to the contract are relatively simple. These are charged to the contract account. These can be seen in the contract account shown on the next page.

Architects' certificates have been received during the year amounting to £14,000. It is assumed for this example that the certificates related to all work done up to the year end. A retention of 10 per cent is to be made, and the Blankshire County Council has paid £12,600. The £14,000 has been credited to a holding account called an Architects' Certificates Account and debited to the Blankshire County Council Account. The total of the Architects' Certificates Account now needs transferring to the Contract 44 account. It is, after all, the 'sale' price of the work done so far, and the contract account is a type of trading account. The £12,600 received has been debited to the Cash Book and credited to Blankshire County Council Account, which now shows a balance of £1,400 that is equal to the retention money.

The cost of the stock of the materials on the site unused is not included in the value of the architects' certificates and is therefore carried forward to the next year at cost price. The value of the plant at the end of the year is also carried forward. In this case the value of the cost of the plant not yet used is £1,400. This means that £2,000 has been debited for the plant and £1,400 credited, thus effectively charging £600 for depreciation. Assume that the stock of unused materials cost £800.

The Contract 44 account will now appear as follows:

Contract 44

	£		£
Wages – labour on site	5,000	Architects' certificates	14,000
Wages – foreman and clerks on the site	600	Stock of unused materials c/d	800
Materials	4,000	Value of plant c/d	1,400
Subcontractors on the site	900		
Other site expenses	300		
Hire of special machinery	400		
Plant bought for the contract	2,000		

Activity 15.2

What is the profit on Contract 44?

15.6 Profit estimation

In order to estimate the profit or loss on Contract 44, more information is needed beyond the values shown in the contract account. The contract is only part-completed, and costly snags may crop up which would dissipate any potential profit earned, or problems may have

developed already, such as subsidence which has remained unnoticed as yet. It is not possible to identify all known factors of this type. To minimise the risk of profits being overstated or losses understated, the concept of prudence is applied and the profit is reduced according to an 'appropriate' modifier.

Before SSAP 9 was revised in 1988, the custom developed of multiplying the profit shown on the contract account by two-thirds and then multiplying the result by the proportion of work certified for which cash had been received. While the SSAP 9 approach must be adopted in practice, this approach is an excellent example of the prudence concept and is still used in examinations. You will, therefore, need to learn how to apply it. It is relatively straightforward to apply, as shown in the following example:

$$\text{Apparent profit} \times \frac{2}{3} \times \frac{\text{Cash received}}{\text{Work certified}} = \text{Amount available for dividends, etc.}$$

For example:

$$£3,000 \times \frac{2}{3} \times \frac{12,600}{14,000} = £1,800$$

On the basis of the £1,800 profit calculated above, the Contract 44 Account can now be completed.

Profit and Loss Account

	£
Profits from contracts:	
Contract 43	–
Contract 44	1,800
Contract 45	–

Contract 44

	£		£
Wages – labour on site	5,000	Architects' certificates	14,000
Wages – foreman and clerks on the site	600	Stock of unused materials c/d	800
Materials	4,000	Value of plant c/d	1,400
Subcontractors on the site	900		
Other site expenses	300		
Hire of special machinery	400		
Plant bought for the contract	2,000		
Profit to the profit and loss account	1,800		
Reserve (the part of the apparent profit not yet recognised as earned) c/d	1,200		
	16,200		16,200
Stock of unused materials b/d	800	Reserve b/d	1,200
Value of plant b/d	1,400		

15.7 Anticipated losses

In the case shown, there has been an apparent profit of £3,000 but the action would have been different if, instead of revealing such a profit, the contract account had shown a loss of £3,000. In such a case it would not be two-thirds of the loss to be taken into account but the whole of it. Thus £3,000 loss would have been transferred to the profit and loss account. This is in accordance with the concept of prudence which states that profits may be underestimated but never losses.

It is not always the case that an engineer or architect will certify the work done up to the financial year end. He or she may call several days earlier than the year end. The cost of work done, but not certified at the year end, will therefore need carrying down as a balance to the next period when certification will take place.

15.8 Long-term contracts and SSAP 9

When a revised version of SSAP 9: *Stocks and long-term contracts* was issued in 1988, this custom-based *rule of thumb* was replaced with a far more complex calculation that focuses upon turnover and the work certified valued in relation to the overall contract amount.

According to SSAP 9, long-term contracts should be assessed on a contract by contract basis. They should be reflected in the profit and loss account by recording turnover and related costs as contract activity progresses. Turnover should be ascertained in a manner appropriate to the stage of completion of the contract, the business and the industry in which it operates. Where the outcome of the contract can be assessed with reasonable accuracy, profit should be recognised (so far as prudence permits) as the difference between recognised turnover and related costs. Any foreseeable losses identified should be immediately recognised.

The amount of long-term contracts, at costs incurred, net of amounts transferred to cost of sales, after deducting foreseeable losses and payments on account not matched with turnover should be classified as 'long term contract balances' and disclosed separately within the balance sheet heading of 'stocks'. The balance sheet note should disclose separately the balances of 'net cost less foreseeable losses' and 'applicable payments on account'.

Profit recognition

SSAP 9 provides two definitions relevant to any consideration of long-term contracts: those of 'attributable profit' and 'foreseeable losses'.

Attributable profit is that part of total profit currently estimated to arise over the duration of the contract, after allowing for estimated remedial and maintenance costs and increases in costs (so far as not recoverable under the terms of the contract), that fairly reflects the profit attributable to that part of the work performed at the accounting date. There can be no attributable profit until the outcome of the contract can be assessed with reasonable certainty.

Foreseeable losses are those losses estimated to arise over the duration of the contract, after allowing for estimated remedial and maintenance costs and increases in costs (so far as not recoverable under the terms of the contract), *whether or not* work has commenced, and irrespective of both the proportion of work completed and profits expected on other contracts.

SSAP 9 does not prescribe a point at which profit on long-term contracts should start to be recognised. The requirement that a contract's outcome must be capable of being assessed with reasonable certainty before any profit should be recognised, leaves it entirely to individual judgement. One company may recognise profit after the first six months, while another may wait until a year has passed. As a result, interfirm comparability is impaired. However, the standard does assist in intrafirm comparison from one year to the next as it requires consistent application of the method of ascertaining attributable profit both within the business, and from year to year.

Clearly, future costs must be estimated in arriving at a figure for attributable profit or foreseeable losses. Unfortunately, no two people are likely to independently arrive at exactly the same amount. Thus, the profits and losses recognised are likely to vary considerably from one company to another and interfirm comparability is further impaired.

Turnover valuation

Turnover should be ascertained in a manner suitable to the industry and the specific contracts concerned. It is suggested that valuation of work carried out may be used to derive a value for turnover; and that profit should be regarded as earned in relation to the *amount* of work performed to date. These two approaches could often produce different results, but the profit taken up needs to reflect the proportion of the work carried out and to take into account any known inequalities of profitability in the various stages of a contract. Consequently, when there is a work certified value, this should be used as the turnover value and the costs incurred in achieving that turnover charged to cost of sales.

Where no work certified figure exists, costs to date as a proportion of total expected costs should be applied to the contract value in order to determine the figure for turnover. Where the work certified value is not available for all work completed, a combination of the two approaches would be appropriate. One further point regarding turnover concerns settlements of claims against the purchaser arising from circumstances not foreseen in the contract: these should only be incorporated when there is sufficient evidence that payment will be received.

Complexity

The standard is extremely complex and it is beyond the scope of this book, where this topic is being introduced rather than developed in detail, to extend coverage to the level of complexity that would be required in order to cover the SSAP 9 rules adequately. Students who require a sound understanding of the SSAP 9 rules concerning long-term contracts should refer to the standard, where the appendix covers the topic in detail, or to a specialised text on the subject.

From the perspective of the review questions that follow at the end of this chapter, apart from question 15.5A, *unless otherwise indicated in the question*, you should apply the two-thirds rule of thumb given above. Doing so will develop an awareness of the complexity of contract accounts without the added complexity of applying the SSAP 9 rules. By adopting this approach, students will be well placed to progress to an understanding of the SSAP 9 rules, knowing well the underlying factors involved in contract accounts. The answer to question 15.5A is based on the SSAP 9 rules, and is provided for the benefit of any student who chooses to study those rules independently of this book.

Learning outcomes

You should now have learnt:

1 That a separate contract account should be opened in respect of every contract.

2 That profits or losses on each uncompleted contract must be estimated at the end of each accounting period.

3 That losses should be written off immediately they are identified.

4 That an appropriate amount of any profit should be included in the financial statements.

5 Some of the definitions and requirements of SSAP 9 relating to long-term contracts.

6 That the rule of thumb profit/loss ascertainment approach adopted in this chapter is necessarily simplified in order to ensure the topic is well understood; SSAP 9 should be consulted for the definitive approach to adopt when preparing financial statements.

Answers to activities

15.1 While it is ongoing, each contract represents an asset or liability. The separate determination concept – see Section 10.6 in *Business Accounting 1* – requires that the amount of each individual asset or liability be determined separately from all other assets and liabilities. Maintaining a separate contract account for each contract enables compliance with this fundamental accounting concept.

15.2 The difference between the two sides (Credit side £16,200; Debit side £13,200) is £3,000. At this stage, as the contract is incomplete, the £3,000 simply reflects the excess of potential revenue over expenditure to date on the contract. It does not necessarily mean that the contract will ultimately result in a profit and it certainly does not mean that there is a profit to date of £3,000 on the contract – the stock, for example, would need to be sold for precisely the amount shown and the plant disposed at the amount it is valued at, neither of which is particularly likely to be the case.

REVIEW QUESTIONS

15.1 The financial statements of Diggers Ltd are made up to 31 December in each year. Work on a certain contract was commenced on 1 April 20X5 and was completed on 31 October 20X6. The total contract price was £174,000, but a penalty of £700 was suffered for failure to complete by 30 September 20X6.
The following is a summary of receipts and payments relating to the contract:

	During 20X5	During 20X6
Payments		
Materials	25,490	33,226
Wages	28,384	45,432
Direct expenses	2,126	2,902
Purchases of plant on 1 April 20X5	16,250	–
Receipts		
Contract price (*less* penalty)	52,200	121,100
Sale, on 31 October 20X6, of all plant purchased on 1 April 20X5	–	4,100

The amount received from the customer in 20X5 represented the contract price of all work certified in that year less 10 per cent retention money.

When the financial statements for 20X5 were prepared it was estimated that the contract would be completed on 30 September 20X6, and that the market value of the plant would be £4,250 on that date. It was estimated that further expenditure on the contract during 20X6 would be £81,400.

For the purposes of the financial statements, depreciation of plant is calculated, in the case of uncompleted contracts, by reference to the expected market value of the plant on the date when the contract is expected to be completed, and is allocated between accounting periods by the straight line method.

Credit is taken, in the financial statements, for such a part of the estimated total profit, on each uncompleted contract, as corresponds to the proportion between the contract price of the work certified and the total contract price.

Required:
Prepare a summary of the account for this contract, showing the amounts transferred to profit and loss account at 31 December 20X5 and 31 December 20X6.

15.2 Stannard and Sykes Ltd are contractors for the construction of a pier for the Seafront Development Corporation. The value of the contract is £300,000, and payment is by engineer's certificate subject to a retention of 10 per cent of the amount certified; this is to be held by the Seafront Development Corporation for six months after the completion of the contract.
The following information is extracted from the records of Stannard and Sykes Ltd.

	£
Wages on site	41,260
Materials delivered to site by supplier	58,966
Materials delivered to site from store	10,180
Hire of plant	21,030
Expenses charged to contract	3,065
Overheads charged to contract	8,330
Materials on site at 30 November 20X8	11,660
Work certified	150,000
Payment received	135,000
Work in progress at cost (not the subject of a certificate to date)	12,613
Wages accrued to 30 November 20X8	2,826

Required:

Prepare the Pier Contract Account to 30 November 20X8, and suggest a method by which profit could be prudently estimated.

(Association of Chartered Certified Accountants)

15.3A Cantilever Ltd was awarded a contract to build an office block in London and work commenced at the site on 1 May 20X5.

During the period to 28 February 20X6, the expenditure on the contract was as follows:

	£
Materials issued from stores	9,411
Materials purchased	28,070
Direct expenses	6,149
Wages	18,493
Charge made by the company for administration expenses	2,146
Plant and machinery purchased on 1 May 20X5, for use at site	12,180

On 28 February 20X6, the stock of materials at the site amounted to £2,164 and there were amounts outstanding for wages £366 and direct expenses £49.

Cantilever Ltd has received on account the sum of £64,170 which represents the amount of Certificate No. 1 issued by the architects in respect of work completed to 28 February 20X6, after deducting 10 per cent retention money.

The following relevant information is also available:

(a) the plant and machinery has an effective life of five years, with no residual value, and
(b) the company only takes credit for two-thirds of the profit on work certified.

Required:

(a) prepare a contract account for the period to 28 February 20X6, and
(b) show your calculation of the profit to be taken to the credit of the company's profit and loss account in respect of the work covered by Certificate No 1.

(Institute of Chartered Accountants)

15.4A You are required to prepare the contract account for the year ended 31 December 20X0, and show the calculation of the sum to be credited to the profit and loss account for that year.

On 1 April 20X0 MN Ltd commenced work on a contract which was to be completed by 30 June 20X1 at an agreed price of £520,000.

MN Ltd's financial year ended on 31 December 20X0, and on that day expenditure on the contract totalled £263,000 made up as under:

	£
Plant	30,000
Materials	124,000
Wages	95,000
Sundry expenses	5,000
Head office charges	9,000
	263,000

Cash totalling £195,000 had been received by 31 December 20X0 representing 75 per cent of the work certified as completed on that date, but in addition, work costing £30,000 had been completed but not certified.

A sum of £9,000 had been obtained on the sale of materials which had cost £8,000 but which had been found unsuitable. On 31 December 20X0 stocks of unused materials on site had cost £10,000 and the plant was valued at £20,000.

To complete the contract by 30 June 20X1 it was estimated that:

(a) the following additional expenditures would be incurred:

	£
Wages	64,000
Materials	74,400
Sundry expenses	9,000

(b) further plant costing £25,000 would be required;
(c) the residual value of all plant used on the contract at 30 June 20X1 would be £15,000;
(d) head office charges to the contract would be at the same annual rate plus 10 per cent.

It was estimated that the contract would be completed on time but that a contingency provision of £15,000 should be made. From this estimate and the expenditure already incurred, it was decided to estimate the total profit that would be made on the contract and to take to the credit of the profit and loss account for the year ended 31 December 20X0, that proportion of the total profit relating to the work actually certified to that date.

(*Chartered Institute of Management Accountants*)

Note: The next question requires the application of the rules contained in SSAP 9.

15.5A *General information on the Lytax group of companies*

Lytax Ltd is a company in the building construction industry.

It has three regional offices, North Borders, Midlands and South Downs, which are constituted as separate units for accounting purposes.

On 25 May 20X0 Lytax Ltd acquired 90 per cent of the ordinary share capital of Ceprem Ltd, a company which manufactures building materials.

Lytax Ltd has for 3 years held 15 per cent of the ordinary share capital of Bleco plc. This company carries out specialist research and development activities into building and construction materials, technology and techniques. It then sells the results of these activities to other companies.

Details of long-term contract work undertaken by Lytax Ltd
At 31 October 20X0, Lytax Ltd was engaged in various contracts including five long-term contracts, details of which are given below:

	1	2	3	4	5
	£000	£000	£000	£000	£000
Contract price	1,100	950	1,400	1,300	1,200
At 31 October 20X0:					
Cumulative costs incurred	664	535	810	640	1,070
Estimated further costs to completion	106	75	680	800	165
Estimated cost of post-completion					
guarantee/rectification work	30	10	45	20	5
Cumulative costs incurred					
transferred to cost of sales	580	470	646	525	900
Progress payments					
Cumulative receipts	615	680	615	385	722
Invoiced:					
Awaiting receipt	60	40	25	200	34
Retained by contractee	75	80	60	65	84

It is not expected that any contractees will default on their payments.

Up to 31 October 20X9, the following amounts had been included in the turnover and cost of sales figures.

	1	2	3	4	5
	£000	£000	£000	£000	£000
Cumulative turnover	560	340	517	400	610
Cumulative costs incurred					
transferred to cost of sales	460	245	517	400	610
Foreseeable loss transferred to cost of sales	–	–	–	70	–

It is the accounting policy of Lytax Ltd to arrive at contract turnover by adjusting contract cost of sales (including foreseeable losses) by the amount of contract profit or loss to be regarded as recognised, separately for each contract.

Required:

(a) Calculate the amounts to be included within the turnover and cost of sales figures of the profit and loss account of Lytax Ltd for the year ended 31 October 20X0, in respect of the long-term contracts.

(b) Prepare extracts from the balance sheet of Lytax Ltd at 31 October 20X0 incorporating the financial effects of the long-term contracts.

Your answer should comply with the requirements of SSAP 9 (Stocks and Long-Term Contracts) and should include any supporting notes required by that standard.

Workings for individual contracts which build up to the total for each item must be shown.
All calculations should be made to the nearest £1,000.

(Association of Chartered Certified Accountants)

PART 3

Groups

Introduction

This part is concerned with group financial statements: how they are prepared, how various transactions should be dealt with, and how their presentation is regulated by the Companies Acts and accounting standards.

CHAPTER 16

Group financial statements: an introduction

Learning objectives

After you have studied this chapter, you should be able to:

- explain the difference between a parent undertaking and a subsidiary undertaking
- explain why it is important to produce consolidated financial statements
- describe some of the alternative methods whereby control can be acquired by one company over another
- explain the relevance of 'dominant influence' to the identification of a parent–subsidiary relationship
- explain the relevance of 'significant influence' to the identification of the existence of an 'associated undertaking'

Introduction

In this chapter you'll learn about the three rights of shareholders, about groups, how they come about and of the need for consolidated financial statements.

16.1 Shareholders and their rights

The owners of a company are its shareholders. When someone buys ordinary shares in a company then they are usually given three rights. These are:

1 voting rights at shareholders' meetings;
2 a right to an interest in the net assets of the company;
3 a right to an interest in the profits earned by the company.

Preference shareholders do not normally have such voting rights, but sometimes they can have such power. This could be when their dividends are in arrears, or their special rights are being changed by the company. Debenture holders have no rights at all to vote at general meetings.

By using their voting rights at shareholders' meetings, the shareholders are able to show their approval, or disapproval, of the election of directors. It is the directors who manage the affairs of the company. Therefore any group of shareholders, who between them own more than 50 per cent of the voting shares of the company, can control the election of directors. As a consequence they can control the policies of the company through the directors. This would also be true if any one shareholder owned more than 50 per cent of the voting shares.

One company may hold shares in another company. Therefore if one company wishes to obtain control of another company it can do so by obtaining more than 50 per cent of the voting shares in that company.

> ### Activity 16.1
> Why don't preference shareholders have the same voting rights as ordinary shareholders?

16.2 Parent undertakings and subsidiary undertakings

- S Ltd has an issued share capital of 1,000 ordinary shares of £1 each.
- On 1 January 19X6, P Ltd buys 501 of these shares from Jones, a shareholder, for £600.
- P Ltd will now have control of S Ltd because it has more than 50 per cent of the voting shares.
- P Ltd is now called the 'parent undertaking'.
- S Ltd is now called the 'subsidiary undertaking' of P Ltd.

Just because the identity of S Ltd's shareholders has changed it does not mean that the balance sheet of S Ltd will be drafted in a different fashion. Looking only at the balance sheet of S Ltd no one would be able to deduce that P Ltd owned more than 50 per cent of the shares, or even that P Ltd owned any shares at all in S Ltd. After obtaining control of S Ltd both P Ltd and S Ltd will continue to maintain their own sets of accounting records and to draft their own balance sheets. If the balance sheets of P Ltd and S Ltd are looked at, both before and after the purchase of the shares, any differences can be noted.

Exhibit 16.1

(a) Before P Ltd acquired control of S Ltd.

P Ltd Balance Sheet as at 31 December 19X5	£	£	S Ltd Balance Sheet as at 31 December 19X5	£	£
Fixed assets		2,000	Fixed assets		400
Current assets			Current assets		
Stock-in-trade	2,900		Stock-in-trade	400	
Debtors	800		Debtors	200	
Bank	1,300		Bank	100	
		5,000			700
		7,000			1,100
Share capital		5,000	Share capital		1,000
Profit and loss account		2,000	Profit and loss account		100
		7,000			1,100

(b) After P Ltd acquired control of S Ltd the balance sheets would appear as follows before any further trading took place:

P Ltd Balance Sheet as at 1 January 19X6	£	£	S Ltd Balance Sheet as at 1 January 19X6	£	£
Fixed assets		2,000	Fixed assets		400
Investment in subsidiary undertaking		600	Current assets		
Current assets			Stock-in-trade	400	
Stock-in-trade	2,900		Debtors	200	
Debtors	800		Bank	100	
Bank	700				700
		4,400			1,100
		7,000	Share capital		1,000
			Profit and loss account		100
					1,100
Share capital		5,000			
Profit and loss account		2,000			
		7,000			

The only differences can be seen to be those in the balance sheets of P Ltd. The bank balance has been reduced by £600, this being the cost of shares in S Ltd, and the cost of the shares now appears as 'Investment in subsidiary undertaking £600'. The balance sheets of S Ltd are completely unchanged.

We shall see later that FRS 2: *Accounting for subsidiary undertakings* gives a much wider meaning to 'subsidiary undertaking' than we have seen so far. This has been deliberately excluded up to this point to let you see the basic structure without complicating it.

16.3 Profit and loss account

From the profit and loss account point of view, the appropriation section of S Ltd would also be completely unchanged after P Ltd takes control. However, P Ltd would see a change in its profit and loss account when a dividend is received from S Ltd – in this case, the dividends received would be shown as investment income in the profit and loss account. Remember that dividends payable are charged to the appropriation section of the paying company's profit and loss account, while dividends received are in the main part of the receiving company's profit and loss account.

The terms 'parent undertaking' and 'subsidiary undertaking' have been in use for only a short time. Previously, a parent undertaking was called a holding company, and a subsidiary undertaking was a subsidiary company. In Chapter 26 we will see why the terms were changed. One of the reasons was that consolidated financial statements used to be concerned only with companies. Now, subsidiary undertakings can include unincorporated businesses as well.

In the chapters which follow, 17 to 25 inclusive, we will show the consolidations only of companies, to demonstrate the principles involved. In addition we will often simply call a parent undertaking by the title of 'parent' and a subsidiary undertaking may also be shortened to 'subsidiary'.

In Chapter 26 we will examine FRS 2 which covers the accounting needed for parent and subsidiary undertakings. This book, in the chapters which follow, fully complies with all the requirements of FRS 2.

16.4 The need for consolidated financial statements

Imagine being a shareholder of P Ltd. Each year you would receive a set of P Ltd's financial statements. After P's acquisition of the shares in S Ltd then £600 would appear as an asset in the balance sheet of P Ltd. It would be normal for it to be shown at cost £600, using the cost concept.

When you looked at the profit and loss account of P Ltd you would see the dividends received from S Ltd. This plus the cost of the investment in the balance sheet would therefore be the only things you would know about the subsidiary.

However, you have invested in P Ltd, and because of its majority shareholding in S Ltd you have in effect also invested in S Ltd as well. Just as you want to know how the assets and liabilities in P Ltd change over the years, you will now also like to know exactly the same for S Ltd.

You are not, however, a shareholder of S Ltd, and therefore you would not be sent a copy of its financial statements. If the situation were to stay like that, you could not get a proper view of your investment.

This would be even worse if in fact P Ltd was a parent undertaking with twenty subsidiaries, and held a different percentage stake in each of them. It would also be almost certain that the companies would trade with each other, and owe money to one another or be owed money by them. This would also raise complications.

Fortunately there is a remedy for this sort of problem. The Companies Acts provide for parent undertakings distributing to their shareholders a set of consolidated financial statements. These bring together all of the financial statements for the parent undertaking and its subsidiaries in such a way that the shareholders can get an overall view of their investments.

16.5 Different methods of acquiring control of one company by another

So far the acquisition of control in S Ltd was by P Ltd buying more than 50 per cent of the shares in S Ltd from Jones, i.e. buying shares on the open market. This is by no means the only way of acquiring control, so by way of illustration some of the other methods are now described.

1 S Ltd may issue new shares to P Ltd amounting to over 50 per cent of the voting shares. P Ltd pays for the shares in cash.
2 P Ltd could purchase over 50 per cent of the voting shares of S Ltd on the open market by exchanging for them newly issued shares of P Ltd.

Or, acting through another company:

3 P Ltd acquires more than 50 per cent of the voting shares in S1 Ltd for cash, and then S1 Ltd proceeds to acquire all of the voting shares of S2 Ltd. S2 Ltd would then be a sub-subsidiary of P Ltd.

These are only some of the more common ways by which one company becomes a subsidiary of another company.

16.6 Control by dominant influence

The issue of FRS 2 in 1992 introduced a further way of looking at whether or not one company had control of another. If one company has 'the right to exercise a dominant influence' over another undertaking, then the company with the dominating influence is deemed to have control of the other. **It is not necessary to have over 50 per cent of the voting share capital of a company in order to be able to exercise a dominant influence.** A dominant influence means that the holder of it has a right to give directions with regard to the operating and financial policies of another undertaking, and that the directors of that latter undertaking are obliged to comply, whether or not those directions are for the benefit of the undertaking.

In other words, if one undertaking can tell another undertaking what to do, both from an operating and a financial point of view, and the directors of that latter undertaking have to carry out such instructions, then such an undertaking will be a subsidiary undertaking. This is a much wider definition than merely looking at the amounts of the shareholdings.

Activity 16.2
How can an entity have a dominant influence when it does not own over 50 per cent of the voting share capital?

16.7 The nature of a group

Wherever two or more companies are in the relationship of parent and subsidiary undertakings, a 'group' is said to exist. When such a group exists then, besides the financial statements of the parent undertaking itself, to comply with legal requirements, there must be a set of financial statements prepared in respect of the group as a whole. These group financial statements are usually known as **consolidated financial statements**, because the financial statements of all the companies have had to be consolidated together to form one set of financial statements.

Sometimes parent undertakings carry on trading as well as investing in their subsidiaries. There are, however, other parent undertakings that do not trade at all, the whole of their activities being concerned with investing in other companies.

16.8 Subsidiary undertakings which are not limited companies

At one time, group financial statements consolidated only those financial statements which belonged to limited companies. In 1992, FRS 2 widened this so that a subsidiary undertaking can be other than a limited company. Share of ownership or the dominant influence approach will determine whether or not an entity is a subsidiary undertaking. If so, its financial statements are then consolidated in a similar fashion to those of limited companies.

Other forms of entity – associates and joint ventures – are not subsidiaries and are not consolidated. They are included in the financial statements according to the rules contained in FRS 9. These rules are dealt with in Chapter 26.

16.9 FRS 2: Accounting for subsidiary undertakings

The main changes brought about by FRS 2 were as follows:

1 The concept of 'dominant influence' widened the scope of which companies could be seen as subsidiary undertakings, rather than relying on share ownership.
2 Unincorporated businesses (i.e. not companies) were brought into its scope and came to be classed as subsidiary undertakings which have to have their financial statements consolidated with the rest of the group.

16.10 Teaching method

The method used in this book for teaching consolidated financial statements is that of showing the reader the adjustments needed on the face of the consolidated balance sheet, together with any workings necessary shown in a normal arithmetical fashion. The reasons why this method of illustrating consolidated financial statements has been chosen are as follows:

1 The authors believe that it is their job to try to help the reader understand the subject, and not just to be able to perform the necessary manipulations. They believe that, given understanding of what is happening, then the accounting entries necessary follow easily enough. Showing the adjustments on the face of the balance sheet gives a 'bird's-eye view' so that it is easier to see what is happening, rather than having to laboriously trace one's way through a complex set of double-entry adjustments made in ledger accounts.

2 This would be a much lengthier and more costly book if all of the double entry accounts were shown. It is better for a first look at consolidated financial statements to be an introduction to the subject only, rather than both an introduction and a very detailed survey of the subject. If students can understand the consolidated financial statements shown in this book, they will have a firm foundation which will enable them to tackle the more difficult and complicated aspects of the subject.

Learning outcomes

You should now have learnt:

1 Ordinary shareholders generally have voting rights, a right in the net assets of the company, and a right to an interest in profits earned.

2 Preference shareholders do not usually have any voting rights.

3 Ordinary shareholders receive copies of the financial statements for the company whose shares they hold, but not for any company whose shares are owned by the company they hold their shares in.

4 Consolidated financial statements provide shareholders in parent undertakings with financial statements incorporating the relevant data for all companies in the group – not just the parent company's own accounts data.

5 The status of 'subsidiary undertaking' is dependent upon the existence of control over that undertaking by another entity.

6 'Control' is determined by whether 'dominant influence' can be exerted, not simply by the level of investment in the company.

Answers to activities

16.1 Preference shareholders have far less risk in their investment than ordinary shareholders. In exchange for the greater risk they experience, the ordinary shareholders get voting rights that permit them to influence the decision-making of the company.

16.2 It could have a dominant influence by virtue of some agreement made with the company. For example, a bank may have dominant influence over the major decisions of a company in exchange for a loan it has granted to the company. Dominant influence is generally able to exist because of agreements between shareholders that result in one of the shareholders being granted the dominant influence.

REVIEW QUESTIONS

16.1 What determines whether or not one company is a subsidiary undertaking of another company?

16.2 How are incorporated businesses affected by the provisions of FRS 2?

16.3 What benefits accrue to the investor in a parent undertaking by the use of consolidated financial statements?

16.4 How did FRS 2 change the way in which consolidated financial statements should be drawn up?

CHAPTER 17

Consolidation of balance sheets: basic mechanics (I)

Learning objectives

After you have studied this chapter, you should be able to:

- explain the principle of cancellation that is adopted when preparing consolidated financial statements
- explain why goodwill may arise on consolidation
- calculate goodwill and include it in the consolidated balance sheet
- explain what is meant by the term 'minority interest'
- explain how the existence of reserves at the time of acquisition affects the preparation of consolidated financial statements

Introduction

In this chapter you'll learn how to consolidate financial statements where a subsidiary is wholly owned or partially owned, how to calculate and include positive goodwill in the consolidated balance sheet, and how to consolidate subsidiaries with reserves. Finally, you'll learn how to include negative goodwill in the consolidated financial statements.

17.1 Background

This chapter is concerned with the basic mechanics of consolidating balance sheets. The figures used will be quite small, as there is no virtue in obscuring the principles involved by bringing in large amounts. For the sake of brevity, some abbreviations will be used. As the consolidation of the financial statements of either two or three companies, but no more, will be attempted, then the abbreviations will be P for the parent undertaking, S1 the first subsidiary undertaking, and S2 the second subsidiary undertaking. Where there is only one subsidiary undertaking it will be shown as S. Unless stated to the contrary, all the shares will be ordinary shares of £1 each.

It will make the problems of the reader far easier if relatively simple balance sheets can be used to demonstrate the principles of consolidated financial statements. To this end, the balance sheets which follow in the next few chapters will usually have only two sorts of assets those of stock and cash at bank. This will save a great deal of time and effort. If every time a consolidated balance sheet were to be drawn up the reader had to deal with assets of land, buildings, patents, motor vehicles, plant and machinery, stock, debtors and bank balances, then they would not be using their time productively.

17.2 The principle of cancellation

The various financial statements of the parent undertaking and its subsidiary undertakings have to be brought together and consolidated into one set of financial statements for the whole of the group. Some items in one of the original sets of financial statements will also be found to refer to exactly the same transactions in one of the other sets of original final accounts.

Let us look at some of the more common examples:

1 An item which is a debtor in one balance sheet may be shown as a creditor in another balance sheet. If P Ltd had sold goods to S Ltd, its subsidiary, but S Ltd had not yet paid for them, then the item would be shown as a debtor in the balance sheet of P Ltd and as a creditor in the balance sheet of S Ltd.
2 Sales by one of the group to another company in the group will appear as sales in one company's accounts and purchases in another company's accounts.
3 Shares bought in one of the subsidiary undertakings by the parent undertaking will be shown as an investment on the assets side of the parent undertaking's balance sheet. In the balance sheet of the subsidiary, exactly those same shares will be shown as issued share capital.
4 Dividends paid by a subsidiary undertaking to its parent undertaking will be shown as paid dividends in the final accounts of the subsidiary, and as dividends received in the final accounts of the parent undertaking.

The group or consolidated financial statements are supposed to show how the group as a whole has dealt with the world outside. Transactions which are simply within the group do not represent dealings with the outside world. When all of the separate accounts of the companies within the group are put together such items need to be deleted, and will not appear in the consolidated financial statements of the group.

This therefore is the principle of cancellation. Similar things in different final accounts within the group should be cancelled out from each to arrive at the group's final accounts. All of the items already listed will therefore not appear in the consolidated financial statements.

This can be shown in the form of the diagram in Exhibit 17.1.

Exhibit 17.1 Consolidation of financial statements of a group

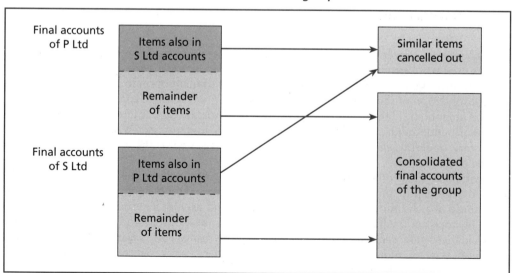

This means that a consolidated set of financial statements, where the subsidiaries are 100 per cent owned by the parent undertaking, will appear as follows:

Group Balance Sheet as at . . .

	£	£
Fixed assets (*less* Cancelled items)		XXXX
Current assets (*less* Cancelled items)	XXXX	
Less Current liabilities (*less* Cancelled items)	(XXXX)	
		XXXX
		XXXX
Financed by:		
Share capital (of the parent undertaking only, as the purchase		
of shares in the subsidiaries have cancelled out)		XXXX
Reserves (*less* Cancelled items)		XXXX
		XXXX

17.3 Rule 1

In consolidation, the first rule, therefore, is that like things cancel out each other. In fact, **cancellation accounts** are what consolidation financial statements are all about. It also helps the reader to see the issue more clearly if the consolidated balance sheet is constructed immediately after P has bought the shares in S. In fact, this may not be done in practice, but it is useful to use the method from a teaching point of view.

Exhibit 17.2

100 per cent of the shares of S bought at balance sheet value.

P has just bought all the shares of S. Before consolidation the balance sheets of P and S appear as follows:

P Balance Sheet

		£
Investment in subsidiary S	(A)	6
Bank		4
		10
Share capital		10
		10

S Balance Sheet

		£
Stock		5
Bank		1
		6
Share capital	(B)	6
		6

Now the consolidated balance sheet can be drawn up. The rule about like things cancelling out each other can now be applied. As can be seen, item A in P's balance sheet and item B in S's balance sheet are concerned with exactly the same thing, namely the 6 ordinary shares of S, and for the same amount, for the shares are shown in both balance sheets at £6. These are cancelled out when the consolidated balance sheet is drafted.

P & S Consolidated Balance Sheet

	£
Stock	5
Bank (£4 + £1)	5
	10
Share capital	10
	10

Exhibit 17.3

100 per cent of the shares of S bought for more than balance sheet value.

P Balance Sheet

		£
Investment in subsidiary S: 6 shares	(C)	9
Bank		1
		10
Share capital		10
		10

S Balance Sheet

		£
Stock		5
Bank		1
		6
Share capital	(D)	6
		6

Now (C) and (D) refer to like things, but the amounts are unequal. What has happened is that P has given £3 more than the book value for the shares of S. In accounting, where the amount paid (or 'consideration') for something exceeds the stated value, the difference is known as **goodwill**; and, when the consideration is less than the stated value, the difference is known as **negative goodwill**. (In practice, the accounting standards require that 'fair values', rather than book values are used – *see* Section 22.3; however, for the sake of clarity, unless otherwise indicated, the book values will be used throughout this book.) The consolidated balance sheet is therefore:

P and S Consolidated Balance Sheet

	£
Goodwill (C) £9 – (D) £6	3
Stock	5
Bank (£1 + £1)	2
	10
Share capital	10
	10

Exhibit 17.4

100 per cent of the shares of S bought for less than balance sheet value.

P Balance Sheet

		£
Investment in subsidiary S: 6 shares	(E)	4
Stock		5
Bank		1
		10
Share capital		10
		10

S Balance Sheet

		£
Stock		5
Bank		1
		6
Share capital	(F)	6
		6

P has bought all the shares of S, but has given only £4 for £6 worth of shares at balance sheet values. The £2 difference is negative goodwill. The uninitiated might look upon the £2 as being 'profit' but your knowledge of company financial statements should tell you that this difference could never be distributed as cash dividends. This negative goodwill is treated as a minus entry in the Goodwill section of the balance sheet under FRS 10: *Goodwill and intangible assets*.

Under FRS 10, the consolidated balance sheet appears as:

P and S Consolidated Balance Sheet

	£
Goodwill: negative goodwill (E) £4 – (F) £6	(2)
Stock (£5 + £5)	10
Bank (£1 + £1)	2
	10
Share capital	10

17.4 Cost of control

The expression **cost of control** could be used instead of 'goodwill'. This expression probably captures the essence of the purchase of the shares rather than calling it goodwill. It is precisely for the sake of gaining control of the assets of the company that the shares are bought. However, the expression 'goodwill' is more widely used and is correspondingly the one that will be used through the remainder of this book. Details of how to record entries in a 'cost of control' account can be seen in Section 23.4.

You can now attempt Review Questions 17.1, 17.2 and 17.3.

17.5 Rule 2

Rule 2 states that, although the whole of the shares of the subsidiary have not been bought, nonetheless the whole of the assets of the subsidiary (subject to certain intercompany transactions described later) will be shown in the consolidated balance sheet.

This rule comes about because of the choice made originally between two possible methods that could have been chosen. Suppose that P bought 75 per cent of the shares of S then the balance sheets could be displayed in one of two ways:

P and S Consolidated Balance Sheet (Method 1)

	£
Goodwill	xxxx
Assets of P: 100 per cent	xxxx
Assets of S: 75 per cent	xxxx
	xxxx
Share capital of P	xxxx
	xxxx

P and S Consolidated Balance Sheet (Method 2)

	£
Goodwill	XXXX
Assets of P: 100 per cent	XXXX
Assets of S: 100 per cent	XXXX
	XXXX
Share capital of P	XXXX
Claims of outsiders which equal 25 per cent of the assets of S	XXXX
	XXXX

It can be seen that both balance sheets show the amount of assets which P owns by virtue of its proportionate shareholding. On the other hand the second balance sheet gives a fuller picture, as it shows that P has control of all of the assets of S, although in fact it does not own all of them. The claims of outsiders come to 25 per cent of S and obviously they cannot control the assets of S, whereas P, with 75 per cent, can control the whole of the assets even though they are not fully owned by it. The second balance sheet method gives rather more meaningful information and is the method that is used for consolidated financial statements in accordance with FRS 2.

Assume that S has 6 shares of £1 each and that it has one asset, namely stock £6. P buys 4 shares for £1 each, £4. If the whole of the assets of S £6 are to be shown on the assets side of the consolidated balance sheet, and the cancellation of only £4 is to take place on the other side, then the consolidated balance sheet would not balance. Exhibit 17.5 shows this in detail before any attempt is made to get the consolidated balance sheet to balance.

Exhibit 17.5

P Balance Sheet

	£
Investment in subsidiary: 4 shares (bought today)	4
Stock	5
Bank	1
	10
Share capital	10
	10

S Balance Sheet

	£
Stock	6
Share capital	6

Now as the two extra shares have not been bought by P then they cannot be brought into any calculation of goodwill or negative goodwill. P has in fact bought four shares with a balance sheet value of £1 each, £4, for precisely £4. There is therefore no element of goodwill or negative goodwill. On the other hand, the consolidated balance sheet per Rule 2 must show the whole of the assets of S. This gives a consolidated balance sheet as follows:

P and S Consolidated Balance Sheet

	£
Stock (£5 + £6)	11
Bank	1
Share capital	10

Quite obviously, if you now inserted the totals, they would differ by £2. What is this £2? On reflection it can be seen to be the £2 shares not bought by P. These shares belong to outsiders, they are not owned by the group. These outsiders also hold less than 50 per cent of the voting shares of S. In fact, if they owned more, then S would probably not be a subsidiary company. The title given to the outside shareholders is the apt one therefore of **minority interest**. As the whole of the assets of S are shown in the consolidated balance sheet then part of these assets are owned by the minority interest. This claim against the assets is therefore shown on the capital side of the consolidated balance sheet. The consolidated balance sheet becomes:

P and S Consolidated Balance Sheet

	£
Stock (£5 + £6)	11
Bank	1
	12
Share capital	10
Minority interest	2
	12

This therefore is the convention of showing the whole of the assets of the subsidiary (less certain intercompany transactions) in the consolidated balance sheet, with the claim of the minority interest shown on the other side of the balance sheet.

Exhibit 17.6

Where less than 100 per cent of the subsidiary's shares are bought at more than book value.

P Balance Sheet

		£
Investment in subsidiary: 6 shares	(G)	8
Stock		11
Bank		1
		20
Share capital		20
		20

S Balance Sheet

		£
Stock		7
Bank		3
		10
Share capital	(I)	10
		10

P has bought 6 shares only, but has paid £8 for them. As the book value of the shares is £6, the £2 excess must therefore be goodwill. The cancellation is therefore £6 from (G) and £6 from (I), leaving £2 of (G) to be shown as goodwill in the consolidated balance sheet. The remaining £4 of (I) is in respect of shares held by the minority interest.

P and S Consolidated Balance Sheet

	£
Goodwill	2
Stock (£11 + £7)	18
Bank (£1 + £3)	4
	24
Share capital	20
Minority interest	4
	24

Exhibit 17.7

Where less than 100 per cent of the shares in the subsidiary are bought at less than book value.

P Balance Sheet

		£
Investment in subsidiary: 7 shares	(J)	5
Stock		13
Bank		2
		20
Share capital		20
		20

S Balance Sheet

		£
Stock		9
Bank		1
		10
Share capital	(K)	10
		10

Seven shares of S have now been bought for £5. This means that £5 of (J) and £5 of (K) cancel out with £2 shown as negative goodwill. The remaining £3 of (K) is in respect of the shares held by the minority interest and will be shown as such in the consolidated balance sheet.

P and S Consolidated Balance Sheet

	£
Goodwill: negative goodwill	(2)
Stock (£13 + £9)	22
Bank (£2 + £1)	3
	23
Shares	20
Minority interest	3
	23

You can now attempt Review Questions 17.6 and 17.7.

17.6 Taking over subsidiaries with reserves

So far, for reasons of simplification, the examples given have been of subsidiaries having share capital but no reserves. When reserves exist, as they do in the vast majority of firms, it must be remembered that they belong to the ordinary shareholders. This means that if P buys all the 10 shares of S for £15, and S at that point of time has a credit balance of £3 on its profit and loss account and a general reserve of £2, then what P acquires for its £15 is the full entitlement/rights of the 10 shares measured by/shown as:

	£
10 Shares	10
Profit and loss	3
General reserve	2
	15

This means that the £15 paid and the £15 entitlements as shown will cancel out each other and will not be shown in the consolidated balance sheet. This is shown by the balance sheets shown in Exhibit 17.8.

Exhibit 17.8

Where 100 per cent of the shares are bought at book value when the subsidiary has reserves.

P Balance Sheet

		£
Investment in subsidiary: 10 shares	(L)	15
Stock		11
Bank		2
		28
Share capital		20
Profit and loss		5
General reserve		3
		28

S Balance Sheet

		£
Stock		9
Bank		6
		15
Share capital	(M1)	10
Profit and loss	(M2)	3
General reserve	(M3)	2
		15

P and S Consolidated Balance Sheet

	£
Stock (£11 + £9)	20
Bank (£2 + £6)	8
	28
Share capital	20
Profit and loss	5
General reserve	3
	28

The cost of the shares (L) £15 is cancelled out exactly against (M1) £10 + (M2) £3 + (M3) £2 = £15. These are therefore the only items cancelled out and the remainder of the two balance sheets of P and S are then combined to be the consolidated balance sheet.

Exhibit 17.9

Where 100 per cent of the shares are bought at more than book value when the subsidiary has reserves.

P Balance Sheet

		£
Investment in subsidiary: 10 shares	(N)	23
Stock		7
Bank		5
		35
Share capital		20
Profit and loss		9
General reserve		6
		35

S Balance Sheet

		£
Stock		15
Bank		2
		17
Share capital	(O1)	10
Profit and loss	(O2)	4
General reserve	(O3)	3
		17

P paid £23 (N) for the entitlements (O1) £10 + (O2) £4 + (O3) £3 = £17, so that a figure of £6 will be shown in the consolidated balance sheet for Goodwill.

P and S Consolidated Balance Sheet

	£
Goodwill	6
Stock (£7 + £15)	22
Bank (£5 + £2)	7
	35
Share capital	20
Profit and loss	9
General reserve	6
	35

Exhibit 17.10

Where 100 per cent of the shares in the subsidiary are bought at below book value when the subsidiary has reserves.

P Balance Sheet

		£
Investment in subsidiary: 10 shares	(Z)	17
Stock		10
Bank		8
		35
Share capital		20
Profit and loss		6
General reserve		9
		35

S Balance Sheet

		£
Stock		16
Bank		5
		21
Share capital	(Q1)	10
Profit and loss	(Q2)	8
General reserve	(Q3)	3
		21

P has paid £17 (Z) for the benefits of (Q1) £10 + (Q2) £8 + (Q3) £3 = £21. This means that there will be negative goodwill of £21 − £17 = £4 in the consolidated balance sheet, while (Z), (Q1), (Q2) and (Q3), having been cancelled out, will not appear.

P and S Consolidated Balance Sheet

	£
Goodwill: negative goodwill	(4)
Stock (£10 + £16)	26
Bank (£8 + £5)	13
	35
Share capital	20
Profit and loss	6
General reserve	9
	35

Exhibit 17.11

Where less than 100 per cent of the shares are bought in a subsidiary which has reserves, and the shares are bought at the balance sheet value.

P Balance Sheet

		£
Investment in subsidiary: 8 shares	(R)	24
Stock		15
Bank		6
		45
Share capital		20
Profit and loss		17
General reserve		8
		45

S Balance Sheet

		£
Stock		21
Bank		9
		30
Share capital	(T1)	10
Profit and loss	(T2)	5
General reserve	(T3)	15
		30

The items (R) and the parts of (T1), (T2) and (T3) which are like things need to be cancelled out. The cancellation takes place from the share capital and reserves of S as follows:

	Total at acquisition date £	Bought by P 80 per cent £	Held by minority interest £
Share capital	10	8	2
Profit and loss	5	4	1
General reserve	15	12	3
	30	24	6

The amount paid by P was £24, and as P acquired a total of £24 value of shares and reserves the cancellation takes place without there being any figure of positive or negative goodwill. The consolidated balance sheet therefore appears:

P and S Consolidated Balance Sheet

	£
Stock (£15 + £21)	36
Bank (£6 + £9)	15
	51
Share capital	20
Profit and loss	17
General reserve	8
Minority interest	6
	51

Activity 17.1

What are the two rules of consolidation?

17.7 Partial control at a price not equal to balance sheet value

In Exhibit 17.11 the amount paid for the 80 per cent of the shares of S was equal to the balance sheet value of the shares in that it amounted to £24. Rarely will it be so, as the price is normally different from balance sheet value. If an amount paid is greater than the balance sheet value then the excess will be shown as goodwill in the consolidated balance sheet; while if a smaller amount than balance sheet value is paid then the difference is negative goodwill and will be shown as such in the consolidated balance sheet. Using the balance sheet figure of S in Exhibit 17.11, if P had paid £30 for 80 per cent of the shares of S then the consolidated balance sheet would show a goodwill figure of £6. If, instead, £21 only had been paid then the consolidated balance sheet would show £3 negative goodwill.

When the acquisition of two subsidiaries brings out in the calculations a figure of goodwill in respect of the acquisition of one subsidiary, and a figure for negative goodwill in respect of the acquisition of the other subsidiary, the two figures should be shown separately in the consolidated balance sheet, followed by the net figure. For instance if P had acquired two subsidiaries S1 and S2 where the calculations showed a figure of £10 for goodwill on the acquisition of S1 and a figure of £4 negative goodwill on the acquisition of S2, then the consolidated balance sheet would show a figure for goodwill of £10 and a figure for negative goodwill of £4.

The final exhibit in this chapter is a composite one, bringing in most of the points already shown.

Exhibit 17.12

Where two subsidiaries have been acquired, both with reserves, full control being acquired of one subsidiary and a partial control of the other subsidiary.

P Balance Sheet

		£
Investment in subsidiaries:		
S1 10 shares	(U)	37
S2 7 shares	(V)	39
Stock		22
Bank		2
		100
Share capital		40
Profit and loss		50
General reserve		10
		100

S1 Balance Sheet

		£
Stock		19
Bank		11
		30
Share capital	(W1)	10
Profit and loss	(W2)	12
General reserve	(W3)	8
		30

S2 Balance Sheet

		£
Stock		42
Bank		18
		60
Share capital	(X1)	10
Profit and loss	(X2)	30
General reserve	(X3)	20
		60

With the acquisition of S1 P has paid £37 for (W1) £10 + (W2) £12 + (W3) £8 = £30, giving a figure of £7 for goodwill. With the acquisition of S2 P has given £39 for $^{7}/_{10}$ of the following: (X1) £10 + (X2) £30 + (X3) £20 = £60 × $^{7}/_{10}$ = £42, giving a figure of £3 for negative goodwill. The two figures should be shown separately in the consolidated balance sheet.

P and S1 and S2 Consolidated Balance Sheet

		£
Goodwill		7
Negative goodwill		(3)
		4
Stock (£22 + £19 + £42)		83
Bank (£2 + £11 + £18)		31
		118
Share capital		40
Profit and loss		50
General reserve		10
Minority interest:		
$^{3}/_{10}$ of (X1)	3	
$^{3}/_{10}$ of (X2)	9	
$^{3}/_{10}$ of (X3)	6	
		18
		118

Now work through Review Questions 17.10 and 17.11.

Learning outcomes

You should now have learnt:

1 Some items in the financial statements of one of the group companies will refer to exactly the same transactions as in the financial statements of one of the other group companies and they will need to be cancelled out when the consolidated financial statements are prepared (*Rule 1*).

2 Where the consideration exceeds the balance sheet value acquired, goodwill arises.

3 Where the consideration is less than the balance sheet value acquired, the negative goodwill is treated as a negative entry in the Goodwill section of the balance sheet under FRS 10.

4 The treatment of goodwill is governed by FRS 10. (*See* Chapter 10.)

5 Minority interests exist when less than 100 per cent of the share capital of a subsidiary is owned at the balance sheet date.

6 All the assets of a subsidiary are included in the consolidated financial statements, even where less than 100 per cent of the share capital has been acquired (*Rule 2*).

7 When a subsidiary has reserves at the date of acquisition, those reserves are treated as part of the capital acquired and the calculation of goodwill includes the relevant proportion of the reserves.

8 When goodwill arises in respect of consolidation of one subsidiary and a negative goodwill arises on another, the two amounts should be shown separately in the consolidated financial statements.

Answers to activities

17.1 Rule 1: items in the financial statements of one of the group companies that refer to exactly the same transactions as in the financial statements of one of the other group companies need to be cancelled out when the consolidated financial statements are prepared.

Rule 2: all the assets of a subsidiary are included in the consolidated financial statements, even where less than 100 per cent of the share capital has been acquired.

REVIEW QUESTIONS

17.1 The following balance sheets were drawn up immediately P Ltd had acquired control of S Ltd. You are to draw up a consolidated balance sheet.

P Balance Sheet

	£
Investment in S: 100 shares	110
Stock	60
Bank	30
	200
Share capital	200
	200

S Balance Sheet

	£
Stock	80
Bank	20
	100
Share capital	100
	100

17.2 You are to draw up a consolidated balance sheet from the following balance sheets of P Ltd and S Ltd which were drawn up immediately P Ltd had acquired the shares in S Ltd.

P Balance Sheet

	£
Investment in S Ltd: 3,000 shares	2,700
Fixed assets	2,000
Stock	800
Debtors	400
Bank	100
	6,000
Share capital	6,000
	6,000

S Balance Sheet

	£
Fixed assets	1,800
Stock	700
Debtors	300
Bank	200
	3,000
Share capital	3,000
	3,000

17.3   Draw up a consolidated balance sheet from the following balance sheets which were drawn up as soon as P Ltd had acquired control of S Ltd.

P Balance Sheet

	£
Investment in S Ltd: 60,000 shares	60,000
Fixed assets	28,000
Stock	6,000
Debtors	5,000
Bank	1,000
	100,000
Share capital	100,000
	100,000

S Balance Sheet

	£
Fixed assets	34,000
Stock	21,000
Debtors	3,000
Bank	2,000
	60,000
Share capital	60,000
	60,000

17.4A   P Ltd acquires all the shares in S Ltd and then the following balance sheets are drawn up. You are to draw up a consolidated balance sheet.

P Balance Sheet

	£
Investment in S Ltd	29,000
Fixed assets	5,000
Stock	4,000
Debtors	3,000
Bank	1,000
	42,000
Share capital	42,000
	42,000

S Balance Sheet

	£
Fixed assets	12,000
Stock	6,000
Debtors	4,000
Bank	2,000
	24,000
Share capital	24,000
	24,000

17.5A Draw up a consolidated balance sheet from the balance sheets of P Ltd and S Ltd that were drafted immediately the shares in S Ltd were acquired by P Ltd.

P Balance Sheet

	£
Investment in S Ltd: 63,000 shares	50,000
Fixed assets	18,000
Stock	5,000
Debtors	4,000
Bank	3,000
	80,000
Share capital	80,000
	80,000

S Balance Sheet

	£
Fixed assets	48,000
Stock	6,000
Debtors	5,000
Bank	4,000
	63,000
Share capital	63,000
	63,000

17.6 P Ltd acquires 60 per cent of the shares in S Ltd. Balance sheets are then drafted immediately. You are to draw up the consolidated balance sheet.

P Balance Sheet

	£
Investment in S Ltd: 1,200 shares	1,500
Fixed assets	900
Stock	800
Debtors	600
Bank	200
	4,000
Share capital	4,000
	4,000

S Balance Sheet

	£
Fixed assets	1,100
Stock	500
Debtors	300
Bank	100
	2,000
Share capital	2,000
	2,000

17.7   P Ltd acquires 95 per cent of the shares of S Ltd. The following balance sheets are then drafted. You are to draw up the consolidated balance sheet.

P Balance Sheet

	£
Investment in S: 2,850 shares	2,475
Fixed assets	2,700
Stock	1,300
Debtors	1,400
Bank	125
	8,000
Share capital	8,000
	8,000

S Balance Sheet

	£
Fixed assets	625
Stock	1,700
Debtors	600
Bank	75
	3,000
Share capital	3,000
	3,000

17.8A   P Ltd buys $66^2/_3$ per cent of the shares in S Ltd. You are to draw up the consolidated balance sheet from the following balance sheets constructed immediately control had been achieved.

P Balance Sheet

	£
Investment in S: 600 shares	540
Fixed assets	1,160
Stock	300
Debtors	200
Bank	100
	2,300
Share capital	2,300
	2,300

S Balance Sheet

	£
Fixed assets	400
Stock	200
Debtors	240
Bank	60
	900
Share capital	900
	900

17.9A   After P Ltd acquired 75 per cent of the shares of S Ltd the following balance sheets are drawn up. You are to draw up the consolidated balance sheet.

P Balance Sheet

	£
Investments in S Ltd: 1,200 shares	1,550
Fixed assets	2,450
Stock	1,000
Debtors	800
Bank	200
	6,000
Share capital	6,000
	6,000

S Balance Sheet

	£
Fixed assets	800
Stock	400
Debtors	250
Bank	150
	1,600
Share capital	1,600
	1,600

17.10 Immediately after P Ltd had acquired control of S1 Ltd and S2 Ltd the following balance sheets were drawn up. You are to draw up a consolidated balance sheet.

P Balance Sheet

	£
Investments in subsidiaries:	
S1 Ltd (3,000 shares)	3,800
S2 Ltd (3,200 shares)	4,700
Fixed assets	5,500
Current assets	2,500
	16,500
Share capital	10,000
Profit and loss account	6,500
	16,500

S1 Balance Sheet

	£
Fixed assets	2,200
Current assets	1,300
	3,500
Share capital	3,000
Profit and loss account	400
General reserve	100
	3,500

S2 Balance Sheet

	£
Fixed assets	4,900
Current assets	2,100
	7,000
Share capital	4,000
Profit and loss account	1,000
General reserve	2,000
	7,000

17.11   Immediately after P Ltd had acquired control of S1 Ltd and S2 Ltd the following balance sheets were drawn up. You are to draw up a consolidated balance sheet.

P Balance Sheet

	£
Investment in subsidiaries:	
S1 Ltd (1,800 shares)	4,200
S2 Ltd (2,000 shares)	2,950
Fixed assets	4,150
Current assets	2,100
	13,400
Share capital	10,000
Profit and loss account	2,000
General reserve	1,400
	13,400

S1 Balance Sheet

	£
Fixed assets	3,500
Current assets	2,500
	6,000
Share capital	3,000
Profit and loss account	1,200
General reserve	1,800
	6,000

S2 Balance Sheet

	£
Fixed assets	1,800
Current assets	1,400
	3,200
Share capital	2,000
Profit and loss account	500
General reserve	700
	3,200

17.12A   Immediately after P Ltd had achieved control of S1 Ltd and S2 Ltd the following balance sheets are drawn up. You are to draw up the consolidated balance sheet.

P Balance Sheet

	£
Investments in subsidiaries:	
S1 Ltd 4,000 shares	6,150
S2 Ltd 6,000 shares	8,950
Fixed assets	3,150
Current assets	2,050
	20,300
Share capital	15,000
Profit and loss account	2,000
General reserve	3,300
	20,300

S1 Balance Sheet

	£
Fixed assets	5,300
Current assets	1,200
	6,500
Share capital	4,000
Profit and loss account	1,100
General reserve	1,400
	6,500

S2 Balance Sheet

	£
Fixed assets	6,000
Current assets	3,450
	9,450
Share capital	7,000
Profit and loss account	1,400
General reserve	1,050
	9,450

17.13A The following balance sheets of P Ltd, S1 Ltd and S2 Ltd were drawn up as soon as P Ltd had acquired the shares in both subsidiaries. You are to draw up a consolidated balance sheet.

P Balance Sheet

	£
Investments in subsidiaries:	
S1 Ltd 3,500 shares	6,070
S2 Ltd 2,000 shares	5,100
Fixed assets	2,030
Current assets	1,400
	14,600
Share capital	11,000
Profit and loss account	1,000
General reserve	2,600
	14,600

S1 Balance Sheet

	£
Fixed assets	4,800
Current assets	2,400
	7,200
Share capital	5,000
Profit and loss account	900
General reserve	1,300
	7,200

S2 Balance Sheet

	£
Fixed assets	2,800
Current assets	900
	3,700
Share capital	2,000
Profit and loss account	1,400
General reserve	300
	3,700

CHAPTER 18

Consolidation of balance sheets: basic mechanics (II)

Learning objectives

After you have studied this chapter, you should be able to:

- explain the implications when the date of acquisition and the group balance sheet date do not coincide
- explain that the calculation of goodwill is performed as at the date of acquisition
- describe the difference in treatment between pre- and post-acquisition reserves of subsidiary undertakings

Introduction

In this chapter you'll learn that goodwill is calculated on the basis of the financial position at the date of acquisition and that it does not change thereafter. You'll also learn that reserves acquired are not available for distribution and you'll learn how to show post-acquisition profits and losses in the consolidated balance sheet.

18.1 Background

In the previous chapter, the consolidation of balance sheets was looked at as if the consolidated balance sheets were drawn up immediately the shares in the subsidiary had been acquired. This is rarely the case in practice. However, even though the consolidation will likely be performed at the end of the accounting period and some time after the acquisition, it must also be looked *at as at the time the acquisition occurred*. Correspondingly, the balance on the profit and loss account of the subsidiary, and possibly the balances on the other reserve accounts, will have altered when compared with the figures at the date of acquisition.

18.2 Goodwill in later years' financial statements

In Chapter 17 the goodwill, positive or negative, was calculated at the date of acquisition, and this calculation remains unchanged as the years go by. It is important to understand this. Say, for instance, that the calculation of goodwill was made on an acquisition made on 31 December 20X3 and that the figure was £5,000. Even if the calculation were made one year later, on 31 December 20X4, then the calculation must refer to the reserves etc. as on 31 December 20X3 as this is when they were acquired, and so the figure of goodwill will still be £5,000. This would be true even if five years went by before anyone performed the calculation.

In practice, therefore, once the figure of goodwill has been calculated there is absolutely no need to recalculate it every year. However, in examinations the goodwill figure will still have to be calculated even though the consolidated balance sheet being drawn up is 5, 10 or 20 years after the company became a subsidiary. This has to be done because the previous working papers are not available to an examinee.

18.3 Capital reserves

Since 1981, companies have had the power to purchase their own shares, previous holders of the shares ceasing to be shareholders upon completion of the transaction. However, unless special permission were granted by the court, it is outside the law for any company to otherwise return its capital to the shareholders. If a parent undertaking were to pay its money in order to acquire a company as a subsidiary, and then distributed as dividends the assets that it had bought, this would really be the same as returning its capital to its shareholders. The situation described can best be illustrated by a simple example. P pays £15 to acquire 100 per cent of the shares of S, and the share capital of S consists of £10 of shares and £5 profit and loss account. Thus to acquire a capital asset, i.e. ownership of S, the holding company has parted with £15. If the balance of the profit and loss account of S were merely added to the profit and loss balance of P in the consolidated balance sheet, then the £5 balance of S could be regarded as being distributable as cash dividends to the shareholders of P. As this £5 of reserves has been bought as a capital asset then a dividend payment that was in part funded by this £5 of reserves would amount to a return of capital to the shareholders of P.

To prevent this, the balance of the profit and loss account of S on acquisition is capitalised, i.e. it is brought into the balance sheet through the calculation of goodwill and is not shown in the consolidated balance sheet as a profit and loss account balance. On the other hand, the whole of any profit made by S since acquisition will clearly belong to P's shareholders as P owns 100 per cent of the shares of S.

Activity 18.1

Why do you think it would be a 'bad' thing to distribute as dividends the reserves acquired in this way?

Exhibit 18.1

Where the parent undertaking holds 100 per cent of the subsidiary undertaking's shares.

P acquires the shares on 31 December 20X4. The balance sheets one year later are as follows:

P Balance Sheet as at 31 December 20X5

		£
Investment in subsidiary: 10 shares bought 31.12.20X4	(A)	18
Stock		11
Bank		3
		32
Share capital		20
Profit and loss		12
		32

S Balance Sheet as at 31 December 20X5

	£	£
Stock		14
Bank		2
		16
Share capital	(B)	10
Profit and loss:		
As at 31.12.20X4	(C)	5
Profit for 20X5	(D)	1
		6
		16

The shares were acquired on 31 December 20X4, therefore the calculation of the goodwill is based on the financial position of those firms at that date. Thus P obtained the following for (A) £18 at 31 December 20X4: shares (B) £10 and profit and loss (C) £5 = £15. Goodwill therefore amounted to £3. The profit made by S during 20X5 was obviously made after acquisition and does not therefore come into the goodwill calculation. The figure of (D) £1 is a reserve which belongs wholly to P, as P in fact owns all of the shares of S. This (D) £1 is added to the reserves shown in the consolidated balance sheet.

P Consolidated Balance Sheet as at 31 December 20X5

	£
Goodwill	3
Stock (£11 + £14)	25
Bank (£3 + £2)	5
	33
Share capital	20
Profit and loss (P £12 + S £1)	13
	33

Exhibit 18.2

Where the parent holds 100 per cent of the shares of the subsidiary and there is a post-acquisition loss.

P Balance Sheet as at 31 December 20X5

	£	£
Investment in subsidiary:		
10 shares bought 31.12.20X4	(E)	19
Stock		10
Bank		4
		33
Share capital		20
Profit and loss:		
As at 31.12.20X4	7	
Add Profit 20X5	6	
		13
		33

S Balance Sheet as at 31 December 20X5

	£	£
Stock		9
Bank		2
		11
Share capital	(F)	10
Profit and loss		
As at 31.12.20X4	(G) 4	
Less Loss 20X5	(I) (3)	
		1
		11

In calculating goodwill, the items (F) £10 and (G) £4 are cancelled against the amount paid (E) £19, thus the goodwill is £5. The loss (I) has been incurred since acquisition. A profit since acquisition, as in Exhibit 18.1, adds to the reserves in the consolidated balance sheet, therefore a loss must be deducted.

P Consolidated Balance Sheet as at 31 December 20X5

	£
Goodwill	5
Stock (£10 + £9)	19
Bank (£4 + £2)	6
	30
Share capital	20
Profit and loss (£13 – (I)£3)	10
	30

Exhibit 18.3

Where the parent acquires less than 100 per cent of the shares of the subsidiary and there is a post-acquisition profit.

P Balance Sheet as at 31 December 20X5

		£	£
Investment in subsidiary: 8 shares bought 31.12.20X4	(J)		28
Stock			7
Bank			3
			38
Share capital			20
Profit and loss			
As at 31.12.20X4		10	
Add Profit 20X5		8	
			18
			38

S Balance Sheet as at 31 December 20X5

		£	£
Stock			28
Bank			2
			30
Share capital	(K)		10
Profit and loss			
As at 31.12.20X4	(L)	15	
Add Profit 20X5	(M)	5	
	(N)		20
			30

P has given (J) £28 to take over 80 per cent of (K) + (L), i.e. 80 per cent of (£10 + £15) = £20. Therefore goodwill is £8. The profit for 20X5 (M) £5 is also owned 80 per cent by P = £4, and as this has been earned since the shares in S were bought the whole of this belongs to the shareholders of P and is also distributable to them, therefore it can be shown with other profit and loss account balances in the consolidated balance sheet.

The minority interest is 20 per cent of (K) £10 + (N) £20 = £6. It must be pointed out that, although the holding company splits up the profit and loss account balances into pre-acquisition and post-acquisition, there is no point in the minority interest doing likewise. It would, however, amount to exactly the same answer if they did, because 20 per cent of (K) £10 + (L) £15 + (M) £5 still comes to £6, i.e. exactly the same as 20 per cent of (N) £20 + (K) £10 = £6.

P Consolidated Balance Sheet as at 31 December 20X5

	£
Goodwill	8
Stock (£7 + £28)	35
Bank (£3 + £2)	5
	48
Share capital	20
Profit and loss (P £18 + £4)	22
Minority interest (shares £2 + profit and loss £4)	6
	48

If there had been a post-acquisition loss, then this would have been deducted from P's profit and loss account balance of £18 when the consolidated balance sheet was drawn up.

Learning outcomes

You should now have learnt:

1 Goodwill must be calculated on the basis of the fair values at the date of acquisition of the consideration given and the net assets acquired.

2 Once calculated, there is no point in recalculating the goodwill on an acquisition at a future balance sheet date as the value determined will not alter.

3 Pre-acquisition reserves of a subsidiary are part of the capital acquired and are cancelled out on consolidation; they are not treated as reserves of the group.

4 Pre-acquisition reserves acquired are not available for distribution to the shareholders of the parent company.

5 The group's share of a subsidiary undertaking's post-acquisition profits and losses are included on consolidation with the reserves of the rest of the group.

Answers to activities

18.1 The £5 reserves acquired by P on acquisition of S were not earned by P and do not represent profits made by P. As such, it would be inappropriate to distribute them in this way.

REVIEW QUESTIONS

18.1 P Ltd buys 100 per cent of the shares of S Ltd on 31 December 20X5. The balance sheets of the two companies on 31 December 20X6 are as shown. You are to draw up a consolidated balance sheet as at 31 December 20X6.

P Balance Sheet as at 31 December 20X6

	£	£
Investment in subsidiary:		
4,000 shares bought 31.12.20X5		5,750
Fixed assets		5,850
Current assets		2,400
		14,000
Share capital		10,000
Profit and loss account:		
As at 31.12.20X5	1,500	
Add Profit for 20X6	2,500	
		4,000
		14,000

S Balance Sheet as at 31 December 20X6

	£	£
Fixed assets		5,100
Current assets		1,500
		6,600
Share capital		4,000
Profit and loss account:		
As at 31.12.20X5	800	
Add Profit for 20X6	1,800	
		2,600
		6,600

18.2   P Ltd buys 70 per cent of the shares of S Ltd on 31 December 20X8. The balance sheets of the two companies on 31 December 20X9 are as follows. You are to draw up a consolidated balance sheet as at 31 December 20X9.

P Balance Sheet as at 31 December 20X9

	£	£
Investment in S Ltd:		
7,000 shares bought 31.12.20X8		7,800
Fixed assets		39,000
Current assets		22,200
		69,000
Share capital		50,000
Profit and loss account:		
As at 31.12.20X8	4,800	
Add Profit for 20X9	9,200	
		14,000
General reserve		5,000
		69,000

S Balance Sheet as at 31 December 20X9

	£	£
Fixed assets		8,400
Current assets		4,900
		13,300
Share capital		10,000
Profit and loss account:		
As at 31.12.20X8	1,700	
Less Loss for 20X9	(400)	
		1,300
General reserve (unchanged since 20X5)		2,000
		13,300

18.3A   P Ltd bought 55 per cent of the shares in S Ltd on 31 December 20X6. From the following balance sheets you are to draw up the consolidated balance sheet as at 31 December 20X7.

P Balance Sheet as at 31 December 20X7

	£	£
Investment in S Ltd: 2,750 shares *Nc*		4,850
Fixed assets		13,150
Current assets		13,500
		31,500
Share capital		30,000
Profit and loss account:		
As at 31.12.20X6	900	
Add Profit for 20X7	600	
		1,500
		31,500

S Balance Sheet as at 31 December 20X7

	£	£
Fixed assets		4,600
Current assets		3,100
		7,700
Share capital		5,000
Profit and loss account:		
As at 31.12.20X6	700	
Add Profit for 20X7	500	
		1,200
General reserve (unchanged since 20X6)		1,500
		7,700

18.4   P buys shares in S1 and S2 on 31 December 20X4. You are to draft the consolidated balance sheet as at 31 December 20X5 from the following:

P Balance Sheet as at 31 December 20X5

	£	£
Investment:		
S1: 6,000 shares		8,150
S2: 8,000 shares		11,400
Fixed assets		21,000
Current assets		12,000
		52,550
Share capital		40,000
Profit and loss account:		
As at 31.12.20X4	2,350	
Add Profit for 20X5	5,200	
		7,550
General reserve		5,000
		52,550

S1 Balance Sheet as at 31 December 20X5

	£	£
Fixed assets		9,900
Current assets		4,900
		14,800
Share capital		10,000
Profit and loss account:		
As at 31.12.20X4	1,100	
Add Profit for 20X5	1,700	
		2,800
General reserve (same as 31.12.20X4)		2,000
		14,800

S2 Balance Sheet as at 31 December 20X5

	£	£
Fixed assets		6,000
Current assets		4,000
		10,000
Share capital		8,000
Profit and loss account:		
As at 31.12.20X4	500	
Less Loss for 20X5	(300)	
		200
General reserve (same as 31.12.20X4)		1,800
		10,000

18.5A P Ltd bought 40,000 shares in S1 Ltd and 27,000 shares in S2 Ltd on 31 December 20X2. The following balance sheets were drafted as at 31 December 20X3. You are to draw up a consolidated balance sheet as at 31 December 20X3.

P Balance Sheet as at 31 December 20X3

	£	£
Investments in subsidiaries		
S1 Ltd 40,000 shares		49,000
S2 Ltd 27,000 shares		30,500
Fixed assets		90,000
Current assets		80,500
		250,000
Share capital		200,000
Profit and loss account:		
As at 31.12.20X2	11,000	
Add Profit for 20X3	16,000	
		27,000
General reserve		23,000
		250,000

S1 Balance Sheet as at 31 December 20X3

	£	£
Fixed assets		38,200
Current assets		19,200
		57,400
Share capital		50,000
Profit and loss account:		
As at 31.12.20X2	3,000	
Less Loss for 20X3	(1,600)	
		1,400
General reserve (as at 31.12.20X2)		6,000
		57,400

S2 Balance Sheet as at 31 December 20X3

	£	£
Fixed assets		31,400
Current assets		14,600
		46,000
Share capital		36,000
Profit and loss account:		
As at 31.12.20X2	4,800	
Add Profit for 20X3	3,400	
		8,200
General reserve (as at 31.12.20X2)		1,800
		46,000

18.6A   The following information relates to Heather Limited and its subsidiary, Thistle Limited.

1 *Heather Limited*
   Retained profits as at 31 March 20X8 £700,000.
   80,000 ordinary shares were purchased in Thistle Limited on 1 April 20X1 for £150,000.

2 *Thistle Limited*
   Retained profits as at 1 April 20X1 £50,000.
   Retained profits as at 31 March 20X8 £120,000.
   There were no other capital or revenue account balances at either of these dates.
   Issued share capital: 100,000 ordinary shares of £1 each.

3 Goodwill arising on consolidation is written off immediately on acquisition against reserves.

Required:
Make the following calculations:
(a) the goodwill arising on the acquisition of Thistle Limited;
(b) the retained profits to be shown in the Heather Group balance sheet as at 31 March 20X8;
(c) the minority interest in the Heather Group as at 31 March 20X8.

(Association of Accounting Technicians)

CHAPTER 19

Intercompany dealings: indebtedness and unrealised profit in stocks

After you have studied this chapter, you should be able to:
- explain how to treat intragroup indebtedness upon consolidation
- explain how to treat unrealised intragroup profits upon consolidation

Introduction

In this chapter you'll learn how to deal with intragroup debts and unrealised profits in stocks sold between companies in a group.

19.1 Intragroup debts

When a subsidiary owes money to the parent, then the amount owing will be shown as a debtor in the parent's balance sheet and as a creditor in the subsidiary's balance sheet. Such debts in fact have to be shown separately from other debts so as to comply with the Companies Acts. Such a debt between these two companies is, however, the same debt and, following the rule that like things cancel out, the consolidated balance sheet will show neither debtor nor creditor for this amount as cancellation will have taken place. The same treatment would apply to debts owed by the parent to the subsidiary, or to debts owed by one subsidiary to another subsidiary. The treatment is exactly the same whether the subsidiary is 100 per cent owned or not.

Exhibit 19.1

Where the subsidiary owes money to the parent.

P Balance Sheet

		£	£
Investment in subsidiary: 10 shares			10
Stock			13
Debtors:			
Owing from subsidiary	(A)	4	
Other debtors		7	
			11
Bank			1
			35
Share capital			20
Profit and loss			6
Creditors			9
			35

S Balance Sheet

		£	£
Stock			6
Debtors			13
Bank			3
			22
Share capital			10
Creditors:			
Owing to parent	(B)	4	
Other creditors		8	
			12
			22

P & S Consolidated Balance Sheet

	£
Stock (£13 + £6)	19
Debtors (£7 + £13)	20
Bank (£1 + £3)	4
	43
Share capital	20
Profit and loss	6
Creditors (£9 + £8)	17
	43

19.2 Unrealised profit in stock-in-trade

It is possible that companies in a group may not have traded with each other. In that case the stocks-in-trade at the balance sheet date will not include goods bought from another member of the group.

It is also possible that the companies may have traded with each other but, at the balance sheet date, all of the goods traded with each other have been sold to firms outside the group. The result is that none of the companies in the group will have any of such goods included in its stock-in-trade.

However, it is also possible that the companies have traded with each other, and that one or more of the companies has goods in its stock-in-trade at the balance sheet date which have been bought from another group member. If the goods have been traded between members of the group at cost price, the goods would be included in the purchasing company's stock-in-trade in its balance sheet. In this circumstance, the consolidated balance sheet will not be altered just because the location of stock-in-trade has moved from one group company to another. Because the goods were transferred at cost price it will not offend accounting practice to add together all of the stock figures in the group company balance sheets and show the total in the consolidated balance sheet, as the total will represent the total cost to the group of the unsold goods within the group.

However, goods are usually sold between members of a group at prices above the original cost price paid by the first member of the group to acquire them. If one or more of the companies in a group has goods in its stock-in-trade at the balance sheet date which have been bought from another group member at above cost price, the goods would be included at the higher price in the purchasing company's stock-in-trade in its balance sheet. You can't then simply add together all of the stock figures in the group company balance sheets and show the total in the consolidated balance sheet. The total derived would not represent the total cost of the unsold goods held within the group.

> ### Activity 19.1
> If the amount at which the stock is included in the balance sheet of each company is the amount the stock cost that company, why would the total derived not represent the total cost of the unsold goods within the group?

Suppose that the parent owns all the shares in S, the subsidiary, and that P had sold to S for £20 goods which had cost it £12. Assume in addition that S had sold none of these goods by the balance sheet date. In the balance sheet of S the goods will be included in stock-in-trade at £20, while the profits made by P will include the £8 profit recorded in buying the goods for £12 and selling them for £20. Although this is true from each company's point of view, it most certainly is not true from the group viewpoint. The goods have not passed to anyone outside the group, and therefore the profit of £8 has not been realised by the group.

> ### Activity 19.2
> Why do you think this intragroup profit must be eliminated upon consolidation?

> ### Activity 19.3
> What could be the benefit to a group if companies within the group were to sell goods to other companies in the group at below cost?

19.3 Realisation of profits

Going back to the basic accounting concepts, the realisation concept states that profit should not be recognised until the goods have been passed to the customer. As the consolidated accounts are concerned with an overall picture of the group, and the profits have not been realised by the group, then such profits should be eliminated. Accordingly the figure of £8 should be deducted from the profit and loss account of P on consolidation, and the same amount should be deducted from the stock-in-trade of S on consolidation. This cancels an unrealised intragroup profit.

If P had sold goods which had cost it £12 to S, a 100 per cent owned subsidiary, for £20, and S had sold ³/₄ of the goods for £22 by the balance sheet date then the picture would be different. P will have shown a profit in its profit and loss account for these sales of £8. In addition S will have shown a profit in its profit and loss account for the sales made of £7, i.e. £22 − ³/₄ of £20. The two profit and loss accounts show total profits of £8 + £7 = £15. So far, however, looking at the group as a whole, these goods have cost the group £12. Three-quarters of these have been sold to firms outside the group, so that the cost of goods sold outside the group is ³/₄ of £12 = £9, and as these were sold by S the profit realised by the group is £22 − £9 = £13. This is £2 less than that shown by adding up the separate figures for each company in the group.

Thus the group figures would be overstated by £2 if the separate figures were merely added together without any adjustment. In addition, the stock-in-trade would be overvalued by £2 if the two separate figures were added together because the remaining stock-in-trade of S includes one-quarter of the goods bought from P, i.e. ¹/₄ of £20 = £5, but the original cost to the group was ¹/₄ of £12 = £3. The adjustment needed is that in the consolidation process £2 will be deducted from the profit and loss balance of P and £2 will be deducted

from the stock-in-trade of S, thus removing any unrealised intragroup profits. This could be expressed in tabular form as:

		£
(a)	Cost of goods to P	12
(b)	Sold to S for	20
(c)	Sold by S, $^3/_4$ for	22
(d)	Stock of S at balance sheet date at cost to S $^1/_4$ of (b)	5
(e)	Stock of S at balance sheet date at cost to P $^1/_4$ of (a)	3
(f)	Excess of S balance sheet value of stock over cost to group (d) – (e)	2

(g) Profit shown in P profit and loss account (b) – (a) = £8
(h) Profit shown in S profit and loss account (c) £22 – $^3/_4$ of (b) = £7
(i) Profit shown in the profit and loss accounts of P and S = (g) + (h) = £15
(j) Actual profit made by the group dealing with outsiders (c) £22 less [$^3/_4$ of (a) £12] £9 = £13
(k) Profit recorded by individual companies exceeds profit made by the group's dealing with outsiders (i) – (j) = £2

The action needed for the consolidated balance sheet is therefore to deduct (f) £2 from the combined stock figure, and to deduct (k) £2 from the combined profit and loss account figure.

Exhibit 19.2

Where the stock-in-trade of one company includes goods bought from another company in the group.

P Balance Sheet as at 31 December 20X3

		£	£
Investment in subsidiary:			
10 shares bought 31.12.20X2			16
Stock-in-trade			24
Bank			6
			46
Share capital			20
Profit and loss account:			
As at 31.12.20X2		8	
Profit for 20X3	(C)	18	
			26
			46

S Balance Sheet as at 31 December 20X3

		£	£
Stock-in-trade	(D)		22
Bank			3
			25
Share capital			10
Profit and loss account:			
As at 31.12.20X2		6	
Profit for 20X3		9	
			15
			25

During the year, P sold to S for £28 goods which had cost it £16, recording a profit for P of £12. Of these goods, two-thirds had been sold by S at the balance sheet date, leaving one-third in stock-in-trade. This means that the stock-in-trade of S (D) includes £4 unrealised profit ($^1/_3 \times$ £12). The figure of P's profit for the year (C) £18 also includes £4 unrealised profit. When consolidating the two balance sheets therefore, £4 needs to be deducted from each of those figures.

In Exhibit 19.2 the subsidiary was wholly owned by the parent. The final figures would have been exactly the same if it had been the subsidiary which had sold the goods to the parent instead of vice versa.

P Consolidated Balance Sheet as at 31 December 20X3

	£
Stock-in-trade (S £22 – £4 + P £24)	42
Bank (P £6 + S £3)	9
	51
Share capital	20
Profit and loss accounts (S £9 + P £8 + £18 – £4)	31
	51

19.4 Partially-owned subsidiaries and unrealised profits

In Exhibit 19.2 the subsidiary was 100 per cent controlled and the unrealised profit in stock-in-trade was £4. A few years ago there were three possible methods of dealing with the adjustments needed, two of the methods taking into account the actual percentage of shares owned. However, with FRS 2 the elimination of intragroup profits or losses is to be made in full.

This means that if in Exhibit 19.2 S had been owned 75 per cent by P it would still be the full inter-group profit of £4 that would be deducted from the stock-in-trade in the consolidated balance sheet, and the full £4 would also be deducted from the profit and loss account of P when it is consolidated, there being no adjustment for minority interest.

Activity 19.4
Why do you think the rules were changed upon the introduction of FRS 2?

Learning outcomes

You should now have learnt:

1 Intragroup indebtedness must be eliminated upon consolidation, irrespective of the proportion of the holding in the subsidiary undertaking(s) involved.

2 Unrealised intragroup profits must be eliminated upon consolidation, irrespective of the proportion of the holding in the subsidiary undertaking(s) involved.

Answers to activities

19.1 Because the original cost when they were first purchased by a group company was lower. For example, imagine S1 bought £10 of goods from a company that was not part of the group and then sold them to S2 for £12. At the end of the accounting period, S2 still had all those goods in stock so its stock figure in the balance sheet is £12, which is £2 more than the goods cost the group.

19.2 If it wasn't eliminated, groups could show far greater profits than they are actually making. For example, imagine S1 bought £10 of goods from a company that was not part of the group and then sold them to S2 for £12. At the end of the accounting period, S2 still had all those goods in stock so its stock figure in the balance sheet is £12. S1 would include a profit of £2 on these goods in its profit for the period. S2 would include the £12 in its purchases and in its closing

stock, resulting in no effect upon its profit. On consolidation, the group would include the £2 profit made by S1 in the group profit for the period.

19.3 They could show far less profits by selling within the group at below cost, so delaying paying tax on some of their profits for a further 12 months.

19.4 By definition, subsidiaries are members of a group because the parent company can exercise a dominant influence over them. Unscrupulous parent companies could, therefore, require less than 100 per cent subsidiaries to purchase goods at above or below cost from other companies in the group and could require them not to sell those goods. Prior to the release of FRS 2, this power could be abused to manipulate profits of the group, as the minority share of the profits and losses could have been included in the profits and losses of the subsidiary and thus the group, making the group appear more or less profitable than it actually was. The change made when FRS 2 was issued eliminated the possibility of including such unrealised profits and losses in the consolidated financial statements.

REVIEW QUESTIONS

19.1 You are to draw up a consolidated balance sheet from the following details as at 31 December 20X9.

P Balance Sheet as at 31 December 20X9

	£	£
Investment in subsidiary: 1,000 shares bought 31.12.20X8		2,800
Fixed assets		1,100
Stock		1,200
Debtors		2,100
Bank		200
		7,400
Share capital		2,000
Profit and loss account:		
As at 31.12.20X8	1,500	
Profit for 20X9	2,200	
		3,700
General reserve		800
Creditors		900
		7,400

S Balance Sheet as at 31 December 20X9

	£	£
Fixed assets		1,200
Stock		900
Debtors		1,400
Bank		300
		3,800
Share capital		1,000
Profit and loss account:		
As at 31.12.20X8	950	
Profit for 20X9	1,150	
		2,100
Creditors		700
		3,800

During the year, P had sold goods which had cost £150 to S for £240. None of these goods had been sold by the balance sheet date.

At the balance sheet date P owes S £220.

19.2 Draw up a consolidated balance sheet as at 31 December 20X4 from the following:

P Balance Sheet as at 31 December 20X4

	£	£
Investment in subsidiary: 6,000 shares bought 31.12.20X3		9,700
Fixed assets		9,000
Stock		3,100
Debtors		4,900
Bank		1,100
		27,800
Share capital		20,000
Profit and loss account:		
As at 31.12.20X3	6,500	
Less Loss for 20X4	(2,500)	
		4,000
Creditors		3,800
		27,800

S Balance Sheet as at 31 December 20X4

	£	£
Fixed assets		5,200
Stock		7,200
Debtors		3,800
Bank		1,400
		17,600
Share capital		10,000
Profit and loss account:		
As at 31.12.20X3	3,500	
Profit for 20X4	2,000	
		5,500
Creditors		2,100
		17,600

At the balance sheet date S owes P £600.

During the year P sold goods which had cost £300 to S for £500. Three-quarters of these goods had been sold by S by the balance sheet date.

19.3 Draw up a consolidated balance sheet from the following details as at 31 December 20X8.

P Balance Sheet as at 31 December 20X8

	£	£
Investment in subsidiaries:		
S1 30,000 shares bought 31.12.20X7		39,000
S2 25,000 shares bought 31.12.20X7		29,000
Fixed assets		22,000
Stock		26,000
Debtors		13,000
Bank		5,000
		134,000
Share capital		100,000
Profit and loss account		
As at 31.12.20X7	14,000	
Add Profit for 20X8	9,000	
		23,000
General reserve		2,000
Creditors		9,000
		134,000

S1 Balance Sheet as at 31 December 20X8

	£	£
Fixed assets		22,000
Stock		11,000
Debtors		8,000
Bank		3,000
		44,000
Share capital		30,000
Profit and loss account:		
As at 31.12.20X7	8,000	
Less Loss for 20X8	(5,000)	
		3,000
General reserve (as at 31.12.20X7)		4,000
Creditors		7,000
		44,000

S2 Balance Sheet as at 31 December 20X8

	£	£
Fixed assets		21,000
Stock		9,000
Debtors		7,000
Bank		1,000
		38,000
Share capital		30,000
Profit and loss account:		
As at 31.12.20X7	1,200	
Add Profit for 20X8	1,800	
		3,000
Creditors		5,000
		38,000

At the balance sheet date S2 owed S1 £500 and P owed S2 £900.

During the year, P had sold to S1 for £2,800 goods costing £2,000. Of these goods, one-half had been sold by the year end. P had also sold goods costing £500 to S2 for £740, of which none had been sold by the year end.

19.4A You are presented with the following information from the Seneley group of companies for the year to 30 September 20X6:

	Seneley plc £000	Lowe Ltd £000	Wright Ltd £000
Tangible fixed assets	225	300	220
Investments			
Shares in group companies:			
Lowe Ltd	450	–	–
Wright Ltd	130	–	–
	580	–	–
Current assets			
Stocks	225	150	45
Trade debtors	240	180	50
Cash at bank and in hand	50	10	5
	515	340	100
Creditors: amounts falling due within one year			
Trade creditors	(320)	(90)	(70)
Net current assets	195	250	30
	1,000	550	250
Capital and reserves			
Called-up share capital	800	400	200
Profit and loss account	200	150	50
	1,000	550	250

Additional information:

(a) The authorised, issued and fully paid share capital of all three companies consists of £1 ordinary shares.

(b) Seneley purchased 320,000 shares in Lowe Ltd on 1 October 20X3, when Lowe's profit and loss account balance stood at £90,000.

(c) Seneley purchased 140,000 shares in Wright Ltd on 1 October 20X5, when Wright's profit and loss account balance stood at £60,000.

(d) During the year to 30 September 20X6, Lowe had sold goods to Wright for £15,000. These goods had cost Lowe £7,000, and Wright still had half of these goods in stock as at 30 September 20X6. Minority interests are not charged with their share of any unrealised stock profits.

(e) Included in the respective trade creditor and trade debtor balances as at 30 September 20X6 were the following inter-company debts:
  • Seneley owed Wright £5,000;
  • Lowe owed Seneley £20,000; and
  • Wright owed Lowe £25,000.

(f) Seneley does not amortise goodwill arising on consolidation.

Required:
Prepare the Seneley group's consolidated balance sheet as at 30 September 20X6. Your workings should be submitted.

(Association of Accounting Technicians)

19.5A You are to draw up a consolidated balance sheet as at 31 December 20X3 from the following:

P Balance Sheet as at 31 December 20X3

	£	£
Investment in subsidiaries:		
S1 75,000 shares bought 31.12.20X2		116,000
S2 45,000 shares bought 31.12.20X2		69,000
Fixed assets		110,000
Stock		13,000
Debtors		31,000
Bank		6,000
		345,000
Creditors		(23,000)
		322,000
Share capital		300,000
Profit and loss account:		
As at 31.12.20X2	22,000	
Less Loss for 20X3	(7,000)	
		15,000
General reserve (as at 31.12.20X2)		7,000
		322,000

S1 Balance Sheet as at 31 December 20X3

	£	£
Fixed assets		63,000
Stock		31,000
Debtors		17,000
Bank		3,000
		114,000
Creditors		(16,000)
		98,000
Share capital		75,000
Profit and loss account:		
As at 31.12.20X2	11,000	
Add Profit for 20X3	12,000	
		23,000
		98,000

S2 Balance Sheet as at 31 December 20X3

	£	£
Fixed assets		66,800
Stock		22,000
Debtors		15,000
Bank		4,000
		107,800
Creditors		(11,000)
		96,800
Share capital		80,000
Profit and loss account:		
As at 31.12.20X2	12,800	
Less Loss for 20X3	(2,400)	
		10,400
General reserve (as at 31.12.20X2)		6,400
		96,800

At the balance sheet date S1 owed P £2,000 and S2 £500, and P owed S2 £1,800.
   P had sold goods which had cost £2,000 to S2 for £3,200, and of these goods one-half had been sold by S2 by the year end.

19.6   The following summarised information relates to the Pagg group of companies.

Balance Sheet at 31 March 20X0

	Pagg plc £000	Ragg Ltd £000	Tagg Ltd £000
Tangible fixed assets at net book value	2,000	900	600
Investments			
800,000 ordinary shares in Ragg Ltd	3,000	–	–
300,000 ordinary shares in Tagg Ltd	1,000	=	=
	4,000	=	=
Current assets			
Stocks	1,300	350	100
Debtors	3,000	200	300
Cash	200	20	50
	4,500	570	450
Current liabilities			
Creditors	(4,000)	(270)	(400)
	6,500	1,200	650
Capital and reserves			
Called-up share capital (all ordinary shares of £1 each)	5,500	1,000	500
Profit and loss account	1,000	200	150
	6,500	1,200	650
		✗ 20%	✗ 40%

Additional information:

1 Pagg acquired its shareholding in Ragg Ltd on 1 April 20X5. Ragg's profit and loss account balance at that time was £600,000. ✗ 80% = 480
2 The shares in Tagg Ltd were acquired on 1 April 20X9 when Tagg's profit and loss account balance was £100,000. ✗ 60% = 60
3 All goodwill arising on consolidation is amortised in equal amounts over a period of 20 years commencing from the date of acquisition of each subsidiary company.
4 At 31 March 20X0, Ragg had in stock goods purchased from Tagg at a cost to Ragg of £60,000. These goods had been invoiced by Tagg at cost plus 20 per cent. Minority interests are not charged with any intercompany profit.
5 Intercompany debts at 31 March 20X0 were as follows: Pagg owed Ragg £200,000 and Ragg owed Tagg £35,000.

Required:
In so far as the information permits, prepare the Pagg group of companies' consolidated balance sheet as at 31 March 20X0 in accordance with the Companies Acts and standard accounting practice.

Note: Formal notes to the accounts are NOT required, although detailed working must be submitted with your answer.

(Association of Chartered Certified Accountants)

19.7A   You are presented with the following summarised information relating to Block plc for the year to 30 September 20X8:

	Block plc £000	Chip Ltd £000	Knot Ltd £000
Fixed assets	8,900	3,240	2,280
Investments			
Shares in group companies:			
Chip Ltd	2,500	–	–
Knot Ltd	1,600	–	–
	4,100	–	–
Current assets			
Stocks	300	160	80
Trade debtors	1,600	130	50
Cash at bank and in hand	400	110	120
	2,300	400	250
Creditors: amounts falling due within one year			
Trade creditors	(200)	(90)	(110)
Proposed dividend	(100)	(50)	(20)
	(300)	(140)	(130)
	15,000	3,500	2,400
Capital and reserves			
Called-up share capital (ordinary shares of £1 each)	10,000	3,000	2,000
Profit and loss account	5,000	500	400
	15,000	3,500	2,400

Additional information:

1 Block purchased 80 per cent of the share capital of Chip on 1 October 20X3 when Chip's profit and loss account balance was £200,000 credit.
2 On 1 October 20X7 Block purchased 60 per cent of the share capital of Knot. Knot's profit and loss account balance at that date was £500,000 credit.
3 Goodwill is not amortised.
4 During the year to 30 September 20X8, Block sold goods costing £200,000 to Chip for £300,000. Half of these goods remained in stock at the year end.
5 Intercompany debts at the year end were as follows:

	£000
Chip owed Block	20
Knot owed Chip	30

Required:
Prepare the Block plc group of companies' consolidated balance sheet as at 30 September 20X8. Formal notes to the accounts are NOT required, although detailed working should be submitted with your answer.

(Association of Chartered Certified Accountants)

CHAPTER 20

Consolidated financial statements: acquisition of shares in subsidiaries at different dates

After you have studied this chapter, you should be able to:

- calculate goodwill when an interest in a subsidiary undertaking was acquired in blocks over a period of time
- calculate goodwill when a subsidiary undertaking was acquired part-way through its accounting period

Introduction

In this chapter you'll learn how to deal with piecemeal acquisitions, i.e. those situations where a subsidiary is acquired through a series of transactions. You will also learn how to calculate goodwill and pre-acquisition profits when a subsidiary is acquired part-way through its accounting period.

20.1 Shares bought at different dates

Up to this point the shares in subsidiaries have all been bought at one point in time for each company. However, it is a simple fact that shares are often bought in blocks at different times, and that the first purchase may not give the buyer a controlling interest.

There used to be two possible methods of calculating pre-acquisition profits, and therefore goodwill. However, FRS 2 states that only one method should be used, and this is the method used in this book. FRS 2 requires that the consolidation be based on the fair values at the date the undertaking actually becomes a subsidiary, even though the acquisition has been made in stages.

Activity 20.1
Why do you think you are not allowed to calculate goodwill at each stage of acquisition?

For instance, a company, S, has an issued share capital of 100 ordinary shares of £1 each. The only reserve of S is the balance on the profit and loss account which was £50 on 31 December 20X4, and two years later on at 31 December 20X6 it was £80. P buys 20 shares on 31 December 20X4 for £36, and a further 40 shares on 31 December 20X6 for £79. The date that S became a subsidiary was therefore 31 December 20X6. The calculation of goodwill becomes:

	£	£
Shares bought (20 + 40)	60	
Profit and loss account of subsidiary, 60 per cent × £80 (date control achieved)	48	
		(108)
Paid 31.12.20X4	36	
Paid 31.12.20X6	79	
		115
Goodwill		7

20.2   Shares bought during an accounting period

In addition it has been conveniently assumed so far that all shares have been bought exactly on the last day of an accounting period. This will just not be so, most shares being bought part-way through an accounting period. Unless specially audited financial statements are drawn up as at the date of acquisition there is no up-to-date figure of profit and loss account as at the date of acquisition. As this is needed for the calculation of goodwill or negative goodwill, the figure has to be obtained somehow. Naturally enough, specially audited financial statements would be the ideal for the purpose of the calculation, but if they are not available a second-best solution is necessary. In this instance the profit and loss balance according to the last balance sheet before the acquisition of the shares is taken, and an addition made (or deduction – if a loss) corresponding to the proportion of the year's profits that had been earned before acquisition took place. This is then taken as the figure of pre-acquisition profits for goodwill and capital reserve calculations.

Exhibit 20.1

Calculation of pre-acquisition profits, and goodwill, where the shares are bought part-way through an accounting period.

P bought 20 of the 30 issued ordinary shares of S for £49 on 30 September 20X5. The financial statements for S are drawn up annually to 31 December. The balance sheet of S as at 31 December 20X4 showed a balance on the profit and loss account of £24. The profit and loss account of S for the year ended 31 December 20X5 disclosed a profit of £12.

	£	£
Shares bought		20
Profit and loss account:		
Balance at 31.12.20X4	24	
Add Proportion of 20X5 profits before acquisition $^9/_{12} \times £12$	9	
	33	
Proportion of pre-acquisition profits		
20 shares owned out of 30, $^2/_3 \times £33$		22
		42

Paid for shares £49
Therefore goodwill is £49 – £42 = £7

Learning outcomes

You should now have learnt:

1 When an interest in a subsidiary undertaking is acquired in blocks over a period of time, goodwill is calculated as if all the blocks had been purchased at the date when control was achieved.

2 When a subsidiary undertaking is acquired part-way through its accounting period, in the absence of specially audited financial statements, the proportion of profit (or loss) applicable to that part of the financial period that preceded the acquisition date should be treated as being part of the pre-acquisition reserves for the calculation of goodwill upon consolidation.

Answers to activities

20.1 The subsidiary was actually acquired only when control passed to the parent company. As goodwill is to be calculated when that happens, it would be inappropriate to calculate parts of it at an earlier date.

REVIEW QUESTIONS

20.1 On 31 December 20X4 S Ltd had share capital of £40,000 ordinary £1 shares and reserves of £24,000. Two years later the share capital has not altered but the reserves have risen to £30,000. The following shares were bought by P Ltd: 10,000 on 31 December 20X4 for £23,500, and on 31 December 20X6 14,000 for £31,000. You are to calculate the figure of goodwill for the consolidated balance sheet as at 31 December 20X6.

20.2A On 31 December 20X6, S Ltd had share capital of £400,000 ordinary £1 shares and reserves of £260,000. Three years later the share capital is unchanged but the reserves have risen to £320,000. The following shares were bought by P Ltd: 100,000 on 31 December 20X6 for £210,000, and 200,000 on 31 December 20X9 for £550,000. Calculate the figure of goodwill for the consolidated balance sheet as at 31 December 20X9.

20.3 P Ltd bought 50,000 of the 80,000 issued ordinary £1 shares of S Ltd for £158,000 on 31 August 20X8. S Ltd financial statements are drawn up annually to 31 December. The balance sheet of S Ltd on 31 December 20X7 showed a balance on the profit and loss account of £36,000. The profit and loss account of S Ltd for the year ended 31 December 20X8 showed a profit of £42,000. Calculate the figure for the goodwill to be shown in the consolidated balance sheet as at 31 December 20X8.

20.4A On 1 January 20X1 S Ltd had a share capital of £300,000, a profit and loss account balance of £28,000 and a general reserve of £20,000. During the year ended 31 December 20X1 S Ltd made a profit of £36,000, none of which was distributed. P Ltd bought 225,000 shares on 1 June 20X1 for £333,000. Calculate the figure of goodwill to be shown in the consolidated balance sheet as at 31 December 20X1.

CHAPTER 21

Intragroup dividends

Learning objectives

After you have studied this chapter, you should be able to:

- explain how to treat intragroup dividends
- explain how to treat dividends from a newly acquired subsidiary undertaking that were proposed prior to the acquisition date
- explain how to treat dividends proposed by subsidiary undertakings at the balance sheet date

Introduction

In this chapter you'll learn how to treat dividends received from a subsidiary and dividends proposed by a subsidiary but not received at the end of the accounting period. You'll learn how to deal with dividends paid by a subsidiary out of pre-acquisition profits as compared with dividends paid by a subsidiary out of post-acquisition profits. You will also learn how to treat dividends proposed by a subsidiary at the acquisition date. Finally, you will learn how to treat dividends paid and proposed by non-wholly-owned subsidiaries.

21.1 Dividends paid from post-acquisition profits

Intragroup dividends are dividends paid by one member of a group to another, i.e. from one company in the group to another in the same group. They will, therefore, be shown in the receiving company's own profit and loss account as investment income, with a subsequent increase in the bank balance. From the point of view of the paying company's financial statements, it will show the dividend as a charge against its own profit and loss account, thus reducing the final balance on that account. Also, when paid, there will be a reduction in the bank balance of that company.

If the dividend has been proposed, but not paid at the end of the accounting period, the proposed dividend will be shown as a current liability in the subsidiary's balance sheet, and as a current asset on the parent undertaking's balance sheet (as a dividend owing from the subsidiary).

From the point of view of the consolidated balance sheet, if the dividend is paid entirely from post-acquisition profits, no action is needed. The two aspects of the dividend (current liability in the subsidiary's balance sheet and a current asset in the parent company's balance sheet) automatically cancel each other out when drafting the consolidated balance sheet.

Activity 21.1

What would be the impact upon the consolidated financial statements if the dividend had been paid before the end of the subsidiary's accounting period?

21.2   If paid from pre-acquisition profits

In Chapter 18, the company law principle that dividends should not be paid out of capital was reiterated. To prevent this happening, the pre-acquisition profits were capitalised and brought into the goodwill calculation. A company cannot circumvent the principle by buying the shares of a company, part of the purchase price being for the reserves of the subsidiary, and then utilising those reserves by paying itself dividends, and consequently adding those dividends to its own profits and then declaring an increased dividend itself. The next two exhibits illustrate this.

Exhibit 21.1

Dividends paid from post-acquisition profits.

P buys 100 per cent of the shares of S on 31 December 20X4. In 20X5, S pays a dividend of 50 per cent = £5 which P receives. To simplify matters the dividend is declared for 20X5 and paid in 20X5.

P Balance Sheet as at 31 December 20X5

	£	£
Investment in subsidiary:		
10 shares bought 31.12.20X4		23
Stock		11
Bank		1
		35
Share capital		20
Profit and loss account:		
As at 31.12.20X4	7	
Add Profit for 20X5 (including dividend of £5 from S)	8	
		15
		35

S Balance Sheet as at 31 December 20X5

	£	£	£
Stock			19
Bank			7
			26
Share capital			10
Profit and loss account:			
As at 31.12.20X4		12	
Profit for 20X5	9		
Less Dividend paid to P	(5)		
		4	16
			26

The dividend is £5 out of profits made since the acquisition of £9. The dividend can be treated as being from post-acquisition profits, and can therefore be shown in the profit and loss account of P as investment income and so swell the profits of P available for dividend purposes.

P Consolidated Balance Sheet as at 31 December 20X5

	£
Goodwill (£23 − £10 − £12)	1
Stock (P £11 + S £19)	30
Bank (P £1 + S £7)	8
	39
Share capital	20
Profit and loss account:	
(P £7 + £8 + S £4)	19
	39

Exhibit 21.2

Dividends paid from pre-acquisition profits.

P Balance Sheet as at 31 December 20X4

	£
Investment in subsidiary:	
10 shares bought 31.12.20X4	23
Stock	7
Bank	1
	31
Share capital	20
Profit and loss account	11
	31

S Balance Sheet as at 31 December 20X4

	£
Stock	14
Bank	3
	17
Share capital	10
Profit and loss account	7
	17

P Consolidated Balance Sheet as at 31 December 20X4
(*immediately after acquisition*)

	£
Goodwill (P £23 – S £10 – S £7)	6
Stock	21
Bank (P £1 + S £3)	4
	31
Share capital	20
Profit and loss account	11
	31

The consolidated balance sheet already shown was drafted immediately after acquisition. The following balance sheets show the position one year later. It is helpful to remember that the calculation of goodwill does not alter.

P Balance Sheet as at 31 December 20X5

	£	£
Investment in subsidiary:		
(£23 originally calculated less dividend from pre-acquisition profits £7)		16
Stock		18
Bank		5
		39
Share capital		20
Profit and loss account:		
As at 31.12.20X4	11	
Add Profit for 20X5 (does not include the dividend from S)	8	
		19
		39

S Balance Sheet as at 31 December 20X5

	£	£
Stock		8
Bank		2
		10
Share capital		10
Profit and loss account:		
As at 31.12.20X4	7	
Add Profit for 20X5 Note	0	
Less Dividend paid	(7)	
		–
		10

Note: For simplicity, the profit of S for 20X5 is taken as being exactly nil.

P Consolidated Balance Sheet as at 31 December 20X5

	£
Goodwill	6
Stock	26
Bank	7
	39
Share capital	20
Profit and loss	19
	39

It will be noticed that when a dividend is paid by a subsidiary out of pre-acquisition profits it is, in fact, a return of capital to the parent company. Accordingly, the dividend is deducted from the original cost of the investment – it is a return of the purchase money – rather than treated as investment income of the holding company.

A common practice of many examiners – or 'trick', if you prefer to call it that – is to treat the receipt as investment income instead of as a refund of capital. Thus the balance sheet of P as at 31 December 20X5 in this exhibit would have read 'Profit and loss account £26' instead of 'Profit and loss account £19', and the investment would be shown at £23 instead of £16. This means that the examiner really wants the examinee to adjust what is, in fact, an incorrect balance sheet; the only way to do this is to adjust the parent's balance sheet before proceeding with the consolidation of the balance sheets of P and S.

21.3 Proposed dividend at date of acquisition of shares

Quite frequently there will be a proposed dividend as at the date of the acquisition of the shares, and the holding company will receive the dividend even though the dividend was proposed to be paid from profits earned before acquisition took place. The action taken is similar to that in Exhibit 21.2, in that it will be deducted from the price paid for the shares in order that the net effective price is calculated.

Exhibit 21.3

Shares acquired in a subsidiary at a date when a proposed dividend is outstanding.

P Balance Sheet as at 31 December 20X3

	£	£
Investment in subsidiary:		
10 shares bought 31.12.20X2	22	
Less Dividend from pre-acquisition profits	(6)	
		16
Stock		11
Bank		2
		29
Share capital		20
Profit and loss account:		
As at 31.12.20X2	4	
Profit for 20X3	5	
		9
		29

S Balance Sheet as at 31 December 20X3

	£	£
Stock		19
Bank		4
		23
Share capital		10
Profit and loss account:		
As at 31.12.20X2 (after deducting the proposed dividend £6)	5	
Add Profit for 20X3	8	
		13
		23

P Consolidated Balance Sheet as at 31 December 20X3

	£	£
Goodwill (*see Workings*)		1
Stock		30
Bank		6
		37
Share capital		20
Profit and loss account: (P £9 + S £8)		17
		37

Calculation of goodwill	£	£
Paid		22
Less Shares taken over	10	
Less Profit and loss balance at 31.12.20X2	5	
Less Dividend paid from pre-acquisition profits	6	
		(21)
Goodwill		1

21.4 Proposed dividends and minority interests

When a dividend is proposed by a company it will be shown as a current liability in its balance sheet. As mentioned in Section 21.1, this is just as true for a subsidiary company as it would be for a company which is not controlled by another company. The parent company

then shows the proposed dividend from the subsidiary as being receivable in the same accounting period. Thus, the subsidiary shows the proposed dividend as a current liability and the parent company shows it as a current asset. However, as this is merely another form of intragroup indebtedness, the amounts owing must be cancelled out when drawing up the consolidated balance sheet. Where the subsidiary is owned 100 per cent by the parent then the two items will cancel out fully.

When the subsidiary is only part-owned, there is the question of the minority interest. The cancellation of the part of the proposed dividend payable to the parent is done, and the remainder of the proposed dividend of the subsidiary will be that part owing to the minority interest. This can be dealt with in two ways, both of which are acceptable:

1 The part of the proposed dividend due to the minority interest is added back to the minority interest figure in the consolidated balance sheet.
2 The part of the proposed dividend due to the minority interest is shown as a current liability in the consolidated balance sheet.

Activity 21.2
Which of these two methods do you think is the more appropriate one to use?

It must be borne in mind that nothing that has been said refers in any way to the proposed dividends of the parent. These will simply be shown as a current liability in the consolidated balance sheet.

Exhibit 21.4
Where a subsidiary has proposed a dividend, and there is a minority interest share in the subsidiary.

This will be shown using method 2 just described.

P Balance Sheet as at 31 December 20X3

	£
Investment in subsidiary: 6 shares bought 31.12.20X1	17
Stock	19
Proposed dividend receivable from S	3
Bank	1
	40
Share capital	20
Profit and loss account	11
Proposed dividend (of the holding company)	9
	40

S Balance Sheet as at 31 December 20X3

	£
Stock	23
Bank	7
	30
Share capital	10
Profit and loss account	15
Proposed dividend	5
	30

Note: At the date of acquisition of the shares on 31 December 20X1 the profit and loss account balance of S was £10, and there were no proposed dividends at that date.

P Consolidated Balance Sheet as at 31 December 20X3

	£	£
Goodwill (see Workings)		5
Stock		42
Bank		8
		55
Share capital		20
Profit and loss account (see Workings)		14
Minority interest		
Shares	4	
Profit and loss ²/₅	6	
		10
Current liabilities		
Proposed dividends of parent	9	
Owing to minority interest	2	
		11
		55

Workings:	£	£	£
Profit and loss account:			
P's profit and loss balance			11
S's profit and loss balance		15	
Less Owned by minority interest: ²/₅ of £15	6		
Less Pre-acquisition profits at 31.12.20X1 bought by			
parent: ³/₅ of £10	6		
		(12)	
			3
			14

Goodwill:			
Paid			17
Less Shares bought		6	
Pre-acquisition profits ³/₅ of £10		6	
			(12)
			5

If method 1 had been used, the consolidated balance sheet would be as shown except for Minority interest and Current liabilities. These would have appeared:

	£	£
Minority interest		
Shares	4	
Profit and loss	8	
		12
Current liabilities		
Proposed dividend		9

Learning outcomes

You should now have learnt:

1 Intragroup dividends paid out of post-acquisition reserves will not appear in the consolidated financial statements, the entries in the individual company financial statements cancelling out upon consolidation.

2 Dividends from a newly acquired subsidiary that were declared prior to the date of acquisition are treated as repayment of capital and the investment in the subsidiary in the parent company balance sheet is reduced by the amount received.

3 Where a subsidiary undertaking is 100 per cent owned, dividends proposed by the subsidiary undertaking that are unpaid at the balance sheet date will be cancelled out upon consolidation.

4 Where a subsidiary undertaking is not 100 per cent owned, dividends proposed by the subsidiary undertaking that are unpaid at the balance sheet date will be cancelled out upon consolidation to the extent that ownership is held; the remainder of the dividend (that relates to the minority interest in the subsidiary undertaking) is shown as either an addition to the minority interest figure in the consolidated balance sheet, or as a current liability in the consolidated balance sheet.

Answers to activities

21.1 If the dividend has been paid, so far as the balance sheets are concerned the bank balance of the subsidiary has decreased while the bank balance of the parent has increased and the profit and loss account reserve of the subsidiary has been reduced while the profit and loss account reserve of the parent has risen. These all offset each other and have no impact upon the consolidated financial statements.

21.2 Method 2 would seem to be the better method. It gives a more complete view of the position. For instance, when considering the working capital or liquidity of the group it is essential that all current liabilities due to external parties should be brought into the calculation. If the proposed dividend soon to be paid to persons outside the group were excluded, this could render the calculations completely invalid.

REVIEW QUESTIONS

21.1 The following balance sheets were drawn up as at 31 December 20X7. The person drafting the balance sheet of P Ltd was not too sure of an item and has shown it as a suspense amount.

P Balance Sheet as at 31 December 20X7

	£	£
Investment in subsidiary:		
20,000 shares bought 31.12.20X6		29,000
Fixed assets		40,000
Current assets		5,000
		74,000
Share capital		50,000
Profit and loss account:		
As at 31.12.20X6	8,000	
Add Profit for 20X7	11,000	
		19,000
Suspense*		5,000
		74,000

*The suspense item consists of the dividend received from S in January 20X7.

S Balance Sheet as at 31 December 20X7

	£	£
Fixed assets		17,000
Current assets		10,000
		27,000
Share capital		20,000
Profit and loss account:		
As at 31.12.20X6*	3,000	
Add Profit for 20X7	4,000	
		7,000
		27,000

*The balance of £3,000 is after deducting the proposed dividend for 20X6 of £5,000.

Required:
Draw up the consolidated balance sheet as at 31 December 20X7.

21.2A The following balance sheets of P Ltd and S Ltd were drawn up as at 31 December 20X4. Draw up the consolidated balance sheet as at that date.

P Balance Sheet as at 31 December 20X4

	£	£
Investment in subsidiary:		
100,000 shares bought 31.12.20X3		194,000
Fixed assets		250,000
Current assets		59,000
		503,000
Share capital		400,000
Profit and loss account:		
As at 31.12.20X3	39,000	
Add Profit for 20X4*	64,000	
		103,000
		503,000

*The profit figure for 20X4 includes the dividend of £20,000 received from S Ltd for the year 20X3.

S Balance Sheet as at 31 December 20X4

	£	£
Fixed assets		84,000
Current assets		49,000
		133,000
Share capital		100,000
Profit and loss account:		
As at 31.12.20X3*	11,000	
Add Profit for 20X4	22,000	
		33,000
		133,000

*The balance of £11,000 is after deducting the proposed dividend for 20X3 £20,000.

21.3 Draw up a consolidated balance sheet as at 31 December 20X9 from the following information.

P Balance Sheet as at 31 December 20X9

	£	£
Investment in subsidiary: 30,000 shares bought 31.12.20X8		47,000
Fixed assets		44,000
Current assets		12,000
		103,000
Share capital		80,000
Profit and loss account:		
As at 31.12.20X8	14,000	
Add Profit for 20X9	9,000	
		23,000
		103,000

S Balance Sheet as at 31 December 20X9

	£	£
Fixed assets		36,000
Current assets		21,000
		57,000
Share capital		40,000
Profit and loss account:		
As at 31.12.20X8	4,000	
Add Profit for 20X9	7,000	
		11,000
Proposed dividend for 20X9		6,000
		57,000

The proposed dividend of S has not yet been brought into the financial statements of P Ltd.

21.4A The balance sheets of P Ltd and S Ltd are as follows:

P Balance Sheet as at 31 December 20X4

	£	£
Investment in subsidiary: 120,000 shares bought 31.12.20X3		230,000
Fixed assets		300,000
Current assets		75,000
		605,000
Share capital		500,000
Profit and loss account:		
As at 31.12.20X3	64,000	
Add Profit for 20X4	41,000	
		105,000
		605,000

S Balance Sheet as at 31 December 20X4

	£	£
Fixed assets		203,000
Current assets		101,000
		304,000
Share capital		200,000
Profit and loss account:		
As at 31.12.20X3	51,000	
Add Profit for 20X4	13,000	
		64,000
Proposed dividend for 20X4		40,000
		304,000

The proposed dividend of S has not yet been brought into the financial statements of P Ltd. Draw up the consolidated balance sheet as at 31 December 20X4.

21.5 The following are the summarised balance sheets of P Ltd and S Ltd at 31 December 20X6.

	P Limited		S Limited	
	£	£	£	£
Tangible fixed assets (see Note (a))		320,000		360,000
Loan to S Ltd		50,000		
Investment in S Ltd		250,000		
Current assets				
Stocks	110,000		50,000	
Debtors	100,000		40,000	
Bank	30,000		10,000	
	240,000		100,000	
Creditors: amounts falling due within one year				
Trade creditors	190,000		22,000	
Proposed preference dividend	–		8,000	
		(190,000)		(30,000)
Total assets *less* current liabilities		670,000		430,000
Capital and reserves:				
Ordinary shares of £1 each, fully paid		500,000		200,000
8% preference shares of £1 each, fully paid		–		100,000
Reserves		170,000		80,000
Loan from P Ltd		–		50,000
		670,000		430,000

Notes:

(a) *Tangible fixed assets*
   P Limited

	Cost	Cumulative depreciation	WDV
	£	£	£
Buildings	120,000	10,000	110,000
Plant and machinery	200,000	40,000	160,000
Motor vehicles	80,000	30,000	50,000
	400,000	80,000	320,000

   Tangible fixed assets
   S Limited

	Cost	Cumulative depreciation	WDV
	£	£	£
Buildings	300,000	100,000	200,000
Plant and machinery	120,000	30,000	90,000
Motor vehicles	130,000	60,000	70,000
	550,000	190,000	360,000

There were no additions or disposals of fixed assets by the group during the year.

(b) P Limited acquired its holding on 1 January 20X6, when the balance on S Limited's reserves stood at £50,000. The investment consists of 150,000 ordinary shares of £1 each, fully paid, purchased for £250,000.

(c) P Limited credited to its profit and loss account a dividend of £7,500 from S Limited in March 20X6, in respect of the shares acquired on 1 January 20X6. S Limited does not intend to pay an ordinary dividend for the year ended 31 December 20X6.

Required:

Prepare a consolidated balance sheet for P Limited and its subsidiary S Limited at 31 December 20X6.

Note: Ignore taxation.

(Chartered Institute of Management Accountants)

21.6   X plc acquired 80 per cent of the ordinary share capital of Y plc on 1 January 20X6 for £300,000.

The lists of balances of the two companies at 31 December 20X6 were as follows:

	X plc £000	Y plc £000
Called-up share capital:		
400,000 ordinary shares of £1 each, fully paid	400	
300,000 ordinary shares of £0.50 each, fully paid		150
Reserves as at 1 January 20X6	220	90
Retained profits for 20X6	20	18
Trade creditors	130	80
Taxation	30	14
Proposed final dividend	20	10
Depreciation provisions:		
Freehold property	12	6
Plant and machinery	40	12
Current account		14
	872	394
Tangible fixed assets:		
Freehold property, at cost	120	160
Plant and machinery, at cost	183	62
Investment in Y plc	300	
Stocks	80	70
Debtors	160	90
Bank	10	12
Current account	19	
	872	394

Notes:

(a) A remittance of £2,000 from Y plc to X plc in December 20X6 was not received by X plc until January 20X7.

(b) Goods, with an invoice value of £3,000, were despatched by X plc in December 20X6 but not received by Y plc until January 20X7. The profit element included in this amount was £400.

(c) Included in the stock of Y plc at 31 December 20X6 were goods purchased from X plc for £10,000. The profit element included in this amount was £2,000.

(d) It is group policy to exclude all profit on any intra-company transactions.

(e) No interim dividend was paid in 20X6 by either company.

(f) Goodwill is not amortised.

Required:
Prepare a consolidated balance sheet for X plc and its subsidiary Y plc as at 31 December 20X6.

(Chartered Institute of Management Accountants)

21.7A P plc acquired 80 per cent of the ordinary share capital of S plc for £150,000 and 50 per cent of the issued 10 per cent cumulative preference shares for £10,000, both purchases being effected on 1 May 20X7. There have been no changes in the issued share capital of S plc since that date. The following balances are taken from the books of the two companies at 30 April 20X8:

	P plc £000	S plc £000
Ordinary share capital (£1 shares)	300	100
10% cumulative preference shares (50p shares)	–	20
Share premium account	20	10
General reserve	68	15
Profit and loss account	50	35
Trade creditors	35	22
Taxation	50	30
Proposed dividends	15	10
Depreciation		
Freehold property	40	15
Plant and machinery	100	48
	678	305
Freehold property at cost	86	55
Plant and machinery at cost	272	168
Investment in S plc	160	–
Stocks	111	65
Debtors	30	15
Cash	19	2
	678	305

The following additional information is available:

(a) Stocks of P plc include goods purchased from S plc for £20,000. S plc charged out these stocks at cost plus 25 per cent.

(b) Proposed dividend of S plc includes a full year's preference dividend. No interim dividends were paid during the year by either company.

(c) Creditors of P plc include £6,000 payable to S plc in respect of stock purchases. Debtors of S plc include £10,000 due from P plc. The holding company sent a cheque for £4,000 to its subsidiary on 29 April 20X8 which was not received by S plc until May 20X8.

(d) At 1 May 20X7 the balances on the reserves of S plc were as follows:

	£000
Share premium	10
General reserve	20
Profit and loss account	30

(e) Goodwill is not amortised.

Required:

(a) Prepare a consolidated balance sheet for P plc and its subsidiary S plc at 30 April 20X8. Notes to the accounts are not required. Workings must be shown.

(b) Explain what is meant by the term 'cost of control' and justify your treatment of this item in the above accounts.

(Chartered Institute of Management Accountants)

CHAPTER 22

Consolidated balance sheets: sundry matters

Learning objectives

After you have studied this chapter, you should be able to:

- calculate goodwill on the purchase of preference shares
- treat unrealised profits and losses on intragroup asset sales
- describe the effect of 'fair value' on the calculation of goodwill and on the preparation of the consolidated financial statements

Introduction

In this chapter you'll learn how to calculate goodwill on preference shares and how to treat it in the consolidated financial statements. You'll also learn what to do with profits and losses on the sale of fixed assets between companies in the same group. Finally, you will learn what is meant by 'fair value' and how to calculate and incorporate it into consolidated financial statements.

22.1 Preference shares

It should be remembered that preference shares do not carry voting powers under normal conditions, nor do they possess a right to the reserves of the company. Contrast this with ordinary shares which, when bought, will give the parent company voting rights and also a proportionate part of the reserves of the company.

This means that the calculation of goodwill on the purchase of preference shares is very simple indeed. If 9 preference shares of £1 each are bought for £12 then goodwill will be £3, while if 20 preference shares of £1 each are bought for £16 then the negative goodwill will be £4. The amount of goodwill on the purchase of preference shares is not shown separately from that calculated on the purchase of ordinary shares. Instead the figures will be amalgamated to throw up one figure only on the consolidated balance sheet.

Preference shares owned by the minority interest are simply shown as part of the minority interest figure in the consolidated balance sheet, each share being shown at nominal value.

22.2 Sale of fixed assets between members of the group

There is obviously nothing illegal in one company in the group selling items in the nature of fixed assets to another company in the group. If the sale is at the cost price originally paid

for it by the first company, then no adjustment will be needed in the consolidated balance sheet. Rather more often, the sale will be at a price different from the original cost price. The intragroup unrealised profit must be eliminated in a similar fashion to that taken for the unrealised profit in trading stock as described in Chapter 19.

If the fixed asset is shown at its cost to the group in the consolidated balance sheet rather than at the cost to the particular company, then obviously the depreciation figure on that fixed asset should be adjusted to that based on the group cost rather than on the cost of the particular company.

Exhibit 22.1

P Balance Sheet as at 31 December 20X6

	£	£
Investment in S:		
50 shares bought 31.12.20X5		95
Fixed assets	78	
Less Depreciation	(23)	
		55
Current assets		20
		170
Share capital		100
Profit and loss account:		
As at 31.12.20X5	30	
For the year 20X6	40	
		70
		170

S Balance Sheet as at 31 December 20X6

	£	£
Fixed assets	80	
Less Depreciation	(20)	
		60
Current assets		35
		95
Share capital		50
Profit and loss account:		
As at 31.12.20X5	20	
For the year 20X6	25	
		45
		95

During the year, P Ltd had sold to S Ltd for £28 a fixed asset which had cost it £20. Of the figure of £20 depreciation in the balance sheet of S, £7 refers to this asset and £13 to the other assets. The rate of depreciation is 25 per cent. The £8 profit is included in the figure of £40 profit for 20X6 in the balance sheet of P.

This means that the figure of £8 needs cancelling from the asset costs in the consolidated balance sheet and from the profit and loss account balance. In addition the figure of depreciation needs adjusting downwards, from the £7 as shown on the balance sheet of S, to the figure of £5, i.e. 25 per cent depreciation based on the cost of the asset to the group. This in turn means that the figure of profit for S, £25, needs increasing by £2, as, instead of the expense of £7 depreciation, there will now be a reduced expense of £5. The consolidated balance sheet becomes:

P and S Consolidated Balance Sheet as at 31 December 20X6

	£	£
Goodwill		25
Fixed assets	150	
Less Depreciation	(41)	
		109
Current assets		55
		189
Share capital		100
Profit and loss account: (P £70 – £8 + S £25 + £2)		89
		189

22.3 Fair values in acquisition accounting

The consolidated balance sheet should give a picture that is not clouded by the method of drafting consolidated financial statements. The consolidation process is looked at from the point of view that the parent undertaking acquires shares in a company, and thereby achieves control of that company. In addition, it is recognised that the reserves are also taken over.

It has been said previously that the economic view is that of taking over the assets of another company – after all one does not buy such shares just to possess the share certificates. Rather, the exercise is undertaken for the assets which are taken over and used. The consolidated balance sheet should therefore give the same picture as that which would have been recorded if, instead of buying shares, the assets themselves had been bought directly.

Prior to the issue of FRS 6: *Acquisitions and mergers* and FRS 7: *Fair values in acquisition accounting* in September 1994, the way in which acquisitions were accounted for varied from case to case. One of the areas of greatest diversity was in the revaluation of assets and liabilities to 'fair values'. 'Fair value' is defined as the amount for which an asset or liability could be exchanged in an arm's length transaction (i.e. in an exchange between strangers).

Generally, acquiring companies set their own 'fair values' on the assets and liabilities acquired, and then follow the FRS 10: *Goodwill and intangible assets* rules that the amount to be attributed to purchased goodwill should be the difference between the 'fair value' of the consideration given and the aggregate of the 'fair values' of the separable net assets acquired. Where assets are revalued, this should apply to all the assets, including those attributable to minority interests.

Under acquisition accounting, the investment is shown at cost (which equals the 'fair value' given) in the parent company's own financial statements. On consolidation, if the fair value of the net assets (excluding goodwill) acquired is less than the fair value of the purchase consideration, FRS 10 requires that the difference should be treated as goodwill and capitalised and, normally, amortised. If the fair value of the net assets (excluding goodwill) acquired exceeds the fair value of the purchase consideration, the difference should be treated as negative goodwill. This is similar to the treatment that has been adopted throughout the previous few chapters, the only difference being that fair values should be used rather than the values as shown in the balance sheet of the acquired company.

FRS 7 seeks to ensure that upon acquisition, all assets and liabilities that existed in the acquired entity at that date are recorded at fair values reflecting their condition at that date. In addition, it seeks to ensure that all changes to the acquired assets and liabilities, and the resulting gains and losses that arise after control of the acquired entity has passed to the acquirer, are reported as part of the post-acquisition financial performance of the reporting group.

There are a number of rules given in FRS 7 governing the determination of the appropriate fair value.

1 The fair value of *tangible fixed assets* should be based upon either *market value* (if assets similar in type and condition are bought and sold on an open market) or *depreciated replacement cost* (reflecting the acquired business's normal buying process and the sources of supply and prices available to it). However, the fair value should not exceed the recoverable amount (i.e. the greater of the net realisable value and the value in use) of the asset.

2 The fair value of *intangible assets* should be based on their *replacement cost*, which is normally their estimated market value.

3 *Stocks*, including commodity stocks, that the acquired entity trades on a market in which it participates as both a buyer and seller should be valued at *current market prices*.

4 *Other stocks and work in progress* should be valued at the lower of *replacement cost* and *net realisable value*. As with the use of *depreciated replacement cost* for *tangible fixed assets*, *replacement cost* for stock should be the cost at which it would have been replaced by the acquired entity, reflecting the acquired business's normal buying process and the sources of supply and prices available to it. The standard suggests that this is synonymous with 'the current cost of bringing the stocks to their present location and condition'.

5 *Quoted investments* should be valued at *market price*.

6 *Monetary assets and liabilities*, including accruals and provisions, should take into account their timing and the amounts expected to be received and paid. The *fair value* should be determined by reference to *market prices*, or by discounting to present value.

7 *Contingencies* should be measured at *fair values* where these can be determined, using reasonable estimates of the expected outcome if necessary.

The 'cost of acquisition' is defined in FRS 7 as the amount of cash paid and the fair value of other purchase consideration given by the acquirer, together with the expenses of the acquisition.

The effect of the use of fair values can be seen from what would occur if fair values were used by the acquiring company in arriving at the price it wished to pay, but then were never incorporated into the financial statements. For instance, if P buys all the 10 shares of S for £18 when the reserves are £5, then the goodwill calculation if fair values are not used is:

	£	£
Cost		18
Less Shares	10	
Less Reserves	5	
		(15)
Goodwill		3

However, P might have bought the shares of S because it thought that the fair value of the net assets of S was £17.

Activity 22.1

What would be wrong with P recording goodwill as £3 in this case?

The revaluation upwards of the fixed assets by £2, and the consequent reduction of the goodwill figure by £2 brings the figures into line with how P views them. Where there are depreciation charges on the revalued assets, this will also require to be adjusted.

Exhibit 22.2

P Balance Sheet as at 31 December 20X6

	£	£
Investment in subsidiary:		
30 shares bought 31.12.20X5		56
Fixed assets	80	
Less Depreciation for the year	(16)	
		64
Current assets		26
		146
Share capital		100
Profit and loss account:		
As at 31.12.20X5	20	
Add Profit 20X6	26	
		46
		146

S Balance Sheet as at 31 December 20X6

	£	£
Fixed assets	50	
Less Depreciation for the year	(10)	
		40
Current assets		14
		54
Share capital		30
Profit and loss account:		
As at 31.12.20X5	3	
Add Profit 20X6	21	
		24
		54

At the time when P bought the shares in S, the assets in S were shown at a value of £33 in the balance sheet of S. In fact, however, P valued the fixed assets as being worth £20 higher than that shown. The consolidated balance sheet will therefore show them at this higher figure. In turn the depreciation, which is at the rate of 20 per cent, will be £4 higher. The consolidated balance sheet therefore appears:

P and S Consolidated Balance Sheet as at 31 December 20X6

	£	£
Goodwill		3
Fixed assets (£80 + £70)	150	
Less Depreciation (£16 + £14)	(30)	
		120
Current assets		40
		163
Share capital		100
Profit and loss account:		
(P £46 + S £21 – increased depreciation £4)		63
		163

You should now have learnt:

1 Goodwill on the purchase of preference shares is the difference between their nominal value and the amount paid.

2 Unrealised profit on the sale of fixed assets between companies in a group must be eliminated upon consolidation.

3 'Fair values' at the time of acquisition should be used in the calculation of goodwill, rather than the value shown in the balance sheet of the subsidiary, and the consolidation of the subsidiary undertaking should also be based on those fair values.

4 Fair value is dependent upon the nature of the item being valued. However, the general rule is that it represents the amount for which an asset or liability could be exchanged in an arm's length transaction, i.e. in an exchange between strangers.

Answers to activities

22.1   In P's eyes, it is giving £18 for physical assets worth £17 and the goodwill figure is correspondingly £18 – £17 = £1. Assuming that the difference is in the recorded value of fixed assets, then the consolidated balance sheet will not be showing a true and fair view if it shows goodwill £3 and assets £15. The assets should be valued at £17 and goodwill recorded as £1.

REVIEW QUESTIONS

22.1   From the following balance sheets and further information you are to draw up a consolidated balance sheet as at 31 December 20X8.

P Balance Sheet as at 31 December 20X8

	£	£
Investment in S:		
200,000 shares bought 31.12.20X7		340,000
Fixed assets	300,000	
Less Depreciation	(100,000)	
		200,000
Current assets		103,000
		643,000
Share capital		500,000
Profit and loss account:		
As at 31.12.20X7	77,000	
Add Profit for 20X8	66,000	
		143,000
		643,000

S Balance Sheet as at 31 December 20X8

	£	£
Fixed assets	210,000	
Less Depreciation	(40,000)	
		170,000
Current assets		102,000
		272,000
Share capital		200,000
Profit and loss account:		
As at 31.12.20X7	40,000	
Add Profit for 20X8	32,000	
		72,000
		272,000

During the year P Ltd had sold to S for £50,000 a fixed asset which had cost it £40,000. S has written off 20 per cent, i.e. £10,000, as depreciation for 20X8.

22.2A From the following balance sheets and supplementary information you are to draw up a consolidated balance sheet as at 31 December 20X5.

P Consolidated Balance Sheet as at 31 December 20X5

	£	£
Investment in S: 10,000 shares bought 31.12.20X4		23,000
Fixed assets	84,000	
Less Depreciation	(14,000)	
		70,000
Current assets		20,000
		113,000
Share capital		75,000
Profit and loss account:		
As at 31.12.20X4	15,000	
Add Profit for 20X5	23,000	
		38,000
		113,000

S Balance Sheet as at 31 December 20X5

	£	£
Fixed assets	26,000	
Less Depreciation	(10,000)	
		16,000
Current assets		12,000
		28,000
Share capital		10,000
Profit and loss account:		
As at 31.12.20X4	6,000	
Add Profit for 20X5	7,000	
		13,000
General reserve (as at 31.12.20X4)		5,000
		28,000

During the year P sold a fixed asset to S. It had cost P £3,000 and it was sold to S for £5,000. S had written off £500 as depreciation during 20X5.

22.3

P Balance Sheet as at 31 December 20X7

	£	£
Investment in S: 60,000 shares bought on 31.12.20X6		121,000
Fixed assets	90,000	
Less Depreciation for year	(24,000)	
		66,000
Current assets		40,000
		227,000
Share capital		150,000
Profit and loss account:		
As at 31.12.20X6	44,000	
Add Profit for 20X7	33,000	
		77,000
		227,000

S Balance Sheet as at 31 December 20X7

	£	£
Fixed assets	70,000	
Less Depreciation for year	(7,000)	
		63,000
Current assets		28,000
		91,000
Share capital		60,000
Profit and loss account:		
As at 31.12.20X6	17,000	
Add Profit for 20X7	14,000	
		31,000
		91,000

When P Ltd bought the shares of S Ltd it valued the fixed assets at £95,000 instead of the figure of £70,000 as shown in the balance sheet of S.

Draw up a consolidated balance sheet as at 31 December 20X7.

22.4A

P Balance Sheet as at 31 December 20X5

	£	£
Investment in S: 30,000 shares bought 31.12.20X4		53,400
Fixed assets	60,000	
Less Depreciation for year	(6,000)	
		54,000
Current assets		10,600
		118,000
Share capital		80,000
Profit and loss account:		
As at 31.12.20X4	27,000	
Add Profit for 20X5	11,000	
		38,000
		118,000

S Balance Sheet as at 31 December 20X5

	£	£
Fixed assets	40,000	
Less Depreciation for year	(4,000)	
		36,000
Current assets		11,000
		47,000
Share capital		30,000
Profit and loss account:		
As at 31.12.20X4	8,000	
Add Profit for 20X5	9,000	
		17,000
		47,000

When P Ltd took control of S Ltd it valued the fixed assets at 31.12.20X4 at £50,000 instead of £40,000 as shown.

Draw up the consolidated balance sheet as at 31 December 20X5.

CHAPTER 23

Consolidation of the financial statements of a vertical group of companies

Introduction

In this chapter you'll learn how to account for situations where there are layers of subsidiaries beneath one overall parent company. You will learn about the exemption that wholly owned subsidiaries have from preparing consolidated financial statements; and you will learn how to treat dividends when preparing consolidated financial statements.

23.1 Subsidiaries that control other companies

So far we have considered the case of parent undertakings having a direct interest in their subsidiary undertakings. In each case, the parent itself has bought the shares in its subsidiaries. In each case, over 50 per cent of the voting shares have been bought. In a straightforward case, where the parent company, P1, has bought shares in subsidiaries S1 and S2, it could be represented by a diagram (Exhibit 23.1).

Exhibit 23.1

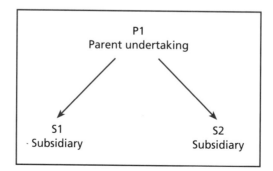

Suppose instead that P2 bought 100 per cent of the shares in S3, and that S3 then itself bought 100 per cent of the shares in S4. Because P2 controls S3 completely, and S3 controls S4 completely, P2 controls both S3 and S4. This is shown as Exhibit 23.2.

If P3 owned S5 100 per cent, but S5 only owned 80 per cent of S6, then we can say that P3 owns 100 per cent of 80 per cent of S6 = 80 per cent (Exhibit 23.3). Similarly if in another case P4 owned 75 per cent of S7, and S7 owns 80 per cent of S8, then P4 owns 75 per cent × 80 per cent = 60 per cent of S8 (Exhibit 23.4).

Exhibit 23.2   *Exhibit 23.3*   *Exhibit 23.4*

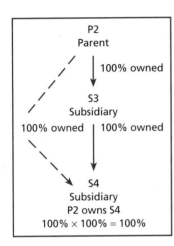
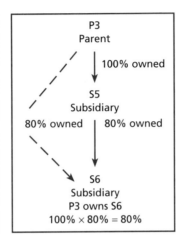
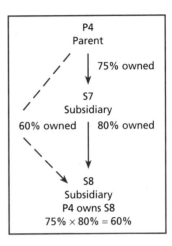

As can be seen in Exhibits 23.2, 23.3 and 23.4, the eventual ownership by P of each subsidiary's subsidiary exceeds 50 per cent.

There will be cases where the ownership of the subsidiary of a subsidiary by the parent is less than 50 per cent. Exhibit 23.5 shows where P5 owns 80 per cent of S9, and S9 owns 60 per cent of S10. This means that P5 owns 80% × 60% = 48% of S10. Exhibit 23.6 similarly shows where P6 owns 60 per cent of S11 and S11 owns 55 per cent of S12. Therefore P6 owns 60% × 55% = 33% of S12.

Exhibit 23.5   *Exhibit 23.6*

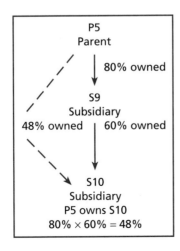
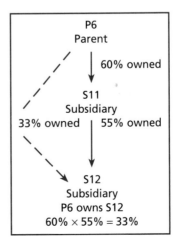

It might look as though S10 is not a subsidiary of P5, because P5 owns less than 50 per cent of S10. However, P5 controls S9 as its ownership is over 50 per cent, and in turn S9 controls S10 as it owns more than 50 per cent. In effect, therefore, P5 controls S10 and so S10 is its subsidiary.

Activity 23.1
Would P6 be considered the ultimate parent company of S12?

23.2 Legal exemptions from preparing consolidated financial statements

Section 228 of the Companies Act 1985 exempts a wholly owned subsidiary from preparing consolidated financial statements. For instance, in Exhibit 23.2 the subsidiary S3 would not have to prepare consolidated financial statements; neither would S5 in Exhibit 23.3.

In each of cases S7, S9 and S11 in Exhibits 23.4, 23.5 and 23.6, there are minority shareholders. In practice, therefore, those subsidiary companies may have to prepare consolidated financial statementss (for example, consolidating S7 and S8 in Exhibit 23.4) if sufficient of the minority interests demand it. See also Chapter 26 for FRS 2 regarding exemptions.

Activity 23.2
Why do you think wholly owned subsidiaries are exempted from preparing consolidated financial statements?

23.3 Methods of consolidating accounts

There are two methods of consolidating the financial statements.

1 The 'indirect' or 'single-stage' method follows the reasoning already given in this chapter, i.e. computing the parent's interest in the subsidiaries and their subsidiaries and taking that percentage of the capital and reserves of these companies into the consolidation process. For instance, in Exhibit 23.5 the capital and reserves would give 100% of P5 + 80% of S9 + 48% of S10.
2 The 'multi-stage' method first consolidates the balance sheets of the subsidiary and its subsidiary, and when that is done it is then consolidated with the balance sheet of the holding company. This recognises the fact that subsidiaries with minority interests have to produce consolidated financial statements and is more generally used in practice than the indirect method.

For an examination, method 1 is to be preferred. It is a quicker method, and usually you will be short of time in an examination. Also an examination question will almost certainly ask for consolidation for all the companies and therefore there will be no need to do the intermediate consolidation. This book will therefore use method 1 only.

23.4 The indirect method consolidation technique

The **indirect method** follows mainly the same techniques as described in earlier chapters, but two points need stressing:

1 The entry for the cost of investment in the cost of control account:
   (a) *For subsidiaries*: debit the total cost of investment to the cost of control account.
   (b) *For subsidiaries of subsidiaries*: debit only **the proportion of the cost concerned with the parent's share in the subsidiary which controls the subsidiary** to the cost of control account. Debit the minority interest account with the balance.

If P invests £20,000 to buy 80 per cent of the shares of S1 and S1 then invests £10,000 to buy 60 per cent of the shares of S2, the entries in the cost of control account of the P group would be:

Cost of Control		
	£	
Cost of shares in S1	20,000	
Cost of shares in S2 (80%)	8,000	

The remaining proportion of investment by S1 is then debited to a minority interest account.

Minority Interest		
	£	
Cost of shares in S2 (20%)	2,000	

2 The apportionment of share capital and reserves to the cost of control account and to the minority interest account:
   (a) *Cost of control*: take only the group's ultimate share of the subsidiary of subsidiary's share capital and reserves.
   (b) *Minority interest*: include the balance of the subsidiary of subsidiary's share capital and reserves.

In the illustration given in 1(*b*) where P bought 80 per cent of S1, and S1 bought 60 per cent of S2, the ultimate share of the group is $80\% \times 60\% = 48\%$. Therefore, in the consolidated financial statements 48 per cent should come into group calculations and 52 per cent shown in minority interest workings.

The double entry from the cost of control account when preparing the consolidated financial statements is:

Dr (appropriate) Reserve account
   Cr Cost of control account

23.5 A worked example (without proposed dividends)

Exhibit 23.7

P Ltd owns 80 per cent of the ordinary share capital of S1 Ltd. In turn S1 Ltd owns 75 per cent of the ordinary share capital of S2 Ltd. Both investments had been acquired on 31 December 20X4, one year previous to the following balance sheets:

Balance Sheets as at December 20X5

	P Ltd £000	P Ltd £000	S1 Ltd £000	S1 Ltd £000	S2 Ltd £000	S2 Ltd £000
Fixed assets		40		4		27
Investments						
Shares in S1		41				
Shares in S2				25		
Net current assets		19		6		28
		100		35		55
Share capital		40		10		20
Profit and loss						
As at 31.12.20X4	24		5		15	
Add Profit 20X5	36		10		20	
		60		15		35
General reserve at 31.12.20X4				10		
		100		35		55

Ownership of P can be seen to be 80 per cent of S1 and 80% x 75% = 60 per cent of S2. Any goodwill on acquisition to be written off to profit and loss.

We now will prepare a consolidated balance sheet on 31 December 20X5, one year after both acquisitions. In previous chapters the illustrations have been given on the face of the balance sheets. In this more complicated example we will use double entry accounts for the main items.

P Ltd and its subsidiaries
Consolidated Balance Sheet as at 31 December 20X5

	£000
Fixed assets	71
Net current assets	53
	124
Share capital	40
Profit and loss (*see* account below)	60
	100
Minority interest (*see* account below)	24
	124

In the accounts which follow, 1(a), 1(b), 2(a) and 2(b) refer to consolidation techniques described in Section 23.4.

Cost of Control

	£000		£000
Cost of shares in S1 (1(a))	41	Share capital S1 80% × 10	8
Cost of shares in S2 80% (1(b))	20	Share capital S2 60% × 20 (2(a))	12
		Pre-acquisition reserves:	
		Profit and loss S1 80% × 5	4
		Profit and loss S2 60% × 15	9
		General reserve S1 80% × 10	8
		Profit and loss: goodwill written off	20
	61		61

Minority Interest

	£000		£000
Cost of shares in S2 20% (1(b))	5	Share capital S1 20%	2
Balance to consolidated balance sheet	24	Share capital S2 40% (2(b))	8
		Profit and loss S1 20%	3
		Profit and loss S2 40% (2(b))	14
		General reserve S1 20% × 10	2
	29		29

Profit and Loss

	£000		£000
Minority interest S1	3	P	60
Minority interest S2	14	S1	15
Cost of control S1: pre-acquisition	4	S2	35
Cost of control S2: pre-acquisition	9		
Cost of control: goodwill written off	20		
Balance to consolidated balance sheet	60		
	110		110

General Reserve

	£000		£000
Cost of control 80% × 10	8	S1 balance b/d	10
Minority interest 20% × 10	2		
	10		10

23.6 A worked example (with proposed dividends)

Take the same companies as in Exhibit 23.7 but in this case the companies have proposed dividends at 31 December 20X5 of P Ltd £16,000; S1 Ltd £5,000; S2 Ltd £20,000. The balance sheets would have appeared:

Balance Sheets as at 31 December 20X5

	P Ltd		S1 Ltd		S2 Ltd
	£000		£000		£000
Fixed assets	40		4		27
Investments					
Shares in S1	41				
Shares in S2			25		
Net current assets (as before)	19		6		28
Dividends to be received	(80% of S1) 4	(75% of S2)	15		
	104		50		55
	£000		£000	£000	
Share capital	40		10		20
Profit and loss as at 31.12.20X4	24		5	15	
Retained profits for 20X5					
(*see below*)	24		20	–	
	48		25		15
General reserve			10		
Proposed dividends	16		5		20
	104		50		55

Note:

	P	S1	S2
Retained profit			
Net profits 20X5	36	10	20
Less Proposed dividends	(16)	(5)	(20)
	20	5	–
Add Dividends receivable			
P 80% of S1 × 5	4		
S1 75% of S2 × 20		15	
	24	20	

Now a consolidated balance sheet can be drawn up:

P Ltd and its subsidiaries
Consolidated Balance Sheet as at 31 December 20X5

	£000
Fixed assets	71
Net current assets	53
	124
Share capital	40
Profit and loss (*see* account below)	44
	84
Minority interest (*see* account below)	24
Proposed dividend	16
	124

The cost of control figures and goodwill in this exhibit are the same as for Exhibit 23.7 as circumstances at dates of acquisition had not changed.

Profit and Loss

	£000		£000
Minority interest:		Balances P	48
S1 20% × 25	5	S1	25
S2 40% × 15	6	S2	15
Cost of control (as before) S1	4		
Cost of control (as before) S2	9		
Cost of control: goodwill written off	20		
Balance to consolidated balance sheet	44		
	88		88

Minority Interest

	£000		£000
Cost of shares in S2 (20%)	5	Profit and loss S1	5
Balance to consolidated balance sheet	24	Profit and loss S2	6
		General reserve 20%	2
		Share capital S1 20%	2
		Share capital S2 40%	8
		Proposed dividends S1	1
		Proposed dividends S2 (Note (*a*))	5
	29		29

Proposed Dividends

	£000		£000
Minority interest S1	1	P	16
Minority interest S2 (25%)	5	S1	5
Consolidated balance sheet (P)	16	S2	20
Cancel against dividends receivable	19		
	41		41

Dividends Receivable

	£000		£000
P	4	Cancel against proposed dividends	
S1	15	(Note (*b*))	19
	19		19

Notes:
(*a*) Credit is given to minority for 25 per cent of S2 dividend, not 40 per cent. This is because 25 per cent is the amount actually received by them, while 75 per cent is received by S1, and the minority interest in this dividend is automatically calculated when we calculate the S1 minority interest in profit and loss balance £25,000 at 20 per cent. As the £25,000 figure already includes the dividend from S2 it should not be double-counted.
(*b*) The balances on dividends proposed and receivable cancel out, so nothing appears in the consolidated balance sheet.

(c) It would have been possible to show the proposed dividends applicable to minority shareholders, S1 £1,000 and S2 £5,000, as a current liability in the consolidated balance sheet, rather than show it as part of minority interest. As discussed in Activity 21.2, this would seem to be the better method. For instance, when considering the working capital or liquidity of the group it is essential that all current liabilities due to external parties should be brought into the calculation. If the proposed dividend soon to be paid to persons outside the group were excluded, this could render the calculations completely invalid.

Learning outcomes

You should now have learnt:

1 A company that is the subsidiary of another is also a subsidiary of its parent's own parent undertaking, even where the ultimate parent's shareholding is below 50 per cent.

2 There are two recognised methods of consolidating the financial statements of groups that contain subsidiaries of subsidiaries:
   (a) the multi-stage method is generally more common in practice, but
   (b) the indirect single-stage method is recommended for examinations.

3 The indirect method involves computing the parent undertaking's interest in the subsidiaries and their subsidiaries and taking that percentage of the capital and reserves of these companies into the consolidation process.

Answers to activities

23.1 Yes. Although P6 has effective ownership of only 33% of S12, it can exercise a dominant influence over S11, as it owns 60% of the company. S11, in turn, can exercise a dominant influence over S12 through its 55% ownership. Consequently, P has dominant influence over both S11 and, through S11, of S12 and so P is the ultimate parent of S12.

23.2 There is no shareholder who would want to read them, other than the parent company, and it has access to far more detailed financial information about the subsidiary and its own subsidiaries than would ever be contained in the subsidiary's consolidated financial statements.

REVIEW QUESTIONS

23.1 From the following balance sheets you are to draft a consolidated balance sheet for the group of P, S1 and S2.

P Balance Sheet as at 31 December 20X7

	£	£
Investment in S1:		
9,000 shares bought 31.12.20X6		23,000
Fixed assets		99,000
Current assets		25,000
		147,000
Share capital		100,000
Profit and loss account:		
As at 31.12.20X6	15,000	
Add Profit for 20X7	22,000	
		37,000
General reserve		10,000
		147,000

S1 Balance Sheet as at 31 December 20X7

	£	£
Investment in S2:		
3,500 shares bought 31.12.20X6		6,000
Fixed assets		22,000
Current assets		5,000
		33,000
Share capital		10,000
Profit and loss account:		
As at 31.12.20X6	7,000	
Add Profit for 20X7	16,000	
		23,000
		33,000

S2 Balance Sheet as at 31 December 20X7

	£	£
Fixed assets		6,000
Current assets		3,000
		9,000
Share capital		5,000
Profit and loss account:		
As at 31.12.20X6	1,000	
Add Profit for 20X7	3,000	
		4,000
		9,000

23.2A From the following balance sheets prepare a consolidated balance sheet for the group of P, S1 and S2.

P Balance Sheet as at 31 December 20X9

	£	£
Investment in S1:		
16,000 shares bought 31.12.20X8		39,000
Fixed assets		200,000
Current assets		40,000
		279,000
Share capital		200,000
Profit and loss account:		
As at 31.12.20X8	43,000	
Add Profit for 20X9	36,000	
		79,000
		279,000

S1 Balance Sheet as at 31 December 20X9

	£	£
Investment in S2:		
7,000 shares bought 31.12.20X8		13,000
Fixed assets		16,000
Current assets		4,000
		33,000
Share capital		20,000
Profit and loss account:		
As at 31.12.20X8	6,000	
Add Profit for 20X9	4,000	
		10,000
General reserve (as at 31.12.20X8)		3,000
		33,000

S2 Balance Sheet as at 31 December 20X9

	£	£
Fixed assets		10,500
Current assets		5,500
		16,000
Share capital		10,000
Profit and loss account:		
As at 31.12.20X8	1,000	
Add Profit for 20X9	5,000	
		6,000
		16,000

23.3   On 1 April 20X1 Machinery Limited bought 80 per cent of the ordinary share capital of Components Limited and on 1 April 20X3 Machinery Limited was itself taken over by Sales Limited who purchased 75 per cent of the ordinary shares in Machinery Limited.

The balance sheets of the three companies at 31 October 20X5 prepared for internal use showed the following position:

	Sales Ltd £	Sales Ltd £	Machinery Ltd £	Machinery Ltd £	Components Ltd £	Components Ltd £
Fixed assets						
Freehold land at cost		89,000		30,000		65,000
Buildings at cost	100,000		120,000		40,000	
Less						
Accumulated depreciation	(36,000)		(40,000)		(16,400)	
		64,000		80,000		23,600
Plant and equipment at cost	102,900		170,000		92,000	
Less						
Accumulated depreciation	(69,900)		(86,000)		(48,200)	
		33,000		84,000		43,800
		186,000		194,000		132,400
Investments						
Shares in Machinery at cost		135,000				
Shares in Components at cost				96,000		
Current assets						
Stocks	108,500		75,500		68,400	
Debtors	196,700		124,800		83,500	
Cash at bank	25,200		–		25,400	
		330,400		200,300		177,300
		651,400		490,300		309,700
Current liabilities						
Creditors	160,000		152,700		59,200	
Bank overdraft	–		37,400		–	
Corporation tax	57,400		47,200		24,500	
Proposed dividends	80,000		48,000		12,000	
		(297,400)		(285,300)		(95,700)
		354,000		205,000		214,000
Ordinary shares		200,000		120,000		100,000
10% preference shares		–		–		40,000
Revenue reserves		154,000		85,000		74,000
		354,000		205,000		214,000

Additional information:

(a) All ordinary shares are £1 each, fully paid.

(b) Preference shares in Components Ltd are 50p each fully paid.

(c) Proposed dividends in Components Ltd are:

on ordinary shares £10,000;

on preference shares £2,000.

(d) Proposed dividends receivable by Sales Ltd and Machinery Ltd are included in debtors.

(e) All creditors are payable within one year.

(f) Items purchased by Machinery Ltd from Components Ltd and remaining in stock at 31 October 20X5 amounted to £25,000. The profit element is 20 per cent of selling price for Components Ltd.

(g) Depreciation policy of the group is to provide for:

    (i) buildings – at the rate of 2 per cent on cost each year;

    (ii) plant and equipment – at the rate of 10 per cent on cost each year including full provision in the year of acquisition.

These policies are applied by all members of the group.

Included in the plant and equipment of Components Ltd is a machine purchased from the manufacturers, Machinery Ltd, on 1 January 20X4 for £10,000. Machinery Ltd recorded a profit of £2,000 on the sale of the machine.

(h) Intragroup balances are included in debtors and creditors respectively and are as follows:

			£
Sales Ltd	Creditors –	Machinery Ltd	45,600
	–	Components Ltd	28,900
Machinery Ltd	Debtors –	Sales Ltd	56,900
Components Ltd	Debtors –	Sales Ltd	28,900

(i) A cheque drawn by Sales Ltd for £11,300 on 28 October 20X5 was received by Machinery Ltd on 3 November 20X5.

(j) At 1 April 20X1, reserves in Machinery Ltd were £28,000 and in Components Ltd £20,000. At 1 April 20X3 the figures were £40,000 and £60,000 respectively.

Required:

Prepare a group balance sheet at 31 October 20X5 for Sales Ltd and its subsidiaries complying, so far as the information will allow, with the accounting requirements of the Companies Acts.

(*Association of Chartered Certified Accountants*)

23.4A Bryon Ltd has held 1,500,000 shares in Carlyle Ltd for many years. At the date of acquisition, the reserves of Carlyle Ltd amounted to £800,000. On 31 March 20X6 Carlyle Ltd bought 400,000 shares in Doyle Ltd for £600,000 and a further 400,000 shares were purchased on 30 June 20X6 for £650,000.

At 30 September 20X6 the balance sheets of the three companies were:

	Bryon Ltd £	Bryon Ltd £	Carlyle Ltd £	Carlyle Ltd £	Doyle Ltd £	Doyle Ltd £
Freehold land and buildings						
– cost		950,000		1,375,000		300,000
Plant and equipment						
Cost	500,000		10,000,000		750,000	
Depreciation	(280,000)		(7,500,000)		(500,000)	
		220,000		2,500,000		250,000
		1,170,000		3,875,000		550,000
Investments						
1,500,000 shares in						
Carlyle Ltd		1,600,000				
800,000 shares in						
Doyle Ltd				1,250,000		
Stocks	50,000		2,050,000		850,500	
Debtors	325,000		2,675,000		1,700,000	
Cash at bank	25,500		–		16,500	
		400,500		4,725,000		2,567,000
		3,170,500		9,850,000		3,117,000
Creditors under 1 year	91,500		2,385,750		1,395,800	
Proposed dividend	200,000					
Bank overdraft	–		1,450,850		–	
		(291,500)		(3,836,600)		(1,395,800)
		2,879,000		6,013,400		1,721,200
10% debenture		–		(2,000,000)		–
		2,879,000		4,013,400		1,721,200

	£	£	£
Ordinary shares of			
£1 each	2,000,000		1,200,000
50p each		1,000,000	
8% redeemable preference			
shares of £1 each		2,000,000	
Reserves	879,000	1,013,400	521,200
	2,879,000	4,013,400	1,721,200

Proposed dividends have not yet been provided for on the shares in Carlyle Ltd and Doyle Ltd although Bryon Ltd has included dividends of 5p per share as receivable from Carlyle Ltd in debtors. Dividends on the preference shares were paid for one-half year on 1 April 20X6; the next payment date was 1 October 20X6. Dividends on the ordinary shares in Doyle Ltd are proposed at the rate of 10p per share and on Carlyle's shares as anticipated by Bryon.

Profits for the year in Doyle Ltd were £310,000, before making any adjustments for consolidation, accruing evenly through the year.

The directors of Bryon Ltd consider that the assets and liabilities of Carlyle Ltd are shown at fair values, but fair values for Doyle Ltd for the purposes of consolidation are:

	£	£
Freehold land and building		500,000
Plant and equipment – Valuation	968,400	
– Depreciation	639,600	
		328,800

Other assets and liabilities are considered to be at fair values in the balance sheet.

Additional depreciation due to the revaluation of the plant and equipment in Doyle Ltd amounts to £40,000 for the year to 30 September 20X6.

Included in stocks in Carlyle Ltd are items purchased from Doyle Ltd during the last three months of the year, on which Doyle Ltd recorded a profit of £80,000.

On 30 September 20X6 Carlyle Ltd drew a cheque for £100,000 and sent it to Doyle Ltd to clear the current account. As this cheque was not received by Doyle Ltd until 3 October, no account was taken of it in the Doyle Ltd balance sheet.

Required:
Prepare a balance sheet as at 30 September 20X6 for Bryon Ltd and its subsidiaries, conforming with the Companies Acts so far as the information given will permit.

Ignore taxation.

(*Association of Chartered Certified Accountants*)

CHAPTER 24

Consolidated profit and loss accounts

After you have studied this chapter, you should be able to:

- prepare consolidated profit and loss accounts for groups with wholly-owned subsidiaries
- prepare consolidated profit and loss accounts for groups with partly-owned subsidiaries

Introduction

In this chapter you'll learn how to prepare consolidated profit and loss accounts for groups with either wholly-owned subsidiaries, partly-owned subsidiaries, or both.

24.1 Wholly-owned subsidiaries

The consolidated profit and loss account is drawn up to show the overall profit (or loss) of the companies in the group, treating the group as a single entity. If all of the subsidiaries are owned 100 per cent, and there are no intragroup dividends or unrealised profits in stock, then it is simply a case of adding together all of the separate profit and loss accounts to form the consolidated profit and loss account. However, such a situation would very rarely be found in practice.

Exhibit 24.1 shows the framework for a consolidated profit and loss account giving details of the adjustments needed. It builds on many of the items you have covered in Chapters 19 to 23.

Activity 24.1
Why can't we simply add together all of the separate profit and loss accounts to form the consolidated profit and loss account when the subsidiaries are partly owned and there is no intragroup dividends or unrealised profits on stock?

Exhibit 24.1

Specimen Profit and Loss Account for the Year ended . . .

		£000	£000	
Turnover	(a)		200	Parent plus
Cost of sales	(b)		120	subsidiaries
Gross profit			80	less cancellation
Distribution costs		10		of intragroup
Administrative expenses		20	30	items
Profit on ordinary activities before taxation			50	
Tax on profit on ordinary activities	(c)		14	
Profit on ordinary activities after taxation			36	
Minority interest	(d)		4	
Profit for the financial year			32	
Retained profits from last year	(e)		7	
			39	
Proposed dividend	(f)	15		Parent only
Transfer to reserves	(g)	8	23	
Retained profits carried to next year			16	

Notes:

(a) Turnover. Intragroup sales to be deducted.

(b) Cost of sales: (*i*) Intragroup purchases. This is the same figure as for (a), as the price at which sales are made by one group company is the same figure at which the other group company has bought them. (*ii*) Adjust for unrealised profit in stock, by reducing closing stock. As cost of sales = opening stock + purchases – closing stock, any reduction in closing stock will increase 'cost of sales'. The balance sheet stock figure will be reduced by unrealised profits.

(c) Tax on profit on ordinary activities. This is the sum of tax for all companies within the group.

(d) Minority interest:

(*i*) If ordinary shares only issued by subsidiary: take requisite percentage of subsidiary's profits after taxation.

(*ii*) If preference shares also issued by subsidiary found by:

Minority interest percentage of preference share capital × total preference dividend for the year

plus

Minority interest percentage of ordinary share capital × balance of profits (i.e. after preference dividend) for the year, e.g.

  Total preference shares £1,000: Minority interest £400.
  Total ordinary shares £2,000: Minority interest £500.
  Total preference dividend for year £150.
  Profit of subsidiary after tax but before dividend: £950.

Therefore, the minority interest is:		£
Share of preference dividend: 40% × £150	=	60
Share of balance of profits: 25% × (£950 – £150)	=	200
		260

(e) This is parent's retained profits plus group's share of post-acquisition profit of subsidiaries.

(f) In respect of parent only.

(g) Those of the parent plus the group's share of the subsidiary's transfers to reserves.

We can now look at two examples:

1 Exhibit 24.2: consolidation of financial statements where the subsidiary is wholly owned.

2 Exhibit 24.3: consolidation where there is a minority interest in the subsidiary company.

Exhibit 24.2

P Ltd owns 100 per cent of shares in S Ltd. Profit and loss accounts of these companies for the year to 31 December 20X4 are as follows:

Profit and loss accounts	P Ltd		S Ltd	
	£000	£000	£000	£000
Turnover		400		280
Cost of sales		270		190
Gross profit		130		90
Distribution costs	20		10	
Administrative expenses	30		15	
		(50)		(25)
Profit on operating activities		80		65
Dividend receivable		30		–
Profit on ordinary activities before taxation		110		65
Tax on profit on ordinary activities		(17)		(11)
Profit on ordinary activities after taxation		93		54
Retained profits from last year		11		7
		104		61
Proposed dividend	40		30	
Transfer to reserves	5		2	
		(45)		(32)
Retained profits carried to next year		59		29

Notes:

(a) P Ltd had sold goods costing £10,000 to S Ltd for £15,000.
(b) At the balance sheet date 40 per cent of the goods in (a) had not been sold by S Ltd.
(c) Of the £7,000 retained profits from last year for S Ltd, £3,000 is in respect of post-acquisition profits.

The consolidated profit and loss of the group can now be drawn up.

P Ltd and subsidiary S Ltd
Consolidated Profit and Loss Account for the year ended 31 December 20X4

	£000	£000
Turnover (W1)		665
Cost of sales (W2)		(447)
Gross profit		218
Distribution costs	30	
Administrative expenses	45	
		(75)
Profit on ordinary activities before taxation		143
Tax on profit on ordinary activities		(28)
Profit on ordinary activities after taxation		115
Retained profits from last year (W3)		14
		129
Proposed dividend (W4)	40	
Transfer to reserves (W5)	7	
		(47)
Retained profits carried to next year		82

Workings:

Letters (a) to (g) refer to the descriptions given above and in Exhibit 24.1.

(W1) P 400 + S 280 – 15 intercompany sales = 665 (a).
(W2) P 270 + S 190 – 15 intercompany purchases + unrealised profit in stock (40% × 5 = 2) = 447 (b) (i) and (ii).
(W3) P 11 + S 3 = 14. Only post-acquisition profits of S included. (See (e) in Exhibit 24.1.)
(W4) Only dividend of P included as S dividend will be received by P and will cancel out. (See (f) in Exhibit 24.1.)
(W5) P 5 + S (100%)2 = 7. (See (g) in Exhibit 24.1.)

24.2 Partly-owned subsidiaries

Exhibit 24.3

P Ltd owns 80 per cent of shares in S Ltd. Profit and loss accounts of the companies for the year to 31 December 20X2 are as follows:

Profit and loss accounts	P Ltd		S Ltd	
	£000	£000	£000	£000
Turnover		640		330
Cost of sales		(410)		(200)
Gross profit		230		130
Distribution costs	35		20	
Administrative expenses	70		55	
		(105)		(75)
Profit on operating activities		125		55
Dividend receivable		28		–
Profit on ordinary activities before taxation		153		55
Tax on profit on ordinary activities		(26)		(10)
Profit on ordinary activities after taxation		127		45
Retained profits from last year		29		35
		156		80
Proposed dividend	60		35	
Transfers to reserves	22		10	
		(82)		(45)
Retained profits carried to next year		74		35

Notes:

(a) S Ltd had sold goods costing £20,000 to P Ltd for £30,000.

(b) At the balance sheet date, 30 per cent of the goods in (a) had not been sold by P Ltd.

(c) Of the £35,000 retained profits of S Ltd brought forward, £15,000 is post-acquisition profits.

P Ltd and subsidiary S Ltd

Consolidated Profit and Loss Account for the year ending 31 December 20X2

	£000	£000
Turnover (W1)		940
Cost of sales (W2)		(583)
Gross profit		357
Distribution costs	55	
Administrative expenses	125	
		(180)
Profit on ordinary activities before taxation		177
Tax on profit on ordinary activities		(36)
Profit on ordinary activities after taxation		141
Minority interest (W3)		(9)
Profit for the financial year		132
Retained profits from last year (W4)		41
		173
Proposed dividend (W5)	60	
Transfer to reserves (W6)	30	
		(90)
Retained profits carried to next year		83

Workings:

Letters (*a*) to (*g*) refer to the descriptions given above and in Exhibit 24.1.

(W1) P 640 + S 330 – intercompany sales 30 = 940 (*a*).

(W2) P 410 + S 200 – intercompany purchases 30 + unrealised profit in stock (30% × 10 = 3)
= 583 (b) (i) and (ii).

(W3) 20 per cent × 45: profit after taxation of S Ltd = 9 (d) (i).

(W4) P 29 + S (80% × 15 = 12) = 41 (e).

(W5) Only the dividend of P shown. See (f).

(W6) P 22 + S (80% × 10 = 8) = 30 (g).

Learning outcomes

You should now have learnt:

1 When consolidating profit and loss accounts for groups with wholly-owned subsidiaries with no intra-group transactions or indebtedness, it is simply a case of adding together all the separate profit and loss accounts to form the consolidated profit and loss account.

2 When consolidating profit and loss accounts, adjustments for unrealised profits on intra-group transactions and for intra-group indebtedness must be made where they exist (as per Chapters 19, 21, and 22).

3 When consolidating profit and loss accounts for groups with partly-owned subsidiaries, the approaches detailed in Chapters 17 and 23 should be followed.

Answers to activities

24.1 You need to deduct the minority interest in the profits or losses of the subsidiary when combining the figures for profits and/or losses of the companies for the period.

REVIEW QUESTIONS

24.1 The following information relates to the Brodick group of companies for the year to 30 April 20X7:

	Brodick plc £000	Lamlash Ltd £000	Corrie Ltd £000
Turnover	1,100	500	130
Cost of sales	(630)	(300)	(70)
Gross profit	470	200	60
Administrative expenses	(105)	(150)	(20)
Dividend from Lamlash Ltd	24	–	–
Dividend from Corrie Ltd	6	–	–
Profit before tax	395	50	40
Taxation	(65)	(10)	(20)
Profit after tax	330	40	20
Interim dividend	(50)	(10)	–
Proposed dividend	(150)	(20)	(10)
Retained profit for the year	130	10	10
Retained profits brought forward	460	106	10
Retained profits carried forward	590	116	40

Additional information:

(a) The issued share capital of the group was as follows:
Brodick plc: 5,000,000 ordinary shares of £1 each;
Lamlash Ltd: 1,000,000 ordinary shares of £1 each; and
Corrie Ltd: 400,000 ordinary shares of £1 each.

(b) Brodick plc purchased 80 per cent of the issued share capital of Lamlash Ltd in 20X0. At that time, the retained profits of Lamlash amounted to £56,000.

(c) Brodick plc purchased 60 per cent of the issued share capital of Corrie Ltd in 20X4. At that time, the retained profits of Corrie amounted to £20,000.

(d) Brodick plc recognises dividends proposed by other group companies in its profit and loss account.

Required:
In so far as the information permits, prepare the Brodick group of companies' consolidated profit and loss account for the year to 30 April 20X7 in accordance with the Companies Acts and related accounting statements. (*Note:* Notes to the profit and loss account are not required, but you should append a statement showing the make-up of the 'retained profits carried forward', and your workings should be submitted.)

(*Association of Accounting Technicians*)

24.2   You are presented with the following summarised information for Norbreck plc and its subsidiary, Bispham Ltd:

Profit and Loss Accounts for the year to 30 September 20X7

	Norbreck plc £000	Bispham Ltd £000
Turnover	1,700	450
Cost of sales	(920)	(75)
Gross profit	780	375
Administration expenses	(300)	(175)
Income from shares in group company	120	–
Profit on ordinary activities before taxation	600	200
Tax on profit on ordinary activities	(30)	(20)
Profit on ordinary activities after taxation	570	180
Dividends: paid	(90)	(50)
proposed	(270)	(100)
Retained profit for the year	210	30
Retained profit brought forward	220	70
Retained profit carried forward	430	100

Balance Sheets at 30 September 20X7

	Norbreck plc £000	Bispham Ltd £000
Fixed tangible assets	1,280	440
Investments: Shares in group company	400	–
Current assets		
Stocks	300	250
Debtors (including, for Norbreck plc, the dividend proposed by the subsidiary)	280	150
Cash at bank and in hand	40	10
	620	410
Creditors (amounts falling due within one year)		
Trade creditors	(80)	(160)
Other creditors, taxation and social security	(160)	(70)
Proposed dividend	(270)	(100)
	(510)	(330)
Net current assets	110	80
Total assets *less* current liabilities	1,790	520
Provisions for liabilities and charges		
Taxation, including deferred taxation	(460)	(20)
	1,330	500

	Norbreck plc £000	Bispham Ltd £000
Capital and reserves		
Called-up share capital (ordinary shares of £1 each)	900	400
Profit and loss account	430	100
	1,330	500

Additional information:

(a) Norbreck plc acquired 80 per cent of the shares in Bispham Ltd on 1 October 20X4. Bispham's profit and loss account balance as at that date was £40,000.

(b) Goodwill arising on acquisition is to be written off against the group's retained profits.

(c) Norbreck takes credit within its own books of account for any dividends receivable from Bispham.

Required:

Prepare Bispham plc's consolidated profit and loss account for the year to 30 September 20X7 and a consolidated balance sheet as at that date.

Note: Formal notes to the account are not required, although detailed workings should be submitted with your answer. You should also append to the consolidated profit and loss account your calculation of earnings per share and a statement showing the make-up of 'retained profits carried forward'.

(*Association of Accounting Technicians*)

24.3A The following figures for the year to 30 April 20X6 have been extracted from the books and records of three companies which form a group:

	Old plc £	Field Ltd £	Lodge Ltd £
Revenue reserves at 1 May 20X5	30,000	40,000	50,000
Stocks at 1 May 20X5	90,000	150,000	80,000
Sales	1,250,000	875,000	650,000
Purchases	780,000	555,000	475,000
Distribution expenses	125,000	85,000	60,000
Administration expenses	28,000	40,000	72,000
Interim dividends:			
Paid 31 July 20X5, ordinary	45,000	35,000	15,000
Paid 31 October 20X5, preference		4,000	
Share capital – fully paid ordinary shares of £1 each	450,000	350,000	200,000
8% preference shares of £1 each		100,000	
Stocks at 30 April 20X6	110,000	135,000	85,000

Profits are deemed to accrue evenly throughout the year.

Other information:

(a) Corporation tax of the following amounts is to be provided on the profits of the year:

Old plc	£125,000
Field Ltd	£75,000
Lodge Ltd	£20,000

(b) Final dividends proposed are:

Old plc	15p per share
Field Ltd	12.5p per share on the ordinary shares and a half-year's dividend on the preference shares
Lodge Ltd	7.5p per share

(c) Field Ltd sells goods for resale to both Old plc and Lodge Ltd. At 30 April 20X6, stocks of goods purchased from Field Ltd are:

in Old plc	£40,000
in Lodge Ltd	£28,000

The net profit percentage for Field Ltd on sales of these goods is 25 per cent.
Old plc has £36,000 of these goods in stock at 1 May 20X5.
Total sales in the year by Field Ltd to Old plc were £150,000 and to Lodge Ltd £120,000.

(d) Old plc acquired the whole of the ordinary shares in Field Ltd many years ago. 50,000 of the preference shares were acquired on 1 August 20X5. Old plc acquired 120,000 shares in Lodge Ltd on 1 August 20X5.

Required:
A consolidated profit and loss account for Old plc and its subsidiaries for the year ended 30 April 20X6, together with any relevant notes.

(*Association of Chartered Certified Accountants*)

24.4A The following are the trial balances of ATH Ltd, GLE Ltd, and FRN Ltd as at 31 December 20X8.

	ATH Ltd	GLE Ltd	FRN Ltd
	£	£	£
Ordinary share capital (shares of £1 each, fully paid)	100,000	30,000	20,000
7 per cent cumulative preference share capital (shares of £1 each, fully paid)	–	–	5,000
Profit and loss account – balance at 31.12.20X7	15,600	6,000	1,900
Current liabilities	20,750	15,900	18,350
Sales	194,000	116,000	84,000
Dividend received from GLE Ltd	1,200		
	331,550	167,900	129,250
Fixed assets	45,000	29,000	25,000
Current assets	46,000	27,500	22,500
24,000 ordinary shares in GLE Ltd at cost	33,700	–	–
20,000 ordinary shares in FRN Ltd at cost	21,250	–	–
Cost of goods sold	153,000	87,000	63,000
General expenses	32,600	22,900	18,750
Dividend for 20X8, paid on 31.12.20X8	–	1,500	–
	331,550	167,900	129,250

ATH Ltd acquired the shares in FRN Ltd on 31 December 20X6, when the credit balance on the profit and loss account of FRN Ltd was £700, and acquired the shares in GLE Ltd on 31 December 20X7. No dividend was paid by either ATH Ltd or GLE Ltd for the year 20X7.

No dividend has been paid by FRN Ltd for the years 20X6, 20X7 and 20X8 and none is proposed. The directors of ATH Ltd propose to pay a dividend of £7,000 for 20X8.

The sales of GLE Ltd for 20X8 (£116,000) include £1,000 for goods sold to FRN Ltd and this amount has been debited to purchases account in the books of FRN Ltd.

All these goods were sold by FRN Ltd during 20X8.

Required:
A consolidated trading and profit and loss account for the year 20X8 and a consolidated balance sheet as on 31 December 20X8 (not necessarily in a form for publication).

Ignore depreciation of fixed assets and taxation.

(*Institute of Chartered Secretaries and Administrators*)

CHAPTER 25

Consolidated financial statements – FRS 6: acquisitions and mergers

After you have studied this chapter, you should be able to:

- explain when merger accounting should be used
- explain the difference between the acquisition and the merger methods of preparing consolidated financial statements

Introduction

In this chapter you'll learn about the two accounting methods used to account for the combination of two companies into one permanent organisation: acquisition accounting and merger accounting.

25.1 Methods of combination of companies

When two limited companies are going to combine together in some way, then it is obvious that the shares must come under common ownership. There are two main methods of achieving this, with different possible methods of accounting for the combination: acquisition accounting, which would normally be applied (and which has been assumed throughout Chapters 16 to 24); and merger accounting, which is restricted to specific circumstances. Acquisition accounting is dealt with in FRS 2: *Accounting for subsidiary undertakings*, FRS 6: *Acquisitions and mergers* and FRS 7: *Fair values in acquisition accounting*. FRS 6 presents the merger accounting approach.

Examples of combinations where it would be appropriate to adopt acquisition accounting

A common approach to the formation of new business combinations is for one company, A, to purchase the shares of another company, B. Often this is achieved by A's making a cash payment to shareholders in B. In accepting the cash, the shareholders sever their links with the company. Company A shareholders now control both companies.

Another common approach is where company A issues debentures (loan stock) to company B's shareholders in exchange for their shareholdings in B: the new debenture holders would have no voting power in the new group, which would be controlled by the shareholders of A.

In both of these cases, **acquisition accounting** should be used.

Exhibit 25.1 *Requirements to be met if merger accounting is to be used*

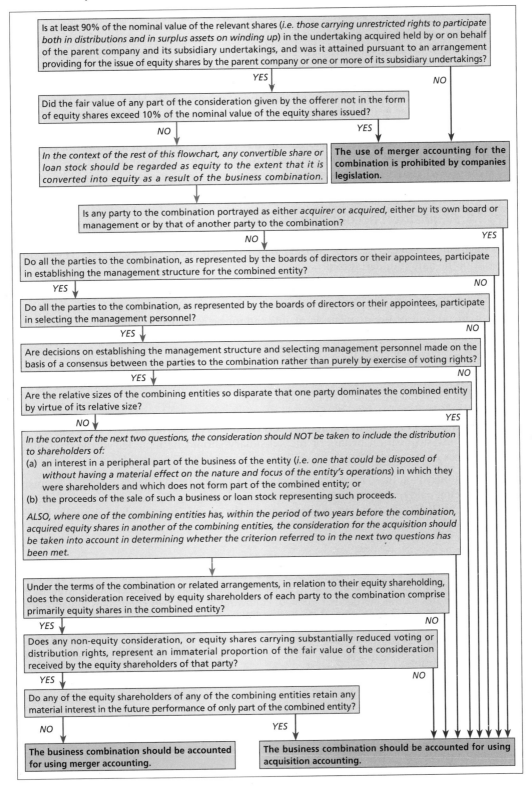

Examples of combinations where it would be appropriate to adopt merger accounting

When company A does not pay cash or issue debentures to the old shareholders of company B but, instead, issues them with new equity (ordinary voting) shares, this means the shareholders of A and B have 'merged' into one and, between them, have a joint interest in the new group. It is often called a 'pooling of interest'.

A variation on this is the 'new entity' method of combination. Here a new company, C, is formed to take over A and B, giving the old shareholders of A and B new shares in C. Once again the shareholders have 'merged' into one.

In both these cases, **merger accounting** may be used, but only if a number of conditions contained in FRS 6 are met. Otherwise, acquisition accounting must be used.

Exhibit 25.1 shows the conditions to be considered if merger accounting is to be used.

25.2 Acquisition accounting method

As mentioned above, this is the method that has been assumed in Chapters 16–24. In the books of the parent undertaking:

(a) shares purchased in a subsidiary should be shown at cost less dividends received out of pre-acquisition profits;
(b) dividends out of pre-acquisition profits cannot be regarded as available for distribution as dividends by the parent.

In the consolidated financial statements:

(c) assets and liabilities of the subsidiary at the date of acquisition should be shown in the balance sheet at their fair value at that date;
(d) the difference at the date of acquisition between the fair value of the purchase consideration and the fair value of the net assets is treated as goodwill, positive or negative;
(e) only post-acquisition profits of the subsidiary should be included in the consolidated reserves of the group.

The idea underlying these rules is to stop capital receipts, i.e. dividends from pre-acquisition profits, being paid out as dividends.

The consolidation of balance sheets using the *acquisition* method is now shown in Exhibit 25.2.

Exhibit 25.2

A Ltd has just made an offer of £270,000 for the whole of the share capital of B Ltd and this has been accepted. Payment to be by cash. The fair value placed on the tangible fixed assets of B Ltd for the purposes of the merger is £148,000. Following are the two companies' balance sheets, immediately before the merger on 31 December 20X3.

	A Ltd £000	A Ltd £000	B Ltd £000	B Ltd £000
Tangible fixed assets		400		120
Current assets	450		200	
Less Current liabilities	(130)		(90)	
		320		110
		720		230
Ordinary shares £1		500		150
Revenue reserves		220		80
		720		230

The balance sheets of A Ltd, and of the group, immediately following the merger, are as follows:

Balance Sheet at 31 December 20X3

		A Ltd			Group	
		£000	£000		£000	£000
Fixed assets						
Intangible (goodwill)		–		(W2)	12	
Tangible		400		(W3)	548	
Investments		270			–	
			670			560
Current assets	(W1)	180		(W4)	380	
Less Current liabilities		(130)			(220)	
			50			160
			720			720
Share capital			500			500
Reserves			220			220
			720			720

Workings (£000):
(W1)   Original current assets 450 – cash paid 270 = 180

(W2) Paid for shares		270
Less Net assets of B at takeover date	230	
Add Increase in value of fixed assets of B to a 'fair value' 148 – 120 =	28	
		(258)
Goodwill (intangible fixed asset)		12

(W3)   Fixed assets A Ltd 400 + B Ltd 148 = 548
(W4)   A Ltd (after payment) 180 + B Ltd 200 = 380

25.3 Merger accounting method

1 Shares issued by the parent are merely the means of achieving the merger in a technical sense. Consequently, no share premium arises. They are shown in the parent's balance sheet (A Ltd) at nominal value, as addition to share capital.

2 As share premium is not recognised in 1 above, the cost of the investment in the parent's balance sheet (A Ltd) is the nominal value of shares issued. If the nominal value of the shares is not the same as the stock exchange or similar market valuation then, obviously, the 'true' value of the subsidiary is not shown in the 'cost' of the investment.

3 Any dividends received by the parent (A Ltd) from the subsidiary (B Ltd) can be distributed in full by the parent. This means that the whole of the subsidiary's reserves can be included in the consolidated balance sheet reserves.

4 The assets of the subsidiary are not revalued at 'fair value' at the date of merger. It would not make sense to revalue B Ltd's assets while leaving A Ltd's assets valued at the old amounts. Sometimes, however, under the 'new entity' method of merger, described in Section 25.1, both companies revalue their assets.

5 Where the total nominal value of the shares issued by the parent, A Ltd, is more than the total nominal value of the shares of B Ltd, the difference is deducted from group reserves. If the total is less, then the shortfall becomes a non-distributable group reserve.

6 Any existing balance on the share premium account or capital redemption reserve of the new subsidiary undertaking should be brought in by being shown as a movement on other reserves.

7 Merger expenses should be charged to the profit and loss account of the combined entity at the effective date of the merger, as *reorganisation or restructuring expenses*.

Exhibit 25.3

Taking the same firms, A Ltd and B Ltd, as in Exhibit 25.2, but instead of a cash offer of £270,000 the offer is 200,000 ordinary shares of £1 each at a stock exchange value of £270,000.

The balance sheets of A Ltd and the group immediately after the merger are now:

	A Ltd £000	A Ltd £000	Group £000	Group £000
Fixed assets				
Tangible	400		520	
Investments	200		–	
		600		520
Current assets	450		650	
Less Current liabilities	(130)		(220)	
		320		430
		920		950
Share capital		700		700
Reserves		220		250
		920		950

Workings:

Reserve	A Ltd	220	
	B Ltd	80	
			300
Less Excess of nominal value shares issued by A Ltd over those exchanged of B Ltd, i.e. 200 – 150			(50)
			250

25.4 The advantages of merger accounting to a group

Merger accounting has a number of advantages from the perspective of the investing group:

1 The subsidiary's results are included in the group for the whole accounting period, not just for the post-acquisition period. Consequently, the group can appear to the casual reviewer as more profitable than it was. However, as the amounts relating to pre- and post-merger must be disclosed, this is not as great an advantage as it may appear.

2 The parent company can appear misleadingly successful if it is in receipt of pre-acquisition dividends which it treats as revenue income. (The investment is normally recorded at the nominal value of the holding company shares issued, plus any other consideration given, and is unlikely to need to be reduced to account for the pre-acquisition distribution.)

3 Assets may be understated (compared with equivalent situations where *acquisition accounting* has been applied), providing an opportunity for instant earnings by selling assets, and resulting in higher returns on capital.

4 Lower depreciation charges and an absence of goodwill will result in a correspondingly higher return on capital employed than would be the case were the acquisition accounting approach adopted.

5 Most importantly, all the pre-acquisition distributable reserves of the companies involved are available for distribution to the group's shareholders (though this may be subject to a reduction resulting from the nominal value of the new shares exceeding the nominal value of the shares received).

However, despite these advantages, the merger method has only been used infrequently in the UK. Furthermore, with the release in September 1994 of FRS 6, which significantly tightened the restriction on its use, future adoption of merger accounting in the UK is likely to be very rare indeed.

25.5 Final points concerning FRS 6

Under *merger accounting* per FRS 6, it is not necessary to adjust values of the subsidiaries' assets and liabilities to fair values. However, adjustments should be made to achieve uniformity of accounting policies within the group.

Remember that *in a merger* there is no such thing as *pre-acquisition profits*. The distribution of pre-acquisition profits is not restricted in the way it is under *acquisition accounting*.

Finally, while *acquisition accounting* will generally give rise to goodwill (positive or negative), *merger accounting* never does – not because a difference cannot arise between the consideration given and the value received, but because such differences arising under the merger accounting approach do not conform to the fair-value-based definition of goodwill given in FRS 10.

Activity 25.1

Given a choice, why would most companies prefer to adopt acquisition accounting?

Learning outcomes

You should now have learnt:

1 Merger accounting should be used only when certain conditions are met, and must be used when they are.

2 Otherwise, acquisition accounting should be used.

3 Under merger accounting, assets and liabilities do not require to be stated at their fair values on acquisition.

4 Goodwill can arise only under acquisition accounting.

5 No distinction is made between pre- and post-acquisition reserves under merger accounting.

6 That double entry follows the rules of the accounting equation.

Answers to activities

25.1 It may not be so much that they would prefer to adopt acquisition accounting as that they have little choice but to do so. Merger accounting really does involve companies merging. Effectively, they must lose their independent identities in order to merge – the last question on the flowchart shown in Exhibit 25.1 highlights this point. Other questions on the flowchart provide further evidence of this. It is most unlikely that this would be desirable to all parties and is, in itself, sufficient to prevent merger accounting from being a feasible option, if they truly had a choice. In other words, if they really were engaged in a merger, they would probably prefer to adopt merger accounting as the advantages of doing so appear far greater than the advantages of adopting acquisition accounting.

REVIEW QUESTIONS

25.1 Large plc, a manufacturer and wholesaler, purchased 600,000 of the 800,000 issued ordinary shares of a smaller company, Small Ltd, on 1 January 20X5 when the retained earnings account of Small Ltd had a credit balance of £72,000.

The latest accounts of the two companies are:

Summary Profit and Loss Accounts for the year to 30 September 20X6 (£000s)

	Large plc		Small Ltd	
Credit sales		10,830		2,000
Cost of sales and production services		(3,570)		(1,100)
Gross profit		7,260		900
Administrative and marketing expenses (including				
depreciation, audit fee and directors' remuneration)		(2,592)		(180)
Operating profit		4,668		720
Dividend received from Small Ltd		180		–
Net profit before tax		4,848		720
Taxation	2,304		200	
Net dividend	2,400		240	
		(4,704)		(440)
Profit retained		144		280
Brought forward from last year		1,200		192
Carried forward to next year		1,344		472

Summary Balance Sheets at 30 September 20X6 (£000)

	Large plc	Small Ltd
Intangible assets:		
Research and development:		
– pure research	20	–
– applied research	30	–
– development	180	–
Goodwill – purchased (at cost less amounts written off)	48	–
– unpurchased	50	–
Fixed assets at cost less depreciation	3,920	728
Investment in Small Ltd	525	–
Current account with Large plc	–	75
Stock	594	231
Debtors	2,250	370
Bank	99	24
	7,716	1,428
Less Current account with Small Ltd	(75)	(–)
Creditors for goods and services	(297)	(156)
	7,344	1,272
Share capital	6,000	800
Retained earnings	1,344	472
	7,344	1,272

Notes:
The intangible asset section of the balance sheet of Large plc has not yet been amended prior to consolidation to take account of the provisions of the Companies Acts or the recommendations contained in accounting standards regarding intangible assets.

The stock of Large plc contained goods valued at £108,000 purchased from Small Ltd at production cost plus 50 per cent.

Required:
(a) Prepare the consolidated profit and loss account of Large plc and its subsidiary Small Ltd for the year to 30 September 20X6 using the acquisition (purchase) method of consolidation.
(b) Prepare the consolidated balance sheet of Large plc and its subsidiary Small Ltd at 30 September 20X6 using the acquisition method of consolidation.
(c) What would the reserves of the group be if the merger method of consolidation were used instead of the acquisition method? Briefly explain why there is a difference between the values of the reserves arising from the two methods of consolidation.

(Institute of Chartered Secretaries and Administrators)

CHAPTER 26

Standards covering subsidiary and associated undertakings

Learning objectives

After you have studied this chapter, you should be able to:

- explain the importance of the control concept
- describe the circumstances under which a parent/subsidiary relationship is recognised
- describe the conditions whereby companies are exempt from preparing consolidated financial statements
- describe the conditions under which a subsidiary company should not be included in the consolidated financial statements
- describe what to do when a company has investments in associated undertakings but does not prepare consolidated financial statements because it has no investments in subsidiary undertakings

Introduction

In this chapter you'll learn about the various accounting standards that regulate the preparation of accounting information relating to subsidiaries and associate undertakings. These regulations have changed considerably in recent years and are now more standardised than in the past, enabling far greater comparability than was previously the case.

26.1 Background

The whole field of accounting relating to consolidated financial statements and groups in general has recently undergone considerable changes. FRS 2 has been introduced to clarify and extend business operations for which consolidated financial statements are needed, and to define those situations where exemptions from their preparation should apply; FRS 9 has updated the requirements concerning associates, and introduced regulations relating to joint ventures; and FRS 10 has replaced SSAP 22 as the accounting standard relating to goodwill.

26.2 FRS 2: Accounting for subsidiary undertakings

FRS 2 superseded SSAP 14: *Group accounts*. While it must comply with the Companies Acts, it redefines the legal requirements by reducing the number of alternatives and making the requirements and definitions more precise, thereby, improving the standardisation and hence comparability of financial statements.

Main changes recently have concerned consolidated financial statements. Specifically:

(a) the definitions of parents and subsidiaries are now based upon control, rather than on ownership;

(b) instead of 'company' the term 'undertaking' is used. This means that unincorporated bodies are now covered;

(c) there are now more exemptions available from the need to prepare consolidated financial statements.

In the remainder of this chapter the more important provisions are discussed. As Chapters 16 to 25 have already incorporated the mechanics of implementing FRS 2, those points will not be looked at again. While this chapter is concerned with the other important aspects of FRS 2 and of FRS 9, it does not cover every detail. Such detail would be needed only at a later stage in your studies.

Activity 26.1

Why do you think control is now the key factor in determining the relationship between related companies, rather than ownership?

26.3 Parent and subsidiary relationship

In general terms, the main test as to the existence of a parent/subsidiary relationship is one of control. A group consists of all the various enterprises, including unincorporated businesses as well as companies, under the control of the parent. If you understand that, the detail contained in FRS 2 and the Companies Acts will become much clearer. In fact, control and ownership usually go together, but it is the exceptions to this that have brought about the need for the changes that have been made to the Companies Acts and that have led to the issue of replacement accounting standards.

FRS 2 states that an undertaking is a parent undertaking of another undertaking (this being the subsidiary undertaking) if any of the following can apply to it:

1 It holds a majority of the voting rights (i.e. shares carrying a right to vote) in the undertaking.

2 It is a member of the undertaking and has the right to appoint or remove directors holding a majority of the voting rights at meetings of the board on substantially all matters.

3 It has the right to exercise a 'dominant influence' over the undertaking. This could be by virtue of provisions in the undertaking's memorandum or articles, or by a control contract which must be in writing and be legally valid. By 'dominant influence' is meant influence that can be exercised to achieve the operating and financial policies desired by the holder of the influence, not withstanding the rights or influence of any other party – in other words, it has the right to give directions as to the functioning of the operating and financial policies of the undertaking, whether or not they are to the benefit of that undertaking.

4 It is a member of the undertaking and controls alone a majority of the voting rights by agreement with other members.

5 It has a 'participating interest' (i.e. an interest in the shares of the undertaking which is held for the long term for the purpose of securing a contribution to its activities by the exercise of control or influence arising from that interest – this would normally be a holding of more than 20 per cent of the shares of the undertaking) and either (a) it exercises a dominant influence over the undertaking, or (b) it and the undertaking are managed on a

unified basis (i.e. where the whole of the operations of the undertakings are integrated and they are managed as a single unit).

6 A parent undertaking is also treated as the parent undertaking of the subsidiary undertakings of its subsidiary undertakings.

Points 1 and 6 above are the more traditional and more usual ways of establishing the existence of a parent/subsidiary relationship in the UK.

26.4 Exemption from preparing consolidated financial statements

The Companies Act 1989 contains provisions which exempt some groups from having to prepare consolidated financial statements. Exactly the same provisions are contained in FRS 2. The main points contained therein are as follows:

1 Small and medium-sized groups can claim exemption on the grounds of size. They must comply with at least two of the following criteria:

	Small	*Medium-sized*
Aggregate turnover not more than	£2.8 million net/ £3.36 million gross	£11.2 million net/ £13.44 million gross
Aggregate gross assets not more than	£1.4 million net/ £1.68 million gross	£5.6 million net/ £6.72 million gross
Aggregate employees not more than	50	250

(This exemption does not apply to groups whose members include a plc, a bank, an insurance company, or an authorised person under the Financial Services Act 1986.)

In the past, small and medium-sized companies could file modified group financial statements. This is no longer possible. Small and medium-sized companies now have to choose between filing *full* consolidated financial statements or *individual* company financial statements.

2 Except for companies who have any of their securities listed on any stock exchange in the European Union, any parent undertaking that is itself a wholly-owned subsidiary whose immediate parent is established in the European Union does not have to prepare consolidated financial statements. Individual company financial statements must still be prepared for the parent and they must include the name of its own parent undertaking; the country where its own parent is incorporated, if it is not the UK; and the fact that it is exempt from preparing group financial statements. As well as this, a copy of the audited consolidated financial statements of its own parent must be filed with its own individual company financial statements. (This exemption can be overturned by minority shareholders who can require that consolidated financial statements are prepared.)

3 If all of the subsidiary undertakings are permitted or required to be excluded from consolidation under the Companies Acts, consolidated financial statements are not required.

26.5 Exemption from the inclusion of a subsidiary in consolidated financial statements

There are three grounds for exclusion of a subsidiary given in FRS 2:

(a) where severe long-term restrictions substantially hinder the rights of the parent undertaking over the assets or management of the subsidiary undertaking;

(b) where the interest in the subsidiary undertaking is held exclusively for subsequent resale; and

(c) where activities are so different from those of other undertakings to be included in the consolidation that their inclusion would be incompatible with the obligation to give a true and fair view.

A subsidiary that is excluded on the grounds of long-term restriction should be treated as a fixed asset investment. However, if the parent still exercises significant influence it should be treated as an associated undertaking.

Subsidiaries excluded on the grounds that they are being held exclusively for resale should be included as current assets at the lower of cost and net realisable value.

Where exclusion is due to the activities of the subsidiary being so different from those of other undertakings to be included in the consolidation that their inclusion would be incompatible with the obligation to give a true and fair view, they should be accounted for using the equity method.

26.6 SSAP 1: Accounting for associated companies

This accounting standard was replaced by FRS 9: *Associates and joint ventures* in November 1997.

26.7 FRS 9: Associates and joint ventures

FRS 9 updated and expanded the content of SSAP 1 to encompass joint ventures, which it defines as entities in which the reporting entity holds an interest on a long-term basis and which are jointly controlled by the reporting entity and one or more other venturers under a contractual arrangement.

SSAP 1 said that B Ltd would be considered as an associate of A Ltd if A Ltd could *significantly* influence the financial and operating decisions of B Ltd. FRS 9 amended this definition of an associate to include entities only where the investing entity *exercises* a significant influence, rather than one that is *in a position to exercise* significant influence. Hence, fewer entities should be defined as associates under FRS 9 than was the case under SSAP 1. At the same time, the amount of disclosure required in the financial statements was increased.

Activity 26.2
Why do you think this change was made?

No change was made to the treatment of associates in the balance sheet, 'investments in associates' appearing as a line under fixed asset investments. In the profit and loss account, the share of the associate's results are shown as a separate line under group operating profit. (Under SSAP 1, they were shown as part of the group profit before tax.)

If one company has invested in another company, and can *significantly influence* the affairs of that company, then ordinary investment accounting (which shows just the income from dividends) is not suitable. SSAP 1 introduced 'equity accounting' by which, rather than simply showing dividends received as a measure of income, the investing company's *full* share of the profit of that company was incorporated in the investing company's financial statements.

FRS 9 introduced the 'gross equity' method of accounting, which is a form of equity accounting applicable to joint ventures under which the investor's share of the aggregate gross assets and liabilities of the joint venture is shown on the face of the balance sheet and the investor's share of the joint venture's turnover is noted in the profit and loss account.

26.8 Equity accounting

Equity accounting is a modified form of consolidation that requires similar adjustments to be made as apply under FRS 2: *Accounting for subsidiary undertakings* for full, acquisition-accounting-based consolidations. In the consolidated profit and loss account, the investing company should take into account the whole of its share of the earnings of the associate, whether or not the associate has distributed the earnings as dividends. In the consolidated balance sheet the investment is shown at cost, adjusted each year by the share of retained profits belonging to the investor, subject to an adjustment for any goodwill arising on acquisition written off.

We will shortly see how this is carried out. You will note that there are considerable differences between equity accounting and consolidation accounting of a subsidiary's results. With subsidiary accounting, the group would take credit for the whole of the turnover, cost of sales, etc. and then make a one-line adjustment to remove any minority share. With equity accounting, the associated undertaking's turnover, cost of sales, etc. are not amalgamated with those of the group. Instead, only the items concerned with the group's share of the associated undertaking's results are brought into account.

As it would be quite rare for the investing company not to have subsidiaries, we will use an example that brings the necessary equity accounting into a consolidated set of financial statements.

Effect upon consolidated profit and loss account

Take out:
(a) dividends received or receivable from the associate.

Include instead the group's share of the associate's:
(b) pre-tax profit
(c) taxation charge
(d) post-acquisition retained profits brought forward.

Effect upon consolidated balance sheet

Rather than   the cost of the investment
Show instead   the cost of the investment
                       plus
                 the group's share of associate's post-acquisition retained profit

Exhibit 26.1 shows how the associated undertaking's results are incorporated into a set of consolidated financial statements.

Exhibit 26.1

A Ltd is a holding company with subsidiaries. It also has 25 per cent of the equity share capital of B Ltd. This was bought for £100,000 three years ago when B Ltd had reserves (retained profits) of £20,000.

Profit and Loss Accounts for the year ending 31 December 20X3

	A Ltd & Subsidiaries (consolidated)		B Ltd (associated co.)	
	£000	£000	£000	£000
Turnover		540		200
Cost of sales		(370)		(130)
Gross profit		170		70
Distribution costs	20		3	
Administrative expenses	40		7	
		(60)		(10)
		110		60
Dividends receivable from B Ltd	(A)	10		–
Profit on ordinary activities before taxation		120	(B)	60
Tax on profit on ordinary activities		(28)	(C)	(16)
Profit on ordinary activities after taxation		92		44
Retained profits from last year		43		40
		135		84
Proposed dividends		(60)		(40)
Retained profits carried to next year		75		44

Balance Sheet as at 31 December 20X3 (abbreviated)

	£000	£000
Fixed assets	145	130
Investment in B Ltd at cost	100	–
Net current assets	180	114
	425	244
Share capital (ordinary shares)	350	200
Reserves	75	44
	425	244

Now we can move to the consolidation of B Ltd with A Ltd. As you have already been told the items needing adjusting are:

Take out: (A) Dividends receivable

Include: (B) Group share of pre-tax profit
(C) Group share of taxation
(D) Group's share post-acquisition retained profit brought forward.

The answer is:

A Ltd Group
Consolidated Profit and Loss Account for the year ending 31 December 20X3

		£000	£000
Turnover			540
Cost of sales			(370)
			170
Distribution costs		20	
Administrative expenses		40	
			(60)
			110
Share of profit of associated undertaking (W1)	(B)		15
Profit on ordinary activities before taxation			125
Tax on profit on ordinary activities (W2)	(C)		(32)
Profit on ordinary activities after taxation			93
Retained profits from last year (W3)	(D)		48
			141
Proposed dividend			(60)
Retained profits carried to next year			81

Consolidated Balance Sheet as at 31 December 20X3

	£000
Fixed assets	145
Investment in B Ltd (W4)	106
Net current assets	180
	431
Share capital	350
Reserves (W5)	81
	431

Workings:

(W1) 25% of profit before taxation of B Ltd x £60 = £15

(W2) A £28 + 25% of B £16 = £32

(W3) A £43 + 25% of B's post-acquisition profits (£40 – £20) £20 = £48

(W4) Cost of 25% share in B =   100

Add Retained profits B c/d	44	
Less Pre-acquisition profits	(20)	
Post-acquisition profits	24	
25% share		6
		106

(W5) Reserves A   75

Add 25% of post-acquisition profit of B (*see* W4)	6
	81

26.9 Investing companies without subsidiaries

If no consolidated financial statements are produced by the investing company and that company is not exempt from preparing consolidated statements, or would not be if it had subsidiaries, a separate profit and loss account (or a supplement to the investing company's own profit and loss account) should be prepared showing the information that would have been included in respect of the associated undertaking had consolidated financial statements been prepared. Similar requirements apply to the balance sheet. An example of a supplementary statement incorporating the results of associated undertakings is shown in Exhibit 26.2.

Exhibit 26.2

Example of a profit and loss account of a company without subsidiaries:

Profit and Loss Account of an Investing Company

	£000	£000
Turnover		2,000
Cost of sales		(1,400)
Gross profit		600
Distribution costs	175	
Administrative expenses	125	
		(300)
Profit on ordinary activities before taxation		300
Tax on profit on ordinary activities		(85)
Profit on ordinary activities after taxation		215
Dividends – proposed		(80)
Amount set aside to reserves		135

Supplementary statement incorporating results of associated undertakings:

	£000
Share of profits less losses of associated undertakings	50
Less Tax	(15)
Share of profits after tax of associated undertakings	35
Profit on ordinary share activities after taxation (as above)	215
Profit attributable to members of the investing company	250
Dividends – proposed	(80)
Net profit retained (£35,000 by associated undertakings)	170

Note: The earnings per share figure would be based on £250,000.

26.10 The control concept

The control concept underlies the presentation of consolidated financial statements for a group as a single economic entity. While the list given in Section 26.3 can be used to identify a parent/subsidiary relationship, it may result in more than one undertaking being classified as the parent. However, FRS 2 states that control can only be held by one parent, and that the control that identifies undertakings as parent and subsidiary undertakings should be distinguished from shared control, for example as in a joint venture. If more than one undertaking is identified as the parent, their interests in the subsidiary are, in effect, interests in a joint venture, and no parent/subsidiary relationship exists.

On the other hand, one or more of these parents may exercise a non-controlling but significant influence over the company in which it has invested. In that case it would be appropriate to account for it as an associate undertaking.

Learning outcomes

You should now have learnt:

1 The existence of a parent/subsidiary relationship depends upon whether the 'parent' undertaking can exercise *dominant* influence over the 'subsidiary' undertaking.

2 The existence of a parent/associate relationship depends upon whether the 'parent' undertaking actually exercises *significant* influence over the 'associate' undertaking.

3 There are some circumstances where groups are exempted from the preparation of consolidated financial statements.

4 Equity accounting is used when including associate undertakings in consolidated financial statements.

5 When a company has investments in associated undertakings but does not prepare consolidated financial statements because it has no investments in subsidiary undertakings, it should prepare a supplement to its financial statements detailing the information that would have been included in respect of the associated undertaking had consolidated financial statements been prepared.

6 Subsidiary undertakings can have only one parent; however, more than one parent may have a significant influence over an associated undertaking.

Answers to activities

26.1 Control is far more all-encompassing. Control in some cases can be exercised with very little ownership. It depends entirely upon the circumstances and may, in fact, depend on contractual agreements, as between lender and borrower, rather than equity ownership. By shifting the

emphasis from ownership to control, the substance of the relationship is identified as the main deciding factor. As a result, parent/subsidiary relationships (and parent/associate relationships) are much more realistically defined, thus providing a more meaningful basis for the preparation of group financial statements.

26.2 Associate undertakings are those over which a *significant* influence can be exerted. They are only marginally different from subsidiaries, for which a *dominant* influence is the key. Associate undertakings are clearly part of the group of companies in which they are given the status of 'associate undertaking'. Hence, it is appropriate to include their results under the group operating profit.

REVIEW QUESTIONS

26.1 Q plc has three subsidiaries: L Ltd, M Ltd, and N Ltd. All three were acquired on 1 January at the start of the financial year which has just ended. Q has a 55 per cent, 70 per cent and 95 per cent holding respectively and holds a majority of the voting equity in L and M. It has changed the composition of both these companies' boards since they were acquired. However, despite its 95 per cent holding in N Ltd, it has only a 45 per cent holding of the voting equity and has so far failed in all its attempts to have a director appointed to the board. How should these three investee companies be treated in the Q group consolidated financial statements?

26.2 At the end of 20X5, a parent company, P plc, with one subsidiary had a holding representing 10 per cent of the equity of R Ltd, a clothing company. It had cost £80,000 when purchased at the start of 20X4. At the time of that investment, R Ltd had net assets of £560,000 which increased to £840,000 by the end of that year. At the start of the current year, the investment was increased by a further 11 per cent of the equity at a cost of £110,000.

Required:
(a) How would the investment be shown in the financial statements if it were treated as a *trade investment*?
(b) How would the investment be shown in the financial statements if it were treated as an *associated undertaking*?

26.3A Relevant balance sheets as at 31 March 20X4 are set out below:

	Jasmin (Holdings) plc £000	Kasbah plc £000	Fortran plc £000
Tangible fixed assets	289,400	91,800	7,600
Investments			
Shares in Kasbah (at cost)	97,600		
Shares in Fortran (at cost)	8,000		
	395,000		
Current assets			
Stock	285,600	151,400	2,600
Cash	319,000	500	6,800
	604,600	151,900	9,400
Creditors: amounts falling due within one year	(289,600)	(238,500)	(2,200)
Net current assets	315,000	(86,600)	7,200
Total assets less current liabilities	710,000	5,200	14,800
Capital and reserves:			
Called up share capital			
Ordinary £1 shares	60,000	20,000	10,000
10% £1 Preference shares		4,000	
Revaluation reserve	40,000		1,200
Profit and loss reserve	610,000	(18,800)	3,600
	710,000	5,200	14,800

You have recently been appointed chief accountant of Jasmin (Holdings) plc and are about to prepare the group balance sheet at 31 March 20X4. The following points are relevant to the preparation of those accounts.

(a) Jasmin (Holdings) plc owns 90 per cent of the ordinary £1 shares and 20 per cent of the 10 per cent £1 preference shares of Kasbah plc. On 1 April 20X3 Jasmin (Holdings) plc paid £96 million for the ordinary £1 shares and £1.6 million for the 10 per cent £1 preference shares when Kasbah's reserves were a credit balance of £45 million.

(b) Jasmin (Holdings) plc sells part of its output to Kasbah plc. The stock of Kasbah plc on 31 March 20X4 includes £1.2 million of stock purchased from Jasmin (Holdings) plc at cost plus one-third.

(c) The policy of the group is to revalue its tangible fixed assets on a yearly basis. However, the directors of Kasbah plc have always resisted this policy, preferring to show tangible fixed assets at historical cost. The market value of the tangible fixed assets of Kasbah plc at 31 March 20X4 is £90 million. The directors of Jasmin (Holdings) plc wish to follow the requirements of FRS 2 'Accounting for Subsidiary Undertakings' in respect of the value of tangible fixed assets to be included in the group accounts.

(d) The ordinary £1 shares of Fortran plc are split into 6 million 'A' ordinary £1 shares and 4 million 'B' ordinary £1 shares. Holders of 'A' shares are assigned 1 vote and holders of 'B' ordinary shares are assigned 2 votes per share. On 1 April 20X3 Jasmin (Holdings) plc acquired 80 per cent of the 'A' ordinary shares and 10 per cent of the 'B' ordinary shares when the profit and loss reserve of Fortran plc was £1.6 million and the revaluation reserve was £2 million. The 'A' ordinary shares and 'B' ordinary shares carry equal rights to share in the company's profit and losses.

(e) The fair values of Kasbah plc and Fortran plc were not materially different from their book values at the time of acquisition of their shares by Jasmin (Holdings) plc.

(f) Goodwill arising on acquisition is amortised over five years.

(g) Kasbah plc has paid its preference dividend for the current year but no other dividends are proposed by the group companies. The preference dividend was paid shortly after the interim results of Kasbah plc were announced and was deemed to be a legal dividend by the auditors.

(h) Because of its substantial losses during the period, the directors of Jasmin (Holdings) plc wish to exclude the financial statements of Kasbah plc from the group accounts on the grounds that Kasbah plc's output is not similar to that of Jasmin (Holdings) plc and that the resultant accounts therefore would be misleading. Jasmin (Holdings) plc produces synthetic yarn and Kasbah plc produces garments.

Required:

(a) List the conditions for exclusion of subsidiaries from consolidation for the directors of Jasmin (Holdings) plc and state whether Kasbah plc may be excluded on these grounds.

(b) Prepare a consolidated balance sheet for Jasmin (Holdings) Group plc for the year ending 31 March 20X4. (All calculations should be made to the nearest thousand pounds.)

(c) Comment briefly on the possible implications of the size of Kasbah plc's losses for the year for the group accounts and the individual accounts of Jasmin (Holdings) plc.

(*Association of Chartered Certified Accountants*)

26.4A Huge plc acquired a holding of 600,000 of the 800,000 ordinary £1 shares of Large plc on 1 October 20X5 when the revenue reserves of Large stood at £320,000.

On 1 October 20X6, the directors of Medium plc agreed to appoint the commercial manager of Huge as one of its directors to enable Huge to participate in its commercial, financial and dividend policy decisions. In exchange, Huge agreed to provide finance to Medium for working capital. On the same day, Huge acquired its holding of 100,000 of the 400,000 ordinary £1 shares of Medium when the revenue reserves of Medium were £150,000. Three months later, the directors of Small plc, who supplied materials to Large, heard of the arrangement between Huge and Medium and suggested that they would be pleased to enter into a similar relationship. The board of Huge were interested in the proposal and showed their good faith by acquiring a 10 per cent holding in Small which at that time had a debit balance of £2,000 on its profit and loss account.

Balance Sheets of the four companies on 30 September 20X7

	Huge £000	Large £000	Medium £000	Small £000
Property, plant and machinery	2,004	780	553	85
Investment in Large	650			
Investment in Medium	180			
Investment in Small	12			
Current a/c Medium	40			
Current a/c Small		10		
Stocks	489	303	72	28
Debtors	488	235	96	22
Bank/cash	45	62	19	5
	3,908	1,390	740	140
Less Liabilities due in one year: Creditors	(318)	(170)	(90)	(10)
	3,590	1,220	650	130
Ordinary share capital	2,400	800	400	80
Revenue reserves	1,190	420	210	40
Current a/c Huge			40	
Current a/c Large				10
	3,590	1,220	650	130

Required:

(a) Identify which of the four companies should be included in a group consolidation, explaining how and why the treatment of one company in the consolidation may be different from another. Mention any appropriate accounting standards or legislation applicable.

(b) Prepare the consolidated balance sheet of the group at 30 September 20X7 using the acquisition method of accounting.

(Institute of Chartered Secretaries and Administrators)

PART 4

Financial analysis

Introduction

This part considers how accounting information is traditionally analysed and used.

Accounting ratios

After you have studied this chapter, you should be able to:

- describe various groups of accounting ratios, where they would be used, why they would be of interest, and to whom they would be of interest
- calculate a number of commonly used accounting ratios
- describe some of the difficulties that may arise in the calculation and interpretation of accounting ratios
- describe the dangers in overtrading and how ratio analysis can be used to identify it

Introduction

In this chapter you'll revise what you learnt in *Business Accounting 1* concerning ratios and be introduced to more of the commonly used ones. You will also learn about overtrading and about how ratios can be used in order to minimise the risk of its occurring.

27.1 Background

Accounting ratios and the interpretation of financial statements were introduced in Volume 1. This chapter takes that material forward, re-examining the material for reinforcement, and developing greater depth of knowledge and understanding.

Information is data organised for a purpose. Information contained in financial statements is organised to enable users of the financial statements to draw conclusions concerning the financial well-being and performance of the reporting entity. In the case of the financial statements of companies, independent auditors review the manner in which the data has been presented and provide a filter mechanism attesting to the reliability of the information presented. For partnerships and sole traders, there is generally no such independent review. However, as the financial statements are generally subject to review by the tax authorities, there is some justification in assuming that they are a reasonable reflection of reality.

Yet, being 'reasonably assured' of their reliability is not generally sufficient for tax authorities and they will review the financial statements of partnerships and sole traders to determine whether there may be cause to doubt their reliability. One of the key instruments at their disposal is ratios, and they use ratio analysis to compare those found in the entity under review with those typically existing in that sector of the economy. Hence, through ratio analysis, factors can be identified that would not otherwise be apparent.

As you learnt in *Business Accounting 1*, ratio analysis can also be used to review trends and compare entities with each other. A number of commercial organisations specialise in this service, providing detailed ratio analysis of the financial statements of plcs to subscribers

and enabling analysts to see, at a glance, how one entity is performing, or how its financial structure compares with that of others of a similar nature.

Without ratios, financial statements would be largely uninformative to all but the very skilled. With ratios, financial statements can be interpreted and usefully applied to satisfy the needs of the reader.

There are, however, a vast number of parties interested in analysing financial statements: shareholders, lenders, customers, suppliers, employees, government agencies and competitors are just some of the groups who may all be interested in the financial statements of an entity. Yet, in many respects they will be interested in different things, and so there is no definitive, all-encompassing list of points for analysis that would be useful to all the groups.

Nevertheless, it is possible to construct a series of ratios that together will provide all these groups with something that they will find relevant, and from which they can choose to investigate further, if necessary. **Ratio analysis is a first step in assessing an entity. It removes some of the mystique surrounding the financial statements and makes it easier to pinpoint items which it would be interesting to investigate further.**

Exhibit 27.1 shows some of categories of ratios and indicates some of the groups that would be interested in them. You will recall a similar list in *Business Accounting 1*. However, note that the term 'solvency' has been substituted for 'liquidity' in the list here. 'Solvency' is a broader term and more clearly indicative of precisely what we are trying to identify when we consider the ratios that fall within its group. Note, however, that **many examiners use the term 'liquidity' when referring to this group of ratios**.

Exhibit 27.1

Ratio category	Examples of interested groups
Profitability	Shareholders, management, employees, creditors, competitors, potential investors
Solvency	Shareholders, suppliers, creditors, competitors
Efficiency	Shareholders, potential purchasers, competitors
Shareholder	Shareholders, potential investors
Capital structure	Shareholders, lenders, creditors, potential investors

27.2 Profitability

These measures indicate whether the company is performing satisfactorily. They are used, among other things, to measure the performance of management, to identify whether a company may be a worthwhile investment opportunity, and to determine a company's performance relative to its competitors.

There are a large number of these ratios. You will recall that we covered three in *Business Accounting 1 – gross profit : sales, net profit : sales* and *return on capital employed*. We shall review them once more and add some of the others that are commonly used.

Gross profit : Sales

If gross profit is £120,000 and sales are £480,000, the ratio would be 25 per cent. (This should not be confused with the gross margin : cost of sales ratio which compares the gross profit to the cost of sales which, in this case, would have a value of 33.33 per cent.)

Net profit after tax : Sales

If net profit is £38,400 and sales are £480,000, the ratio would be 8 per cent. It indicates how much safety there is in the price, i.e. current prices could be reduced by up to 8 per cent without causing the company to make a loss. Of course, it is much more complex than this. As

any student of economics knows only too well, if a commodity's price falls, generally demand for it rises. This could result in costs increasing (if unexpected demand has to be met in a hurry) or falling (as bulk discounts become available that were not previously obtainable owing to the lower level of demand). Nevertheless, as a general guide, it is a sensible indicator of safety, as well as an indicator of success.

While a high value for this ratio may suggest successful performance, it is not always the case. It is possible for selling prices to be so high that demand is reduced causing overall profitability to be significantly lower than it could be were a lower price being used. In this circumstance, the ratio would produce a high percentage, but performance would certainly not be as good as it ought to have been.

Return on capital employed

This is such an important ratio that we will first remind you of what you learnt in *Business Accounting 1*. An adequate return on capital employed is why people invested their money in a business in the first place.

(i) Sole traders

In this chapter, we will use the average of the capital account as the figure for capital employed, i.e. (opening balance + closing balance) ÷ 2.

In businesses C and D in Exhibit 27.2 the same amount of net profit has been made, but the capitals employed are different.

Exhibit 27.2

Balance Sheets

	C	D
	£	£
Fixed + Current assets – Current liabilities	10,000	16,000
Capital accounts		
Opening balance	8,000	14,000
Add Net profit	3,600	3,600
	11,600	17,600
Less Drawings	(1,600)	(1,600)
	10,000	16,000

Return on capital employed (ROCE) is:

$$\text{ROCE} = \frac{\text{Net Profit}}{\text{Capital employed}} \times 100$$

therefore,

$$C \qquad \frac{3,600}{(8,000 + 10,000) \div 2} \times \frac{100}{1} = 40\% \qquad D \qquad \frac{3,600}{(14,000 + 16,000) \div 2} \times \frac{100}{1} = 24\%$$

The ratio illustrates that what is important is not simply how much profit has been made but how well the capital has been employed. Business C has made far better use of its capital, achieving a return of £40 net profit for every £100 invested, whereas D has received only a net profit of £24 per £100.

(ii) Limited companies

There is no universally agreed definition of **capital employed** for companies. The main ones used are:

(a) return on capital employed by ordinary shareholders
(b) return on capital employed by all long-term suppliers of capital

Let's now look at each of these:

(a) In a limited company this is known as 'return on owners' equity' (ROOE) or, more commonly, 'return on shareholders' funds' (ROSF). From now on, we shall use the second of these terms, 'return on shareholders' funds' but you will need to remember that when you see 'return on owners' equity', it is the same as ROSF.

The word 'return' is the net profit for the period. The term 'shareholders' funds' means the book value of all things in the balance sheet that describe the owners' capital and reserves. 'Owners' are the holders of the *ordinary* share capital. This is calculated: ordinary share capital + all reserves including profit and loss account.

(b) This is often known simply as 'return on capital employed' (ROCE). The word 'return' in this case means net profit + any preference share dividends + debenture and long-term loan interest. The word 'capital' means ordinary share capital + reserves including profit and loss account + preference shares + debentures and long-term loans.

Given the following balance sheets and profit and loss accounts of two companies, P Ltd and Q Ltd, the calculations of ROSF and ROCE can be attempted.

Balance Sheets as at 31 December

	P Ltd £ 20X8	P Ltd £ 20X9	Q Ltd £ 20X8	Q Ltd £ 20X9
Fixed assets	5,200	5,600	8,400	9,300
Net current assets	2,800	3,400	1,600	2,700
	8,000	9,000	10,000	12,000
10% debentures	–	–	(1,200)	(1,200)
	8,000	9,000	8,800	10,800
Share capital (ordinary)	3,000	3,000	5,000	5,000
Reserves	5,000	6,000	3,800	5,800
	8,000	9,000	8,800	10,800

Profit and Loss Accounts for years to 31 December 20X9

	P Ltd £	Q Ltd £
Net profit	2,200	3,800
Dividends	(1,200)	(1,800)
	1,000	2,000

Return on Shareholders' Funds (ROSF)

P Ltd
$$\frac{2,200}{(8,000 + 9,000) \div 2} \times \frac{100}{1} = 25.9\%$$

Q Ltd
$$\frac{3,800}{(8,800 + 10,800) \div 2} \times \frac{100}{1} = 38.8\%$$

Return on Capital Employed (ROCE)

P Ltd
Same as ROSF[Note 1] = 25.9%

Q Ltd
$$\frac{3,800 + 120^{Note\ 2}}{(10,000 + 12,000) \div 2} \times \frac{100}{1} = 35.6\%$$

Note 1: The return on capital employed by all long-term sources of capital (in Q Ltd's case, the shareholders' funds and the debentures) is the same as the ROSF in the case of P Ltd, as it has no debentures.

Note 2: The debenture interest (i.e. 10% of £1,200 = £120) must be added back, as it was an expense in calculating the £3,800 net profit.

To summarise: return on capital employed is one of the more awkward ratios to deal with. Unlike the current ratio there is no widely agreed definition for ROCE. Hence, care must be taken when comparing this ratio as calculated for one company and as reported for another. Use of financial analysis bureaux that use the same formula to calculate the ratios of all the companies they consider is one way around this difficulty. Another is to ensure that the formula used by the companies being compared against is known and, where necessary, the result is revised to bring it into line with the internally calculated ratio.

Note: A problem you face as a student is that you will never be quite sure what an examiner wants if the exam paper refers to this ratio. You will need to remember to write down the formula you are using on your exam script.

Unless otherwise indicated, use the definition for ROCE given above. The ratio compares the profit earned (usually *before* interest and tax) to the funds used to generate that return (often the total of shareholders' funds at the beginning of the accounting period plus long-term creditors – most simply defined as total assets minus current liabilities). Were the profit before interest and tax £40,000 and the opening capital employed shown in the balance sheet £800,000 the return on capital employed would be 5 per cent. In theory, the higher the ratio, the more profitably the resources of the company have been used.

Return on share capital

As with ROCE, there are a number of different ways in which return on share capital may be calculated. One is the comparison of profit on ordinary activities before tax with share capital and reserves. For example, if profit on ordinary activities before tax were £40,000 and the share capital and reserves at the start of the accounting period £720,000 the return on share capital (ROSC) would be 5.56 per cent. In theory, the higher the ratio, the more profitably the shareholders' investment in the company has been used, and it is often used to compare performance between accounting periods, rather than to draw comparison with the ROSC of other companies.

Net profit after tax : Total assets

Net profit after tax is compared with the total of all assets other than current assets, plus working capital (i.e. current assets less current liabilities). If working capital is £20,000 and all non-current assets total £820,000, total assets are £840,000. If net profit after tax is £30,000, the ratio is £30,000/£840,000, i.e. 3.57 per cent.

There are problems with the integrity of this ratio: some items of expenditure that are relevant, e.g. interest on debentures, will have been charged against the profit in arriving at the figure for profit after tax. Strictly speaking, these other payments to investors and creditors ought to be reviewed and included in the profit figure used in the ratio, otherwise the profit may be significantly understated, giving a less healthy view than would be appropriate to present.

Intangible assets, e.g. goodwill, are included in the value of total assets used in the ratio. However, many would argue that this is inappropriate as there is not an agreed view on how such assets should be valued, thus intercompany comparisons may be difficult.

Net operating profit : Operating assets

This is an alternative to net profit after tax : total assets. It takes the net profit before interest, taxes and dividends, and before inclusion of any investment income. This is then compared with the assets other than intangibles and investments outside the company. Working capital would be included, but bank overdrafts would be excluded from the current liabilities on the

basis that they are not generally short term in nature. If net operating profit before interest, tax and dividends is £36,000, tangible fixed assets excluding investments made outside the company are £600,000, working capital is £20,000, and there is a bank overdraft of £5,000, the ratio is:

$$\frac{£36,000}{£625,00} = 5.76\%$$

27.3 Solvency

Being solvent means having sufficient resources to meet your debts when due. Your resources must be sufficiently liquid to do so, hence the frequent use of the term, 'liquidity' when referring to this group of ratios. As you learnt in *Business Accounting 1*, the solvency of individuals is often performed through credit checks undertaken by credit rating agencies. Some lenders, such as banks, use a checklist of questions concerning financial status before they will lend or grant credit to a private individual. For companies, information can be purchased that indicates their solvency, i.e. whether they are liable to be bad credit risks. Such information is usually based, at least in part, upon a ratio analysis of their financial statements.

When it comes to the solvency of a business, both its own ability to pay it debts when due and the ability of its debtors to pay the amount they owe to the business are of great importance. Ratio analysis that focuses upon solvency (or liquidity) of the business generally starts with a look at two ratios that are affected most by these two aspects of liquidity: the **current ratio** and the **acid test ratio**.

Current ratio

The **current ratio** compares total current assets to total current liabilities and is intended to indicate whether there are sufficient short-term assets to meet the short-term liabilities. Traditionally, in order to provide some general guide, a value is given that may generally be taken to be the norm. This has become increasingly less meaningful and is really more misleading (as it instils undue confidence) than helpful – the ratio is so sector-dependent as to be incapable of being defined as 'generally best if around x'. Consequently, no such guidance will be given here. Rather, a set of factors will be suggested that ought to be considered:

1 What is the norm in this industrial sector?
2 Is this company significantly above or below that norm?
3 If so, can this be justified after an analysis of the nature of these assets and liabilities, and of the reasons for the amounts of each held?

The ratio when calculated may be expressed as either a ratio to 1, with current liabilities being set to 1, or as a 'number of times', representing the relative size of the amount of total current assets compared with total current liabilities.

Example

If total current assets are £40,000 and total current liabilities are £20,000, the current ratio could be expressed as either:

$$£40,000 : £20,000 = 2 : 1$$

or as:

$$\frac{£40,000}{£20,000} = 2 \text{ times}$$

Acid test ratio

As with the current ratio, there is little benefit in suggesting a norm for the value to expect. The only difference in the items involved between the two ratios is that the **acid test ratio** (or 'quick' ratio) does not include stock. Otherwise, it is identical to the current ratio, comparing current assets, excluding stock, with current liabilities. Stock is omitted as it is considered to be relatively illiquid, because it depends upon prevailing and future market forces and may be impossible to convert to cash in a relatively short time.

Many companies operate with acid test ratios below 1 : 1; that is, they have insufficient liquid assets to meet their short-term liabilities. The great majority of companies in this situation have no problem paying their creditors when due. Consideration of a simple example should explain how this is possible.

Activity 27.1

The only difference between the current and acid test ratios is that stock is omitted from the acid test ratio. Why is it appropriate to remove stock from the analysis in this way?

Example

If total current assets, including stock of £22,000, are worth £40,000 and total current liabilities stand at £20,000, the acid test ratio will be £18,000 : £20,000 = 0.9 : 1 (or 0.9 times). This means that at the balance sheet date, had all current liabilities been due for payment, it would not have been possible to do so without converting some assets (e.g. stock, or fixed assets) into cash that were likely only to be convertible into cash at a discount on their true value. In other words, the company would have had to pay a premium in order to meet its obligations, and would not be able to continue to do so indefinitely.

However, the reality is generally that the current liabilities are due for payment at varying times over the coming financial period and some, for example a bank overdraft, may not, in reality, ever be likely to be subject to a demand for repayment.

The current assets, on the other hand, are within the control of the company and can be adjusted in their timing to match the due dates for payment to creditors. They can be renewed many times before one or other of the current liabilities is due for payment. For example, debtors may be on a 10-day cycle while trade creditors are paid after 90 days' credit has expired. Clearly, in this case, receipts from nine times the balance sheet debtors' figure could be received and available to meet the trade creditor figure shown in the balance sheet.

As with the current ratio, the acid test ratio should be compared with the norms for the industrial sector, and then the underlying assets and liabilities should be considered to determine whether there is any cause for concern in the result obtained.

Activity 27.2

If stock is removed from the analysis when calculating the acid test ratio, why isn't the figure for debtors also removed? Debtors can be just as difficult to turn into cash.

27.4 Efficiency ratios

Profitability is affected by the way that the assets of a business are used. If plant and machinery are used only for a few hours a day, the business is failing to utilise these assets efficiently. This may be because there is limited demand for the product produced. It could

be due to the business restricting supply in order to maximise profitability per unit produced. On the other hand, it could be that there is a shortage of skilled labour and that there is no one to operate the plant and machinery the rest of the time. Alternatively, it could be that the plant and machinery is unreliable, breaking down a lot, and that the limited level of use is a precautionary measure designed to ensure that production targets are met.

In common with all accounting ratios, it is important that the results of efficiency ratio computations are not treated as definitively good or bad. They must be investigated further through consideration both of the underlying variables in the ratios, and of the broader context of the business and its relation to the industrial sector in which it operates.

Efficiency ratios include the following.

Asset turnover

Asset turnover is a measure of how effectively the assets are being used to generate sales. It is one of the ratios that would be considered when interpreting the results of profitability ratio analyses like ROCE, but is of sufficient importance to be calculated and analysed irrespective of that fact. The calculation involves dividing sales by total assets less current liabilities.

As a general guide, where a company's asset turnover is significantly lower than that of its competitors, it suggests there may be overinvestment in assets which could, in turn, make the company vulnerable to takeover by a company interested in selling off any surplus assets while otherwise retaining the business in its current form. However, considerable care must be taken when interpreting this ratio: the assets may be much newer than those of other companies; the company may use a lower rate of depreciation than its competitors; or the company may purchase its plant and machinery, whereas the industry norm is to lease them. On the other side of the ratio, the result may be high because selling prices are being suppressed in order to maximise volume.

Stock turnover

Included in virtually every case where accounting ratios are being calculated, stock turnover measures the number of times (approximately) that stock is replenished in an accounting period. If stock is £100,000 and cost of sales are £800,000, the stock turnover ratio would be 8 times. The ratio can also be expressed as a number of days – the number of days stock held. In this example, 365 would be divided by 8 producing a result of 45.6 days.

There are two major difficulties in computing the stock turnover ratio: if cost of sales is not available, it is tempting to use sales instead. This should not be done. Sales are expressed at selling prices; stock is expressed at cost price. Use of sales instead of cost of sales in the equation will not be comparing like with like.

In addition, there are at least three possible stock values that could be used: opening, closing and the average of these figures. The average figure would be the more commonly used, but use of any of the three can be justified.

Whichever approach is taken, the result will, at best, be a crude estimate. Due to seasonality of the business, stock, as shown in the balance sheet for example, may not be representative of the 'normal' level of stock. However, it is still useful for comparing trends over time and should be used mainly for that purpose. The result it produces needs careful consideration. A rising stock turnover may indicate greater efficiency, or it may be an indicator that stocks are being run down and that there may be problems in meeting demand in future. A falling stock turnover may indicate lower efficiency, perhaps with a build-up of obsolete stocks, or it could indicate higher stock volumes are being held because stock purchasing has become more efficient and the higher stock levels are financially beneficial for the company. In addition, it is important not to overlook that any change in the ratio may have nothing to do with the stock, but be due to changes in factors relating to the sales for the period.

Debtor days

Debtor days indicates how efficient the company is at controlling its debtors. If debtors are £50,000 and sales £800,000, debtors are taking, on average, 22.8 days credit, i.e.

$$\frac{£50,000}{£800,000} \times 365 = 22.8$$

Strictly speaking, the two figures are not comparable. Debtors includes the VAT on sales; the figure for sales excludes VAT. However, the adjustment is not difficult to make if required for clarity.

As with stock, the amount shown in the balance sheet for debtors may not be representative of the 'normal' level. Nevertheless, this is generally a useful ratio to calculate and comparison with that of other companies in the same industrial sector may be very interesting. However, as with stock turnover, its strength lies in trend analysis between periods.

Creditor days

Creditor days ratio indicates how the company uses short-term financing to fund its activities, and further investigation will reveal whether or not the result is due to efficiency. It is calculated by dividing creditors by purchases, and multiplying the result by 365. The purchases figure is not usually available in published financial statements, and the cost of sales amount would be used in its place. As with stock turnover and debtor days, its strength lies in trend analysis between periods.

27.5 Shareholder ratios

Shareholder ratios are those most commonly used by anyone interested in an investment in a company. They indicate how well a company is performing in relation to the price of its shares and other related items including dividends and number of shares in issue. The ratios usually calculated are described below.

Dividend yield

Dividend yield measures the real rate of return by comparing the dividend paid to the market price of a share. It is calculated as:

$$\frac{\text{Gross dividend per share}}{\text{Market price per share}}$$

Earnings per share (EPS)

EPS is the most frequently used of all the accounting ratios and is generally felt to give the best view of performance. It indicates how much of a company's profit can be attributed to each ordinary share in the company. FRS 14: *Earnings per share* provides the formula to be used when calculating this ratio:

$$\frac{\text{Net profit or loss attributable to ordinary shareholders}}{\text{The weighted average number of ordinary shares outstanding during the period}}$$

Dividend cover

Dividend cover compares the amount of profit earned per ordinary share with the amount of dividend paid, thereby showing the proportion of profits that could have been distributed and were. It differs from EPS only in having a different denominator. The formula is:

$$\frac{\text{Net profit or loss attributable to ordinary shareholders}}{\text{Net dividend on ordinary shares}}$$

Price earnings (P/E) ratio

The P/E ratio relates the earnings per share to the market price of the shares. It is calculated as:

$$\frac{\text{Market price}}{\text{Earnings per share}}$$

and is a useful indicator of how the stock market assesses the company. It is also very useful when a company proposes an issue of new shares, in that it enables potential investors to better assess whether the expected future earnings make the share a worthwhile investment.

27.6   Capital structure

There are a number of ratios that can be used to assess the way in which a company finances its activities. One, creditor days, was referred to in the last section. The ratios discussed in this section differ in that they are longer-term in nature, being concerned more with the strategic rather than with the operational level of corporate decision-making. Some of the more commonly analysed ratios of this type are described below.

Net worth : Total assets

This ratio indicates the proportion of fixed and current assets that are financed by net worth (the total of shareholders' funds, i.e. share capital plus reserves). If fixed assets are shown at a value of £500,000, current assets £100,000 and net worth is £300,000, then 50 per cent of total assets are financed by shareholders' funds. As with many accounting ratios, it is the trend in this ratio between periods that is important.

Fixed assets : Net worth

This ratio focuses on the longer-term aspects of the net worth : total assets ratio. By matching long-term investment with long-term finance it is possible to determine whether borrowing has been used to finance some long-term investment in assets. Where this has occurred, there may be a problem when the borrowing is to be repaid (as the fixed assets it was used to acquire cannot be readily converted into cash). Again, this ratio is of most use when the trend over time is analysed.

Fixed assets : Net worth + long-term liabilities

This ratio focuses on whether sufficient long-term finance has been obtained to meet the investment in fixed assets.

Debt ratio

This ratio compares the total debts to total assets and is concerned with whether the company has sufficient assets to meet all its liabilities when due. For example, if total liabilities

are £150,000 and total assets are £600,000, the debts represent 25 per cent of total assets. Whether this is good or bad will, as with all accounting ratios, depend upon the norm for the industrial sector in which the company operates and on the underlying items within the figures included in the ratio.

Capital gearing ratio

This ratio provides the proportion of a company's total capital that has a prior claim to profits over those of ordinary shareholders. Prior claim (or prior charge) capital includes debentures, other long-term loans, and preference share capital and is any capital carrying a right to a fixed return. Total capital includes ordinary share capital and reserves, preference shares and long-term liabilities.

Debt : Equity ratio

This is the ratio of prior charge capital to ordinary share capital and reserves.

Borrowing : Net worth

This ratio indicates the proportion that borrowing represents of a company's net worth. If long-term liabilities are £100,000 and current liabilities are £50,000, then total borrowing is £150,000. If net worth is £300,000, the ratio is 1 : 2, or 50 per cent.

This and the debt : equity ratio indicate the degree of risk to investors in ordinary shares in a company. The higher these ratios are, the greater the possibility of risk to ordinary shareholders – both in respect of expectations of future dividends (especially in times of depressed performance where much of the profits may be paid to the holders of prior charge capital), and from the threat of liquidation should there be a slump in performance that leads to a failure to meet payments to holders of prior charge capital. Whether these risks may be relevant can be investigated by reference to the next ratio.

Interest cover

This ratio shows whether enough profits are being earned to meet interest payments when due. It is calculated by dividing profit before interest and tax by the interest charges. Thus, the interest cover is 20 times if profit before interest and tax is £400,000 and the total interest charges are £20,000. In this case, there would be little cause for immediate concern that there was any risk of the company's failing to meet its interest charges when due. However, just because a company is making profits does not guarantee that there will be sufficient cash available to make the interest charge payments when due.

27.7 Overtrading

A very high proportion of new businesses fail within the first two years of trading. This can occur because there was insufficient demand for the goods or service provided, because of poor management, or a number of other reasons of which possibly the most common to arise would be **overtrading**. However, unlike the other common causes of business failure, overtrading often arises when a business is performing profitably. Furthermore, overtrading can just as easily affect established businesses as new businesses.

Overtrading occurs when insufficient control over working capital results in there being insufficient liquid funds to meet the demands of creditors. As the cash dries up, so do the sources of supply of raw materials and other essential inputs – sources will not continue to supply a business that fails to settle its bills when due. Overtrading is generally the result of

sales growth being at too fast a rate in relation to the level of trade debtors, trade creditors and stock.

Take an example where, over a twelve-month period, profits increased by 20 per cent, sales doubled from £1 million to £2 million, trade debtors doubled from £80,000 to £160,000, trade creditors quadrupled from £60,000 to £240,000, stock quadrupled from £50,000 to £200,000, and the bank balance moved from positive £20,000 to an overdraft of £80,000. No changes occurred during the period in long-term financing of the business, though £100,000 was spent on some new equipment needed as a result of the expansion.

Working capital was 2.5 : 1; now it is 1.125 : 1 and the acid test ratio is now 0.5 : 1 from 1.67 : 1. Liquidity appears to have deteriorated significantly (but may have been high previously compared with other businesses in the same sector). Debtor days are unchanged (as the ratio of sales to debtors is unaltered). However, creditor days have probably doubled (subject to a slight reduction due to some cheaper purchasing costs as a result of the higher volumes involved). If the bank overdraft is currently at its limit, the business would be unable to meet any requests from creditors for immediate payment, never mind pay wages and other regular expenses.

This situation can be addressed by raising long-term finance, or by cutting back on the expansion – clearly, the first option is likely to be the more attractive one to the business.

Signals suggesting overtrading include:

(a) significant increases in the volume of sales;
(b) lower profit margins;
(c) deteriorating debtor, creditor and stock turnover ratios;
(d) increasing reliance on short-term finance.

27.8 Summary of ratios

Profitability

Gross profit : Sales
$$\frac{\text{Gross profit}}{\text{Sales}}$$

Net profit after tax : Sales
$$\frac{\text{Net profit after tax}}{\text{Sales}}$$

Return on capital employed
$$\frac{\text{Profit before interest and tax}}{\text{Total assets} - \text{Current liabilities}}$$

Return on share capital
$$\frac{\text{Profit before tax}}{\text{Share capital} + \text{Reserves}}$$

Net profit after tax : Total assets
$$\frac{\text{Net profit after tax}}{\text{Fixed and other non-current assets} + \text{Working capital}}$$

Net operating profit : Operating assets
$$\frac{\text{Net profit before interest, tax, dividends, and investment income}}{\text{Tangible fixed assets} - \text{Outside investments} + \text{Working capital} + \text{Bank overdraft}}$$

Solvency

Current ratio
$$\frac{\text{Current assets}}{\text{Current liabilities}}$$

Acid test ratio
$$\frac{\text{Current assets} - \text{Stock}}{\text{Current liabilities}}$$

Efficiency

Asset turnover

$$\frac{\text{Sales}}{\text{Total assets} - \text{Current liabilities}}$$

Stock turnover

$$\frac{\text{Cost of goods sold}}{\text{Average stock}}$$

Debtor days

$$\frac{\text{Debtors}}{\text{Sales}} \times 365$$

Creditor days

$$\frac{\text{Creditors}}{\text{Purchases}} \times 365$$

Shareholder ratios

Dividend yield

$$\frac{\text{Gross dividend per share}}{\text{Market price per share}}$$

Earnings per share

$$\frac{\text{Net profit or loss attributable to ordinary shareholders}}{\text{Weighted average number of ordinary shares outstanding during the period}}$$

Dividend cover

$$\frac{\text{Net profit or loss attributable to ordinary shareholders}}{\text{Net dividend on ordinary shares}}$$

Price/earnings ratio

$$\frac{\text{Market price}}{\text{Earnings per share}}$$

Capital structure

Net worth : Total assets

$$\frac{\text{Shareholders' funds}}{\text{Total assets}}$$

Fixed assets : Net worth

$$\frac{\text{Fixed assets}}{\text{Shareholders' funds}}$$

Fixed assets :
Net worth + long-term liabilities

$$\frac{\text{Fixed assets}}{\text{Shareholders' funds} + \text{Long-term liabilities}}$$

Debt ratio

$$\frac{\text{Total liabilities}}{\text{Total assets}}$$

Capital gearing ratio

$$\frac{\text{Prior charge capital}}{\text{Total capital}}$$

Debt : Equity ratio

$$\frac{\text{Prior charge capital}}{\text{Ordinary share capital and reserves}}$$

Borrowing : Net worth

$$\frac{\text{Total borrowing}}{\text{Shareholders' funds}}$$

Interest cover

$$\frac{\text{Profit before interest and tax}}{\text{Interest charges}}$$

You should now have learnt:

1 There are many different categories of accounting ratios and many different ratios within each category.

2 Ratios that are of interest to one group of readers of financial statements may not be of interest to another.

3 Ratios may be used in order to review reliability of financial statements.

4 Ratios may be used to review trends between periods for the same company.

5 Ratios may be used to compare a company to others in the same industrial sector.

6 Some ratios are in wide use for which there is no agreed 'correct' formula to calculate them. This makes comparison between analysis reported elsewhere of limited value unless the formula used can be identified.

7 The ratios derived can be misleading if taken at face value. It is essential that they are placed in context and that interpretation goes beyond a superficial comparison to general norms.

8 Used casually, accounting ratios can mislead and result in poor quality decision making.

9 Used carefully, accounting ratios can provide pointers towards areas of interest in an entity, and provide a far more complete picture of an entity than that given by the financial statements.

10 Overtrading can be financially disastrous for a business and ratios can be used to help detect it.

Answers to activities

27.1 Stock is sometimes very difficult to convert into cash, particularly at the value placed upon it in the balance sheet. Because it can be difficult to generate liquid funds through the sale of stock, it is inappropriate to consider it when looking at the issue of whether an organisation is able to pay its debts quickly.

27.2 Debtors can be very difficult to turn into cash. However, there are three aspects of debtors that make them less problematic than stock in this context. Firstly, specialist financial agencies called 'factors' will take over debts in many instances in exchange for a percentage of the amount owing. Through this medium, organisations can convert some of their debtors into cash quickly and at relatively little cost. Secondly, debtors can be pursued through the courts. Thus, when an organisation urgently needs money owing from debtors that is already overdue, it can threaten legal action, thereby accelerating the receipt of the money due. Finally, most debtors do eventually pay their debts; stock may never be sold.

In the context of the cash it will generate, stock is usually sold at above the value placed upon it in the balance sheet while, apart from overestimation of doubtful debts, debtors never realise more than the value shown for them in the balance sheet. However, so far as the acid test ratio is concerned, the key difference is that money owing by debtors will generally be received more quickly than money tied up in stock.

REVIEW QUESTIONS

27.1   Five categories of accounting ratios are described in this chapter. What are they?

27.2A   Why should different groups of people be interested in different categories of accounting ratios?

27.3   Describe two ratios from each of the five groups of ratios, including how to calculate them.

27.4A   What is the purpose in using each of the following ratios:

(*a*) current ratio
(*b*) net profit after tax : sales
(*c*) asset turnover
(*d*) interest cover
(*e*) dividend cover?

27.5   If you wished to assess the efficiency of a company, which of these ratios would you use:

(*a*) stock turnover
(*b*) interest cover
(*c*) return on capital employed
(*d*) acid test ratio
(*e*) dividend yield?

27.6A   A company has capital of 1 million ordinary shares of £1 each. It pays a dividend of 6 per cent out of its profits after tax of £480,000 on sales of £4 million. The market price of the shares is £2.40. What is the:

(*a*) net profit after tax : sales
(*b*) dividend yield
(*c*) earnings per share
(*d*) price earnings ratio?

27.7   In respect of each of the following events, select all the effects resulting from that event that are shown in the list of effects:

(*i*)   a bad debt written off;
(*ii*)   an increase in the bank overdraft;
(*iii*) a purchase of six months' stock;
(*iv*)   payment of all amounts due to trade creditors that had been outstanding for longer than 90 days;
(*v*)   an offer of 5 per cent discount to all customers who settle their accounts within two weeks.

Effects
(*a*) increased current ratio
(*b*) reduced current ratio
(*c*) increased acid test ratio
(*d*) reduced acid test ratio.

27.8A Using the following balance sheet and profit and loss accounts, calculate and comment on ten accounting ratios (ignore taxation):

Balance Sheet as at 31 December 20X1 (£000)

Fixed assets

Equipment at cost		6,000
Less Depreciation to date		(2,000)
		4,000
Current assets		
Stock	600	
Debtors	60	
Bank	–	
	660	
Less Current liabilities		
Creditors	90	
Dividends payable	80	
Bank overdraft	450	
	(620)	
		40
		4,040
Long-term liabilities		
10% debentures		(500)
		3,540
Financed by:		
Share capital – £1 ordinary shares		2,000
Reserves		
General reserve		800
Profit and loss account		740
		3,540

Profit and Loss Account for period ending 31 December 20X1 (£000)

Sales		8,000
Less Cost of sales		
Opening stock	500	
Add Purchases	1,300	
	1,800	
Less Closing stock	(600)	
		(1,200)
Gross profit		6,800
Less Depreciation	800	
Other expenses	5,500	
		(6,300)
Net operating profit		500
Less Debenture interest		(50)
Net profit		450
Add Balance b/d		490
		940
Less Appropriations		
General reserve	120	
Dividend	80	
		(200)
		740

27.9 You are to study the following financial statements for two similar types of retail store and then answer the questions which follow.

Summary of Financial Statements

Balance Sheets	A		B	
	£	£	£	£
Fixed assets				
Equipment at cost	10,000		20,000	
Less Depreciation to date	(8,000)		(6,000)	
		2,000		14,000
Current assets				
Stock	15,000		17,500	
Debtors	25,000		20,000	
Bank	5,000		2,500	
	45,000		40,000	
Less Current liabilities				
Creditors	(5,000)		(10,000)	
		40,000		30,000
		42,000		44,000
Financed by:				
Capitals				
Balance at start of year		38,000		36,000
Add Net profit		10,000		15,000
		48,000		51,000
Less Drawings		(6,000)		(7,000)
		42,000		44,000
Trading and Profit and Loss Account				
Sales		80,000		(120,000)
Less Cost of goods sold				
Opening stock	25,000		22,500	
Add Purchases	50,000		91,000	
	75,000		113,500	
Less Closing stock	(15,000)		(17,500)	
		(60,000)		(96,000)
Gross profit		20,000		24,000
Less Depreciation	1,000		3,000	
Other expenses	9,000		6,000	
		(10,000)		(9,000)
Net profit		10,000		15,000

Required:
(a) Calculate the following ratios:
    (i)   gross profit as percentage of sales;
    (ii)   net profit as percentage of sales;
    (iii) expenses as percentage of sales;
    (iv) stockturn;
    (v)   rate of return of net profit on capital employed (use the average of the capital account for this purpose);
    (vi) current ratio;
    (vii) acid test ratio;
    (viii) debtor : sales ratio;
    (ix) creditor : purchases ratio.
(b) Drawing upon all your knowledge of accounting, comment upon the differences and similarities of the accounting ratios for A and B. Which business seems to be the most efficient? Give possible reasons.

27.10A Study the following accounts of two companies and then answer the questions which follow. Both companies are stores selling textile goods.

Trading and Profit and Loss Accounts

	R Ltd		T Ltd	
	£	£	£	£
Sales		250,000		160,000
Less Cost of goods sold				
Opening stock	90,000		30,000	
Add Purchases	210,000		120,000	
	300,000		150,000	
Less Closing stock	(110,000)		(50,000)	
		(190,000)		(100,000)
Gross profit		60,000		60,000
Less Expenses				
Wages and salaries	14,000		10,000	
Directors' remuneration	10,000		10,000	
Other expenses	11,000		8,000	
		(35,000)		(28,000)
Net profit		25,000		32,000
Add Balance from last year		15,000		8,000
		40,000		40,000
Less Appropriations				
General reserve	2,000		2,000	
Dividend	25,000		20,000	
		(27,000)		(22,000)
Balance carried to next year		13,000		18,000

Balance Sheets

	R Ltd		T Ltd	
Fixed assets				
Equipment at cost	20,000		5,000	
Less Depreciation to date	(8,000)		(2,000)	
		12,000		3,000
Motor lorries	30,000		20,000	
Less Depreciation to date	(12,000)		(7,000)	
		18,000		13,000
		30,000		16,000
Current assets				
Stock	110,000		50,000	
Debtors	62,500		20,000	
Bank	7,500		10,000	
	180,000		80,000	
Less Current liabilities				
Creditors	(90,000)		(16,000)	
		90,000		64,000
		120,000		80,000
Financed by:				
Issued share capital		100,000		50,000
Reserves				
General reserve	7,000		12,000	
Profit and loss	13,000		18,000	
		20,000		30,000
		120,000		80,000

Required:

(a) Calculate the following ratios for each of R Ltd and T Ltd:

(*i*)   gross profit as percentage of sales;
(*ii*) net profit as percentage of sales;
(*iii*) expenses as percentage of sales;
(*iv*) stockturn;
(*v*)   rate of return of net profit on capital employed
        (for the purpose of this question only, take
        capital as being total of share capitals + reserves
        at the balance sheet date);

(*vi*)   current ratio;
(*vii*) acid test ratio;
(*viii*) debtor : sales ratio;
(*ix*)   creditor : purchases ratio.

(b) Comment briefly on the comparison of each ratio as between the two companies. State which company appears to be the most efficient, giving what you consider to be possible reasons.

27.11 The directors of L Ltd appointed a new sales manager towards the end of 20X2. This manager devised a plan to increase sales and profit by means of a reduction in selling price and extended credit terms to customers. This involved considerable investment in new machinery early in 20X3 in order to meet the demand which the change in sales policy had created.

The financial statements for the years ended 31 December 20X2 and 20X3 are shown below. The sales manager has argued that the new policy has been a resounding success because sales and, more importantly, profits have increased dramatically.

Profit and loss accounts	*20X2*	*20X3*
	£000	*£000*
Sales	900	2,800
Cost of sales	(360)	(1,680)
Gross profit	540	1,120
Selling expenses	(150)	(270)
Bad debts	(18)	(140)
Depreciation	(58)	(208)
Interest	(12)	(192)
Net profit	302	310
Balance b/fwd	327	629
	629	939

Balance sheets	*20X2*		*20X3*	
	£000	*£000*	*£000*	*£000*
Fixed assets				
Factory		450		441
Machinery		490		1,791
		940		2,232
Current assets				
Stock	30		238	
Debtors	83		583	
Bank	12		–	
	125		821	
Current liabilities				
Creditors	(36)		(175)	
Bank	–		(11)	
	(36)		(186)	
Current assets *less* Current liabilities		89		635
		1,029		2,867
Borrowings		(100)		(1,600)
		929		1,267
Share capital		300		328
Profit and loss		629		939
		929		1,267

(a) **You are required to** explain whether you believe that the performance for the year ended 31 December 20X3 and the financial position at that date have improved as a result of the new policies adopted by the company. You should support your answer with appropriate ratios.

(b) All of L Ltd's sales are on credit. The finance director has asked you to calculate the immediate financial impact of reducing the credit period offered to customers. Calculate the amount of cash which would be released if the company could impose a collection period of 45 days.

(*Chartered Institute of Management Accountants*)

CHAPTER 28

Interpretation of financial statements

Learning objectives

After you have studied this chapter, you should be able to:

- explain the importance of trend analysis when analysing financial statements
- explain that there is no such thing as a generally 'good' or 'bad' value for any ratio
- describe the need to compare like with like if attempting to assess the quality of the result found from ratio analysis
- explain the pyramid of ratios that can be used in order to enhance the view obtained from ratio analysis
- explain that different groups of users of financial statements have access to different sources of information that may help in developing an understanding of and explanation for the results of ratio analysis

Introduction

In this chapter you'll learn more about ratio analysis and how to use it effectively. You'll revisit comparisons between organisations and the need for effective and appropriate comparitors in order to make valid and worthwhile use of ratios. You'll also learn about the relationships between ratios and look in greater detail at return on capital employed.

28.1 Background

When shareholders receive the annual financial statements of a business, many simply look to see whether the business has made a profit, and then put the document away. They are aware of only one thing – that the company made a profit of £x. They do not know if it was a 'good' profit. Nor do they know whether it was any different from the profit earned in previous years. (Even if they had noticed the previous period's profit figure in the comparative column, they would be unaware of the equivalent figures for the periods that preceded it.) In addition, they would have no perception of how the performance compared with that of other companies operating in the same sector.

In order that performance within a period can be assessed, ratio analysis may be undertaken, as explained in Chapter 27. However, as you learnt in *Business Accounting 1*, such analysis is relatively useless unless a similar task is undertaken on the financial figures for previous periods. Trend analysis is very important in the interpretation of financial statements, for it is only then that the relative position can be identified, i.e. whether things are improving, etc.

Of similar importance if financial statements are to be usefully interpreted is comparison of the position shown with that of other companies operating in the same sector.

28.2 Sector relevance

Analysis and interpretation of any phenomenon is all very well if conducted in isolation of the rest of the world, but can be of only limited use without comparitors with which to develop an understanding of what is being examined. Even then, it is important that the comparitors are valid – there is not much point in comparing the performance of a Rolls-Royce with that of a bicycle. Like must be compared with like. Racing bike to racing bike, mountain bike to mountain bike, Premiership football team to Premiership football team, and so on. **For companies, the easiest way to ensure like is being compared with like is to compare companies that operate in the same sector.**

The importance of ensuring that any comparison of analysis between companies is between companies in the same sector can best be illustrated through an extreme example: that of the contrast between service companies and manufacturing companies.

Stating the obvious, a firm of consultants who advise their clients on marketing strategies will have far fewer tangible assets than a company with the same turnover which manufactures forklift trucks. The service industry will need premises, but these could easily be rented and, in addition, would need very little in the way of machinery. Some computer equipment and office equipment as well as (perhaps) some motor cars would be all that would be needed.

Compared with the service industry firm, a manufacturing company, such as that making forklift trucks, would need a great deal of machinery as well as lorries and various types of buildings, and so on. The manufacturing firm would also have stocks of materials and unsold forklift trucks. The service firm would have very little in the way of stocks of tangible assets.

> *Activity 28.1*
> What effect would these types of differences have on the ratios of the two businesses?

Especially with service industries, it is also likely that the number of people working for the firm, but who do most, sometimes all, of their work in their homes will grow apace. The need for people to turn up at offices at given times every day is falling dramatically with the wider use of computers and advances in telecommunications.

All of this has an effect on the ratios of performance calculated from the financial statements of manufacturers and service industry firms. The figure of return on capital employed for a service firm, simply because of the few tangible assets needed, may appear to be quite high. For a manufacturing firm the opposite may well be the case.

If this distinction between these completely different types of organisation is understood, then the interpreter of the financial statements will judge them accordingly. Failure to understand the distinction will bring forth some very strange conclusions.

28.3 Trend analysis

Looking internally at one organisation, sensible comparisons can be made between the situation it was in at various points in time.

> *Activity 28.2*
> What two things does an inward-looking analysis of this type NOT tell you?

In *Business Accounting 1*, the example was introduced of two companies, G and H. The example is now reintroduced and further developed: Exhibit 28.1 presents four ratios derived from the financial statements of G over the past five periods.

Exhibit 28.1

Year:	1	2	3	4	5 (now)
Gross profit as % of sales	40	38	36	35	34
Net profit as % of sales	15	13	12	12	11
Net profit as % of capital employed	13	12	11	11	10
Current ratio	3.0	2.8	2.6	2.3	2.0

If the trends in these four ratios are considered, it is clear that they are all deteriorating, but there is no indication whether there should be cause for concern as a result. For example, the industry may be becoming more competitive, causing margins to shrink, and the falling current ratio may be due to an increase in efficiency over the control of working capital.

A company with this trend of figures could state that these were the reasons for the decline in margins and for the reduction in liquidity. A reader of the financial statements could then accept the explanation and put the calculations away. However, there is no guarantee that an explanation of this kind actually indicates a beneficial situation, whether or not it is accurate. In order to gain a fuller view of the company, comparison with other comparable companies in the same sector is needed. Exhibit 28.2 presents the information from Exhibit 28.1 for company G plus information on another company of similar size operating in the same sector, company H.

Exhibit 28.2

		Years				
		1	2	3	4	5 (current)
Gross profit as % of sales	G	40	38	36	35	34
	H	30	32	33	33	34
Net profit as % of sales	G	15	13	12	12	11
	H	10	10	10	11	11
Net profit as % of capital employed	G	13	12	11	11	10
	H	8	8	9	9	10
Current ratio	G	3	2.8	2.6	2.3	2.0
	H	1.5	1.7	1.9	1.0	2.0

Another way in which these results may be compared is through graphs, as shown by the example in Exhibit 28.3 which compares the trend in gross profit as a percentage of sales of the two companies. (Note that the vertical axis does not show the percentage below 30 as there is no percentage below that amount. Omitting the lower figures on the graph allows for a more informative display of the information.)

Exhibit 28.3 The trend of gross profit as a percentage of sales

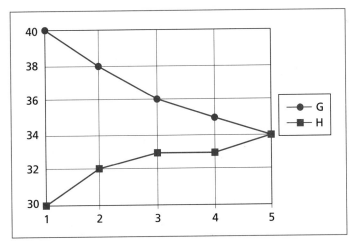

The companies have identical ratios for the current period – does that make them equally desirable as investments? Given one year's financial statements it appears so, but the five-year trend analysis reveals a different picture.

From these figures, G appears to be the worse investment for the future, as the trend for it appears to be downwards, while that of H is upwards. It suggests that the explanation made earlier for the falling margins may not be valid. If the trend for G is continued it could be in a very dangerous financial situation in a year or two's time. H, on the other hand, is strengthening its position all the time.

While it would be ridiculous to assert that H will continue on an upward trend, or that G will continue downwards, a consistent trend of this type does suggest that the situation may well continue into the foreseeable future. It is certainly cause for further investigation.

28.4 Comparisons over time

As shown in the previous section, one of the best ways of using ratios is to compare them with the ratios for the same organisation in respect of previous years. Take another example, the net profit percentage of a company for the past six years, including the current year 20X8:

	20X3	20X4	20X5	20X6	20X7	20X8	(now)
Net profit %	5.4	5.2	4.7	4.8	4.8	4.5	

This could be graphed as in Exhibit 28.4.

Exhibit 28.4

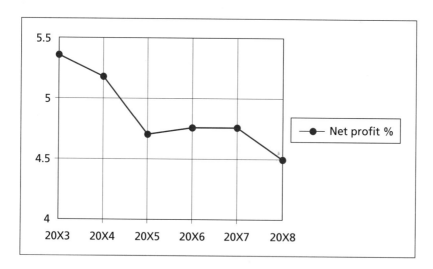

It is obvious that there is a long-term decline in net profit percentage. This prompts us to examine why this should be so. Without measuring against past years our understanding of the direction in which the business seems to be heading would be much diminished.

We would not only look at the long-term changes in net profit percentages, but also compare similar long-term figures in relation to other aspects of the business.

In considering trends, problems may arise from the use of the historical cost accounting concept during a period of significant price increases because of inflation.

28.5   Comparisons with other businesses

No one can say in isolation that a firm is very profitable. It could be the case that it has made £6 million a year, which to most people may seem profitable. On the other hand, if firms of a similar size in the same type of industry are making £20 million a year, then the firm making £6 million cannot be said to be very profitable.

Ideally we would like to be able to compare the results of one firm with those of similar firms in the same sort of industry. Then, and only then, would we be able to judge how well, or how badly, that firm was doing.

The size of firm can have an important effect upon ratios. Just as we would not try to compare a chemist's shop with a building firm, it would also be wrong to judge a small supermarket against Sainsbury's, which owns hundreds of supermarkets.

Interfirm comparisons are also sometimes misleading because of the different accounting treatment of various items, and the location and ages of assets. Some industries have, however, set up interfirm comparisons with guidelines to the companies to ensure that the figures have been constructed using the same bases so that the information is comparable. The information does not disclose data which can be traced to any one firm, ensuring that full confidentiality is observed.

The information available may take the form shown in Exhibit 28.5.

Exhibit 28.5 Published ratios for the widget industry (extract)

	Solvency		Efficiency			
	Current	Acid test	Asset T/O	Stock T/O	Debtor days	Creditor days
20X6	2.4	0.7	5.4	8.2	56.4	80.4
20X7	2.2	0.8	5.7	9.3	52.6	66.8

The equivalent figures for the company being assessed can then be tabulated alongside the industry figures to enable comparisons to be made, as in Exhibit 28.6.

Exhibit 28.6

	Company ratios		Industry ratios	
	20X6	20X7	20X6	20X7
Current ratio	2.9	2.8	2.4	2.2
Acid test ratio	0.5	0.6	0.7	0.8
Asset turnover	5.2	5.3	5.4	5.7
Stock turnover	4.4	4.7	8.2	9.3
Debtor days	65.9	65.2	56.4	52.6
Creditor days	58.3	56.8	80.4	66.8

The financial status of the company is now much clearer. What appeared to be a situation of improving liquidity and efficiency is now shown to be an increasingly poorer liquidity and efficiency position compared with the industry as a whole.

However, it should be borne in mind that the industry figures probably include many companies that are either much larger or much smaller than the company being assessed. To obtain a more complete picture, information is needed concerning companies of a similar size, such as in the comparison between G and H earlier in this chapter (Section 28.3). This information may be available from the source of the interfirm comparison. If not, other sources would need to be used, for example the published financial statements of appropriate companies.

The other information missing from the above comparison is data from previous periods. While not so relevant to the current position, it can be useful in explaining why a situation has developed, and in determining whether the current position is likely to persist.

Activity 28.3

When an organisation operates in more than one sector, how do you identify other appropriate organisations with which to compare it?

28.6 Pyramid of ratios

Once ratios have been analysed and compared, explanations must be sought for the results obtained. Sometimes it will be obvious why a certain result was obtained – for example, if a company has moved from traditional stock-keeping to a just-in-time system during the period, its stock turnover will bear no resemblance to that which it had in the previous period.

For those inside the company – its directors and management – the management accounting records are available to assist in finding explanations, as are the company's staff. Outsiders – shareholders, analysts, lenders, suppliers, customers, etc. – do not have access to all this internal information (though some of these user groups will have access to more internal information than others – banks, for example, can usually obtain copies of a company's management accounts upon request). They must fall back upon other sources of information – newspaper reports and industry publications, for example. One source of additional information available to everyone is the **pyramid of ratios**. Most ratios can be further subdivided into secondary ratios, which themselves can also be subdivided. By following through the pyramid of a given ratio, the source of the original ratio can often be isolated, enabling a far more focused investigation than would otherwise be possible.

For example, one of the most important ratios is the return on the capital employed (ROCE). This ratio has not happened by itself. If the ratio of net profit to sales had not been a particular figure and the ratio of sales to capital employed had not been a particular figure, then the ROCE would not have turned out to be the figure that it is.

Thus, the ROCE comes about as a result of all the other ratios which have underpinned it. It is the final summation of all that has happened in the various aspects of the business. The ROCE pyramid of ratios is shown in Exhibit 28.7.

Exhibit 28.7

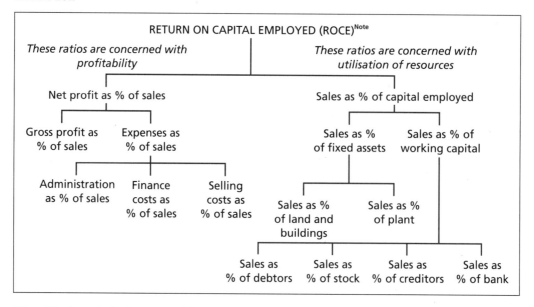

Note: The formula for ROCE used here is a simplified version of the formula used in Chapter 27. It is, in effect, the same.

By itself, the pyramid of ratios may not tell you much. It comes into full effect when compared with similar figures of the ratios for previous years, or with pyramids in respect of other firms. If the ROCE has been falling over the past year then a study of the pyramids for the previous two years may enable you to pinpoint exactly where the changes have been made to bring about the worsening position. Investigation of these matters may then give you some indication of action to be taken.

28.7 Return on capital employed: company policy

The pyramid of ratios in Exhibit 28.7 illustrates the interdependence of each ratio. This can be examined in greater detail by investigating the policies of two companies to achieve their desired return on capital employed.

The first part of the pyramid tells us that the ROCE is dependent on both net profit as a percentage of sales and also sales as a percentage of capital employed. This means that:

$$\text{ROCE} = \frac{\text{Net profit}}{\text{Capital employed}}$$

which by splitting the equation between profitability ratios and resource utilisation ratios means also that:

$$\text{ROCE} = \frac{\text{Net profit}}{\text{Sales}} \times \frac{\text{Sales}}{\text{Capital employed}}$$

This interrelationship of the subsidiary ratios can be illustrated through an example. At the same time, it can be seen that the result of computing a primary ratio is dependent upon the items comprising it; and that there is no guarantee that a value of x will be 'good', and y 'bad'. Whether the result obtained is 'good' or 'bad' depends on the underlying factors that give rise to the result obtained (what, for example, is the company's policy on depreciation and replacement of assets, as this can significantly affect the ROCE?), the sector in which the business operates and its relative size. Without knowledge of these items, comparison of the ratio analysis of two companies is likely to be misleading at best.

Two companies, both in the grocery business, may decide to aim for the same ROCE of 10 per cent. This can be achieved in completely different ways by the two companies.

A Ltd is a large company operating a supermarket. It seeks to attract customers by offering low prices and makes a net profit of only 1.25 per cent on sales. Its sales for the year are £8,000,000 on which its net profit is £100,000. Its capital employed is £1,000,000. The ROCE is, therefore, 10 per cent (i.e. £100,000 net profit on capital employed of £1,000,000). This can also be expressed as:

$$\text{ROCE} = \frac{\text{Net profit}}{\text{Sales}} \times \frac{\text{Sales}}{\text{Capital employed}}$$

$$= \frac{£100,000}{£8,000,000} \times \frac{£8,000,000}{£1,000,000}$$

$$= 10\%$$

B Ltd by comparison, is a small local retailer. It seeks a higher margin per £100 sales, but because of higher prices it will achieve a lower volume of business. It makes a net profit of 5 per cent on sales. Its sales for the year amount to £200,000 on which it makes a net profit

of £10,000. The capital employed is £100,000. The ROCE is therefore 10 per cent (i.e. £10,000 on capital employed of £100,000). This can also be expressed as:

$$\text{ROCE} = \frac{\text{Net profit}}{\text{Sales}} \times \frac{\text{Sales}}{\text{Capital employed}}$$

$$= \frac{£10,000}{£200,000} \times \frac{£200,000}{£100,000}$$

$$= 10\%$$

It can be seen that two firms, despite different sizes of business and operating different pricing policies, can have the same ROCE.

Learning outcomes

You should now have learnt:

1 Ratios on their own are frequently misleading – they should not be considered in isolation from similar computations:
   (*a*) in previous periods; and/or
   (*b*) on similar-sized firms in the same sector.

2 The items in the financial statements are affected by company policy – for example, the rate of depreciation to use, and the policy of asset replacement; the policies adopted, therefore, directly affect the ratio analysis.

3 Companies of very different size and in very different sectors can have the same ratio results despite their being different in every respect.

4 The importance and impact of size, sector and company policies upon ratios mean that there is no such thing as a 'good' or 'bad' value that can be treated as a yardstick for any ratio.

5 All ratios are part of one or more pyramids of ratios.

6 When the results of ratio analysis are being investigated further, the relevant pyramid of ratios can be analysed in order to pinpoint the element giving rise to the situation being investigated.

Answers to activities

28.1 The service business will probably have a lower current ratio – it has no stock. Its creditor days are probably near zero. Its return on capital employed is probably much higher. Its asset turnover may be extremely high – it may not have very many fixed assets. Overall, trying to draw any sensible conclusions by comparing the ratios of these two businesses will be a waste of time.

28.2 It won't tell you whether the organisation is or was in a good position relative to its competitors or other organisations in the same sector. Nor will it tell you if changes in the ratios are actually moving in the appropriate direction for the sector in which the organisation operates.

28.3 In this case, you can try to identify other organisations with a similar range of activities. However, it would probably be more beneficial to separate out the data relating to each type of activity and then compare the reduced data against appropriate comparitors.

Advice

Ratio analysis is a topic that causes more marks to be thrown away in exams than probably every other topic combined. No other accounting topic is as concerned with understanding rather than

knowledge, and examiners tend to expect students to be able to demonstrate their understanding rather than simply their ability to prepare the financial statements or calculate the ratios.

There is no one set pattern to the questions, which depend upon the examiner's ingenuity and background experience. The usual shortcomings in the answers handed in by examinees, particularly on questions relating to this topic but also on questions in other areas, can be listed as follows:

1 Not following the instructions as laid down. If the question says 'list the' then the examiner expects a list as an answer, 'Discuss the' means exactly that, 'Write a report' needs a report as the answer, and so on. You will lose a lot of marks for not giving the examiner exactly what has been asked for.

2 Very often all the ratios etc. are calculated, but then the candidate does not offer any comments even though they have been asked for. *Make certain you cover this part of the question in an appropriate amount of detail.*

3 Even where students have written something about the ratios, they often repeat what the calculations are and offer nothing else, e.g. 'you can see that the gross profit ratio has increased from 18 to 20 per cent' and the answer has finished there. The examiner can already see from your calculations that the gross profit percentage has increased, and wants you to write about *why* it might have increased, what conclusions, if any, can be arrived at, or what further information may be needed to discover why it has changed.

4 Remember that when the examiner asks you 'what other information you would like to have' about a firm when trying to interpret the financial statements so as to give advice to someone then, ideally, you would like to know more about the plans for the future of the business, how it compares with others in the same industry, whether or not there are going to be changes in the management and so on. We should not limit ourselves to information about the past, we really need to know as much about the future as we possibly can.

5 Do not restrict your examination answers to what you have read in a textbook. Keep your eyes and ears open as you go shopping, visit factories, work, buy petrol at the filling station, go to the theatre, and so on. Reading a 'quality' newspaper helps, as there are quite a lot of items about business. Bring all of this sort of knowledge and experience into your answers. You will impress the examiners. They are extremely bored of reading regurgitations of textbook learning with nothing added.

6 Quite a few questions will concern the type of business of which you will have first-hand experience, so you can introduce personal knowledge into your answer. A typical instance would be comparing two grocery businesses. One would be a large supermarket and the other would be a small corner shop. The policies of the two firms would be quite different. The supermarket would have decided on a policy of attracting new customers by lowering sales margins and yet boosting ROCE. The corner shop might have a policy of high margins, but remain open on Sundays and late at nights, and thus be a 'convenience shop', i.e. customers might well go there when other shops are closed or are too far away to be worth the extra cost in petrol, etc. when compared with the extra cost of shopping at the corner shop.

7 Last, but not least, *show your workings*. If you make a mistake in your calculations and do not show your workings you cannot be awarded any credit for a partially incorrect calculation. Consider how much longer it takes to show the detail contained in Section 28.7 above, rather than simply the result of the calculation – maybe 30 seconds. *Now consider whether you would rather spend five minutes in an exam showing the workings of ten ratio calculations, or six months studying to retake the exam you failed because you made a mistake in two of your calculations and lost five marks because the examiner could not tell why you got the answer wrong.*

REVIEW QUESTIONS

28.1 Adrian Frampton was considering the purchase of one of two businesses. However, Frampton had only been provided with limited information about the businesses, as follows:

Summarised Financial Information for the year ended 31 December 20X9

Information	Business X	Business Y
Cost of goods sold	£400,000	£600,000
Administrative expenses	£50,000	£60,000
Average stock at cost	£40,000	£50,000
Working capital as at 31 December 20X9	£90,000	£250,000
Selling and distribution expenses	£15,000	£35,000
Proprietor's capital at 1 January 20X9	£200,000	£350,000
Gross profit percentage mark-up on cost	20	25

Additional information:

1 Average stock had been calculated by using the year's opening and closing stocks. Subsequently it was discovered that Business Y had overvalued its stock on 31 December 20X9 by £10,000.
2 Business X's administrative expenses included a payment for rent of £15,000 which covered a three-year period to 31 December 20X1.
3 A sum of £2,500 was included in the administrative expenses of Business Y in respect of a holiday taken by the owner and his family.
4 Cash drawings for the year ended 31 December 20X9 were:

	£
Business X	20,000
Business Y	25,000

5 The owners of the businesses had stipulated the following prices for their businesses:

	£
Business X	190,000
Business Y	400,000

Required:
(a) Based on the information available prepare comparative trading and profit and loss accounts for the year ended 31 December 20X9.
(b) Using the information provided and the accounting statements prepared in (a), calculate relevant accounting ratios in order to give Frampton a basis for assessing the performances of the two businesses. Comment on the results.
(c) What additional information is needed in order to assess more accurately
  (i) the liquidity of the businesses;
  (ii) the future prospects of the businesses?

(AQA (Associated Examining Board): GCE A-level)

28.2 Three companies have the capital structures shown below.

Company	A £000	B £000	C £000
Ordinary shares	600	400	50
12% debentures	–	200	550
	600	600	600

The return on capital employed was 20 per cent for each firm in 20X4, and in 20X5 was 10 per cent. Corporation tax in both years was assumed to be 55 per cent, and debenture interest is an allowable expense against corporation tax.

(a) Calculate the percentage return on the shareholders' capital for each company for 20X4 and 20X5. Assume that all profits are distributed.
(b) Use your answer to explain the merits and the dangers of high gearing.

(Edexcel: University of London GCE A-level)

28.3A Martha is the accountant of a trading business. During the past year she produced interim accounts for the six months ended 30 November 20X5, and draft final accounts for the year ended 31 May 20X6, as follows:

	Interim accounts	Draft final accounts
	£	£
Sales (all on credit terms)	140,000	336,000
Cost of sales (Note 1)	42,000	112,000
Gross profit	98,000	224,000
Less Expenses	56,000	168,000
Net profit	42,000	56,000
Fixed assets	70,000	63,000
Current assets (Note 2)	42,000	71,000
Current liabilities (Note 3)	(22,000)	(30,000)
	90,000	104,000
Share capital	30,000	30,000
Retained earnings	60,000	74,000
	90,000	104,000

Notes:

1 Average stock was £14,000 during the first six months.

2 Current assets were:

	30 Nov 20X5	31 May 20X6
	£	£
Stock	16,000	25,000
Debtors	24,000	28,000
Bank	2,000	18,000
	42,000	71,000

3 Current liabilities consisted entirely of trade creditors.

Martha informs you that the business leased additional premises from 1 December 20X5, and that sales arising therefrom totalled £70,000 for the six months to 31 May 20X6, with an average mark-up on cost prices of 150 per cent being made on those goods.

Expenses relating to these additional premises totalled £21,000 for the period. Two-fifths of the closing stock of the business was located at these premises.

Prepare a report, using appropriate accounting ratios, to explain the changes in the financial situation of the business during the year ended 31 May 20X6.

(*Edexcel: University of London GCE A-level*)

28.4 John Jones is considering purchasing shares in one of two companies and has extracted the following information from the balance sheet of each company.

	Company A Plc £000	Company B Plc £000
Authorised share capital		
£1 ordinary shares	600	1,000
8% £1 preference shares	400	
Issued share capital		
£1 ordinary shares	300	800
8% £1 preference shares	200	
Reserves		
Share premium	300	400
Retained earnings	400	200
Loan capital		
10% debentures (20X0)		200
12% debentures (20X6)	400	

Required:
(a) Define the term 'gearing' stating clearly what is meant by a low gearing ratio.
(b) Calculate the gearing factor for each company.
(c) Explain to John Jones the significance of gearing to an ordinary shareholder in each of the companies above.
(d) Assuming for each company a trading profit of £200,000 before interest and an ordinary dividend of 15 per cent complete the profit and loss appropriation account for a year for each company. You should ignore taxation.

(AQA (Associated Examining Board): GCE A-level)

28.5A The following are extracts from the balance sheets as at 31 March 20X4 and 31 March 20X5 of Glebe Ltd:

	31 March 20X4		31 March 20X5	
	£	£	£	£
Current assets				
Stocks	20,000		25,000	
Trade debtors	10,000		17,000	
Cash	5,000		3,000	
		35,000		45,000
Less				
Current liabilities				
Trade creditors	12,000		16,000	
Proposed dividends	6,000		5,000	
Bank overdraft	7,000		29,000	
		(25,000)		(50,000)
		10,000		(5,000)

Required:
(a) Calculate for each of the two years two ratios that indicate the liquidity position of the company.
(b) (i) From the information given, give reasons for the changes which have occurred in the working capital.
   (ii) What other information regarding the current assets and current liabilities would you consider necessary to assess the ability of the business to continue in operation?
(c) Discuss any other information available from a balance sheet that may affect an assessment of the liquidity of a business.

(AQA (Associated Examining Board): GCE A-level)

28.6 Colin Black is considering investing a substantial sum in the ordinary shares of Jacks Ltd. Having some accounting knowledge he has extracted the following information from the accounts for the last two financial years.

	As at 31 March 20X4	As at 31 March 20X5
	£	£
Issued share capital		
£1 ordinary shares, fully paid	100,000	150,000
Reserves		
Share premium	10,000	60,000
Retained earnings	140,000	160,000
Loan capital		
10% debentures 20X7–X9	40,000	40,000

	For year ended 31 March 20X4	For year ended 31 March 20X5
	£	£
Net profit after tax	60,000	70,000

Because he was disappointed with the result he obtained when he calculated the return on the equity capital employed, Colin Black has asked for your advice.

Required:

(a) Calculate the figures which prompted Colin Black's reaction.

(b) Prepare a memorandum to Colin Black pointing out other information to be considered when comparing the return on equity capital employed over two years as a basis for his investment decision.

(c) Explain why a company builds up and maintains reserves.

(AQA (Associated Examining Board): GCE A-level)

28.7A The following information has been extracted from the accounts of Witton Way Ltd:

Profit and Loss Account for the year to 30 April

	20X5	20X6
	£000	£000
Turnover (all credit sales)	7,650	11,500
Less Cost of sales	(5,800)	(9,430)
Gross profit	1,850	2,070
Other expenses	(150)	(170)
Loan interest	(50)	(350)
Profit before taxation	1,650	1,550
Taxation	(600)	(550)
Profit after taxation	1,050	1,000
Dividends (all ordinary shares)	(300)	(300)
Retained profits	750	700

Balance Sheet at 30 April

	20X5	20X6
	£000	£000
Fixed assets		
Tangible assets	10,050	11,350
Current assets		
Stocks	1,500	2,450
Trade debtors	1,200	3,800
Cash	900	50
	3,600	6,300
Creditors: Amounts falling due within one year	(2,400)	(2,700)
Net current assets	1,200	3,600
Total assets less current liabilities	11,250	14,950
Creditors:		
Amounts falling due after more than one year		
Loans and other borrowings	(350)	(3,350)
	10,900	11,600
Capital and reserves		
Called-up share capital	5,900	5,900
Profit and loss account	5,000	5,700
	10,900	11,600

Additional information:

During the year to 30 April 20X6, the company tried to stimulate sales by reducing the selling price of its products and by offering more generous credit terms to its customers.

Required:

(a) Calculate six accounting ratios specifying the basis of your calculations for each of the two years to 30 April 20X5 and 20X6 respectively which will enable you to examine the company's progress during 20X6.

(b) From the information available to you, including the ratios calculated in part (a) of the question, comment upon the company's results for the year to 30 April 20X6 under the heads of 'profitability', 'liquidity', 'efficiency' and 'shareholders' interests'.

(c) State what additional information you would require in order to assess the company's attempts to stimulate sales during the year to 30 April 20X6.

(*Association of Accounting Technicians*)

28.8 You are presented with the following information for three quite separate and independent companies:

Summarised Balance Sheets at 31 March 20X7

	Chan plc £000	Ling plc £000	Wong plc £000
Total assets *less* current liabilities	600	600	700
Creditors: amounts falling due after more than one year			
10% debenture stock	–	–	(100)
	£600	£600	£600
Capital and reserves:			
Called-up share capital			
Ordinary shares of £1 each	500	300	200
10% cumulative preference shares of £1 each	–	200	300
Profit and loss account	100	100	100
	£600	£600	£600

Additional information:

1 The operating profit before interest and tax for the year to 31 March 20X8 earned by each of the three companies was £300,000.
2 The effective rate of corporation tax for all three companies for the year to 31 March 20X8 is 30 per cent. This rate is to be used in calculating each company's tax payable on ordinary profit.
3 An ordinary dividend of 20p for the year to 31 March 20X8 is proposed by all three companies, and any preference dividends are to be provided for.
4 The market prices per ordinary share at 31 March 20X8 were as follows:

	£
Chan plc	8.40
Ling plc	9.50
Wong plc	10.38

5 There were no changes in the share capital structure or in long-term loans of any of the companies during the year to 31 March 20X8.

Required:
(a) In so far as the information permits, prepare the profit and loss account for each of the three companies (in columnar format) for the year to 31 March 20X8 (formal notes to the accounts are not required);
(b) calculate the following accounting ratios for each company:
    (i) earnings per share;
    (ii) price earnings;
    (iii) gearing (taken as total borrowings (preference share capital and long-term loans) to ordinary shareholders' funds); and
(c) using the gearing ratios calculated in answering part (b) of the question, briefly examine the importance of gearing if you were thinking of investing in some ordinary shares in one of the three companies assuming that the profits of the three companies were fluctuating.

(*Association of Accounting Technicians*)

28.9A The chairman of a family business has been examining the following summary of the accounts of the company since it began three years ago.

Balance Sheet (at 30 June) £000

	20X4 Actual		20X5 Actual		20X6 Actual	
Freehold land and buildings		150		150		150
Plant	150		150		450	
Less: Depreciation	(15)		(30)		(75)	
		135		120		375
		285		270		525
Stock and work in progress	20		45		85	
Debtors	33		101		124	
Bank and cash	10		15		–	
	63		161		209	
Less: Creditors	(20)		(80)		(35)	
Taxation	(4)		(17)		(6)	
Overdraft	(–)		(–)		(25)	
		39		64		143
		324		334		668
Less: Loan		(–)		(–)		(200)
		324		334		468
Ordinary share capital (£1 shares)		300		300		400
General reserve		17		25		45
Deferred tax account		7		9		23
		324		334		468

Profit and Loss Account (for year to 30 June) £000

	20X4 Actual		20X5 Actual		20X6 Actual	
Sales		260		265		510
Trading profit		53		50		137
Depreciation	15		15		45	
Loan interest	–		–		43	
		(15)		(15)		(88)
Net profit		38		35		49
Taxation (including transfer to or from deferred tax account)		(11)		(15)		(15)
Net profit after tax		27		20		34
Dividend (proposed*)		(10)		(12)		(14)*
Retained		17		8		20

The company's products are popular in the locality and in the first two years sales could have been higher if there had been extra machine capacity available.

On 1 January 20X6, additional share and loan capital was obtained which enabled extra machinery to be purchased. This gave an immediate increase in sales and profits.

Although 20X5/X6 showed the best yet results, the chairman is not very happy; the accountant has suggested that a dividend should not be paid this year because of the overdraft. The accountant has, however, shown a proposed dividend of £14,000 (£2,000 up on last year) for purposes of comparison pending a decision by the directors.

Naturally, the chairman is displeased and wants some explanations from the accountant regarding the figures in the accounts. He specifically asks:

(*i*) Why, if profits are the best ever and considering the company has obtained extra capital during the year, has the company gone into overdraft? Can there really be a profit if there is no cash left in the bank to pay a dividend?

(*ii*) Why is the freehold still valued at the same price as in 20X4? The real value seems to be about £225,000. Why is this real value not in the balance sheet?

Required:
Write a report to the chairman:
(a) commenting on the state and progress of the business as disclosed by the accounts and the above information, supporting your analysis by appropriate key accounting ratios, and
(b) giving reasoned answers, in the context of recognised accounting law, rules and practices, to each of the questions raised by the chairman.

(*Institute of Chartered Secretaries and Administrators*)

28.10 The following information is provided for Bessemer Ltd which operates in an industry subject to marked variations in consumer demand.

(*i*) Shareholders' equity at 30 September 20X5:	£000
Issued ordinary shares of £1 each fully paid	5,000
Retained profits	1,650
	6,650

There were no loans outstanding at the balance sheet date.

(*ii*) Profit and loss account extracts: year to 30 September 20X5:	£000
Net profit before tax	900
Less Corporation tax	270
	630
Less Dividends	600
Retained profit for the year	30
Retained profit at 1 October 20X4	1,620
Retained profit at 30 September 20X5	1,650

(*iii*) The directors are planning to expand output. This will require an additional investment of £2,000,000 which may be financed either by issuing 1,000,000 ordinary shares each with a nominal value of £1, or by raising a 12 per cent debenture.

(*iv*) Forecast profits before interest charges, if any, for the year to 30 September:

	£000
20X6	1,800
20X7	500
20X8	2,200

A corporation tax rate of 30 per cent on reported profit before tax may be assumed; the directors plan to pay out the entire post-tax profit as dividends.

Required:
(a) The forecast profit and loss appropriation accounts for each of the next three years and year-end balance sheet extracts, so far as the information permits, assuming that the expansion is financed by:
(i) issuing additional shares, or
(ii) raising a debenture.
(b) Calculate the forecast return on shareholders' equity, for each of the next three years, under the alternative methods for financing the planned expansion.
(c) An assessment of the merits and demerits of the alternative methods of finance based on the calculations made under (a) and (b) and any other relevant methods of comparison.

(*Institute of Chartered Secretaries and Administrators*)

28.11A An investor is considering the purchase of shares in either AA plc or BB plc whose latest accounts are summarised below. Both companies carry on similar manufacturing activities with similar selling prices and costs of materials, labour and services.

Balance Sheets at 30 September 20X7 (£000)

	AA plc		BB plc	
Freehold property at revaluation 20X5		2,400		–
Plant, machinery and equipment:				
at cost	1,800		1,800	
depreciation	1,200		400	
		600		1,400
Goodwill		–		800
Stocks: finished goods		400		200
work in progress		300		100
Debtors		800		500
Bank deposit		–		400
		4,500		3,400
Less Liabilities due within one year				
Creditors	600		900	
Overdraft	200		–	
	800		900	
Liabilities due after one year	1,400		1,000	
		(2,200)		(1,900)
		2,300		1,500
Ordinary £1 shares		1,000		500
Reserves		1,300		1,000
		2,300		1,500

Profit and Loss Accounts – Year to 30 September 20X7 (£000)

	AA plc		BB plc	
Sales		2,500		2,500
Operating profit		400		600
Depreciation – plant, machinery and equipment	180		180	
Loan interest	150		160	
		(330)		(340)
		70		260
Bank interest		–		100
		70		360
Taxation		(20)		(90)
Available to ordinary shareholders		50		270
Dividend		(40)		(130)
Retained		10		140
Price/earnings ratio	30		5	
Market value of share	£1.50		£2.70	

Required:
(a) write a report to the investor, giving an appraisal of the results and state of each business, and
(b) advise the investor whether, in your opinion, the price/earnings ratios and market price of the shares can be justified in the light of the figures in the accounts, giving your reasons.

(Institute of Chartered Secretaries and Administrators)

28.12 The following are the summarised accounts for B Limited, a company with an accounting year ending on 30 September.

Summarised Balance Sheets for	20X5/6		20X6/7	
	£000	£000	£000	£000
Tangible fixed assets – at cost				
Less Depreciation		4,995		12,700
Current assets:				
Stocks	40,145		50,455	
Debtors	40,210		43,370	
Cash at bank	12,092		5,790	
	92,447		99,615	
Creditors: amounts falling due within one year:				
Trade creditors	32,604		37,230	
Taxation	2,473		3,260	
Proposed dividend	1,785		1,985	
	36,862		42,475	
Net current assets		55,585		57,140
Total assets less current liabilities		60,580		69,840
Creditors: amounts falling due after more than one year:				
10% debentures 20X6/20X9		(19,840)		(19,840)
		40,740		50,000
Capital and reserves:				
Called-up share capital of £0.25 per share		9,920		9,920
Profit and loss account		30,820		40,080
Shareholders' funds		40,740		50,000

Summarised Profit and Loss Accounts for	20X5/6	20X6/7
	£000	£000
Turnover	486,300	583,900
Operating profit	17,238	20,670
Interest payable	(1,984)	(1,984)
Profit on ordinary activities before taxation	15,254	18,686
Tax on profit on ordinary activities	(5,734)	(7,026)
Profit for the financial year	9,520	11,660
Dividends	(2,240)	(2,400)
	7,280	9,260
Retained profit brought forward	23,540	30,820
Retained profit carried forward	30,820	40,080

You are required to:

(a) calculate, for each year, two ratios for each of the following user groups, which are of particular significance to them: (i) shareholders; (ii) trade creditors; (iii) internal management;

(b) make brief comments upon the changes, between the two years, in the ratios calculated in (a) above.

(*Chartered Institute of Management Accountants*)

28.13A The following are the financial statements of D Limited, a wholesaling company, for the year ended 31 December:

Profit and Loss Accounts	20X4	20X4	20X5	20X5
	£000	£000	£000	£000
Turnover – credit sales	2,200		2,640	
cash sales	200		160	
		2,400		2,800
Cost of sales		(1,872)		(2,212)
Gross profit		528		588
Distribution costs		(278)		(300)
Administration expenses		(112)		(114)
Operating profit		138		174
Interest payable		–		(32)
Profit on ordinary activities before tax		138		142

Balance Sheets as at 31 December	20X4 £000	20X4 £000	20X5 £000	20X5 £000
Tangible fixed assets		220		286
Current assets: Stocks	544		660	
Debtors	384		644	
Cash at bank	8		110	
	936		1,414	
Creditors: amounts falling due within one year:				
Trade creditors	(256)		(338)	
Net current assets		680		1,076
Total assets *less* current liabilities		900		1,362
Creditors: amounts falling due after more than one year:				
Debenture loans		–		(320)
Shareholders' funds		900		1,042

The following information should be taken into consideration.

1 You may assume that:
   (i) the range of products sold by D Limited remained unchanged over the two years;
   (ii) the company managed to acquire its products in 20X5 at the same prices as it acquired them for in 20X4;
   (iii) the effects of any inflationary aspects have been taken into account in the figures.
2 Ignore taxation.
3 All calculations must be shown to one decimal place.

You are required, using the information above, to assess and comment briefly on the company, from the point of view of:
(a) profitability;
(b) liquidity.

(*Chartered Institute of Management Accountants*)

28.14 G plc is a holding company with subsidiaries that have diversified interests. G plc's board of directors is interested in the group acquiring a subsidiary in the machine tool manufacturing sector. Two companies have been identified as potential acquisitions, A Ltd and B Ltd. Summaries of both these companies' accounts are shown below:

Profit and Loss Accounts for the year ended 30 April 20X8

	A Ltd £000	B Ltd £000
Turnover	985	560
Cost of goods sold		
Opening stock	150	145
Materials	255	136
Labour	160	125
Factory overheads	205	111
Depreciation	35	20
Closing stock	(155)	(140)
	650	397
Gross profit	335	163
Selling and administration expenses	(124)	(75)
Interest	(35)	(10)
Profit before taxation	176	78
Taxation	65	25
Profit after taxation	111	53

Balance Sheets at 30 April 20X8

	A Ltd		B Ltd	
	£000	£000	£000	£000
Fixed assets		765		410
Current assets				
Stock	155		140	
Debtors	170		395	
Bank	50		45	
	375		580	
Current liabilities				
Trade creditors	235		300	
Other	130		125	
	(365)		(425)	
Net current assets		10		155
Debentures		(220)		(70)
		555		495
Share capital		450		440
Profit and loss account		105		55
		555		495

You are required to prepare a report for the board of G plc assessing the financial performance and position of A Ltd and B Ltd. Your report should be prepared in the context of G plc's interests in these two companies and should be illustrated with financial ratios where appropriate. You should state any assumptions you make as well as any limitations of your analysis.

(*Chartered Institute of Management Accountants*)

28.15A J plc supplies and fits car tyres, exhaust pipes and other components. The company has branches throughout the country. Roughly 60 per cent of sales are for cash (retail sales). The remainder are credit sales made to car hire companies and large organisations with fleets of company cars (business sales). Business sales tend to be more profitable than retail and the company is keen to expand in this area. There is, however, considerable competition. Branch managers are responsible for obtaining business customers and have some discretion over terms of trade and discounts.

The company's computerised accounting system has recently produced the following report for the manager of the Eastown branch for the six months ended 30 September 20X4:

	Eastown Branch	Average for all branches
Return on capital employed	22%	16%
Gross profit	38%	45%
Selling and promotion costs/sales	9%	6%
Wages/sales	19%	14%
Debtors turnover (based on credit sales only)	63 days	52 days
Stock turnover	37 days	49 days

The Eastown branch manager has only recently been appointed and is unsure whether his branch appears well managed. He has asked for your advice.

You are required to compare the performance of the Eastown branch with the average for all branches. Suggest reasons for the differences you identify.

(*Chartered Institute of Management Accountants*)

28.16A Company managers are aware that the readers of financial statements often use accounting ratios to evaluate their performance. **Explain** how this could lead to decisions which are against the company's best interests.

(*Chartered Institute of Management Accountants*)

PART 5

Issues in financial reporting

Introduction

This part looks at the theories upon which accounting practice is based, considers issues affecting accounting and financial reporting, and reviews the place of accounting information in the context of the environment in which business entities operate.

Accounting theory

After you have studied this chapter, you should be able to:

- explain that there is no one overall accepted general theory of accounting
- describe some of the possible valuation alternatives to historical cost
- explain the difference between current purchasing power and current cost accounting
- describe the characteristics of useful information
- describe problems relating to the production of accounting information

Introduction

This chapter is in three parts: general accounting theory; accounting for changing price levels; and the objectives of financial statements. You will learn about asset valuation, the concept of wealth measurement, the needs of the users of accounting information, and about the problems inherent in the production of accounting information.

PART I: GENERAL ACCOUNTING THEORY

29.1 Background

To many students it will seem strange that a discussion of accounting theory has been left until this late stage of the book. Logically you could argue that it should have preceded all the practical work.

The reason for not dealing with theory at the beginning is simple. From a teaching point of view, it could easily have confused you, and made it more difficult to assimilate the basic rules of accounting. The terms used in theory, such as what is meant in accounting by capital, liabilities, assets, net profit and so on, would not then have been understood. Leaving it until now, if theory points out what is wrong with accounting methods, at least you know those methods. Theory taught in a vacuum is counterproductive for most students.

In the discussion which follows, we want you to remember that this is your first proper look at accounting theory. We do not intend it to be an exhaustive examination, but simply an introduction to give you an overall appreciation. If you carry your studies to a higher level you will have to study accounting theory in much greater depth.

29.2 An overall accepted theory?

It would not be surprising if you were expecting to read here exactly what the overall accepted theory of accounting is, and then proceed to examine the details later. Unfortunately, there is no such 'accepted' theory. This is much regretted by those accountants who have

chosen an academic life. To practising accountants, accounting is what accountants do, and they feel theory has little place in that. Such a narrow view is to be deprecated. The reality, however, is that accounting theory provides a general frame of reference by which accounting practices can be judged, and it also guides the way to the development of new practices and procedures.

The lack of an accepted theory of accounting does not mean that it has not been attempted; there have been numerous attempts. At first an inductive approach was tried – i.e. one that tried to create a theory from a few examples. For example, if you saw a white swan, you might induce the theory that all swans are white (which they are not). The practices of accountants were observed and analysed to see if any consistent behaviour could be detected. This was done in the hope that if a general principle was identified, everyone could be led towards applying it. The inductive approach failed.

It was impossible to find consistent patterns of behaviour amongst the mass of practices that had developed over the years. Also, such an approach would not have brought about any important improvements in accounting practices, as it looked at 'what accountants do' rather than 'what accountants should be doing'.

A different approach emerged in the 1950s. It was a **normative approach**, in that it aimed to improve accounting practice. It looked at what accountants should be doing rather than at what they did. However, it also included elements of the inductive approach in attempting to derive rules based on logical reasoning when given a set of objectives. The combination of these approaches has been promising, but the main problem has been a lack of a general agreement as to the objectives of accounting.

As you might expect, attention then switched towards a less ambitious approach. This is based, first, on identifying the users of financial statements, and then finding out what kind of information they require. Such an approach was used in *The Corporate Report*, sponsored by the government and published in 1975. We will look later at the user groups which were identified. The other important report using this approach was that of the Sandilands Committee (also sponsored by the government and published in 1975). This will also be considered more fully later.

Activity 29.1

Should accountants give the user groups the information they are asking for, or the information for which they should be asking?

Another point which will be considered later is whether only one report should be issued for all user groups, or whether each group should have its own report.

Having had an overall look at how theory construction is proceeding, we can now turn to look at theory in more detail.

29.3 Measurement of income

The syllabus uses the word 'income', but the words 'net profit' mean exactly the same. In this book the calculation of net profit is done within fairly strict guidelines. Chapter 10 in *Frank Wood's Business Accounting 1* provided guidance on the overall concepts ruling such calculations. However, just because the business world and the accounting profession use this basic approach does not mean it is the only one available. We will now consider possible alternatives to the basic method.

Let us start by looking at the simplest possible example of the calculation of profit, where everyone would agree with the way it is calculated. John is starting in business, his only

asset being cash £1,000. He rents a stall in the market for the day, costing him £40. He then buys fruit for cash £90, and sells it all during the day for cash £160. At the end of the day John's only asset is still cash: £1,000 − £40 − £90 + 160 = £1,030. Everyone would agree that his profit for that day was £30, i.e. £160 sales − £90 purchases − £40 expenses = £30. In this case his profit equals the increase in his cash.

Suppose that John now changes his style of trading. He buys the market stall, and he also starts selling nuts and dried fruit, of which he can keep a stock from one day to another. If we now want to calculate profit we cannot do it simply in terms of cash, we will also have to place a value both on the stock of fruit and nuts and on his stall, at both the beginning and the end of each day.

The argument just put forward assumes that we can all agree that profit represents an increase in wealth. It assumes that John will make a profit for a period if either:

(a) he is better off at the end of the period than he was at the beginning; or
(b) he would have been better off at the end than at the beginning had he not consumed some of the profits by taking drawings.

The Nobel prize winning economist Sir John Hicks expressed the view that profit was the maximum value which a person could consume during a period and still be as well off at the end of the period as at the beginning. You will learn later about the rules governing the calculation of profit. In a sense, profit is very much the same as income – what you have left after you subtract all your expenses from your receipts is your 'income'. (Accountants call it 'net income' or 'net profit' but, for simplicity, let's just call it 'income' for the time being.)

In terms of a limited company, the Sandilands Committee, which will be mentioned in greater detail later, said that a company's profit for the year is the maximum value which the company can distribute as dividends during the year, and still be as well off at the end of the year as it was at the beginning. There are some important questions here which need answering. They are:

1 How can we measure wealth at the beginning and end of a period?
2 How do we measure the change in wealth over a period?
3 Having measured wealth over a period, how much can be available for consumption and how much should not be consumed?

There are two main approaches to the measurement of wealth of a business:

(a) By finding the values of the individual assets of a business and then subtracting from them the value of the individual liabilities of the business.
(b) By measuring the expectation of future benefits. (This involves calculating something known as the 'present value of expected future net cash flows'. You will be covering this topic in Chapters 43 and 44.)

From these, you can see that in order to measure wealth, you must first identify the value of your assets and liabilities or the value of your future net cash flows.

Activity 29.2
If you paid £1,000 for a computer, what value would you say it had?

Arriving at an acceptable value for a fixed asset is not nearly as simple as it appears. Firstly, you need to know what the term 'value' means. It is rather more than just the amount paid or the amount something is sold for. You need to consider the context – a glass of water has a lot more value in a desert than in London. If you have studied any economics, you will know that the availability of something dictates its value to the purchaser. And, from an accounting perspective, once you own something, the value you place on it

may not be what you paid for it and the basis of valuation that you use needs to be acceptable in the context of accounting.

Let's now look at the different methods that can be used to value assets.

29.4 Asset valuation alternatives

1 Historical cost

This is the most commonly applied method and you will be using it throughout your accounting studies. The principles underpinning it are quite simple. An asset is valued at what it cost, less an amount representing the effect of its use so far upon that value.

Taking the computer costing £1,000 as an example. Let's assume it was expected to be used for four years before being scrapped. As it would last four years, each year its value would reduce by a quarter of what was paid for it. That is, it would be reduced by £250 every year. At the end of two years, it would have a value of £500. (£1,000 − £250 − £250).

This seems quite simple, except that someone needs to decide by how much to reduce its value by each year. Why was four years chosen for the useful economic life of the computer? Why not three or five? Why was it assumed that it would lose value equally each year? This depreciation adjustment is just one example of how imprecise accounting can be in relation to arriving at a value for something. There is no one 'true' answer; the choice of method, expected length of use of the asset, etc., is quite arbitrary.

Let's look at a couple of other examples.

(a) Stocks to be used during the period can be charged out at FIFO (first in, first out), LIFO (last in, first out), AVCO (average cost method) for stock valuation, and so on. There is no one 'true' figure.

(b) Suppose we buy a block of assets, e.g. we take over the net assets of another organisation. How do we allocate the cost exactly? There is no precise way, we simply use a 'fair value' for each asset. As you know, any difference between the cost and total of the fair values is treated as goodwill.

2 Adjusted historical cost

Because of the changes in the value or purchasing power of money, the normal historical cost approach can be very unsatisfactory. Take the case of a buildings account. In it we find that two items have been debited. One was a warehouse bought in 1970 for £100,000 and the other an almost identical warehouse bought in 1995 for £400,000. These two figures are added together to show cost of warehouses £500,000 – quite clearly a value which has little significance.

To remedy this defect, the original historical cost of an asset is adjusted for the changes in the value or purchasing power of money over the period from acquisition to the present balance sheet date. The calculations are effected by using a price index.

This method does not mean that the asset itself is revalued. What is revalued is the money for which the asset was originally bought. This method forms the basis of what is known as **current purchasing power** accounting, abbreviated as CPP. During the early 1980s when inflation in the UK was high, many companies produced financial accounting information based on CPP.

The method does not remove the problem of the 'true' cost. All it does is to assume the original historical cost was accurate and then adjust the value of the business (and, hence, the owner's wealth) to allow for the different timings.

To illustrate how it works, let's take an instance which works out precisely, just as the proponents of CPP would wish.

A machine which will last for five years, depreciated using the straight line method, was bought on 1 January 20X4 for £5,000. On 1 January 20X6 exactly the same kind of machine (there have been no technological improvements) is bought for £6,000. The price index was 100 at 1 January 20X4, 120 at 1 January 20X6 and 130 at 31 December 20X6. The machines would appear in the balance sheet at 31 December 20X6 as follows, the workings being shown in the box alongside.

	Historical cost £	Conversion factor £		Balance sheet CPP at 31 Dec 20X6 £
Machine 1	5,000	130/100	6,500	
Machine 2	6,000	130/120	6,500	13,000
Less Depreciation				
Machine 1	3,000	130/100	3,900	
Machine 2	1,200	130/120	1,300	(5,200)
				7,800

You can see that the CPP balance sheet shows two exactly similar machines at the same cost, and each has been depreciated £1,300 for each year of use. In this particular case CPP has achieved exactly what it sets out to do, namely put similar things on a similar basis.

Underlying this method are the problems inherent in the price index used to adjust the historical cost figures. Any drawbacks in the index will result in a distortion of the adjusted historical cost figures.

Activity 29.3
To summarise, what are the potential flaws in this method?

3 Replacement cost

Replacement cost, abbreviated as RC, is the estimated amount that would have to be paid to replace the asset at the date of valuation. You will often see it referred to as an 'entry value' as it is the cost of an asset entering the business.

How do we 'estimate' the replacement cost? As we are not in fact replacing the asset we will have to look at the state of the market at the date of valuation. If the asset is exactly the same as those currently being traded, perhaps we can look at suppliers' price lists.

Even with exactly the same item, there are still problems. Until you have actually negotiated a purchase it is impossible to say how much discount you could get – you might guess but you could not be certain. Also, if the asset consists of, say, ten computers, how much discount could you get for buying ten computers instead of one?

And that's the 'easy' one! What do you do when you are trying to find out these figures for assets that are no longer available? Technological change has greatly speeded up in recent years. If there is a second-hand market, it may be possible to get a valuation. However, in second-hand markets the price is often even more subject to negotiation. It becomes even more complicated when the original asset was specially made and there is no exactly comparable item, new or second-hand.

The difficulties outlined above mean that solutions to valuation can be sought under three headings:

(a) **Market prices.** There will often be a market, new or second-hand, for the assets. For instance, this is particularly true for motor vehicles. However, if your asset differs in some way from the one you found the price of, an adjustment may be necessary to the value, thus decreasing the reliability of the value you place on the asset.

(b) **Units of service.** Where a market price cannot be found, a value can be placed based upon the units of service (or output) which the asset can provide.

For example, take a machine that it is estimated will be able to produce another 1,000 items before it is scrapped. A new but different machine would be expected to produce 5,000 of the same items before being scrapped. The old machine can be given a value equal to one-fifth of the cost of the new machine. However, if the costs of operating the two machines differ, this would need to be taken into account when arriving at the valuation figure for the old machine.

(c) **Cost of inputs.** If the asset was made or constructed by the owner, it may be possible to calculate the cost of replacing it at the balance sheet date. Present rates of labour and materials costs could be worked out to give the replacement cost.

Activity 29.4
What flaw can you see in this method?

---

4 Net realisable value

Net realisable value means the estimated amount that would be received from the sale of the asset less the estimated costs on its disposal. The term **exit value** is often used as it is the amount receivable when an asset leaves the business.

A very important factor affecting such a valuation is the conditions under which the assets are to be sold. To realise in a hurry would often mean accepting a very low price. Look at the sale prices received from stock from bankruptcies – usually very low figures. The standard way of approaching this problem is to value as though the realisation were 'in the normal course of business'. This is not capable of a precise valuation, as economic conditions change and the firm might never sell such an asset 'in the normal course of business'.

The difficulties of establishing an asset's net realisable value are similar to those of the replacement value method when similar assets are not being bought and sold in the marketplace. However, the problems are more severe as the units of service approach cannot be used, since that takes the seller's rather than buyer's viewpoint.

5 Economic value (present value)

As any economist would be delighted to tell you, they would value an asset as the sum of the future expected net cash flows associated with the asset, discounted (adjusted) to its present value (what the cash flows would be worth today). For example, £20 in a year's time might only be able to buy goods that today could be purchased for £19. The technicalities of discounting are discussed in Chapters 43 and 44.

Certainly, if you really did know (not guess) the future net cash flows associated with the asset and you had the correct discount rate, your valuation would be absolutely correct. The trouble is that it is impossible to forecast future net cash flows with certainty, neither will we necessarily have chosen the correct discount rate. It is also very difficult to relate cash flows to a particular asset, since a business's assets combine together to generate revenue.

Before considering the next method, you may find it helpful to see four of these methods compared in the contexts of time and valuation base.

Exhibit 29.1 Four methods of valuation in the contexts of time and valuation basis

	Past	Present	Future
Entry value	Historical Cost	Replacement cost	
Exit value		Realisable value	Present value

6 Deprival value

The final concept of value is based on ideas propounded in the USA by Professor Bonbright in the 1930s, and later developed in the UK for profit measurement by Professor W T Baxter.

Deprival value is based on the concept of the value of an asset being the amount of money the owner would have to receive to compensate him exactly for being deprived of it. We had better point out immediately that the owner does not have to be deprived of the asset to ascertain this value, it is a hypothetical exercise. This leads to a number of consequences.

(a) Deprival value cannot exceed replacement cost, since if the owner were deprived of the asset he could replace it for a lesser amount. Here we will ignore any costs concerned with a delay in replacement.
(b) If the owner feels that the asset is not worth replacing, its replacement cost would be more than its deprival value. The owner simply would not pay the replacement cost, so the value to the owner is less than that figure.
(c) If the asset's deprival value is to be taken as its net realisable value, that value must be less than its replacement cost. It would otherwise make sense for someone to sell the asset at net realisable value and buy a replacement at a lower cost. Again, delays in replacement are ignored.
(d) Take the case where an owner would not replace the asset, but neither would he sell it. It is possible to envisage a fixed asset which has become obsolete but might possibly be used, for example, when other machines break down. It is not worth buying a new machine, as the replacement cost is more than the value of the machine to the business. Such a machine may well have a very low net realisable value. The benefit to the business of keeping such a machine can be said to be its 'value in use'. This value must be less than its replacement cost, as pointed out above, but more than its net realisable value, for otherwise the owner would sell it.

It is probably easier to summarise how to find deprival value by means of the diagram in Exhibit 29.2.

Exhibit 29.2 Deprival value

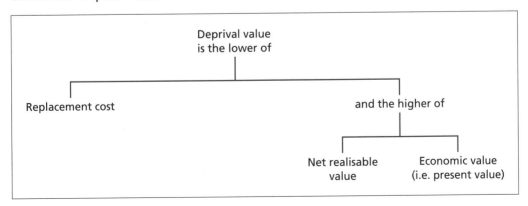

Deprival values can be illustrated by a few examples, using assets A, B and C.

	Asset A	Asset B	Asset C
	£	£	£
Replacement cost (RC)	1,000	800	600
Net realisable value (NRV)	900	500	400
Economic value (EV)	2,000	700	300

The deprival values can be explained as follows. Check them against Exhibit 29.2.

(a) *Asset A.* If the firm were deprived of asset A, what would it do? As economic value is greater than replacement cost it would buy another asset A. The deprival value to the business is therefore £1,000, i.e. replacement cost.

(b) *Asset B.* If deprived of asset B, what would the firm do? It would not replace it, as RC £800 is greater than its value to the business – its economic value £700. If deprived, the firm would therefore lose the present value of future cash flows, i.e. economic value £700. This then is the deprival value for asset B.

(c) *Asset C.* With this asset there would be no point in keeping it, as its economic value to the firm is less than the firm could sell it for. Selling it is the logical way, so the deprival value is net realisable value £400.

29.5 Capital maintenance

Let's go back to Sir John Hicks's definition of income (profit): 'A man's income is the maximum value which he can consume during a week, and still expect to be as well off at the end of the week as he was at the beginning.'

We've looked at the different ways assets may be valued so that they can be added together to find the wealth or 'well-offness' of a business at a particular date. Now, let's examine the problems of measuring the maintenance of wealth over a period. This is called *capital maintenance.*

Capital maintenance is the basic method of measuring maintenance of wealth used in accounting. If a business has a value (called its 'net worth') according to its financial statements of £100,000 on 1 January 20X1 it must also have a value in its financial statements of £100,000 at 31 December 20X1 to be as well off at the end of the period. Take the example of a company that has neither issued (sold) nor redeemed (bought back) any of its share capital (shares) and has paid no dividends. If it started with a value according to its financial statements of £100,000 on 1 January 20X2 and finished with a value in its financial statements of £170,000 on 31 December 20X2, it must have made a profit of £70,000.

This approach is known as 'money capital maintenance'. It would be acceptable to everyone in a period when there is no change in price levels. However, most people would agree that it is not satisfactory when either prices in general, or specific prices affecting the business, are changing. In these two cases, to state that £70,000 profit has been made in 20X2 completely ignores the fact that the £100,000 at 1 January 20X2 and the £100,000 at 31 December 20X2 do not have the same value. That is, the purchasing power of £100,000 has changed between the two dates.

From this we can see the possibilities of three different concepts.

1 **Money capital maintenance.** The traditional system of accounting as already described.
2 **Real capital maintenance.** This concept is concerned with maintaining the general purchasing power of the equity shareholders. This takes into account changes in the purchasing power of money (i.e. inflation) as measured by the retail price index.

3 **Maintenance of specific purchasing power of the capital of the equity.** This uses a price index which is related to the specific price changes of the goods in which the firm deals.

From these we can look at the following example, which illustrates three different figures of profit being thrown up for a firm.

29.6 A worked example

A company has only equity share capital. Its net assets on 1 January 20X5 are £1,000, and on 31 December 20X5 £1,400. There have been no issues or withdrawal of share capital during the year. The general rate of inflation, as measured by the retail price index, is 10 per cent, whereas the specific rate of price increase for the type of goods in which the company deals is 15 per cent. The profits for the three measures are as follows:

	(a) Money maintenance of capital	(b) Real capital maintenance	(c) Maintenance of specific purchasing power
	£	£	£
Net assets 31 Dec 20X5	1,400	1,400	1,400
Less What net assets would have to be at 31 Dec 20X5 to be as well off on 1 Jan 20X5			
(a) Money maintenance	(1,000)		
(b) Real capital £1,000 + 10%		(1,100)	
(c) Specific purchasing power maintenance £1,000 + 15%			(1,150)
Profit	400	300	250

Note that under the three methods:

(a) here the normal accounting method gives £400 profit;
(b) this case recognises that there has been a fall in the purchasing power of money;
(c) this takes into account that it would cost £1,150 for goods whose value at the start of the year was £1,000.

29.7 Combinations of different values and capital maintenance concepts

We have just looked at three ways of calculating profits based on historical cost allied with three capital maintenance concepts. This can be extended by using replacement cost or net realisable value instead. Each of these, when adjusted by each capital maintenance concept, will give three separate figures for profit. Together the three different means of valuation, multiplied by three different concepts of capital maintenance, will give us nine different profit figures.

At this stage in your studies it will be difficult to understand how such different profit measures could be useful for different purposes. We can leave this until your studies progress to more advanced examinations. However, we can use one simple example to illustrate how using only the traditional way of calculating profits can have dire consequences.

29.8 Another worked example

A company has net assets on 1 January 20X7 of £100,000 financed purely by equity share capital. During 20X7 there has been no injection or withdrawal of capital. At 31 December 20X7 net assets have risen to £115,000. Both the retail price index and the specific price index for the goods dealt in have risen by 25 per cent. Taxation, based on traditional historical cost calculations (maintenance of money capital), is at the rate of 40 per cent. The profit may be calculated as follows.

	Maintenance of money capital	Maintenance of real capital and of specific purchasing power
	£	£
Net assets on 31 Dec 20X7	115,000	115,000
Less Net assets needed to be as well off at 31 Dec 20X7 as with £100,000 on 1 Jan 20X7		
(a) Money capital	(100,000)	
(b) Both real capital and specific purchasing power £100,000 + 25%		(125,000)
Profit/loss	15,000	(10,000)

Tax payable is £15,000 × 40% = £6,000. Yet the real capital or that of specific purchasing power has fallen by £10,000. When tax is paid, that would leave us with net assets of £115,000 – £6,000 = £109,000. Because of price changes, £109,000 could not finance the amount of activity financed by £100,000 one year before. The operating capacity of the company would therefore be reduced.

Obviously it is not equitable for a company to have to pay tax on what is in fact a loss. It is only the traditional way of measuring profits that has thrown up a profit figure.

29.9 Operating capital maintenance concept

This approach looks at the output which could be generated by the initial holding of assets. A profit will only be made if the assets held at the end of the period are able to maintain the same level of output.

A simple example of this is that of a newspaper seller who sells newspapers on a street corner. The only costs the newspaper seller incurs are those of buying the newspapers. No other products are sold and the newspaper seller has no assets apart from the newspapers. In this case the operating capital consists solely of newspapers.

Under historical cost, a newspaper seller will recognise a profit if the revenue from the sale of newspapers is greater than the historical cost of the newspapers. Using the operating capital maintenance concept, the newspaper seller will recognise a profit only if the revenue from the sale is greater than the cost of buying the newspapers to replace the newspapers sold.

29.10 Summary

You should now be aware that there are a large number of alternative ways in which wealth can be measured. Accounting has tended always to use the simplest: historical cost. However, there have been occasions – during periods of high inflation, for example – when another method has been used. Another exception to historical cost is that net realisable value and replacement cost are both used when businesses need to value their unsold goods for resale at the end of periods.

PART II: ACCOUNTING FOR CHANGING PRICE LEVELS

29.11 Background

As you have seen already in this chapter, changes in price levels can lead to both profit and asset valuation figures being far from reality if simple historical cost figures are used. This is not a recently observed phenomenon. As far back as 1938, Sir Ronald Edwards wrote several classic articles which were published in *The Accountant*. You can find these in the book *Studies in Accounting Theory*, edited by W T Baxter and S Davidson and published by the Institute of Chartered Accountants (London, 1977).

The greater the rate of change in price levels, the greater the distortion. The clamour for changes to simple historical cost accounting is noticeably greater when the inflation rate is high – at such times the deficiencies of historical cost financial statements are most obvious. If there were a period of deflation, however, the historical cost financial statements would be still misleading.

In certain countries the annual rate of inflation in recent years has been several hundred per cent. Historical cost financial statements in those countries would certainly be at odds with financial statements adjusted for inflation. In the UK the highest rate in recent years, based on the RPI, was 17.8 per cent for 1979, falling to less than 5 per cent in some years.

We can now look, in outline only, at suggestions made in the UK since 1968 as to methods which could be used to adjust financial statements for changing price levels.

29.12 Current purchasing power (CPP)

This proposal is something you have already read about. It is the adjustment of historical cost accounting figures by a price index figure to give figures showing what we called real capital maintenance. It will convey more of the problems and uncertainties facing the accounting profession in this regard, if we look at the history of the various proposals.

First came *Accounting for Stewardship in a Period of Inflation*, published in 1968 by the Research Foundation of the Institute of Chartered Accountants in England and Wales (ICAEW). Stemming from this came Exposure Draft No 8 (ED 8), published in 1973. ED 8 contained the proposal that companies should be required to publish, in addition to their conventional financial statements, supplementary statements which would be, in effect, their final financial statements amended to conform to CPP principles. In May 1974 a Provisional Statement of Standard Accounting Practice No 7 ([P]SSAP 7) was published. Notice the sign of uncertainty; it was a *provisional* standard – the only one yet published. Compared with ED 8, which said that a company should be *required* to publish CPP financial statements, [P]SSAP 7 simply *requested* them to publish such financial statements. Many companies would not accede to such a request.

[P]SSAP 7 stipulated that the price index to be used in the conversion of financial statements from historical cost should be the retail price index (RPI). As the actual price index relating to the goods dealt in by the firm might be quite different from RPI, the CPP financial statements could well be distant from the current values of the firm itself.

The exact nature of the calculations needed for CPP financial statements is not part of your syllabus, and we will not repeat the calculations here.

Many people, including the government, were completely dissatisfied with the CPP approach. After ED 8 was issued the government set up its own committee of inquiry into inflation accounting. The chairman of the committee was Sir Francis Sandilands. The report, known as the Sandilands Report, was published in September 1975.

29.13 Current cost accounting (CCA)

The Sandilands Committee's approach was quite different from ED 8 and [P]SSAP 7. The committee recommended a system called **current cost accounting** (CCA). This basically approved the concept of capital maintenance as the maintenance of operating capacity.

After the Sandilands Report appeared, the accounting bodies, as represented by their own Accounting Standards Committee (ASC), abandoned their proposals in [P]SSAP 7. A working party, the Inflation Accounting Steering Group (IASG), was set up to prepare a Statement of Standard Accounting Practice based on the Sandilands Report.

This group published ED 18: *Current cost accounting* in November 1976. It was attacked by many members of the ICAEW, whose members passed, in July 1977, a resolution rejecting compulsory use of CCA. However, the government continued its support, and in November 1977 the accounting profession issued a set of interim recommendations called the Hyde Guidelines (named after the chairman of the committee). The second exposure draft, ED 24, was issued in April 1979, followed by SSAP 16 in March 1980. SSAP 16 was to last three years to permit the evaluation of the introduction of CCA. After this, ED 35 was published in July 1984.

In November 1986 the CCAB Accounting Standards Committee published its handbook, *Accounting for the Effects of Changing Prices*. At the same time presidents of five of the leading accountancy bodies issued the following statement:

> The presidents of five of the leading accountancy bodies welcome the publication by the CCAB Accounting Standards Committee of its Handbook on *Accounting for the effects of changing prices*.
>
> The presidents endorse the CCAB Accounting Standards Committee's view that, where a company's results and financial position are materially affected by changing prices, historical cost accounts alone are insufficient and that information on the effects of changing prices is important for an appreciation of the company's results and financial position. The presidents join the Accounting Standards Committee in encouraging companies to appraise and, where material, report the effects of changing prices.
>
> The five bodies have proposed that SSAP 16, 'Current cost accounting', which was made non-mandatory by all the CCAB bodies in June 1985, should now be formally withdrawn. They take the view, however, that the subject of accounting for the effects of changing prices is one of great importance. Accordingly, they support the Accounting Standards Committee in its continuing work on the subject and agree that an acceptable accounting standard should be developed.
>
> *The Institute of Chartered Accountants in England and Wales; The Institute of Chartered Accountants of Scotland; The Institute of Chartered Accountants in Ireland; The Chartered Institute of Management Accountants; The Chartered Institute of Public Finance and Accountancy*

So once again the idea of forcing companies to produce financial statements adjusted for changing prices was rejected. The emphasis is now on encouragement, rather than trying to force companies to do it.

The reason why, at this early stage in your studies, we have given you some of the history behind the efforts to compel companies to produce CCA financial statements is to illustrate the conflicts that have taken place inside and outside the accountancy profession. Opinions on the merits of CCA financial statements are widely divided. You will study this in greater detail in the later stages of more advanced examinations, but it should be made clear at the outset that it is a controversial topic.

29.14 Handbook on *Accounting for the Effects of Changing Prices*

We can now look at the main outline of this handbook. The ASC encouraged companies to co-operate in an attempt to produce financial statements suitable for the effects of changing price levels. In doing this it did not try to recommend any one method, or even recommend one way only of publishing the results. The handbook says that the information may be presented:

(a) as the main financial statements, or
(b) in the notes to the financial statements, or
(c) as information supplemental to the financial statements.

The handbook first examines the problems.

29.15 Problems during a period of changing price levels

Obviously, the greater the rate of change, the greater will be the problems. We can now list some of them.

1 **Fixing selling prices.** If you can change your prices very quickly, an extreme case being a market trader, this problem hardly exists. For a company setting prices which it is expected to maintain for a reasonably long period, the problems are severe. It dare not price too highly, as early demand may be reduced by an excessive price; on the other hand, the company has to guess how prices are going to change over a period so that sufficient profit is made.
2 **Financial planning.** As it is so difficult to guess how prices are going to change over a period, planning the firm's finances becomes particularly trying. Obviously, it would be better if the plans were revised frequently as conditions changed.
3 **Paying taxation and replacing assets.** We have seen earlier how, during a period of inflation, traditional historical accounting will tend to overstate profits. Such artificial profits are then taxed. Unless various supplementary tax allowances are given, the taxation paid is both excessive and more than true profits, adjusted for inflation, can bear easily. This tends to lead to companies being short of cash, too much having been taken in tax. Therefore, when assets which have risen in price have to be replaced, adequate finance may not be available.
4 **Monetary assets.** If stocks of goods are held, they will tend to rise in money terms during a period of inflation. On the other hand, holding monetary assets, e.g. cash, bank and debtors, will be counterproductive. A bank balance of £1,000 held for six months, during which the purchasing power of money has fallen 10 per cent, will in real terms be worth only 90 per cent of its value six months before. Similarly, in real terms, debt of £5,000 owed continually over that same period will have seen its real value fall by 10 per cent.
5 **Dividend distribution.** Just as it is difficult to calculate profits, so is it equally difficult to decide how much to pay as dividends without impairing the efficiency and operating capability of the company. At the same time the shareholders will be looking to payment of adequate dividends.

29.16 Solutions to the problems

The handbook recommends the use of one of two concepts. These will now be examined fairly briefly, in as much detail as is needed at this stage of your examinations.

1 Profit under the operating capital maintenance concept

This has been mentioned previously, with a simple example given of a trader buying and selling newspapers. Under this concept several adjustments are needed to the profit calculated on the historical cost basis. Each adjustment is now considered.

Adjustment 1: holding gains and operating gains

Nearly all companies hold fixed assets and stocks. For each of these assets the opportunity cost will bear little relationship to its historical cost. Instead it is the asset's value to the business at date of consumption, and this is usually the replacement cost of the asset.

Accordingly the historical cost profit, which was based on money capital maintenance, can be divided into two parts.

1 Current cost profit, or operating gains. This is the difference between sales revenue and the replacement cost of the assets.
2 Holding gains. This is the replacement cost of the assets less the historical cost of those assets.

For example, a company buys an asset for £1,000 on 1 January 20X4. It holds it for one year and sells it for £1,600 when the replacement cost is £1,200. There has been a historical cost profit of £600. This can be analysed as in Exhibit 29.3.

Exhibit 29.3

Profit for 20X4	
	£
Historical cost profit (£1,600 – £1,000)	600
Less Holding gain (£1,200 – £1,000)	(200)
Current cost profit (or operating gain)	400

To put it another way, the company makes £200 historical profit by simply holding the asset from when its replacement cost (i.e. original cost) was £1,000, until the date of sale when its replacement cost was £1,200. The actual current cost profit at point of sale must reflect conditions at the date of sale, i.e. the company has sold for £1,600 something which would currently cost £1,200 to replace. The current cost profit is therefore £400.

The holding gains are often described as a cost of sales adjustment (COSA).

Adjustment 2: depreciation

Depreciation is to be adjusted to current replacement cost values. Without going into complicated examples, this means that if the historical cost of depreciation is £4,000 and the current cost of depreciation, based on current replacement cost values, is £7,000, then the adjustment should be £3,000 as follows:

	£
Depreciation based on historical cost	4,000
Adjustment needed to bring depreciation charge to CCA basis	3,000
CCA depreciation	7,000

Adjustment 3: monetary working capital adjustment

The monetary working capital needed to support the operating capability of the business will be affected by inflation. An adjustment will be needed to the historical profits in respect of this.

Adjustment 4: gearing adjustment

If we borrow £1,000 now, and have to pay back exactly £1,000 in five years' time, we will gain during a period of inflation. We will be able to put the £1,000 to use at current purchasing power. In five years' time, if £1 now is worth only 60p then, we will have gained because we will only be giving up £600 of current purchasing power now. The gearing adjustment is an attempt to adjust current cost operating profits for this factor.

2 Profit and loss account based on the operating capital maintenance concept

A general idea of how such a profit and loss account could appear can now be given.

RST Ltd

*Profit and Loss Account incorporating Operating Capital
Maintenance Concept adjustments*

	£	£
Profit on the historical cost basis, before interest and taxation		100,000
Less Current cost operating adjustments:		
(1) Holding gains (COSA)	15,000	
(2) Depreciation	10,000	
(3) Monetary working capital	5,000	
		(30,000)
Current cost operating profit		70,000
(4) Gearing adjustment	(2,000)	
Interest payable less receivable	6,000	
		(4,000)
Current cost profit before taxation		66,000
Taxation		(25,000)
Current cost profit attributable to shareholders		41,000
Dividends		(30,000)
Retained current cost profit for the year		11,000

3 Profit under the financial capital maintenance concept

According to the handbook, this method is sometimes known as the 'real terms' system of accounting. The steps by which the profit is calculated can be summarised as:

(a) calculate shareholders' funds at the beginning of the period, based on current cost asset values; then
(b) restate that opening amount in terms of pounds at the end of the period, by adjusting (a) by the relevant change in a general price index (e.g. RPI); then
(c) calculate shareholders' funds at the end of the period, based on current cost values.

Assuming that there have been no introductions or withdrawals of capital, including dividends, if (c) is greater than (b) a 'real terms' profit will have been made. Otherwise a loss will have been incurred.

Allowance will have to be made in steps (a) to (c) above where there have been introductions or withdrawals of capital, or where there have been dividends.

The calculation of 'real terms' profit, as described, has been by way of comparing opening and closing balance sheets. Suppose that the 'real terms' profit figure had been £10,000, it could in fact have been calculated in the following manner:

	£	£
Historical cost profit		7,800
Add Holding gains: the amount by which the current costs of the assets have increased over the period	3,400	
Less Inflation adjustment: the amount by which general inflation has eroded shareholders' funds	(1,200)	
Real holding gains		2,200
Total real gains		10,000

The balance sheet approach was described first, as it is probably the easier to understand in the first instance. Obviously the link between opening and closing balance sheets can be traced to total real gains, which can also be explained using the profit and loss account concept.

4 Current cost balance sheet

The two main differences between a current cost balance sheet and a historical cost balance sheet are as follows:

1 Assets are shown at value to the business on the balance sheet date, rather than at any figure based on historical cost or at any previous revaluation.
2 Obviously the balance sheet would not balance if asset values were altered without an amendment somewhere else. A current cost reserve account is opened, additions to historical cost account values are debited to each asset account, while a credit will be made in the current cost reserve account. Entries are also made here to complete the double entry in respect of the four adjustments in the current cost profit and loss account. As a result, all double entry adjustments are made in this account and so the balance sheet will now balance.

29.17 More on current cost accounting

Chapter 30 further explores this topic.

PART III: OBJECTIVES OF FINANCIAL STATEMENTS

29.18 Background

In any consideration of asset valuation and wealth measurement, it is important to remember why the calculations are being made. At the end of the day, the reason is that the users of the accounting information wish them to be done.

29.19 Users of financial statements

The main users of published financial statements of large companies are now identified with the main reasons they require the financial statements.

1 **Shareholders of the company,** both existing and potential, will want to know how effectively the directors are performing their stewardship function. They will use the financial statements as a base for decisions to dispose of some or all of their shares, or to buy some.

2 **The loan-creditor group.** This consists of existing and potential debenture and loan stock holders, and providers of short-term secured funds. They will want to ensure that interest payments will be made promptly and capital repayments will be made as agreed. Debenture and loan stock holders, whether redeemable or irredeemable, will also want to be able to assess how easily they may dispose of their debentures or loan stocks, should they so wish.

3 **Employee groups**, including existing, potential and past employees. These can include trade unions whose members are employees. Past employees will be mainly concerned with ensuring that any pensions, etc., paid by the company are maintained. Present employees will be interested in ensuring that the company is able to keep on operating, so maintaining their jobs and paying them acceptable wages, and that any pension contributions are maintained. In addition, they may want to ensure that the company is being fair to them, so that they get a reasonable share of the profits accruing to the firm from their efforts. Trade unions will be upholding the interests of their members, and will possibly use the financial statements in wage and pension negotiations. Potential employees will be interested in assessing whether or not it would be worth seeking employment with the company.

4 **Bankers.** Where the bank has not given a loan or granted an overdraft, there will be no great need to see the financial statements. Where money is owed to the banks, they will want to ensure that payments of interest will be made when due, and that the firm will be able to repay the loan or overdraft at the correct time.

5 **The business contact group.** This includes trade creditors and suppliers, who will want to know whether or not they will continue to be paid, and the prospects for a profitable future association. Customers are included, since they will want to know whether or not the company is a secure source of supply. Business rivals in this group will be trying to assess their own position compared with the firm. Potential takeover bidders, or those interested in a merger will want to assess the desirability of any such move.

6 **The analyst/adviser group.** These will need information for their clients or their readers. Financial journalists need information for their readers. Stockbrokers need it to advise investors. Credit agencies want it to be able to advise present and possible suppliers of goods and services to the company as to its creditworthiness.

7 **The Inland Revenue** will need the financial statements to assess the tax payable by the company.

8 **Other official agencies.** Various organisations concerned with the supervision of industry and commerce may want the financial statements for their purposes.

9 **Management.** In addition to the internally produced management accounts the management is also vitally concerned with any published financial statements. It has to consider the effect of such published financial statements on the world at large.

10 **The public.** This consists of groups such as ratepayers, taxpayers, political parties, pressure groups and consumers. The needs of these parties will vary accordingly.

29.20 Characteristics of useful information

From the various reports which have appeared since 1975 the following characteristics have been noted.

1 **Relevance.** This is regarded as one of the two main qualities. The information supplied should be that which will satisfy the needs of its users.

2 **Reliability.** This is regarded as the other main quality. Obviously, if such information is also subject to an independent check, such as that of the auditor, this will considerably enhance the reliance people can place on the information.

3 **Objectivity.** Information which is free from bias will increase the reliance people place on it. It is, therefore, essential that the information is prepared as objectively as possible. Management may often tend to give a better picture of its own performance than is warranted, and is therefore subjective. It is the auditor's task to counter this view, and to ensure objectivity in the financial statements.

4 **Ability to be understood.** Information is not much use to a recipient if it is presented in such a manner that no one can understand it. This is not necessarily the same as simplicity.

5 **Comparability.** Recipients of financial statements will want to compare them both with previous financial statements of that company and with the results of other companies. Without comparability the financial statements would be of little use.

6 **Realism.** This can be largely covered by the fact that financial statements should show a 'true and fair' view. It has also been contended that financial statements should not give a sense of absolute precision when such precision cannot exist.

7 **Consistency.** This is one of the basic concepts, but it is not to be followed slavishly if new and improved accounting techniques indicate a change in methods.

8 **Timeliness.** Up-to-date information is of more use to recipients than outdated news.

9 **Economy of presentation.** Too much detail can obscure the important factors in financial statements and cause difficulties in understanding them.

10 **Completeness.** A rounded picture of the company's activities is needed.

29.21 Problems of information production in accounting

You have seen that a company's profit and loss account and balance sheet produced for general publication is a multi-purpose document. The present state of the art of accounting is such that we have not yet arrived at producing specific financial reports for each group of users, tailored to their special needs.

At times, companies do produce special reports for certain groups of users. A bank, for instance, will almost certainly want to see a forecast of future cash flows before granting a loan or overdraft. The Inland Revenue will often require various analyses in order to agree the tax position. Some companies produce special reports for the use of their employees. In total, such extra reports are a very small part of the reports which could be issued.

Of course, producing reports is not costless. To produce special reports, tailored to every possible group of users, would be extremely costly and time-consuming. It is hardly likely that any company would wish to do so. There is, however, no doubt that this is the way things are moving and will continue to move.

For the present, however, most companies produce one set of financial statements for all the possible users, with the exception that management will have produced its own management accounts for its own internal purposes. Obviously such a multi-purpose document cannot satisfy all the users. In fact, it will almost certainly not fully satisfy the needs of any one user group – save that it must satisfy the legal requirements of the Companies Act.

Published financial statements are, therefore, a compromise between the requirements of users and the maintenance of accounting concepts, subject to the overriding scrutiny of the auditor. Judgement has a major impact on the information presented. It can be said that if two large companies operating in the same industry and in the same location had identical share capitals, liabilities, numbers of employees, assets, turnover, costs, transactions, and so on, the published financial statements of the two companies would not be identical. Differences would arise for a number of reasons. For example, depreciation methods and policies may vary, as may stock valuation assessments, bad debt provisions, figures for revaluation of properties, etc. There will also probably be rather more subtle distinctions, many of which you will come across in the later stages of your studies.

You should now have learnt:

1 That there is no one overall accepted general theory of accounting.

2 Changing price levels distort historical cost values and that various approaches have been suggested to deal with this issue.

3 Some of the possible valuation alternatives to historical cost.

4 The difference between current purchasing power and current cost accounting.

5 The characteristics of useful information.

6 About problems relating to the production of accounting information.

7 A wide range of user groups require accounting information for a variety of reasons, resulting in its being impossible to satisfy all user groups with one set of financial statements.

Answers to activities

29.1 This isn't a problem for management accounting (which is concerned with providing information for internal use) – management and the management accountants agree on what should be produced and the management accountants do what they can to provide it. With financial accounting information, there is no such close relationship between the accountant and the user groups. There are also the legal and other regulations governing financial reports that the accountant must observe. It would not be appropriate to give all users what they want – some user groups, such as competitors, would prefer information that is sensitive to the business. At the same time, no one can foretell what information a particular user should be asking for at a given time.

29.2 This may appear to be an easy question. If you said it was £1,000 because that is what it cost, you would be correct so far as its *cost* to you was concerned, but no accountant would say that that was its *value*. It may have cost you that amount but do you really believe you could get someone else to pay you £1,000 for it? And how much would it cost to replace it? More, or less than £1,000?

29.3 CPP does not remove the problem of the 'true' cost. All it does is to assume the original historical cost was accurate and then adjust the value of the business to allow for the different timings. Also, any inaccuracies, inconsistencies, inappropriateness or other drawbacks inherent in the price index used to adjust the historical cost figures will result in a distortion of the adjusted historical cost figures.

29.4 Replacement cost rarely arrives at asset values that everyone would agree upon. It can be very subjective and can often be easy to dispute.

CHAPTER 30

Current cost accounting

Learning objectives

After you have studied this chapter, you should be able to:

- explain why historical cost financial statements are deficient in times of rising prices
- describe different valuation methods
- describe the purposes of specific price indices for assets and liabilities
- explain the adjustments necessary in order to convert historical costs to current costs
- prepare a current cost balance sheet and current cost profit and loss account

Introduction

In this chapter you'll learn about the issues behind the development of current cost accounting and how to prepare current cost financial statements according to the procedures laid down in SSAP 16.

30.1 Background

Accounts have traditionally been prepared for two main purposes, stewardship and decision making. The Accounting Standards Board's Exposure Draft: Statement of Principles, published in 1991, outlined several user groups with varying needs, all of whom are interested in financial information. Shareholders are interested in different information than trade creditors. This information has traditionally been provided by financial statements prepared under the historical cost convention. However, there are circumstances when financial statements prepared under this traditional approach can present financial information in a misleading way.

Consider the following example. On 1 January 20X4, a company invests in 500 widgets for £1,000 i.e. £2 per unit. Shortly before the year end, when the replacement cost of a widget is £2.20 per unit, the stock is sold for £1,200. On a historical cost basis, the profit is recorded as follows:

	£
Sales	1,200
Cost of Sales	(1,000)
Profit	200

However, in order to maintain the same operating capacity, the company will need to invest in more widgets at a cost of £1,100 (500 × £2.20). If the company distributes the £200 as a dividend, it will only be left with £1,000 and cannot make this investment.

Activity 30.1

If you replaced the £1,000 cost of the stock in the above calculation of profit with the £1,100 it will cost to replace it, does it remind you of any of the alternatives to historical cost accounting you learnt about in Chapter 29?

From this simple example, one of the major criticisms of historical cost accounting is evident – its inability to reflect the effects of changing prices. Obviously, this criticism is dependent upon the level of inflation at the time.

An acceptable alternative to historical cost accounting has been sought by the accountancy profession in the UK for several years. The attempts of the Accounting Standards Committee (ASC) to introduce a system of inflation accounting, which are outlined in Chapter 29, failed.

The culmination of great effort and numerous exposure drafts and standards was the ASC handbook, *Accounting for the Effects of Changing Prices*, published in 1986. In Chapter 29, you started looking at some of the aspects covered in the handbook. In this chapter, we'll consider several of the issues dealt with in the handbook in the context of the preparation of a set of current cost accounts.

It is worth noting that the ASB recognises that the present system of historical cost accounting, modified by voluntary revaluations of certain assets, is unsatisfactory. The ASB aims to tackle the issue, and current values are once again on the agenda. It is unlikely, however, that a system of current cost accounting will be introduced without difficulty, particularly when inflation is at and has been at a low level in the UK for quite some time.

30.2 Valuation

Under historical cost accounting, assets and liabilities are recorded at their actual cost at the date of transaction. For example, when a new machine is purchased, the price per the invoice can be recorded in the books of the business. While this is a familiar and reasonably cheap method of recording the assets and liabilities of an entity, its main advantage is its objectivity. The historical cost of an item is an objective, verifiable fact that can easily be ascertained from the records of the business.

It is worth remembering that there is some degree of subjectivity in the preparation of historical cost financial statements. Consider, for example, the choice of suitable depreciation method for a fixed asset which is left to the discretion of the directors of the company. The size of the bad debts provision is also dependent upon the exercise of judgement. Notwithstanding this, it is fair to say that historical values have a high degree of reliability.

Activity 30.2

Apart from the subjectivity in some of the adjustments made to the original figures, such as for depreciation, if you were asked for the main disadvantage of historical cost accounting, especially in times of rising prices, what would you say it was?

Current value accounting considers the following valuation methods which were covered in Chapter 29: economic value, value to the business (i.e. deprival value), replacement cost, net realisable value and recoverable amount.

To recap what you learnt in Chapter 29, the **economic value** of an asset is the sum of the future expected net cash flows associated with the asset, discounted to its present value.

Value to the business, or **deprival value**, can be considered an appropriate valuation basis for accounting purposes. If a business were deprived of an asset, it could either replace it, or choose not to. If the asset were replaced, then its current value to the business is its net current **replacement cost**. This is normally the current cost of a fixed asset, except where it has suffered a permanent diminution in value, in which case it will be written down to its **recoverable amount**. This may happen, for example, because there is no longer a market for the product. Alternatively, if the business chooses not to replace the asset, then it would sell it and its current cost is its **net realisable value**, i.e. the price at which it can be sold in the market.

How are these values determined by a business? The replacement cost of an asset can be approximated using a relevant index. Indices, published for example by the UK Government Statistical Service, are usually specific to a class of asset. A company may prepare its own index based on experience or, where it is not appropriate to use an index, a valuer may be relied upon. This is usual in the case of revaluing property. The index will indicate the change in value of the asset or class of asset.

Consider the following example. A machine was purchased on 1 January 20X2 for £75,000 when the relevant specific price index was 90. Its current value at 31 December 20X4, when the relevant specific price index is 120, is:

$$\frac{\text{Index at accounting date}}{\text{Index at date of purchase}} \times £75,000 = \frac{120}{90} \times £75,000 = £100,000$$

Replacement does not necessarily mean replacement of the asset with a similar asset. Rather, it focuses on replacement of the service potential of the asset and its contribution to the business.

Net realisable value is the price at which the asset could be sold in an arm's length transaction. A problem may arise where no market exists for the asset. The main problem with current values is the level of subjectivity involved in ascertaining valuations. A business may need to spend considerable time and effort ascertaining current values for its assets and liabilities.

Let's now look in detail at current cost accounting.

30.3 Current cost financial statements

In order to prepare current cost financial statements, a number of adjustments to the historical cost figures must be made. Specifically, **adjustments are needed relating to**:

- fixed assets
- depreciation
- stock
- cost of sales
- monetary working capital
- gearing.

Other than the gearing adjustment, no adjustment is made to monetary assets, such as debtors, bank and cash, or to monetary liabilities such as creditors or long-term loans.

We shall use Hillcrest Ltd to show how these adjustments are made.

The directors of Hillcrest Ltd are interested in preparing current cost accounts to reflect changing prices. They have prepared a historical cost balance sheet and profit and loss account (Exhibit 30.1). The relevant price indices for plant and machinery, stock, debtors and creditors, are given in Exhibit 30.2.

Exhibit 30.1

Hillcrest Ltd
Balance Sheet as at 30 June (£000)

	20X5		20X4	
Fixed assets				
Plant and machinery				
Cost		800		800
Depreciation		(320)		(240)
Net book value		480		560
Current assets				
Stock	250		200	
Trade debtors	180		110	
Cash	105		75	
	535		385	
Current liabilities				
Trade creditors	(90)		(100)	
Net current assets		445		285
		925		845
10% loan stock		(310)		(310)
		615		535
Financed by:				
Ordinary shares		200		200
Reserves		415		335
		615		535

Hillcrest Ltd
Profit and Loss Account for year ending 30 June 20X5 (£000)

Sales		1,700
Cost of sales		
Opening stock	200	
Purchases	1,375	
	1,575	
Less Closing stock	(250)	
		(1,325)
Gross profit		375
Interest	31	
Depreciation	80	
Other expenses	184	
		(295)
Net profit		80

Exhibit 30.2

Price index for stock at the end of each month:					
March	20X4	109			
April	20X4	112			
June	20X4	114			
December	20X4	116			
March	20X5	122			
April	20X5	126			
June	20X5	130			
Average for the year ending 30 June 20X5		126			
Plant and machinery index			*Debtors and creditors index*		
June	20X1	80	June	20X4	110
June	20X2	90	June	20X5	200
June	20X3	100			
June	20X4	105			
June	20X5	110	Average for	20X5	155

In order to prepare current cost accounts, the first step is to calculate current values for the assets. Hillcrest Ltd's plant and machinery was purchased for £800,000 on 1 July 20X1. The current value of the plant and machinery at 30 June 20X5 is:

$$\text{Plant and machinery at cost} \times \frac{\text{Index at balance sheet date}}{\text{Index at date of purchase}}$$

$$= £800,000 \times \frac{110}{80}$$

$$= £1,100,000$$

The accumulated depreciation of £320,000 charged in the historical cost financial statements, representing 40 per cent of the asset which has been consumed, is also restated. The current value of the depreciation is:

$$£320,000 \times \frac{110}{80} = £440,000$$

On average, Hillcrest Ltd's stock was acquired three months before the year end. Hence, its current value, rounded to the nearest £000, at 30 June 20X5 is:

$$£250,000 \times \frac{130}{122} = £266,393$$

Monetary assets, for example trade debtors and cash, and monetary liabilities, including trade creditors, are not restated. These items have a fixed monetary value which does not change. For example, if you borrow £1,000 today under an agreement to repay in 12 months' time, the monetary value of the amount borrowed will not change, that is you will repay £1,000. However, in times of rising prices, the market value of the amount will decrease. This gain will be dealt with later in this chapter.

30.4 Current cost reserve

Having revalued both plant and machinery and stock to their current values, the following revaluation gains are recorded:

	Plant & machinery (£)	Stock (£)	Total (£)
Current book value	660,000[Note]	266,393	
Historical book value	(480,000)	(250,000)	
Surplus on revaluation	180,000	16,393	196,393

Note: Plant at current cost less accumulated depreciation, i.e. £1,100,000 – £440,000

The total gain of £196,393 is not a gain which has been realised through a transaction, for example, sale of goods at a profit. In addition, Hillcrest Ltd cannot distribute this revaluation gain as a dividend if it wishes to maintain its operating capacity. In this example the gain of £196,393 will be credited to a non-distributable reserve called the current cost reserve. The balance sheet incorporating these revaluations is shown in Exhibit 30.3.

Exhibit 30.3

Hillcrest Ltd
Balance Sheet as at 30 June 20X5 (£000)

Plant and machinery		
Current value		1,100
Depreciation		(440)
Net book value		660
Current assets		
Stock	266	
Debtors	180	
Cash	105	
	551	
Current liabilities		
Trade creditors	(90)	
Net current assets		461
		1,121
10% loan stock		(310)
		811
Financed by:		
Ordinary shares		200
Reserves		415
Current cost reserve		196
		811

Exhibit 30.3, however, does not incorporate the effect of changing prices on the profit for the year. The reserves figure of £415,000 includes historical cost profit of £80,000 for the year ended 30 June 20X5. We will now consider adjustments necessary in order to calculate the current cost profit for Hillcrest Ltd for the year.

30.5 Cost of sales adjustment

In calculating the profit for an accounting period, the cost of the goods sold (or cost of sales) is charged against sales. In Exhibit 30.1, sales of £1,700,000 are recorded at their invoiced prices during the year to 30 June 20X5. Likewise, purchases of £1,375,000 are recorded at their actual cost prices during the year. If we assume that activity occurs evenly throughout the year, a reasonable assumption unless trade is seasonal, then these figures will reflect the average prices for the period. The opening and closing stock valuations, in times of rising prices, will not reflect average prices under the historical cost convention. It is therefore necessary to adjust these figures in order to calculate the current cost of sales. This is carried out using an averaging method.

Using the price index for stock, the current cost of sales for Hillcrest Ltd is:

$$£$$

Opening stock at average prices: $£200,000 \times \dfrac{130}{109}$ =		238,532
Purchases (assume occur evenly through year) =		1,375,000
		1,613,532
Closing stock at average prices: $£250,000 \times \dfrac{130}{122}$ =		(266,393)
Current cost of sales =		1,347,139

The cost of sales adjustment is the difference between the current cost of sales of £1,347,139 and the historical cost of sales of £1,325,000, i.e. £22,139. This is charged to the historical

cost profit and loss account as an adjustment in order to arrive at the current cost profit. A corresponding amount will be credited to the current cost reserve.

30.6 Depreciation adjustment

Depreciation charged in the profit and loss account should be based on the value of the asset as stated in the balance sheet. Hence, an adjustment is necessary where depreciation has been based on the historical cost of a fixed asset.

Consider the following example in which the depreciation charge is based on the value of the asset at the year end. A fixed asset is purchased on 1 January 20X3 for £10,000 when the relevant price index is 100. It is planned to depreciate this asset on a straight line basis at 20 per cent per annum. At the end of 20X3, when the index has moved to 110, the current value of the asset is:

$$£10,000 \times \frac{110}{100} = £11,000$$

and depreciation based on current cost of the asset is:

$$£10,000 \times \frac{110}{100} \times 20\% = £2,200$$

The net book value of the asset as stated in the current cost balance sheet is:

	£
Asset at current value	11,000
Accumulated depreciation	(2,200)
	8,800

At the end of 20X4 the relevant index is 120, and the current value of the asset is:

$$£10,000 \times \frac{120}{100} = £12,000$$

and the depreciation charge based on current cost is:

$$£10,000 \times \frac{120}{100} \times 20\% = £2,400$$

Hence, at the end of 20X4, the net book value of the asset in the current cost balance sheet is:

	£
Asset at current value	12,000
Accumulated depreciation	(4,600)
	7,400

While 40 per cent of the value of the asset has been consumed at 31 December 20X4, it is noted that £4,600 is not 40 per cent of £12,000. This is due to an undercharge of £200 depreciation in 20X3 in current value terms. Hence, as the original cost of the asset is altered to reflect current values, so too must the aggregate depreciation.

The term given to depreciation relating to earlier years is **backlog depreciation**. Backlog depreciation is not charged against this period's profit. As we saw in the Hillcrest example, only an adjustment for this year's depreciation is charged against profit. Backlog depreciation is charged to the current cost reserve.

For Hillcrest Ltd, depreciation charged at 10 per cent on the current value of the plant and machinery of £1,100,000 is £110,000. Comparing this with the historical cost depreciation charge in the historical cost profit and loss account of £80,000 gives an additional, i.e. backlog depreciation adjustment of £30,000. This is a charge in arriving at current cost profit for the year, the corresponding credit going to the current cost reserve.

30.7 Monetary working capital adjustment

The effect of changing prices on stock values has already been considered. In addition, during inflationary periods, the market value of monetary assets, e.g. trade debtors, trade creditors and cash, will change. In order for a business to maintain its operating capacity, this change needs to be reflected in the accounts. The monetary working capital adjustment represents the increase (or decrease) in finance necessary to provide an appropriate level of monetary working capital due to price changes, rather than a change in the volume of working capital.

Cash is usually excluded from the calculation as the amount of cash held by a business may not relate to its operating activities. For example, cash may be held in order to make a capital investment. However, in the case of a bank, cash balances which are required to support daily operations are included in the **monetary working capital adjustment**.

Calculation of the monetary working capital adjustment is similar to the calculation of the cost of sales adjustment.

The index for debtors should reflect changes in the cost of goods or services sold which are included in debtors. Likewise, the index for creditors should reflect changes in the cost of goods or services purchased which are included in creditors. A single index may be appropriate, and in some businesses, a fair approximation may be the index used for stock. Consider the following example:

	31 December 20X4 £	31 December 20X5 £
Trade debtors	9,000	12,000
Trade creditors	(7,500)	(11,000)
Monetary working capital	1,500	1,000

Relevant indices applicable to the business are:

31 December 20X4	100
31 December 20X5	200
Average for the year	150

The monetary working capital at 31 December 20X4 in the historical cost financial statements is £1,500 (£9,000 – £7,500). Stating this at average values for the year gives:

$$£1,500 \times \frac{150}{100} = £2,250$$

The monetary working capital at 31 December 20X5 in the historical cost financial statements is £1,000 (£12,000 – £11,000). Stating this at average values for the year gives:

$$£1,000 \times \frac{150}{200} = £750$$

The historical cost financial statements show a decrease in monetary working capital over the year of £500. However, at average values for the year, the monetary working capital is reduced by £1,500 (£2,250 – £750).

> ### Activity 30.3
> What does the difference between the change under the historical cost convention and under the current cost convention of £1,000 (£1,500 – £500) – the monetary working capital adjustment – represent?

Now, let's do the same thing for Hillcrest Ltd. The monetary working capital adjustment is calculated as follows:

	20X5	20X4
	£	£
Trade debtors	180,000	110,000
Trade creditors	(90,000)	(100,000)
Net monetary working capital	90,000	10,000

Hence, the increase in monetary working capital in historical cost terms is £80,000 (£90,000 – £10,000).

Restating opening monetary working capital at average prices gives (to the nearest £000):

$$£10,000 \times \frac{155}{110} = £14,000$$

The value of closing monetary working capital at average prices is (to the nearest £000):

$$£90,000 \times \frac{155}{200} = £70,000$$

The increase in monetary working capital which is due to change in volume is £56,000 (£70,000 – £14,000). The increase due to price changes – the monetary working capital adjustment – is £24,000 (£80,000 – £56,000).

30.8 Current cost operating profit

Hillcrest Ltd's current cost operating profit, having applied the above adjustments, is given in Exhibit 30.4.

Exhibit 30.4

Hillcrest Ltd
Current Cost Operating Profit for year ending 30 June 20X5 (£000)

Sales		1,700
Net profit		80
Add Interest		31
		111
Adjustments		
Cost of sales adjustment	22	
Monetary working capital adjustment	24	
Additional depreciation adjustment	30	
		(76)
Current cost operating profit		35

From the point of view of a business and maintenance of its operating capacity, the current cost operating profit is relevant. However, maintenance of financial capital is also relevant where a business is not financed solely by equity. In this case, account should be taken of the capital structure of the business.

30.9 Gearing adjustment

If a company is financed by debt, and prices increase, whilst the monetary value of the loan has not changed, the market value has reduced. This gain for shareholders is recorded by making a gearing adjustment. The gearing adjustment is calculated in the following way.

Firstly, a gearing proportion is calculated. This is:

Average net borrowings for the year (L) : Shareholders' interest (S) + L

For Hillcrest Ltd, its net borrowings for the two years to 30 June 20X5 are:

	20X5	20X4
	£	£
Loan stock	310,000	310,000
Cash	(105,000)	(75,000)
Net borrowing	205,000	235,000

Hence, average net borrowings for the year to 30 June 20X5 are:

$$\frac{£205,000 + £235,000}{2} = £220,000$$

Shareholders' interest for both years are:

	20X5	20X4
	£	£
Ordinary shares	200,000	200,000
Reserves	415,000	335,000
	615,000	535,000

Average shareholders' interest (S) for the year to 30 June 20X5 is:

$$\frac{£615,000 + £535,000}{2} = £575,000$$

The gearing proportion is:

$$\frac{L}{L + S} = \frac{£220,000}{£220,000 + £575,000} = 27.67\%$$

To calculate the gearing adjustment, this proportion is applied to the sum of the current cost adjustments for the year, that is:

	£
Cost of sales adjustment	23,000
Depreciation adjustment	30,000
Monetary working capital adjustment	24,000
	77,000

The gearing adjustment for Hillcrest Ltd (to the nearest £000) is:

$$27.67\% \times £77,000 = £21,000$$

Exhibit 30.5 shows the current cost reserve having made the above adjustments.

Exhibit 30.5

	£000
Current cost reserve	
Surplus on revaluation of plant and machinery	180
Additional depreciation adjustment	30
Surplus on revaluation of stock	16
Cost of sales adjustment	22
Monetary working capital adjustment	24
Gearing adjustment	(21)
Balance at 30 June 20X5	251

The current cost profit for the year to 30 June 20X5 is given in Exhibit 30.6.

Exhibit 30.6

Hillcrest Ltd
Current Cost Profit and Loss Account for year ending 30 June 20X5

		£000
Sales		1,700
Trading profit (after adding back interest)		111
Adjustments		
Cost of sales adjustment	22	
Monetary working capital adjustment	24	
Additional depreciation adjustment	30	
		(76)
Current cost operating profit		35
Gearing adjustment	21	
Less Interest payable	(31)	
		(10)
Current cost profit		25

The balance sheet for Hillcrest Ltd for 30 June 20X5, based on current costs, is given in Exhibit 30.7.

Exhibit 30.7

Hillcrest Ltd
Current Cost Balance Sheet as at 30 June 20X5

		£000
Plant and machinery		
Cost		1,100
Depreciation		(440)
Net book value		660
Current assets		
Stock	266	
Debtors	180	
Cash	105	
	551	
Current liabilities		
Trade creditors	(90)	
Net current assets		461
		1,121
10% loan stock		(310)
		811
Financed by:		
Ordinary shares		200
Reserves (335 + 25)		360
Current cost reserve		251
		811

You should now have learnt:

1 During inflationary periods, one of the main criticisms of historical cost accounting is its inability to reflect changing prices.

2 Deprival value is a suitable valuation basis for accounting purposes.

3 One of the major difficulties with current cost accounting is the level of subjectivity which can be involved in converting historical costs to current costs.

4 Relevant price indices, specific to an asset or class of assets, can approximate replacement cost.

5 The purpose of the cost of sales adjustment is to restate historical cost of sales in current cost terms by including opening and closing stock at average prices.

6 The depreciation adjustment ensures that the depreciation charge in the current cost profit and loss account is based on the current value of the asset as stated in the current cost balance sheet.

7 The monetary working capital adjustment reflects the change in the market value of monetary assets and liabilities, usually trade debtors and trade creditors, in the current cost accounts.

8 Gains or losses for shareholders, which arise due to debt financing in times of changing prices, are accounted for in the gearing adjustment.

9 Surpluses and deficits on revaluations are credited or charged to the current cost reserve, which is a non-distributable reserve.

Answers to activities

30.1 Substituting the £1,100 it would cost to replace the stock in place of the £1,000 the stock cost would produce a profit of £100. This is an example of the concept of 'maintenance of specific purchasing power' you learnt about in Section 29.5.

30.2 The main disadvantage of historical cost accounting, particularly in times of changing prices, is its relevance to decision-making. This was demonstrated in the widget example in the previous section, when any business that relied purely on the historical cost-based profit calculation to determine how much profit was available for distribution could find it impossible to replace all the stock it had sold.

30.3 The change in working capital due to price changes during the year.

REVIEW QUESTIONS

30.1 State whether you consider the following statements to be true or false:

(a) During inflationary periods, historical cost financial statements do not reflect a true and fair view.

(b) The preparation of historical cost financial statements does not involve subjectivity.

(c) Current cost accounting involves estimating future events.

(d) An index number must relate to a specific asset in order to be useful in converting historical cost accounts to current cost accounts.

(e) Where no market exists for an asset, conversion from historical cost to current cost can be difficult.

30.2A State whether you consider the following statements to be true or false:

(a) The current cost of plant and machinery is likely to be its net realisable value.
(b) A company should distribute dividends from the current cost reserve.
(c) The market value of a monetary asset, for example trade debtors, will decrease during inflationary periods.
(d) A gearing adjustment is necessary where a company is financed solely by equity capital.
(e) Backlog depreciation is charged to the current cost reserve.

30.3A What are the practical difficulties a company may encounter in ascertaining the current values of its assets?

30.4 Plant and machinery was purchased on 1 January 20X3 for £30,000, when the relevant specific price index was 90. What is the current cost value of the asset at 31 December 20X4 if the index at that date is 120?

30.5A The plant and machinery, details of which are given in question 30.4, is depreciated on a straight line basis at 10 per cent per annum. The depreciation charge is based on year end values. What is the current cost depreciation charge for the year ended 31 December 20X5, if the index at that date is 160?

30.6 Calculate backlog depreciation at 31 December 20X5 for the plant and machinery whose details are given in question 30.5A.

30.7A A firm purchased machinery on 1 January 20X4 for £40,000, at which date the relevant price index for machinery was 100. Depreciation is charged on a straight line basis at 25 per cent per annum. The index at 31 December 20X4 had moved to 150, and at 31 December 20X5 it was 200. Show the current cost balance sheet entries for machinery at 31 December 20X4 and 31 December 20X5. Calculate the adjustments to the current cost reserve in respect of machinery.

30.8 The historical cost of sales figure for Apple Ltd for the year ended 31 December 20X3 is calculated as follows:

	£
Opening stock	50,000
Purchases	450,000
	500,000
Closing stock	(70,000)
Cost of sales	430,000

Price indices for stock are as follows:

Index at date of purchase of opening stock	80
Index at date of purchase of closing stock	120
Average index for 20X3	100
Index at 31 December 20X3	130

Required:
Assuming that purchases occur evenly throughout the year, calculate the cost of sales adjustment for Apple Ltd for 20X3.

30.9A The balance sheet of Seafield Ltd at 31 December 20X4 shows the following balances:

	31 December 20X4	31 December 20X3
	£	£
Trade debtors	35,000	30,000
Trade creditors	25,000	23,000

The relevant price indices for trade debtors and trade creditors are:

31 December 20X3	120
31 December 20X4	180
Average for the year ending 31 December 20X4	150

Required:
Using the above information, calculate the monetary working capital adjustment at 31 December 20X4 for Seafield Ltd.

30.10 If the relevant price indices for trade debtors and trade creditors are as follows, calculate the monetary working capital adjustment for Seafield Ltd, using the details given in question 30.9A.

31 December 20X3	200
31 December 20X4	280
Average for the year ending 31 December 20X4	240

30.11A The information given below has been extracted from the accounting records of Cedarwood Ltd for the year ended 30 June 20X4. Prepare a statement showing the current cost operating profit to 30 June 20X4.

	£
Sales	2,500,000
Historical cost operating profit	1,400,000
Current cost adjustments	
Additional depreciation adjustment	500,000
Cost of sales adjustment	750,000
Monetary working capital adjustment	25,000

30.12 The balance sheet for Cremore Ltd at 31 December 20X3 is given below (£000):

	20X3		*20X2*	
Plant and machinery				
Cost		800		800
Depreciation		(320)		(160)
		480		640
Current assets				
Stock	210		130	
Debtors	100		60	
Cash	145		50	
	455		240	
Current liabilities				
Trade creditors	(80)		(60)	
Net current assets		375		180
10% loan stock		(200)		(200)
		655		620
Financed by:				
Ordinary shares		250		250
Reserves		370		340
Current cost reserve		35		30
		655		620

Required:
Using the above information, calculate the gearing adjustment percentage:

$$\frac{L}{L+S}$$

30.13A The following information has been extracted from the accounting records of Sycamore Ltd for the year ended 30 June 20X3.

	£
Sales	9,000,000
Historical cost trading profit	4,000,000
Interest payable	500,000
Corporation tax charge for the year	1,500,000
Ordinary dividend	600,000
Additional depreciation adjustment	200,000
Cost of sales adjustment	800,000
Monetary working capital adjustment	370,000
Gearing adjustment: $\dfrac{L}{L+S}$	20%

Required:

Prepare a current cost profit and loss account for Sycamore Ltd for the year ended 30 June 20X3.

30.14 During a period of inflation, many accountants believe that financial reports prepared under the historical cost convention are subject to the following major limitations:

1 stocks are undervalued;
2 depreciation is understated;
3 gains and losses on net monetary assets are undisclosed;
4 balance sheet values are unrealistic; and
5 meaningful periodic comparisons are difficult to make.

Required:

Explain briefly the limitations of historical cost accounting in periods of inflation with reference to each of the items listed above.

(*Association of Accounting Technicians*)

30.15A You are presented with the following information relating to Messiter plc:

Year to 31 December	20X4	20X5
	£m	£m
Profit and loss accounts:		
Turnover, all on credit terms	1,300	1,400
Cost of sales	650	770
Gross profit	650	630
Profit before taxation	115	130
Balance sheets at 31 December:		
Fixed assets at cost	850	850
Less Accumulated depreciation	510	595
Net book value	340	255
Stock at cost	105	135
Trade debtors	142	190

Required:

(a) Using the historical cost financial statements and stating the formulae you use, calculate the following accounting ratios for both 20X4 and 20X5:
  (*i*)   Gross profit percentage;
  (*ii*) Net profit percentage;
  (*iii*) Stock turnover, stated in days;
  (*iv*) Trade debtor collection period, stated in days; and
  (*v*)   Fixed asset turnover.

(b) Using the following additional information:

  (i) Restate the turnover for 20X4 and 20X5 incorporating the following average retail price indices:

Year to 31.12.20X4	85
Year to 31.12.20X5	111

  (ii) Calculate the additional depreciation charge required to finance the replacement of fixed assets at their replacement cost. The company's depreciation policy is to provide 10 per cent per annum on original cost, assuming no residual value.

  The replacement cost of fixed assets at 31 December was as follows:

	£ millions
20X4	1,140
20X5	1,200

  (iii) Based upon these two inflation adjustments, why may it be misleading to compare a company's results for one year with that of another without adjusting for changes in general (RPI) or specific inflation?

(Association of Accounting Technicians)

Social accounting

After you have studied this chapter, you should be able to:
- explain the term social 'accounting'
- describe the implications of social accounting for the accounting function
- describe some of the difficulties in the measurement of qualitative factors
- describe the conflict between shareholders' interests and social considerations

Introduction

In this chapter you'll learn about some of the issues underlying the development of social accounting, of five general areas to which social accounting has been applied, and of the extent to which social accounting is becoming part of company reporting.

31.1 Background

Over time, the objective of financial statements has changed. In addition to reporting to shareholders of the company, directors are aware of a wide range of other user groups who are interested in accounting information. These user groups include employees of the company and, more controversially, the public at large. The controversy arises when considering whether or not organisations are responsible for 'social actions', that is actions which do not have purely financial implications.

31.2 Costs and measurement

One of the problems associated with actions of this type is the difficulty of identifying costs and measuring the effects of (often intangible) factors that contribute to the 'value' of an organisation. It is obvious that employee loyalty and commitment to quality performance increase this value, but how are such intangibles to be measured using objective and verifiable techniques?

Activity 31.1
How would you value employee loyalty?

Some of the input costs of 'social' activities can be evaluated reasonably accurately. Providing 'social' information required under the Companies Act 1985 is not particularly

difficult – it requires information regarding employees to be presented in the financial statements, including numbers of employees, wages and salaries data, and details regarding the company's policy on disabled persons. Also, even where 'social' actions are required by legislation, they can often be costed reasonably accurately. For example, there are a large number of European Union directives which have been implemented in the UK relating to social and environmental policies, including the monitoring and control of air and water pollution.

The costs of complying with these disclosure requirements and operational control measures can be high and, as the number of regulations increase, these costs will become a basic and essential part of financial statements. It will become increasingly important that not only the costs are reported, but also the benefits, and this is where the difficulties arise – how can the benefits of controlling pollution from a factory be evaluated? Indeed, should an attempt be made to evaluate them at all? Would they be better reported in qualitative or non-financial quantitative terms?

As soon as a company seeks to incorporate social criteria alongside other, more traditional performance measures, problems of objectivity, comparability and usefulness arise. For example, social criteria for a paper manufacturer may include environmental issues concerning reforestation; and an oil extraction company would include the environmentally safe disposal of oil rigs at the end of their useful economic lives among its social criteria.

However, issues of this type become problematical when viewed using conventional capital appraisal techniques. Not only may the measurable financial payback be so long as to be immaterial – as in the case of an environmental project such as reforestation – it may be virtually non-existent, as in the case of the disposal of obsolete oil rigs. Assessment of issues of this type require different techniques from those traditionally used, and organisations' accounting information systems will need to take this into account, not just in terms of using more qualitative value criteria, but also in selecting the information which is sought in order to assist in the decision-making process.

31.3 The pressure for social actions and social accounting

Despite the existence of many environmental laws, much of the pressure for social actions comes from pressure groups like Greenpeace. These groups can have an enormous impact upon an organisation's profitability, in ways that governments have singularly failed to do. For example, an air pollution law may concentrate on monitoring the quality of air around a factory, rather than on measuring emissions from the factory, making it far more difficult to enforce action against the factory, as it can always argue that another factory is the cause of any pollution found. Also, powerful cartels can influence legislation to create enormous delays in introducing socially responsible legislative controls. On the other hand, a pressure group can stop demand for a company's products, make it difficult for it to send its products to its customers, and may give it so much negative publicity that it can find its public image materially and irreversibly altered in a very short time.

While pressure groups are not a new phenomenon, their power is now far greater than it has ever been. Organisations need to be aware of the social, particularly the environmental, issues inherent in and/or related to their activities, and must be in a position to assess how best to approach these issues. They can only do so if they identify all the variables, both quantitative and qualitative, and both the inputs (costs) and the outputs (effects) of these variables, and determine methods with which to determine what actions to take.

Social accounting is concerned with how to report upon the application of the social policies adopted by an organisation, and upon how they have impacted upon the organisation and its environment. An organisation that does so effectively will not only be providing user groups with rich information from which to form a view concerning its social ethos, it will

also be enhancing its ability to take decisions appropriate for its own longer-term survival and prosperity.

31.4 Corporate social reporting

The reporting of the social effects of a company's activities became an issue in the UK in the 1970s. The reporting of non-financial information usually takes the form of narrative disclosure, sometimes supported by a statistical summary. As much social reporting is non-mandatory, comparison with other companies is difficult, if not pointless and misleading. This is partially due to a positive bias in what is reported – most companies tend to report only 'good news' in their social reports. It is also due to the lack of standards governing what to include and how to present social reports.

Environmental issues have been firmly on the political agenda since the early 1980s and large corporations have responded to public demands for more information about 'green issues'. Oil companies, in particular, produce a notable amount of additional information in their annual reports. This environmental information usually includes details about the company's waste disposal practices, attitudes towards pollution and natural resource depletion, as well as the overall corporate environmental policy. However, many continue to avoid any non-mandatory social reporting, and many instances have been reported of organisations claiming to be socially responsible, when they were, in fact, anything but.

31.5 Types of social accounting

Social accounting can be divided into five general areas:

(a) national social income accounting
(b) social auditing
(c) financial social accounting in profit-oriented organisations
(d) managerial social accounting in profit-oriented organisations
(e) financial and/or managerial social accounting for non-profit organisations.

31.6 National social income accounting

National social income accounts have now been in existence for many years. The measure of the nation's productivity recorded in the accounts – basically in sales terms – gives an income called the gross national product, usually referred to as GNP.

To an outsider, an increase in GNP would seem to indicate a betterment or progress in the state of affairs existing in the country. This is not necessarily so. The following example illustrates this point.

A new chemical factory is built in a town. Fumes are emitted during production which cause houses in the surrounding areas to suffer destruction of paintwork and rotting woodwork, and it also causes extensive corrosion of bodywork on motor vehicles in the neighbourhood. In addition it also affects the health of the people living nearby. An increase in GNP results because the profit elements in the above add to GNP. These profit elements include:

- to construction companies and suppliers of building materials: profit made on construction of plant
- to house paint dealers and paint manufacturers, painters and decorators, joiners and carpenters: profit made on all work effected in extra painting, woodwork, etc.

- to garages and car paint manufacturers: profit made on all extra work needed on motor vehicles
- to chemists and medical requirement manufacturers: profit made on dealing with effects on residents' health, because of extra medical purchases, etc.

However, in real terms one can hardly say that there has been progress. Obviously the quality of life has been seriously undermined for many people.

As national income accounts do not record the 'social' well-being of a country, other national measures have been proposed. The one most often mentioned is a system of 'social indicators'. These measure social progress in such ways as:

- national life expectancies
- living conditions
- levels of disease
- nutritional levels
- amount of crime
- road deaths.

Thus if national life expectancies rose, or road deaths per 100,000 people decreased, etc. there could be said to be social progress, while the converse would apply were the opposite signals found to be occurring.

The main difficulty with this approach is that (given present knowledge and techniques) it cannot be measured in monetary terms. Because of this, the national social income accounts cannot be adjusted to take account of social indicators. On the level of an individual organisation, however, social indicators similar to the above are used in planning, programming, budgeting systems (PPBS). This will be discussed later.

31.7 Social auditing

While national social accounting would measure national social progress, many individuals and organisations are interested in their own social progress. This form of social progress is usually called 'social responsibility'.

To identify activities to be measured, a 'social audit' is required, investigating:

(a) which of their activities contribute to, or detract from, being socially responsible;
(b) measurement of those activities;
(c) a report on the results disclosed by the investigation.

An example of this might be to discover how the organisation had performed in respect of such matters as:

- employment of women
- employment of disabled people
- occupational safety
- occupational health
- benefits at pensionable age
- air pollution
- water pollution
- charitable activities
- help to developing countries.

Social audits may be carried out by an organisation's own staff or by external auditors. The reports may be for internal use only or for general publication.

31.8 Financial social accounting in profit-oriented organisations

Financial social accounting is an extension to normal financial accounting. The objective may either be to show how the social actions have affected financial performance, or otherwise to put a social value on the financial statements of the organisations. The two main types of financial social accounting envisaged to date are those of human resource accounting and how the organisation has responded to governmental or professional bodies' regulations concerning environmental matters.

Human resource accounting

One of the main limitations of 'normal' financial accounting is the lack of any inclusion of the 'value' of the workforce to an organisation. The value may be determined by:

(a) capitalising recruitment and training costs of employees and apportioning value over employees' period of employment; or

(b) calculating the 'replacement cost' of the workforce and taking this as the value of human resources; or

(c) extending either of the above to include the organisation's suppliers and customers.

It is contended that such measurements have the benefits that (1) financial statements are more complete, and (2) managerial decisions can be made with a fuller understanding of their implications.

For instance, suppose that a short-term drop in demand for a firm's goods led to a manufacturer laying off part of the workforce. This might mean higher profits in the short term, because of wages and salaries saved. In the long term, it could do irreparable damage, as recruitment could then be made difficult, or because of the effect on the morale of the rest of the workforce, or changes in attitudes of suppliers and customers.

Compliance costs of statutory/professional requirements

As the effects of organisations upon societies are more widely recognised there will be more and more regulations with which to comply. The costs of compliance will obviously then become a basic and essential part of financial statements.

31.9 Managerial social accounting in profit-oriented organisations

All that has been described has an effect upon the information systems of an organisation. They will have to be established on an ongoing basis, rather than be based purely on adjustments such as those made to the financial accounts at the year end.

The information will be used to affect the day-to-day decisions needed to run the organisation.

Activity 31.2
Why is an ongoing information system required in order to do this?

31.10 Financial and/or managerial social accounting for non-profit organisations

As profit is not a measure in these organisations it can be difficult to measure how well they are performing. Two approaches to measurement have been used, **planning, programming, budgeting systems (PPBS)** and **social programme measurement**.

Both of these approaches can be said to be part of what politicians in recent years have called 'value for money'. The general attitude is that while there may be a need for all sorts of social programmes, including health, there is a great need for ensuring that money is not wasted in doing this. The demand is that we should ensure that we get 'value for money' in that the outputs from such schemes should be worth the amount of money expended in carrying them out.

Planning, programming, budgeting systems (PPBS)

It has been said that in the past there was a great deal of confusion between planning and budgeting. Annual budgeting takes a short-term financial view. Planning, on the other hand, should be long term and also be concerned with strategic thinking.

PPBS enables management of non-profit organisations to make decisions on a better informed basis about the allocation of resources to achieve their overall objectives. PPBS works in four stages:

1 Review organisational objectives.
2 Identify programmes to achieve objectives.
3 Identify and evaluate alternative ways of achieving each specific programme.
4 On the basis of cost/benefit principles, select appropriate programme.

PPBS necessitates the drawing up of a long-term corporate plan. This shows the objectives which the organisation is aiming to achieve. Such objectives may not be in accord with the existing organisational structure.

For instance, suppose that the objective of a local government authority, such as a city, is the care of the elderly. This could include providing:

● services to help them keep fit
● medical services when they are ill
● old people's housing
● sheltered accommodation
● recreational facilities
● educational facilities.

These services will usually be provided by separate departments, e.g. housing, welfare, education. PPBS relates the total costs to the care of the elderly, rather than to individual departmental budgets.

Management is therefore forced by PPBS to identify exactly which services or activities should be provided, otherwise the worthiness of the programme could not be evaluated. PPBS also provides information which enables management to assess the effectiveness of their plans, such as giving them a base to decide whether, for every thousand pounds, they are giving as good a service as possible.

As the structure of the programme will not match up with the structure of the organisation, e.g. the services provided will cut across departmental borders, a specific individual must be made responsible for controlling and supervising the programme.

Social programme measurement

The idea that governmental social programmes should be measured effectively is, as yet, in its infancy.

A government auditor would determine whether the agency had complied with the relevant laws, and had exercised adequate cost controls. The auditor would determine whether or not the results expected were being achieved and whether there were alternatives to the programmes at a lower cost.

There should be cost/benefit analyses to show that the benefits are worth the costs they incur. However, the benefit side of the analysis is often very difficult to measure. How, for instance, do you measure the benefits of not dumping a particular substance or an obsolete oil rig into the sea?

As a consequence, most social programmes do not measure results (benefits). Instead they measure 'outputs', e.g. how many prosecutions for dumping waste: a high number of prosecutions is 'good', a low number 'bad'. This is hardly a rational way of assessing results, and quite a lot of research is going into better methods of audit.

31.11 Conflict between shareholders' interests and social considerations

Obviously, an organisation has to come to a compromise about how far it should look after the interests of its shareholders and how far it should bother about social considerations. For instance, a company could treat its employees so well in terms of pay, pensions and welfare that the extra costs would mean very low profits or even losses.

On the other hand there must be instances that, no matter what the effects on profits, the expenses just have to be incurred. If the company has a chemical plant which could easily explode, causing widespread destruction and danger to people, then there cannot be any justification for not spending the money either to keep the plant safe or to demolish it. The full severity of the law must bear down on transgressors of the law in such cases of wilful neglect.

All the facts of the particular case must be brought into account. Let us look at a typical case where the answer may seem obvious, but perhaps there may be other factors which may make the answer not so obvious. Workers in underdeveloped countries are usually paid far lower wages than those in the developed countries. What happens if a large multinational company pays its workers in a given country three or four times as much as home-based companies? Immediately everyone wants to work for the multinational company, which can afford high wages, and leave the home-based companies which cannot. Is that sensible? What chance is there for the development of the country's own home-based industries if the outside companies constantly take all the best brains and most able people?

In such a case it would probably make more sense for the multinational company to pay wages more in keeping with the particular economy, and to help that country in other ways such as by improving the health care generally for all, better education for all, and so on. Obviously a topic such as this will engender discussions and arguments for some considerable time.

31.12 Reports from companies

Companies, mainly those based in the USA, have begun to declare their philosophy towards such matters as the environment. This is usually included in the annual reports which accompany their financial statements.

For example, a company may have decided to have the following ten principles of environmental policy:

1 To comply with both governmental and community standards of environmental excellence.
2 To use only materials and packaging selected to be good for the health of consumers, and for the safety and quality of the environment.
3 To keep energy use per unit of output down to a low level.
4 To minimise waste.
5 To get to as low a level as possible the discharge of pollutants.
6 To use other firms which have shown commitment to environmental excellence.
7 To research fully the ecological effect of the company's products and packaging.
8 To carry on business operations in an open, honest and co-operative manner.
9 To make certain that on the board of directors there would be scientifically knowledgeable directors, and ensure that they were regularly provided with environmental reports.
10 To ensure that all the above principles are fully observed and that challenges posed by the environment are vigorously and effectively pursued.

Learning outcomes

You should now have learnt:

1 To whom organisations are responsible is a controversial area, and there is no exact definition of 'social accounting'.
2 That social indicators measure social progress, but as yet, given their inability to measure progress in monetary terms, they cannot be incorporated into social income accounts.
3 That a social audit will test the social responsibility of an organisation, including compliance with regulations, for example legislation relating to employees.
4 If an organisation wishes to take account of social and environmental factors, these items need to be incorporated into its accounting information system.
5 That there is a conflict between shareholders' interests, for example profit maximisation, and social considerations.
6 That corporate social reporting is the reporting of a company's activities and how they are related to social, including environmental, issues.
7 That there are five areas into which social accounting can be divided:
   (a) national social income accounting;
   (b) social auditing;
   (c) financial social accounting in profit-oriented organisations;
   (d) managerial social accounting in profit-oriented organisations;
   (e) financial and/or managerial social accounting for non-profit organisations.
8 That social accounting is as yet in its infancy. There is obviously a great difficulty in trying to put money values on the various aspects of being better off or worse off. There are also problems connected with exactly what 'better off' and 'worse off' mean. One person's worsening in some way may be someone else's betterment.

Answers to activities

31.1 There isn't a correct answer to this question but there are examples of values being placed on employee loyalty, for example, clocks for 25 years' service, gold watches for 50 years' service, etc.

But, do acts like this actually place a value on employee loyalty? Hardly – what is the cost per year of a clock costing £25 that is presented to an employee for 25 years' loyal service to the organisation: £1 per year. Professional footballers who stay longer than the norm with one club are entitled to a testimonial match where all the proceeds are given to the loyal player. Similar schemes also exist in cricket though, in cricket, it is usually a 'benefit year' where lots of events are held for the benefit of an individual player. Yet, there have been cases where footballers have ended up out-of-pocket because the gifts they gave all the players who took part in the testimonial match (they don't get paid) and other expenses were greater than the income from the game – hardly a case of loyalty being rewarded.

Clearly, organisations don't tend to put a value on loyalty in such a way as to directly reward the loyal individual. They also cannot include a figure for employee loyalty in the balance sheet as an asset. However, when a business is sold, employee loyalty is one of the factors that will be taken into account when deciding what the business is worth.

Just about the only way a business can recognise loyalty and endeavour to give it a value is to publicise it. This can be done through the media (tv, radio, newspapers, internet, etc). It can also be done in the annual report, the document containing all the financial statements and accompanying reports that is sent to shareholders each year. The share price may rise slightly as a result but, even if it does, it is hardly the same as the company placing a value of the loyalty of its employees.

31.2 Being socially aware means that you monitor constantly the extent to which you are achieving your social-related goals. You can't simply check once a year whether you are putting too much pollution in the local river or whether your employees are being loyal and are happy, or whether your supplies are coming from companies that do not employ child labour. If an organisation becomes socially aware and adopts social accounting, its information system needs to be amended to reflect the change. It is not necessarily the case that its accounting information system will be affected – that depends upon whether the company's social policies are to be reported by the company along with its financial information.

REVIEW QUESTIONS

31.1 Describe how an increase in gross national product may not have a positive effect on the well-being of the country.

31.2 What types of measure could be used to measure social well-being? What difficulties would be discovered in trying to use accounting in measuring these?

31.3 What aspects of an organisation's activities could be measured in a social audit?

31.4 Describe how there could be conflicts between short-term and long-term benefits.

31.5 Describe how PPBS may conflict with departmental budgets.

31.6A Review a set of company financial statements for social disclosures. Consider the usefulness of such disclosures to different user groups.

31.7 Why has the traditional model of income measurement failed to account for the impact of business activities on the environment?

(*Association of Chartered Certified Accountants*)

CHAPTER 32

Accounting for management control

Learning objectives

After you have studied this chapter, you should be able to:

- describe some of the deficiencies of financial accounting if it were used for management control purposes
- describe the need to avoid potential conflicts between alternative or competing objectives that may be adopted within an organisation
- explain that decision making should involve more than just the financial figures involved
- explain that the information needs of organisations are, in part at least, a function of their size
- describe the difference between the three areas in which management operates, and their different information needs
- explain that accounting information is only one part of the overall system in which organisations operate
- describe how the accounting system is affected by the surrounding environment both inside and outside the organisation in which it operates

Introduction

In this chapter you'll learn about the deficiencies of financial accounting information for decision-making. You'll also learn about the impact of organisational objectives, people and organisation size upon decision-making and about the three-part role of management. Finally, you will learn about the manner in which the accounting system interacts with its environment and of the relationship between quantitative and qualitative data and formal and informal information systems.

32.1 The part played by financial accounting

So far your studies have been concerned primarily with the recording function of accounting, often called bookkeeping, and the drafting of the final accounts of different types of organisations, such as partnerships or limited companies. The term generally used for your studies up to this point is that of **financial accounting**. Much of it is concerned with legal requirements, such as complying with the provisions of the Companies Acts when drafting final accounts, or keeping an accounting record of a customer's legal indebtedness, i.e. a debtor's account.

With companies the final accounts represent the account given to the shareholders by the directors of their running of the company during a particular year, in other words it is a statement of the directors' 'stewardship'. These accounts are also given to other interested parties such as the bankers to the firm, creditors, inspectors of taxes, etc.

While financial accounting is necessary from a legal point of view, it cannot be said to be ideal from the point of view of controlling the activities of a firm. Your studies would therefore be incomplete if you had seen only the 'stewardship' function of accounting. The use of accounting for controlling the activities of a firm is probably more important. In this chapter, we shall briefly consider accounting for 'management control' purposes.

The word 'management' does not necessarily mean that the firm is a limited company, although most of the large organisations in the private sector of industry would in fact be limited companies. It means instead the people who are managing the affairs of the firm, whether they are directors, partners, sole traders or 'managers' classified as those employees who are in charge of other employees.

32.2 Deficiencies of financial accounting

Before starting to examine accounting for management control let us look first at the deficiencies of financial accounting when we want to control the activities of an organisation.

The first deficiency of financial accounting is that it deals with operations that have already occurred. It deals with the past, not the future. It is possible to control something while it is happening, and control can be arranged for something that is going to happen but, when it has already happened without being controlled, the activity has ended and we are too late to do anything about control. For example, if a company incurs a loss and we do not realise it until long after the event, the loss obviously cannot be prevented.

What we really want to do is to control affairs so that a loss is not incurred if at all possible, and we should be able to call on accounting techniques to help in the control of activities. However, it certainly does not mean that we are not interested in the past. We can learn lessons from the past which can be very useful in understanding what is going on now, and what is likely to be happening in the future.

The second deficiency of financial accounting is that it is concerned with the whole of the firm. Thus the trading account of a firm may show a gross profit of £60,000, and while it is better to know that than to have no idea at all of what the gross profit is, it does not tell management much about past transactions. Suppose that the firm manufactures three products – watches, pens and cigarette lighters. Some possibilities of how much profit (or loss) was attributable to each of the products might be as in Exhibit 32.1.

Exhibit 32.1

	Various possibilities of profits and loss for each product (£s)			
	1	2	3	4
Watches	20,000	5,000	30,000	(30,000)[Note]
Pens	20,000	70,000	28,000	65,000
Lighters	20,000	(15,000)[Note]	2,000	25,000
Total gross profit	60,000	60,000	60,000	60,000

Note: Losses are shown in brackets

These are only some of the possible figures of profit and loss for each product which could result in an overall gross profit of £60,000. Just the figure of total gross profit would give you very few clues as to what lessons can be learnt from studying the past to help you control the firm in the future. If possibility number 2 was in fact the correct solution then it would stimulate further discussion and investigation as to why these results had occurred. It

could result in the closing down of the section of the firm which makes cigarette lighters if, after investigation, it was found to be in the interests of the firm to cease manufacturing them. Many more lessons can therefore be learnt from events if the firm's activities can be examined for each part of its activities instead of just the whole of its activities.

This means that financial accounting is of little use by itself for management control purposes. It does not mean that it is of no use at all for control purposes – the financial accounting system may reveal that the debtors at a point in time are £50,000, something that management need to know if they are to control their finances properly – but much financial accounting information is of little use in controlling the business.

Activity 32.1

Imagine we bought a building in 1980 for £40,000 that is now worth £120,000. If we rented a similar building now it might cost us £30,000 a year. What use would you make of the knowledge that the building originally cost £40,000 when deciding whether or not to rent a similar building now, or buy another one for £120,000?

32.3 Objectives of the firm

If we want to discuss management control we must first of all ask ourselves what is its purpose. We can only have control if it is for a particular purpose, otherwise how can we possibly draw up any plans?

It might seem obvious to you that the objectives of an organisation should be spelled out clearly and unambiguously. In fact the writing down of objectives is not done by quite a few organisations. This means that all the employees of the firm could well be pulling in different directions, as they all have different ideas of the firm's objectives.

Let us look at some of the possible objectives an organisation may have:

- To ensure that the maximum profit is made. This still is not clear; do we mean profits in the long term or the short term?
- To obtain a given share of the market for our sort of goods or services.
- To be the largest organisation of its type in terms of sales revenue.
- To achieve a high quality in the goods being manufactured or services offered.
- To ensure that our customers are fully satisfied with our goods and services.
- To ensure full employment for our employees.
- To ensure that our employees' welfare is maintained at a high level, in terms of such things as back-up facilities and adequate pension schemes.
- To ensure that our employees receive the best training and are kept fully up to date with the latest technology for our sort of business.
- To cause as little damage as possible ecologically.

Activity 32.2

What other objectives can you think of? Try to think of another two.

32.4 Conflicts between objectives

Each objective of the firm is not mutually exclusive. By that we mean that one objective may affect another objective, and that no objective cannot be considered completely on its own.

Let us take the case of the objective of maximum profit with that of causing as little damage as possible ecologically. We could have to spend a lot of money ensuring that dangerous chemical substances are not released into the atmosphere. This could mean lower profits. There would be a conflict here if the improvements were being made voluntarily by the firm instead of being forced on it by the authorities. Even where it was being forced on the firm, it would raise a conflict as the firm would want to do so in the cheapest possible way so as to maintain its objective of profit maximisation. Cheapness may be achieved by relaxing controls so that a small but noticeable level of emission still occurred which just happened to be within the limit set by the government.

Activity 32.3
Both these examples have something in common relating to the timeframe in which the actions taken can be justified. What is it?

Similarly, to maintain a very high quality of goods could mean lower profits if a large number of items manufactured are scrapped because they are not up to this standard. Lowering the quality could possibly increase profits.

It is thus essential to ensure that the objectives are very clearly spelled out *and prioritised.* Otherwise people will easily misunderstand them and because of this the firm may not proceed in the direction that is desired. **It is also essential that an appropriate timeframe is considered when resolving conflicting objectives.**

32.5 People and management control

It is important to note that the most important resource of any firm is the people who work in it. A danger exists that a great deal of care and attention may be given to designing a management control system and operating it, but this is of absolutely no use to management if it does not result in action by the human beings in the firm. Systems and figures do not themselves do anything; instead it is the people in the firm who take (or do not take) the necessary action.

You must bear in mind that figures thrown up by systems are only part of the evidence available when a decision has to be made as to the necessary action. A particular department may be incurring losses now, but the sales manager may give as his considered opinion that sales will increase soon and that the department will become profitable. **If people accepted accounting figures as the only criteria on which action should be based then there would be some very poor decisions taken by management.** Many very successful products have started off by incurring losses in the early stages, but have eventually proved successful because the firm has had faith in the product and persevered with it.

If it was possible to have exactly the same system of management control in three different firms, it might be found in firm A that the control system was useless because no one acted on the data produced. In firm B the control system might result in damage being done to the firm because management used the data as though it were the only criterion in gauging the actions it should take. In firm C it might be an extremely good system because the management saw the data as a useful guide in the planning and control of the firm, and had also made certain that the rest of the organisation took the same view.

How human beings use and react to a management control system is therefore at the heart of the problem of ensuring that an effective management control system is in use.

32.6 Different sizes of organisations and the decision-making process

Part of this book is about information which is intended to be used by the management of an organisation. For a small and simple organisation the information needs of management may be limited and can be obtained by direct observation – using eyes to look and the voice to ask questions.

For example, a person managing a greengrocery stall on a market can often operate effectively without formal records to help him. What he buys is determined by the goods available in the local wholesale market and his personal knowledge of what his customers are prepared to buy at a given price. His records will probably centre around the recording of cash – the details of his sales and expenditures in order to prepare financial accounts. However, apart from the essential requirement of maintaining proper cash levels, these records do not help him in the day-to-day management of his business operations.

In contrast, if we look at the manager responsible for buying fresh fruit and vegetables for a large supermarket chain, certain differences emerge. The basic decision about what to buy at a given price remains the same. However, a large organisation has a much wider choice of where and how to buy than a small one. The buyer from the large organisation may, for example, be able to enter into contracts directly with growers and to enter forward contracts for the supply of produce (for example, a farmer agrees to sell all his potatoes at the end of the summer to the firm at a fixed price).

In the large organisation the buyer will not be in direct contact with the many different sales outlets and therefore needs written information to keep him in touch with demand. He does not have to listen to complaining customers! Similarly because the sources of supply are likely to be much wider for the big firm, he needs more formal information to keep him in touch with market prices.

One of the other features about the large organisation which distinguishes it from the small is that responsibility for running the business is shared between many different people. In order to ensure that the operations of the firm are carried out efficiently and effectively there needs to be some criterion to measure the performance of the managers. In a small firm the inadequate proprietor will either make a very poor living or become a bankrupt. Thus his success or failure is clearly his own responsibility. In a large firm the same things can happen overall, but the situation may be obscured by a swings and roundabouts effect of some good sections making up for some bad. A management information system should help identify these problems in an organisation.

32.7 The management process

The way that management operates in an organisation may be conveniently described by a division into three areas:

(a) forecasting and planning
(b) controlling operations
(c) evaluating performance.

Forecasting and planning

Forecasting and planning is the process by which senior management decide on major overall issues concerning what the business is going to do, and how it is going to do it. It involves an assessment of information about the future which is called forecasting. When the forecast has been prepared, the company can plan how to achieve the objectives set by management. Planning is the process of co-ordinating the resources available to attain an objective.

Controlling operations

Controlling operations involves management in a number of processes and requires several different kinds of information. It involves converting top management plans into an operating pattern which matches the parts into which a company is divided. This changes the overall plan into detailed operating plans which relate to the management structure of the company. This process is called budgeting.

When actual events occur, then the information recording the events needs to be measured in such a way that it can be compared with the plan. This important process of management gives a feedback on the success of the plan to those who set it up in the first instance.

Controlling operations effectively also requires information designed to help managers take the decisions which their jobs require. For example, information about the profit produced by one product as compared to another will enable a decision about how many of each product to make.

Evaluating performance

Evaluating performance involves the analysis and assessment of actual results. This is partly a process of comparison with plans but not exclusively. The information on which plans were based may have been wrong. Thus the analysis of performance, while involving comparison of actual with planned results, needs considerable judgement as to what the plans should have been had all the facts been known in advance.

The three elements we have described are by no means completely independent. One way of looking at them is as a cycle in which information is circulating continually from one area to another as in Exhibit 32.2.

Exhibit 32.2

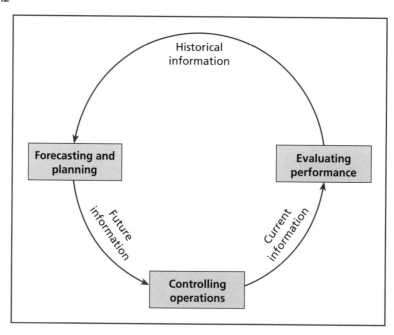

In this diagram information is shown to flow around from one part into the other. Thus, for example, forecasts in one period may be improved by taking account of the analysis of what happened last period.

It is also useful, as in Exhibit 32.2, to include a time dimension in the diagram. Forecasting and planning must relate to the future. Controlling operations relates to concurrent events – the here and now. Evaluating performance can only be concerned with the past.

The diagram we have just considered only looks at internal information. Exhibit 32.3 takes into account that information is being fed into the process from outside, both from the general environment in which the organisation operates and as a result of interactions between the organisation and its operating environment. Top management will have to take into account all the information it can about the outside environment such as competition, economic cutbacks, etc. Controlling operations also receives information about actual business events, e.g. sales activity, purchasing activity, etc.

Exhibit 32.3

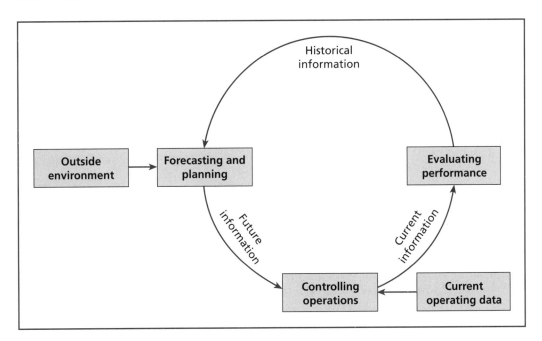

32.8 Types of management information

So far in this chapter no attempt has been made to describe the nature of the information which management requires. Information may come in many shapes and forms. In this book we are concerned with information which is capable of being expressed in numerical terms. That is, with information that can be quantified. Information of a more general nature about people's feelings or views may be very useful to management but cannot be quantified. It is, therefore, usually part of the informal rather than the formal information system of an organisation.

Activity 32.4
Apart from what is said above, what do you think is the difference between formal and informal information systems?

Within the body of quantified information it is normal to identify that part which can be measured in money terms. This is the part of the information system which is called accounting information. Accounting information is a very important element in the whole system since the organisation is basically an economic unit which must survive in conditions of economic scarcity and competition. In other words, an organisation which does not meet its economic objectives will eventually fail or be taken over, hence the central importance of accounting information.

However, other quantified information may be very important for management. For example, if you are a farmer you will measure the yield of milk from your cows in the first instance as litres. A production manager will be very concerned to monitor the tonnages produced on his machines. A supermarket will want to know how long customers have to queue at the checkout (and whether customers are being lost because it takes too long).

32.9 Quantitative methods in the information system

A modern management information system collects all the data together (into what is called a database) and, after appropriate processing, issues that information which is important to each manager. Thus the distinction between accounting and other types of management information has tended to become less meaningful in modern data processing systems. The techniques of quantitative analysis (or statistics) apply to all the data in this system whether it be accounting data or not.

Learning outcomes

You should now have learnt:

1 Financial accounting fulfils a stewardship function by reporting past performance and financial position.

2 Financial accounting information is of only limited use for management control purposes, for which other forms of data and information are required.

3 It is important that organisational objectives are clearly defined and that the financial accounting information system is designed to meet and support those objectives in the most efficient and effective way.

4 Management is concerned with three areas of activity:
   (a) forecasting and planning;
   (b) control;
   (c) evaluating performance.

5 The financial accounting information system does not exist in a vacuum, it interacts with and is affected by the environment in which it is operating and must be designed accordingly.

Answers to activities

32.1 The original cost is now completely irrelevant for decision-making purposes, whether at this time or at some point in the future. Yet, in many cases, it is the £40,000 that will appear in the current year's balance sheet and, in that case, the £40,000 is included in the amounts used to calculated ROCE and other key profitability and efficiency ratios. This is one of the reasons why FRS 15 allows fixed assets such as buildings to be revalued on a regular basis.

32.2 (i) To be identified as the most innovative company in the field and (ii) to have the lowest rate of staff turnover in the industry are two, neither of which can be demonstrated through the financial accounting information.

32.3 Lowering the standard of pollution control or the quality of product could possibly increase the profits in the short term, but it could mean lower profits in the long term if our customers deserted us because we had a reputation for causing pollution or our goods were considered to be second-rate. Short-termism can be very counterproductive and lead to the wrong decisions being taken. In the pollution example, by eliminating pollution the firm may be able to enhance its reputation sufficiently to recoup the additional cost through increased revenues and, thus, profits.

32.4 At its simplest, an informal information system is one that operates without rules and procedures. Information gets passed through it virtually accidentally, in the same way as you may learn what someone did last weekend during a casual conversation. An informal information system has no firm structure. It does not have a hierarchy and information does not undergo any uniform or routine transformation as it passes around the information system. Information is not constrained by the nature of the information system and can be both qualitative and quantitative.

A formal information system is everything an informal information system is not. It has rules, procedures, a hierarchy, a routing system for data and information flow, and set procedures for data and information processing. The data and information within it tends to be quantitative, though this is changing as computer systems become capable of greater storage. One key aspect of the formal information system is that nothing gets into it that isn't identified beforehand as an appropriate form of input. Formal information systems also tend to be fairly inflexible and slow to change compared with informal ones. Thus, for example, if the VAT rate changes and the information system cannot be easily or quickly amended to accept the new VAT rate, it may be some time before the necessary changes can be made and the information adjusted to reflect the change.

REVIEW QUESTIONS

32.1 'Financial accounting looks behind, whilst management accounting looks ahead.' To what extent does this quotation accurately reflect the role of the two branches of accountancy?

(*Edexcel: GCE A-level*)

32.2 'Financial accounting is non-dynamic, backward looking, conservative, as objective as possible, and subject to statutory and other regulation. Management accounting is future oriented, is dynamic, produces forward looking figures, should not be too concerned with objectivity, and is not generally subject to external regulation.' (Prof. Michael Bromwich)
Justify this statement, giving examples to illustrate your answer.

(*Edexcel: GCE A-level*)

32.3 What are some of the deficiencies of financial accounting?

32.4 Why is it important that the employees of an organisation should clearly understand what the objectives of the organisation are?

32.5 How can there be a conflict between the various objectives of an organisation?

32.6 Describe how the management process is carried out.

PART 6

Costing

Introduction

This part looks at what constitutes cost and at four techniques used to derive cost.

CHAPTER 33

Elements of costing

After you have studied this chapter, you should be able to:

- explain why information must fit the purpose for which it is prepared
- discuss why the costs of obtaining information should be less than the benefits of having the information
- describe the flow of costs through financial accounts
- describe the flow of costs through a manufacturing company
- classify expenses appropriately
- explain the importance of an effective costing system
- explain the importance of cost allocation in the context of control

Introduction

In this chapter you'll learn how costs flow through financial accounts and through a manufacturing company's accounting system into its manufacturing account. You will also be introduced to and reminded of terminology relating to costs and expenses and learn the difference between them through an exercise in cost classification.

33.1 Management accounting

So far you have learnt about bookkeeping and the preparation of financial statements. In accounting, these are the two components of what is known as financial accounting. As you learnt in Chapter 32, the information that is produced by financial accounting is usually historic, backward-looking and (mainly) for the use of decision-makers external to the organisation to which the data relates.

There is a second side to accounting. This one is generally forward-looking or capable of being used to aid managerial control, forecasting and planning. It also consists of two components. One where costs are recorded and one where the data is processed and converted into reports for managers and other decision-makers. The cost recording component is called **cost accounting** and the processing and reporting component is called **management accounting**, which is also the name used to refer to this side of accounting. It is also sometimes referred to as 'managerial accounting'.

Cost accounting data also feeds into financial accounting. However, the two branches of accounting use the data and information differently. Referring once more to the third exhibit in Chapter 32, reproduced here as Exhibit 33.1, you can follow the flow of data and information within it and see how and where management accounting information is used.

Exhibit 33.1

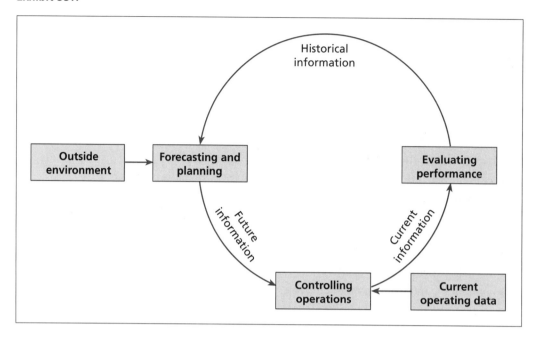

Management accounting produces the financial forecasts that guide planning. It embeds controls into the flow of operating data and uses them to control activities within the context of the plans. It evaluates performance and uses the information that is produced in order to underpin the forecasts that guide planning. As you can tell, while it is frequently looking backwards in order to gather information, its main emphasis is on producing information for control over current operations and in order to forecast and plan for the future.

Activity 33.1
Which aspects of this exhibit also relate to financial accounting?

For financial accounting and management accounting to operate effectively, they both need the raw data that is then built up and processed into the information they produce. As mentioned earlier, the process whereby this data is gathered is known as cost accounting.

33.2   Costs for different purposes

Cost accounting is needed so that there can be an effective management accounting system and an effective financial accounting system. Without a study of costs, such systems could not exist. Before entering into any detailed description of costs it is better if we ask ourselves first of all what use we are going to make of information about costs in the business.

This can best be done by referring to something which is not accounting, and then relating it to accounting. Suppose that your employer asked you to measure the distance between Manchester and London, but walked away from you without giving any further information. As you thought about his request the following thoughts might go through your head:

1 *HOW* does he want the distance measured? Some possibilities are:
   (a) from the southern outskirts of Manchester to the northern outskirts of London;
   (b) from the accepted geographical centre of London to the accepted geographical centre of Manchester;
   (c) to the centres of the two cities calculated as mathematically precise points;
   (d) by road – this could be just major roads, just minor roads, or could be a mixture of both – the main requirement being the quickest route by road;
   (e) by canal;
   (f) by train;
   (g) by air; allowance may or may not be made for the distance covered by the aircraft which would include climbing to an altitude of 5,000 feet or perhaps 40,000 feet, or might ignore the distance travelling in achieving an altitude.

2 The *COST* of obtaining the information. Measuring distances (or measuring costs) is not costless itself. Using very sophisticated instruments to get accurate measurement can be very expensive indeed. On the other hand it might just be a matter of measuring the distance on a map with a rule and converting it into miles – this would cost hardly anything at all.

3 What is the *PURPOSE* for which the measurement will be used? This has been deliberately left as the last point, but in fact it should have been the first question that came into your mind. Illustrations of the use could have been as follows:
   (a) he is going to drive from Manchester to London by car and wants a rough idea of the mileage so that he can gauge what time to set off if he is to arrive before it gets dark in London;
   (b) he might conceivably want to walk it;
   (c) he might be submitting a tender for the building of a motorway by the shortest possible route, cutting tunnels through ranges of hills;
   (d) perhaps he wants to send goods by canal;
   (e) maybe he wants to arrive as close as possible to an underground station;
   (f) he might be an amateur pilot who wants to fly from Manchester Airport to London Airport.

The lesson to be learnt from this is that measurement depends entirely on the use that is to be made of the data. Too often, businesses make measurements of financial and other data without looking first at the use that is going to be made of it. In fact, it could be said that 'information' is useful data that is provided for someone.

Data given to someone which is not relevant to the purpose for which it is required is just not information. Data which is provided for a particular purpose, and which is completely wrong for the purpose, is worse than having no data at all. At least when there is no data, the manager knows the best that can be done is to guess.

Activity 33.2
Apart from the obvious fact that it is irrelevant, why is useless data such a bad thing?

Having discovered what information is required, you need to look at the costs. You need to consider the following:

1 *What is the data on costs wanted for?* It might be needed for the financial accounts, for management control or for decision-making. Different data on costs are wanted for different purposes.

2 *How are the costs to be measured?* Only when the purpose for which the costs are to be used has been decided can the measurement process be decided. Financial accounting, for instance, needs a certain precision in calculating costs which is often not needed in management accounting, where sometimes the nearest thousand pounds will be good enough for the purpose.

3 *The cost of obtaining costing data should not exceed the benefits to be gained from having it.* This does not refer to some cost data which is needed to comply with various provisions of the law. We can, however, look at several cases to illustrate the cost/benefit factor:

(a) Spending £100 to obtain costs which will be used as a basis for pricing many of the products of the firm. If the costs had been 'guessed' an error could have meant large losses for the firm.

(b) Spending £10,000 to find data on sales which the sales manager will toss into the wastebasket because it is not the sort of data he wants, is obviously money wasted.

(c) Spending a lot of time and money to find out that the stock values on a particular day were £2,532,198, when such precision was not needed. Perhaps the chairman was having a general chat with the bank manager, and all he needed to know was an approximate figure for stock of £2,500,000. The approximate figure could have been found easily and at little cost, so here costs have exceeded benefits.

When it is known what the costs are for, and how much is to be spent on studying them, the appropriate method for measuring them can be decided.

33.3   Past costs in trading companies

There are many classifications of cost. As we go through the rest of this chapter, we'll summarise briefly those that you already know about. The first of these is historical cost.

Historical costs

These are the foundation of financial accounting. Exhibit 33.2 shows costs flowing through the financial accounting system.

Exhibit 33.2

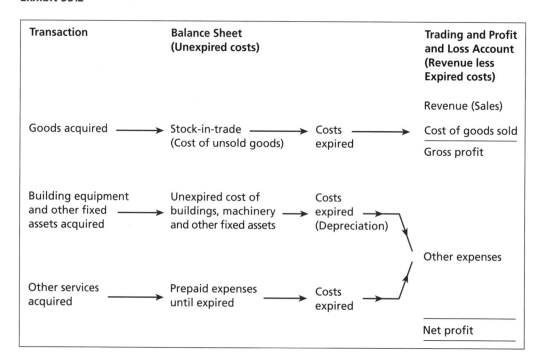

33.4 Past costs in manufacturing companies

You have probably already covered the topic of manufacturing accounts earlier when studying *Business Accounting 1*. In this chapter we will examine some of the detailed aspects of them a little further, as this is essential for a study of costing. First, a couple of definitions:

Product costs

These are the costs attributed to the units of goods manufactured. They are charged up to the cost of goods manufactured in the trading account, and would normally be part of the valuation of unsold goods if the goods to which they refer had not been sold by the end of the period. Product costs are therefore matched up against revenue as and when the goods are sold and not before.

Period costs

Period costs are those of a non-manufacturing nature and represent the selling and distribution, administration and the financial expenses. They are treated as expenses of the period in which they were incurred irrespective of the volume of goods sold.

Combining all this, you arrive at manufacturing accounts. Exhibit 33.3 shows the flow of costs through a manufacturing company to finished products.

Exhibit 33.3

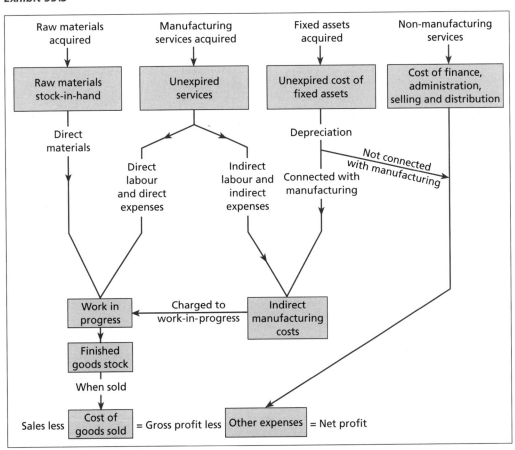

Exhibits 33.2 and 33.3 show what you use cost information for in financial accounting: to produce the information you need in order to prepare the financial statements. In management accounting, there is a different emphasis, some of which overlaps with the needs of financial accounting, but some of which is for something quite different.

33.5 Further costs defined

The following is a more detailed description of costs than you will have encountered previously.

- *Direct materials* are those materials which become part of the finished goods, subject to the proviso that the expense involved in tracing the cost is worth while. Some items, usually of insignificant amounts, are treated as indirect materials even though they are part of the finished product because the cost cannot be ascertained easily.
- *Direct labour* is those labour costs which are applied to convert the direct materials into the finished goods, also subject to the proviso that the expense involved in tracing this cost is worth while.
- *Direct expenses* are those expenses which can be traced directly to the product being manufactured. These are fairly rare, but an instance would be a royalty where the production of each item resulted in, say, £1 being due to the owner of a patent.
- *Prime cost*: the total of direct materials + direct labour + direct expenses is called prime cost. Naturally there will be disagreement between accountants as to whether certain costs are worth tracing as being of a direct type, as it will often be a matter of judgement which defies any easy proof whether or not the expense of tracing the cost exceeds the benefit from so doing. You should get used to the idea in accounting that disagreement will often occur, which will only be settled by a compromise or appeal to someone in higher authority to settle the argument. This relates to many things in accounting besides the decision as to whether an item is of a direct type or not.
- *Indirect manufacturing costs, factory indirect expenses or manufacturing overheads* are all those other expenses concerned with the manufacturing process which have not been treated as being of the direct type. Because there is no easily traceable direct connection with the goods being manufactured, these costs must be apportioned between the goods being manufactured in a logical fashion.
- *Production cost*: the total of prime cost + indirect manufacturing costs is called production cost.
- *Administration, selling and distribution and finance expenses* are common to both trading and manufacturing firms.
- *Total cost*: If we add together production cost and administration, selling and distribution, and finance expenses, the resultant figure is known as total cost. To summarise:

	Direct materials
ADD	Direct labour
ADD	Direct expenses
Gives:	PRIME COST
ADD	Indirect manufacturing costs
Gives:	PRODUCTION COST
ADD	Administration expenses
ADD	Selling and distribution expenses
ADD	Finance expenses
Gives:	TOTAL COST

Activity 33.3

Here is a list of typical types of expenses found in a manufacturing firm. These can be analysed as to whether they are direct materials, direct labour, direct expenses, factory indirect expenses, administration expenses, selling and distribution expenses, or finance expenses. In the right-hand column, write down what type of expense each item is.

Cost	Cost analysis
1 Raw materials for goods – identifiable with product made.	1 _____
2 Rent of factory buildings.	2 _____
3 Sales staff salaries.	3 _____
4 Wages of machine operators in factory.	4 _____
5 Wages of accounting machine operators in office.	5 _____
6 Depreciation of lathes in factory.	6 _____
7 Depreciation of typewriters in office.	7 _____
8 Depreciation of fixtures in sales showrooms.	8 _____
9 Supervisors' wages in factory.	9 _____
10 Royalty paid for each item manufactured.	10 _____
11 Works manager's salary: he reckons that he spends $3/4$ of his time in the factory and $1/4$ in general administration of the firm.	11 _____
12 Raw materials incorporated in goods sold, but too difficult to trace to the goods being made.	12 _____
13 Depreciation of motor vehicles used for delivery of finished goods to customers.	13 _____
14 Interest on bank overdraft.	14 _____
15 Wages of crane drivers in factory.	15 _____
16 Discounts allowed.	16 _____
17 Company secretary's salary.	17 _____
18 Advertising.	18 _____
19 Wages of staff of canteen used by factory staff only.	19 _____
20 Cost of hiring special machinery for use in manufacturing one special item.	20 _____

33.6 Advantages of a costing system

You have now looked at the various elements of cost as far as the whole of the firm is concerned. Such a classification of costs is necessary so that the overall production cost can be ascertained in the case of a manufacturing company with its effect on the valuation of the closing stock of finished goods and of work in progress.

What most businesses want to know is how much each item has cost to make. This means that the total costs for the whole business are not sufficient, and so these costs must be analysed further. They also want to know what costs are likely to be in the future. Again, more analysis is needed. Cost accounting is the process of measuring and recording all these costs.

Any costing system must bring about the better control of the firm in guiding it towards its objectives, and the benefits to be derived from the costing system must be greater than the expense of operating the costing system. We must, therefore, look at the possible advantages to be gained in carrying on further analyses of cost:

1 Because expenditure is traced down to each item produced, or each batch of items, it becomes possible to ascertain the contribution of each item to the profitability of the business. The desirability of stopping unprofitable activities can then be assessed.

2 Once the profitability of each item is known, the reasons for increases or decreases in profits can be seen more clearly.

3 It becomes easier to forecast future results if we know more about the operations of all the various parts of the business. When forecast results are not achieved it becomes possible to highlight the reasons for the failure to achieve the forecast results.

4 Estimates and tenders can be prepared in future with far greater confidence – previously such calculations as were done must have been largely guesswork. Fewer errors should be made because of the greater knowledge gained via the costing system.

5 Improvements in various activities of the firm may come about because of the more relevant information that can be supplied. Thus a machine which had always been thought to be quite cheap to use may turn out to be very expensive to use. This may bring about an investigation which would not otherwise have happened, and it may consequently be found that a simple attachment to the machine costing £10 brings about a saving of £100 a year.

6 As we will see, a very important advantage is the control of expenditure, and it can be achieved because an individual can be made responsible for the expenditure under his/her control.

Many advantages are gained by having a cost accounting system that provides this detail of cost information. **It is, however, now a convenient point to remind you that accounting techniques themselves do not solve problems, people are needed to do that.** When armed with the cost information that management accounting techniques can provide, managers and other internal decision-makers are far more able to make sensible decisions about what should be done to aid the progress of the business towards its objectives.

For example, imagine trying to decide which item to stop producing out of twelve items made by a business if you have little information as to the amount each item contributes towards the profitability of the business. Very often the solution will be that a new layout in the factory is needed; special training given to certain employees; changes made in the system of remunerating employees; and so on. The information provided by accounting is, therefore, only one part of the whole story for any problem requiring a decision to be made. Sometimes *it will be the least important information* available, as far as the decision-maker is concerned.

33.7 The control of costs

One of the most important features of cost accounting is its use for control purposes meaning, in this context, the control of expenditure. But control of expenditure is possible only if you can trace the costs down to employees who are responsible for such costs. A convenient and frequently adopted approach to collecting costs is through **cost centres** – production or service locations, functions, activities, or items of equipment. Costs are collected from cost centres for individual **cost units** – units of product or service. For example, in a manufacturing firm all direct materials, direct labour and direct expenses are traced to cost centres. (In this case, they may be known as 'product centres'.)

A cost centre may be such as a single machine used for jobbing work, i.e. quite a lot of separate jobs performed specially to conform with the customer's specifications. It could, however, be a group of similar machines or a production department. Thus, if a firm makes metal boxes on one machine, all the costs incurred directly relating to that machine (cost centre) would be gathered and then shared (allocated) among all the metal boxes (cost units) made by that machine.

By comparison, factory indirect expenses are 'indirect' expenses and so cannot be traced (or it is not worth while tracing them) to product centres. Instead, these are traced to cost centres which give service rather than being concerned with work directly on the products, and such cost centres are, therefore, known as **service centres**. Examples of service centres would be the factory canteen or the maintenance department. The costs from these service centres will then need apportioning to the product centres in a logical fashion – for example, canteen costs may be allocated to product cost centres according to the number of employees working at each of them.

In practice there are a number of possible ways of attributing costs to cost centres. What must not be lost sight of is the endeavour to trace costs to a person responsible for the expenditure so that the costs can be controlled.

33.8 Costing: manufacturing firms compared with retailing or wholesale firms

It is quite wrong to think that costing is concerned only with manufacturing firms. Both textbooks and examination papers often give the impression that only in manufacturing is costing needed or found. This is quite incorrect. Costing is just as relevant to retailing and wholesaling firms and service industries as it is to those in manufacturing. It is simply that manufacturing, which usually has more complex sorts of activities because of the manufacturing element, has attracted greater attention than other types of firms. There are, in addition, many other forms of organisations such as farming, shipping, banking and even charitable organisations where costing can aid management control. It would indeed be difficult to find any organisation which could not use some form of costing system profitably.

Learning outcomes

You should now have learnt:

1 Cost accounting is needed for there to be an effective management accounting system.

2 The benefits of operating a costing system should always outweigh the costs of operating it.

3 To be useful, information must be 'fit for purpose'.

4 When it is known what costs are for, and how much is to be spent on studying them, the appropriate method for measuring them can be decided.

5 In the case of a manufacturing company, classifying costs appropriately is necessary so that the overall production cost can be ascertained and so enable appropriate valuation of the closing stock of finished goods and of work in progress.

6 Accounting techniques themselves do not solve problems; it is people within the firm who, when armed with the information that accounting techniques can provide, are far more able to make sensible decisions about what should be done to aid the progress of the firm towards its objectives.

7 Appropriate cost allocation is very important for control.

8 When costs are assigned to an individual cost centre, they are 'allocated'; when they are assigned to two or more cost centres, they are 'apportioned'.

Answers to activities

33.1 Financial accounting gathers data relating to current performance in ledger accounts and then summarises it in order to evaluate performance through the preparation of financial statements which convey historic performance information to stakeholders in the organisation and other interested parties. It has no involvement in forecasting and planning and no interest in future information. In addition, the evaluation of performance conducted by financial accounting is very different from that undertaken by management accounting.

33.2 When useless data is collected it has cost money to collect, in itself a waste of money. Secondly, it is often assumed to be useful and so misleads a manager into taking decisions that are completely inappropriate. Third, it clogs up the communication system within a business, so that other data is not acted on properly because of the general confusion that has been caused.

33.3

Cost	*Cost analysis*
1 Raw materials for goods – identifiable with product made.	1 Direct materials
2 Rent of factory buildings.	2 Factory indirect expenses
3 Sales staff salaries.	3 Selling and distribution
4 Wages of machine operators in factory.	4 Direct labour
5 Wages of accounting machine operators in office.	5 Administration expenses
6 Depreciation of lathes in factory.	6 Factory indirect expenses
7 Depreciation of typewriters in office.	7 Administration expenses
8 Depreciation of fixtures in sales showrooms.	8 Selling and distribution expenses
9 Supervisors' wages in factory.	9 Factory indirect expenses
10 Royalty paid for each item manufactured.	10 Direct expenses
11 Works manager's salary: he reckons that he spends $3/4$ of his time in the factory and $1/4$ in general administration of the firm.	11 $3/4$ Factory indirect expenses $1/4$ Administration expense
12 Raw materials incorporated in goods sold, but too difficult to trace to the goods being made.	12 Factory indirect costs
13 Depreciation of motor vehicles used for delivery of finished goods to customers.	13 Selling and distribution expenses
14 Interest on bank overdraft.	14 Finance expenses
15 Wages of crane drivers in factory.	15 Factory indirect expenses
16 Discounts allowed.	16 Finance expenses
17 Company secretary's salary.	17 Administration expenses
18 Advertising.	18 Selling and distribution expenses
19 Wages of staff of canteen used by factory staff only.	19 Factory indirect expenses
20 Cost of hiring special machinery for use in manufacturing one special item.	20 Direct expenses

REVIEW QUESTIONS

33.1 Analyse the following costs between:

(*i*)   Direct materials
(*ii*) Direct labour
(*iii*) Factory indirect expenses
(*iv*) Administration expenses
(*v*)   Selling and distribution expenses
(*vi*) Finance expenses

  (*a*) Wages for staff maintaining machines in factory
  (*b*) Wages for staff maintaining accounting machinery
  (*c*) Expenses of canteen run exclusively for factory workers
  (*d*) Expenses of canteen run exclusively for administrative workers

(e) Grease used for factory machinery
(f) Cost of raw materials
(g) Carriage inwards on fuel used in factory boiler-house
(h) Carriage inwards on raw material
(i) Wages of managing director's chauffeur
(j) Wages of cleaners in factory
(k) Discounts allowed
(l) Rent of salesrooms
(m) Wages of lathe operators in factory
(n) Wages of security guards; the area of the factory buildings is four times as great as the other buildings
(o) Debenture interest
(p) Rent of annexe used by accounting staff
(q) Managing director's remuneration
(r) Sales staff salaries
(s) Running costs of sales staff cars
(t) Repairs to factory buildings
(u) Audit fees
(v) Power for machines in factory
(w) Rates: $3/4$ for factory buildings and $1/4$ for other buildings
(x) Rent of internal telephone system in factory
(y) Bank charges
(z) Costs of advertising products on television.

33.2A Analyse the following costs between:

(i) Direct materials
(ii) Direct labour
(iii) Factory indirect expenses
(iv) Administration expenses
(v) Selling and distribution expenses
(vi) Finance expenses

(a) Interest on bank overdraft
(b) Factory storekeepers' wages
(c) Hire of Rolls-Royce for managing director's use
(d) Repairs to factory roof
(e) Hotel bills incurred by sales staff
(f) Motor tax for vans used for delivering goods to customers
(g) Chief accountant's salary
(h) Lubricants for factory machinery
(i) Cost of disks for firm's computer
(j) Helicopter hire charges re special demonstration of company's products
(k) Debt collection costs
(l) Costs of painting advertising signs on London buses
(m) Cost of airplane tickets for sales staff
(n) Wages of painters engaged in production
(o) Wages of timekeepers in factory
(p) Postal charges for letters
(q) Wages of office boy in general office
(r) Postal charges – parcels sent to customers
(s) Repairs to vans used for taking goods to customers
(t) Cost of raw materials included in product
(u) Wages for cleaners engaged in administration block
(v) Carriage inwards on raw materials
(w) Repairs to neon sign in Piccadilly Circus
(x) Advertising agency fees
(y) Wages of crane drivers in factory
(z) Power costs of accounting machinery.

33.3 From the following information work out:

(a) Prime cost
(b) Production cost
(c) Total cost.

	£	£
Wages and salaries of employees:		
In factory (70 per cent is directly concerned with units being manufactured)		220,000
Salaries: Sales staff		8,000
Commission on sales paid to sales staff		1,400
Salaries of administrative staff		72,000
Travelling expenses:		
Sales staff	2,900	
Factory workers not directly concerned with production	100	
Administrative staff	200	
		3,200
Haulage costs on raw material bought		4,000
Carriage costs on goods sold		7,800
Depreciation:		
Factory machinery	38,000	
Accounting and office machinery	2,000	
Motor vehicles:		
Sales staff cars	3,800	
Administrative staff	1,600	
Sales display equipment	300	
		45,700
Royalties payable per unit of production		1,600
Canteen costs used by all the workers, $2/3$ work in the factory, $1/3$ in other parts of the firm		6,000
Raw materials:		
Stock at start of period		120,000
Stock at close of period		160,000
Bought in the period		400,000
Interest on loans and overdrafts		3,800
Other factory indirect expenses		58,000
Other administrative expenses		42,000
Other selling expenses		65,000

33.4A From the following information work out:

(a) Prime cost
(b) Production cost
(c) Total cost

	£	£
Wages and salaries of employees:		
In factory (60 per cent is directly concerned with units being manufactured)		150,000
In salesforce		15,000
In administration		26,000
Carriage costs:		
On raw materials brought into the firm		1,800
On finished goods delivered to customers		1,100
Rent and rates:		
Of factory block	4,900	
Of sales department and showrooms	1,000	
Of administrative block	1,100	
		7,000
Travelling expenses:		
Sales staff	3,400	
Administrative staff	300	
Factory workers not connected directly with production	200	
		3,900
Raw materials:		
Stock at start of period		11,400
Bought in the period		209,000
Stock at close of the period		15,600
Royalties: payable per unit of production		400
Depreciation:		
Sales staff cars	500	
Vehicles used for deliveries to customers	300	
Cars of administrative staff	400	
Machinery in factory	1,800	
Office machinery	200	
		3,200
Interest costs on borrowed money		800
Other factory indirect expenses		6,000
Other administrative expenses		4,000
Other selling expenses		1,000

33.5A

(a) The terms *cost behaviour* and *analysis of total cost* are regularly used in cost accounting to classify costs. Distinguish between the two terms.
(b) Explain how the following costs will:
   (i) behave;
   (ii) be analysed.
   - Factory power and lighting
   - Production line workers' wages
   - Sales manager's salary
   - Office rent.

(Edexcel: GCE A-level)

CHAPTER 34

Absorption and marginal costing

Learning objectives

After you have studied this chapter, you should be able to:

- explain why the costs relevant for decision-making are often different from those used for the calculation of net profit
- explain the difference between fixed, variable, semi-variable, and step-variable costs
- explain the difference between absorption and marginal costing
- discuss various factors underlying the pricing policy adopted by an organisation
- explain why marginal costing, not absorption costing, should be used when deciding how to utilise spare capacity through additional production
- explain what is meant by 'full cost pricing'
- explain the importance of contribution to pricing, production, and selling decisions
- explain what is meant by activity-based costing (ABC)
- discuss the advantages and limitations of ABC

Introduction

In this chapter you'll learn about the nature of different types of costs, including fixed, variable and semi-variable costs. You will learn how costs may be attributed to goods and services in order to arrive at a cost per unit that can then be used to set an appropriate selling price for the good or service. Two contrasting approaches – absorption (or full) costing and marginal costing – are reviewed and the concept of contribution is introduced and its importance in pricing and production decisions is explored. Finally, you will learn about another approach to cost attribution: activity based costing.

34.1 Allocation of indirect manufacturing costs

The most commonly accepted cost accounting theory used for purposes of the determination of profit is where all the indirect manufacturing costs are allocated to the products manufactured. The indirect manufacturing costs are seen as adding to the value of work in progress and thence to finished goods stock. The production cost of any article thus comprises direct materials, direct labour, any direct expenses and a share of factory indirect expenses.

After the end of the financial period, it is possible to look back and calculate exactly what the indirect manufacturing costs were. This means that this figure is used when calculating the valuation of the closing stock. Consider a firm which had produced 1,000 units, of which 200 units have not yet been sold, and a total production cost of £100,000. The closing stock valuation becomes:

$$\frac{\text{Unsold units}}{\text{Total units produced}} \times \text{Production cost of goods completed} = \frac{200}{1,000} \times £100,000$$

$$= £20,000 \text{ closing stock valuation}$$

Cost data is, however, used for purposes other than that of valuing stock. The question is, therefore, whether or not this method is suitable for all costing purposes. The method we have just used above, of allocating all indirect manufacturing costs to products, is known as **absorption costing**, sometimes called full costing.

34.2   Absorption costing: effect upon future action

We can now look at a decision we might have to come to about a future action. Exhibit 34.1 shows a firm which has to make a decision about whether or not to take on an extra order.

Exhibit 34.1

Donald Ltd's factory has been making 1,000 units annually of a particular product for the past few years. Last year, costs were:

	£
Direct labour	2,000
Direct materials	3,000
Indirect manufacturing costs	4,000
Production cost	9,000
Administration and other expenses	1,500
	10,500

The 1,000 units had been sold for £12 each = £12,000

The production cost per unit can be seen to be $\dfrac{£9,000}{1,000} = £9$.

The current year is following exactly the same pattern of production and costs. Suddenly, part-way through the year, a foreign buyer says he will take 200 units if the price for him can be cut from £12 each to £8 each. A meeting is held and the managing director says, 'What a pity. This could have been our first export order, something we have been waiting to happen for several years. The selling price overseas has no bearing on our selling price at home. But it costs us £9 a unit in production costs alone. We just cannot afford to lose money so as to export. Our shareholders would not tolerate the profits of the company falling to less than £1,500.'

'I think that you are wrong,' says John the accountant. 'Let's look at this year's results (a) if we do not accept the order and (b) if the order is accepted.' He then drafts the following:

	(a) Order not taken		(b) Order taken	
	£	£	£	£
Sales 1,000 × £12		12,000		
1,000 × £12 + 200 × £8				13,600
Less Expenses:				
Direct labour	2,000		2,400	
Direct materials	3,000		3,600	
Indirect manufacturing costs	4,000		4,200	
Other expenses	1,500		1,500	
		(10,500)		(11,700)
Net profit		1,500		1,900

'More profit. This means that we take the order,' says the sales director enthusiastically.

'Surely you've got your figures wrong, John,' says the managing director. 'Check your arithmetic.'

'There's nothing wrong with my arithmetic,' says John; 'but perhaps it will be a little more enlightening if I draft (b), Order taken, more fully.'

	(a) Order not taken		(b) Order taken	
	£	£	£	£
Sales		12,000		13,600
Less Costs which vary with production: Direct labour. The workers are on piece-work, i.e. they are paid according to how much they produce). In this case, this means 20 per cent more production brings 20 per cent more wages (i.e. £2,000 for 1,000 units, £2,400 for 1,200 units)	2,000		2,400	
Direct materials. 20 per cent greater production gives 20 per cent more materials (£3,000 + £600)	3,000		3,600	
Indirect manufacturing costs: Some would not change at all, e.g. factory rent, factory rates. Some would alter, e.g. cost of electric power because machines are used more. Of the indirect manufacturing costs, one-quarter is variable. For this variable part, £1,000 costs for 1,000 units becomes £1,200 costs for 1,200 units.	1,000		1,200	
Marginal cost		(6,000)		(7,200)
Sales *less* Variable costs		6,000		6,400
Costs: i.e. costs which will not alter at all if 200 more units are produced:				
Indirect manufacturing costs; fixed part	3,000		3,000	
Administration and other expenses	1,500		1,500	
		(4,500)		(4,500)
Net profit		1,500		1,900

'We can do all this without borrowing any money,' says the managing director, 'so I'll phone now to tell them we will start production immediately. By the way, John, come to my office this afternoon and tell me more about variable and fixed costs.'

34.3 The lesson to be learnt

We must not get lost in the technicalities of accounting. It is easy to think that calculations which look complicated must give the right answer. Logic must be brought to bear on such problems. This last case shows that **the costs needed when making decisions about the future will often be different from those which were used for calculating profit earned in the past**. In the example, £9 per unit had been taken for stock valuation, but this case proves that a firm could still manufacture units and sell at less than £9 each and still increase profits. The reason for this state of affairs is the very essence of the differences between fixed and variable costs which we will now consider.

34.4 Fixed and variable costs

The division of costs into those that are fixed and those that are variable is not an easy matter. Even factory rent is not always a fixed cost, for if production had to be increased to a certain figure the firm might have to rent further premises. Such a change would not usually happen in the short term: it would take a while to rent and set up a new factory or extra premises before production could start. **When fixed costs are mentioned it is normally assumed that this means costs which are fixed in the short term.**

In the firm Donald Ltd, Exhibit 34.1 assumed that variable costs were 100 per cent variable, by this meaning that if production rose 20 per cent then the cost would rise 20 per cent, if the production rose 47 per cent then the cost would also rise 47 per cent. This is not necessarily true. The cost of power may rise 20 per cent if production rose 20 per cent, but the cost of repairing and maintaining the machines may rise by only 10 per cent if production rose 20 per cent. In this case, the machine maintenance would be a semi-variable cost, this being the term for a cost which varies with production but not at a proportionate rate.

34.5 Cost behaviour

Appropriate cost planning and control is dependent on the knowledge of how costs behave under certain conditions. What is important is how costs behave in a particular firm. There is no substitute for experience in this respect.

Raw materials are examples of variable costs which normally vary in strict proportion to the units manufactured. Labour costs, on the other hand, usually move in steps, thus the name 'step-variable' costs. For instance, a job may be done by two people, and then a slight increase in activity means that the two people cannot manage it so that a third person is added. In fact it may represent only $2^{1}/_{3}$ people's work, but **the acquisition of workers come in indivisible chunks**. There can still be a further increase in activity without any more workers, but then the time will come when a fourth person is needed. This is shown on the two graphs in Exhibit 34.2.

Exhibit 34.2

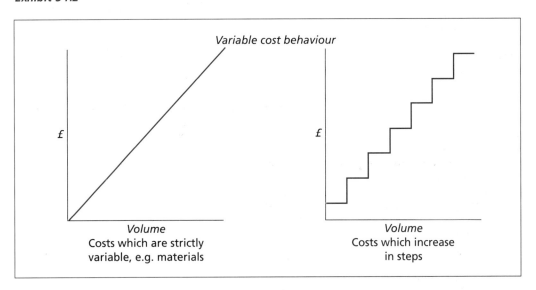

Variable cost behaviour

£   £

Volume   Volume
Costs which are strictly   Costs which increase
variable, e.g. materials   in steps

34.6 Marginal costing and absorption costing contrasted

Where costing is used which takes account of the variable cost of products rather than the full production cost, then this is said to be **marginal costing**. We have seen that a marginal costing approach to the decision whether or not to accept the foreign order by Donald Ltd gave us the answer which increased the firm's profitability, whereas to use absorption costing of £9 a unit in a blind fashion would have meant our rejecting the order and therefore

passing up the chance to increase profits and break into the foreign market. Let us look now at what would happen if we used either marginal costing or absorption costing in the calculation of profits for a whole firm, i.e. income determination.

Exhibit 34.3

The financial statements of a firm, Burke Ltd, are now shown drafted as if (A) marginal costing had been used, and (B) absorption costing had been used. The following information is available:

1 All fixed manufacturing costs amounted to £4,000 per annum.
2 Variable overheads amounted to £2 per unit.
3 Direct labour and direct materials total £3 per unit.
4 Sales remain constant at 1,000 units per annum at £12 per unit.
5 Production in year 1 is 1,200 units, year 2 is 1,500 units and year 3 is 900 units.

Year 1	(A) Marginal costing		(B) Absorption costing	
	£	£	£	£
Sales		12,000		12,000
Less Variable costs:				
Direct labour and material, 1,200 × £3	3,600		3,600	
Variable overheads, 1,200 × £2	2,400		2,400	
Total variable cost	6,000			
Less in (A) Valuation of closing stock				
$\frac{200}{1,200} \times £6,000$	(1,000)Note			
Marginal cost of goods sold	5,000			
Fixed manufacturing costs	4,000		4,000	
		(9,000)		
Total production costs			10,000	
Less in (B) Valuation of closing stock				
$\frac{200}{1,200} \times £10,000$			(1,666)Note	
				(8,334)
Gross profit		3,000		3,666

Year 2	(A) Marginal costing		(B) Absorption costing	
	£	£	£	£
Sales		12,000		12,000
Less Variable costs:				
Direct labour and material 1,500 × £3	4,500		4,500	
Variable overheads, 1,500 × £2	3,000		3,000	
Total variable cost	7,500			
Add in (A) Opening stock b/fwd	1,000			
	8,500			
Less in (A) Closing stock				
$\frac{700}{1,500} \times £7,500$	(3,500)Note			
Marginal cost of goods sold	5,000			
Fixed manufacturing costs	4,000		4,000	
		(9,000)		
Total production costs			11,500	
Add opening stock in (B) b/fwd			1,666	
			13,166	
Less Closing stock in (B)				
$\frac{700}{1,500} \times £11,500$			(5,366)Note	
				(7,800)
Gross profit		3,000		4,200

Year 3	(A) Marginal costing		(B) Absorption costing	
	£	£	£	£
Sales		12,000		12,000
Less Variable costs:				
Direct labour and material, 900 × £3	2,700		2,700	
Variable overheads, 900 × £2	1,800		1,800	
Total variable cost	4,500			
Add in (A) Opening stock b/fwd	3,500			
	8,000			
Less in (A) Closing stock $\frac{600}{900}$ × £4,500	(3,000)Note			
Marginal cost of goods sold	5,000			
Fixed manufacturing costs	4,000		4,000	
		(9,000)		
			8,500	
Add in (B) Opening stock b/fwd			5,366	
			13,866	
Less in (B) Closing stock $\frac{600}{900}$ × £8,500			5,666Note	
				(8,200)
Gross profit		3,000		3,800

Note:
The closing stock each year for (A) is made up of:

$$\frac{\text{Unsold units}}{\text{No. of units produced in year}} \times \text{Total variable cost of that year}$$

Units produced year 1   1,200 – 1,000 = Closing stock 200 units
Units produced year 2   1,500 + 200 opening stock – sales 1,000 = Closing stock 700 units
Units produced year 3   900 + 700 opening stock – sales 1,000 = Closing stock 600 units

So in year 1 unsold units are 200 units; units produced 1,200; total variable cost is £6,000; therefore stock valuation is:

$$\frac{200}{1,200} \times £6,000 = £1,000$$

The closing stock each year for (B) is made up of:

$$\frac{\text{Unsold units}}{\text{No. of units produced in year}} \times \text{Total production cost of that year}$$

So in year 1 stock valuation becomes $\frac{200}{1,200} \times £10,000 = £1,666.$

Exhibit 34.4 shows in diagrammatic form the reported gross profits shown in Exhibit 34.3.

Exhibit 34.4

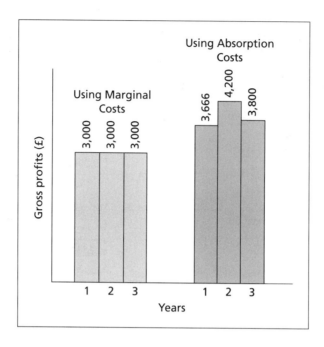

34.7 Comparison of reported profits – constant sales and uneven production

Exhibits 34.3 and 34.4 have illustrated that Burke Ltd, a firm which has had the same amount of sales each year at the same prices, and the same variable costs per unit, shows quite different gross profit figures using a marginal costing approach compared with absorption costing. As these were the gross profits that were calculated let us assume that the selling, distribution, administration and finance expenses were £1,000 for each of these years. The net profits would therefore be as follows:

	(A) *Marginal costing* £	(B) *Absorption costing* £
Year 1	2,000	2,666
Year 2	2,000	3,200
Year 3	2,000	2,800

Because of the absorption costing approach, year 2 shows the biggest profit. As sales etc. are the same, only production being different, this means that the year which has the greatest closing stock has shown the greatest profit. Because of greater production, the amount of fixed factory overhead per unit is less. For instance in Year 1 with 1,200 units produced and £4,000 fixed factory overhead this means:

$$\frac{£4,000}{1,200} = £3.3 \text{ per unit; Year 2 } \frac{£4,000}{1,500} = £2.7 \text{ per unit; Year 3 } \frac{£4,000}{900} = £4.4 \text{ per unit}$$

(taken to only one decimal place).

Calculating the value of closing stock to include the fixed factory overhead means that less gets charged per unit for fixed factory overhead when production is greatest, and thus a greater gross profit is shown.

Of course the situation gets more complicated because the closing stock of one year is the opening stock of the next year and, under absorption costing, the values of units of stock will vary. Fixed manufacturing cost, year 3: the opening stock of 700 units is shown as £5,366 = £7.7 per unit approximately; the closing stock of 600 units is shown as £5,666 = £9.4 per unit approximately. Yet these are exactly the same kinds of thing, and because we have made costs the same each year we have been ignoring inflation. **To show a higher profit in a year when the closing stock is higher than usual may often give a false sense of security.**

Activity 34.1
Why?

Many experts have argued for or against the marginal and the absorption approach in the context of profit calculation. The marginal approach assumes that fixed factory overhead is a function of time and should not be carried forward to the next period by including it in stock valuations. The absorption approach assumes that such overhead is concerned with production and, therefore, that the goods produced in that year but not yet sold should include it in the calculation of their value carried forward to the next period.

Do such costs 'attach' to the product or to time? They attach to time. It does seem that the marginal approach is more appropriate for closing stock valuation.

Of course, **during the life of a business, the recorded profits of a firm will be the same in total whichever method is in use.** If Burke Ltd exists for 20 years before it closes down, the profits as calculated for each year using the different methods will result in different recorded profits year by year (except by coincidence). The total profit during the complete life of the business of (say) £20 million will be the same. However, the intermediate reporting of profits may induce decisions which may change the pattern of activities and, therefore, affect the future profitability of the business. Use of an inappropriate basis for calculating profits could lead to inappropriate decisions being made.

34.8 Pricing policy

One thing is clear: **in the long term the revenues of a firm must exceed its costs or else the firm will go out of business.** If it was a company, it would have to be liquidated. If it was a firm run by a sole trader, he might conceivably become bankrupt. On the other hand, firms may find that, in the short term, costs sometimes exceed revenues. In other words, the firm makes a net loss. Many firms do make losses from time to time without being forced out of business.

This being so, the way in which the prices are determined of the goods sold by the firm is of paramount importance. You may well expect that there are some definite rules which will be observed by a firm when it fixes its prices, and that these rules are followed by all businesses. Your expectations would, however, be quite wrong.

With pricing, each firm has certain features which may not apply to other firms, and this will affect its pricing policy. For instance, taking a simple illustration, let us look at the price of sugar sold by three different businesses dealing in groceries. The first business (A) is a grocer's shop in a village, it is the only grocer's shop, and the next shop at which the villagers can buy sugar is thirty miles away. The second shop (B) is a grocer's shop in a town where there are plenty of other shops selling sugar. The last business (C) is a very large supermarket in a city, in a street where there are other large supermarkets. For a bag of sugar you might have to pay, at (A) 90p, (B) 80p, (C) 60p. The sugar may well be of exactly the same quality

and be manufactured by the same company. Firm (A) buys in small quantities; consequently it pays a higher price than (B) or (C) for its sugar, but it knows that none of its customers want to go thirty miles for sugar. The owner does not want to lose self-respect by over-charging anyway, so he settles for 90p. He always reflects that if he charged more, his customers might well buy sugar in large quantities when they went to the market town to shop. Firm (B) makes hardly any profit at all out of its sugar sales; it fears that if its regular customers were to go elsewhere for their sugar they might well decide to buy other things as well, so that (B) would lose not only its sugar sales but also a great deal of its other sales. Supermarket (C) sells sugar at a loss – it does this quite deliberately to tempt in customers who come to buy cheap sugar, and then buy other items on which the supermarket makes reasonable profits.

If there can be such differences in the selling price of a bag of sugar when sold by three firms, none of which had, in fact, produced the sugar, then how much more complex is the position where firms manufacture goods and then have to fix prices. This is where a study of economics helps to get this in better perspective. Along with other economic factors, the elasticity of demand must be considered as well as whether or not the firm has a monopoly. Economics will give you a framework for your thinking but it is not the purpose of this book to be an economics text. Still, you can see that the thinking behind pricing relies on economic analysis. We will content ourselves with accepting that this is so, and will merely look at how accounting portrays it.

34.9 Full cost pricing

Although there may be no clearly defined rules on pricing, it can at least be said that views of pricing can be traced to one of two attitudes. These are:

1 Ascertain the cost of the product and then add something to that for profit, the sum being the selling price. This is usually known as **full cost pricing**.
2 Ascertain the price at which similar products are selling, and then attempt to keep costs below that level so as to make a profit.

Many of the problems connected with full cost pricing are those concerned with absorption costing and marginal costing.

> **Activity 34.2**
> What are these problems of absorption costing and marginal costing?

Nevertheless, a considerable number of firms use the full cost basis, very probably because it is easy to apply. This is of itself not meant as a criticism – after all, the accounting that is used should be the simplest method of achieving the desired ends. There is certainly no virtue in using complicated methods when simple ones would suffice.

Complicated methods mean that the accounting system costs more to operate and, if the benefits are no greater than those derived from the simple system, the accounting system should be scrapped and replaced by the simple system. Using methods just because they are simple can, however, be harmful if they give the wrong data.

The information shown in Exhibit 34.5 has been drawn up on a full cost basis, using the following philosophy. The simple system of full cost pricing is to find the cost of direct materials and direct labour and then add relevant amounts to represent overheads and profit. The selling price is calculated in a manner similar to the following:

	£
Cost of direct materials and direct labour	10
Add Variable manufacturing overhead	5
Add Share of fixed manufacturing overhead	1
Absorption cost	16
Add Percentage (say 50 per cent in this case) for selling, administration and finance costs	8
Full cost	24
Add Percentage for profit (in this case, say, 25 per cent)	6
Selling price	30

The 50 per cent for selling, administration and finance costs is probably based on the figures for the previous year, when, as a total for the year, they would have approximated to 50 per cent of the total of direct materials + direct labour + variable manufacturing overhead + fixed manufacturing overhead (i.e. in this case it would have amounted to £16 for one unit). Therefore, taking 50 per cent of that figure (£8) as an addition is really saying that the basic situation is similar to the previous year.

Remember that this was an example. Full cost pricing is not always done in exactly the same manner, but the example just shown is a typical one. As we have seen already in an earlier chapter, the allocation of fixed costs is very arbitrary, yet here the selling price is based upon figures produced as a direct consequence of such arbitrary allocation.

34.10 Example of full cost pricing

We can now look at Exhibit 34.5. Three firms are making identical products. For the purpose of illustration, we will assume that the variable and fixed costs for each firm are the same. Different accountants use different methods of allocating fixed overhead between products even though, in each case, the allocation may seem to be quite rational. There is usually no one 'right' way of allocating fixed overhead. Instead, there are 'possible' ways. In this exhibit, each of the three firms manufactures two products and, because of the different ways in which they have allocated fixed overhead, they have come up with different selling prices for their products.

Exhibit 34.5

	Blue Ltd Products A	B	Green Ltd Products A	B	Red Ltd Products A	B
	£	£	£	£	£	£
Direct labour and materials	10	12	10	12	10	12
Variable overhead	16	10	16	10	16	10
Marginal cost	26	22	26	22	26	22
Fixed overhead	6	26	22	10	14	18
Full cost	32	48	48	32	40	40
Add Profit: 12.5 per cent of full cost	4	6	6	4	5	5
	36	54	54	36	45	45

In real life, once the selling prices have been calculated the market prices of similar goods are looked at, and the price fixed on the basis of competition, etc. In this case, the price might well be adjusted to £45 for both products A and B. By a coincidence – the allocation of fixed overhead has been done on an arbitrary basis – Red Ltd has managed to get its selling prices calculated to exactly the average market price.

Suppose the firms had really placed their faith in their selling price calculations but now realised they would have to fix selling prices at £45. Blue might think that as the full cost of product B was £48 then it would lose £3 for every unit sold of product B. Green Ltd might, on the other hand, think that as the full cost of product A is £48 it would lose £3 on every unit sold of product A. Blue Ltd might decide to cease production of B, and Green Ltd decide to cease production of A.

If the plans had been for each firm to sell 100 of each of products A and B, then the plans have now altered to Blue Ltd to produce and sell 100 of A only, Green Ltd to sell 100 of B only, and Red Ltd to sell both 100 of A and 100 of B. The summarised profit and loss accounts will now be as shown in Exhibit 34.6.

Exhibit 34.6

	Blue Ltd £	Green Ltd £	Red Ltd £
Sales: 100 of A @ £45	4,500		4,500
100 of B @ £45		4,500	4,500
Total revenue	4,500	4,500	9,000
Less Costs: Direct labour and materials			
Product A 100 × £10	1,000		1,000
Product B 100 × £12		1,200	1,200
Variable overhead:			
Product A 100 × £16	1,600		1,600
Product B 100 × £10		1,000	1,000
Fixed overhead: does not change			
Because of cessation of production in			
Blue Ltd and Green Ltd (see text)	3,200	3,200	3,200
Total costs	5,800	5,400	8,000
Net profit			1,000
Net loss	(1,300)	(900)	

Exhibit 34.6 shows that Blue Ltd and Green Ltd would incur losses if they ceased production of product B and product A respectively. Yet, if they had not ceased production they would both have made profits of £1,000 as Red Ltd has done. After all, they are *similar* firms with *exactly* the same costs – the only difference was the way they allocated fixed costs. The fixed costs in each firm totalled £3,200. Blue allocated this between products as A £6, B £26. Green allocated it A £22, B £2. Red allocated it A £14, B £18. With 100 units of each product this amounted to an allocation of £3,200 for each firm. Fixed overhead does not change just because of ceasing production of one type of product. The factory rent and rates will remain the same, so will the secretaries' salaries and other fixed costs.

34.11 Contribution

The question arises therefore as to which approach, absorption or marginal costing, is relevant in deciding whether to continue the manufacture of a certain product. The answer to this is that the *marginal cost* figure – i.e. the variable cost – is the one that is relevant. If the marginal cost is less than the selling price, then the difference will make a **contribution** towards fixed overheads, thus reducing the burden of the fixed overhead on the other products.

This can be seen in the following example concerning which of the two products we introduced in Section 34.10, A and B, to make when there is some spare production capacity. As absorption costing includes an element of fixed cost, it is not appropriate to use it when considering decisions of this type:

	Product A	Product B
	£	£
Selling price	45	45
Marginal cost	26	22
Contribution towards fixed overhead and profit	19	23

Either product could be usefully considered, both making a positive contribution towards fixed costs. However, all other things being equal, product B would appear the better option. Thus, if there is spare capacity, and an opportunity arises to use some of it, marginal costing would be used in order to determine whether the projected income exceeds the marginal cost. If it does, it would be appropriate to consider taking on the work. This is based on an important rule:

$$\text{Contribution} = \text{Selling Price} - \text{Variable Cost}$$

Contribution is also the basis of another important rule for decision-making:

$$\text{Break-even point} = \frac{\text{Fixed costs}}{\text{Selling price per unit} - \text{Variable costs per unit}}$$

Break-even point is the volume of sales required in order to make neither a profit nor a loss. You'll learn more about these rules when you look at break-even analysis (also called cost–volume–profit analysis) in Chapter 42.

Note: Marginal costing uses variable costs. The variable cost is often referred to as the marginal cost. They are, effectively, the same thing.

34.12 Using marginal costs

Let's test this out using a firm that produces five products and has the following cost and selling information. The firm would sell 100 of each product it manufactured. Total fixed overhead is £4,800, allocated A £5 (100), B £7 (100), C £11 (100), D £15 (100), E £10 (100), i.e. £4,800 total. Exhibit 34.7 presents this in tabular form.

Exhibit 34.7

Violet Ltd	Products				
	A	B	C	D	E
Cost per unit:	£	£	£	£	£
Direct labour and materials	8	9	16	25	11
Variable overhead	7	8	10	13	14
Marginal cost	15	17	26	38	25
Fixed overhead	5	7	11	15	10
Full cost	20	24	37	53	35
Selling price per unit	30	21	31	80	20

On the full-cost basis only A and D would seem to be profitable. Should production of B, C and E be discontinued? According to what has been said, production should cease only when the selling price is less than marginal cost. In Exhibit 34.8 we will see if following our own advice brings about the greatest profit. We will also see what would have happened if production was not cut at all.

Exhibit 34.8

	(1) Following full-cost pricing, cease producing B, C and E £	(2) Using marginal costing, cease producing E only £	(3) Ignore costing altogether and produce all items £
Sales: A 100 × £30	3,000	3,000	3,000
B 100 × £21		2,100	2,100
C 100 × £31		3,100	3,100
D 100 × £80	8,000	8,000	8,000
E 100 × £20			2,000
Total revenue	11,000	16,200	18,200
Less Costs:			
Direct labour and materials:			
100 × cost per product	(£33) 3,300	(£58) 5,800	(£69) 6,900
Variable cost: 100 × cost per product	(£20) 2,000	(£38) 3,800	(£52) 5,200
Fixed overhead (does not change)	4,800	4,800	4,800
Total costs	10,100	14,400	16,900
Net profit	900	1,800	1,300

The £s figures in brackets show the cost of each product, e.g. in (1) the direct labour and materials are A £8 + D £25 = £33.

As you can see from Exhibit 34.8, it would be just as well if we followed our own advice. This would give a profit of £1,800 compared with £900 using the full-cost method or £1,300 if we disregarded costing altogether. Sometimes the full-cost method will give far better results than ignoring costing altogether, but this case shows that in fact **the wrong kind of costing can be even worse than having no costing at all.** The marginal costing approach will, however, give the better answer in this sort of situation.

There is, however, a danger in thinking that if the marginal cost of each product is less than the selling price then activities will be profitable. This is certainly not so, and full consideration must be given to the fact that the total contributions from all the products should exceed the fixed costs, otherwise the firm will incur an overall loss. Different volumes of activity will affect this. Exhibit 34.9 looks at a two-product firm making products A and B at different volumes of activity. Product A has a marginal cost of £10 and a selling price of £14. Product B has a marginal cost of £6 and a selling price of £8. Fixed costs are £1,400.

Exhibit 34.9

	Profit, or loss, at different volumes of activity							
	A	B	A	B	A	B	A	B
Units sold	100	100	200	200	300	300	400	400
	£	£	£	£	£	£	£	£
Contribution (Selling price *less* Marginal cost) A £4 per unit, B £2 per unit	400	200	800	400	1,200	600	1,600	800
Total contributions	600		1,200		1,800		2,400	
Fixed overhead	(1,400)		(1,400)		(1,400)		(1,400)	
Net loss	800		200					
Net profit					400		1,000	

Here the selling price always exceeds marginal cost, but if activity is low the firm will incur a loss. This is shown where activity is only 100 or 200 units of each product.

The main lessons to be learned about selling prices are that:

(a) a product should make a positive contribution (unless there is some overriding matter which makes the product a kind of loss-leader). That is, selling prices should exceed marginal costs; and
(b) the volume of sales should be sufficient so that in the long term (it may be different in the short term) the fixed overheads are more than covered by the total of all the contributions.

34.13 Maximisation of total contribution

It should be stressed that it is the maximisation of the total contribution from a product that is important. In this, the volumes of activity cannot be disregarded. Suppose, for instance, that a firm could only manufacture two products in future, whereas to date it had manufactured three. It may be that per unit the contribution may well have been (A) £10, (B) £8 and (C) £6. If a decision was made on this basis only then (C) would be discontinued. However, if the volumes were (A) 20, (B) 15 and (C) 30, then the total contributions would be (A) $20 \times £10$ = £200: (B) $15 \times £8 = £120$: (C) $30 \times £6 = £180$. As (B) has the lowest *total* contribution it should be (B) that is discontinued, not (C).

Where there is a limit of one of the items used in production of the product, the contribution per product per unit of that limiting factor (or key factor) should be used as the basis for the decision taken.

Take, for example, a situation where there are only 200 spare hours of machine capacity available and a choice has to be made between increasing current production levels of a range of products. The contribution per machine hour of each product is: A £2; B £3; C £5; D £1. Product C should be produced. It will generate the greatest amount of contribution. If there is any spare capacity remaining after all of product C has been produced (for example, if there is only enough material available to make a few of product C) then product B should be produced, etc.

34.14 Activity-based costing (ABC)

A single measure of volume is used for each production/service cost centre when traditional overhead absorption is in use. For example:

- machine hours
- direct labour hours
- direct materials cost
- direct labour cost.

These bases are often unjustifiable when the nature of the activity at the cost centre and, more particularly, the nature of the item that is absorbing the cost is considered. In reality, the amount of overhead incurred may depend on any of a range of factors. **An appropriate basis for cost absorption ought to adopt a basis that as truly as possible reflects the changes in overhead arising from the activities undertaken.**

Cost drivers

Cost drivers are activities that generate cost. They are the factors that cause overhead to be incurred. A cost driver may be related to a short-term variable overhead (e.g. machine running costs) – where the cost is driven by production volume and the cost driver will be volume-based, e.g. machine hours. Alternatively, it could be related to a long-term variable

overhead (e.g. quality inspection costs) – where the cost is driven by the number of occasions the relevant activity occurs and where the cost driver will be transaction-based, e.g. the number of quality inspections.

Activity-based costing is the process of using cost drivers as the basis for overhead absorption. Costs are attributed to cost units on the basis of benefit received from indirect activities, e.g. ordering, setting up, assuring quality.

While this sounds more appropriate than absorption costing, the information required to apply ABC is not generally available from the traditional accounting records and organisations that embrace ABC often require to develop a new information system to provide that information.

Cost pools

A cost pool is a collection of individual costs within a single heading and in traditional overhead absorption, cost pools are production cost centres. Under ABC, a cost pool is created for each activity area. Then, in order to attribute costs held in a cost pool to an item, the cost pool is divided by the appropriate quantity of the related cost driver. This process of cost attribution is very similar to that used in traditional absorption costing – it is the terminology, the manner in which costs are built up, and the type of basis used for cost attribution that differ.

ABC vs. absorption costing

It is claimed that traditional overhead absorption underallocates overheads to lower-volume products and overallocates overheads to higher-volume products – that is, it produces potentially misleading information at the two extremes. ABC directs attention to matters of interest that traditional overhead absorption is insufficiently sensitive to identify. It should, therefore, be capable of producing more useful information for decision-making than traditional overhead absorption.

Because administration, selling and distribution overheads are excluded from financial accounting inventory and cost of sales calculations, traditional overhead absorption stops at the edge of the factory floor. A full analysis of product profitability requires consideration of these non-production overheads, which is one reason why some organisations have chosen to adopt ABC, which does include these overheads. When companies that use ABC to evaluate stock and cost of sales have to produce their financial statements, it should be straightforward to remove these non-production overheads from the calculated figures.

Limitations of ABC

While it is usually possible to implement an ABC system, in many cases it is not worthwhile:

1 The costs of implementing and operating such a system often outweigh the benefits for smaller organisations.
2 It can often be the case that the additional precision and accuracy that ABC brings is immaterial in the context of managerial decision-making.
3 For single-product or single-service organisations, ABC is of little benefit.
4 Because of the need to exclude adminstration, selling and distribution overheads from stock and cost of sales in financial statements, many organisations that implement ABC operate an absorption costing accounting system in parallel with it. This simply adds to the complexity of the accounting system and is liable to confuse non-accounting-aware managers when they have two different 'cost' figures for the same product or item of stock.

However, where organisations have multiple products or services, ABC can prove to be a worthwhile and cost-effective way of increasing the reliability of managerial decision-making.

Learning outcomes

You should now have learnt:

1 Why different costs are often relevant for decision-making rather than those used for the calculation of net profit.

2 The costs needed when making decisions about the future will often be different from those used when calculating profit in the past.

3 The difference between fixed, variable, semi-variable and step-variable costs.

4 The difference between absorption and marginal costing.

5 How various factors underlie the pricing policy adopted by an organisation.

6 Why marginal cost, not full (or absorption cost), is the relevant cost when considering a change in what and/or how much is produced.

7 What is meant by full cost pricing.

8 The importance of contribution to pricing, production and selling decisions.

9 That selling prices should exceed marginal costs. (Almost the only exception to this would be where a product was being promoted as a loss-leader.)

10 That, in the long term, the total contributions at given volumes must exceed the fixed costs of the firm.

12 What is meant by activity-based costing (ABC).

13 The advantages and limitations of ABC.

Answers to activities

34.1 The stock may be rising because we cannot sell the goods; we are really getting into trouble, yet the financial statements sublimely show a higher profit.

34.2 In absorption costing the whole of the fixed costs were allocated to products, whereas in marginal costing the 'contribution' was found (i.e. revenue *less* variable cost) out of which fixed costs would have to come, leaving the profit as the difference. The problem is how to decide the amount of fixed cost per unit to arrive at 'full cost'.

REVIEW QUESTIONS

34.1 Drake Ltd's costs and revenues for the current year are expected to be:

	£	£
Direct labour		6,000
Direct materials		7,000
Indirect manufacturing costs:		
Variable	4,500	
Fixed	500	
		5,000
Administration expenses		1,200
Selling and distribution expenses		600
Finance expenses		200
		20,000

It was expected that 2,000 units would be manufactured and sold, the selling price being £11 each.
   Suddenly during the year two enquiries were made at the same time which would result in extra production being necessary. They were:

(A) An existing customer said that he would take an extra 100 units, but the price would have to be reduced to £9 per unit on this extra 100 units. The only extra costs that would be involved would be in respect of variable costs.
(B) A new customer would take 150 units annually. This would mean extra variable costs and also an extra machine would have to be bought costing £1,500 which would last for 5 years before being scrapped. It would have no scrap value. Extra running costs of this machine would be £600 per annum. The units are needed for an underdeveloped country and owing to currency difficulties the highest price that could be paid for the units was £10 per unit.

   On this information, and assuming that there are no alternatives open to Drake Ltd, should the company accept or reject these orders? **Draft the memo** that you would give to the managing director of Drake Ltd.

34.2A   Hawkins Ltd expects its cost per unit, assuming a production level of 100,000 per annum, to be:

	£
Direct materials	2.8
Direct labour	2.4
Indirect manufacturing costs: Variable	0.8
Fixed	0.4
Selling and distribution expenses	0.2
Administration expenses	0.3
Finance	0.1
	7.0

Selling price is £7.5 per unit.
   The following propositions are put to the managing director. Each proposition is to be considered on its own without reference to the other propositions.

(a) If the selling price is reduced to £7.4 per unit, sales could be raised to 120,000 units per annum instead of the current 100,000 units. Apart from direct materials, direct labour and indirect fixed manufacturing costs, there would be no change in costs.
(b) If the selling price is put up to £7.7 per unit, sales would be 80,000 per annum instead of 100,000. Apart from variable costs there would also be a saving of £2,000 per annum in finance costs.
(c) To satisfy a special order, which would not be repeated, 5,000 extra units could be sold at £6.3 each. This would have no effect on fixed expenses.
(d) To satisfy a special order, which would not be repeated, 3,000 extra units could be sold for £5.9 each. This would have no effect on fixed expenses.

   Draft a memo stating what you would advise the managing director to do, giving your reasons and workings.

34.3   Assume that by coincidence two firms have exactly the same costs and revenue, but that Magellan Ltd uses a marginal costing approach to the valuation of stock-in-trade in its final accounts, while Frobisher Ltd has an absorption cost approach. **Calculate** the gross profits for each company for each of their first three years of operating from the following:

(a) All fixed manufacturing cost is £9,000 per annum.
(b) Direct labour costs over each of the three years – £3 per unit.
(c) Direct material costs over each of the three years – £5 per unit.
(d) Variable overheads which vary in direct ratio to production were £2 per unit.
(e) Sales are: Year 1 900 units: Year 2 1,200 units: Year 3 1,100 units.
   The selling price remained constant at £29 per unit.
(f) Production is at the rate of: Year 1 1,200 units: Year 2 1,300 units: Year 3 1,250 units.

34.4A Your firm has been trading for three years. It has used a marginal costing approach to the valuation of stock-in-trade in its final accounts. Your directors are interested to know what the recorded profits would have been if the absorption cost approach had been used instead. **Draw up the three year's accounts using both methods.**

(a) Fixed manufacturing cost is £16,000 per annum.
(b) Direct labour costs per unit over each of the three years £4 per unit.
(c) Direct material costs over each of the three years £3 per unit.
(d) Variable overheads which vary in direct ratio to production were £5 per unit.
(e) Sales are: Year 1 9,000 units; Year 2 10,000 units; Year 3 15,000 units. All at £16 per unit.
(f) Production is at the rate of: Year 1 10,000 units; Year 2 12,000 units; Year 3 16,000 units.

34.5 Greatsound Ltd manufactures and sells compact disc players, the cost of which is made up as follows:

	£
Direct material	74.80
Direct labour	18.70
Variable overhead	7.50
Fixed overhead	30.00
Total cost	131.00

The current selling price is £187.

Greatsound Ltd works a day shift only, at present producing 120,000 compact disc players per annum, and has no spare capacity.

Market research has shown that there is a demand for an additional 60,000 compact disc players in the forthcoming year. However, these additional sales would have a selling price of £150 each. One way of achieving the extra production required is to work a night shift. However, this would increase fixed costs by £2,500,000 and the labour force would have to be paid an extra 20 per cent over the day shift rate.

The company supplying the materials to Greatsound Ltd has indicated that it will offer a special discount of 10 per cent on total purchases if the annual purchases of materials increase by 50 per cent.

The selling price and all other costs will remain the same.

Assuming that the additional purchases will only be made if the night shift runs, **you are required to:**

(a) Advise Greatsound Ltd whether it should proceed with the proposal to commence the night shift, based on financial considerations.
(b) Calculate the minimum increase in sales and production required to justify the night shift.
(c) Give **four** other matters which should be taken into consideration when making a decision of this nature.

(AQA (Northern Examinations and Assessment Board): GCE A-level)

34.6A
(a) What is meant by the terms *contribution* and *marginal cost*?

(b) Barton & Co Ltd make and sell 2,000 units per month of a product 'Barco'. The selling price is £65 per unit, and unit costs are: direct labour £8; direct materials £17; variable overheads £11. Fixed costs per month are £29,400.

The company receives two export orders for completion in September 20X2. Order A requests 600 items at a special total price of £20,000; order B requires 750 items at a total price of £34,000. Order A will require no special treatment, but order B will demand extra processing at a cost of £6 per item. The company has sufficient capacity to undertake *either* A *or* B in addition to its current production, but only by paying its direct labour force an overtime premium of 25 per cent.

Calculate the company's contribution and the profits for the month if:
(i) normal production only takes place;
(ii) order A is accepted in addition to normal production;
(iii) order B is accepted in addition to normal production.

(c) Use your answer to (b) to demonstrate that a company will normally accept an order which produces a *contribution* towards overheads.

(Edexcel: GCE A-level)

34.7 Arncliffe Limited manufactures two types of product marketed under the brand names of 'Crowns' and 'Kings'. All the company's production is sold to a large firm of wholesalers.

Arncliffe is in something of a crisis because the chief accountant has been taken ill just as the company was about to begin negotiating the terms of future contracts with its customer. You have been called in to help and are given the following information relating to each product for the last year. This information has been prepared by a junior assistant.

Report on revenues/costs for the year just ended:

	Crowns	Kings
	£	£
Sales	60,000	25,000
Floor space costs (rent and rates)	10,000	5,000
Raw materials	8,000	2,000
Direct labour	20,000	10,000
Insurances	400	200
Machine running costs	12,000	3,000
Net profit	9,600	4,800

The junior assistant says in his report, 'As you can see, Crowns make twice as much profit as Kings and we should therefore stop manufacturing Kings if we wish to maximise our profits. I have allocated floor space costs and insurances on the basis of the labour costs for each product. All other costs/revenues can be directly related to the individual product.'

Further investigation reveals the following information:

(i) The wholesaler bought all the 20,000 Crowns and 10,000 Kings produced last year, selling them to their customers at £4 and £3 each respectively. The wholesaler is experiencing an increasing demand for Crowns and intends to raise his price next year to £4.50 each.

(ii) Crowns took 8,000 hours to process on the one machine the company owns, whereas Kings took 2,000 hours. The machine has a maximum capacity of 10,000 hours per year.

(iii) Because all production is immediately sold to the wholesaler no stocks are kept.

Required:

(a) Prepare the revenue/cost statement for the year just ended on a marginal cost basis, and calculate the rate of contribution to sales for each product.

(b) You are told that in the coming year the maximum market demand for the two products will be 40,000 Crowns and 36,000 Kings and that the wholesaler wishes to sell a minimum of 6,000 units of each product. Calculate the best product mix and resulting profit for Arncliffe Limited.

(c) Calculate the best product mix and resulting profit for Arncliffe Limited if another machine with identical running costs and capacity can be hired for £20,000 per annum. Floor space and insurance costs would not change and the maximum and minimum conditions set out in (b) above continue to apply.

(d) What points does Arncliffe Limited need to bear in mind when negotiating next year's contract with the wholesaler?

(Reproduced with the kind permission of OCR: from the University of Cambridge Local Examinations Syndicate)

34.8A Reed Ltd manufactures three products A, B and C. Budgeted costs and selling prices for the three months ending 30 September 20X2 are as follows:

	A	B	C
Sales (units per month)	6,000	8,000	5,000
	£	£	£
Selling price per unit	45	44	37
Unit costs			
Direct labour	6	9	6
Direct materials[Note]	20	24	16
Variable overhead	4	3	2
Fixed overhead	5	5	6

Labour costs are £3 per hour, and material costs are £4 per kilo for all products. The total fixed costs are of a general factory nature, and are unavoidable.

The company has been advised by its supplier that due to a material shortage, its material requirement for the month of September will be reduced by 15 per cent. No other changes are anticipated.

Required:

A A statement to show the maximum net profit for the three months ending 30 September 20X2, taking into account the material shortage for the month of September.

B Explain how the fixed cost element is dealt with in marginal costing and in absorption costing. Briefly explain how this affects any closing stock valuation.

(Reproduced with the kind permission of OCR – University of Oxford Delegacy of Local Examinations: GCE A-level)

Authors' note: Assume that the materials used in each product are of the same kind.

34.9 Paul Wagtail started a small manufacturing business on 1 May 20X8. He has kept his records on the double entry system, and has drawn up a trial balance at 30 April 20X9 before attempting to prepare his first final accounts.

Extract from the Trial Balance of Paul Wagtail at 30 April 20X9

	£	£
Purchases of raw materials	125,000	
Sales		464,360
Selling expenses	23,800	
Insurance	4,800	
Factory repairs and maintenance	19,360	
Carriage on raw materials	1,500	
Heating and lighting	3,600	
Direct factory power	12,430	
Distribution expenses	25,400	
Production wages	105,270	
Factory supervisor's wages	29,600	
Administration expenses	46,700	
Plant and machinery at cost	88,000	
Delivery vehicles at cost	88,000	
Raw materials returned to supplier		2,100

At 30 April 20X9, he has closing stocks of raw materials costing £8,900. He has manufactured 9,500 completed units of his product, and sold 8,900. He has a further 625 units that are 80 per cent complete for raw materials and production labour, and also 80 per cent complete for factory indirect costs.

He has decided to divide his insurance costs and his heating and lighting costs 40 per cent for the factory and 60 per cent for the office/showroom.

He wishes to depreciate his plant and machinery at 20 per cent p.a. on cost, and his delivery vehicles using the reducing balance method at 40 per cent p.a.

He has not yet made up his mind how to value his stocks of work in progress and finished goods. He has heard that he could use either marginal or absorption costing to do this, and has received different advice from a friend running a similar business and from an accountant.

Required:

(a) Prepare Paul Wagtail's manufacturing, trading and profit and loss accounts for the year ended 30 April 20X9 using *both* marginal and absorption costing methods, preferably in columnar format.

(b) Advise Paul Wagtail of the advantages and disadvantages of using each method.

(Reproduced with the kind permission of OCR – University of Oxford Local Delegacy Examinations: GCE A-level)

34.10A The figures given below are all that could be salvaged from the records after a recent fire in the offices of Firelighters Limited. The company manufactures a single product, has no raw materials or work in progress and values its stocks at marginal cost (i.e. at variable manufacturing cost) using the FIFO basis. It is known that the unit closing stock valuation in 20X0 was the same as in 20X9.

	20X0	20X1
Selling price per unit	£10.00	£10.00
Variable manufacturing cost (per unit produced)	£4.00	£4.00
Variable selling cost (per unit sold)	£1.25	?
Quantity sold (units)	100,000	?
Quantity manufactured (units)	105,000	130,000
Contribution	?	£585,000
Fixed manufacturing costs	£105,000	£117,000
Other fixed costs	£155,000	?
Operating profit before interest charges	?	£292,000
Interest charges	£70,000	?
Opening finished stock (units)	?	?
Closing finished stock (units)	20,000	20,000
Net profit for the year	?	£210,000

Required:
Prepare a revenue statement for management showing contribution, operating profit and net profit for each year in as much detail as the information given above permits.

(*Reproduced with the kind permission of OCR: from the University of Cambridge Local Examinations Syndicate*)

34.11A Gainford Ltd is a manufacturing company which produces three specialist products – A, B and C. For costing purposes the company's financial year is divided into thirteen periods of four weeks. There is always sufficient raw material in stock to meet any planned level of production but there is a maximum number of labour hours available to the company. The production of each product requires a different physical layout of the factory equipment although the labour tasks are broadly similar. For this reason the company only produces one type of product at any time, and the decision as to which product to manufacture is taken before each four week period commences.

A forty hour working week is in operation and the following factory staff are employed:

Grade 1   28 staff paid at a rate of £8 per hour
Grade 2   12 staff paid at a rate of £6 per hour

In addition, a limited number of qualified part-time staff can be employed when required. Both full-time and part-time staff are paid at the same rate. The next four week period is number 7 and the following maximum part-time hours are available for that period:

Grade 1   2,240 hours
Grade 2   1,104 hours

The production costs and selling costs per unit for each product are:

	A	B	C
	£	£	£
Direct raw material	147	87	185
Direct labour: Grade 1	64	56	60
Grade 2	24	27	21
Variable overheads	15	10	15
Fixed Overheads	12	12	12
Selling price of each product	400	350	450

There is a strong demand for all three products and every unit produced is sold.

Required:
(a) Explain the terms:
   (i) 'contribution'
   (ii) 'key factor'
(b) Calculate the contribution and profit obtained when **each** product is sold.
(c) Prepare a statement from the available information, for each period number 7 which will assist management to decide which product to produce in order to maximise contribution. This statement should include details of the:
   (i) total production labour hours available
   (ii) number of hours required to produce one unit of **each** type of product
   (iii) maximum production (in units) possible of **each** type of product
   (iv) product which will give the greatest contribution in period number 7
(d) Outline the main steps in the manufacturing decision-making process which ought to be adopted by a business.

(AQA (Associated Examining Board): GCE A-level)

34.12A Vale Manufacturing started in business on 1 April 20X3, and incurred the following costs during its first three years.

Year ending 31 March	20X4	20X5	20X6
	£	£	£
Direct materials	60,000	49,900	52,200
Direct labour	48,000	44,000	45,000
Variable overheads	24,000	30,000	40,000
Fixed costs	40,000	40,600	41,300

Sales during the first three years were all at £20 per unit.

Production each year (units)	16,000	14,000	14,000
Sales each year (units)	14,000	14,000	15,000

Required:
(a) Prepare a statement showing the gross profit for each of the three years if the company used:
   (i) the marginal costing approach to valuing stock;
   (ii) the absorption costing approach to valuing stock.
(b) Advise the company of the advantages and disadvantages of using each method.

(Reproduced with the kind permission of OCR – University of Oxford Delegacy of Local Examinations: GCE A-level)

34.13 Glasses Ltd make four different products, Q, R, S and T. They have ascertained the cost of direct materials and direct labour and the variable overhead for each unit of product. An attempt is made to allocate the other costs in a logical manner. When this is done 10 per cent is added for profit. The cost of direct labour and materials per unit is Q £14; R £28; S £60; T £32. Variable overheads per unit are Q £4; R £8; S £13; T £12. Fixed overhead of £1,900 is allocated per unit as Q £2; R £4; S £7; T £6.

You are required to:
(a) Calculate the prices at which the units would be sold by Glasses Ltd if the full-cost system of pricing was adhered to.
(b) What would you advise the company to do if, because of market competition, prices had to be fixed at Q £33; R £39; S £70; T £49?
(c) Assuming production of 100 units of each item per accounting period, what would be the net profit (i) if your advice given in your answer to (b) was followed; (ii) if the firm continued to produce all of the items?
(d) What would you advise the company to do if, because of market competition, prices had to be fixed at Q £17; R £48; S £140; T £39?
(e) Assuming production of 100 units of each item per accounting period, what would be the net profit (i) if your advice given in your answer to (d) was followed; (ii) if the firm continued to produce all of the items?

34.14A Bottles Ltd makes six different products, F, G, H, I, J and K. An analysis of costs ascertains the following:

Per unit	F	G	H	I	J	K
	£	£	£	£	£	£
Direct labour and direct materials	15	17	38	49	62	114
Variable cost	6	11	10	21	22	23

Fixed costs of £11,400 are allocated per unit as F £4; G £7; H £7; I £10; J £16 and K £13. Using full-cost pricing 20 per cent is to be added per unit for profit.

You are required to:
(a) Calculate the prices that would be charged by Bottles Ltd if the full-cost pricing system was adhered to.
(b) What advice would you give the company if a survey of the market showed that the prices charged could be F £26; G £26; H £66; I £75; J £80; K £220?
(c) Assuming production of 200 units per period of each unit manufactured what would be the profit of the firm, (i) if your advice in (b) was followed, (ii) if the firm continued to produce all of the items?
(d) Suppose that in fact the market survey had revealed instead that the prices charged could be F £30; G £33; H £75; I £66; J £145 and K £130, then what would your advice have been to the company?
(e) Assuming that production of each item manufactured was 200 units per month, then what would have been the profit (i) if your advice in (d) had been followed, (ii) if the company chose to continue manufacturing all items?

34.15A
(a) What are the differences between marginal cost pricing and full cost pricing?
(b) How far is it true to state that marginal cost pricing is a short-term strategy?
(c) A.S. Teriod Ltd makes five different products – Ceres, Eros, Hermes, Icarus and Vesta. The various costs per unit of the products are respectively: direct labour, £14, £8, £22, £18 and £26; direct materials, £8, £10, £13, £12 and £17; variable overheads, £11, £9, £16, £15 and £19.

The fixed expenses for the month of February 20X1 are estimated at £8,200, and this has been allocated to the units produced as Ceres £17, Eros £13, Hermes £19, Icarus £15 and Vesta £18. The company adds 20 per cent on to the total cost of each product by way of profit.

(i) Calculate the prices based upon full cost pricing.
(ii) Advise the company on which products to produce, if competition forces the prices to: Ceres £59, Eros £25, Hermes £80, Icarus £44 and Vesta £92.
(iii) Assuming that output for the month amounts to 100 units of each model: that fixed costs remain the same irrespective of output and that unused capacity cannot be used for other products: calculate the profit or loss if the company continued to produce the whole range at the new prices; AND if the company followed your advice in (ii) above.

(*Edexcel: GCE A-level*)

CHAPTER 35

Job, batch and process costing

After you have studied this chapter, you should be able to:

- explain how indirect costs are apportioned among cost centres
- explain the difference between the accounting treatment of normal and abnormal losses
- explain the difference between scrap, by-products, and joint products
- discuss some of the issues relating to cost allocation between joint products
- describe the system of job costing
- describe the system of process costing
- explain the appropriate treatment for under- and overabsorbed overheads

Introduction

In this chapter you'll learn about the differences between costing for continuous processes and costing for short-term production runs or one-off production activity. You'll learn more about attributing costs to cost centres, in this case, indirect costs such as service centre costs. Finally, you'll learn about how to deal with costs and revenues relating to by-products and joint products.

35.1 Background

The earlier chapters on costing have been concerned mainly with the firm as a whole. You have seen the effects of marginal and absorption costing if applied to the firm, and you have seen the flow of costs through manufacturing and retail businesses. Now we have to consider the use of these concepts in the application of costing in firms. So far there has been a certain amount of simplification just so that the concepts could be seen without too much detail obscuring your view. For instance, it has been assumed in most of the *exhibits* that the firms have been making only one kind of product, and that there has really been only one cost centre. Without stretching your imagination greatly, you will realise that firms manufacture many different types of goods, and that there are many cost centres in most firms.

When looking at the costing systems in use it can be seen that they can usually be divided into two main types, (*a*) **job costing**, and (*b*) **process costing**. These two main types of costing system have either an absorption or marginal costing approach, they use FIFO or LIFO or AVCO methods of pricing issues etc.

It is important to realise that marginal costing is not a costing system; it is, instead, an approach to costing which is used when job or process costing systems are used. The same applies to absorption costing.

35.2   The choice of job costing or process costing

Process costing is relevant where production is regarded as a continuous flow, and would be applicable to industries where production is repetitive and continuous. One example would be an oil refinery where crude oil is processed continually, emerging as different grades of petrol, paraffin, motor oil, etc. Another instance would be a salt works where brine (salt water) is pumped into the works, and the product is slabs or packets of salt. Salt works and oil refineries will have a repetitive and continuous flow of production and would, therefore, use process costing.

Contrasted with this would be production which consisted of separate jobs for special orders which could be just one item or of a batch of items. For instance, where bodies of Rolls-Royce cars are made to each customer's specifications, each car can be regarded as a separate job. Compared with this would be a printer's business where books are printed, so that the printing of say 5,000 copies of a book can also be regarded as a job. The 'job' can thus be one item or a batch of similar items.

Two terms are used to describe this 'specific order' form of costing – 'job costing', when costs are to be attributed to an individual job (a customer order or task of relatively short duration); and **batch costing**, when costs are to be attributed to a specific batch of a product (a group of similar items which is treated as a separate cost unit – a unit of product or service in relation to which costs are ascertained).

In effect, the accounting treatment is the same. For our purposes, we shall focus in this chapter upon job costing. If you are asked to perform batch costing remember, the process is the same. (You will find that Question 35.9 at the end of this chapter is on batch costing.)

We can compare the two approaches by using diagrams of the different types of costing. These are shown as Exhibit 35.1.

Exhibit 35.1

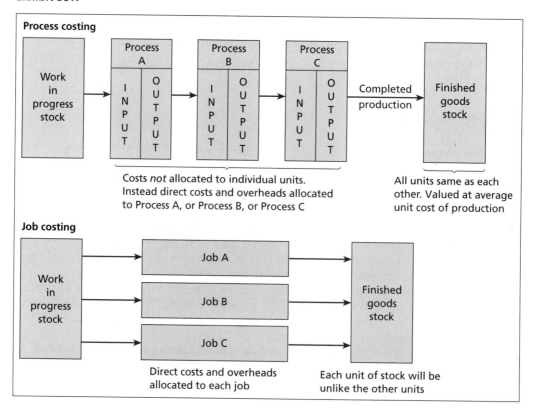

35.3 Job costing

Each job is given a separate job number, and direct materials and direct labour used on the job are charged to the job. The accumulation of the costs is done on a 'job cost sheet'. The materials will be charged to the job on the FIFO, LIFO, or AVCO basis. The direct labour costs will be found by recording the number of direct labour hours of each type of direct worker, and multiplying by the labour cost per hour for each type.

The job is thus the cost centre, and direct labour and direct materials can be charged direct to the cost centre. The indirect expenses cannot be charged direct to the job, such costs are charged instead to a service cost centre and the cost of the service centre is then apportioned between the various jobs to give the cost of each job including indirect expenses.

It is only after the accounting period is over that the exact costs of each service centre are known, but you will want to know how much each job costs as it is finished. You will not want to wait months to find out the cost of each job.

Activity 35.1
How do you think this is done?

Let's consider an example. Suppose there are three jobs being performed and these are in separate production departments, A, B and C. There are also two service centres, G and H. Some of the indirect labour expenses and other indirect expenses can be allocated direct to the production departments – for instance the wages of the foremen of each of departments A, B and C, or items such as lubricating materials if each department used quite different lubricants. Other indirect labour can be traced to the two centres G and H as well as expenses. The problem then is that of apportioning the costs of G and H between departments A, B and C. We can now look at Exhibit 35.2, and see what answer this firm came up with.

Exhibit 35.2

Indirect labour costs and other indirect expenses have been allocated to production departments A, B and C and service departments G and H as follows:

	Production departments			Service departments	
	A	B	C	G	H
Indirect labour	2,000	3,000	4,000	500	1,000
Other expenses	1,000	2,000	3,000	1,500	2,000
	3,000	5,000	7,000	2,000	3,000

The problem is to apportion the costs of G and H to the production departments. G was a department which maintained factory buildings while H maintained factory machinery.

A study of the costs of G produced a very easy answer. There was no doubt that the costs were in direct relationship to the floor space occupied by each department. But it must not be overlooked that department H also needed the attention of G's workforce so that part of the costs of G would have to be apportioned to H.

These costs would then increase the total of costs of department H which would then need apportioning to the production departments. Floor space in square feet was A 2,000, B 4,000, C 3,000 and H 1,000. The £2,000 costs of department G were therefore apportioned:

$$\text{Each department: } \frac{\text{Its floor space}}{\text{Total floor space}} \times £2,000$$

Therefore:

A $\dfrac{2,000}{10,000} \times £2,000 = £400$ B $\dfrac{4,000}{10,000} \times £2,000 = £800$

C $\dfrac{3,000}{10,000} \times £2,000 = £600$ H $\dfrac{1,000}{10,000} \times £2,000 = £200$

(Department H's costs have now increased by £200 and become £3,200.)

Department H's costs presented a far more difficult problem. Consideration was given to apportionment based on numbers of machines, volumes of production and types of machinery. It was, however, felt that there was a high relationship in this case (although this would certainly not always be true in other firms) between the values of machinery in use and the costs of maintaining them. The more costly equipment was very complicated and needed a lot of attention. Consequently it was decided to apportion H's costs between A, B and C on the basis of the value of machinery in each department. This was found to be A £3,000; B £6,000; C £7,000. The costs were therefore apportioned:

$$\frac{\text{Value of machinery in department}}{\text{Total value of machinery in all 3 departments}} \times £3,200$$

Therefore:

A $\frac{3,000}{16,000} \times £3,200 = £600$ B $\frac{6,000}{16,000} \times £3,200 = £1,200$

C $\frac{7,000}{16,000} \times £3,200 = £1,400$

The costs and their apportionment can, therefore, be shown:

	Production departments			Service departments	
	A	B	C	G	H
Indirect labour	2,000	3,000	4,000	500	1,000
Other expenses	1,000	2,000	3,000	1,500	2,000
	3,000	5,000	7,000	2,000	3,000
Department G's costs apportioned	400	800	600	(2,000)	200
					3,200
Department H's costs apportioned	600	1,200	1,400		(3,200)
	4,000	7,000	9,000	–	–

This continuous method of apportioning service department overheads is sometimes called the **repeated distribution method**. (See Question 35.7 for a discussion of this and another method, the elimination method.)

We have now identified the estimated overhead for each department for the ensuing accounting period. We now have another problem – how the overhead is going to be taken into the calculation of the cost of each job in these departments.

After investigation, the conclusion is that in departments A and B there is a direct relationship between direct labour hours and overhead but, in department C, the guiding factor is machine hours.

If the total overheads of departments A and B are divided by the estimated number of direct labour hours this will give the overhead rate per direct labour hour, while in department C, the total overhead will be divided by the estimated machine hours. The calculation of the overhead rates are therefore:

	Production departments		
	A	B	C
Direct labour hours	5,000	4,000	
Machine hours			6,000
Overhead rate per direct labour hour	$\frac{£4,000}{5,000}$	$\frac{£7,000}{4,000}$	
	= £0.8	= £1.75	
Overhead rate per machine hour			$\frac{£9,000}{6,000}$
			= £1.5

We can now calculate the costs of four jobs performed in this factory:

Department A
Job A/70/144   Started 1.7.20X2. Completed 13.7.20X2
Cost of direct materials £130
Number of direct labour hours 100
Cost rate of direct labour per hour £0.9

Department B
Job B/96/121   Started 4.7.20X2. Completed 9.7.20X2
Cost of direct materials £89
Number of direct labour hours 40
Cost rate of direct labour per hour £1.1

Department C
Job C/67/198   Started 8.7.20X2. Completed 16.7.20X2
Cost of direct materials £58
Number of direct labour hours 50
Cost rate of direct labour per hour £1.0
Number of machine hours 40

Departments A and C
Job AC/45/34   Started in A 3.7.20X2. Passed on to C 11.7.20X2. Completed in C 16.7.20X2
Cost of materials £115
Number of direct labour hours (in Dept A) 80
Number of direct labour hours (in Dept C) 90
Cost rate per direct labour hour Dept A £0.9
                                  Dept C £1.0
Number of machine hours, Dept C 70

The job cost sheets for these four jobs are shown below. At no point during this Exhibit has it been stated whether a marginal costing or an absorption costing approach has been adopted. If an absorption costing approach had been used, overhead would include both fixed and variable overhead. If a marginal costing approach had been used, the overhead brought into the calculations of job costs would exclude fixed overhead, so that the overhead rate would be a variable overhead rate.

Job Cost Sheet. Job No. A/70/144			
Started 1.7.20X2		Completed 13.7.20X2	
	Hours	*Rates £*	*£*
Materials			130
Direct labour	100	0.9	90
Factory overhead	100	0.8	80
Total job cost			300

Job Cost Sheet. Job No. B/96/121			
Started 4.7.20X2		Completed 9.7.20X2	
	Hours	*Rates £*	*£*
Materials			89
Direct labour	40	1.1	44
Factory overhead	40	1.75	70
Total job cost			203

Job Cost Sheet. Job No. C/67/198			
Started 8.7.20X2		Completed 16.7.20X2	
	Hours	*Rates £*	*£*
Materials			58
Direct labour	50	1.0	50
Factory overhead	40	1.5	60
Total job cost			168

```
                         Job Cost Sheet. Job No. AC/45/34
Started 3.7.20X2                                       Completed 16.7.20X2
                                              Hours      Rates £        £
Materials                                                              115

Direct labour (Dept A)                          80        0.9          72
Direct labour (Dept C)                          90        1.0          90
Factory overhead (Dept A)                       80        0.8          64
Factory overhead (Dept C)                       70        1.5         105
Total job cost                                                        446
```

35.4 Cost centres – job costing and responsibility

It must be pointed out that a cost centre for job costing is not necessarily the same as tracing the costs down to the individual who is responsible for controlling them. There are two requirements here: (*a*) finding the cost of a job to check on its profitability and (*b*) controlling the costs by making someone responsible for them so that he/she will have to answer for any variations from planned results. Many firms therefore keep separate records of costs to fulfil each of these functions.

35.5 Process costing

Job costing treats production as a number of separate jobs being performed, whereas process costing sees production as a continuous flow. In process costing there is correspondingly no attempt to allocate costs to specific units being produced.

There is, however, usually more than one process in the manufacture of goods. We can take as an example a bakery producing cakes. There are three processes: (*A*) the mixing of the cake ingredients, (*B*) the baking of the cakes, and (*C*) the packaging of the cakes. Each process is treated as a cost centre.

Therefore, costs for (*A*), (*B*) and (*C*) are collected separately. Overhead rates are then calculated for each cost centre in a similar fashion to that in job costing.

In the case of the bakery, each accounting period would probably start and finish without any half-mixed or half-baked cakes, but some types of firms which use process costing have processes which take rather longer to complete than baking cakes. A typical case would be the brewing of beer. At the beginning and end of each period there would be partly processed units. It is a matter of arithmetic to convert production into 'equivalent units produced' (which is also known as **equivalent production**). For instance, production during a particular period may be as in Exhibit 35.3.

Exhibit 35.3

Started in previous year $3/4$ completed then, and $1/4$ completed in current period, 400 units, $400 \times 1/4$	100
Started and completed in current period	680
Started in current period and $1/8$ completed by end of period, 160 units, $160 \times 1/8$	20
Equivalent production	800 units

If the total costs of the cost centre amounted to £4,000 then the unit cost would be:

$$\frac{£4,000}{800} = £5$$

In fact, process costing can become very complicated because some of the part-produced items are complete in terms of, say, materials, but incomplete in terms of labour, or else say $^2/_3$ complete for materials and $^1/_4$ complete for labour. Although the situation becomes complicated, the principles are no different from those described for calculating equivalent production.

We can now look at an example of process costing in Exhibit 35.4. So that we do not get involved in too many arithmetical complications, we will assume that there are no partly completed goods in each process at the start and end of the period considered.

Exhibit 35.4

A bakery making cakes has three processes, process (A) the mixing of the cake ingredients, (B) the baking of the cakes, and (C) the packaging of the cakes.

January activity was as follows:

	£
Materials used:	
Process (A)	4,000
Process (B)	–
Process (C)	1,000
Direct labour:	
Process (A)	1,500
Process (B)	500
Process (C)	800
Factory overhead:	
Variable:	
Process (A)	400
Process (B)	1,300
Process (C)	700
Fixed: (allocated to processes)	
Process (A)	600
Process (B)	500
Process (C)	400

During January 100,000 cakes were made. The process cost accounts will appear as:

Process (A)

	£		£
Materials	4,000	Transferred to process (B)	
Direct labour	1,500	100,000 units at £0.065	6,500
Variable overhead	400		
Fixed overhead	600		
	6,500		6,500

Process (B)

	£		£
Transferred from process (A)		Transferred to process (C)	
100,000 units at £0.065	6,500	100,000 units at £0.088	8,800
Direct labour	500		
Variable overhead	1,300		
Fixed overhead	500		
	8,800		8,800

Process (C)

	£		£
Transferred from process (B)		Transferred to finished goods stock	
100,000 units at £0.088	8,800	100,000 units at £0.117	11,700
Materials	1,000		
Direct labour	800		
Variable overhead	700		
Fixed overhead	400		
	11,700		11,700

35.6 Normal and abnormal losses

There are some losses that are basically part of the production process and cannot be eliminated. For instance, when printing books, losses occur in the cutting of paper; when brewing beer there will be losses due to evaporation, when cutting steel there will be losses. These losses are inevitable, even in the most efficient firms, and as such they are called **normal or uncontrollable losses.**

On the other hand, there are losses which should be avoided if there are efficient operating conditions. Such things as the incorrect cutting of cloth so that it is wasted unnecessarily, not mixing ingredients properly so that some of the product is unusable, and the use of inferior materials so that much of the product cannot pass production tests and is wasted. These are **abnormal or controllable losses.**

The accounting treatment varies between these two sorts of losses:

- **Normal losses.** These are not transferred from the process account but are treated as part of the process costs.
- **Abnormal losses.** These are transferred from out of the process account to an abnormal loss account. The double entry is:

Dr Abnormal loss account
Cr Process account

The abnormal loss is then treated as a period cost.

> ### Activity 35.2
> How do you think this is done?

35.7 Under/overabsorption of overheads

When an overhead rate is based on estimated annual overhead expenditure and estimated activity, it would be very rare for it to be exactly the same as the actual overhead incurred. Either the costs themselves will have changed, or the activity, or both.

If £300,000 has been allocated to the year's production, but actual costs were £298,000 then too much has been allocated. In other words, it is a case of overabsorption of overheads amounting to £2,000.

If, on the other hand, £305,000 had been allocated, but the actual costs were £311,000 then too little has been allocated. This is an underabsorption of overheads amounting to £6,000.

At the closing balance sheet date, the stock-in-trade has been valued and this will include something for overheads. In the case of an underabsorption the question arises as to whether the closing stock valuation should be amended to include something for the underabsorbed overheads. **The accounting answer is that no adjustment should be made to the stock valuation.** Similarly the stock valuation should not be reduced to take account of over-absorption of overheads.

Exhibit 35.5 shows how the costs should be treated.

Exhibit 35.5

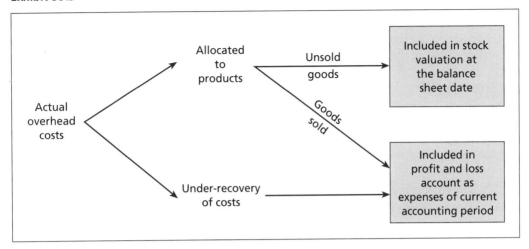

35.8   Other kinds of firm

Process costing is found most often in industries such as oil, canning, paint manufacture, steel, textiles and food processing.

35.9   The problem of joint costs

A manufacturing operation often results in one simple product being produced. Any excess output other than the product is regarded as scrap, and the small cost that could be traced to it is ignored. For example, in the manufacture of a suit, when the cost is traced to the suit, the small unusable bits of cloth that are left over are ignored.

This is not always the case, and **where a group of separate products is produced simultaneously, each of the products having relatively substantial sales values, then the products are called 'joint products'**. Thus, crude oil taken into an oil refinery is processed and the output is in terms of different grades of petrol, paraffin, motor oil, etc. This means that in costing terms the costs of the materials and processes, etc. have to be split between the joint products.

Many problems exist in this area. Perhaps you will see why when the problem of allocating costs between joint products is concerned with the cutting up of a cow for beef. From a cow there is rump steak, the fillet steaks, the T-bone steaks, sirloin, silverside, brisket, etc. If the cow costs the butcher £300, then how would you allocate the cost between all of these various joint products? This gives you some idea of the problem which exists – in many industries this becomes involved with complex technological problems.

> **Activity 35.3**
> How do you think this is done?

In fact, you could allocate the costs on any basis and none would be indisputably 'correct'. With joint products, there is no rational reason or basis for splitting their costs that cannot be argued against.

Sometimes, a minor (i.e. much lower value) but, nevertheless, distinguishable product is produced at the same time as the main product. One example is the sawdust that is created when wood is being converted into furniture. Such a product is known as a **by-product**. One way of dealing with the costs involved is to ignore them and simply credit any income derived from sale of the by-product against the cost of producing the main product.

Learning outcomes

You should now have learnt:

1 That neither marginal costing nor absorption costing are costing 'systems'; rather, they are approaches to costing which are used when job or processing costing systems are used.

2 The differences between job (and batch) costing and process costing.

3 That direct costs can be allocated directly to the relevant cost centre. However, indirect costs have to be apportioned among cost centres on an appropriate basis, as there is no way of knowing precisely how much indirect cost was incurred on each item produced.

4 How indirect costs can be apportioned across cost centres.

5 How to deal with normal and abnormal losses.

6 About the problems relating to cost allocation between joint products.

Answers to activities

35.1 This is solved by estimating the indirect expenses, and then fixing the method of apportioning these estimated expenses.

35.2 It is written off to the debit of the profit and loss account at the end of the period.

35.3 Among the obvious choices, you could allocate the joint costs on the basis of the sale price of each of the joint products, or on the basis of the relative weight or volume of the joint products.

REVIEW QUESTIONS

Advice: Questions on job and process costing are usually fairly easy to answer and it is also relatively simple to gain quite high marks by tackling them.

35.1 In a firm there are four types of jobs performed in separate production departments A, B, C and D. In addition there are three service departments, K, L and M. Costs have been allocated to the departments as follows:

	Production departments				Service departments		
	A	B	C	D	K	L	M
	£	£	£	£	£	£	£
Indirect labour	4,000	6,000	8,000	2,000	1,500	3,000	4,100
Other expenses	2,700	3,100	3,600	1,500	4,500	2,000	2,000

The expenses of the service departments are to be allocated between other departments as follows:

Dept K to Depts A 25 per cent: B 30 per cent: C 20 per cent: D 10 per cent: M 15 per cent.
Dept L to Depts A 60 per cent: C 30 per cent: D 10 per cent.
Dept M to Depts B 30 per cent: C 50 per cent: D 20 per cent.

In departments A and C the job costing is to use an overhead rate per direct labour hour, while in B and D a machine hour rate will be used. The number of direct hours and machine hours per department is expected to be:

	A	B	C	D
Direct labour hours	2,000	4,000	4,450	2,700
Machine hours	1,900	2,600	2,900	2,400

You are required to calculate:
(a) The overhead rates for departments A and C.
(b) The overhead rates for departments B and D.

(Keep your answer – it will be used as a basis for the next question.)

35.2 In the firm mentioned in Question 35.1, what would be the costs of the following jobs given that the direct labour costs per hour are: Dept A £2.1; B £1.7; C £2.4; D £2.3?

Job 351: Dept A	Direct materials cost	£190
	Number of direct labour hours	56
	Number of machine hours	40
Job 352: Dept B	Direct materials cost	£1,199
	Number of direct labour hours	178
	Number of machine hours	176
Job 353: Dept C	Direct materials cost	£500
	Number of direct labour hours	130
	Number of machine hours	100
Job 354: Dept D	Direct materials cost	£666
	Number of direct labour hours	90
	Number of machine hours	64
Job 355: Dept C	Direct materials cost	£560
	Number of direct labour hours	160
	Number of machine hours	150
	Job passed on to Dept B where additional direct materials cost	£68
	Number of direct labour hours	30
	Number of machine hours	20

35.3A In a firm there are five types of job performed in separate production departments P, Q, R, S and T. In addition there are two service departments F and G. Costs have been allocated to the departments as follows:

	Production departments				Service departments		
	P	Q	R	S	T	F	G
	£	£	£	£	£	£	£
Indirect labour	5,000	7,000	3,000	6,000	8,000	10,000	9,000
Other expenses	500	1,800	1,000	1,200	1,300	6,000	7,000

The expenses of the service departments are to be allocated between other departments as follows:

Dept F to Depts P 10 per cent; Q 20 per cent; S 30 per cent; T 15 per cent; G 25 per cent.
Dept G to Depts P 12.5 per cent; Q 20 per cent; R 25 per cent; S 30 per cent; T 12.5 per cent.

In departments R and T the job costing is to use an overhead rate per direct labour hour, while in the other production departments a machine hour rate will be used. The number of direct labour hours and machine hours per department are expected to be:

	P	Q	R	S	T
Direct labour hours	4,000	5,000	3,600	10,000	3,550
Machine hours	3,000	4,000	3,000	8,000	2,800

You are required to calculate:
(a) The overhead rates for departments R and T.
(b) The overhead rates for departments P, Q and S.

(Keep your answer – it will be used for Question 35.4A.)

35.4A In the firm mentioned in Question 35.3A, what would be the costs of the following jobs, given that the direct labour rate per hour is Dept P £1.9; Q £2.5; R £2.0; S £2.7; T £2.4?

Job 701: Dept R	Direct materials cost	£115
	Number of direct labour hours	35
	Number of machine hours	29
Job 702: Dept T	Direct materials cost	£1,656
	Number of direct labour hours	180
	Number of machine hours	160
Job 703: Dept P	Direct materials cost	£546
	Number of direct labour hours	100
	Number of machine hours	90
Job 704: Dept S	Direct materials cost	£65
	Number of direct labour hours	250
	Number of machine hours	60
Job 705: Dept Q	Direct materials cost	£4,778
	Number of direct labour hours	305
	Number of machine hours	280
Job 706: Dept P	Direct materials cost	£555
	Number of direct labour hours	200
	Number of machine hours	180
	Then passed to Dept T for completion where direct materials cost	£11
	Number of direct labour hours	18
	Number of machine hours	2

35.5
(a) Define the term *equivalent production* and state when the principle is used.
(b) During May 20X1, M Wurzel & Co. Limited's output was 4,000 finished items plus 600 partly finished items. There was no work in progress on 1 May 20X1.

	Materials	Labour	Overheads	Total
Total cost (£)	8,172	7,120	5,196	20,488
WIP degree of completion %	90	75	55	–

Calculate for the month of May 20X1:
(i) the total equivalent production for each cost element;
(ii) the cost per complete unit;
(iii) the value of the work in progress.

(*Edexcel: GCE A-level*)

35.6A
(a) What is meant by the term *equivalent production*?
(b) At Earith Industries at the beginning of April there were no partially finished goods on hand. During the month, 6,000 completed units were produced, together with 800 units partially completed. Details of the partially finished items were:

	Total cost (£)	Percentage completed
Materials	12,540	75
Labour	8,476	65
Overheads	7,084	55

Calculate:
(*i*)   the total equivalent production,
(*ii*)   the cost per complete unit,
(*iii*)   the total value of work in progress.

(*Edexcel: GCE A-level*)

35.7
(a) Explain the difference between the terms *overhead allotment*, *overhead apportionment* and *overhead absorption*.
(b) Why are *estimated* figures used in calculating overhead absorption rates?
(c) The following information relates to the Flyby Knight Plc for the six months ended 31 December 20X1:

	Production Departments			Service Departments	
	A	B	C	X	Y
Overheads (£)	14,000	12,000	8,000	4,000	3,000
Overheads to be apportioned:					
Dept X (%)	35	30	20	–	15
Dept Y (%)	30	40	25	5	–

(*i*)   Use the continuous apportionment (repeated distribution) method to apportion the service departments' overheads between each other.
(*ii*)   Apportion the service departments' overheads calculated in (*i*) to the production departments.
(*iii*)   Show how the overheads apportioned to the production departments would have differed if the elimination method had been used for the service departments.
(*iv*)   State how far it is true to say that the elimination method produces an inaccurate answer, and is therefore not to be recommended.

(*Edexcel: GCE A-level*)

35.8A   Kalmo Ltd offers a subcontracting service in assembly, painting and packing. Components are supplied by customers to the company, the required operations are then carried out, and the completed work returned to the customer. The company is labour intensive, with only a relatively small amount of materials purchased.
   Currently, one factory overhead recovery rate is used which is a percentage of total direct labour costs. This is calculated from the following budgeted costs.

Department	Direct labour costs	Direct labour hours	Machine hours	Factory overheads
	£			£
Assembly	450,000	150,000	6,000	180,000
Painting	500,000	140,625	–	225,000
Packing	250,000	100,000	8,000	75,000

The cost sheet for Job 131190 shows the following information:

Department	Direct labour costs	Direct labour hours	Machine hours	Direct material costs
	£			£
Assembly	2,500	1,000	120	100
Painting	2,200	900	–	400
Packing	4,800	960	80	500

General administration expenses of 20 per cent are added to the total factory costs, and then a further 25 per cent of the total cost is added as profit, to arrive at the selling price.
   Although the company has been using the blanket factory overhead recovery rate for a number of years, one of the directors has questioned this method, and asks if it would be possible to apply overhead recovery rates for each department.

Required:

(a) Calculate the current factory overhead recovery rate, and apply this to arrive at the selling price for Job 131190.

(b) In line with the director's comments, calculate overhead recovery rates for each department, using two alternative methods, and apply both to arrive at new selling prices for Job 131190.

(c) Briefly evaluate the methods you have used for the recovery of factory overheads, justifying which one you consider to be most appropriate.

(d) Outline how an unsatisfactory method of overhead absorption can affect the profits of a business.

(Reproduced with the kind permission of OCR (from *University of Oxford Delegacy of Local Examinations*): *GCE A-level*)

35.9

(a) What is meant by the term 'specific order costing'?

(b) In what ways does specific order costing differ from process costing?

(c) The Acme Shelving Co. Ltd manufactures shelving brackets in batches of 300. During May, Batch No. 23 was machined at a rate of 15 per hour. Sixty of the brackets failed to pass inspection, but of these, 40 were thought to be rectifiable. The remaining 20 were scrapped, and the scrap value was credited to the batch cost account. Rectification work took nine hours.

Batch No. 23

	£
Raw materials per bracket	1.60
Scrap value per bracket	0.86
Machinists' hourly rate	4.20
Machine hour overhead rate	3.60
(running time only)	
Setting up of machine: normal machining	21.00
rectification	18.00

Calculate:

(i) the cost of Batch No. 23 in total and per unit, if all units pass inspection;

(ii) the *actual* cost of Batch No. 23, in total and per unit, after crediting the recovery value of the scrapped components, and including the rectification costs;

(iii) the loss incurred because of defective work.

(*Edexcel: GCE A-level*)

35.10A Horden Products Ltd manufactures goods which could involve any or all of three production departments. These departments are simply entitled **A**, **B** and **C**. A direct wages cost percentage absorption rate for the recovery of production overheads is applied to individual job costs.

Details from the company's budgets for the year ended 31 March 20X5 are as follows:

	Dept A	Dept B	Dept C
Indirect materials	£23,000	£35,000	£57,000
Indirect wages	£21,000	£34,000	£55,000
Direct wages	£140,000	£200,000	£125,000
Direct labour hours	25,000	50,000	60,000
Machine hours	100,000	40,000	10,000

The following information is also available for the production departments:

	Dept A	Dept B	Dept C
Area (square metres)	30,000	20,000	10,000
Cost of machinery	£220,000	£160,000	£20,000
Horse power of machinery	55	30	15

	£
Other budgeted figures are:	
Power	120,000
Rent, rates, light, heat	90,000
Insurance (machinery)	20,000
Depreciation	80,000

Machinery is depreciated on the basis of 20% on cost.

Job No. 347 passed through all three departments and incurred the following actual direct costs and times:

	Direct material £	Direct wages £	Direct labour hours £	Machine hours £
Dept A	152	88	35	60
Dept B	85	192	90	30
Dept C	52	105	45	10

A sum amounting to 30% of the production cost is added to every job to enable a selling price to be quoted.

Required:

(a) A statement to show the total production overheads per department and calculate the absorption rate which the company has adopted.

(b) Calculate the selling price to be quoted for Job No. 347.

(c) Using the available data, calculate absorption rates when based on:
    (i) direct labour hour rate;
    (ii) machine hour rate.

(d) Explain clearly the meaning of the following terms relating to overheads:
    (i) allotment;
    (ii) allocation;
    (iii) apportionment.

(AQA (Associated Examining Board): GCE A-level)

35.11A

(a) Explain the following terms as used in process costing:
    (i) normal losses
    (ii) abnormal losses
    (iii) equivalent production
    (iv) joint cost
    (v) split-off point.

(b) In process costing, it is neither the technology nor the costs incurred, but the market price of the item, which determines whether an item is classed as:
    (i) scrap or waste; and
    (ii) a joint product or a by-product.

    How far do you agree?

(Edexcel: GCE A-level)

PART 7

Budgets

Introduction

This part looks at how management can institute a system to support planning, evaluation and control through the use of budgets.

CHAPTER 36

Budgeting and budgetary control

Learning objectives

After you have studied this chapter, you should be able to:
- describe the budgetary process
- explain the importance of budgets for planning and control
- explain how to apply the economic order quantity approach to stock control

Introduction

In this chapter you'll learn about the need for budgeting, how production budgets can be set, both when production is to be at a constant level and when it is to vary according to demand. You will also learn about how to plan when to order new supplies and about alternatives to traditional methods of ensuring that sufficient raw materials and bought-in goods for resale are available for production and for sale when required.

36.1 Background

In Chapters 32 and 33 you learnt that management control is needed to try to ensure that organisations achieve their objectives. Once the objectives have been agreed, plans should be drawn up so that the progress of the organisation can be directed towards the ends specified in the objectives.

It must not be thought that plans can be expressed only in accounting terms. For example, quality of the product might be best shown in engineering terms, or social objectives shown in a plan concerned with employee welfare. But some of the objectives, such as the attainment of a desired profit, or of the attainment of a desired growth in assets can be expressed in accounting terms.

When a plan is expressed quantitatively it is known as a **budget** and the process of converting plans into budgets is known as **budgeting**. In this book, we are concerned primarily with budgets shown in monetary terms, i.e. financial budgets.

The budgeting process may be quite formal in a large organisation with committees set up to perform the task. On the other hand, in a very small organisation the owner may jot down his budget on a piece of scrap-paper or the back of a used envelope. Some even manage without writing anything down at all, they have done the budgets in their heads and can easily remember them. This book is concerned with budgeting in a formal manner.

36.2 Budgets and people

Probably in no other part of accounting is there a greater need for understanding other people than in the processes of budgeting. Budgets are prepared in order to try to guide the

firm towards its objectives. There is no doubt that some budgets that are drawn up are even more harmful to a firm than if none were drawn up at all.

> ### Activity 36.1
> What does this last statement remind you of from earlier chapters?

Budgets are drawn up for control purposes, that is, as an attempt to control the direction that the firm is taking. Many people, however, look upon them, not as a guide, but as a straitjacket. We can look at a few undesirable actions that can result from people regarding budgets as a straitjacket rather than as a guide.

1 The sales manager refuses to let a salesman go to Sweden in response to an urgent and unexpected request from a Swedish firm. The reason: the overseas sales expenses budget has already been spent. The result: the most profitable order that the firm would have received for many years is taken up instead by another firm.

2 The works manager turns down requests for overtime work because the budgeted overtime has already been exceeded. The result: the job is not completed on time, and the firm has to pay a large sum under a penalty clause in the contract which stated that if the job was not finished by a certain date then a penalty of £20,000 would become payable.

3 Towards the end of the accounting period a manager realises that he has not spent all of his budget for a particular item. He then launches on a spending spree, completely unnecessary items being bought on the basis that 'If I don't spend this amount this year they will cut down next year when I will really need the money.' The result: a lot of unusable and unnecessary equipment.

4 The education budget has been spent, therefore the education manager will not let anyone go on courses for the rest of the year. The result: the firm starts to fall behind in an industry which is highly technical, the staff concerned become fed up, and the better ones start to look for jobs in other firms which are more responsive to the need to allow personnel to keep in touch with changing technology.

Studies have shown that the more that managers are brought into the budgeting process, then the more successful budgetary control is likely to be. A manager on whom a budget is imposed, rather than a manager who had an active part in the drafting of his budget, is more likely to pay less attention to the budget and use it unwisely in the control process.

Having sounded the warning that needs to be borne in mind constantly when budgeting, we can now look at the positive end of budgeting – to see the advantages of a good budgetary control system.

36.3 Budgets, planning and control

The methodology of budgetary control is probably accountancy's major contribution to management. Before we get down to the mechanics of constructing budgets we should first of all look at the main outlines of drafting budgets.

When the budgets are being drawn up the two main objectives must be uppermost in the mind of top management, that is that the budgets are for:

1 **Planning.** This means a properly co-ordinated and comprehensive plan for the whole business. Each part must interlock with the other parts.

2 **Control.** Just because a plan is set down on paper does not mean that the plan will carry itself out. Control is exercised via the budgets, thus the name 'budgetary control'. To do this means that the responsibility of managers and budgets must be so linked that the

responsible manager is given a guide to help him to produce certain desired results, and the actual achieved results can be compared against the expected, i.e. actual compared with budget.

36.4 Preparation of estimates

The first thing to establish is what the limiting factors are in a firm. It may well be that sales cannot be pushed above a certain amount, or it might be that the firm could sell as much as it can produce, but the productive capacity of the firm sets a limit. Whatever the limiting factor, there is no doubt that this aspect of the firm will need more attention than probably any other. There would not, for instance, be much point in budgeting for the sale of 1,000 units a year if production could not manufacture more that 700, or to manufacture 2,000 a year if only 1,300 of them could be sold.

There is no doubt that usually the most difficult estimate to make is that of sales revenue. This can be done by using one of two methods:

1 Make a statistical forecast on the basis of the economic conditions applying with reference to the goods sold by the company, and what is known about the actions of competitors.
2 The opposite is to make an internal forecast. This is usually done by asking each salesperson, or group of salespeople, to estimate the sales in their own areas, and then total the estimates. Sometimes, however, they are not asked at all.

Now we should remember that much of the subject matter that you have read about, or are currently reading, in economics is very relevant here. A knowledge of elasticity of demand, whether the product is a complementary product, e.g. the price of egg-cups is linked to the demand for eggs, or whether it is a substitute, e.g. that a rise in the price of butter may induce consumers to turn to other commodities instead, is very relevant in this area. Factors such as whether the firm has a monopoly, whether the firm has many small customers, a few large customers, or even one large customer, are of crucial importance. Estimating sales revenue is very much a matter of taking all the economic factors into account allied to other factors.

The sales budget is, however, more than just a sales forecast. Budgets should show the actions that management is taking to influence future events. If an increase in sales is desired, the sales budget may show extra sales, which may well be an indication of the action that management is going to take by means of extra television advertising, making a better product, or giving retailers better profit margins and pushing up sales in that way.

36.5 The production budget

The production budget stems from the sales budget, but the first question that has to be settled is that of the level of the stock of finished goods which will be held by the firm.

If sales are even over the year, then production can also be in keeping with the sales figure, and the stock figure can remain constant. Suppose that the firm sells 50 units every month, then the firm can produce 50 units per month. In almost every firm, a stock level will have to be maintained, the amount of stock being dependent on factors such as amount of storage space, the estimated amount needed to cater for breakdowns in production or for delays in receiving raw materials, etc. Nonetheless, if the stock level was to be a minimum of 70 units it would still mean that production was at the rate of 50 units per month.

On the other hand sales may not be constant. Sales may average 50 units per month, but the figures may well be as follows:

January	20 units	February	30 units	March	60 units
April	80 units	May	70 units	June	40 units

This would mean that if production levels were kept at 50 units per month, there would be a shortage of 10 units in November – when 70 were demanded but only 60 were available for sale (10 left over from October plus 50 produced in November). An extra 10 units would need to be held to cover this shortfall. If production each month is to be the same, 10 units would need to be held at the beginning of the year.

Any calculation of minimum stock levels must include these 10 units. For example, if minimum stock of 100 is required, stock at the beginning of the year would need to be 110 units.

However, instead of producing the same number of units each month, the monthly production could be set to equal the sales figures. If a minimum stock level of 100 units is required, the number of units held at the beginning of the year would then be 100.

We can now compare the two levels of production in Sections 36.6 and 36.7.

36.6 Even production flow

The problem here is to find the stock level that the firm would need on 1 January if (a) sales are as shown, (b) the stock must not fall below 100 units, (c) production is to be 50 units per month. It can be found by trial and error. For instance, if you decided to see what would happen if the firm started off with 100 units in stock at 1 January, you would find that, after adding production and deducting sales each month, the stock level would fall to 90 units in May. As 100 units of stock is the minimum needed you would need to start off on 1 January with 110 units. The method is that if you start off your calculation with an estimated figure of stock, which must at least be the minimum figure required, then if you find that the lowest figure of stock shown during the period is 10 units less than the minimum stock required, go back and add 10 units to the stock to be held on 1 January. If the lowest figure is 30 units less than required add 30 units to the 1 January stock, and so on. We can now look at the figures in Exhibit 36.1.

Exhibit 36.1

Units	January	February	March	April	May	June
Opening stock	110	140	160	150	120	100
Add Units produced	50	50	50	50	50	50
	160	190	210	200	170	150
Less Sales	(20)	(30)	(60)	(80)	(70)	(40)
Closing stock	140	160	150	120	100	110

Activity 36.2

Sales are expected to be: January 70, February 40, March 50, April 120, May 140 and June 70. The stock level must not fall below 120 units, which is the level at the end of May, and an even production flow of 80 units is required. What stock level would there have to be on 1 January?

It is more important in many firms to ensure a smooth production flow than to bother unduly about stock levels, assuming that the minimum stock level is always attained. If the work is skilled, the labour force may take several years to become trained, and skilled labour in many industries does not take kindly to being sacked and re-employed as the demand for the goods fluctuates. This is not always true with skilled labour. For instance, in the building industry, such craftsmen as bricklayers may go to a builder until they have completed a contract such as building a college, a hospital or a housing estate, and then leave and look for another employer.

On the other hand, a skilled engineer concerned with the manufacture of, say, diesel engines would not expect to be fired and re-employed continuously. The bricklayer has a skill that is easily transferable to many other building employers in an area, whereas the diesel engineer may have only one firm within fifty miles of her home where she can perform her skills properly. A person employed as a labourer might work on a building site in one part of the year and then transfer to an engineering factory as a labourer in another part of the year.

Whether a firm could carry on production with widely uneven production levels depends so much on the type of firm and the type of labour involved. A firm would only sack skilled labour which it needed again shortly if it could persuade the men or women to come back when required. If the people who had been sacked were likely to find other employment, and not return to the firm when required, then this would mean that the firm would probably keep them on its payroll and production would continue and stocks of finished goods would begin to pile up.

Many firms do, in fact, realise their social obligations by only laying off workers when no other alternative is at all reasonable. In some organisations there are probably more workers from time to time than the firm actually needs – this is known as 'organisational slack', so that there is a leeway between the increasing of production and having to take on extra workers.

36.7 Uneven production levels

Some firms, by their very nature, will have uneven production levels, and this will be accepted by their labour force. An ice-cream firm would find its sales at their highest levels in summer, tailing off in winter. It is not really possible to build up stocks of ice-cream very much in the winter for summer sales. Even if it could be done, the costs of refrigerating large quantities of ice-cream for several months could hardly be economical. The large labour force used in the summer months will probably include quite a few students occupying their vacation periods profitably, and not able anyway to work at the job all the year round, even if they wanted to. Such a kind of firm will normally have a far greater relationship between current stock levels and current sales than a firm which has even production levels.

The calculation of the quantity to be produced is then:

$$\text{Sales} - \text{Opening stock} + \text{Closing stock} = \text{Production}$$

This can also be stated as:

$$\text{Opening stock} + \text{Units produced} - \text{Sales} = \text{Closing stock}$$

This means that if the opening stock will be 80 units, the sales are expected to be 100 units and the desired closing stock is 50 units the quantity to be produced becomes:

	Units
	Units
Opening stock	80
Add Production	?
	?
Less Sales	(100)
Closing stock	50

Production will, therefore, be the missing figure, i.e. 70 units (80 + production 70 = 150 for sale less actually sold 100 = closing stock 50).

Exhibit 36.2 shows the units to be produced if the following information is known: stock required 1 January 40, at end of each month, January 60, February 110, March 170, April 100, May 60, June 20. Sales are expected to be January 100, February 150, March 110, April 190, May 70, June 50.

Exhibit 36.2

Units	January	February	March	April	May	June
Opening stock	40	60	110	170	100	60
Production required (?)	120	200	170	120	30	10
	160	260	280	290	130	70
Less Sales	(100)	(150)	(110)	(190)	(70)	(50)
Closing stock	60	110	170	100	60	20

Linked with the production budget will be a materials purchase budget. It may well be that an order will have to be placed in January, received in March and issued to production in April. The purchase of materials will have to be planned as scientifically as possible.

Activity 36.3

What is the relationship between the sales budget, the production budget and the materials purchase budget?

36.8 Stock control

In your first-year studies you will have examined the different methods by which stocks are valued – see *Frank Wood's Business Accounting 1*, ninth edition, Chapter 29. It is also important for an accountant to ensure that the stocks being carried are not greater than they need be.

Let us look at how excessive stocks can have a detrimental effect upon the financial results of a firm:

1 Money tied up in unnecessarily large stocks is not earning anything. If, therefore, an extra £1 million is tied up in stocks which do not have to be so large, then the money which we could have earned from utilising that extra £1 million somewhere else has been lost. If we could have earned 10 per cent return on that money, then the unnecessary stocks have cost us £100,000 a year without any alternative benefit.
2 Too much stock needs extra storage space. Therefore the rent for the extra space, heating, lighting, insurance, wages of extra storekeepers, etc. is all money being spent for no benefit.

One thing that anyone should look for when examining the affairs of a business is to see if stocks are larger than they need be. For someone controlling the business there are three methods of cutting down on unnecessarily high stocks which have become much more popular in recent times. These are:

1 Economic order quantity (EOQ). This is a mathematical method of deciding what is the lowest amount of stock that should be ordered at a time so that the costs of financing and keeping stock are kept down to the minimum.
    The formula for this is:

$$EOQ = \sqrt{\frac{2CO}{S}}$$

where:
C = consumption (usage) per annum in units
O = cost of placing one order
S = cost of storage and holding of one unit per year

S will include the costs of operating the stores, transport and insurance, and also the costs concerned with interest on capital which has been invested in stock. We then take the square root of the above as the answer.

Exhibit 36.3 shows the calculation of the minimum order to be made.

Exhibit 36.3

Annual consumption = 800 units
Cost of reordering = £4
Storage and holding costs per unit = £1

$$\text{EOQ} = \sqrt{\frac{2 \times 800 \times 4}{1}} = \sqrt{\frac{6,400}{1}} = 80 \text{ units (10 orders per year)}$$

2 Just-in-time (JIT). This has been seen as one of the major factors which have resulted in the past success of Japanese manufacturers. It is not just an approach which is concerned with stock levels, but that is part of it.

The JIT approach requires that delivery of materials should occur immediately before their use. If arrangements are made with suppliers for more frequent deliveries then stocks can be cut to a minimum. Getting suppliers to inspect the materials before they deliver them, and getting them to guarantee their quality, also cuts down on costs, including the need to keep larger stocks in case there are deficiencies.

This sort of service is obtained by giving more business to fewer suppliers, and also placing longer-term orders. This enables the supplier to plan ahead more effectively to give you a better service.

3 Optimised production technology (OPT). The object of this new approach to the management of production is to distinguish between 'bottleneck' and 'non-bottleneck' resources. To give an example, the 'bottleneck' resource might be a machine which has a limited capacity. As a result, everything else can only be operated at that same level. Rather than other parts of the business produce more than the 'bottleneck' machine can absorb, a lower overall level of activity takes place. This needs less stocks.

Of course if a 'bottleneck' can be eliminated it will be. The above applies when a bottleneck, for whatever reason, cannot be eliminated.

It is better to have a smooth-running business, operating within its 'bottleneck' capacities, than to have one which operates very irregularly. One run irregularly would have to have parts of the business shut down at times. One running smoothly, besides all the other economies, needs fewer stocks.

Of these three methods, the existence of a formula makes EOQ particularly easy to examine. It is a useful aid to management in ensuring that they are making best use of their stock-related resources. Also, because of the precise nature of the calculation, it lends itself to incorporation within a computerised managerial decision support system.

Learning outcomes

You should now have learnt:

1 That budgets are prepared in order to guide the firm towards its objectives.
2 That they should be drawn up within the context of *planning* and *control*.
3 That while budgets are drawn up for control purposes, a budget should not be seen as a straitjacket.
4 That there are a number of methods or techniques available to management wishing to ensure that excessive stocks are not carried by their organisations. These include economic order quantity (EOQ), just-in-time (JIT), and optimised production technology (OPT).

Answers to activities

36.1 'Data which is provided for a particular purpose, and which is completely wrong for the purpose, is worse than having no data at all.' (Section 33.2)
'The wrong kind of costing can be even worse than having no costing at all.' (Section 34.12)

36.2

Units	January	February	March	April	May	June
Opening stock	140	150	190	220	180	120
Add Units produced	80	80	80	80	80	80
	220	230	270	300	260	200
Less Sales	(70)	(40)	(50)	(120)	(140)	(70)
Closing stock	150	190	220	180	120	130

36.3 The sales budget is used to set the levels of activity required in the production budget which, in turn, is used to set the quantities required to be obtained in the materials purchase budget.

REVIEW QUESTIONS

36.1 What would the production levels have to be for each month if the following data was available:

Units 20X5	Jan	Feb	Mar	Apr	May	June
(a) Stocks levels wanted at the end of each month	690	780	1,100	1,400	1,160	940
(b) Expected sales each month	800	920	1,090	1,320	1,480	1,020

(c) The stock level at 1 January, 20X5 will be 740 units.

36.2 For the year ended 31 December 20X9 the sales of units are expected to be:

January	110	July	70
February	180	August	30
March	170	September	170
April	150	October	110
May	120	November	150
June	100	December	190

The opening stock at 1 January 20X9 will be 140 units. The closing stock desired at 31 December 20X9 is 150 units.

Required:
(a) What will production be per month if an even production flow is required and stock levels during the year could be allowed to fall to zero?
(b) Given the same information plus the constraint that stock levels must never fall below 80 units, and that extra production will be undertaken in January 20X9 to ensure this, what will be the January production figure?

36.3A
(a) For each of the following, state three reasons why a firm may wish to keep:
   (i) a minimum stock level of finished goods, and
   (ii) an even level of production in the face of fluctuating demand.
(b) The sales forecast for Douglas & Co for July–December 20X7 is:

	J	A	S	O	N	D
Units	280	200	260	360	400	420

Produce a production budget showing monthly opening and closing stock figures if the firm wishes to maintain an even level of producing 300 units each month, and a minimum stock level of 150 units.
   What must the opening stock be at 1 July to achieve this?
(c) Under what circumstances, in budgetary control, may a firm's productive capacity prove to be its limiting or key factor?

(AQA (Associated Examining Board): GCE A-level)

CHAPTER 37

Cash budgets

Learning objectives

After you have studied this chapter, you should be able to:

- explain the importance of cash funds to an organisation
- explain what is meant by the term 'cash budget'
- prepare a cash budget
- explain the importance of cash budgeting in the control of cash funds
- explain why a cash budget may be prepared
- explain the difference between profits and cash in the context of organisational survival

Introduction

In this chapter you'll learn how to prepare a cash budget, of the advantages of cash budgets and, in the context of business survival, of the relationship between profit, cash and shortage of cash funds.

37.1 The need for cash budgets

It is no use budgeting for production and for sales if, during the budget period, the firm runs out of cash funds. When talking about cash in budgets we are also usually including bank funds. For that reason, in this book we will not be differentiating between cash and cheque payments or between cash and cheques received.

As cash is so important, it is budgeted for, so that any shortage of cash can be known in advance and action taken to obtain permission for a loan or a bank overdraft to be available then, rather than wait until the shortage or deficiency occurs. Bank managers, or anyone concerned with the lending of money, resent most strongly one of their customers needing a bank overdraft without prior warning, when, in fact, if a cash budget had been prepared the customer could have known well in advance that there would be a need for cash funds on a particular date.

The finance needed may not just be by way of borrowing from a bank or finance house. It may well be a long-term need that can only be satisfied by an issue of shares or debentures. Such issues need planning well in advance, and a cash budget can reveal (*a*) that they will be needed, (*b*) how much is needed and (*c*) when it will be needed.

We can now look at a very simple case. Without being concerned in this first exhibit with exactly what the receipts and payments are for, just to keep matters simple at this stage, we can see the dangers that are inherent in not budgeting for cash.

Exhibit 37.1

Mr Muddlem had a meeting with his accountant on 1 July 20X3. He was feeling very pleased with himself. He had managed to get some very good orders from customers, mainly because he was now allowing them extra time in which to pay their accounts. Sprite, the accountant, said, 'Can you afford to do all that you are hoping to do?'

Muddlem laughed, 'Why, I'll be making so much money I won't know how to spend it.'

'But have you got the cash to finance everything?' asked Sprite.

'If I'm making a good profit then of course I'll have the cash,' said Muddlem. 'I know the bank manager says that any bank overdraft could not be more than £1,000, but I doubt if I need it.'

'Don't let's rely on guesses,' says Sprite. 'Let's work it out.'

After an hour's work the following facts emerge.

(a) Present cash balance (including bank balance) £800.
(b) Receipts from debtors will be: July £2,000, August £2,600, September £5,000, October £7,000, November £8,000, December £15,000.
(c) Payments will be July £2,500, August £2,700, September £6,900, October £7,800, November £9,900, December £10,300.

This is then summarised:

	July £	Aug £	Sep £	Oct £	Nov £	Dec £
Balance at start of the month:	800	300	200			
Deficit at the start of the month:				(1,700)	(2,500)	(4,400)
Receipts	2,000	2,600	5,000	7,000	8,000	15,000
	2,800	2,900	5,200	5,300	5,500	10,600
Payments	2,500	2,700	6,900	7,800	9,900	10,300
Balance at end of the month	300	200				300
Deficit at the end of the month			(1,700)	(2,500)	(4,400)	

'I'm in an awkward position now,' says Muddlem. 'I just cannot borrow £4,400 nor can I cut down on my sales, and anyway I don't really want to as these new sales are very profitable indeed. If only I'd known this, I could have borrowed the money from my brother only last week but he's invested it elsewhere now.'

'Come and see me tomorrow,' says Sprite. 'There may well be something we can do.'

Fortunately for Muddlem his luck was in. He arrived to see his accountant the following morning waving a cheque. 'My wife won £5,000 on a jackpot bingo last night,' he said.

'Thank goodness for that. At least in future you'll learn to budget ahead for cash requirements. You can't be lucky all the time,' says Sprite.

37.2 Timing of cash receipts and payments

In drawing up a cash budget it must be borne in mind that all the payments for units produced would very rarely be at the same time as production itself. For instance, raw materials might be bought in March, incorporated in goods being produced in April, and paid for in May. On the other hand, the raw materials may have been in hand for some time, bought in January, paid for in February, and used in production the following August.

In contrast, the direct labour part of the product is usually paid for almost at the same time as the unit being produced. Even here a unit may be produced in one week and the wages paid one week later, so that a unit might be produced on, say, 27 June and the wages for the direct labour involved paid for on 3 July.

Similarly, except in many supermarkets and retail stores where many of the goods sold are paid for at the time of sale, the date of sale and the date of receipt of cash will not usually be the same. The goods might be sold in May and the money received in August, or even paid for in advance so that the goods might be paid for in February but the goods not

shipped to the buyer until May. This is especially true, at least for part of the goods, when a cash deposit is left for custom-made goods which will take some time to manufacture. A simple example of this would be a made-to-measure suit on which a deposit would be paid at the time of order, the final payment being made when the completed suit is collected by the buyer.

Exhibit 37.2

A cash budget for the six months ended 30 June 20X3 is to be drafted from the following information.

(a) Opening cash balance at 1 January 20X3 £3,200.

(b) Sales, at £12 per unit, cash received three months after sale: in units.

20X2			20X3								
Oct	Nov	Dec	Jan	Feb	Mar	Apr	May	June	July	Aug	Sept
80	90	70	100	60	120	150	140	130	110	100	160

(c) Production: in units.

20X2			20X3								
Oct	Nov	Dec	Jan	Feb	Mar	Apr	May	June	July	Aug	Sept
70	80	90	100	110	130	140	150	120	160	170	180

(d) Raw materials used in production cost £4 per unit of production. They are paid for two months before being used in production.

(e) Direct labour, £3 per unit paid for in the same month as the unit is produced.

(f) Other variable expenses, £2 per unit, $3/4$ of the cost being paid for in the same month as production, the other $1/4$ paid in the month after production.

(g) Fixed expenses of £100 per month are paid monthly.

(h) A van is to be bought and paid for in April for £800.

Schedules of payments and receipts are as follows:

Payments (the month shown in brackets is the month in which the units are produced):

January	£	February	£
Raw materials: 130 (March) × £4	520	140 (April) × £4	560
Direct labour: 100 (January) × £3	300	110 (February) × £3	330
Variable: 100 (January) × $3/4$ × £2	150	110 (February) × $3/4$ × £2	165
90 (December) × $1/4$ × £2	45	100 (January) × $1/4$ × £2	50
Fixed	100	Fixed	100
	1,115		1,205

March	£	April	£
Raw materials: 150 (May) × £4	600	120 (June) × £4	480
Direct labour: 130 (March) × £3	390	140 (April) × £3	420
Variable: 130 (March) × $3/4$ × £2	195	140 (April) × $3/4$ × £2	210
110 (February) × $1/4$ × £2	55	130 (March) × $1/4$ × £2	65
Fixed	100		100
Motor van			800
	1,340		2,075

May	£	June	£
Raw materials: 160 (July) × £4	640	170 (August) × £4	680
Direct labour: 150 (May) × £3	450	120 (June) × £3	360
Variable: 150 (May) × $3/4$ × £2	225	120 (June) × $3/4$ × £2	180
140 (April) × $1/4$ × £2	70	150 (May) × $1/4$ × £2	75
Fixed	100		100
	1,485		1,395

Receipts: (the month shown in brackets is the month in which the sale was made):

				£
January	80	(October)	× £12	960
February	90	(November)	× £12	1,080
March	70	(December)	× £12	840
April	100	(January)	× £12	1,200
May	60	(February)	× £12	720
June	120	(March)	× £12	1,440

Cash Budget

	Jan £	Feb £	Mar £	Apr £	May £	June £
Balance from previous month	3,200	3,045	2,920	2,420	1,545	780
Add Receipts (per schedule)	960	1,080	840	1,200	720	1,440
	4,160	4,125	3,760	3,620	2,265	2,220
Less Payments (per schedule)	(1,115)	(1,205)	(1,340)	(2,075)	(1,485)	(1,395)
Balance carried next month	3,045	2,920	2,420	1,545	780	825

37.3 Advantages of cash budgets

These can be said to be:

1 Having to think ahead and plan for the future and express the plans in figures, focuses the mind in a way that thinking in a general fashion about the future will not do – general optimistic feeling that 'all will be well' often fails to stand up to scrutiny when the views of the future are expressed in a cash budget.

2 Seeing that money will have to be borrowed at a particular date will mean that you can negotiate for a loan in advance, rather than at the time when you have actually run out of cash. Bankers and other lenders do not like someone attempting to borrow money in a panic, and which has to be instantly available.

When borrowing money, you have to give the lender the confidence that the loan will be repaid at the agreed time, plus any interest and charges that may accrue. Last-minute borrowing, unsupported by any calmly thought-out plan, will not inspire such confidence, and will often lead to the loan's being refused as the lender may think that the risk is too great.

Activity 37.1
What other disadvantages do you think there might be in waiting until the last minute to arrange a loan of this type?

3 Knowing about the need to borrow in advance also widens the possible pool of lenders. Such people as friends, relations and businesspeople or investors other than bankers rarely have large sums of cash quickly available. They need time to turn their own investments into cash before they can lend to you.

4 Alternatively, you may find that you will have cash funds surplus to requirements. Knowing this in advance will enable you to investigate properly how you can invest this surplus cash until required, thus earning interest or other investment income. Surplus cash lying in bank current accounts very often earns absolutely no interest at all, no matter how large the amount. Banks often offer deposit accounts linked to current accounts that automatically transfer funds from one to the other so that any surplus fund in the current

account are moved immediately to the deposit account and reversed back to the current account when required.

There are also other sorts of short-term investments which banks and accountants can advise businesses to put their surplus cash into at appropriate times.

37.4 Profits and shortages of cash funds

Just because a business is making good profits does not mean that it will not be short of cash funds. Let's look at how some firms may have good profits and yet still be short of cash funds, possibly having bank overdrafts or loans which are getting steadily bigger.

1 Firm A has increased its sales by 50 per cent, is making the same percentage gross profit and its expenses have hardly increased, yet its overdraft has got bigger. The reason is that it increased its sales by giving all of its customers four months to pay instead of the usual one month. This has attracted a lot of new customers.

  This means that the debtors are increasing by very large amounts, as they can wait another three months in which to pay their bills. Thus, the equivalent of three months' cash receipts have not come into the bank. Meanwhile, the firm is making extra purchases for goods for the new customers, with a consequent outflow of more cash than usual, especially if it has not got longer credit terms from its suppliers. So, hardly any cash is coming in in the short term, while more cash than usual is going out.

  The answer to this is: large increase in profits and fewer cash funds probably resulting in higher bank overdrafts or loans.

2 Firm B has the same sales, purchases and expenses as usual. However, the proprietor is now taking much higher drawings than before. In fact, his drawings are exceeding the profits he is making.

  Such a situation cannot go on for ever. He will start to find his cash funds in the business are decreasing, possibly meaning higher loans or overdrafts being needed.

3 Firm C has just spent a lot of money on fixed assets. It will be several years before the firm recoups the money it has paid out. In the meantime, only the depreciation provisions are charged against profits. However, the cash funds have seen the disappearance of the whole amount paid for fixed assets.

  The net result is that profits may be recorded but the firm is hard-up for cash funds.

4 Firm D is going through a bad patch in that sales are very difficult to make, but it does not want to get rid of any of its workforce. Production is kept going at normal rates, and the products not sold are simply kept in stock. Thus the stock is increasing at an alarming rate.

  If stock is not being sold, then cash is obviously not being received in respect of such production. Meanwhile, all the expenses and wages are still being paid for. This can result in a severe shortage of funds if carried on for long unless further finance is received.

5 A long-term loan has been paid off but no extra finance from anywhere else has been received. This could equally apply to a partner retiring and the balance due to him being paid out of the firm's funds, without a new partner being introduced. A company buying back its shares without a new issue of shares could face the same situation.

  In the long-term, there is a connection between profits and cash funds available, even though it may not be that marked. In the short-term, you can see that there may be no relationship at all. This simple fact is one that surprises most people. It is because the calculation of profits follows one set of concepts, whereas the calculation of cash funds follows a completely different set of rules. You may remember this being discussed when you learnt about overtrading in Section 27.7.

You should now have learnt:

1 The difference between profit and cash funds.

2 When undertaking a cash budget, 'cash' includes both money held in the form of cash and amounts held in the bank.

3 The importance of cash funds to an organisation.

4 What is meant by the term 'cash budget'.

5 The importance of preparing and monitoring a cash budget.

6 How to prepare a cash budget.

7 The difference between profits and cash in the context of organisational survival.

Answers to activities

37.1 It is not only that you risk the loan being refused. Lenders will often realise that they have you at their mercy, and will charge much higher rates of interest and impose other conditions than they would not otherwise have done.

REVIEW QUESTIONS

Advice: Cash budgeting is an extremely important part of accounting. Questions on this topic are relatively easy to do, and high marks can be gained quite easily.

37.1 Ukridge comes to see you in April 20X3. He is full of enthusiasm for a new product that he is about to launch on to the market. Unfortunately his financial recklessness in the past has led him into being bankrupted twice, and he has only just got discharged by the court from his second bankruptcy.

'Look here, laddie,' he says, 'with my new idea I'll be a wealthy man before Christmas.'

'Calm down,' you say, 'and tell me all about it.'

Ukridge's plans as far as cash is concerned for the next six months are:

(a) Present cash balance (including bank) £5.

(b) Timely legacy under a will – being received on 1 May, 20X3, £5,000. This will be paid into the business bank account by Ukridge.

(c) Receipts from debtors will be: May £400, June £4,000, July £8,000, August £12,000, September £9,000, October £5,000.

(d) Payments will be: May £100, June £5,000, July £11,000, August £20,000, September £12,000, October £7,000.

You are required:

(a) To draw up a cash budget, showing the balances each month, for the six months to 31 October 20X3.

(b) The only person Ukridge could borrow money from would charge interest at the rate of 100 per cent per annum. This is not excessive considering Ukridge's past record. Advise Ukridge.

37.2 Draw up a cash budget for N. Morris showing the balance at the end of each month, from the following information for the six months ended 31 December 20X2:

(a) Opening cash (including bank) balance £1,200

(b) Production in units:

20X2									20X3	
Apr	May	June	July	Aug	Sept	Oct	Nov	Dec	Jan	Feb
240	270	300	320	350	370	380	340	310	260	250

(c) Raw materials used in production cost £5 per unit. Of this 80 per cent is paid in the month of production and 20 per cent in the month after production.

(d) Direct labour costs of £8 per unit are payable in the month of production.

(e) Variable expenses are £2 per unit, payable one-half in the same month as production and one-half in the month following production.

(f) Sales at £20 per unit:

20X2

Mar	Apr	May	June	July	Aug	Sept	Oct	Nov	Dec
260	200	320	290	400	300	350	400	390	400

Debtors to pay their accounts three months after that in which sales are made.

(g) Fixed expenses of £400 per month payable each month.

(h) Machinery costing £2,000 to be paid for in October 20X2.

(i) Will receive a legacy £2,500 in December 20X2.

(j) Drawings to be £300 per month.

37.3 Herbert Limited make a single product, whose unit budget details are as follows:

	£	£
Selling price		30
Less Costs		
Direct material	9	
Direct labour	4	
Direct production expenses	6	
Variable selling expenses	4	
		(23)
Contribution		7

Additional information:

1 Unit sales are expected to be:

June	July	August	September	October
1,000	800	400	600	900

2 Credit sales will account for 60 per cent of total sales. Debtors are expected to pay in the month following sale for which there will be a cash discount of 2 per cent.

3 Stock levels will be arranged so that the production in one month will meet the next month's sales demand.

4 The purchases of direct materials in one month will just meet the next month's production requirements.

5 Suppliers of direct materials will be paid in the month following purchase.

6 Labour costs will be paid in the month in which they are incurred. All other expenses will be paid in the month following that in which they are incurred.

7 Fixed expenses are £2,000 per month and include £180 for depreciation.

8 The bank balance at 1 July 20X9 is £3,900 favourable to the business.

Required:

(a) A cash budget for Herbert Limited for the three month period ending on 30 September 20X9 showing the balance of cash at the end of each month.

(b) List and explain **three** ways in which the preparation of a cash flow budget could be of advantage to the management of Herbert Limited.

(AQA (Associated Examining Board): GCE A-level)

37.4A Mtoto Ltd operate as wholesale 'cash and carry' stores and in addition to its main store have two other depots. The company's summarised balance sheet as at 31 August 20X1 was as follows.

	£	£		£	£
Fixed assets			*Authorised and issued capital*		
(at net book value)		549,600	450,000 £1 Ordinary shares		
Current assets			Fully paid		450,000
Stock	399,900		Retained earnings at		
Trade debtors	21,000		1 Sept 20X0	300,000	
		420,900	*Less* Current year ended		
			31 Aug 20X1 loss	(130,000)	
					170,000
			Current liabilities		
			Trade (and other)		
			creditors	110,500	
			Bank overdraft	240,000	
					350,500
		970,500			970,500

- Over the past year the company has experienced increased competition and as a consequence reported a net trading loss for the year ended 31 August 20X1.
- The company has decided that in the new financial year tighter control must be exercised over cash resources.

The following information is available:

1 All goods are purchased by the main store.

Purchases 20X1

	Actual			Forecast		
July	Aug		Sept	Oct	Nov	Dec
£	£		£	£	£	£
55,800	61,200		64,300	41,000	46,000	41,800

- Mtoto Ltd pays suppliers two months after the month of purchase.
- Forecast purchases are being reduced since the managing director regarded current stock levels as too high.
- In addition, shop-soiled stock which cost £20,000 is to be sold for cash in October. It is anticipated that this stock will be sold for £17,000. This sale is not included in the sales of note 2 below.

2 All sales are on a cash basis only except for several important customers who trade only with Mtoto's main store.

Sales 20X1

		Actual			Forecast		
		July	Aug		Sept	Oct	Nov	Dec
		£	£		£	£	£	£
Main store								
Cash sales		21,500	21,600		18,000	26,300	19,200	24,700
Credit sales		24,000	21,000		32,500	26,000	25,400	27,800
Depot	1	15,500	17,400		19,700	18,000	17,600	17,900
Depot	2	21,000	24,000		26,300	19,700	21,000	19,100

3 Mtoto Ltd pays £9,500 fixed overhead costs per month.

4 Wages and salaries are paid each month through a centralised payroll system.

Wages and salaries 20X1

Actual		Forecast			
Aug		Sept	Oct	Nov	Dec
£		£	£	£	£
16,000		17,000	19,000	13,000	12,000

In October, 10 staff were made redundant and are to receive their redundancy compensation of £12,000 in December. This amount is not included in the above figures.

5 Other variable overhead charges are paid by Mtoto Ltd in the month following the month they are incurred.

Variable overhead charges 20X1

	Actual		Forecast			
	Aug		Sept	Oct	Nov	Dec
	£		£	£	£	£
	5,600		6,800	6,100	7,400	6,900

6 Plant surplus to requirement is to be sold in September for £26,500 cash. The plant cost £55,000 and depreciation to date is £20,000.

Required:
(*a*) A detailed cash budget, on a month by month basis, for the first four months of the financial year ending 31 December 20X1 for Mtoto Ltd.
(*b*) A report commenting on:
    (*i*) the current and forecast liquidity position.
    (*ii*) the action that Mtoto Ltd could take to attempt a return to a profit situation.

(AQA (Associated Examining Board): GCE A-level)

37.5 David Llewelyn has been advised by his bank manager that he ought to provide a forecast of his cash position at the end of each month. This is to ensure that his cash inputs will be sufficient to allow a bank loan to be repaid when due and to check that his outgoings are properly controlled. It is estimated that at 30 June 20X0 his current account will be £5,000 in credit, whereas the amount owing in respect of the bank loan taken out on 1 July 20X5 will be £15,000. Monthly deductions from the current account balance amount to £242 including interest charges on account of this loan. In addition to these outgoings, David has to allow for the following:

(*i*)   The payment of wages of £2,000 per month.
(*ii*)   Personal drawings of £500 per month.
(*iii*) On average David earns a margin of 15 per cent (of sales) and expects to sell stocks purchased in the previous month. Of the sales in any one month, 20 per cent are paid for within that month, 70 per cent the following month and the remainder two months after sale. Other receipts from debtors are expected to be £40,000 in July 20X0, £32,000 in August 20X0 and £4,000 in September 20X0.
(*iv*) Purchases of supplies will amount to £38,250 per month from July 20X0 payable one month in arrears. In addition, purchases of £7,500 to increase stocks will be delivered in September 20X0 and must be paid for in October 20X0. Creditors of £34,000 for purchases made in June 20X0 are to be paid in July 20X0.
(*v*)   Monthly payments to the Inland Revenue for the taxation of his employees' earnings will amount to £500 per month.
(*vi*) Rent which has to be paid quarterly in advance amounts to £5,000 per annum. These payments commenced in January 20X0.
(*vii*) Business rates are to be paid in two instalments as due in October 20X0 and in March 20X1. This estimated expenditure will amount to £4,500 per annum.
(*viii*) Payment of Value Added Tax to H.M. Customs and Excise of £5,000 in July 20X0 and every third month thereafter (but see also (*ix*)).
(*ix*) David intends to purchase a van for £8,150 in August 20X0. He will then be entitled to deduct £1,050 from the VAT payment due to H.M. Customs and Excise in October 20X0.

Required:
A forecast cash flow statement in columnar form showing the estimated current account balance at the close of each of the four months ending 31 October 20X0.

(Welsh Joint Examining Board: GCE A-level)

37.6 The managing director of Pumpkin Ltd was reviewing the results of the company for the financial year ended 31 March 20X0. The following summarised information was available:

Balances as at 1 April 20X9	£
Issued ordinary share capital:	
£1 fully paid shares	150,000
Share premium account	100,000
Balance of retained earnings	40,000
Balances as at 31 March 20X0	
Net profit for year 20X9/X0	70,000
Fixed assets	300,000
Bank overdraft	150,000
Other net current assets	210,000

Note: There were no other accounts with balances. The balances as at 1 April 20X9 had remained unchanged throughout the year.

The managing director was pleased that the company had made a good profit, but he was rather concerned that a healthy bank balance at the beginning of the year had now become a large bank overdraft.

Consequently he asked the company accountant to prepare forecast information for 20X0/X1 in order that the cash situation could be improved.

The following information was prepared by the accountant:

1 Company sales – March 20X0 £

	£
Cash sales	30,000
Credit sales	65,000

In each month April to September (inclusive) the sales per month would be:

	£
Cash sales	40,000
Credit sales	70,000

All credit sales are settled the month after the sale.

2 All goods purchased are from a single supplier. The goods are purchased on credit and each month's purchases are paid for three months after the month of purchase.

The following purchase schedule had been prepared for the first 9 months of 20X0:

	January	February	March
Purchases	£60,000	£58,000	£61,000

Purchases in April, May and June
£55,000 in each month
Purchases in July, August and September
£45,000 in each month

Note: The company had successfully negotiated lower prices from its supplier commencing 1 July 20X0.

3 Dividends would be paid as follows:

(*i*) Final ordinary dividend of 5p per share payable on 31 May 20X0 in respect of financial year 20X9/X0.

(*ii*) Interim ordinary dividend of 2p per share payable on 31 July 20X0 in respect of financial year 20X0/X1.

4 Selling and distribution expenses are expected to be 6 per cent of a given month's total sales. They are paid one month in arrears.

5 Administration charges would be incurred as follows:

20X0 February, March, April	£10,000 per month
20X0 May to September (inclusive)	£13,500 per month

Administration charges are settled two months after the month in which they were incurred.

6 The company had decided to make a bonus issue of shares of one share for every three held. The issue would be made on 30 April 20X0. The bonus shares would not qualify for the final dividend of 20X9/X0, but would qualify for the interim dividend to be paid on 31 July 20X0.

Required:
(a) Comment on the liquidity of the company as at 31 March 20X0 and explain to the managing director why a company can apparently make a good profit but have no cash in the bank.
(b) Prepare a cash budget for each of the four months ending 31 July 20X0.
(c) Comment on the forecast bank balance as shown by your cash budget. Identify ways in which the bank overdraft could be reduced over the last five months of 20X0.

(AQA (Associated Examining Board): GCE A-level)

37.7A Belinda Raglan owns a clothing factory. Trading over the last two years has been very successful and she feels that having achieved good results it is now time to request an increase in the overdraft facility.

- In the past the bank has been willing to offer business overdraft facilities and at present there is an agreed limit of £15,000.
- On 1 May 20X4 the overdraft stands at £5,000.
- In order to support her request for the increased facility, she has produced a forecast profit statement for the four months ended 31 August 20X4 as follows:

	\multicolumn{2}{c}{*May*}	\multicolumn{2}{c}{*June*}	\multicolumn{2}{c}{*July*}	\multicolumn{2}{c}{*August*}
	£000	*£000*	*£000*	*£000*	*£000*	*£000*	*£000*	*£000*
Sales		74		28		116		168
Cost of sales		51		12		78		101
Gross Profit		23		16		38		67
Less Rent	4		4		4		4	
Other expenses	8		3		10		14	
Depreciation	5		5		5		5	
		(17)		(12)		(19)		(23)
Net profit		6		4		19		44

Although Belinda thought these figures would be sufficient to satisfy the requirements of the bank, the manager has asked for a cash budget for the period concerned to be submitted.
The following additional information concerning the business is available.

(1) Rent is paid quarterly in advance on the first day of May, August, November and February.
(2) All other expenses are payable in the month in which they are incurred.
(3) Purchases for the period are expected to be – May £60,000; June £120,000; July £40,000 and August £43,000. These will be paid for in the month of purchase. Purchases will be unusually high in May and June because they will be subject to a special reduction of 3% of the amounts quoted.
(4) 80% of the sales are on a credit basis payable two months later. Sales in March and April were £88,000 and £84,000 respectively.
(5) A compensation payment of £10,000 to a former employee for an industrial injury, not covered by insurance, is due to be paid in May.

Required:
(a) Prepare a forecast cash budget on a month by month basis for the period May to August 20X4.
(b) Discuss the advantages and disadvantages of cash budgeting.
(c) Draft notes, to be used by the bank manager for a letter to Ms Raglan, indicating why the request for an increased overdraft facility may be refused.

(AQA (Associated Examining Board): GCE A-level)

37.8A Ian Spiro, formerly a taxi-driver, decided to establish a car-hire business after inheriting £50,000.
His business year would be divided into budget periods each being four weeks.
He commenced business on a Monday the first day of period 1, by paying into a business bank account £34,000 as his initial capital.
All receipts and payments would be passed through his bank account.
The following additional forecast information is available on the first four budget periods of his proposed business venture.

1 At the beginning of period 1 he would purchase 6 saloon cars of a standard type; list price £6,000 each, on which he had negotiated a trade discount of 11 per cent.

2 He estimates that four of the cars will be on the road each Monday to Friday inclusive, and at weekends all six cars will be on the road. Hire charges as follows:

Weekday rate £10 per day per car
Weekend rate £18 per day per car

He estimates that this business trading pattern will commence on the Monday of the second week of period 1, and then continue thereafter.

All hire transactions are to be settled for cash.

Note: a weekend consists of Saturday and Sunday. All remaining days are weekdays.

3 An account was established with a local garage for fuel, and it was agreed to settle the account two periods in arrear. The forecast gallon usage is as follows:

Period 1	Period 2	Period 3	Period 4
200	200	400	500

The fuel costs £1.80 per gallon.

4 Servicing costs for the vehicles would amount to £300 per period, paid during the period following the service. Servicing would commence in period 1.

5 Each of his vehicles would be depreciated at 25 per cent per annum on a reducing balance basis.

6 Fixed costs of £200 per period would be paid each period.

7 He had agreed with a local firm to provide two cars on a regular basis, Monday to Friday inclusive, as chauffeur driven cars. The agreed rate was £60 a day (per car), payment being made in the following period.

This contract would not commence until the first day of period 2, a Monday.

8 Drawings: Periods 1 and 2: £400 a period.
Periods 3 and 4: £800 a period.

9 Wages and salaries:
(a) Initially he would employ 3 staff, each on £320 a budget period. Employment would commence at the beginning of period 1.
(b) On commencement of the contract the two additional staff employed as chauffeurs would each receive £360 a budget period. Payments are to be made at the end of the relevant period.

10 In anticipation of more business being developed he planned to buy a further three cars for cash in period 4. The cars would cost £6,500 each and it was agreed he would be allowed a trade discount of 10 per cent.

Required:
(a) A detailed cash budget for the first four budget periods.
(b) An explanation as to why it is important that a business should prepare a cash budget.
(c) Identify how a sole proprietor may finance a forecast cash deficit distinguishing between internal and external financial sources.

(*AQA (Associated Examining Board): GCE A-level*)

CHAPTER 38

Co-ordination of budgets

Learning objectives

After you have studied this chapter, you should be able to:
- explain the benefits of budgeting to an organisation
- explain the importance of effective co-ordination of budgets for the organisation
- prepare a master budget
- describe the benefits of operating a system of flexible budgeting.

Introduction

In this chapter you'll learn about the process of preparing a budget and how budgets are co-ordinated and used to monitor and identify deviations between them and actual performance. You'll also learn about the importance of investigating variances and of the benefits of adopting a system of flexible budgeting.

38.1 Master budgets

The various budgets have to be linked together to draw up a **master budget**, which is really a budgeted set of financial statements. We have looked at the sales, production and cash budgets. There are, however, many more budgets for parts of the organisation, including:

- a selling budget
- an administration expense budget
- a manufacturing overhead budget
- a direct labour budget
- a purchases budget

and so on. In this book, we do not wish to get entangled in too many details, but in a real firm with a proper set of budgeting techniques there will be a great deal of detailed backing for the figures that are incorporated in the more important budgets.

Now it may be that when all the budgets have been co-ordinated, or slotted together, the master budget shows a smaller profit than the directors are prepared to accept. This will mean recasting budgets to see whether a greater profit can be earned, and if at all possible the budgets will be altered. Eventually there will be a master budget that the directors can agree to. This then gives the target for the results that the firm hopes to achieve in financial terms. **Remember that there are other targets such as employee welfare, product quality, etc. that cannot be expressed in financial terms but which will impact upon and influence the setting of budgets.**

The rest of this chapter is concerned with the drawing up of budgets for an imaginary firm, Walsh Ltd, culminating in the drawing up of the master budget.

Let's start with a look at the last balance sheet of Walsh Ltd, as at 31 December 20X4. This will give us our opening figures of stocks of raw materials, stock of finished goods, cash (including bank) balance, creditors, debtors, etc. Next, we'll produce budgets for the six months ending 30 June 20X5.

Walsh Ltd
Balance Sheet as at 31 December 20X4

Fixed assets		Cost	Depreciation to date	Net
		£	£	£
Machinery		4,000	1,600	2,400
Motor vehicles		2,000	800	1,200
		6,000	2,400	3,600

Current assets		
Stocks: Finished goods (75 units)		900
Raw materials		500
Debtors (20X4 October £540 + November £360 +		
December £450)		1,350
Cash and bank balances		650
		3,400
Less Current liabilities		
Creditors for raw materials		
(November £120 + December £180)	300	
Creditors for fixed expenses (December)	100	
		(400)
Net current assets		3,000
		6,600

Financed by:	
Share capital: 4,000 shares £1 each	4,000
Profit and loss account	2,600
	6,600

The plans for the six months ended 30 June 20X5 are as follows:

(a) Production will be 60 units per month for the first four months, followed by 70 units per month for May and June.

(b) Production costs will be (per unit):

	£
Direct materials	5
Direct labour	4
Variable overhead	3
	12

(c) Fixed overhead is £100 per month, payable always one month in arrears.

(d) Sales, at a price of £18 per unit, are expected to be:

	January	February	March	April	May	June
No. of units	40	50	60	90	90	70

(e) Purchases of direct materials (raw materials) will be:

	January	February	March	April	May	June
	£	£	£	£	£	£
	150	200	250	300	400	320

(f) The creditors for raw materials bought are paid two months after purchase.

(g) Debtors are expected to pay their accounts three months after they have bought the goods.

(h) Direct labour and variable overheads are paid in the same month as the units are produced.

(i) A machine costing £2,000 will be bought and paid for in March.

(j) 3,000 shares of £1 each are to be issued at par in May.

(k) Depreciation for the six months: machinery £450, motor vehicles £200.

We must first of all draw up the various budgets and then incorporate them into the master budget. Some of the more detailed budgets which can be dispensed with in this illustration will be omitted.

Materials Budget

	January	February	March	April	May	June
Opening stock (£)	500	350	250	200	200	250
Add Purchases (£)	150	200	250	300	400	320
	650	550	500	500	600	570
Less Used in production:						
Jan–April 60 × £5	(300)	(300)	(300)	(300)		
May and June 70 × £5					(350)	(350)
Closing stock (£)	350	250	200	200	250	220

Production Budget (in units)

	January	February	March	April	May	June
Opening stock (units)	75	95	105	105	75	55
Add Produced	60	60	60	60	70	70
	135	155	165	165	145	125
Less Sales	(40)	(50)	(60)	(90)	(90)	(70)
Closing stock	95	105	105	75	55	55

Production Cost Budget (in £s)

	January	February	March	April	May	June	Total
Materials cost (£)	300	300	300	300	350	350	1,900
Labour cost (£)	240	240	240	240	280	280	1,520
Variable overhead (£)	180	180	180	180	210	210	1,140
	720	720	720	720	840	840	4,560

Creditors Budget

	January	February	March	April	May	June
Opening balance (£)	300	330	350	450	550	700
Add Purchases (£)	150	200	250	300	400	320
	450	530	600	750	950	1,020
Less Payments (£)	(120)	(180)	(150)	(200)	(250)	(300)
Closing balance (£)	330	350	450	550	700	720

Debtors Budget

	January	February	March	April	May	June
Opening balances (£)	1,350	1,530	2,070	2,700	3,600	4,320
Add Sales (£)	720	900	1,080	1,620	1,620	1,260
	2,070	2,430	3,150	4,320	5,220	5,580
Less Received (£)	(540)	(360)	(450)	(720)	(900)	(1,080)
Closing balances (£)	1,530	2,070	2,700	3,600	4,320	4,500

Cash Budget

	January	February	March	April	May	June
Opening balance (£)	650	550	210			1,050
Opening overdraft (£)				(2,010)	(2,010)	
Received						
(see schedule) (£)	540	360	450	720	3,900	1,080
	1,190	910	660	(1,290)	1,890	2,130
Payments						
(see schedule) (£)	(640)	(700)	(2,670)	(720)	(840)	(890)
Closing balance (£)	550	210			1,050	1,240
Closing overdraft (£)			(2,010)	(2,010)		

Cash Payments Schedule

	January	February	March	April	May	June
Creditors for goods bought two months previously (£)	120	180	150	200	250	300
Fixed overhead (£)	100	100	100	100	100	100
Direct labour (£)	240	240	240	240	280	280
Variable overhead (£)	180	180	180	180	210	210
Machinery (£)			2,000			
	640	700	2,670	720	840	890

Cash Receipts Schedule

	January	February	March	April	May	June
Debtors for goods sold three months previously (£)	540	360	450	720	900	1,080
Shares issued (£)					3,000	
					3,900	

Master Budget
Forecast Operating Statement for the six months ended 30 June 20X5

	£	£	£
Sales			7,200
Less Cost of goods sold:			
Opening stock of finished goods		900	
Add Cost of goods completed		4,560	
		5,460	
Less Closing stock of finished goods		(660)	
			(4,800)
Gross profit			2,400
Less			
Fixed overhead		600	
Depreciation: Machinery	450		
Motors	200		
		650	
			(1,250)
Net profit			1,150

Forecast Balance Sheet as at 30 June 20X5

Fixed assets	Cost £	Depreciation to date £	Net £
Machinery	6,000	2,050	3,950
Motor vehicles	2,000	1,000	1,000
	8,000	3,050	4,950
Current assets			
Stocks: Finished goods		660	
Raw materials		220	
Debtors		4,500	
Cash and bank balances		1,240	
		6,620	
Creditors: amounts falling due within 1 year			
Creditors for goods	720		
Creditors for overheads	100		
		(820)	
Net current assets			5,800
Total assets less current liabilities			10,750
Capital and reserves			
Called-up share capital			7,000
Profit and loss account (2,600 + 1,150)			3,750
			10,750

38.2 Capital budgeting

You'll have noticed that the cash budget included £2,000 for the machine paid for in March. The other side of the double entry will also have been entered in a budget – the **capital budget**. This is where all the plans for the acquisition of fixed assets such as machinery, buildings, etc. are entered. Management will evaluate the various possibilities open to it, and will compare the alternatives. This is a very important part of budgeting. However, for the purposes of demonstrating how budgets are co-ordinated, we shall stick to the budgets we have demonstrated in this example. Suffice to say that the process for the capital budget and others omitted from the detail of this example is broadly similar to those you have seen so far.

38.3 The advantages of budgeting

The process of budgeting with the necessary participation throughout the organisation, finally producing a profit plan, is now a regular feature in all but the smallest firms. Very often budgeting is the one time when the various parts of management can really get together and work as a team rather than as separate parts of an organisation.

> ### Activity 38.1
> Which factor that you learnt about earlier in this book that involved managers across the organisation needs to be 'right' if appropriate budgets are to be agreed?

When budgeting is conducted under favourable conditions, there is no doubt that a firm which budgets will tend to perform rather better than a similar firm that does not budget. Budgeting means that managers can no longer give general answers affecting the running of the firm. They have to put figures to their ideas, and they know that in the end their estimated figures are going to be compared with what the actual figures turn out to be.

It has often been said that the act of budgeting is possibly of more benefit than the budgets which are produced. However, the following benefits can be claimed for good budgeting:

1 The strategic planning carried out by the board of directors or owners can be more easily linked to the decisions by managers as to how the resources of the business will be used to try to achieve the objectives of the business. The strategic planning has to be converted into action, and budgeting provides the ideal place where such planning can be changed into financial terms.

2 Standards of performance can be agreed for the various parts of the business. If sales and production targets are set as part of a co-ordinated plan, then the sales department cannot really complain that production is insufficient if they had agreed previously to a production level and this is being achieved, nor can production complain if its production exceeds the amount budgeted for and it remains unsold.

3 The expression of plans in comparable financial terms. Some managers think mainly in terms of, say, units of production, or of tonnes of inputs or outputs, or of lorry mileage, etc. The effect that each of them has upon financial results must be brought home to them. For instance, a transport manager might be unconcerned about the number of miles that his haulage fleet of lorries covers until the cost of doing such a large mileage is brought home to him, often during budgeting, and it may be then and only then that he starts to search for possible economies. It is possible in many cases to use mathematics to find the best ways of loading vehicles, or to plan routes taken by vehicles so that fewer miles are covered and yet the same delivery service is maintained. This is just one instance of many when the expression of the plans of a section of a business in financial terms sparks off a search for economies, when otherwise such a search may never be started at all.

4 Managers can see how their work slots into the activities of the firm. It can help to get rid of the feeling of 'I'm only a number not a person', because they can identify their positions within the firm and can see that their jobs really are essential to the proper functioning of the firm.

5 **The budgets for a firm cannot be set in isolation.** This means that the situation of the business, the nature of its products and its workforce, etc., must be seen against the economic background of the country. For instance, it is no use budgeting for extra labour when labour is in extremely short supply, without realising the implications, such as having to pay higher than normal wage rates. Increasing the sales target during a credit squeeze needs a full investigation of the effect of the shortage of money upon the demand for the firm's goods and so on.

Activity 38.2

What disadvantages you've already learnt about earlier in this book may arise if an organisation's managers are not allowed to vary their activity from budget?

Too many budgets are set at one level of sales or production when, in fact, flexible budgets (discussed below) ought to be used. It is very often the case that budgeting is forced upon managers against their will. Instead the firm should really set out first of all to do a 'selling job' to convince managers that budgets are not the monsters so often thought. A trial run for part of a business is far superior to starting off by having a fully detailed budget set up right away for the whole of the business.

Learning to use budgets is rather like learning to swim. Let a child get used to the water first and remove its fear of the water, then it will learn to swim fairly easily. For most children (but not all), if the first visit to the baths meant being pushed into the deep end immediately, then reaction against swimming would probably set in. Let managers become used to the idea of budgeting during a trial period, without the fear of being dealt with severely. Most managers will then accept it and participate appropriately and effectively.

38.4   The use of computers in budgeting

Years ago, budgeting was a task which most accountants hated doing. It was not the concept of budgeting that accountants disliked. Far from it, it suited their needs perfectly. Rather, it was the multitude of numerical manipulations that had to be performed that made the task both boring and formidable.

Those of you who have done some of the exercises in this book manually know the feeling when, after a lot of work, your answer simply will not balance. Searching through to find the error(s) can be a daunting prospect. Imagine how much more complicated it is in a real firm dealing with real figures, rather than with the simple sets of data which form your exercises. Also imagine the feeling when the managing director used to say to the accountant 'What if we increased our prices by 5 per cent and took an extra month to pay creditors?' The accountant would then have to plough his way through a large number of extra calculations.

Most of that is now a thing of the past. Computers are used instead. They either have software specially written for the task, or else spreadsheets can be used. By keying in the necessary basic figures or 'what if' amendments, the computer will automatically produce the budgets or the amended budgets within a very short space of time.

This enables management to see the results that would be expected from many separate propositions, thus enhancing the chance of choosing the best solution. Also, as the accounting period unfolds, the changes that have occurred since the period started can be incorporated very easily so as to adjust the budgets as the accounting period progresses.

38.5 Flexible budgets

So far in this book, budgets have been drawn up on the basis of one set of expectations, based on just one level of sales and production. Later, when the actual results are compared with the budgeted results expected in a fixed budget, they will have deviated for two reasons:

1 While the actual and budgeted volumes of production and sales may be the same there may be a difference on actual and budgeted costs.
2 The volumes of actual and budgeted units of sales and production may vary, so that the costs will be different because of different volumes.

The variations, or as they are more commonly known, **variances** are usually under the control of different managers in the organisation. Variances coming under 1 will probably be under the control of the relevant department. On the other hand, variances under 2 are caused because of variations in plans brought about by changing sales, or at least the expectation of changing sales.

Budgets are used for control purposes. A manager does not take kindly to being held responsible for a variance in his spending if he is working to a fixed budget and the variance is caused by a type 2 occurrence. The answer to this is to construct budgets at several levels of volume, and to show what costs etc. they should incur at these different levels.

For example, if a budget had been fixed at a volume of 500 units and the actual volume is 550, the manager would undoubtedly feel aggrieved if his costs for producing 550 units were compared with the costs he should have incurred for 500 units. Budgets which do allow for changing levels are called **flexible budgets**.

To draft a full set of flexible budgets is outside the scope of this book, but an instance of one department's flexible budget for manufacturing overhead is shown in Exhibit 38.1.

Exhibit 38.1

Data Ltd
Budget for Manufacturing Overhead, Department S[Note]

Units	400	450	500	550	600
	£	£	£	£	£
Variable overhead	510	550	600	680	770
Fixed overhead	400	400	400	400	400
Total overhead (A)	910	950	1,000	1,080	1,170
Direct labour hours (B)	200	225	250	275	300
Overhead rates (A) divided by (B)	£4.55	£4.22	£4.00	£3.92	£3.90

Note: In real life, this would be in greater detail.

Notice in Exhibit 38.1 that the variable costs in this case do not vary in direct proportion to production. Once 500 units production have been exceeded, they start to climb rapidly. The flexible budget makes far greater sense than a fixed budget. For instance, if a fixed budget had been agreed at 400 units, with variable overhead £510, then if production rose to 600 units, the manager would think the whole system unfair if he were expected to incur only £510 variable overhead (the figure for 400 units). On the contrary, if the comparison was on a flexible budget then costs at 600 units production would instead be compared with £770 (the figure at 600 units).

You should now have learnt:

1 There are a number of budgets that together comprise the master budget and they must all reconcile to each other and to the master budget.

2 That budget preparation is often an iterative process as the master budget is focused more and more tightly to the objectives of the organisation.

3 How to prepare a master budget.

4 That flexible budgeting permits managers to adjust their budgets in the light of variations in plan, often involving items over which they have no control.

Answers to activities

38.1 The various objectives of each of the functional areas and departments need to be compatible with each other and with the overall goals of the organisation. (Section 32.3)

38.2 Budgets that are too rigorously applied generate a situation of inflexibility that can be extremely counterproductive. There must be scope for managers to depart from budget when it is in the best interests of the organisation to do so. (Section 36.2)

REVIEW QUESTIONS

Note: In many ways, drawing up a budgeted set of final accounts is very much like drawing up accounts from single-entry records. Accounts from single-entry records concern the past; budgeted accounts are based on estimates and concern the future.

38.1 Richard Toms has agreed to purchase the business of Norman Soul with effect from 1 August 20X7. Soul's budgeted working capital at 1 August 20X7 is as follows:

	£	£	£
Current assets			
Stock at cost	13,000		
Debtors	25,000		
		38,000	
Current liabilities			
Creditors	10,000		
Bank overdraft	20,000		
		(30,000)	
			8,000

In addition to paying Soul for the acquisition of the business, Toms intends to improve the liquidity position of the business by introducing £10,000 capital on 1 August 20X7. He has also negotiated a bank overdraft limit of £15,000. It is probable that 10 per cent of Soul's debtors will in fact be bad debts and that the remaining debtors will settle their accounts during August subject to a cash discount of 10 per cent. The opening creditors are to be paid during August. The sales for the first four months of Toms' ownership of the business are expected to be as follows: August £24,000, September £30,000, October £30,000 and November £36,000. All sales will be on credit and debtors will receive a two-month credit period. Gross profit will be at a standard rate of 25 per cent of selling price. In addition, in order to further improve the bank position and to reduce his opening stock, Toms intends to sell on 1 August 20X7 at cost price £8,000 of stock for cash. In order to operate within the overdraft limit Toms intends to control stock levels and to organise his purchases to achieve a monthly rate of stock turnover of 3. He will receive one month's credit from his suppliers.

General cash expenses are expected to be £700 per month.

Required:

(a) A stock budget for the four months ending 30 November 20X7 showing clearly the stock held at the end of each month.

(b) A cash budget for the four months ending 30 November 20X7 showing clearly the bank balance at the end of each month.

(AQA (Associated Examining Board): GCE A-level)

38.2A A company's estimated pattern of costs and revenues for the first four months of 20X7 is as follows:

Cost and Revenues: January–April 20X7 (£000)

Month	Sales	Materials	Wages	Overheads
January	410.4	81.6	16.2	273.6
February	423.6	84.8	16.8	282.4
March	460.8	93.6	18.3	306.7
April	456.3	91.2	18.6	304.5

1 One-quarter of the materials are paid for in the month of production and the remainder two months later: deliveries received in November 20X6 were £78,400, and in December 20X6 £74,800.

2 Customers are expected to pay one-third of their debts a month after the sale and the remainder after two months: sales expected for November 20X6 are £398,400, and for December 20X6, £402,600.

3 Old factory equipment is to be sold in February 20X7 for £9,600. Receipt of the money is expected in April 20X7. New equipment will be installed at a cost of £38,000. One-half of the amount is payable in March 20X7 and the remainder in August 20X7.

4 Two-thirds of the wages are payable in the month they fall due, and one-third a month later: wages for December 20X6 are estimated at £15,900.

5 £50,000 of total monthly overheads are payable in the month they occur, and the remainder one month later: total overheads for December 20X6 are expected to be £265,200.

6 The opening bank balance at 1 January 20X7 is expected to be an overdraft of £10,600.

Required:

(a) Using the information above, prepare the firm's cash budget for the period January–April 20X7.

(b) Provide a statement to show those items in part (a) which would appear in a budgeted balance sheet as at 30 April 20X7.

(Edexcel: GCE A-level)

38.3 D. Smith is to open a retail shop on 1 January 20X4. He will put in £25,000 cash as capital. His plans are as follows:

(i)   On 1 January 20X4 to buy and pay for premises £20,000, shop fixtures £3,000, motor van £1,000.

(ii) To employ two assistants, each to get a salary of £130 per month, to be paid at the end of each month. (PAYE tax, National Insurance contributions, etc., are to be ignored.)

(iii) To buy the following goods (shown in units):

	Jan	Feb	Mar	Apr	May	June
Units	200	220	280	350	400	330

(iv) To sell the following number of units:

	Jan	Feb	Mar	Apr	May	June
Units	120	180	240	300	390	420

(v) Units will be sold for £10 each. One-third of the sales are for cash, the other two-thirds being on credit. These latter customers are expected to pay their accounts in the second month following that in which they received the goods.

(*vi*)   The units will cost £6 each for January to April inclusive, and £7 each thereafter. Creditors will be paid in the month following purchase. (Value stock-in-trade on FIFO basis.)

(*vii*)   The other expenses of the shop will be £150 per month payable in the month following that in which they were incurred.

(*viii*)   Part of the premises will be sub-let as an office at a rent of £600 per annum. This is paid in equal instalments in March, June, September and December.

(*ix*)   Smith's cash drawings will amount to £250 per month.

(*x*)   Depreciation is to be provided on shop fixtures at 10 per cent per annum and on the motor van at 20 per cent per annum.

You are required to:

(*a*) Draw up a cash budget for the six months ended 30 June 20X4, showing the balance of cash at the end of each month.

(*b*) Draw up a forecast trading and profit and loss account for the six months ended 30 June 20X4 and a balance sheet as at that date.

38.4A   B. Cooper is going to set up a new business on 1 January 20X8. He estimates that his first six months in business will be as follows:

(*i*)   He will put £10,000 into a bank account for the firm on 1 January 20X8.

(*ii*)   On 1 January 20X8 he will buy machinery £2,000, motor vehicles £1,600 and premises £5,000, paying for them immediately out of the business bank account.

(*iii*)   All purchases will be effected on credit. He will buy £2,000 goods on 1 January and he will pay for these in February. He will purchase another £3,200 of goods in January and £4,000 of goods each month during February, March, April, May and June. Other than the £2,000 worth bought in January all other purchases will be paid for two months after purchase.

(*iv*)   Sales (all on credit) will be £4,000 for January and £5,000 for each month after that. Debtors will pay for the goods in the third month after purchase by them.

(*v*)   Stock-in-trade on 30 June 20X8 will be £2,000.

(*vi*)   Wages and salaries will be £150 per month and will be paid on the last day of each month.

(*vii*)   General expenses will be £50 per month, payable in the month following that in which they were incurred.

(*viii*)   He will receive a legacy of £5,500 on 21 April 20X8. This will be paid into the business bank account immediately.

(*ix*)   Insurance covering the 12 months of 20X8 will be paid for by cheque on 30 June 20X8, £140.

(*x*)   Rates will be paid as follows: for the three months to 31 March 20X8 by cheque on 28 February 20X8: for the 12 months ended 31 March 20X9 by cheque on 31 July 20X8. Rates are £360 per annum.

(*xi*)   He will make drawings of £80 per month by cheque.

(*xii*)   He has substantial investments in public companies. His bank manager will give him any overdraft that he may require.

(*xiii*)   Depreciate motors 20 per cent per annum, machinery 10 per cent per annum.

You are required to:

(*a*) Draft a cash budget (includes bank) month by month showing clearly the amount of bank balance or overdraft at the end of each month.

(*b*) Draft the projected trading and profit and loss account for the first six months' trading, and a balance sheet as at 30 June 20X8.

38.5A

(*a*) What is meant by the terms:
   (*i*)   Budget
   (*ii*)   Operating budget
   (*iii*)   Master budget?

(*b*) The information below relates to the business of Madingley Ltd:

Balance Sheet as at 30 May 20X0 (£000)

	Cost	Aggregate depreciation	Book value
Fixed assets			
Land and buildings	134.00	–	134.00
Plant and machinery	9.40	3.76	5.64
Fixtures and fittings	2.30	1.05	1.25
	145.70	4.81	140.89
Current assets			
Stocks: Raw materials	91.70		
Finished goods	142.40		
Debtors	594.40		
Bank	12.40		
		840.90	
Less Current liabilities			
Creditors: Raw materials	82.20		
Overheads	127.40		
		(209.60)	
Working capital			631.30
			772.19
Financed by:			
Share capital		500.00	
Profit and loss account		272.19	
			772.19

The following is a schedule of the budgeted income and expenditure for the six months ended 30 November 20X0 (£000):

	Sales	Materials	Wages	Overheads
June	193.20	41.20	7.60	123.00
July	201.40	42.40	7.90	119.20
August	216.10	49.60	8.80	131.40
September	200.50	31.40	6.10	91.50
October	190.30	21.20	3.70	59.30
November	183.70	19.80	2.60	42.60

Notes:
(i)   Generally, materials are paid for two months after receipt, and customers pay on average after three months.
(ii) Payments outstanding for materials at 1 June 20X0 were: April £38,500; May £43,700.
(iii) Debtors were: March £194,300; April £203,600; May £196,500.
(iv) Wages are to be paid in the month in which they fall due.
(v)   Overheads are to be paid one month after they are incurred: the figure for May was £127,400.
(vi) Stocks of raw materials are to be kept at £91,700.
(vii) The stocks of finished goods at 30 November 20X0 are to be £136,200.
(viii) There are no stocks of semi-finished items on 31 May 20X0, and none are expected in stock on 30 November.
(ix) Forty per cent of the overheads are to be considered as fixed.
(x)   Depreciation on plant and machinery is to be allowed at 10 per cent *per annum* on cost; the fixtures and fittings are thought to have a value at 30 November of £980.
(xi) There are no sales of finished goods or purchases of raw materials for cash planned during the period.

Prepare:
(a) A forecast operating statement for the period June to November 20X0; and
(b) A forecast balance sheet as at 30 November 20X0.

(Edexcel: GCE A-level)

38.6 The following information has been extracted from the books of Issa Ltd for the financial year ended 31 December 20X0.

Trading and Profit and Loss Account
for the year ended 31 December 20X0

	£000		£000
Opening stock	90	Sales	750
Purchases	490		
	580		
Less Closing stock	80		
Cost of goods sold	500		
Gross profit	250		
	750		750
Administration expenses	60	Gross profit	250
Selling and distribution expenses	50		
Financial charges	20		
Depreciation of fixed assets	20		
Net profit	100		
	250		250

Balance Sheet as at 31 December 20X0

	£000	£000		£000	£000
Fixed assets at cost		750	£1 Ordinary shares fully paid		200
Less Aggregate			9% £1 Preference shares,		
depreciation		144	fully paid		100
		606			
Current assets			Share premium		150
Stock		80	Retained earnings		350
Trade debtors	75				
Less Provision for			*Current liabilities*		
doubtful debtors	5	70	Trade creditors	50	
Balance at bank	100	250	Accrued expenses	6	56
		856			856

The company had commenced the preparation of its budget for the year ending 31 December 20X1 and the following information is the basis of its forecast.

1 An intensive advertising campaign will be carried out in the first six months of 20X1 at a cost of £15,000. It is anticipated that as a result of this, sales will increase to £900,000 in 20X1.
2 The gross profit/sales ratio will be increased to 35 per cent.
3 A new stock control system is to be installed in 20X1 and it is expected that the stock level will be reduced by £15,000 as compared to the 20X0 closing stock.
4 Land and buildings which cost £50,000 (nil depreciation to date) will be sold in 20X1 for £200,000 cash. Half of the proceeds will be used to buy ordinary shares in another company, Yates Ltd, at an agreed price of £4 per share. (Ignore share commission etc.)
5 The company planned to capitalise some of its reserves on 1 April 20X1. New ordinary shares are to be issued on a 1 for 2 basis. Half the funds required will be drawn from the share premium account and the remainder will be taken from retained earnings.
6 Preference share dividends will be paid on 1 May 20X1 and 1 November 20X1. The company planned to pay an interim ordinary share dividend on the increased share capital of 2.5p per share on 1 July 20X1. No final dividend is proposed.
7 Owing to inflation revenue expenses are expected to rise as follows:
Administration expenses will increase by 6 per cent.
Selling and distribution expenses will increase by 8 per cent.
The advertising campaign expenses are in addition to the increase above.
Financial charges will increase by 4 per cent.
These percentage increases are based on the figures for the year ended 31 December 20X0.

8 With the projected sales increases trade debtors are expected to rise to £100,000 by 31 December 20X1. The provision for doubtful debts is to be adjusted to $7\frac{1}{2}$ per cent of forecast trade debtors.

9 Other forecast figures as at 31 December 20X1.

	£000
Balance at bank	350.1
Trade creditors	56.0
Expense creditors	15.0

10 Depreciation of 10 per cent per annum on cost is to be provided on £600,000 of the company's fixed assets.

Required:
(a) A budgeted trading, profit and loss and appropriation account for the year ending 31 December 20X1.
   Show the full details of the trading account.
(b) A budgeted balance sheet as at 31 December 20X1.
(c) What advantages accrue to a business by preparing a budget with respect to
   (i) forecast profitability;
   (ii) forecast liquidity?

(AQA (Associated Examining Board): GCE A-level)

38.7   The balance sheet of Gregg Ltd at 30 June 20X6 was expected to be as follows:

Balance Sheet 30 June 20X6 (£)

Fixed assets	Cost	Depreciation to date	Net
Land and buildings	40,000	–	40,000
Plant and machinery	10,000	6,000	4,000
Motor vehicles	6,000	2,800	3,200
Office fixtures	500	220	280
	56,500	9,020	47,480

Current assets		
Stock-in-trade: Finished goods	1,800	
Raw materials	300	
Debtors (20X6 May £990 + June £900)	1,890	
Cash and bank balances	7,100	11,090
		£58,570

Financed by:	
Share capital	50,000
Profit and loss account	7,820
	57,820

Current liabilities		
Creditors for raw materials (April £240 + May £140 + June £160)	540	
Creditors for variable overhead	210	750
		£58,570

The plans for the six months to 31 December 20X6 can be summarised as:

(i)   Production costs per unit will be:

	£
Direct materials	2
Direct labour	5
Variable overhead	3
	10

(ii) Sales will be at a price of £18 per unit for the three months to 30 September and at £18.5 subsequently. The number of units sold would be:

	Jul	Aug	Sept	Oct	Nov	Dec
Units	60	80	100	100	90	70

All sales will be on credit, and debtors will pay their accounts two months after they have bought the goods.

(iii) Production will be even at 90 units per month.
(iv) Purchases of direct materials – all on credit – will be:

	Jul	Aug	Sept	Oct	Nov	Dec
	£	£	£	£	£	£
	220	200	160	140	140	180

Creditors for direct materials will be paid three months after purchase.
(v) Direct labour is paid in the same month as production occurs.
(vi) Variable overhead is paid in the month following that in which the units are produced.
(vii) Fixed overhead of £90 per month is paid each month and is never in arrears.
(viii) A machine costing £500 will be bought and paid for in July. A motor vehicle costing £2,000 will be bought and paid for in September.
(ix) A debenture of £5,000 will be issued and the cash received in November. Interest will not start to run until 20X7.
(x) Provide for depreciation for the six months: Motor vehicles £600, Office fixtures £30, Machinery £700.

You are required to draw up as a minimum:
(a) Cash budget, showing figures each month.
(b) Debtors budget, showing figures each month.
(c) Creditors budget, showing figures each month.
(d) Raw materials budget, showing figures each month.
(e) Forecast operating statement for the six months.
(f) Forecast balance sheet as at 31 December 20X6.

In addition you may draw up any further budgets you may wish to show the workings behind the above budgets.

38.8 The following information relates to the actual sales of Griffton Ltd during the last four months of its financial year.

	March	April	May	June
Quantity (units)	900	900	900	1,000
Price each	£55	£55	£55	£55

The budgeted information below relates to the next financial year commencing 1 July 20X2:

(i) The company forecasts that sales quantity will decrease in July by 10 per cent of the level in June. The reduced quantity will remain for August and September, but will then increase by 10 per cent in October, and remain fixed for the next three months.

The sales price will remain at £55 each until 1 September when it will be increased to £60 per unit, this price will be effective for a minimum of six months.

50 per cent of sales are on a cash basis and attract a 2 per cent cash discount, the remaining 50 per cent of sales are paid two months in arrears.

The company arranges its purchases of raw materials such that the closing stock at the end of each month exactly meets the requirement for the following month's sales. Each unit sold requires 2 kg of material at £15 per kg; this price is fixed until December 20X3.

(ii) As a separate exercise, the managing director asks for stock levels to be reviewed, and asks you about the use of economic order quantities at some time in 20X3. The following budgeted data would apply to this exercise:

Material	2,000 kg per month
Price	£15 per kg
Stockholding costs	20% p.a. on average stock value
Ordering costs	£10 per order

Required:
A Draw up monthly budgets for the four-month period commencing 1 July 20X2 for:
   (a) Debtors in £s;
   (b) Raw material purchases in kg.
B From the budgeted information given in note (ii) calculate the economic order quantity for the company. Briefly outline the limitations of this ordering method.

(Reproduced with the kind permission of OCR: from *University of Oxford Delegacy of Local Examinations: GCE A-level*)

38.9 Bedford Ltd is a manufacturing business with several production departments. Benjamin Kent, the manager of the machining department, submitted the following figures for the firm's annual budget for his department:

Units produced (normal production level)	64,000
	£
Raw materials	294,400
Direct labour	236,800
Power	38,400
Repairs and maintenance (25% variable at this level of budgeted cost)	51,200
Insurance	1,300
Heating and lighting	1,250
Indirect wages (15% variable at this level of budgeted cost)	64,000
Total cost	687,350
Total capacity for machining department	80,000 units

Actual production for the period is 68,000 units, and costs are:

Materials	310,750
Labour	249,100
Power	39,800
Repairs and maintenance	53,050
Insurance	1,350
Heating and lighting	1,200
Indirect wages	65,250
Total cost	720,500

Benjamin is being criticised for overspending £33,150 compared with his normal budget. It is appreciated that he has made a saving on heating and lighting, but concern is being expressed over the spending on materials and labour. Benjamin feels that he has been able to control the department's costs efficiently.

Required:
A Construct a flexible budget for 60 per cent, 70 per cent, 75 per cent, 85 per cent and 90 per cent of production capacity, calculate any savings or overspending by Benjamin's department and comment on its efficiency.
B Describe the operation of an efficient system of budgetary control.

(Reproduced with the kind permission of OCR: from *University of Oxford Delegacy of Local Examinations: GCE A-level*)

38.10A The summarised balance sheet of Newland Traders at 30 May 20X7 was as follows:

	£000	£000
Fixed assets at cost		610
Less depreciation		264
		346
Current assets		
Stocks	210	
Debtors	315	
Cash at bank and in hand	48	
	573	
Less Current liabilities		
Creditors	128	445
		791
Capital and reserves		
Issued capital		600
General reserve		150
Profit and loss account		41
		791

Selling and materials prices at 30 May 20X7 provide for a gross profit at the rate of 25 per cent of sales.

The creditors at 30 May 20X7 represent the purchases for May 20X7, and the debtors the sales for April of £150,000 and May of £165,000.

Estimates of sales and expenditure for the six months to 30 November 20X7 are as follows:

(i) Sales for the period at current prices will be £800,000. Sales for the months of September and October will each be twice those of the sales in each of the other months.

(ii) Stock at the end of each month will be the same as at 30 May 20X7 except that at 30 November 20X7 it will be increased to 20 per cent above that level.

(iii) Creditors will be paid one month after the goods are supplied and debtors will pay two months after the goods are supplied.

(iv) Wages and expenses will be £20,000 a month and will be paid in the month in which they are incurred.

(v) Depreciation will be at the rate of £5,000 a month.

(vi) There will be capital expenditure of £80,000 on 1 September 20X7. Depreciation, in addition to that given in (v) above, will be at the rate of 10 per cent per annum on cost.

(vii) There will be no changes in issued capital, general reserve or prices of sales or purchases.

Required:

(a) Sales and purchases budgets and budgeted trading and profit and loss accounts for the six months ended 30 November 20X7.

(b) A budgeted balance sheet as at 30 November 20X7.

(c) A cash flow budget for the six months ended 30 November 20X7 indicating whether or not it will be necessary to make arrangements for extra finance and, if so, your recommendation as to what form it should take.

Show all your calculations.

(Welsh Joint Education Committee: GCE A-level)

38.11A Len Auck and Brian Land trade as partners in Auckland Manufacturing Company making components for minicomputers. To cope with increasing demand the partners intend to extend their manufacturing capacity but are concerned about the effect of the expansion on their cash resources during the build-up period from January to April 20X6.

The following information is available.

(a) The balance sheet of Auckland Manufacturing Company at 31 December 20X5 is expected to be:

	£	£
Fixed assets		
Plant and machinery at cost		65,000
Less depreciation		28,000
		37,000
Current assets		
Stocks – raw materials	10,500	
– finished goods	18,500	
Debtors	36,000	
Cash at bank	4,550	
	69,550	
Current liabilities		
Creditors	27,550	
		42,000
		79,000
Partners' capital accounts		
Len Auck		40,000
Brian Land		39,000
	£	79,000

(b) Creditors at 31 December 20X5 are made up of:

Creditors for materials supplied in November and December at	
£13,000 per month	26,000
Creditors for overheads	1,550
	27,550

(c) New plant costing £25,000 will be delivered and paid for in January 20X6.

(d) Raw material stocks are to be increased to £12,000 by the end of January 20X6, thereafter raw material stocks will be maintained at that level. Payment for raw materials is made two months after the month of delivery. Finished goods stocks will be maintained at £18,500 throughout the period. There is no work in progress.

(e) Sales for the four months are expected to be:

	£
January	18,000
February	22,000
March	22,000
April	24,000

Sales for several months prior to 31 December had been running at the rate of £18,000 per month. It is anticipated that all sales will continue to be paid for two months following the month of delivery.

(f) The cost structure of the product is expected to be:

	%
Raw materials	50
Direct wages	20
Overheads, including depreciation	$17\frac{1}{2}$
Profit	$12\frac{1}{2}$
Selling price	100

(g) Indirect wages and salaries included in overheads amount to £900 for the month of January and £1,000 per month thereafter.

(h) Depreciation of plant and machinery (including the new plant) is to be provided at £700 per month and is included in the total overheads.

(i) Wages and salaries are to be paid in the month to which they relate; all other expenses are to be paid for in the month following the month to which they relate.

(j) The partners share profits equally and drawings are £400 per month each.

(k) During the period to April an overdraft facility is being requested.

Required:
(a) A forecast profit and loss account for the four months January to April 20X6 and a balance sheet as at 30 April 20X6.
(b) A month by month cash forecast for the four months showing the maximum amount of finance required during the period.
(c) A calculation of the month in which the overdraft facility would be repaid on the assumption that the level of activity in April is maintained.

For the purposes of this question, taxation and bank interest may be ignored.

(*Association of Chartered Certified Accountants*)

PART 8

Standard costing and variance analysis

Introduction

This part looks at how budgetary control can be exercised in a timely manner through the establishment of estimates for cost and income and the subsequent monitoring of those estimates against the actual costs and income as they arise.

CHAPTER 39

Standard costing

Learning objectives

After you have studied this chapter, you should be able to:
- explain the difference between a standard costing system and an actual cost system
- explain the advantages of adopting a standard costing system
- distinguish between ideal standards and attainable standards
- explain the importance of selecting appropriate standards

Introduction

In this chapter you'll learn about standard costing, its benefits, and the difference between 'ideal' and 'attainable' standards.

39.1 Comparison with actual costs

A cost accounting system can be said to be either an actual cost system or a standard cost system. The difference is not in the systems themselves but rather in the kinds of costs that are used. In the costing systems already shown, we have seen that they have consisted of the actual costs for direct materials and direct labour, and that overhead has been charged by reference to a predetermined overhead rate. Standard costing uses instead the costs that *should have been incurred*. So standard costing has costs that should have been incurred, while other systems use costs that have been incurred.

In an actual cost accounting system, costs are traced through the records as product costs. On the other hand, **standard costing** uses standards of performance and of prices derived from studying operations and of estimating future prices. Each unit being produced can have a standard material cost, a standard direct labour cost and a standard overhead cost. As with any form of management accounting, this does not in fact have to be carried out fully, for instance some companies will use standard labour and standard overhead costs but may use actual material costs. In the rest of this chapter, we will consider firms that use standard costing system for all items.

As with all management accounting techniques, the benefits flowing from using standard costing should exceed the costs of operating it, so that there should be advantages accruing from having a standard costing system. These are as follows:

1 Usually a standard costing system is simpler and needs less work than an actual cost system. This is because once the standards have been set they are adhered to, and the standard costs will remain unchanged for fairly long periods. Other systems need constant recalculations of cost. For instance, the average cost method of pricing issues of materials needs a recalculation of the price each time there are further receipts, whereas standard cost of

materials will remain at a constant figure. This can bring about a reduction in the costs of clerical work.

2 The unit costs for each identical product will be the same, whereas this may not be the same with actual costing systems. For instance, in an actual cost system two people making identical units may be paid at different wage rates, the materials issued to one person may have come from a slightly later lot of raw materials received which cost more than the previous lot and therefore the issue price may be higher, and so on. In a standard costing system the same amount would be charged for each of these people until such time as the standards were altered.

3 A standard cost system provides a better means of checking on the efficiency with which production is carried on, in that the differences between the standard costs and the actual costs, i.e. the **variances**, throw up the changes in efficiency.

4 One important advantage may be that standard costing might make faster reporting available. This is certainly important, as generally the later that information is received the less useful it is. Standard costing has a great deal of predetermined data when compared with an actual costing system; therefore entering up job order sheets, job sheets and many other tasks can be speeded up if the actual costs do not have to be awaited.

The costs that will have been flowing through the standard costing system is that of standard costs and as actual costs will normally be different, then the difference or variance if adverse (i.e. actual costs have exceeded standard costs) will be debited to the profit and loss account. If the variance is a favourable one (i.e. actual costs have been less than standard costs) then this would be credited to the profit and loss account. This must be done, as all the costs used for the calculation of gross profit, etc. have been standard costs, and if the variances were not put in the profit and loss account then the net profit would not be the net profit actually made.

39.2   Setting standards

Standard costing is a classic case of the use of the principle of 'management by exception'. Put roughly, this means that when things are going according to plan leave them alone, and concentrate instead on the things that are deviating from planned results. With standard costing, the actual results that conform to the standards require little attention. Instead, management's interest is centred on the exceptions to standards. The approach whereby this information is given to management is known as 'exception reporting'.

Getting the 'right' standards is, therefore, of prime importance. If the 'wrong' standards are used, not only will a lot of time and money have been wasted, but it may bring worse results than if no standard had been set at all.

Activity 39.1
What does this last statement remind you of from earlier chapters?

Standards may be unsuitable because they were not set properly, or because conditions have changed greatly since they were set.

Standards of one of two types can be used: ideal standards and maintainable standards. These are as follows:

1 **Ideal standards.** These are set at a maximum level of efficiency, and thus represent conditions that can rarely be attained. This approach can be seriously objected to, in that if standards are too high, employees who might otherwise be motivated by standards which are possible to achieve may become discouraged.

2 **Attainable standards.** It is simple for someone to say that individuals will be motivated to attain standards that they are capable of, that they will not exert very much effort to exceed standards, and that standards outside their capabilities will not motivate them. From this follows the easy conclusion that standards should be neither 'too easy' nor 'too difficult' but should be 'just right'. The difficult part of this is in saying what the 'just right' figures are. There is no doubt that the work of behavioural scientists in this area has brought about a far greater insight into such problems. In a very large firm, such specialists may be members of the team setting the standards.

The standards for materials and for labour can be divided between those which are concerned with (*a*) prices and (*b*) quantities. Standard overhead costs are divided between standard variable overhead costs and standard fixed overhead costs. The standard fixed overhead costs will be used in absorption costing only, as marginal costing does not bring the fixed costs into its figures.

Activity 39.2

Think back to Activity 39.1. What message have you taken from these four statements:

1 'Data which is provided for a particular purpose, and which is completely wrong for the purpose, is worse than having no data at all.' (Section 33.2)
2 'The wrong kind of costing can be even worse than having no costing at all.' (Section 34.12)
3 'Some budgets that are drawn up are even more harmful to a firm than if none were drawn up at all.' (Section 36.2)
4 'If the "wrong" standards are used, not only will a lot of time and money have been wasted, but it may bring worse results than if no standard had been set at all.' (Section 39.1)

Learning outcomes

You should now have learnt:

1 That standard costing is based upon costs that should have been incurred, while other costing systems are based upon actual costs, i.e. costs that have been incurred.

2 About the benefits of standard costing.

3 That under a standard costing system, management focuses upon the exceptions to the standards.

4 That it is essential that the standards adopted are appropriate and attainable.

Answers to activities

39.1 'Data which is provided for a particular purpose, and which is completely wrong for the purpose, is worse than having no data at all.' (Section 33.2)
'The wrong kind of costing can be even worse than having no costing at all.' (Section 34.12)
'Some budgets that are drawn up are even more harmful to a firm than if none were drawn up at all.' (Section 36.2)

39.2 In order to obtain maximum benefit from the costing and management accounting systems, it is vitally important that appropriate data and management accounting techniques are used and that they are used in an appropriate and effective manner. Failing to do so is both directly wasteful of resources and can be not just counterproductive but harmful to the organisation.

REVIEW QUESTIONS

Note: This is a chapter giving background information only. You will not find many computational questions limited to the contents of the chapter.

39.1 Rimham plc prepares its budgets annually and as the accountant you are responsible for this task. The following standard data is available:

Material content	Product X kg	Product Y kg	Product Z kg
Material 1	–	18	24
Material 2	4	14	–
Material 3	12	10	6
Material 4	8	–	18

Material prices	Price per kg £
Material 1	0.1
Material 2	0.15
Material 3	0.25
Material 4	0.05

Labour content	Product X hours	Product Y hours	Product Z hours
Department A	2.5	1.5	3
Department B	2.5	1.5	3

Labour rates	Rate per hour £
Department A	1.6
Department B	1.2

Additional budgeted information

Direct labour hours	635,000
Production overheads	£1,143,000

- Production overheads are absorbed on the direct labour hour rate method.
- Administration and selling overheads are absorbed as a percentage of production cost at the rates of 50 per cent and 25 per cent, respectively.
- Profit is estimated at 12½ per cent on budgeted selling price.
- Sales, at standard selling price, for the following year are budgeted as follows:

Product	£
X	800,000
Y	1,280,000
Z	2,400,000

- In order to meet the needs of an expansion programme the company considers it necessary to increase stocks as follows:

Material 1	90,000 kg
Material 2	36,000 kg
Material 3	42,000 kg
Material 4	54,000 kg

Finished goods	
Product X	5,000 units
Product Y	10,000 units
Product Z	10,000 units

You are required to prepare the following:

(a) A schedule giving a detailed standard cost and standard selling price per unit for **each** product.

(b) The sales budget in units.

(c) The production budget in units.
(d) The direct material purchases budget in both units and value.

(*Northern Examinations and Assessment Board: GCE A-level*)

39.2A   Define the terms:

(*i*)   standard costing
(*ii*) standard cost
(*iii*) standard hours
(*iv*) variance

(*Edexcel Foundation, London Examinations: GCE A-level*)

CHAPTER 40

Materials and labour variances

Learning objectives

After you have studied this chapter, you should be able to:

- explain the difference between a favourable and an adverse variance
- calculate materials usage and price variances
- calculate labour efficiency and wage rate variances
- explain the similarity between the calculation of the materials usage variance and the labour efficiency variance
- explain the similarity between the calculation of the materials price variance and the wage rate variance
- suggest possible explanations for variances

Introduction

In this chapter you'll learn about two of the main groups of variances, those relating to materials and labour, and how to calculate them.

40.1 Background

Variance analysis is a means of assessing the difference between budgeted and actual amounts. These can be monetary amounts or physical quantities.

Properly used, variance analysis can improve the operating efficiency of a business by, first of all, setting up the predetermined standard cost structures and, then, measuring actual costs against them in order to measure efficiency.

Variance analysis makes use of the principle of management by exception. When things are going according to plan they can be left alone. Management can then concentrate on the things that deviate from the planned results and, as mentioned in Chapter 39, can adopt exception reporting in order to do so.

40.2 Adverse and favourable variances

The difference between standard cost and actual cost has already been stated to be a variance. Remember these are classified:

- Adverse: actual amount *greater* than standard amount.
- Favourable: actual amount *less* than standard amount.

The use of the words 'favourable' and 'adverse' should not be confused with their meaning in ordinary language, they are technical terms. Whether a variance is 'good' or 'bad' can only be determined after the causes of the variance have been fully investigated and ascertained.

40.3 Computation of variances

There is a great deal of difference between the *computation* of the variances and their *analysis*. The computation is simply the mathematical calculation of the variance. The analysis of the variance is a matter requiring a fair amount of judgement, which cannot be performed in a mechanical fashion.

We can now look at some computations of variances. In fact, there are many variances which can be computed, but we will concentrate on a few of the more important ones. In order that sense can be made of the computations and a reasonable job of analysis done, it will be assumed that the standards set were calculated on a rational basis.

Note: In the computations of variances which follow, there are exhibits to illustrate the variances which have been calculated. The lines drawn on the exhibits will be as follows:
Representing standard costs – – – – – – – – – – – –
Representing actual costs ································
Where actual costs and standard costs are the same — · —— · —— · —— · — · —
The shaded part(s) of each diagram represent the variance.

1 Materials price variances

Favourable variance

Material J	
Standard price per metre	£4
Standard usage per unit	5 metres
Actual price per metre	£3
Actual usage per unit	5 metres

Usage is the same as standard, therefore the only variance is that of price calculated:

	£
Actual cost per unit 5 × £3	15
Standard cost per unit 5 × £4	20
Variance (favourable)	5

Exhibit 40.1 shows the variance represented by the shaded area. This is £1 by a quantity of 5, therefore the variance is £5. The variance extends to the price line and not the quantity line. It is, therefore, a price variance.

Exhibit 40.1

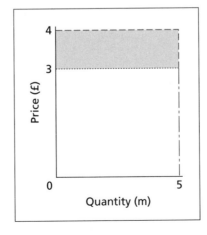

Adverse variance

Material K

Standard price per metre	£9
Standard usage per unit	8 metres
Actual price per metre	£11
Actual usage per unit	8 metres

Exhibit 40.2

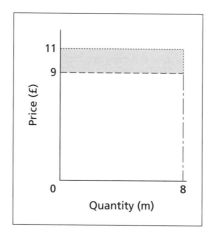

Variance computed:	£
Actual cost per unit 8 × £11	88
Standard cost per unit 8 × £9	72
Variance (adverse)	16

The shaded part of Exhibit 40.2 is the variance. This extends £2 times a quantity of 8. Therefore, the variance is £16. Notice that the shaded area is outside the lines marked – – – – – – – – – – – – representing standard costs.

Note: In the exhibits, when the variance is outside the standard cost area as marked by the standard cost lines, it will be an adverse variance. When it is inside the standard cost area as marked by the standard cost lines, it will be a favourable variance.

2 Materials usage variances

Favourable variance

Material L

Standard price per tonne	£5
Standard usage per unit	100 tonnes
Actual price per tonne	£5
Actual usage per unit	95 tonnes

Cost is the same as standard, therefore the only variance is that of usage calculated:

	£
Actual cost per unit 95 × £5	475
Standard cost per unit 100 × £5	500
Variance (favourable)	25

Exhibit 40.3

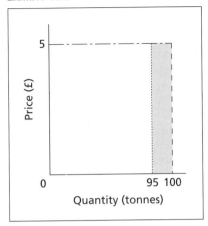

Adverse variance

Material M

Standard price per centimetre	£8
Standard usage per unit	11 cm
Actual price per centimetre	£8
Actual usage per unit	13 cm

Exhibit 40.4

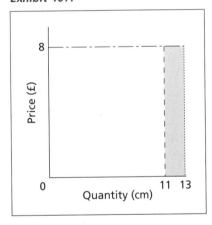

Variance computed:	£
Actual cost per unit 13 × £8	104
Standard cost per unit 11 × £8	88
Variance (adverse)	16

Here again the variances for materials L and M are shown in exhibits by means of shaded areas. The variances extend to the quantity lines and are, therefore, usage variances. With material L, the variance is shown inside the standard cost area, and is, therefore, a favourable variance, whereas material M shows an adverse variance as it is outside the standard cost area.

3 Combinations of materials price and usage variances

Most variances are combinations of both materials price and usage variances. Sometimes one variance will be favourable while the other is adverse; sometimes both will be adverse variances; and at other times both will be favourable variances.

Favourable and adverse variances combined

Material N

Standard price per metre	£6
Standard usage per unit	25 m
Actual price per metre	£7
Actual usage per metre	24 m

The net variance is calculated as:

	£
Actual cost per unit 24 × £7	168
Standard cost per unit 25 × £6	150
Variance (adverse)	18

Exhibit 40.5

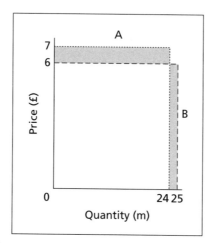

As Exhibit 40.5 shows, this is in fact made up of two variances. The first variance, shown as the shaded portion A, is an adverse price variance (i.e. it is outside the standard cost lines, therefore actual cost has exceeded standard cost). The second variance, shown as the shaded portion B, is a favourable usage variance (i.e. it is inside the standard cost lines, therefore actual usage has been less than standard usage).

The adverse price variance can therefore be seen to be £1 by a quantity of 24 = £24. The favourable usage variance can be seen to be a length of 1 metre by a price of £6 = £6. The net (adverse) variance is therefore made up:

	£
Adverse material price variance	24
Favourable materials usage variance	6
Net (adverse) variance	18

Both adverse variances combined

Material O

Standard price per kg	£9
Standard usage per unit	13 kg
Actual price per kg	£11
Actual usage per unit	15 kg

The net variance is computed:

	£
Actual cost per unit 15 × £11	165
Standard cost per unit 13 × £9	117
Variance (adverse)	48

Exhibit 40.6

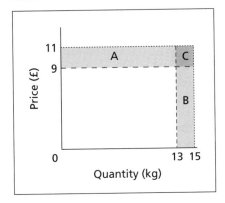

Exhibit 40.6 shows the shaded area A which is definitely a price variance of £2 × 13 = £26 adverse. Shaded area B is definitely a usage variance of 2 × £9 = £18 adverse. This makes up £44 of the variance, but there is the double-shaded area, C, of 2 × £2 = £4. This is really an area which is common to both usage and price. Sometimes, although not very often, this would be treated as a separate variance, but as detail is necessarily limited, in this book we will just add it to the price variance, making it £26 + £4 = £30, the usage variance being left at £18.

Both favourable variances combined

Material P

Standard price per tonne	£20
Standard usage per unit	15 tonnes
Actual price per tonne	£19
Actual usage per unit	13 tonnes

The net variance is computed:

	£
Actual cost per unit 13 × £19	247
Standard cost per unit 15 × £20	300
Variance (favourable)	53

Exhibit 40.7

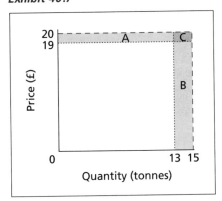

Exhibit 40.7 shows the shaded area A which is definitely a price variance of £1 × 13 = £13 favourable. Shaded area B is a usage variance of 2 × £19 = £38 favourable. The double-shaded area C of £1 × 2 = £2, making up the total variance of 53 would normally be added to the usage variance to make it £38 + £2 = £40.

40.4 Materials variances – analysis

1 Price variances

The price variance is a simple one in that it is obvious that the purchasing department has not been able to buy at the anticipated price. How far this is completely outside the powers of the purchasing department depends entirely on the facts. It may simply be that the rate of inflation is far greater than it had been possible to foresee, or that special forms of extra taxes have been introduced by the government. No one can surely blame the purchasing department for not knowing the secrets of the government's budget each year.

On the other hand, it may have been that poor purchasing control has meant that orders for materials have been placed too late for the firm to manage to get the right price in the market, or that materials which ought to have been bought in bulk have, in fact, been bought in small lots at uneconomic prices. If there are regular suppliers, a short-term gain by buying a cheaper lot from somewhere else could militate against the firm's benefit in the long run if the firm's regular suppliers took umbrage.

Buying the cheapest materials does not always result in the greatest possible profit being attained.

> *Activity 40.1*
> Why do you think this is the case?

In the end, after all the variance analysis has been undertaken, there must be someone to whom the responsibility for the price variance can be traced and who is then accountable for it. However, as Activity 40.1 illustrated, care must be taken not to give praise blindly or to criticise unfairly.

2 Usage variances

There are many reasons for excessive use of materials. Inferior materials can bring about a lot of waste, so can workers who are not as skilled as they ought to be. Perhaps the machinery is not suitable for the job, or there might even be deliberate wastage of material, e.g. wood wasted so that it can be taken home by workers as fuel etc. The theft of material obviously aggravates a usage variance. Here again responsibility must be traced.

> *Activity 40.2*
> When you prepare one of these variance diagrams, there are two simple rules you can use to identify the type (price or usage) and nature (favourable or adverse) of the variance. What are they?

40.5 Key questions of variances

Before we look at the computation or analysis of any further variances this is a convenient point to raise some fundamental questions about variances. They are:

1 Why do we wish to calculate this particular variance?
2 When it has been calculated, what action are we going to take based on it?
3 If we are not going to make an effective use of the variance, then why bother to calculate it?

40.6 Formulae for materials variances

We have deliberately waited until now to give you the formula for calculating each variance. We wanted you to understand what the variances were, rather than simply give you the formula to calculate them. They are as follows:

Materials price variance = (Standard price − Actual price per unit) × Quantity purchased
$$= (SP − AP) × QP$$

Materials usage variance = (Standard quantity required − Actual quantity) × Standard price
$$= (SQ − AQ) × SP$$

40.7 Inventory records under standard costing

It is worth noting at this point that when a firm adopts a standard costing system it avoids the difficulties involving FIFO, LIFO or average stock methods. In a standard costing system all materials received and issued are valued at the standard cost in the inventory account. There is no recording problem associated with changing prices during the period since they are separately recorded as variances.

Provided that standards are reviewed sufficiently often this system should ensure that the values of inventories are maintained close to their current value.

40.8 Disposition of variances

The question arises as to how the variances are to be brought into the final accounts of the business. There are, in fact, several methods of dealing with them.

They can be treated entirely as costs (if adverse variances) which are period costs and are, therefore, not included in the valuation of closing stocks of finished goods or work in progress. Alternatively they may be brought in as product costs and therefore used in the valuation of closing stocks. Another variation is to treat those variances which are controllable as period costs, but the uncontrollable variances be treated as product costs.

All of these methods are acceptable for the financial statements which are used for external reporting.

Before you read further, attempt Questions 40.1 and 40.2A.

40.9 Costing for labour

Before looking at labour variances, we first need to consider the range of basis upon which labour may be paid. There is no exact definition of 'wages' and 'salaries'. In general, it is accepted that wages are earnings paid on a weekly basis, while salaries are paid monthly.

The methods can vary widely between employers and also as regards different employees in the same organisation. The main methods are:

1 Fixed amount salaries or wages – these are an agreed annual amount.
2 Piece rate – based on the number of units produced by the employee.

3 Commission – a percentage based on the amount of sales made by the employee.
4 Basic rate per hour – a fixed rate multiplied by number of hours worked.

Arrangements for rewarding people for working overtime (time exceeding normal hours worked) will vary widely. The rate will usually be in excess of that paid during normal working hours. People being paid salaries will often not be paid for overtime.

In addition, bonuses may be paid on top of the above earnings. Bonus schemes will also vary widely and may depend on the amount of net profit made by the company, or on the amount of work performed or production achieved, either by the whole company or else the department in which the employee works.

It is important that the nature of payment to the employees is known before attempting to interpret the results of labour variance calculations. There will be significant differences in the possible explanations when employees are on salaries as opposed to basic rate as opposed to overtime, etc.

40.10 Labour variances

The computation of labour variances is similar to that of material variances. With labour variances the analysis can be broken down into:

(*a*) wage rate variances
(*b*) labour efficiency variances.

Note: As you read and work through this section, you will notice great similarity between the labour variance formulae and the materials variance formulae. In actual fact, the only difference is a terminological one. The wage rate formula is identical in method to the materials price formula; and the labour efficiency formula is similarly identical to the materials usage formula. This is something that students frequently fail to grasp. In effect, it means that you need only learn one of the pairs of formulae, along with the terminology for the other pair. You can then complete any variance computation on both pairs of formulae.

Because the computation of labour variances is so similar to those of materials variances only a few examples will be given.

1 Wage rate variance

Product A	
Standard hours to produce	100
Actual hours to produce	100
Standard wage rate per hour	£0.9
Actual wage rate per hour	£1.0

Exhibit 40.8

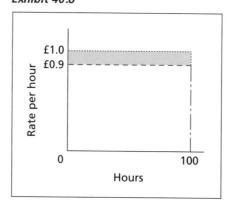

As the actual and standard hours are the same, then the only variance will be a wage rate variance, computed as follows:

	£
Actual cost per unit 100 × £1.0	100
Standard cost per unit 100 × £0.9	90
Variance (adverse)	10

Exhibit 40.8 illustrates this in that the variance is represented by the shaded area. This is £0.1 by a quantity of 100, therefore the variance is £10. The variance extends to the wage rate line and it is thus a wage rate variance, and as the shaded area is outside the standard cost lines, indicated by lines marked – – – – – –, then it is an adverse variance.

2 Labour efficiency variance

Product B	
Standard hours to produce	400
Actual hours to produce	370
Standard wage rate per hour	£1.0
Actual wage rate per hour	£1.0

Exhibit 40.9

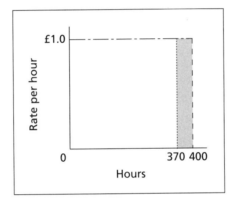

As the actual and standard wage rates are the same, then the only variance will be a labour efficiency variance, computed as follows:

	£
Actual cost per unit 370 × £1.0	370
Standard cost per unit 400 × £1.0	400
Variance (favourable)	30

Exhibit 40.9 illustrates this in that the variance is represented by the shaded area. This is a quantity of 30 by a rate of £1.0, therefore the variance is £30. The variance extends to the time line, therefore this is an efficiency variance, as the job has been completed in a different number of hours from standard. As the shaded area is inside the standard cost lines indicated by lines marked – – – – – –, it is a favourable variance.

3 Combined wage rate and efficiency variance

Product C	
Standard hours to produce	500
Actual hours to produce	460
Standard wage rate per hour	£0.9
Actual wage rate per hour	£1.1

Exhibit 40.10

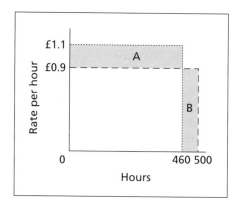

The net variance can be computed as:

	£
Actual cost per unit 460 × £1.1	506
Standard cost per unit 500 × £0.9	450
Variance (adverse)	56

Exhibit 40.10 shows that this is made up of two variances. The first variance, shown as the shaded portion A, is an adverse wage rate variance (it is outside the standard cost lines, therefore it is an adverse variance because actual cost for this has exceeded standard cost). The second variance, shown as the shaded portion B, is a favourable labour efficiency variance (it is inside the standard cost lines, therefore actual hours have been less than standard hours).

The adverse wage rate variance can, therefore, be seen to be £0.2 by a quantity of 460 = £92. The favourable efficiency variance is a quantity of 40 by a price of £0.9 = £36. The net adverse variance is, therefore, made up of:

	£
Adverse wage rate variance	92
Favourable labour efficiency variance	36
	56

40.11 Labour variances – analysis

Labour wage rates will probably be set in conjunction with the trade unions involved, so that this variance may not really be subject to control at any other level other than at the bargaining table with the unions involved. Nevertheless such a variance could arise because a higher grade of labour was being used than was necessary, even taking into account trade union needs. It might reflect a job running behind schedule that had to be finished off quickly even though higher grade labour was used. It might have been a rush job that also meant bringing in a higher grade of labour as well. The staffing policy of the firm may have come adrift because the firm had not recruited sufficient numbers of the various grades of labour.

Labour efficiency variances can be caused by a great number of things. Using unsuitable labour, unsuitable machinery, workers trying to slow work up so that more overtime rates of pay are earned, the day after a bank holiday, or the day before it, can affect performance. The morale of workers, the physical state of workers, using poor materials which slows up

production, hold-ups because of bottlenecks in production, and so on. The possibilities are almost endless. At the same time, if the variance was worth calculating, some form of action should follow. Otherwise, there is no point at all in calculating such variances.

40.12 Formulas for labour variances

Wage rate variance   = (Standard wage rate per hour – Actual wage rate) × Actual hours worked

= (SR – AR) × AH

Labour efficiency variance = (Standard labour hours for actual production – Actual labour hours worked) × Standard wage rate per hour

= (SH – AH) × SR

Don't forget, if you compare these formulae to the materials variance formulae, you will see that they are actually the same, only the terminology is different, i.e. 'wage rate' instead of 'price'; 'efficiency' instead of 'usage'.

Learning outcomes

You should now have learnt:

1 Variance analysis can improve the operating efficiency of a business by pinpointing items in need of investigation.

2 Adverse variances are not necessarily 'bad'. They result from more having been used or spent than was anticipated. Similarly, favourable variances are not necessarily 'good'. It is the reason for the variance, not the effect, that determines whether it is 'good' or 'bad'.

3 The materials usage variance formula is identical to the labour efficiency variance formula. Only the terminology differs.

4 The materials price variance formula is identical to the wage rate variance formula. Only the terminology differs.

Answers to activities

40.1 Buying cheaply may produce a favourable variance for the purchasing manager. This makes that individual appear efficient. However, doing so may result in poor quality materials being used, resulting in more wastage, a greater amount of labour time because the workers take longer to do the job with inferior materials, and a product made up of poor materials may well damage the image of the firm because its products do not last as long as they used to. This will make the production manager look inefficient. Clearly, it is not fair that the production manager takes the blame while the purchasing manager is congratulated for a job well done. This is one very good reason why it is important that overall variances are broken down into their constituent parts. Only then can blame be attributed to the correct individual and praise given to those that deserve it.

40.2 Rule 1: if the shaded box is horizontal, it is a price variance; if vertical, it is a usage variance.
Rule 2: if the shaded box lies inside the standard cost line, the variance is favourable; if it lies outside, it is adverse.

REVIEW QUESTIONS

Advice: Work carefully through Questions 40.1 and 40.3. If you have any difficulty, repeat them after 24 hours. Once you get into the swing of doing this type of question, it is quite easy to tackle them and get high marks.

40.1 Calculate the materials variances from the following data.

(*i*)   Material Q:
Standard price per tonne	£20	
Standard usage per unit	34	tonnes
Actual price per tonne	£18	
Actual usage per unit	37	tonnes

(*ii*) Material R:
Standard price per metre	£17	
Standard usage per unit	50	metres
Actual price per metre	£19	
Actual usage per unit	46	metres

(*iii*) Material S:
Standard price per metre	£12	
Standard usage per unit	15	metres
Actual price per metre	£14	
Actual usage per unit	18	metres

(*iv*) Material T:
Standard price per roll	£40	
Standard usage per unit	29	rolls
Actual price per roll	£37	
Actual usage per unit	27	rolls

(*v*)   Material U:
Standard price per kilo	£7	
Standard usage per unit	145	kg
Actual price per kilo	£8	
Actual usage per unit	154	kg

(*vi*) Material V:
Standard price per litre	£25	
Standard usage per unit	10,000	litres
Actual price per litre	£22	
Actual usage per unit	9,850	litres

40.2A Calculate the materials variances from the following data.

(*i*)   Material E:
Standard price per metre	£6	
Standard usage per unit	88	metres
Actual price per metre	£6	
Actual usage per unit	85	metres

(*ii*) Material F:
Standard price per tonne	£117	
Standard usage per unit	30	tonnes
Actual price per tonne	£123	
Actual usage per unit	30	tonnes

(*iii*) Material G:
Standard price per litre	£16	
Standard usage per unit	158	litres
Actual price per litre	£16	
Actual usage per unit	165	litres

(*iv*) Material H:
Standard price per foot	£16	
Standard usage per unit	92	feet
Actual price per foot	£19	
Actual usage per unit	92	feet

(v) Material I:

Standard price per tonne	£294
Standard usage per unit	50 tonnes
Actual price per tonne	£300
Actual usage per unit	50 tonnes

(vi) Material J:

Standard price per kilo	£27.5
Standard usage per unit	168 kg
Actual price per kilo	£27.5
Actual usage per unit	156 kg

40.3   Calculate the labour variances from the following data:

		Standard hours	Actual hours	Standard wage rate	Actual wage rate
(i)	Job A	220	218	£2.1	£2.1
(ii)	Job B	115	115	£1.7	£1.9
(iii)	Job C	200	240	£1.8	£1.8
(iv)	Job D	120	104	£2.0	£2.0
(v)	Job E	68	68	£1.8	£1.5
(vi)	Job F	30	34	£1.7	£1.7
(vii)	Job G	70	77	£1.6	£1.6
(viii)	Job H	100	100	£1.9	£2.0

40.4A   Calculate the labour variances from the following data:

		Standard hours	Actual hours	Standard wage rate	Actual wage rate
(i)	Job I	150	142	£2.0	£2.2
(ii)	Job J	220	234	£1.9	£1.7
(iii)	Job K	50	48	£2.0	£1.9
(iv)	Job L	170	176	£2.0	£2.2
(v)	Job M	140	149	£2.1	£1.8
(vi)	Job N	270	263	£1.6	£2.0

40.5   The company for which you are the accountant manufactures three related, but different, products. These are dishwashers, washing machines and refrigerators. Each product has a standard time per unit of production. These are:

dishwashers	10 hours
washing machines	12 hours
refrigerators	14 hours

In the month of March the actual production was:

dishwashers	150
washing machines	100
refrigerators	90

and the labour details were:

actual hours worked	4,100
standard hourly rate of pay	£4
actual wages incurred	£18,450

You are required to:
(a) Explain the term 'standard hour'
(b) Calculate the standard hours produced in the month of March
(c) Calculate the following variances, using the above data:
   (i)   total direct labour variance
   (ii) direct labour rate variance
   (iii) direct labour efficiency variance
(d) Give **two** possible causes for **each** of the labour rate and efficiency variances in (c).

(AQA (Northern Examinations and Assessment Board): GCE A-level)

40.6A Central Grid plc manufactures tungsten parts which pass through two processes, machining and polishing, before being transferred to finished goods. The management of the company have in operation a system of standard costing and budgetary control. The standard cost and budget information for April 20X8 has been established by the management accountant as follows:

Standard Cost and Budget Details for April 20X8

	Machining	Polishing
Standard cost per unit		
Direct material	£5	–
Direct labour	£12	£4.50
Budgeted output – units	16,000	16,000
(See Note below)		
Budgeted direct labour hours	48,000	24,000

Note: Output passes through both processes and there is no opening or closing work in progress.

Additional information:

1 The actual production costs and details for April 20X8 are as follows:
   (*i*) The output that passed through the two processes was 12,000 units and there was no opening or closing work in progress.
   (*ii*) Direct material used at standard prices was £64,150.
   (*iii*) Direct material used at actual prices was £60,390.
   (*iv*) The direct wages bill and the direct labour hours clocked for the machining department were:

	£	Hours
Machining department	153,000	34,000

2 Variances for the polishing department have been calculated and reveal the following:

Labour efficiency variance	£3,000 Adverse
Labour rate variance	Nil

Required:
(*a*) Calculate the total direct materials variance and its analysis into:
   (*i*) direct materials usage variance
   (*ii*) direct materials price variance.
(*b*) Calculate the overall direct labour variance for the machining department and analyse this variance into:
   (*i*) direct labour efficiency variance
   (*ii*) direct labour rate variance.
(*c*) Identify the possible reasons for each of the variances calculated for the machining department in (*a*) and (*b*) above and also for the variances given for the polishing department.
(*d*) Discuss possible interrelationships between these variances.

(AQA (Associated Examining Board): GCE A-level)

40.7 Borrico Ltd manufacture a single product and they had recently introduced a system of budgeting and variance analysis. The following information is available for the month of July 20X1:

1	Budget	Actual
	£	£
Direct materials	200,000	201,285
Direct labour	313,625	337,500
Variable manufacturing overhead	141,400	143,000
Fixed manufacturing overhead	64,400	69,500
Variable sales overhead	75,000	71,000
Administration costs	150,000	148,650

2 Standard costs were:
   Direct labour 48,250 hours at £6.50 per hour.
   Direct materials 20,000 kilograms at £10 a kilogram.

3 Actual manufacturing costs were:
Direct labour 50,000 hours at £6.75 per hour.
Direct materials 18,900 kilograms at £10.65 a kilogram.

4 Budgeted sales were 20,000 units at £50 a unit.
Actual sales were
   15,000 units at £52 a unit
   5,200 units at £56 a unit

5 There was no work in progress or stock of finished goods.

Required:
(a) An accounting statement showing the budgeted and actual gross and net profits or losses for July 20X1.
(b) The following variances for July 20X1.
   (i) Direct materials cost variance, direct materials price variance and direct materials usage variance.
   (ii) Direct labour cost variance, direct labour rate variance and direct labour efficiency variance.
(c) What use can the management of Borrico Ltd make of the variances calculated in (b) above?

(AQA (Associated Examining Board): GCE A-level)

40.8A
(a) How does a system of standard costing enable a business to operate on the principle of management by exception?
(b) Some of the following materials and labour variances have been wrongly calculated, although the figures used are correct. Recalculate the variances, showing clearly the formulae you have used, and state whether the variances are adverse or favourable.

   (i) *Total Materials Variance*
   (Standard price – Actual price)   (Standard quantity – Actual quantity)
   = (£8.42 – £8.24)   (1,940 litres – 2,270 litres)
   = (£0.18)   (– 330 litres)
   = £59.40 *adverse*

   (ii) *Materials Price Variance*
   (Standard price – Actual price)   Standard quantity
   = (£8.42 – £8.24)   1,940
   = £349.20 *favourable*

   (iii) *Materials Usage Variance*
   (Standard quantity – Actual quantity)   Standard price
   = (1,940 – 2,270)   £8.42
   = £2,778.6 *adverse*

   (iv) *Total Labour Variance*
   (Actual hours – Standard hours)   (Actual rate – Standard rate)
   = (860 – 800)   (£6.14 – £6.53)
   = (60 hours)   (–£0.39)
   = £23.4 *adverse*

   (v) *Wage Rate Variance*
   (Standard rate – Actual rate)   Actual hours
   = (£6.53 – £6.14)   860
   = £335.4 *favourable*

   (vi) *Labour Efficiency Variance*
   (Actual hours – Standard hours)   Standard rate
   = (860 – 800)   £6.53
   = £391.80 *favourable*

(Edexcel: GCE A-level)

40.9A Makers Ltd assembles computer games machines. Standard costs have been prepared as follows:

	Gamesmaster £	Gotchya £
Standard cost:		
Direct material: boards	5	10
components	20	30
Direct labour: assembly	5	5
testing	5	10
Overheads charged at 200%	20	30
	55	85
Profit margin	11	15
Standard selling price	66	100

The standard direct labour rate is £5 per hour.
During May 20X5, 5,000 Gamesmasters were sold at £60 each and 2,000 Gotchyas at £110 each. Actual costs were incurred as follows:

	£
5,050 Gamesmaster boards	26,000
5,060 sets Gamesmaster components	75,000
2,010 Gotchya boards	28,390
2,025 sets Gotchya components	56,409
10,000 assembly labour hours @ £4.90	49,000
7,000 testing labour hours at £5.10	35,700
Overheads	160,000
	430,499

There are no opening or closing stocks.

Required:
A schedule of direct materials and direct labour variances for the month.

(Welsh Joint Education Committee: GCE A-level)

40.10A The following diagram reflects costs under a standard costing system. Assume that all the variances are *unfavourable*. State, with reasons, which rectangle(s) represent:

(*i*) the standard cost
(*ii*) the actual cost
(*iii*) the total labour cost variance
(*iv*) the efficiency variance
(*v*) the wage rate variance.

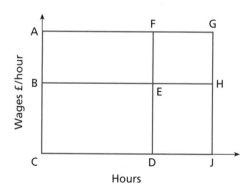

(Edexcel: GCE A-level)

CHAPTER 41

Overhead and sales variances

Learning objectives

After you have studied this chapter, you should be able to:

- calculate overhead expenditure variances, volume variances, efficiency variances, and capacity variances
- calculate sales price, volume and mix variances
- describe the similarities between the variable production overhead efficiency variance and both the labour efficiency variance and the materials usage variance
- identify appropriate reasons why variances found have occurred

Introduction

In this chapter you'll learn about another two groups of variances: those relating to overheads, both variable and fixed, and sales, and how to calculate them and interpret the results.

41.1 Management overheads

In Chapter 35, the problem of allocating manufacturing overheads to jobs or processes, was introduced. In the first instance the costs were collected in cost centres – normally recognisable departments of the organisation. The total costs of these centres is then applied to products or jobs as they pass through the operations of the cost centre.

Suppose that a firm collects costs into three manufacturing departments, and that the results are as shown in Exhibit 41.1.

Exhibit 41.1

	Department		
	A	B	C
	£	£	£
Fixed overhead cost	50,000	40,000	20,000
Variable overhead cost	30,000	35,000	40,000
Total overhead	80,000	75,000	60,000
Direct labour hours	10,000	30,000	15,000
Direct labour cost	£22,000	£59,000	£35,000
Machine hours	20,000	2,000	10,000

A decision has to be taken as to which activity, either labour or machine time, is the dominant factor in the department and will, therefore, provide the most appropriate basis for allocating the overheads.

In the case of department A, machine hours appear to be the major factor. Overheads will, therefore, be charged on the basis £80,000/20,000 hours = £4 per machine hour. The firm will record for each job or process the number of machine hours taken and the overheads will be allocated on this total of hours at £4 per hour.

In department B, labour appears to be the dominant feature. Overheads will, therefore, be charged on a labour hour rate calculated at £75,000/30,000 hours = £2.50 per hour.

Department C does not exhibit any dominant activity and could be expressed in either a machine hour rate or a labour hour rate. Some firms, where rates of pay in a department are stable and the mix of labour at different rates of pay stays the same, prefer to express the overheads as a percentage of labour cost. In department C it could be £60,000/£35,000 = 171 per cent. Thus the labour cost for all work going through department C would be collected and overheads allocated at 171 per cent of the labour cost figure.

41.2 Predetermined rates

The usual procedure, whether using standard costing or not, is to predetermine the overhead absorption rates using budgeted figures for both the overhead costs and the activity measure, whether machine or labour hours, or cost. This process has a number of advantages. It not only allows appropriate current estimates to be made for things such as price quotations, but also avoids the problem of fluctuating overhead rates at different times of the year due to seasonal variations.

For example, an ice-cream manufacturer is likely to be much more active in the summer months than in the winter. Because activity is low in winter, the rate of absorption is likely to rise steeply, as costs will not reduce proportionately. It makes more sense to view the overheads in this type of business on an annual cycle and recover the same amount of overhead in both summer and winter.

41.3 Variances in overhead recovery

As in all situations where budgeted figures are used, there are almost certainly going to be variances at the end of a period. Let's take figures from Exhibit 41.1 for Department A as the budget, and compare them with actual performance. This is shown in Exhibit 41.2.

Exhibit 41.2

	Department A	
	Budget figures	Actual figures
	£	£
Fixed overhead	50,000	52,000
Variable overhead	30,000	37,000
Total overhead	80,000	89,000
Machine hours	20,000	25,000
Machine hour rate £4		

The actual machine hours worked of 25,000 will have been used to allocate overheads to production at the rate of £4 per hour. As a result, £100,000 will have been allocated. Compared to actual overheads of £89,000 this represents an overabsorption of £11,000. The recovery would only have been exactly equal to actual overhead costs if 22,250 machine hours had been worked, i.e. 22,250 × £4 = £89,000.

In a cost accounting system not using standard costing the over- or underabsorption of overheads would be either:

(a) transferred wholly to cost of goods sold in the profit and loss account for the period;
(b) allocated between closing inventories and cost of goods sold; or
(c) carried forward to the next period.

The first choice would be used if the difference was felt to represent a shortfall in achievement; for example, if the number of hours worked had dropped due to bad management planning. The second would be applied if the differences were felt to be due to poor estimates of the original budgets. The third would apply only to interim financial statements, not those prepared at a period end.

Activity 41.1

Why?

Analysing the variances

The £11,000 variance between the amount recovered of £100,000 and the actual overhead cost of £89,000 can be analysed into a number of constituent variances in the normal manner of standard costing. In the example we have used, the variance can be due to

(a) the prices paid for goods and services being different from original estimates or standards – an 'expenditure' variance (sometimes called a 'budget' variance – both terms mean the same thing); or
(b) the volume of activity during the period being different from the original estimate – a 'volume' variance (for fixed overheads) or an 'efficiency' variance (for variable overheads).

Expenditure variance

An expenditure variance represents the difference between the actual cost of overhead and the budgeted overhead cost adjusted to the actual level of operational activity. From Exhibit 41.2 the budget figures need to be increased to take account of the fact that activity measured in machine hours has increased from 20,000 to 25,000 hours. This will not, of course, increase the fixed overhead – only the variable overheads which we will assume increase by 25 per cent in line with the hours. (You can see from Exhibit 41.1 that the £4 overhead recovery rate comprised 5/8 i.e. £2.50 for the fixed element and 3/8 i.e. £1.50 for the variable element.) This adjusted budget is shown in Exhibit 41.3.

Exhibit 41.3

	a Original budget	*b* Adjusted budget	*c* Actual	*b – c* Variance
		Department A		
Fixed overhead	50,000	50,000	52,000	(2,000)
Variable overhead	30,000	37,500	37,000	500
	80,000	87,500	89,000	(1,500)

The actual expenditure exceeds the adjusted budget by £1,500 which represents an adverse fixed overhead expenditure variance of £2,000 and a favourable variable expenditure variance of £500.

Volume variance

Apart from the cost of the overheads, the other factor that was budgeted in developing the predetermined standard was the number of machine hours. In the example, we estimated

that 20,000 machine hours would be worked. In fact, 25,000 machine hours were actually worked. This difference would not matter if *all* the overheads were variable, since the rate per hour would be constant at different activities. However, where fixed costs are concerned, increasing the activity will increase the amount recovered above the level required and, if activity is below budget, insufficient fixed overhead will be recovered.

In the example the rate is split:

$$\text{Fixed} \qquad \frac{50,000}{20,000} = \quad £2.50$$

$$\text{Variable} \qquad \frac{30,000}{20,000} = \quad \frac{£1.50}{\underline{4.00}}$$

When the machine hours increase from 20,000 to 25,000 we recover $5,000 \times £2.50 = £12,500$ more than required for the fixed overheads.

An alternative way of viewing this is to compare the amount of overheads recovered at 25,000 hours with the flexible budget for this level of activity:

		Total	*Fixed*	*Variable*
Recovered 25,000 × £4 =		100,000	62,500	37,500
Budget variable cost 25,000 × £1.50	37,500			(37,500)
Fixed cost	50,000		(50,000)	
		(87,500)		
Volume variance		12,500	12,500	–

This variance shows that by increasing the utilisation of the fixed resources in a business considerable savings are made. The £12,500 is a favourable variance in terms of the original standard.

Summary of variances

The analysis so far shows:

	£	£
Standard overhead recovered at actual level of activity (25,000 × £4)		100,000
Total fixed overhead variance at this level of activity – adverse	2,000	
Total variable overhead variance at this level of activity – favourable	(500)	
		1,500
		101,500
Volume variance – favourable		(12,500)
Actual level of manufacturing overheads		89,000

If this were the limit of the analysis, the variances to be investigated would be the adverse fixed cost variance of £2,000 and the favourable variable cost variance of £500. The remaining £12,500 volume variance is due to the increase in activity and it has been eliminated from further investigation when the budget was adjusted for the change in activity. (This is known as 'flexing' the budget.)

Nevertheless, while it does not require further investigation, it does require to be dealt with. As it stands, £12,500 too much has been recovered. That is, production has been charged with £12,500 too much. If you are not operating a standard costing system, you would need to deal with it using the second of the three approaches described earlier in this section – by allocating it between closing inventories and cost of goods sold.

However, you need to do more than simply find the difference between what it should have cost at the actual level of activity (i.e. the flexed budget) and what it actually cost. You need to look at what was actually produced and use that information to identify precisely what the variances to be investigated are.

41.4 Assessing variances

In an organisation where products are being manufactured that has adopted a standard costing system, it is common for the cost of the overheads to be related to the product. For example, if a Superwidget is manufactured in department A and it is estimated that it requires 2 machine hours per Superwidget, the standard cost of overhead per Superwidget will be 2 × £4 = £8.

If in the actual period, a Superwidget takes less than two hours to make there will be a favourable variance which will be costed at £4 per hour. Similarly, if more than two hours are taken, there will be an adverse (i.e. unfavourable) variance costed on the same basis.

Let's use the example from Exhibit 41.1, and assume department A manufactures only Superwidgets, that the original budget is to make 10,000 Superwidgets, and that the actual production of Superwidgets is 12,000. This is shown in Exhibit 41.4.

Exhibit 41.4

	Department A	
	Original budget	*Actual*
	£	£
Total overhead	80,000	89,000
Machine hours	20,000	25,000
Hours per Superwidget	2	
Number of units	10,000	12,000

Note that we are no longer using the machine hours to flex the budget. Instead, we are using the output, the number of Superwidgets produced. Immediately we do this, we identify another variance: to produce 12,000 widgets should take 24,000 hours at the standard rate. Since the actual hours are 25,000 there is an adverse variance of 1,000 hours which costs £4 per hour (note, this is made up of both fixed *and* variable overhead, as it is money wasted through operating at below expected efficiency).

Relating this adverse £4,000 variance to the other overhead variances, we get a standard overhead recovery at the actual level of output of £96,000 (i.e. 12,000 Superwidgets at 2 machine hours each equals 24,000 machine hours at £4 per hour). Actual costs were £89,000. The total variance is, therefore, £7,000. This can be broken down as follows:

	£
Standard cost of overheads for 12,000 actual Superwidgets produced × £8 =	(96,000)
Variable production overhead expenditure variance – favourable (*see below*)	500
Variable production overhead efficiency variance – adverse (*see below*)	(1,500)
Fixed production overhead expenditure variance – adverse (*see below*)	(2,000)
Fixed production overhead volume variance – favourable (*see below*)	10,000
Actual level of manufacturing overhead	(89,000)

41.5 Formulae for variances

The formula for each overhead variance is as follows:

Variable overhead
expenditure variance = Actual cost − (Actual hours worked × Standard rate)
$$= AC - (AH \times SR)$$
$$= £37,000 - (25,000 \times £1.50) = £500 \text{ favourable}$$

Variable overhead
efficiency variance $= $ (Actual hours worked $-$ Actual production in
$\qquad$ standard hours) $\times$ Standard rate
$= (AH - APSH) \times SR$
$= (25{,}000 - 24{,}000) \times £1.50 = £1{,}500$ adverse[Note 2]

Fixed overhead
expenditure variance $=$ Budgeted fixed production overheads $-$ Actual fixed
$\qquad$ production overheads
$= BFPO - AFPO$
$= £50{,}000 - £52{,}000 = £2{,}000$ adverse

Fixed overhead
volume variance[Note 1] $= $ (Actual production in standard hours $\times$ Standard rate)
$\qquad - $ Budgeted fixed production overheads
$= (APSH \times SR) - BFPO$
$= (24{,}000 \times £2.50) - £50{,}000 = £10{,}000$ favourable

The fixed overhead volume variance can be further divided into:

Fixed overhead
efficiency variance[Note 1] $= $ (Actual hours worked $-$ Actual production in
$\qquad$ standard hours) $\times$ Standard rate
$= (AH - APSH) \times SR$
$= (25{,}000 - 24{,}000) \times £2.50 = £2{,}500$ adverse

Fixed overhead
capacity variance[Note 1] $= $ (Actual hours worked $-$ Budgeted hours to be worked)
$\qquad \times$ Standard rate
$= (AH - BH) \times SR$
$= (25{,}000 - 20{,}000) \times £2.50 = £12{,}500$ favourable

Note 1: The last three variances – the fixed overhead volume, efficiency and capacity variances – are only calculated when absorption costing is being used. When the basis of the costing system is marginal costing, only the first three are used (because you do not link fixed costs to the level of output). In a marginal-costing-based environment, the total standard overhead cost for the 12,000 Superwidgets would be 12,000 at £3.00 variable overhead cost per Superwidget (= £36,000) plus the budgeted fixed cost of £50,000.

Rather than simply calculate the fixed overhead volume variance, you should normally calculate the efficiency and capacity variances. However, you need to be aware that together they represent the fixed overhead volume variance and should be able to calculate it if required. Replacing the favourable fixed overhead volume variance of £10,000 in the Superwidgets example produces the following breakdown of costs and variances:

	£
Standard cost of overheads for 12,000 actual Superwidgets produced × £8 =	(96,000)
Variable production overhead expenditure variance – favourable	500
Variable production overhead efficiency variance – adverse	(1,500)
Fixed production overhead expenditure variance – adverse	(2,000)
Fixed production overhead efficiency variance – adverse	(2,500)
Fixed production overhead capacity variance – favourable	12,500
Actual level of manufacturing overhead	(89,000)

Obviously, the variable overhead efficiency variance is the same formula as for the fixed overhead efficiency variance, the labour efficiency variance and the material usage variance.

Note 2: Efficiency variances are adverse when less is recovered than should have been.

41.6 A comprehensive example

The firm in this example operates standard costing based on absorption costing. The data set out below refers to a cost centre for a particular period:

Budget

Variable overheads (extract)

	Output	Cost
In units	In standard hours	£
9,800	49,000	98,000
9,900	49,500	99,000
10,000	50,000	100,000
10,100	50,500	101,000
10,200	51,000	102,000

Fixed overheads   150,000

Budgeted volume of production 10,000 units

Standard labour hours per unit = 5

Actual

Variable overhead	£104,000	
Fixed overhead	£160,000	
Direct labour hours worked	49,000	hours
Units of production	9,900	units

The 9,900 units of production is the equivalent of $9,900 \times 5 = 49,500$ standard direct labour hours.

Before making the variance calculations it will be helpful to make some observations on the data given. The flexible budget shows that each unit of production has a standard variable overhead cost of £10. Alternatively, this can be expressed as $£10 \div 5 = £2$ per standard hour of labour. It should not be assumed that this rate of £2 would also apply to levels of production outside the range shown. There may well be step costs, such as additional supervision, which would alter the standard variable overhead rate at higher levels of output.

The fixed costs are thought likely to remain fixed provided the range of output does not extend too far above or below the budgeted volume of production. The fixed standard rate is $£150,000 \div 50,000 = £3$ per standard hour of labour, or $£150,000 \div 10,000 = £15$ per unit.

The standard unit cost for overhead is thus $£10 + £15 = £25$ per unit or $£2 + £3 = £5$ per labour hour.

This budgeted volume of production is likely to be the level of output thought of as being normal and acceptable in the long run. It is referred to as the normal volume of production or, more commonly, as the 'normal level of activity'.

Calculation of variances

Firstly, it is helpful to calculate the net variance which is to be analysed. This is developed from the standard cost of the actual units produced:

Actual total overhead costs		264,000
Standard cost of actual production 9,900 × £25 =		247,500
Total variance	Adverse	(16,500)

This is broken down into the five variances as follows.

Variable overhead expenditure variance

Actual cost			104,000
Actual hours worked at standard rate = 49,000 × £2			98,000
Variable expenditure variance		Adverse	(6,000)

Variable overhead efficiency variance

Actual hours worked	49,000			
Actual production in standard hours	49,500			
Variable efficiency variance	500	× £2	Favourable	1,000

Fixed overhead expenditure variance

Budgeted fixed production overheads			150,000
Actual fixed production overheads			160,000
Fixed expenditure variance		Adverse	(10,000)

Fixed overhead efficiency variance

Actual hours worked	49,000			
Actual production in standard hours	49,500			
Variable efficiency variance	500	× £3	Favourable	1,500

Fixed overhead capacity variance

Actual hours worked	49,000			
Budgeted hours to be worked	50,000			
Fixed volume variance	1,000	× £3	Adverse	(3,000)

Summary of variances

Variable expenditure	Adverse	(6,000)
Variable efficiency	Favourable	1,000
Fixed expenditure	Adverse	(10,000)
Fixed efficiency	Favourable	1,500
Fixed capacity	Adverse	(3,000)
	Net Adverse	(16,500)

Reconciliation of standard and actual cost

Standard cost of actual production 9,900 units × £25	(247,500)
Variable expenditure – adverse	(6,000)
Efficiency variance – favourable	1,000
Fixed expenditure – adverse	(10,000)
Fixed efficiency variance – favourable	1,500
Fixed capacity variance – adverse	(3,000)
Actual cost of overheads	(264,000)

41.7 Variances and management action

The calculation of variances and their explanation to managers is of no value unless the information so revealed is put to use in making decisions which change subsequent activities. The question then arises as to whether every variance needs some form of action. It is not possible to be dogmatic here; it really does depend on circumstances. In some cases, a fairly large variance may be insignificant, whereas in others even a small amount may call for urgent action.

There is no doubt that variance calculations of the right type, transmitted to the right people at the right time, and which have an effect upon subsequent operations, can be of immense use. On the other hand, much of the effort put into variance calculation in many firms just goes to waste, as managers do not act on the information. This is very often because a poor 'selling' job has been done by the accounting staff to the managers concerned, in that either they have not been able to convince the managers that variance analysis is worthwhile or, possibly, the information provided is not really what the managers require to enable them to tackle their jobs properly.

41.8 Sales variances

The analysis of the difference between budgeted sales levels and actual levels can have an important bearing on the understanding of results. The main factors which are important in analysing sales are:

(a) selling price variances
(b) volume variances
(c) mix variances.

The selling price variance measures the overall profit difference caused by budgeted unit selling price and actual unit selling price being different. If the budget was to sell 100 widgets at £5 each and the actual sales were 100 widgets of £4.50 each, there will be a profit reduction of £50 due to the adverse selling price variance of 50p per unit on the 100 units sold.

The volume variances in sales will be measured in terms of the difference in the total quantity being sold between budget and actual. The impact of changes in volume of sales on profit can only be measured if we know the profitability of the sales. This will be dealt with at gross profit level. Thus if the budget is to sell 100 widgets with a unit gross margin of £2 and the actual sales achieved are only 90 widgets then there is an adverse variance of 10 units at the margin of £2 which represents a loss of profit of £20. If several products are being sold, the variance will be worked on total units actually sold in the proportion originally budgeted.

Exhibit 41.5

Product	Budget sales units	%	Budget gross margin £	Total budget margin £	Actual sales units	Actual sales in budget %
X	200	33.3	1.00	200	250	240
Y	200	33.3	1.50	300	190	240
Z	200	33.3	3.50	700	280	240
	600	100.0		1,200	720	720

The volume variance is calculated by comparing actual sales in budget percentage mix with the original budget at budget margins:

Product	Budget sales units	Actual sales in budget % units	Variance units	Budget margin £	Volume variances £
X	200	240	40	1.00	40.00
Y	200	240	40	1.50	60.00
Z	200	240	40	3.50	140.00
	600	720	120		240.00

The mix variance arises where more than one product is being sold and the different products have differing profit margins. If the proportions in which the actual sales of the products varies from budget then the overall profit will vary as a consequence.

In the example on volume variance the original budget was compared with actual sales split in the budget mix. For the mix variance these figures of actual sales in budget mix are compared with the actual sales and the differences evaluated at the budgeted gross profit margin.

Product	Actual sales in budget % units	Actual sales units	Variance units	Budget gross margin £	Mix variance £
X	240	250	10	1.00	10
Y	240	190	(50)	1.50	(75)
Z	240	280	40	3.50	140
	720	720	–		75

The difference in mix between budget and actual has increased profit by £75 due to the influence of more sales of product Z, i.e. there is a favourable mix variance of £75.

Exhibit 41.6

			Budget				Actual		
Product	%	Units	Unit selling price £	Unit gross profit £	Total profit £	Units	Unit selling price £	Unit gross profit £	Total profit £
A	16.7	100	20	5	500	90	21	6	540
B	33.3	200	25	10	2,000	220	24	9	1,980
C	50	300	10	2	600	350	10	2	700
	100	600			3,100	660			3,220

Total variance =	Actual profit	3,220
	Budget profit	3,100
	Favourable variance	120

Firstly eliminate the price variance using the actual units sold as the basis.

	Actual units sold 1	Budget price 2 £	Actual price 3 £	Unit variance 3 – 2 = 4 £	Total price variance 1 × 4 = 5 £
A	90	20	21	1	90
B	220	25	24	(1)	(220)
C	350	10	10	–	–
				Adverse price variance	(130)

Secondly eliminate the volume variance using the unit budgeted gross profit to evaluate the variance.

	Actual units sold 1	Actual units in budget (%) 2	Budget units sold 3	Variance in units 2 – 3 = 4	Budget unit gross profit 5 £	Total value variance 4 × 5 = 6 £
A	90	110	100	10	5	50
B	220	220	200	20	10	200
C	350	330	300	30	2	60
	660	660	600	60		
					Favourable volume variance	310

Finally, eliminate the mix variance. This is done by comparing the actual total units sold in the mix as originally budgeted with the actual sales.

	Budget % 1	Actual total sales split in budget % 2	Actual sales units 3	Difference units 3 – 2 = 4	Budget unit gross profit 5	Mix variance 4 × 5 = 6
A	16.7	110	90	(20)	5	(100)
B	33.3	220	220	–	10	–
C	50.0	330	350	20	2	40
		660	660			
					Adverse mix variance	(60)

Summary of variance:

Adverse price variance	(130)
Favourable volume variance	310
Adverse mix variance	(60)
Favourable total sales variance	120

The gross profit margin may change for reasons other than changes in sales – for example, if the cost of materials varies from budgets or wage rates change. This type of variance has, however, already been dealt with under materials and labour variances.

Learning outcomes

You should now have learnt:

1 How to calculate overhead and sales variances.

2 The similarities between the variable production overhead efficiency variance and both the labour efficiency variance and the materials usage variance.

3 How to identify appropriate reasons why variances found have occurred.

4 That the calculation of variances and their explanation to managers is of no value unless the information so revealed is put to use in making decisions which change subsequent activities.

Answers to activities

41.1 Because they are period costs that must be charged to profit and loss during the accounting period.

REVIEW QUESTIONS

Advice: Remember that the overhead variances consist of the difference between the standard costs at the actual level of activity and the actual costs. Remember also that sales variances consist of those for price, volume and mix.

It is important that you answer the parts of the questions that ask you to comment on exactly what might be behind the variances and what action is needed.

41.1 **You are required to** calculate the overhead variances from the following data.

(a) Budgeted for £6,000 variable overhead and 1,000 machine hours.

Actual overhead	£5,840
Actual machine hours	1,000

(b) Budgeted for £20,000 variable overhead and 5,000 machine hours.

Actual overhead	£21,230
Actual machine hours	5,000

(c) Budgeted for £12,000 fixed overhead and the actual overhead is found to be £11,770.
(d) Budgeted for £40,000 fixed overhead and the actual overhead is found to be £41,390.
(e) Budgeted production of 2,000 units in 8,000 hours. Standard variable overhead rate is £3 per hour. In fact 2,000 units are produced in 7,940 hours.
(f) Budgeted production of 5,000 units in 15,000 hours. Standard variable overhead rate is £4 per hour. In fact 4,860 units are produced in 15,000 hours.

41.2A You are required to calculate the overhead variances in the following cases:

(a) Budgeted for £37,000 fixed overhead. The actual fixed overhead turns out to be £36,420.
(b) Budgeted for production of 500 units in 250 hours. The variable overhead rate is £6 per hour. In fact 500 units are produced in 242 hours.
(c) Budgeted for £18,000 variable overhead and 9,000 machine hours. Actual overhead is £18,000 and actual machine hours 8,820.
(d) Budgeted for £9,000 variable overhead and 3,000 machine hours. Actual overhead is £8,790 and actual machine hours 3,000.
(e) Budgeted for £120,000 fixed overhead. The actual fixed overhead turns out to be £129,470.
(f) Budgeted for production of 10,000 units in 30,000 hours. Standard variable overhead rate is £8 an hour. In fact 9,880 units are produced in 30,000 hours.

41.3 You are required to calculate the overhead variances of Joseph Ltd. The budget is prepared as:

(a) Total budgeted variable overhead £400,000.
(b) Total budgeted fixed overhead £160,000.
(c) Budgeted volume of production 80,000 direct labour hours for 40,000 units.

The actual results turn out to be:

(d) Actual variable overhead £403,600.
(e) Actual fixed overhead £157,200.
(f) Actual volume 78,500 direct labour hours which resulted in 42,000 units of production.

41.4A You are required to calculate the overhead variances of Raymond Ltd. The budget is prepared as:

(a) Total budgeted variable overhead £100,000.
(b) Total budgeted fixed overhead £125,000.
(c) Budgeted volume of production 50,000 direct labour hours of 250,000 units.

The actual results turn out to be:

(d) Actual variable overhead £96,500.
(e) Actual fixed overhead £129,400.
(f) Actual volume 52,000 direct labour hours which resulted in 244,000 units.

41.5 The Grange Company had the following results for the year to 31 March 20X1. A single product – a toggle – was made by the company.

	Budget	Actual
Sales in units	125,000	150,000
Sales in £	312,500	356,250

The standard cost of manufacturing each unit was £1.50.

What are the price and volume variances on sales in 20X1?

41.6A Corporec PLC manufactures a detergent in one of its plants. The information for the year to 30 September 20X2 was as follows:

	Budget	Actual
Sales in litres	180,000	170,000
Sales in £	540,000	527,000

The standard cost of manufacturing a litre was £2.

Calculate the price and volume variances for 20X2.

41.7 The following data was collected for Molton Ltd for the year ended 31 March 20X3.

Product	Budget selling price £	Budget sales units	%	Budget gross profit per unit £	Budget gross profit total £	Actual selling price £	Actual sales unit	%	Actual gross profit per unit £	Actual gross profit total £
M	5	800	25	1.00	800	5.10	840	30	0.90	756
N	8	1,600	50	1.50	2,400	7.90	1,680	60	1.40	2,352
P	7	800	25	1.20	960	7.30	280	10	1.20	336
		3,200	100		4,160		2,800	100		3,444

Calculate price, volume and mix variances for 20X3.

41.8A The following information relates to Burton Company for the year to 30 June 20X6:

Product	Budget units	Sales %	Budget selling price per unit £	Budget gross profit per unit £	Actual units	Sales %	Actual unit selling price £	Actual unit gross profit £
A	400	14.3	30	5	500	20.8	29	4
B	600	21.4	25	4	400	16.7	27	5
C	1,800	64.3	40	10	1,500	62.5	39	9
	2,800	100.0			2,400	100.0		

Calculate price, volume and mix variances for 20X6.

41.9 Singleton has been operating for some years as a manufacturer of a single product, and after several years' growth has decided to form a company Singleton Ltd.

His accountant advised him that in an increasingly competitive world he really should achieve greater financial control of his business, and to assist Singleton in this objective the accountant prepared a simple manufacturing budget for the financial year ending 31 August 20X9.

The following schedule provides the detail of the budget and the actual results for the year ended 31 August 20X9. The actual results have been extracted from the ledger as at that date without any adjustments made.

	Budget £	Actual £
Raw materials consumed	80,000	90,000
Factory rent	10,000	12,500
Factory maintenance expenses	6,700	6,100
Heating and lighting	2,900	3,000
Direct labour wages	120,000	110,500
Direct expenses	5,800	6,000
Depreciation of plant and machinery	8,900	10,500
Wages, maintenance labour	18,000	24,000
Other factory overheads	12,700	9,600

Additional information:

1 At 31 August 20X9 the following amounts were still owing:

	£
Direct labour wages	5,100
Heating and lighting	900
Other factory overhead	400

2 The factory rent paid covered the period from 1 September 20X8 to 30 November 20X9.
3 During the year the firm sold 90,000 units of its product at £4.50 a unit.
4 There was no work-in-progress. The stocks of finished goods were:

	£
1 September 20X8	28,900
31 August 20X9	35,000

Required:
(a) What is variance analysis and how can it contribute to the operating efficiency of Singleton's business?
(b) For the year ended 31 August 20X9 prepare:
  (i) A manufacturing account and a schedule of the relevant variances;
  (ii) A trading account.
(c) Write a report to advise Singleton whether the principles of budgeting can be applied to:
  (i) Non-manufacturing costs;
  (ii) The control of cash resources.

Your report should indicate in each case the potential benefits that the firm could achieve through extending its use of budgeting.

(AQA (Associated Examining Board): GCE A-level)

41.10A Flint Palatignium Ltd calculates the prices of its output by adding a mark-up of 15 per cent to standard costs. These standard costs are arrived at by reference to budgeted outputs and estimated direct costs as follows:

	£ each	Standard price/rate
Materials	5.00	£1 per unit
Direct labour	2.50	£1.25 per hour
Overheads	7.50	£3.75 per direct labour hour
	15.00	
Mark-up	2.25	
Selling price	17.25	

Management accounts for April, 20X8 provide an analysis of operations as follows:

	£
Sales – at standard price	534,750
Standard margin on sales	69,750
Favourable sales price variance	8,691
	78,441
Other favourable variances	
Material price	4,662
Labour rate	600
Overhead expenditure	147
	83,850
Adverse variances	
Material usage	(1,743)
Labour efficiency	(292)
Overhead capacity	(9)
Actual operating profit	81,806

Materials in stock are valued at standard cost. At 1 April, 1,000 units of material were held, whereas at 30 April the stock of this material increased to 1.750 units.

Required:
(*i*) A trading account for the month of April 20X8 comparing the budgeted income and expenditure appropriate to actual output, to actual income and expenditure.
(*ii*) An explanation of the value of standard costing and variance analysis to a service business whose custom is to negotiate fixed price contracts.

(*Welsh Joint Education Committee: GCE A-level*)

(*Note: The following question covers material from both Chapters 40 and 41.*)

41.11A   HGW Limited produces a product called a Lexton. The standard selling price and the manufacturing costs of this product are as follows:

		£
Standard selling price per unit		<u>86</u>
Standard production costs:		
Direct material	1.5 kilos at £12 per kilo	18
Direct labour	4.4 hours at £7.50 per hour	33
Variable overheads	4.4 hours at £5 per hour	<u>22</u>
		<u>73</u>

The projected production and sales for March 20X4 were 520 units.

On 1 April 20X4 the following actual figures were determined.

Sales	550 units at £85 each
Production	550 units
Direct material	785 kilos at £12.40 per kilo
Direct labour	2,400 hours at £7.80 per hour
Overheads	£12,500 (overall variance £400 adverse)

There was no opening stock of the product Lexton.

Required:
(*a*) Prepare an actual profit and loss statement for HGW Ltd for March 20X4
(*b*) Calculate the following variances and their respective sub-variances:
    (*i*)   sales – price and volume
    (*ii*) direct materials – price and usage
    (*iii*) direct labour – rate and efficiency
(*c*) Prepare a statement reconciling the actual profit calculated in part (*a*) with the budgeted profit on actual sales. (Use the variances calculated in part (*b*) and the given overhead variance.)
(*d*) Write a report to the management outlining the factors that need to be considered when standards are being established.

(*AQA (Associated Examining Board): GCE A-level*)

Planning, control and decision making

Introduction

This part looks at how accounting information may be used to guide decision making within an entity, at how the cost of investment is calculated, and at how organisations are beginning to use the information available to them to provide a richer view of the performance of the organisation than is possible from straightforward ratio analysis.

CHAPTER 42

Break-even analysis

Learning objectives

After you have studied this chapter, you should be able to:

- prepare break-even graphs and contribution graphs
- explain what is meant by 'break-even'
- explain the importance of contribution and fixed costs in identifying the break-even level of sales
- use graphs to identify break-even point, the margin of safety, and the contribution for any level of activity
- use break-even graphs to show the impact of changes in costs, volume and selling price upon profitability
- describe some of the limitations of break-even charts
- use a formula in order to calculate the break-even point
- explain the relevance of contribution to decision making

Introduction

In this chapter you'll learn about break-even analysis and, through it, about the relationship between costs, volume, selling price and profit.

42.1 Introduction

The level of activity achieved by a firm is of paramount importance in determining both whether it makes a profit or loss, and the size of such profits or losses. Let's take an example to which the answer is obvious. If a firm has fixed costs of £10,000 and its total revenue is £8,000 then, no matter how much the variable costs are, the firm is bound to make a loss. A firm has to cover both its fixed costs and its variable costs before it can make a profit. With very low revenue, as in this case, a loss is bound to be incurred.

There is, therefore, a great deal of interest in exactly how much revenue (i.e. sales) has to be earned before a profit can be made. If revenue is below fixed costs then a loss will be incurred; if revenue is below total costs (i.e. fixed costs + variable costs) a loss will still be incurred. Where revenue is greater than fixed costs plus variable costs then a profit will have been made. The question then arises, at what point does the firm stop incurring a loss and, with the next unit of revenue, make a profit? That is, at what point does the firm break even or make neither a profit nor a loss?

Fixed costs stay unchanged over stated ranges in the volume of production, but variable costs are those that change in total when the volume of production changes within a stated

range. As revenue increases so do variable costs, so that the only item that remains unchanged is that of fixed costs. Let us look at an example of a firm showing the changing costs and revenue over differing volumes of production.

Apollo Ltd has fixed costs of £5,000. The variable costs are £2 per unit. The revenue (selling price) is £3 per unit. Looking at production in stages of 1,000 units we can see that the figures emerge as in Exhibit 42.1.

Exhibit 42.1

No. of units	Fixed cost	Variable cost	Total cost: Variable + Fixed	Revenue (Sales)	Profit	Loss
	£	£	£	£	£	£
0	5,000	nil	5,000	nil		5,000
1,000	5,000	2,000	7,000	3,000		4,000
2,000	5,000	4,000	9,000	6,000		3,000
3,000	5,000	6,000	11,000	9,000		2,000
4,000	5,000	8,000	13,000	12,000		1,000
5,000	5,000	10,000	15,000	15,000	nil	nil
6,000	5,000	12,000	17,000	18,000	1,000	
7,000	5,000	14,000	19,000	21,000	2,000	
8,000	5,000	16,000	21,000	24,000	3,000	
9,000	5,000	18,000	23,000	27,000	4,000	

With activity of 5,000 units, the firm will break even, it will make neither a profit nor a loss. Above that the firm moves into profit; below that the firm would never make a profit.

We could have calculated the break-even point without drawing up a schedule of costs, etc. as in Exhibit 30.1. Instead we could have said that for one unit the revenue is £3 and the variable cost is £2, so that the remaining £1 is the amount out of which the fixed costs have to be paid, and that anything left over is profit.

The £1 is the 'contribution' towards fixed costs and profit. If the contribution was only just enough to cover fixed costs, there would be no profit, but neither would there be any loss. There are £5,000 fixed costs, so that with a contribution of £1 per unit there would have to be 5,000 units to provide a contribution of £5,000 to cover fixed costs. It could be stated as:

$$\text{Break-even point} = \frac{\text{Fixed costs}}{\text{Selling price per unit} - \text{Variable costs per unit}}$$

i.e. in the case of Apollo Ltd

$$\frac{£5,000}{£3 - £2} = \frac{5,000}{1} = 5,000 \text{ units}$$

Activity 42.1

If fixed costs were £7,000 and the contribution per unit were 2, what would be the break-even level of sales?

42.2 The break-even chart

The information given in Exhibit 42.1 can also be shown in the form of a chart. Many people seem to grasp the idea of break-even analysis rather more easily when they see it in chart form. This is particularly true of people who are not used to dealing with accounting information. We will, therefore, plot the figures from Exhibit 42.1 on a chart which is shown as Exhibit 42.2.

The use of the chart can now be looked at. It would be extremely useful if you could draw the chart as shown in Exhibit 42.2 on a piece of graph paper. The larger the scale that you use, the easier it will be to take accurate readings. Plot the lines from the figures as shown in Exhibit 42.1.

Exhibit 42.2

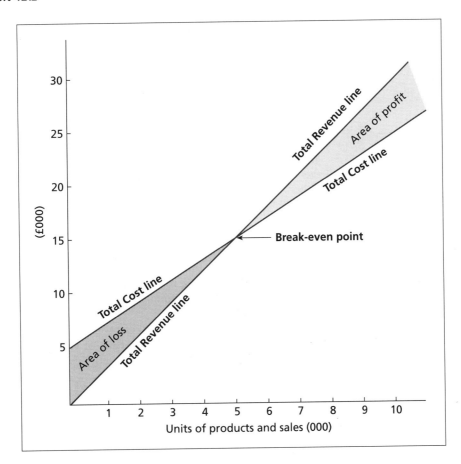

To find the break-even point in terms of units of product, draw a line straight down from the break-even point so that it meets the horizontal axis at right angles. This is shown in Exhibit 42.3 as line A which, when read off, gives units of products and sales as 5,000 units.

Exhibit 42.3

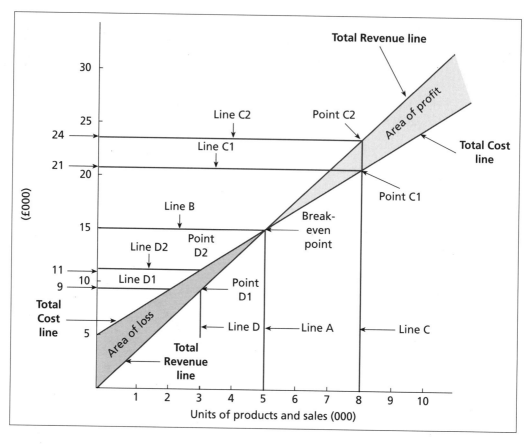

Now draw a line direct to the vertical £s axis so that it meets that at a right angle. This is line B and shows £15,000. This means that according to the chart the break-even point is shown at 5,000 units where both costs and revenue are equal at £15,000. This is, of course, the same answer as given in the table in Exhibit 42.1.

As production and sales go above 5,000 units, the firm makes profits. When production and sales are above 5,000 units, the difference represents the **margin of safety**. This is the number of units in excess of the break-even point. If volume fell by more than the margin of safety, the firm would incur losses.

Activity 42.2

Look at the chart again and, without looking back at what you have just read, attempt to answer the following two questions by taking readings off your chart:

(*i*) What would the total costs of the firm be at (*a*) 2,000 units, (*b*) 7,000 units, (*c*) 8,500 units?

(*Remember*: take a line up from the product line for the figure needed then, from where the cost line is bisected, draw a line to the £s line to meet it at right angles.)

(*ii*) What is the revenue for (*a*) 3,000 units, (*b*) 6,000 units, (*c*) 7,500 units?

Before proceeding further, look at the answers to this activity.

Now we will try to find the amount of profit or loss at various levels by looking at the chart in Exhibit 42.3. First, let's calculate the profit made if 8,000 units are going to be made and sold. Draw a line up from the product line (horizontal axis) at right angles (shown as line C) until it bisects both the Total Cost line and the Total Revenue line, the points of intersection being shown as C1 for the Total Cost line and C2 for the Total Revenue line. Read off the amounts in £s by taking lines across to the £s vertical axis until they meet it at right angles. These are shown as lines C1 and C2. The line from C1 will give a reading of £21,000 and from C2 of £24,000. As the Total Revenue exceeds the Total Costs there is a profit. In this case, the profit is £3,000.

If we now try for 3,000 units, the line drawn up from the product line will meet the Total Revenue line at point D1 and the Total Cost line at D2. Reading off to the £s line D1 shows as £9,000 while D2 shows as £11,000. In this case, the Total Cost exceeds the Total Revenue by £2,000 and there is, therefore, a loss of £2,000.

Activity 42.3

Look at your chart again and use it to find the profit or loss recorded at

(a) 1,000 units, (b) 4,000 units, (c) 6,500 units and (d) 8,500 units.

Before proceeding, look at the answers to this activity at the end of the chapter.

42.3   Changes and break-even charts

The effect of changes on profits can easily be shown by drawing fresh lines on the chart to show the changes, or intended changes, in the circumstances of the firm. Let us first of all consider what factors can bring about a change in the profits of a firm. These are:

(a) the selling price per unit could be increased (or decreased)
(b) a possible decrease (or increase) in fixed costs
(c) a possible decrease (or increase) in variable costs per unit
(d) increase the volume of production and sales.

We will investigate these by starting with some basic information for a firm and then seeing what would happen if each of the changes (a) to (d) were to happen.

The basic information is shown in Exhibit 42.4.

Exhibit 42.4

No. of units	Fixed cost	Variable cost	Total cost: Variable + Fixed	Revenue (Sales)	Profit	Loss
	£	£	£	£	£	£
100	2,000	400	2,400	900		1,500
200	2,000	800	2,800	1,800		1,000
300	2,000	1,200	3,200	2,700		500
400	2,000	1,600	3,600	3,600	nil	nil
500	2,000	2,000	4,000	4,500	500	
600	2,000	2,400	4,400	5,400	1,000	
700	2,000	2,800	4,800	6,300	1,500	
800	2,000	3,200	5,200	7,200	2,000	
900	2,000	3,600	5,600	8,100	2,500	

The table in Exhibit 42.4 shows that variable costs are £4 per unit and selling price £9 per unit. (These figures are found by dividing the variable cost and revenue values at any number of units by that number of units. For example, dividing £400 variable cost by 100 gives £4 variable cost per unit.)

We can draw a chart to incorporate this information before considering the changes being contemplated. This is shown in Exhibit 42.5.

Exhibit 42.5

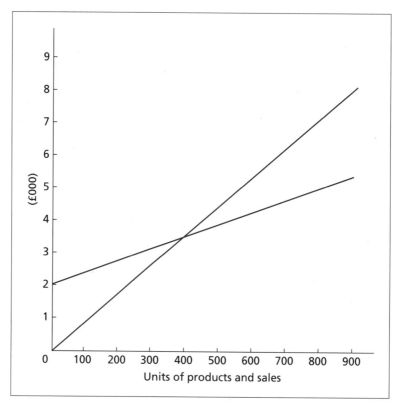

(a) Increase selling price

Taking a copy of the chart shown in Exhibit 42.5 as a base, we can now draw an extra line on it to represent an increase in selling price. Let us suppose that the selling price could be increased by £2 per unit. This can now be shown on a break-even chart in Exhibit 42.6. The line shown as New Total Revenue can then be added. This would mean that the break-even point would change as the increased revenue means that costs can be covered sooner. The dotted area shows the reduction in the loss area that would be incurred at the same volume of sales, while the shaded area shows the increase in profit at the various volumes of sales.

(b) Reduce fixed costs

We can now draw some more lines on the chart shown in Exhibit 42.6, this time to reflect a reduction of £800 in fixed costs. This can be seen in Exhibit 42.7, where a line entitled New Total Costs has been added. The reduction in loss if sales were at a low volume is represented by the dotted area, while the shaded area shows the additional profit at various volumes of activity. The change in profit or loss will be constant at £800 over these volumes.

Exhibit 42.6

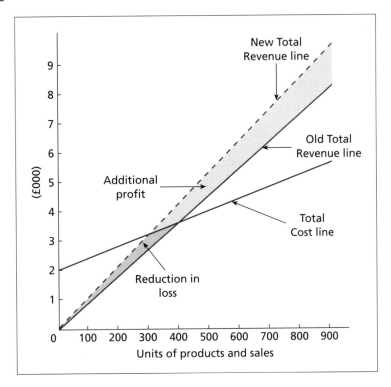

Exhibit 42.7

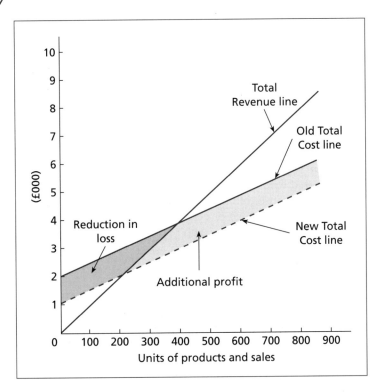

(c) Reduce variable costs

Reverting to the chart shown in Exhibit 42.6 (where the fixed costs are £2,000), we can see what happens if the variable costs per unit are reduced, in this case by £2 per unit. This is shown in Exhibit 42.8, where the dotted area shows the reduction in loss compared with the position if the costs had not changed, while the shaded area shows the additional profit at different levels of activity.

Exhibit 42.8

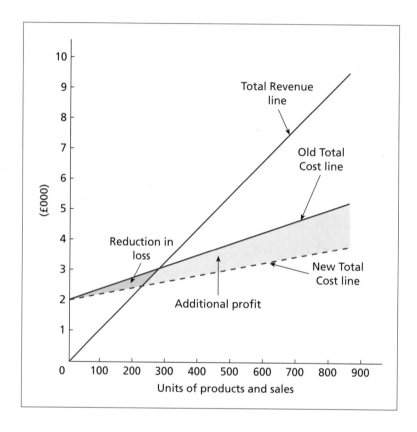

You will recall that an £800 reduction in fixed costs in Exhibit 42.7 showed a constant difference of £800 compared with previously over the whole range of activity. In contrast, a reduction in variable costs (as in Exhibit 42.8) brings about different increases of profit, or reduction of loss, over the whole range of activity. The greater the activity the greater the gain with variable cost savings, whereas the gain remains constant with fixed cost savings.

(d) Increased production and sales

Reverting once more to the original position as shown in Exhibit 42.5, when sales and/or production increase, all that is required is that the lines Total Revenue and Total Costs are extended. Exhibit 42.9 shows Exhibit 42.5 with the level of activity increased by 300 units. The new profit indicated will be greater than the old profit because all extra units are being sold at a profit.

Exhibit 42.9

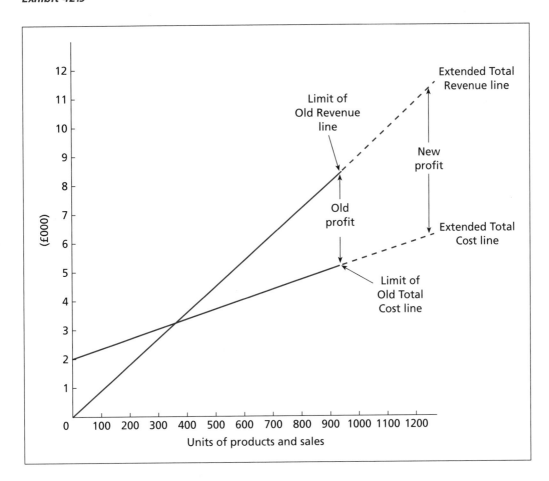

42.4 The limitations of break-even charts

In each of the cases looked at it has been assumed that only one of the factors of variable cost, fixed cost, selling price or volume of sales has altered. This is not usually the case. An increase in price may well reduce the number sold. There may well be an increase in fixed cost which has an effect which brings down variable costs. The changes in the various factors should, therefore, be studied simultaneously rather than separately.

In addition, **where there is more than one product, the proportions in which the products are sold, i.e. the product mix, can have a very important bearing on costs.** Suppose that there are two products, one has a large amount of fixed costs but hardly any variable costs, and the other has a large amount of variable costs but little fixed costs. If the proportions in which each is sold change very much then this could mean that the costs and profit could vary tremendously, even though the total figures of sales stayed constant. An illustration of this can be seen in Exhibit 42.10.

Exhibit 42.10

In considering the break-even analysis we may expect that the following will occur.

Fixed costs £1,000, Variable costs: Product A £5 per unit, B £20 per unit.
Selling prices: A £10 per unit, B £30 per unit.
Expected sales: A 150, B 50. Actual sales: A 30, B 90.

The expected sales are: A 150 × £10 + B 50 × £30 = £3,000.
The actual sales are: A 30 × £10 + B 90 × £30 = £3,000.

The actual sales revenue and expected sales revenue are the same, but the sales mix is different, as are the costs and profit:

			£
Expected:			
Sales			3,000
Less Variable costs:	A 150 × £5 =	750	
	B 50 × £20 =	1,000	
			(1,750)
Contribution			1,250
Less Fixed costs			1,000
Net profit			250
Actual:			
Sales			3,000
Less Variable costs:	A 30 × £5 =	150	
	B 90 × £20 =	1,800	
			(1,950)
Contribution			1,050
Less Fixed costs			(1,000)
Net profit			50

Variable costs are usually taken to be in direct proportion to volume, so that 1,000 units means (say) £5,000 variable costs and therefore 2,000 units would mean £10,000 variable costs, 3,000 units equal £15,000 variable costs and so on. This is often a reasonable estimation of the situation, but may well hold true only within fairly tight limits. For instance 3,100 units could mean £16,000 costs instead of the £15,500 that it would be if a linear relationship existed. This is also true of sales, because to increase sales beyond certain points some units may be sold cheaply. Thus 1,000 units might be sold for £9,000; 2,000 units sold for £18,000; but to sell 2,200 units the revenue might be only £19,100 instead of the £19,800 (2,200 × £9) that might be expected if a linear relationship existed over all ranges.

It is assumed that everything produced is sold, and that stocks-in-trade remain constant. It would be difficult to do otherwise as both sales revenue and costs relate to one and the same measure of volume.

Another limitation, is more of a complication than a hindrance. Organisations considering a change in the level of activity outside the current range may well be faced with changed fixed costs as a result. For example, a new warehouse may need to be leased in order to cope with the extra production. In that case, the break-even graphs produced need to incorporate stepped fixed costs that increase to a new fixed level once the threshold in activity for the higher cost has been reached. This can result in multiple break-even points.

42.5 Contribution graph

Exhibit 42.11 is a redrafting of Exhibit 42.5 that includes the addition of a line representing variable cost. It runs parallel to and below the total cost line. This is an alternative method of presentation. It highlights the total contribution. The vertical gap between the Total Cost

line and the Variable Cost line at any particular number of units represents the contribution at that number of units.

Exhibit 42.11

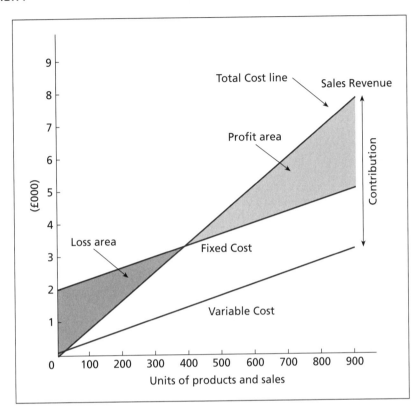

You should now have learnt:

1 How to prepare break-even graphs and contribution graphs.

2 That break-even analysis can be performed using either a formula or a graph.

3 How to use graphs to identify break-even point, the margin of safety and the contribution for any level of activity.

4 How to use a formula in order to calculate the break-even point.

5 That fixed costs are assumed to be fixed for the range of activity being considered, and variable costs per unit and sales revenue per unit are assumed to be constant within that range of activity. It is important to check whether these assumptions are correct when carrying out a break-even analysis. If they are not, the format of the analysis should be adjusted appropriately.

6 How to use break-even graphs to show the impact of changes in costs, volume and selling price upon profitability.

7 How to explain the relevance of contribution to decision making.

Answers to activities

42.1 3,500 units.

42.2 (*i*) (*a*) £9,000 (*b*) £19,000 (*c*) £22,000
(*ii*) (*a*) £9,000 (*b*) £18,000 (*c*) £22,500

42.3 (*a*) Loss £4,000 (*b*) Loss £1,000 (*c*) Profit £1,500 (*d*) Profit £3,500

REVIEW QUESTIONS

Advice: The very important concept of break-even attracts quite a large number of questions. Be careful when drawing any charts, as a faulty chart will give you wrong answers for every part of your answer and you are unlikely to get marks for those wrong answers. You cannot expect examiners to assume that your faulty drawing of a graph was a simple error of draughtsmanship instead of being conceptual.

42.1 Hedges Ltd has fixed costs of £8,000. The variable costs are £4 per unit. The revenue (selling price) is £6 per unit. **You are required** (*i*) to draft a schedule as follows filling in the columns (*a*) to (*f*) for each stage of 1,000 units up to 10,000 units.

No. of units	(a) Fixed cost £	(b) Variable cost £	(c) Total cost £	(d) Revenue £	(e) Profit £	(f) Loss £
0						
1,000						
2,000						
3,000						
4,000						
5,000						
6,000						
7,000						
8,000						
9,000						
10,000						

(*ii*) **You are also required to** draw a break-even chart from the data in this schedule. Draw it carefully to scale on a piece of graph paper. Retain your answer, you will need it for some questions which follow later.

42.2 Cover up the schedule you constructed as your answer to 42.1(*i*) and look instead at the break-even chart constructed as the answer to 42.1(*ii*). **Answer the following**:

(*a*) What are the total costs at production levels of (*i*) 4,000 units; (*ii*) 7,000 units; (*iii*) 9,000 units; (*iv*) 5,500 units?
(*b*) What is the total revenue at (*i*) 3,000 units; (*ii*) 8,000 units; (*iii*) 5,500 units?

42.3A Look at your schedule in answer to 42.1(*i*) and **answer the following**:

(*a*) What are the total costs at production levels of (*i*) 4,000 units; (*ii*) 7,000 units; (*iii*) 9,000 units; (*iv*) 5,500 units? You will have to deduce this amount as it is not shown as a figure on the schedule.
(*b*) What is the total revenue at (*i*) 3,000 units; (*ii*) 8,000 units; (*iii*) 5,500 units?

42.4 From your break-even chart for 42.1(*ii*), **calculate** the profit or loss that will be made at levels of (*i*) 3,000 units; (*ii*) 10,000 units; (*iii*) 4,000 units; (*iv*) 7,000 units; (*v*) 8,500 units.

42.5A From the schedule in 42.1(*i*), **calculate** the profit or loss that would be made at levels of (*i*) 3,000 units; (*ii*) 10,000 units; (*iii*) 4,000 units; (*iv*) 7,000 units; (*v*) 8,500 units (this last figure will have to be deduced as it is not a figure on the schedule).

42.6 Polemic Ltd manufacture and sell a single product. The following information is available for three financial years ending 30 September.

	Price per unit £	Unit volume 000s
Sales		
Actual 19X1	130	50
Forecast 19X2	129	52
Forecast 19X3	128.5	53

	Actual	Forecast	
Costs per unit	19X1	19X2	19X3
Produced	£	£	£
Direct materials	50	55	55
Direct labour	30	31.5	33
Variable production overhead	10	11	12
Direct expenses	5	5	6
Variable sales overhead	15	16	16

	£ 000	£ 000	£ 000
Other costs for the year			
Fixed production overhead	50	55	55
Other fixed overhead	200	220	220

Additional information:

1 When the management of Polemic prepared its direct labour forecast unit cost for 19X2 and 19X3, direct wages were increased only by the forecast rate of inflation.

2 The trade union representatives of the production workers wished to press for a greater wage increase. They suggested that:

(*i*) Direct wages be increased at twice the rate of inflation. The effect of this would be to increase direct labour costs per unit as follows:

	19X2 £	19X3 £
Direct labour	33.0	35.0

(*ii*) Unit selling prices be increased in order to cover the increased labour costs.

3 It is to be assumed that all expense and revenue relationships will be unchanged except where indicated.

Required:

(*a*) A schedule for 19X1, 19X2 and 19X3 for Polemic Ltd showing:
   (*i*) the break-even points;
   (*ii*) the net profit for each year.
   Base your calculations on the original labour costs.

(*b*) A graph showing a break-even point for 19X2.

(*c*) Advise Polemic Ltd's management as to their response to the trade union's claim for higher wages. Include relevant financial analysis.

(*d*) Explain the limitation of break-even analysis.

(*AQA (Associated Examining Board*): *GCE A-level*)

42.7A The relationship between income/cost/volume suggests that there are four ways by which profit can be increased. These are:

1 Increase unit selling price.
2 Decrease unit variable cost.
3 Decrease fixed costs.
4 Increase volume.

Assume that the current situation for a product is as follows:

Sales volume	1,000 units
Selling price	£2 each
Variable cost	£1 per unit
Fixed costs	£500

You are required to:

(a) draw **four** separate break-even charts showing the effect of the following changes on the current situation:
- (i) a 10 per cent increase in volume,
- (ii) a 10 per cent increase in unit selling price,
- (iii) a 10 per cent decrease in unit variable cost,
- (iv) a 10 per cent reduction in fixed costs.

(b) Use your charts to state the additional profit resulting from **each** change.

(AQA (Northern Examinations and Assessment Board): GCE A-level)

42.8 At the monthly senior management meeting of Hampshire plc on 1 May 19X0, various suggestions were made to improve the profit to be made by selling the firm's single product in the last quarter of the year ending 30 September 19X0. The product is not subject to seasonal demand fluctuations, but there are several competitors producing similar items. In the first quarter of the year a suggestion was made that profit could be improved if the selling price were reduced by 5 per cent, and this was put into effect at the beginning of the second quarter. As the new price undercut that of the rival firms, demand increased, and the firm's break-even point was reduced.
  The following suggestions have now been raised:

(i) Differentiate the product from its rivals by giving it a more distinctive shape, colour and packaging. This would increase material costs per unit by £0.30, but selling price would not be raised. Demand is then predicted to rise by 10 per cent;

(ii) Improve the quality of the product by strengthening it and giving it a one-year guarantee – material costs would then increase by £0.15 per unit and labour costs by £0.30 per unit. Selling price would rise by £0.40 per unit, and demand increase by 7 per cent;

(iii) Further reduce the selling price by 10 per cent – demand to rise by 20 per cent;

(iv) Pay commission plus salaries instead of fixed salaries only to all sales staff. Variable selling costs would then rise by £0.20 per unit, but fixed costs would fall by £4,100 per quarter;

(v) Subcontract the making of some components, and close the department responsible, making six staff redundant at an estimated cost to the firm of £12,000. 30,000 components are currently made per quarter. Each component's variable cost is £0.55. They can be bought from a recently established firm for £0.60 per unit. The department's share of the firm's fixed costs is 20 per cent and £2,500 fixed costs per quarter would cease to arise if the department were to be closed.

Data for:	First quarter	Second quarter
Number of units produced and sold	9,000	10,800
	£	£
Selling price per unit	14	13.30
Materials per unit	3.65	3.65
Labour per unit	2.10	2.10
Variable factory overhead per unit	1.40	1.40
Variable selling costs per unit	0.85	0.85
Fixed factory overhead	21,375	21,375
Fixed selling and administration costs	16,125	16,125

Required:

A Calculate the profit made in each of the first and second quarters, showing clearly the contribution per unit in each case.

B Draw one break-even chart showing the total costs and total revenues for the first and second quarters. You should label clearly the two break-even points and margins of safety.

C Taking each suggestion independently, calculate the profit that might be made in the last quarter if each of them were to be implemented.

D Discuss the implications for the firm of undertaking suggestions (*i*)–(*iv*), and for the firm and the local community of undertaking suggestion (*v*).

E Explain to the senior managers how, while break-even analysis is useful, it has limitations.

(Reproduced with the kind permission of the OCR: from *University of Oxford Delegacy of Local Examinations: GCE A-level*)

42.9A You are employed by Monarch Ltd which manufactures specialist hydraulic seals for the aircraft industry. The company has developed a new seal with the following budgeted data.

	£
Variable cost per unit	
Direct materials	8
Direct labour	4
Variable overheads	4
	16

The draft budget for the following year is as follows.

Production and sales	60,000 units

	£
Fixed cost: Production	260,000
Administration	90,000
Selling, marketing and distribution	100,000
Contribution	840,000

Certain departmental managers within the company believe there is room for improvement on the budgeted figures, and the following options have been suggested.

(*i*) The sales manager has suggested that if the selling price was reduced by 10 per cent, then an extra 30 per cent units could be sold. The purchasing manager has indicated that if materials requirements were increased in line, then a materials price reduction of 6.25 per cent could be negotiated. With this additional output, fixed production costs would increase by £30,000, administration by £5,000 and selling, marketing and distribution by £10,000. Other costs would remain unchanged.

(*ii*) The export manager has suggested that if the company increased overseas marketing by £15,000 then exports would increase from 15,000 units to 17,000 units. With this suggestion, distribution costs would increase by £12,000, and all other costs would remain unchanged.

(*iii*) The marketing manager has suggested that if an extra £40,000 were spent on advertising, then sales quantity would increase by 25 per cent. The purchasing manager has indicated that in such circumstances, materials costs would reduce by £0.30 per unit. With this suggestion fixed production costs would increase by £25,000, administration by £4,000 and other selling, marketing and distribution costs by £7,000. All other costs would remain unchanged.

(*iv*) The managing director believes the company should be aiming for a profit of £486,000. He asks what the selling price would be per unit if marketing were increased by £50,000, this leading to an estimated increase in sales quantity of 30 per cent? Other fixed costs would increase by £67,000, whilst material prices would decrease by 6.25 per cent per unit. All other costs would remain unchanged.

Required:
(a) Taking each suggestion independently, compile a profit statement for options (*i*) to (*iii*), showing clearly the contribution per unit in each case. For suggestion (*iv*), calculate the selling price per unit as requested by the managing director.

(b) Calculate the break-even quantity in units if the managing director's suggestion were implemented. Draw a contribution/sales graph to illustrate your calculations.
Read from the graph the profit if 60,000 units were sold.

(c) Whilst marginal costing has a number of applications, it also has disadvantages. In a report to the managing director, outline the main applications of marginal costing and explain its disadvantages.

(Reproduced with the kind permission of the OCR: from *University of Oxford Delegacy of Local Examinations: GCE A-level*)

42.10 Magwitch Limited's finance director produced the following forecast break-even chart for the year ending 31 May 19X1:

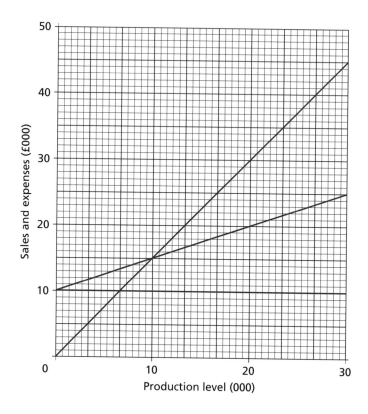

During the year the company produced and sold 20,000 units, and both revenue and expenses were 10 per cent higher than forecast.

Compeyson plc has made an agreed takeover bid for the company at a value of twelve times the net profit for the year ending 31 May 19X1.

Magwitch's assets and liabilities are to be taken over at their balance sheet values, with the exception of fixed assets, which are to be revalued at £40,000.

The summarised balance sheets of Magwitch Limited and Compeyson plc at the takeover date of 31 May 19X1 are as follows:

	Magwitch £000	Compeyson £000
Fixed assets	32	160
Current assets	65	340
Short-term liabilities	(26)	(110)
	71	390
Share capital (£1 shares)	40	200
Reserves	31	190
	71	390

The terms of the takeover are that Compeyson plc will give three of its shares (value £1.80 each) for every two shares in Magwitch Limited, plus a cash payment to make up the total agreed takeover price.

Magwitch Limited will cease to trade on 31 May 19X1, and its assets and liabilities will be assumed by Compeyson plc. Any goodwill arising is to be written off immediately against reserves.

(a) Draw up a summarised profit and loss account for Magwitch Limited for the year ended 31 May 19X1.
(b) Draw up a balance sheet for Compeyson plc after the takeover of Magwitch Limited has taken place.
(c) Calculate how many shares and how much cash would be received by a holder of 6,000 shares in Magwitch Limited as a result of the takeover.

(*Edexcel: GCE A-level*)

42.11A
(a) How far is it true to state that a company's break-even point occurs where the contribution just equals the fixed costs?
(b) A company's detailed information of costs and sales has been destroyed because of a computer malfunction. The following data has, however, been gleaned from various sources:

Sales volume (units)	10,000	12,000
Costs (£):		
direct materials	30,000	36,000
direct labour	28,000	33,000
overheads	20,500	24,100

Selling price per unit at all volumes of output is £12.30

Calculate:
(i)   the cost of an additional 2,000 units of output;
(ii) the variable costs of 10,000 units of output;
(iii) the fixed element – if any – of each component cost;
(iv) the break-even point.

(*Edexcel: GCE A-level*)

CHAPTER 43

Interest, annuities and leasing

Learning objectives

After you have studied this chapter, you should be able to:

- explain the difference between simple and compound interest
- explain what is meant by and be able to calculate the annual percentage rate (APR)
- calculate the present value of a series of cash flows
- describe what an annuity is and be able to calculate the value of ordinary annuities
- describe the difference between operating and finance leases and be able to calculate the relevant figures for use in financial statements

Introduction

In this chapter you'll learn about the nature of interest rates, of the difference between simple interest and compound interest and how to calculate them. You'll also learn how to calculate the annual percentage rate (APR) and how to calculate the cost and value of annuities and leases. Finally, you'll learn about the accounting rules relating to leases.

43.1 Different values

Would you rather be given £10 today or in 12 months' time? As time passes, money loses value due to the effects of inflation. When a transaction involves a delay in payment for the item purchased (e.g. a new car), the loss in value of the amount to be paid will be recovered by the seller's charging the buyer interest. The delay also represents a period during which the seller could have invested the money and earned interest. This 'opportunity cost' of interest lost will also be charged to the buyer. The seller may have had to borrow money in order to provide the item purchased, and the interest cost incurred will be charged to the buyer. The seller will also add interest to the amount due in order to compensate for risk – the risk that the buyer will not pay the debt when due. Thus, the amount the buyer will be required to pay depends upon both the market rate of interest and the degree of risk in the debt, as perceived by the seller.

43.2 Interest rates

If a seller adds 10 per cent interest to a debt of £100, the required payment if made 1 year later is £100 + (10 per cent × £100 = £10) = £110. The interest in this case is known as **simple interest** – 'simple' because the rate (10 per cent) is for one year, which matches the length of the debt. Interest rates generally indicate the percentage of the amount due that will be charged as interest if the debt is unpaid for a year.

If a 10 per cent interest rate is used, but the buyer is given two years to pay the debt, the second year's interest will be based on the amount due at the end of the first year – £110 (i.e. the original debt of £100 plus the £10 interest charged for the first year). The interest for the second year is therefore 10 per cent × £110 = £11, and the amount due at the end of the second year is the original debt (£100) + the first year's interest (£10) + the second year's interest (£11) = £121. This is known as **compound interest** – 'compound' because the amount of interest due for years beyond the first year is calculated on the basis of how much is owed at the start of each year, i.e. the original amount plus all the interest to that date.

If the buyer offers to pay £121 in two years' time, instead of paying £100 today, providing the seller charges debtors 10 per cent interest, the value to the seller of the £121 in two years' time is £100 today. However, if the seller uses a 20 per cent interest rate, the £121 will only be worth £84.03. On the other hand, if the seller uses a 5 per cent interest rate, the £121 will be worth £109.75. These different values can be checked by applying the same approach as with the 10 per cent interest rate.

At 20 per cent, the interest for the first year on a debt of £84.03 will be £16.80, and the amount due at the end of one year will be £100.84. The second year's interest will be 20 per cent of £100.84, i.e. £20.17, and the total due at the end of the second year will be £121.

At 5 per cent, the interest for the first year on a debt of £109.75 will be £5.49, and the amount due at the end of one year will be £115.24. The second year's interest will be 5 per cent of £115.24, i.e. £5.76, and the total due at the end of the second year will be £121.

43.3   Simple interest

Simple interest on a debt of one year is, therefore, calculated using the formula:

$$\text{Amount of interest } (Y) = \text{Amount due } (A) \times \text{Interest rate } (r)$$

However, simple interest also applies to periods of less than a year. In order to calculate the interest on a shorter period, the period in question is expressed as a proportion of a year, and the formula is adjusted to:

$$\text{Amount of interest } (Y) = \text{Amount due } (A) \times \text{Interest rate } (r) \times \text{Fraction of a year } (t)$$

Example

Interest on a debt of £100 is to be charged at 10 per cent per annum. The debt will be repaid after 60 days. The interest due can be calculated using the formula:

$$Y = £100 \times 10\% \times (60/365)$$
$$= £10 \times (60/365)$$
$$= £1.64$$

43.4   Annual percentage rate (APR)

Sometimes, an interest rate that appears to be a 'simple interest' rate does not actually represent the 'real' rate charged. This can arise where, for example, a 10 per cent rate is charged on a debt for a year, but part of the debt must be repaid after six months, and the interest charge ignores the fact that there is early payment of part of the debt. This 'real' rate is known as the **annual percentage rate** (APR). Hire purchase agreements are examples of debts where APR must be calculated in order to determine the 'real' cost incurred by the debtor.

Example

Interest on a debt of £100 is to be charged at 10 per cent per annum. However, £40 must be paid after six months, and the balance plus the interest at the end of the year.

			£
The interest to be paid is	10% of £100	$= Y$	= 10
The amount due is	£100 for ½ year =		50
	£60 for ½ year =		30
The equivalent amount due for a year is		$= q$	= 80
The 'real' rate of interest		$= r$	$= Y/q$
			= 10/80
			= 12.5% = the APR

Another typical example of APR arises when a business is owed money by its customers and it decides to sell the debt to a factor in order to obtain cash now. In these cases, the factor will pay the business an amount equal to the amount of the debt less a discount.

Example

A business is due £10,000 from a customer and the customer has agreed to make the payment in 90 days' time. The business approaches a debt factor who agrees to pay the amount due now, less a discount rate of 10 per cent. Applying the formula for debts of less than one year

Amount of interest (Y) = Amount due (A) × Interest rate (r) × Fraction of a year (t)

the discount charged is:

$$Y = £10,000 \times 10\% \times (90/365)$$
$$= £1,000 \times (90/365)$$
$$= £246.58$$

The debt factor will pay the business £10,000 less £246.58, i.e. £9,753.42. However, £246.58 does not represent a charge based on the amount of the advance (£9,753.42). Rather, it is based on the higher original amount of the customer's debt of £10,000. As a proportion of the £9,753.42 advanced by the debt factor, £246.58 represents an interest rate of 10.25 per cent. This can be seen by rewriting the formula for debts of less than one year to:

$$r = \frac{Y}{A \times t}$$

which, substituting the example values, gives:

$$r = \frac{246.58}{9,753.42 \times (90/365)}$$
$$= 10.25\%$$

A similar approach must be adopted with *bills of exchange* and *trade bill* interest rate calculations.

43.5 Compound interest

As mentioned in Section 43.2, when more than a year is involved, the interest due is compounded, i.e. each year's interest charge is based on the amount outstanding, including all previous years' interest, at the beginning of the year.

The graph shown in Exhibit 43.1 illustrates the difference between two investments of £1,000 at 10 per cent per annum for 20 years. In the first case, the interest is reinvested at the same 10 per cent rate and the final value of the investment is £6,727.50. In the other case, the interest is withdrawn as soon as it is paid, leaving only the original £1,000 invested, which is also the final value of the investment. However, 20 times £100, i.e. £2,000, has been received in interest over the 20 years, resulting in the overall value (ignoring inflation) being £3,000.

Exhibit 43.1

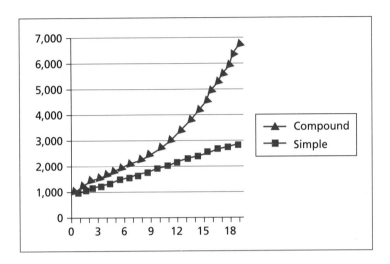

The final value of an investment that is subject to compound interest can be calculated laboriously by calculating the value at the end of the first year, calculating the interest on that amount for the next year, adding that interest to the amount at the start of the year to get the amount at the end of the year, and repeating the process for each year. However, there is a formula which enables the amount to be calculated swiftly:

Final value (V) = Amount invested $(I) \times (1 + r)^n$, where n = the number of years

Example

£1,000 invested today for five years at 10 per cent would have a final value (V) of:

$$V = £1,000 \times (1 + 0.10)^5$$
$$= £1,000 \times (1.1)^5$$
$$= £1,000 \times 1.61051$$
$$= £1,610.51$$

Calculations of this type are easily performed on most calculators, or by the use of tables. Where such calculations are performed regularly, it is quite common for a spreadsheet to be used to perform the calculation, often using the structure of a compound interest table within the spreadsheet to make it clear how the numbers used were derived. A compound interest table is included in Appendix 1, but a shorter example is reproduced in Exhibit 43.2.

Exhibit 43.2   An example of a compound interest table

Compound Interest Table
Period
Length £1 compounded at the end of each period at the interest rate shown

n	1%	2%	3%	4%	5%	6%	7%	8%	9%	10%	n
1	1.010	1.020	1.030	1.040	1.050	1.060	1.070	1.080	1.090	1.100	1
2	1.202	1.040	1.061	1.082	1.103	1.124	1.145	1.166	1.188	1.210	2
3	1.030	1.061	1.093	1.125	1.158	1.191	1.225	1.260	1.295	1.331	3
4	1.041	1.082	1.126	1.170	1.216	1.262	1.311	1.360	1.412	1.464	4
5	1.051	1.104	1.159	1.217	1.276	1.338	1.403	1.469	1.539	1.611	5
6	1.062	1.126	1.194	1.265	1.340	1.419	1.501	1.587	1.677	1.772	6
7	1.072	1.149	1.230	1.316	1.407	1.504	1.606	1.714	1.828	1.949	7
8	1.083	1.172	1.267	1.369	1.477	1.594	1.718	1.851	1.993	2.144	8
9	1.094	1.195	1.305	1.423	1.551	1.689	1.838	1.999	2.172	2.358	9
10	1.105	1.219	1.344	1.480	1.629	1.791	1.967	2.159	2.367	2.594	10

n	11%	12%	13%	14%	15%	16%	17%	18%	19%	20%	n
1	1.110	1.120	1.130	1.140	1.150	1.160	1.170	1.180	1.190	1.200	1
2	1.232	1.254	1.277	1.300	1.323	1.346	1.369	1.392	1.416	1.440	2
3	1.368	1.405	1.443	1.482	1.521	1.561	1.602	1.643	1.685	1.728	3
4	1.518	1.574	1.630	1.689	1.749	1.811	1.874	1.939	2.005	2.074	4
5	1.685	1.762	1.842	1.925	2.011	2.100	2.192	2.288	2.386	2.488	5
6	1.870	1.974	2.082	2.195	2.313	2.436	2.565	2.700	2.840	2.986	6
7	2.076	2.211	2.353	2.502	2.660	2.826	3.001	3.185	3.379	3.583	7
8	2.305	2.476	2.658	2.853	3.059	3.278	3.511	3.759	4.021	4.300	8
9	2.558	2.773	3.004	3.252	3.518	3.803	4.108	4.435	4.785	5.160	9
10	2.839	3.106	3.395	3.707	4.046	4.411	4.807	5.234	5.695	6.192	10

Example

If you want to know how much will be held at the end of seven years if you invest £100 at 6 per cent compound interest per annum, the table in Exhibit 43.2 shows that it would be £100 times 1.504 = £150.40.

Sometimes, interest accumulates more frequently than once a year. It will often be paid every three months. If so, the rate of interest used in the formula must be changed to reflect this. To do this, the number of periods is multiplied by the number of payments being made each year, and the interest rate used is divided by the same amount. The formula can then be used with these adjusted values.

Example

If £100 is invested for two years at 12 per cent compound interest paid quarterly, the interest rate used in the calculation is 3 per cent (i.e. 12 per cent divided by four). The number of periods to use is eight (i.e. two multiplied by four). Looking up the table, the amount accumulated at the end of the two years will be £126.70. Compare that to the compounded amount if interest was paid annually, £125.40. The difference is very small. However, the investment was for a short period of time. Had it been for a longer period, the difference would have become progressively greater. When large amounts of money are being invested over a long period, an increased frequency of interest payments will have a significant effect upon the amount of interest received.

Over time, most investments change their value. Investments in the stock market or in houses, for example, are made without knowing what the rate of return (interest) will be. When the investment is ended and the final amount received is known, it is often useful to know what the rate of return over the period of the investment was.

This can be done using the table. If an investment was made for five years, it is the five year row in the table that would be consulted. In that row, you would search for the number that represented the proportion that the final amount represented of the initial investment. The interest rate column in which that proportion lay would represent the average rate of return on the investment.

Example

If a house were bought for £100,000 on 1 January 20X1 and sold for £140,300 on 31 December 20X5, a five-year investment was made. The proportion that £140,300 represents of the £100,000 invested is 1.403 : 1. Looking up the table in the row where $n = 5$, a value of 1.403 can be seen in the 7 per cent interest rate column. The rate of return is equivalent to 7 per cent compound per annum. Where the proportion calculated is not shown in the table, the table can be used to identify an approximate rate which can then be adjusted in order to arrive at the accurate rate.

Example

If a house were bought for £100,000 on 1 January 20X1 and sold for £160,000 on 31 December 20X4, a four-year investment was made. The proportion that £160,000 represents of the £100,000 invested is 1.6 : 1. Looking up the table in the row where $n = 4$, a value of 1.574 can be seen in the 12 per cent column and 1.630 can be seen in the 13 per cent column. The difference between these two values is 0.056 (i.e. $1.630 - 1.574$). The difference between 1.574 and the amount being searched for of 1.6 is 0.026, which represents 46 per cent of the total difference of 0.056 between the 12 per cent and 13 per cent amounts. Adding 0.46 to 12 produces a percentage return of 12.46 per cent.

Rather than using the tables to identify the rate of return, a formula can be used which is the final value formula [Final value (V) = Amount invested $(I) \times (1 + r)^n$, where $n =$ the number of years] rewritten to identify r:

$$r = \sqrt[n]{(V/I)} - 1$$

Substituting the values from the last example:

$$r = \sqrt[4]{(160,000/100,000)} - 1$$
$$= 12.46\%$$

43.6 Annuities

Annuities are an income-generating investment whereby, in return for the payment of a single lump sum, the 'annuitant' receives regular amounts of income over a predefined term (i.e. number of years). The frequency of the payments to the annuitant will depend upon the agreement reached, but would generally be either monthly, quarterly, six-monthly or annually.

The timing of the payments to the annuitant vary from annuity to annuity. For example, some involve the regular payments to the annuitant being made at the start of each period, others have the payments at the end of each period.

In some cases, the original investment will be repaid at the end of the agreed term, in others it is not. It is also possible for the agreement to include the annuitant making a number of payments, rather than paying everything in a single lump sum.

As this suggests, there is a large range of possible arrangements that can be incorporated into an annuity, and it is not possible to describe how to deal with each of them. However, by concentrating upon one specific form of annuity – one in which equal payments are made to

the annuitant at the end of each period – the basic principles to be applied can be identified. These principles can then be applied to more complex situations and, as a result, there should be very few circumstances when, with a little thought, it should not be possible to perform the appropriate calculation.

Many forms of business transactions are annuity-like, and a knowledge of the calculation of annuities can be useful, for example when considering rental agreements, hire purchase agreements and leases.

43.7 Calculation of the value of ordinary annuities

When calculating the value of an annuity, it can be helpful to think of it as being similar to the calculation of compound interest, but one period in arrears. Thus, when considering compound interest, it would be assumed that an investment of £1,000 in year two was made at the start of the year. For an annuity, all the payments are assumed to arise at the end of a year, and interest on a payment made in year two would only start to accumulate during year three – there would be no interest in year two on that part of the annuity.

The following formula may be used to calculate the value of an annuity:

$$\text{Value} = \text{Annuity per period} \times \frac{(1 + r)^n - 1}{r}$$

It can be applied to calculate the final value of a series of regular payments where a set rate of interest is being earned. For example, if £1,000 is being saved at the end of each year for five years and the interest rate is 10 per cent, the amount accumulated at the end of the fifth year will be:

$$\text{Value} = £1,000 \times \frac{(1 + 0.10)^n - 1}{0.10}$$
$$= £1,000 \times 6.1051$$
$$= £6,105.10$$

This can be confirmed by treating each of the five payments as individual compound interest calculations:

Year	Invested £	Formula	Value £
1	1,000	£1,000 × (1 + 0.10)^4	1,464.10
2	1,000	£1,000 × (1 + 0.10)^3	1,331.00
3	1,000	£1,000 × (1 + 0.10)^2	1,210.00
4	1,000	£1,000 × (1 + 0.10)^1	1,100.00
5	1,000	£1,000 × (1 + 0.10)^0	1,000.00
			6,105.10

Tables can also be used. The one provided in Appendix 1 also confirms that the value of an annuity of £1 for five years at 10 per cent would be £6.105, i.e. £1 times the multiplier of 6.105 given in the table.

Example

As an alternative to calculating the value of an annuity when the amounts paid are known, it can often be useful to know how much should be set aside regularly in order to accumulate a certain amount at the end of a given period. For example, if it was intended to purchase

equipment estimated to cost £10,000 in five years' time, and a 10 per cent interest rate was being offered for regular investments over a five-year period, the annuity formula can be rewritten so as to provide the amount to set aside:

$$\text{Annuity per period} = \frac{\text{Value} \times (r)}{(1 + r)^n - 1}$$

For our example, this gives:

$$\frac{£10,000 \times 0.10}{(1.10)^5 - 1} = £1,637.97$$

As mentioned previously, the multiplier given in the annuity table for a five-year annuity at 10 per cent is 6.105. If £1,637.97 is multiplied by 6.105, it confirms the annuity has a final value (to the nearest £1) of £10,000. It is also possible to confirm the annuity per period does result in the correct final value of £10,000 by creating a payment plus interest table:

Annuity paid	Payment £	Interest £	Increase in fund £	Balance of fund £
end of year 1	1,637.97	–	1,637.97	1,637.97
end of year 2	1,637.97	163.80	1,801.77	3,439.74
end of year 3	1,637.97	343.97	1,981.94	5,421.68
end of year 4	1,637.97	542.17	2,180.14	7,601.82
end of year 5	1,637.97	760.18	2,398.15	9,999.97

43.8 Calculation of the present value of ordinary annuities

If faced with a choice of paying for something now, or paying for it in instalments over the next year, it is useful to know which is the cheaper of the two alternatives. For example, a business may purchase a new computer costing £1,000 and have a choice of paying £1,000 now, or £200 per month for six months. It seems that the second option will be more expensive because £1,200 (i.e. six times £200) would be paid instead of £1,000.

In order to be able to compare the two alternatives, the payments must all be discounted to arrive at their cost expressed in terms of today's money. This is known as their **present values**. Whether it really is more expensive to pay by instalments will depend on the discount rate used in the calculation.

As with the calculation of the value of an ordinary annuity, tables are available for the calculation of the present value of an ordinary annuity. A full table is provided in Appendix 1 and it shows the value now of £1 per period for n periods when an organisation uses a discount rate of r. When payments are made more frequently than once per annum, the discount rate used should be reduced accordingly – that is, if payments are half-yearly, the rate is halved; if they are made every month, the rate is divided by 12.

The formula for calculating the present value of an ordinary annuity is:

$$\text{Present value} = \text{Payment} \times \left[\frac{1 - \dfrac{1}{(1 + r)^n}}{r} \right]$$

If a 12 per cent rate were used with the above example, the rate of 12 per cent would be divided by 12 (because payments are made monthly) for the calculation and the present value would be:

$$\text{Present value} = £100 \times \left[\frac{1 - \dfrac{1}{(1 + 0.01)^6}}{0.01} \right]$$

$$= £579.55$$

The multiplier in the table in Appendix 1 for 1 per cent over 6 periods is 5.795 which, when multiplied by the payment of £100, confirms a present value of £579.50.

It can be shown that this is the amount required if a table of interest and withdrawals is constructed (interest is at the same rate as above – 1 per cent per month):

Period	Balance b/d £	Interest £	Payment £	Balance c/d £
1	579.55	5.80	(100)	485.35
2	485.35	4.85	(100)	390.20
3	390.20	3.90	(100)	294.10
4	294.10	2.94	(100)	197.04
5	197.04	1.97	(100)	99.01
6	99.01	0.99	(100)	–

43.9 Leasing

Under a lease, the lessee agrees to pay a rental to the lessor for use of something for a period of time. Lease rental payments are treated as allowable expenses for tax, whereas assets that are purchased are only eligible for a partial deduction against tax in the form of a capital allowance. The lessor claims the capital allowances on the assets leased. The lessee charges all the lease rental payments against income.

Activity 43.1

Why do you think leasing is usually financially advantageous for both the lessor and the lessee?

An organisation acquiring an asset will often consider whether leasing may be preferable to outright purchase. As the cost, expected useful economic life, anticipated scrap value, and leasing charges can all be identified, it is possible to identify the APR of the lease. That can then be used to assess whether it would be preferable to lease rather than buy the asset.

Example

A printing machine costing £200,000 has an expected useful economic life of ten years. Scrap value of the machine is expected to be zero, as the rate of obsolescence on machinery of this type is very high. The machine could be leased for £32,547 per annum. The APR is the interest rate that is found when the cost of the machine is equal to the present value of the annual rental payments. That is, it is the interest rate for which the ten-year multiplier will convert £32,547 into £200,000.

£200,000 divided by £32,547 is 6.145. In the 10 year row of the annuity table in Appendix 1, 6.145 is the multiplier for an interest rate of 10 per cent which is, therefore, the APR of the lease. If the multiplier being sought lay part-way between two values in the annuity table, the APR would be identified by interpolation, as in the calculation of IRR (internal rate of return – *see* Chapter 44).

Normally, tax would be taken into account in identifying the APR of a lease. Ignoring the time lags inherent in the tax system, as the expense is charged directly against income, if the tax rate is 40 per cent, in the above example the net of tax cost of the lease would be 60 per cent of £32,547 (i.e. £19,528) and the APR would be 60 per cent of 10 per cent, i.e. 6 per cent. This could then be compared to the organisation's cost of capital after tax in order to assess whether to lease or purchase the machine.

So far as the option to purchase is concerned, an annualised cost approach can be used. The cost of £200,000 would be assumed to occur immediately, so its real cost is £200,000. Technically, the cost is said to have occurred at 'year zero'.

If 100 per cent capital allowances were available on the machine, at a tax rate of 40 per cent, there would be a tax saving equivalent to 40 per cent of £200,000 in year one. **Net present value (NPV)** is the sum of the present values of all the cash flows. If the organisation's net of tax cost of capital is 8 per cent, the £80,000 tax saving would be discounted to £74,080 (i.e. £80,000 × 0.926), leaving a net present value of £125,920. The annualised cost is, therefore, £125,920 ÷ 6.710 (which is the annuity multiplier for 10 years at 8 per cent), i.e. £18,766. When compared to the net of tax cost of the lease of £19,528, this suggests that it might be preferable to purchase the machine.

As an alternative to the above approach, the £125,920 net present value of buying the machine (as derived in the annualised cost calculation) can be compared to the NPV of the lease payments. The net of tax NPV of leasing is the net of tax rental (£19,528) multiplied by the present value multiplier of a ten-year annuity at 8 per cent (6.710), i.e. £131,033.

43.10 Financial implications of leasing

Despite the existence of a legal obligation to continue paying rental on a lease, neither the extent of the obligation to the lessor, nor the benefits obtainable under the lease normally appear on the face of the lessee's balance sheet. However, a lease often represents the equivalent of a loan. The equivalent loan is the NPV of the outstanding lease payments discounted at the pre-tax rate of interest. For example, the NPV of a ten-year lease with rental of £32,547 and a pre-tax rate of interest of 10 per cent would be £32,547 × 6.145 = £200,000.

43.11 Accounting for leases

Leases are either finance leases or operating leases. SSAP 21: *Accounting for leases and hire purchase contracts* defines the difference between them. The principal characteristic of a finance lease is that substantially all the risks and rewards of ownership are transferred to the lessee. Various steps are described in SSAP 21 that should be followed in order to determine whether a finance lease exists. These involve determining whether the present value of the minimum lease payments amount to substantially all (normally 90 per cent) of the fair value of the asset.

However, if the substance of the lease is to have the opposite effect, then it should be categorised accordingly. At the end of the day, it is the substance (i.e. what is actually happening to the risks and rewards of ownership) rather than the form of the transaction that decides whether there exists a finance or an operating lease.

Hire purchase contracts will usually be of a financing nature and treated in the same way as finance leases.

When a lease is classified as 'operating', it is deemed to still be an asset of the lessor. Both lessor and lessee take the rentals to the profit and loss account. The lessor should also record the fixed asset and depreciate it over its useful life.

An asset held under a finance lease is deemed to 'belong' to the lessee, who should capitalise it and make a corresponding entry in creditors. The initial value used should be the present value of the minimum lease payments. Depreciation should then be provided over the shorter of the lease term and the asset's useful life, except in the case of a hire purchase contract, under which circumstances the asset should be depreciated over its useful life. As each payment is made, the proportion which relates to the creditor balance should be applied to reduce that balance. The rest of the payment should be treated as a lease charge in the profit and loss account for the period.

Lessors should initially record the amount due under a finance lease as a debtor using the amount of the net investment in the lease. As each payment is received, the proportion which relates to payment of the debtor balance should be applied to reduce that balance. The rest of the receipt should be treated as lease income in the profit and loss account for the period.

Operating leases are accounted for in the same way as most revenue expenditure and income. Finance leases, however, are much more complex. The rental payments comprise a mixture of capital and revenue, and they must be separated and recorded differently. An approach called the actuarial method is generally used. Under this approach, it is first necessary to calculate the real rate of interest implied in the lease. This requires that information is available concerning the rental payments, the lease period and the cash value of the asset at the start of the lease.

Example

Quarterly rental on a leased computer is £400, the lease period is 12 quarters from 1 January 20X4, and the cash value of the computer at 1 January 20X4 is £4,000. The interest rate implied in the lease is that which produces a present value for the 12 payments of £400 equal to £4,000. Note, the first payment is at the start of the lease, yet ordinary annuity calculations relate to payments at the end of periods. In order to bring the example into line with this assumption, the first payment is offset against the cash value, reducing it to £3,600, and the annuity is calculated over 11 periods rather than 12.

$$\text{The factor for 11 periods is } \frac{£3,600}{400} = 9$$

$$\text{From the tables} \quad 3\% \qquad = 9.253$$
$$4\% \qquad = 8.760$$

By interpolation, the gap between 3 per cent and the rate is $253/493 = 0.513$, therefore, the interest rate implied in the lease is 3.513 per cent. This can be verified by substituting the rate and other information into the formula given in Section 43.8:

$$\text{Present value} = \text{Payment} \times \left[\frac{1 - \dfrac{1}{(1 + r)^n}}{r} \right]$$

$$3,600 = 400 \times \left[\frac{1 - \dfrac{1}{(1 + 0.03513)^{11}}}{0.03513} \right]$$

$$3,600 = £400 \times 9$$

Applying the rate of interest of 3.513 to the lease data produces the data in Exhibit 43.4.

Exhibit 43.4 Calculation of the periodic finance charge in the lease

Quarter		Capital sum at start of period £	Rental paid at start of period £	Capital sum during period £	Finance charge (3.513% per quarter) £	Capital sum at end of period £
20X4	−1	4,000	400	3,600	126	3,726
	2	3,726	400	3,326	117	3,443
	3	3,443	400	3,043	107	3,150
	4	3,150	400	2,750	96	2,846
20X5	−1	2,846	400	2,446	86	2,532
	2	2,532	400	2,132	75	2,207
	3	2,207	400	1,807	63	1,870
	4	1,870	400	1,470	51	1,521
20X6	−1	1,521	400	1,121	39	1,160
	2	1,160	400	760	27	787
	3	787	400	387	13	400
	4	400	400	–	–	–
			4,800		800	

The finance charges for each year of the lease are:

		£
20X4 (126 + 117 + 107 + 96)	=	446
20X5 (86 + 75 + 63 + 51)	=	275
20X6 (39 + 27 + 13)	=	79
		800

The overall picture in each of the three years is:

Year	Total rental £	less	Finance charge £	=	Capital repayment £
20X4	1,600		446		1,154
20X5	1,600		275		1,325
20X6	1,600		79		1,521

In the balance sheet of the lessee, the liability under the finance lease would be:

Year	Obligations under finance lease at start of year £	less	Capital repayment £	=	Obligations under finance lease at end of year £
20X4	4,000		1,154		2,846
20X5	2,846		1,325		1,521
20X6	1,521		1,521		–

43.12 The rule of 78

Before spreadsheets became commonplace, these actuarial method lease calculations were often considered too complex and, in their place, a simple rule-of-thumb approach was adopted: the rule of 78.

The '78' is the sum of the numbers 1 to 12, and is used because these calculations originally focused on twelve-month periods. Each month receives a proportion in reverse to its position. Thus, month 1 of 12 would be accorded $^{12}/_{78}$ of the total, and month 12 of 12, $^{1}/_{78}$.

Similarly to the actuarial method, under the rule of 78, earlier periods will carry the majority of the allocation. For the purpose of lease calculations, the proportion is applied to the difference between the total payments under the leasing agreement and the cash value of the asset at the start.

Using the example from Exhibit 43.4, the rule of 78 produces the following:

Quarter	Rental payment number	Rule of 78	Allocation × £800	Annual allocation £
20X4 – 1	1	11	11/66 × £800 = 133	
2	2	10	121	
3	3	9	109	
4	4	8	97	460
20X5 – 1	5	7	85	
2	6	6	73	
3	7	5	61	
4	8	4	49	268
20X6 – 1	9	3	36	
2	10	2	24	
3	11	1	12	
4	–	–	–	72
		66	800	800

(There is no allocation to the final quarter as the payments are made at the start of each quarter.) Comparison of the two methods shows that the rule of 78 provides a general indication of the flows.

Year	Actuarial method £	Rule of 78 £
20X4	446	460
20X5	275	268
20X6	79	72
	800	800

Learning outcomes

You should now have learnt:

1 As time passes, money loses value and this loss of value must be allowed for when considering long-term investments.

2 Interest rates may be simple or compound, and interest may be paid at any appropriate frequency. Compound interest will generate significantly greater values than the same rate of simple interest the longer the time period involved and the greater the frequency of interest payments.

3 How to calculate simple interest, compound interest, APR, annuities and leases.

4 The real rate of interest often differs from the apparent rate and an annual percentage rate (APR) must be calculated in order to compare alternatives.

5 Annuity calculations are useful when considering rental agreements, hire purchase and leases.

6 Operating leases are accounted for differently from finance leases.

Answers to activities

43.1 Leasing exists because both lessee and lessor can benefit from the arrangement as a result of their differing tax positions and capital-raising abilities. A small company may find it very expensive, possibly impossible, to borrow £200,000 for some new equipment, whereas a large leasing company would be able to raise the funds at a very competitive rate.

REVIEW QUESTIONS

43.1
(a) If you were lent £12,000 for 56 days at 9 per cent, how much interest would you pay?
(b) If a debt factor offered to discount a £6,000 bill of exchange at 15 per cent, and if the bill had an outstanding period of 80 days, how much would the debt factor pay for the bill?

43.2A What is the real rate of interest of discounting the bill of exchange in Question 43.1?

43.3 Interest of £1,000 is charged and included in a loan of £3,000. The loan has to be repaid at £750 per quarter over the next 12 months. What is the real rate of interest of the loan?

43.4 If £1,000 is invested for five years at 12 per cent compound per annum, how much interest is earned over the five years?

43.5A If the interest on the investment in Question 43.4 had been compounded every six months, how much interest would have been earned over the five years?

43.6A Shares bought on 1 January 20X2 for £2,000 were sold on 31 December 20X5 for £3,158. What was the rate of annual compound interest on the investment?

43.7 Should you accept an offer of £15,000 for your rights over the next four years to the £4,000 annual rent from shop premises you own and have leased to a local company? You could invest the £15,000 at 10 per cent per annum.

43.8A In relation to the rental income, what rate of interest does the offer made in Question 43.7 represent?

43.9 A condition of a ten-year loan of £20,000 is that the borrower will pay equal annual amounts into a sinking fund so that it accumulates at the end of the ten years to the amount of the loan. The sinking fund will earn interest at 8 per cent per annum. How much should be paid into the sinking fund each year?

43.10A If the interest on the sinking fund in Question 43.9 were at 10 per cent, how much would the annual payments into it be?

43.11 What is the implied interest rate if equipment can be leased for four years at £20,000 per annum and the cash price is £64,800?

43.12 The annual rental payments on a six-year lease are £4,000. If the rate of interest payable on borrowing for this purpose is 16 per cent, what is the capital value of the lease?

CHAPTER 44

Capital expenditure appraisal

Learning objectives

After you have studied this chapter, you should be able to:

- explain why interest rates are important in financial decision making
- calculate and compare the net present value (NPV), internal rate of return (IRR), and payback of a series of cash flows
- choose between alternative projects on the basis of NPV, IRR and payback
- describe and compute the effects of taxation upon capital expenditure appraisal
- calculate the annualised amount of a series of cash flows and select between alternative projects on that basis

Introduction

In this chapter you'll learn how to assess and choose between alternative capital expenditure proposals using a variety of appraisal techniques. You'll also learn about relevant and irrelevant costs, sunk costs, and of the impact of uncertainty and uneven project lengths upon the capital expenditure appraisal decision.

44.1 Present value

You were introduced to the concept of present value in Chapter 43. You will recall that it is the amount that a future cash flow is worth in terms of today's money. £1,000 invested for five years at 10 per cent compound results in a final amount of £1,610.51 but, what would be the value of that £1,610.51 at the date of the initial investment (i.e. today)? If it were known, it would be possible to tell whether the investment might be worthwhile.

To calculate present value, the formula to use has the same variables as that used to calculate compound interest which you learnt about in Section 43.5, but it is rewritten to reflect that it is really the reciprocal of the compound interest formula:

$$\text{Amount invested } (I) = \frac{\text{Final value } (V)}{(1 + r)^n}$$

However, it would be more appropriate to describe the amount calculated as 'present value' rather than 'amount invested' and the formula becomes:

$$\text{Present value } (PV) = \frac{\text{Final value } (V)}{(1 + r)^n}$$

Example

A bank is offering a guaranteed return at the end of five years of £1,500 for every £1,000 invested. If you could usually expect to obtain a rate of interest of 8 per cent on your investments, what would be the present value of investing £1,000 in the bank?

$$PV = \frac{£1,500}{(1.08)^5} = £1,020.87$$

The 8 per cent interest rate used in this example is generally referred to as the **discount rate**, i.e. the rate at which the future flow of cash is discounted to arrive at its present value. As with compound interest, present value tables are generally used, and will often be created and used on spreadsheets. A present value table is included in Appendix 1, but an extract is reproduced in Exhibit 44.1.

Exhibit 44.1 An example of a present value table

Present Value Table
Period
Length PV of £1 discounted over the period at the rate shown

n	1%	2%	3%	4%	5%	6%	7%	8%	9%	10%	n
1	0.990	0.980	0.971	0.961	0.952	0.943	0.935	0.926	0.917	0.909	1
2	0.980	0.961	0.943	0.925	0.907	0.890	0.873	0.857	0.842	0.826	2
3	0.971	0.942	0.915	0.889	0.864	0.840	0.816	0.794	0.772	0.751	3
4	0.961	0.924	0.889	0.855	0.823	0.792	0.763	0.735	0.708	0.683	4
5	0.951	0.906	0.863	0.822	0.784	0.747	0.713	0.681	0.650	0.621	5
6	0.942	0.888	0.838	0.790	0.746	0.705	0.666	0.630	0.596	0.564	6
7	0.933	0.871	0.813	0.760	0.711	0.665	0.623	0.583	0.547	0.513	7
8	0.923	0.853	0.789	0.731	0.677	0.627	0.582	0.540	0.502	0.467	8
9	0.914	0.837	0.766	0.703	0.645	0.592	0.544	0.500	0.460	0.424	9
10	0.905	0.820	0.744	0.676	0.614	0.558	0.508	0.463	0.422	0.386	10

n	11%	12%	13%	14%	15%	16%	17%	18%	19%	20%	n
1	0.901	0.893	0.885	0.877	0.870	0.862	0.855	0.847	0.840	0.833	1
2	0.812	0.797	0.783	0.769	0.756	0.743	0.731	0.718	0.706	0.694	2
3	0.731	0.712	0.693	0.675	0.658	0.641	0.624	0.609	0.593	0.579	3
4	0.659	0.636	0.613	0.592	0.572	0.552	0.534	0.516	0.499	0.482	4
5	0.593	0.567	0.543	0.519	0.497	0.476	0.456	0.437	0.419	0.402	5
6	0.535	0.507	0.480	0.456	0.432	0.410	0.390	0.370	0.352	0.335	6
7	0.482	0.452	0.425	0.400	0.376	0.354	0.333	0.314	0.296	0.279	7
8	0.434	0.404	0.376	0.351	0.327	0.305	0.285	0.266	0.249	0.233	8
9	0.391	0.361	0.333	0.308	0.284	0.263	0.243	0.226	0.209	0.194	9
10	0.352	0.322	0.295	0.270	0.247	0.227	0.208	0.191	0.176	0.162	10

Frequently, the cash flows arising from an investment arise throughout the period of the investment, not simply at the end. To calculate the overall present value of all the cash flows, each is calculated separately, and all the resulting present values are added together.

Example

An investment of £10,000 is made for five years. The net cash flows at the end of each of the five years are:

Period	Amount £
1	2,000
2	3,000
3	4,000
4	3,000
5	1,000

If the discount rate used is 10 per cent, the overall present value of the net cash flows is calculated as:

Period	Amount £	Discount factor 10%	Present value £
1	2,000	0.909	1,818
2	3,000	0.826	2,478
3	4,000	0.751	3,004
4	3,000	0.683	2,049
5	1,000	0.621	621
		Overall present value of cash flows	9,970

When compared to the initial investment of £10,000, it can be seen that this investment would lose £30 (i.e. £10,000 – £9,970). To make it easier to see this figure, these calculations usually incorporate the initial investment (which is not discounted as it is already at today's value) and produce a figure known as the net present value, or NPV. Incorporating the initial investment into this example produces the following table:

Period	Amount £	Discount factor 10%	Present value £
0	(10,000)	1.000	(10,000)
1	2,000	0.909	1,818
2	3,000	0.826	2,478
3	4,000	0.751	3,004
4	3,000	0.683	2,049
5	1,000	0.621	621
		Net present value	(30)

Many businesses have a rate of return that they require to achieve on investments. If a potential investment is not expected to achieve that rate of return, the investment will not be made. It is always possible to adopt the NPV approach in order to determine whether the return exceeds the required rate (which is shown by a positive NPV). However, it is often useful to know what the actual rate of return is – the proposed investment may, for example, require that some additional financing be obtained that would be at a higher rate than the business's normal rate of return.

The actual rate of return is known as the **internal rate of return**, or **IRR**. It is the discount rate that results in an NPV of zero. It can be calculated very easily using a spreadsheet – a table similar to the one above would be written in the spreadsheet, but the discount factor would be left blank. Then, by instigating an appropriate command, the spreadsheet would identify and insert the IRR into the table so as to arrive at an NPV of zero.

However, spreadsheets are not always available and IRR may need to be calculated manually. The method to adopt is similar to that adopted in the final example in Section 43.5 – a guess is made as to an appropriate IRR and the NPV calculation is made using that rate. If the NPV is positive, a higher rate is selected (a lower rate is selected if the NPV is negative) and the NPV is again calculated. This continues until one positive NPV and one negative NPV are identified. The absolute difference between the two NPVs is calculated and the proportion of that difference that represents the difference between the NPV of the lower of the rates involved and zero is added to the lower rate to produce the IRR.

Example

You have been asked if you would be willing to lend £10,000 to a taxi company in order that it may expand its fleet of taxis. The money would be repaid at the rate of £3,000 per annum for four years. What is the IRR?

Step 1 is to select a rate that may be approximately correct. There is no simple way to select such a rate, and what would often be done is that the same rate would be used as the first step with most IRR calculations, and then the choice of the second rate to use would depend on how close to zero the first attempt came, and on whether the NPV it gave was positive or negative. If an 8 per cent rate is used, the following results:

Period	Amount £	Discount factor 8%	Present value £
0	(10,000)	1.000	(10,000)
1	3,000	0.926	2,778
2	3,000	0.857	2,571
3	3,000	0.794	2,382
4	3,000	0.735	2,205
		Net present value	(64)

Using the 8 per cent rate resulted in an NPV that was less than zero. The next rate chosen must, therefore, be less than 8 per cent. A 7 per cent rate produces the following:

Period	Amount £	Discount factor 7%	Present value £
0	(10,000)	1.000	(10,000)
1	3,000	0.935	2,805
2	3,000	0.873	2,619
3	3,000	0.816	2,448
4	3,000	0.763	2,289
		Net present value	161

Therefore, the IRR lies between 7 per cent and 8 per cent. The difference between the two NPVs is 225 (i.e. 64 + 161). A zero NPV will result if the rate is set to 7 per cent plus 161/225 (as 7 per cent is 161 away from zero). Expressed as a decimal, 161/225 = 0.72 and the IRR is, therefore, 7.72 per cent.

44.2   Capital expenditure appraisal

Activity 44.1

If you had £5,000 to spend today and had the choice of investing it in a five-year bond with a bank, or lending it to a friend who had just opened a restaurant and who offered you 10 per cent of the profits for five years, plus the return of your £5,000 at the end of the five years, which alternative would you choose and why?

Organisations make vast numbers of short-term decisions. They make comparatively few long-term decisions. These long-term decisions involve investing resources in something and then receiving the benefits. Examples include:

- building a new production facility
- buying a new delivery truck
- sponsoring a local football team for three years
- building a bridge
- buying an airline
- making a new product
- starting a new business.

Generally, only the incremental cash payments and receipts arising from the decision to invest are relevant. The relevant costs include interest, but not items that normally appear in the calculation of profit but which do not involve cash – depreciation, for example. There are two aspects of the incremental cash flows that should be distinguished: the cash outflows resulting from the decision to invest, and the cash inflows arising as a result of investing. The difference between these two groups of incremental cash flows determines whether or not an investment is made.

The techniques used to aid the selection of the appropriate long-term decision are referred to collectively as **capital expenditure appraisal**. There are three generally acceptable capital expenditure appraisal techniques in common use. Two have already been introduced in Section 44.1 – *net present value* and *internal rate of return*. Collectively, these two are known as **discounted cash flow (DCF)** techniques, as they involve the discounting of future net cash flows of a capital project to find their present value. Both techniques assume that all cash flows occur at the end of a period.

The third technique, **payback**, involves selecting the alternative that repays the initial investment in the shortest time, provided that it does not exceed the business's maximum acceptable payback period – its payback hurdle period. It is useful when cash resources are limited and swift repayment of the investment is vital for the maintenance of working capital. Also, because risks of problems arising increase with the length of an investment, payback reduces the risk by minimising the relevant length of investment. In contrast to the DCF techniques, payback assumes all cash flows occur evenly over a period.

A fourth technique, accounting rate of return (ARR), having once been very popular, is now falling into disuse as technology becomes more sophisticated, and those performing these calculations become more aware of the benefits of using the other three techniques in preference to ARR. The technique uses profits rather than cash flows and it involves dividing the average return by the average investment over the period. For example, if £10,000 is invested and the return is £30,000 over a ten-year period, there would be a return of £3,000 per year (£30,000 ÷ 10). If the £10,000 is repaid at the end of the ten years, the average investment is £10,000 (i.e. [£10,000 + £10,000] ÷ 2). Therefore, the (annual) accounting rate of return is £3,000 divided by £10,000, i.e. 30 per cent.

Although it is generally easy to calculate, ARR produces a percentage figure that is of little practical use. It cannot, for example, be compared with an organisation's cost of capital in order to assess whether a project would achieve a greater return than the cost of the capital that financed it. It also ignores the timing of cash flows – a project whose profits all arose at the start would be rejected in favour of one with a higher ARR whose profits all came at the end, even if inflation meant that those later period profits were worth significantly less in present value terms than the earlier profits of the rejected project.

Example

When considering a capital expenditure (or 'capital project') proposal, the first step is to identify all the incremental cash flows that would arise were the decision taken to proceed with the investment. As most decisions of this type involve cash flows over a number of years, once identified, the cash flows are mapped against the year in which they arise.

A new machine would cost £10,000 and installation would cost a further £1,000. It would replace an existing machine that would be sold for £2,000. The machine would generate cash income of £2,500 per annum for four years, at the end of which it would be sold for £3,000.

The cash flows are:

Period		Amount £
0	purchase + installation – sale proceeds	(9,000)
1	income	2,500
2	income	2,500
3	income	2,500
4	income (including sale proceeds)	5,500
		4,000

If the business's cost of capital is 10 per cent, that would be the discount rate used and the net present value (as previously illustrated in Section 43.6) would be:

Period	Amount £	Discount factor 10%	Present value £
0	(9,000)	1.000	(9,000.00)
1	2,500	0.909	2,272.50
2	2,500	0.826	2,065.00
3	2,500	0.751	1,877.50
4	5,500	0.683	3,756.50
		Overall net present value of cash flows	971.50

As the NPV is positive, the internal rate of return is higher than 10 per cent. A 15 per cent discount factor produces a negative NPV of £144:

Period	Amount £	Discount factor 15%	Present value £
0	(9,000)	1.000	(9,000)
1	2,500	0.870	2,175
2	2,500	0.756	1,890
3	2,500	0.658	1,645
4	5,500	0.572	3,146
		Overall net present value of cash flows	(144)

Interpolating between these two values, as in Section 44.1, the IRR is found to be 14.35 per cent. (The absolute difference is £1,115.50 (i.e. £971.50 + £144), of which approximately 87 per cent (£971.50) is represented by the proportion relating to the 10 per cent NPV. Multiplying the difference between the two discount rates (15% – 10% = 5%) by 87 per cent gives an answer to two decimal places of 4.35 per cent. This is then added to 10 per cent to produce the IRR of 14.35 per cent.) On the basis that the business's cost of capital is 10 per cent, this project will be financially beneficial. Substituting the discount rate of 14.35 per cent into the table produces a net present value of –10, the failure to reach a value of zero being due to rounding.

Period	Amount £	Discount factor 14.35%	Present value £
0	(9,000)	1.000	(9,000.00)
1	2,500	0.875	2,187.50
2	2,500	0.765	1,912.50
3	2,500	0.669	1,672.50
4	5,500	0.585	3,217.50
		Overall net present value of cash flows	(10.00)

These two DCF techniques generally arrive at the selection of the same alternative when faced with a choice between two or more projects. However, they can produce different choices, and when they do, it is the NPV choice that should be selected.

As the following schedule shows, payback on the machine occurs after 3.27 years:

Period	Amount £	Balance £	
0	(9,000)	(9,000)	
1	2,500	(6,500)	
2	2,500	(4,000)	
3	2,500	(1,500)	
4	5,500	–	Payback at 3 plus 1,500/5,500 years = 3.27 years

This will then be compared to the business's hurdle period for payback. If it is later than the hurdle period, the project will be rejected. When cash flow is important, for example when the cost of capital is high, or when the risks in a project increase significantly the longer it runs, payback provides a measure of how quickly the investment in the project will be repaid, any subsequent cash flows being viewed as a bonus. However, it can result in a project being selected that is considerably less profitable than another that happens to take longer to repay the investment in it. It also ignores the time value of money. ('Real' payback will always be later than revealed by calculation as later receipts are not worth so much in today's money as early ones because of inflation.)

Activity 44.2
How could you address these deficiencies to ensure payback was effectively applied?

Closer inspection of the approach reveals that payback ignores everything after the (first) break-even point. Applied blindly, it is not concerned about whether a project breaks even overall, only that the amount invested in a project is reduced to zero at some stage. The fact that a project may break even in three years, but then requires more investment in year five, only finally breaking even in year six, can easily be overlooked when calculating payback.

44.3 Taxation

One factor often overlooked in consideration of capital projects is taxation. Items of equipment acquired will give rise to tax allowances that can be used to reduce tax payable, and any incremental profits arising from a capital project will give rise to payments of tax.

Writing-down allowances are granted in place of depreciation and, when the equipment is sold or scrapped, its tax-written-down value (i.e. cost less writing-down allowances claimed) less any amount received upon its disposal is allowed as a deduction against income for tax purposes.

Once calculated, the impact of taxation on the incremental cash flows is taken into account in the same way as any other item of incremental income or expenditure.

Example

A new machine costing £10,000 has an estimated useful economic life of four years, after which it will be scrapped. During those four years, it is expected to generate sales of £5,000 per annum. Production costs are anticipated to be 40 per cent of sales revenue. Working capital of £3,000 will be required for this activity, all of which will be recovered when the machine is scrapped. Depreciation is by the straight line method, i.e. £2,500 per annum starting in year 1. Corporation tax of 40 per cent is paid nine months after the end of each accounting period. A writing-down allowance of 25 per cent (reducing balance) will be available if the machine is acquired.

The expected annual profit is:

	£	£
Sales		5,000
Production costs	2,000	
Depreciation	2,500	
		(4,500)
		500
Corporation tax		(200)
Net profit after tax		300

The expected cash flows that would be used for the capital expenditure appraisal are:

Investment (£)	Year 1	2	3	4	5
Machine	(10,000)				
Working capital	(3,000)			3,000	
Tax allowance		1,000	750	562.50	1,687.50
	(13,000)	1,000	750	3,562.50	1,687.50
Cash flows (£)					
Sales	5,000	5,000	5,000	5,000	
Production costs	(2,000)	(2,000)	(2,000)	(2,000)	
Tax (40% × £3,000)		(1,200)	(1,200)	(1,200)	(1,200)
	3,000	1,800	1,800	1,800	(1,200)
Net cash flows (£)	(10,000)	2,800	2,550	5,362.50	487.50

(The overall tax allowances are £4,000, which is 40 per cent of the cost of the equipment, for which it has been assumed that there will be no scrap proceeds. Also, the cost of the machine and additional working capital would be treated as having arisen in year 0 for the purposes of the capital expenditure appraisal techniques. They are shown in year 1 in the above table so as to clarify the timing of the tax and tax allowance cash flows.)

44.4 Annualised figures

It can be difficult comparing projects that have different lengths. To overcome this complication, it is possible to use annualised amounts. Notionally, this approach assumes that the comparison would then be made over a period that represented the lowest common multiple of the projects – a twelve-year cycle would be used for two projects, one of three years' duration, the other four. However, as will be seen, once the annualised amounts are calculated, the decision can be taken without reference to any particular length of time.

The first step is to calculate the present value of the projects and then identify the amount of the annuity for the period of each project that has the same present value as that project's NPV. For example, if a discount rate of 10 per cent is used and the NPV of the three-year project is £500, the annuity multiplier (from the table in Appendix 1) is 2.487 and the three-year annuity with a present value of £500 is therefore £201 (i.e. £500 ÷ 2.487). If the four-year project has an NPV of £800, the four-year annuity is £252 (i.e. £800 ÷ 3.170). On the basis of these annualised amounts, the four-year project would be selected.

44.5 Relevant and irrelevant costs

When decision making, some costs and revenues are relevant to a decision that is to be taken, whilst other costs and revenues are not, i.e. they are irrelevant. The **relevant costs** and **relevant revenues** are those costs and revenues of the future that will be affected by the decision, whereas irrelevant costs and revenues will not be so affected.

Take as an example a decision as to whether or not we should telephone a lot of our customers or not in a sales campaign. The cost of the telephone rental is irrelevant in the decision whether or not to conduct the campaign, as we will have to pay exactly the same rental whether or not we engage in the campaign. On the other hand, the cost of making the extra calls will be a relevant cost as they would not have been incurred if the campaign had not gone ahead.

With revenues, take the case of buying a new car for a salesperson. If the revenues he would help create by sales would remain unchanged no matter which car he were to have, then the revenues would be completely irrelevant in taking the decision as to the type of car to be bought.

However, to take the case of a salesperson who sells some of his products to farmers. With a four-wheel drive car he could get to farms which would otherwise be inaccessible to a two-wheel drive car. In this case the revenues would be relevant to the decision as to the type of car to be bought, as they would be affected by the decision.

44.6 Sunk costs

Sunk cost is a term which can be confusing, since it really means an irrelevant cost which has already occurred. It is a past cost, not a future cost.

Let us take the case of a machine which was bought several years ago, and now has a written down value of £10,000. The scrap value is nil. We can either use the machine on a project we are considering or else we can scrap it. Let us suppose that the revenue from the project will be £25,000 and the future relevant costs will be £18,000. If we added the written down value of the machine to the £18,000 costs then we would make a loss of £3,000 (£25,000 – £28,000). Looking at it that way, we would not tackle the project.

However, the cost of the machine was a past cost. If we do not use the machine on this project the only other alternative is to scrap it. Such a past cost is said to be a *sunk cost* and is irrelevant to the decision to be taken. We therefore take on the project (assuming there is no better alternative project) and are better off by £7,000 (£25,000 – £18,000).

44.7 A comparison of the methods

We will now look at a case where each of the methods already described will be used to try to select the best investment. You will see that the different methods can give different answers as to which project should be chosen.

Exhibit 44.2

ABC Ltd is wondering whether or not to invest in one of three possible projects. The initial investment will be £10,000, and the cost of capital is 10 per cent. There is no scrap value for fixed assets used. Details of the net cash inflows are as follows:

	M	N	P
	£	£	£
Year 1	3,000	5,000	4,000
Year 2	6,000	5,000	5,000
Year 3	4,000	2,000	3,000
Year 4	–	1,600	1,000
Year 5	–	–	1,400
	13,000	13,600	14,400

1 Accounting rate of return method:

$$\frac{\text{Average yearly profit}}{\text{Average investment}} \times \frac{100}{1} \qquad \frac{1,000}{5,000} = 20\% \qquad \frac{900}{5,000} = 18\% \qquad \frac{880}{5,000} = 17.6\%$$

2 Payback method:

M	N	P
2.25 years	2 years	2 years

3 Net present value method (cost of capital 10%)

Discount factors per tables		Present values (£)	
	M	N	P
1,000	× (10,000) = (10,000)	× (10,000) = (10,000)	× (10,000) = (10,000)
0.909	× 3,000 = 2,727	× 5,000 = 4,545	× 4,000 = 3,636
0.826	× 6,000 = 4,956	× 5,000 = 4,130	× 5,000 = 4,130
0.751	× 4,000 = 3,004	× 2,000 = 1,502	× 3,000 = 2,253
0.683		× 1,600 = 1,092	× 1,000 = 683
0.621			× 1,400 = 869
Net present values	687	1,269	1,571

4 Internal rate of return:

Stage 1: Use a rate of return which will give negative net present values. In this instance it is taken to be 18%.

Discount factors per tables at 18%		Present values (£)	
	M	N	P
1,000	× (10,000) = (10,000)	× (10,000) = (10,000)	× (10,000) = (10,000)
0.847	× 3,000 = 2,541	× 5,000 = 4,235	× 4,000 = 3,388
0.718	× 6,000 = 4,308	× 5,000 = 3,590	× 5,000 = 3,590
0.609	× 4,000 = 2,436	× 2,000 = 1,218	× 3,000 = 1,827
0.516		× 1,600 = 826	× 1,000 = 516
0.437			× 1,400 = 611
Net present values	(715)	(131)	(68)

Stage 2: Calculate the internal rate of return (IRR), using figures for positive present values already calculated in **3** above.

$$M \quad 10\% + \left(8\% \times \frac{687}{687 + 715}\right) = 13.92\%$$

$$N \quad 10\% + \left(8\% \times \frac{1,269}{1,269 + 131}\right) = 17.25\%$$

$$P \quad 10\% + \left(8\% \times \frac{1,571}{1,571 + 68}\right) = 17.67\%$$

If used on its own, without reference to the other methods:

1 Accounting rate of return would choose project M, as it gives highest rate of 20 per cent.
2 Payback would choose project N, as it pays back in the shortest time of two years.
3 Net present value would choose project P as it gives the highest net present value of £1,571.
4 Internal rate of return would choose project P, as it shows highest return of 17.67 per cent, which is itself higher than the cost of capital.

44.8 Uncertainty

Many of the values used in the calculations and formulae described in this chapter are, at best, objectively based estimates of future cash flows and interest rates. It is, for example, virtually inconceivable that the figures forecast in a capital expenditure appraisal will be confirmed to have been 100 per cent accurate when the project is completed.

Proposers of a course of action tend to be over-optimistic and, in order to avoid the risk of non-achievement of forecasted results, a number of measures have been adopted. The two most common are the adoption of a higher cost of capital rate than is actually required in practice, and reducing estimates of income by a fixed percentage and using the same percentage to increase all costs. However, such arbitrary adjustments can no more guarantee accuracy than the original estimates, and they will often cause the decision taken to be different from that which the original, possibly more meaningful, data would have produced.

A more rational adjustment that can be adopted is to change the amounts forecast according to their subjective probabilities. The probabilities would be provided by the proposers of a project.

Example

Estimated sales × Probability of occurrence =	Expected sales
£	£	
2,000	0.2	400
4,000	0.5	2,000
6,000	0.2	1,200
8,000	0.1	800
	1.0	4,400

In this case, the expected value of £4,400 will be used, rather than the most likely value of £4,000. While this approach appears more rational than the other possible methods of dealing with uncertainty, it is dependent upon the probabilities used being soundly based.

Activity 44.3

If two projects both require the same investment and one has an NPV of £100 and the other an NPV of £240, which should be selected? Would this always be the case?

44.9 Sensitivity analysis

One of the greatest benefits of spreadsheets is the facility to perform unlimited numbers of sensitivity analysis computations on a given set of data. Cash flows can be adjusted marginally to see if the change turns a positive NPV negative; interest rates can be altered to see if the same decision would be made; the timing of cash flows can be altered to see what the impact of doing so is upon NPV. Sensitivity analysis enables information generated using the formulae and methods described in this chapter to be manipulated in order to maximise the understanding of the flexibility and limits of that information.

The importance of discounting has been recognised by the Institute of Chartered Accountants in England and Wales, which has issued Technical Release 773 *The Use of Discounting in Financial Statements*. It is an excellent source of discussion on this topic, and on its application in practice.

You should now have learnt:

1 That as time passes, money loses value and this loss of value must be allowed for when considering long-term investments.

2 That net present value (NPV) and internal rate of return (IRR) usually lead to the same selection being made between mutually exclusive projects. When they differ, it is the NPV selection that should be followed.

3 That accounting rate of return (ARR) is still used, but the rate it produces cannot be compared to the cost of capital and the technique is not recommended.

4 How to calculate NPV, IRR, Payback, and ARR.

5 The relative merits of the four methods.

6 What is meant by relevant and irrelevant costs.

7 What is meant by sunk cost.

8 How to select the 'best' project for an organisation to pursue at a given time from a range of possible alternative projects.

9 How to explain why, from a financial perspective, the selected project is the 'best' one for the organisation to pursue.

10 That where alternative projects are of unequal length, annualised amounts can be calculated to enable comparison.

Answers to activities

44.1 It would depend on many factors, not least the rate of interest you would receive from the bank and the anticipated profits from the restaurant. You would need to consider the probability of the estimates concerning the profitability of the restaurant. You would also need to take into account your relationship with your friend and your own willingness to run the risk that you may not be able to recover your investment without damaging your relationship with your friend should you need the money back before the five years had passed. There are many non-financial factors that often need to be taken into account when considering long-term investments.

44.2 These deficiencies in the payback approach can be addressed by discounting all cash flows to their present values, and by ensuring that the calculation includes a check for there being multiple payback points. While the first is generally sensible, the second is essential if payback is to be effectively applied.

44.3 The project with the higher NPV should normally be chosen. Where the NPV is very small relative to the investment, it may not be so important that the one with the higher NPV is chosen. For example, if the investment required for these NPVs is £7,500 the NPVs are relatively very small indeed. Other factors would be more important, such as the likelihood that the figures would prove to be accurate; the potential impact of each alternative on the general image and reputation of the organisation; whether the projects would involve any opportunity costs that are not accounted for in the NPV calculation (such as employees being unavailable for other work), etc.

REVIEW QUESTIONS

44.1 The following project costs have been estimated relating to the upgrading of some equipment; all the costs are being incurred solely because of the project:

20X2			£
January	1	One year's rent on premises paid	6,000
	31	Equipment purchased	40,000
March	31	Installation of equipment completed and paid	12,000
December	31	Costs incurred in commissioning equipment	18,000
20X3			
January	1	One year's rent on premises paid	6,000
March	31	Additional commissioning costs paid	10,000
May	31	Training costs paid	4,000
June	30	Additional working capital provided	14,000
December	31	Cash proceeds from sale of old equipment	10,000

Ignoring tax, prepare a statement showing the outlays of cash on the project in 20X2 and 20X3. The new facility will be in full use from 1 July 20X3.

44.2 Assume the company in Question 44.1 pays tax at 40 per cent, on 30 September each year, nine months after the end of its financial period. The company receives 25 per cent writing-down allowances on the cost of equipment and will receive the allowances for 20X2 expenditure to be offset against the tax payable on the profits for 20X2. 100 per cent capital allowances were received on the old equipment sold in 20X3 and the receipts from the sale of the old equipment must, therefore, be treated as taxable income of 20X3. Show the impact on the cash flows of these tax items.

44.3 Assuming an interest rate of 10 per cent, what is the net present value of the net of tax cash flows in Question 44.2 for 20X2, 20X3, 20X4 and 20X5?

44.4A The annual profit from a project is forecasted as:

	£	£
Sales		110,000
Labour, materials, and overheads	30,000	
Depreciation	20,000	
		(50,000)
Net profit before tax		60,000
Tax at 40%		(24,000)
Net profit after tax		36,000

Equipment with a five-year useful economic life and no residual value will be purchased on 1 September for £30,000. £15,000 additional working capital, which will be recovered in full at the end of the five years, will be required from 1 September. A 25 per cent writing-down allowance will be available throughout the period of the project. Tax at 40 per cent will be payable on 1 June each year, nine months after the end of the company's financial period on 31 August. Prepare a cash flow budget for the project.

44.5A If the interest rate is 10 per cent, what is the net present value of the net cash flows arising from the project in Question 44.4A?

44.6A If retained, a machine would be depreciated at £2,500 for the next four years, at which point it would be fully written down and scrapped. The machine could be sold at any point in the next year for £15,000, the gain being subject to tax at 40 per cent, payable the following year. If it were sold, a new machine costing £80,000 would be bought. The new machine would receive 25 per cent writing-down allowances to be offset annually against profits. It is estimated that the new machine would save material costs of £25,000 per year. Profits are subject to tax at 40 per cent, payable nine months after the end of the company's financial period. The new machinery would have a four-year life, with a residual value of zero, and would be depreciated straight line over that period. Prepare a cash flow statement for the replacement option, and indicate how the profits reported in the financial statements would be altered were the existing machine to be replaced.

44.7 What is the payback period on the following project cash flows? (Brackets indicate expenditure.)

Year	Net cash flows £
0	(10,000)
1	8,000
2	4,000
3	2,000
4	1,000

44.8 Using a discount rate of 12 per cent, what is the net present value of the project in Question 44.7?

44.9 What is the internal rate of return on the project in Question 44.7?

44.10 What is the annualised amount of the net benefits from the project in Question 44.7?

44.11A What is the payback on a project requiring £60,000 initial investment that has a net cash inflow of £40,000 in year 1, £25,000 in year 2, and £15,000 in year 3?

44.12A Using a discount rate of 10 per cent, what is the net present value of the project in Question 44.11A?

44.13A What is the internal rate of return on the project in Question 44.11A?

44.14A What is the annualised amount of the net benefits from the project in Question 44.11A?

44.15A The annual profit from a project is forecast as:

	£	£
Sales		80,000
Labour, materials, and overheads	20,000	
Depreciation	15,000	
		(35,000)
Net profit before tax		45,000

The project requires that a new machine be purchased for £65,000. It will be depreciated using the straight line method over four years to a residual value of £5,000. The project will cease when the machine is sold for £5,000 at the end of the fourth year. Ignoring taxation, what is the accounting rate of return? (No additional working capital is required for this project.)

44.16A Assuming that all sales are for cash, what is the internal rate of return on the project in Question 44.15A?

44.17 Which of the following two mutually exclusive alternatives should be selected if a 10 per cent interest rate is used for the calculation of net present value?

	Net cash flow Year 0 £	Net cash flow Year 3 £
Machine A project	(12,000)	22,000
Machine B project	(38,000)	66,000

44.18 Using internal rate of return, which of the two projects in Question 44.17 would be preferred?

44.19A Which of the following two mutually exclusive alternatives should be selected if a 12 per cent interest rate is used for the calculation of net present value?

	Net cash flow Year 0 £	Net cash flow Year 1 £	Net cash flow Year 3 £
Project A	(34,000)	16,000	26,000
Project B	(29,000)	22,000	12,000

44.20A Using internal rate of return, which of the two projects in Question 44.19A would be preferred?

44.21 Equipment with an estimated useful economic life of five years has an NPV of £3,100 using a 10 per cent discount rate. What is the annualised equivalent of the £3,100 NPV?

44.22A Two mutually exclusive alternatives are available. Project A will require initial investment of £3,000 and run for two years at a cost of £500 per annum. Project B will require initial investment of £7,000 and last for four years at a cost of £800 for the first three years and £1,000 in the fourth. Calculate the annualised cost of both projects over a four-year period, assuming that reinvestment in project A would cost £2,500 at the end of year two and assuming an interest rate of 8 per cent. Which alternative should be selected?

44.23 A machine with a five-year useful life could be purchased for £60,000. It would have zero residual value at the end of the five years. Alternatively, the machine could be rented at £14,633 per annum for five years. Assuming a tax rate of 40 per cent and that tax relief is obtained in the same period as the payments, what is the implicit interest rate in the lease?

44.24 Roadwheelers Ltd were considering buying an additional lorry but the company had not yet decided which particular lorry to purchase. The lorries had broadly similar technical specifications and each was expected to have a working life of five years.
The following information was available on the lorries being considered:

1

	Lorries		
	BN Roadhog	FX Sprinter	VR Rocket
Purchase price	£40,000	£45,000	£50,000
Estimated scrap value after 5 years	£8,000	£9,000	£14,000
Fixed costs other than depreciation	£	£	£
Year 1	2,000	1,800	1,500
Year 2	2,000	1,800	1,500
Year 3	2,200	1,800	1,400
Year 4	2,400	2,000	1,400
Year 5	2,400	2,200	1,400
Variable costs per road mile	6p	8p	7p

2 The company charges 25p per mile for all journeys irrespective of the length of journey and the expected annual mileages over the five-year period are:

	Miles
Year 1	50,000
Year 2	60,000
Year 3	80,000
Year 4	80,000
Year 5	80,000

3 The company's cost of capital is 10 per cent per annum.
4 It should be assumed that all operating costs are paid and revenues received at the end of year.
5 Present value of £1 at interest rate of 10 per cent per annum:

Year 1	£0.909
Year 2	£0.826
Year 3	£0.751
Year 4	£0.683
Year 5	£0.621

Required:

(a) (i) Appropriate computations using the net present value method for each of the lorries under consideration.

(ii) A report to the directors of Roadwheelers Ltd advising them as to which specific lorry should be purchased.

(b) A brief outline of the problems encountered in evaluating capital projects.

(AQA (Associated Examining Board): GCE A-level)

44.25A Hirwaun Pig Iron Co. operate a single blast furnace producing pig iron. The present blast furnace is obsolete and the company is considering its replacement. The alternatives the company is considering are:

(i) Blast furnace type Exco. Cost £2 million.

This furnace is of a standard size capable of a monthly output of 10,000 tonnes. The company expects to sell 80 per cent of its output annually at £150 per tonne on a fixed price contract. The remaining output will be sold on the open market at the following expected prices:

	20X5	20X6	20X7	20X8
Price per tonne	£150	£140	£140	£160

(ii) Blast furnace type Ohio. Cost £3.5 million.

This large furnace is capable of a monthly output of 20,000 tonnes. A single buyer has agreed to buy all the monthly output at a fixed price which is applicable from 1 January each year. The prices fixed for the next four years are as follows:

	Payments per tonne of output			
	20X5	20X6	20X7	20X8
Price per tonne	£130	£130	£140	£170

Additional information:

1 Blast furnaces operate continuously and the operating labour is regarded as a fixed cost. During the next four years the operating labour costs will be as follows:

Exco £1.2 million per annum
Ohio £2.5 million per annum

2 Other forecast operating payments (excluding labour) per tonne:

	20X5	20X6	20X7	20X8
Exco	£130	£130	£135	£135
Ohio	£120	£120	£125	£125

3 It can be assumed that both blast furnaces will have a life of 10 years.
4 The company's cost of capital is 12 per cent per annum.
5 It should be assumed that all costs are paid and revenues received at the end of each year.
6 The following is an extract from the present value table for £1:

	11%	12%	13%	14%
Year 1	£0.901	£0.893	£0.885	£0.877
Year 2	£0.812	£0.797	£0.783	£0.770
Year 3	£0.731	£0.712	£0.693	£0.675
Year 4	£0.659	£0.636	£0.613	£0.592

Required:

(a) The forecast budgets for each of the years 20X5–20X8 and for each of the blast furnaces being considered. Show the expected yearly net cash flows.

(b) Appropriate computations using the net present value method for each of the blast furnaces, Exco and Ohio, for the first four years.

(c) A report providing a recommendation to the management of Hirwaun Pig Iron Co. as to which blast furnace should be purchased. Your report should include a critical evaluation of the method used to assess the capital project.

(AQA (Associated Examining Board): GCE A-level)

44.26 Moray Ferries Ltd own a single ship which provides a short sea ferry service for passengers, private vehicles and commercial traffic. The present ship is nearing the end of its useful life and the company is considering the purchase of a new ship.

The forecast operating budgets using the present ship are as follows:

	20X5 £m	20X6 £m	20X7 £m	20X8 £m	20X9 £m
Estimated revenue receipts					
Private traffic	2	3	4.5	6	7
Commercial traffic	3	4	4.5	5	6
	5	7	9.0	11	13
Estimated operating payments	4	5	6.5	7.5	9
	1	2	2.5	3.5	4

The ships being considered as a replacement are as described below.

1 Ship A. Cost £10m

This ship is of similar capacity to the one being replaced, but being a more modern ship it is expected that extra business would be attracted from competitors. It is anticipated therefore that estimated revenue receipts would be 10 per cent higher in each year of the present forecast. There would be no change in operating payments.

2 Ship B. Cost £14m

This modern ship has a carrying capacity 30 per cent greater than the present ship. It is expected that private traffic receipts would increase by £$\frac{1}{2}$m a year in each year of the forecast. Commercial traffic receipts are expected to increase by 15 per cent in each of the first two years and by 30 per cent in each of the remaining years.

Operating payments would increase by 20 per cent in each year of the forecast.

Additional information:

3 The company's cost of capital is 15 per cent per annum.
4 It is company policy to assume that ships have a life of 20 years.
5 It should be assumed that all costs are paid and revenues received at the end of each year.
6 The following is an extract from the present value table for £1:

	12%	14%	15%	16%
Year 1	£0.893	£0.877	£0.870	£0.862
Year 2	£0.797	£0.769	£0.756	£0.743
Year 3	£0.712	£0.675	£0.658	£0.641
Year 4	£0.636	£0.592	£0.572	£0.552
Year 5	£0.567	£0.519	£0.497	£0.476

7 All calculations should be made correct to three places of decimals.

Required:

(*a*) Revised operating budgets for 20X5–20X9 for each of the alternatives being considered.
(*b*) Appropriate computations using the net present value method for each of the ships, A and B.
(*c*) A report providing a recommendation to the management of Moray Ferries Ltd as to which course of action should be followed. Your report should include any reservations that you may have.

(AQA (Associated Examining Board): GCE A-level)

44.27A The Rovers Football Club are languishing in the middle of the Premier Division of the Football League. The Club have suffered a loss of £200,000 in their last financial year and whilst receipts from spectators have declined over the last five years, recently receipts have stabilised at approximately £1,000,000 per season. The Club is considering the purchase of the services of one of two new football players, Jimmy Jam or Johnny Star.

Jimmy Jam is 21 years old and considered to be a future international footballer. He is prepared to sign a five-year contract with Rovers for a salary of £50,000 per annum. His present club would require a transfer fee of £200,000 for the transfer of his existing contract. With J. Jam in the team the Rovers Club would expect receipts to increase by 20 per cent.

Johnny Star is 32 years old and a leading international footballer who is prepared to sign for Rovers on a two-year contract before retiring completely from football. He would expect a salary of £200,000 per annum and his present club would require a transfer fee of £100,000 for the transfer of his existing contract. Rovers believe that as a result of signing Star receipts would increase by 40 per cent.

The rate of interest applicable to the transaction is 12 per cent and the following is an extract from the present value table for £1:

	12%
Year 1	0.893
Year 2	0.797
Year 3	0.712
Year 4	0.636
Year 5	0.567

It should be assumed that all costs are paid and revenues received at the end of each year.

Required:

A report, incorporating an evaluation of the financial result of engaging each player by the net present value method, providing the Rovers Football Club with information to assist it in deciding which alternative to adopt. Indicate any other factors that may be taken into consideration.

(AQA (Associated Examining Board): GCE A-level)

CHAPTER 45

The balanced scorecard

Learning objectives

After you have studied this chapter, you should be able to:

- describe the aims of the balanced scorecard
- explain the four perspectives of the balanced scorecard
- explain the two types of measure inherent in the balanced scorecard
- explain the difference between the balanced scorecard and a traditional financial-accounting-based performance appraisal system
- describe some advantages of adopting the balanced scorecard
- describe some of the problems that can arise when the balanced scorecard is adopted

Introduction

In this chapter you'll learn about the balanced scorecard, its four perspectives, its two measures and it advantages compared with more traditional financial-accounting-based performance appraisal systems. You'll also learn about some of the problems that can arise when the balanced scorecard is adopted.

45.1 Background

Much has changed in the way that organisations operate today compared with even five years ago. The change over the past 25 years has been immense. In 1980, only the largest organisations had computers, the spreadsheet had only just been invented, the internet was something only academics and some government employees had heard of, email was used by only a few, the *World Wide Web* was about 10 years away from being invented, electronic commerce was something from science fiction, and most business records were still recorded and maintained by hand.

The business environment of today is far more competitive, far more open, and far more volatile than it has ever been. In order to survive, businesses need to be far more efficient in the use of their resources, have a far better understanding of the needs of their customers, have far better organised internal systems and procedures, and have employees who have a far greater level of interpersonal skills than in the past. Above all, they need to have a well-defined organisational strategy and to have both defined the objectives that ensure the strategy is pursued and identified the measures required in order to ensure that the objectives not only are being achieved but will continue to be achieved in future.

This means that organisations need to look beyond the historical perspective of their traditional financial reporting systems which were mainly backwards looking, focusing upon reporting achievements rather than upon the attainment and pursuit of objectives. They need to incorporate data capture and analysis of non-financial measures, such as customer

profiles, customer satisfaction, employee performance, employee satisfaction, product quality, service quality, organisational transformation and development. They need to pay attention to the long-term and think less about the short-term.

One performance evaluation technique that supports this shift in emphasis and focus has emerged over the last 20 years, Kaplan and Norton's **balanced scorecard.** It bridges the strengths of the traditional financial measures of past performance with the benefits of measuring factors that impact upon or 'drive' future performance. It does so at all levels of the business, not just at the overall level typified by the traditional measures of financial performance.

45.2 The framework of the balanced scorecard

The balanced scorecard assesses performance across a balanced set of four perspectives: customers, internal processes, organisational learning and growth, and financial. It does not replace the traditional focus upon financial measurement as a critical summary of managerial and business performance. Rather, it complements it by the addition of the other three perspectives.

Thus, the traditional financial measures are still there for those that require them and for the purposes to which they are most suited but new measures are provided that enrich the information available at all levels of the organisation and so facilitate the co-ordinated achievement of organisational objectives, particularly in the long-term.

The four perspectives of the balanced scorecard

Exhibit 45.1 shows the relationship between the four perspectives, and organisational vision and strategy.

Exhibit 45.1

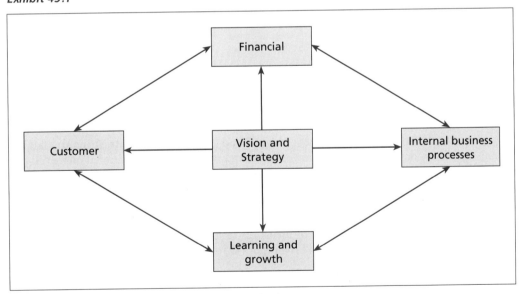

The financial perspective

Here you identify the financial objectives that the organisation wishes to pursue and develop measures that indicate how successful the organisation has been in achieving those objectives. In essence, this is the aspect of the balanced scorecard that accounting has long

been associated with and includes the use of such measures as return on capital employed, earnings per share, and the other financial ratios you learnt about in Chapter 27. It answers the question, how does the organisation appear to its owners?

Examples of possible measures are:

- return on capital employed
- return on net assets
- reduction of administrative expenses
- reduction in bad debts
- reduction in debtor days
- reduction in gearing.

The customer perspective

You must identify the customer and market segments in which the organisation operates. Measurements should then be made of factors such as customer satisfaction, retention, acquisition, customer profitability and market share. It answers the question, how does the organisation appear to its customers?

Examples of possible measures are:

- customer satisfaction
- customer retention
- increasing customer base
- reduction in delivery times
- reduction in rate of goods returned by customers.

The internal business processes perspective

You need to identify and measure the internal processes that are critical to the organisation being able to improve the drivers that will attract and retain customers in targeted markets and satisfy owner expectations concerning financial returns. It answers the question, at what must the organisation excel?

Examples of possible measures are:

- reduction in quality control rejection rate
- reduced production lead times
- increased level of production capacity utilisation.

The learning and growth perspective

This identifies the human relations, technological and general systems infrastructure that the organisation must develop if it is to achieve long-term growth and organisational improvement. Appropriate measures would include those relating to the level of relevant employee skills, how up to date the organisation's IT systems and programs are, and the ability of the organisation's systems architecture to provide the information in an efficient, timely and cost effective way. One of the key aspects in this perspective is appropriate and timely development of people and systems and development of measures to monitor and confirm that this is being done. It answers the question, how will the organisation continue to change and improve?

Examples of possible measures are:

- increased level of spending per head on employee training
- reduced employee absenteeism rate
- reduced staff turnover rate
- increased range of products
- increased proportion of new product sales as a proportion of total sales
- greater reporting flexibility in the information system
- increase in the range of information available on demand from the information system.

45.3 Measures

Two forms of measures are used in the balanced scorecard approach:

(*a*) *outcome measures*, which assess past performance;
(*b*) *performance measures (or drivers)*, which are indicators that drive future performance.

Performance measures need to be aligned to organisation strategy and, therefore, to outcomes. There is no point in having a measure that has no bearing on strategy or its pursuit. Typically, three to five measures for each of the four perspectives should be adequate. Once the organisation strategy has been identified and converted into objectives, those factors that will achieve the desired objectives (i.e. the performance measures) are identified, along with those that can confirm the objectives are being achieved (i.e. the outcome measures).

As a result of articulating the outcomes the organisation desires and the pinpointing the drivers of those outcomes, the energies, abilities and specific knowledge of people throughout the organisation can be aligned to achieve the goals of the organisation.

Once they been established, there is no reason why the measures inherent in the balanced scorecard should remain fixed. Organisational strategy may change at any time. When it does, the objectives will obviously be changed to keep them in line with the revised strategy. Clearly, the measures of both output and performance will also change as appropriate.

45.4 The relationship between the four perspectives

There needs to be a series of cause and effect relationships between the four perspectives and the factors within them. Specifically, there must be clear and logical relationship between each performance driver and one or more of the outcome measures. If there is not, the overall strategy of the organisation cannot be achieved.

Activity 45.1
Why is this the case?

45.5 Benefits of adopting the balanced scorecard

There are a number of benefits to those organisations that adopt the balanced scorecard:

1 *It provides the organisation with a strategic management system that:*
   (*a*) clarifies and encourages consensus about organisational vision and strategy
   (*b*) communicates strategy, objectives, drives and measures of performance
   (*c*) facilitates the linking of strategic objectives to budgets
   (*d*) facilitates strategic reviews, especially periodic but also *ad hoc*
   (*e*) facilitates the identification and promotion of new strategic initiatives
   (*f*) facilitates fine-tuning and amendment of strategy in the light of performance.

In effect, the balanced scorecard provides management with a tool to focus strategy and move the organisation in a co-ordinated and transparent manner towards the achievement of its objectives.

2 *It helps people understand how they can contribute to the strategic success of the organisation.* By making it clear what items are important indicators of success, people become aware of what actually leads to the organisation achieving its objectives. They then know which aspects of their work are vital and know that to focus upon them will be beneficial to the organisation. Previously, they would have had to choose to focus upon one or more of

a range of alternative activities, many of which may have made no worthwhile contribution to the achievement of the organisational goals.

3 *It guides the transformation of the organisation's vision and strategy into a set of performance measures.* The chain of development of the balanced scorecard is quite straightforward. First, the organisation's mission must be established, then its strategy to pursue its mission, then the objectives that will underpin its strategy, then output measures must be defined so that performance can be assessed and the performance measures (or drivers) established so that it can be seen whether the organisation is moving in the right direction. By creating and providing such a framework to management, the balanced scorecard approach supports the organisation's move towards a greater and more consistent performance that is in line with the organisation's objectives and strategy.

45.6 Problems that may arise in introducing the balanced scorecard

There are a number of problems that may arise when introducing the balanced scorecard. Each of them can result in its being less than successful and care needs to be taken to ensure they do not arise, or, if they do arise, that they are eliminated as quickly as possible. The problems include:

1 *A lack of a clearly defined organisational vision or strategy.* It is very difficult to establish objectives if there is no overall organisational vision or strategy. Many organisations have no statement of their mission and many that do have developed no clear organisational strategy. This slows down implementation of the balanced scorecard, as it first requires that a mission, vision and strategy be developed and agreed. Not surprisingly, unless this is done, the balanced scorecard can do little to improve the overall ability of the organisation to achieve its strategic objectives.

2 *Developing and implementing a balanced scorecard before appropriate objectives have been identified.* It can only be wasteful and misleading to develop a balanced scorecard in this case, as there will be aspects of it that are wasteful of resources and other aspects that simply fail to address the appropriate measures. Once the mission, vision and strategy have been developed, it will become obvious that the objectives that existed previously and formed the basis for the development of a balanced scorecard were inappropriate. At that point the incorrect balanced scorecard must be amended and replaced with one that is consistent with the 'real' objectives. As most people are naturally resistant to change, this can create a human relations problems that seriously undermine the effort to install an appropriate balanced scorecard. It is far better to wait for appropriate objectives to be identified before starting to develop the balanced scorecard.

3 *Failing to achieve consensus and acceptance at all levels of the organisation.* In this aspect, there are similarities with the need to ensure all individuals accept, understand and appropriately apply a system of budgetary control. As the extent of the measures and drivers of the four perspectives of the balanced scorecard are far greater than for a budgetary control system, the need for consensus is considerably greater. Dysfunctional responses to the balanced scorecard seriously undermine its potential to motivate development of the organisation in the directions established by the clear definition of the organisational strategy which the balanced scorecard provides.

4 *When first attempted, definition of the objectives inherent in the financial, customer and internal business process perspectives often reveals gaps between the existing capabilities of people, organisational systems and procedures and the objectives that are sought.* Management must close these gaps by retraining employees, improving the organisational systems (often through more effective use of IT), and realigning organisational procedures and routines so that they are more compatible with the systems to which they relate.

5 *The organisational objectives across all four perspectives must be compatible and moving in the same direction in the long-term.* If the balanced scorecard is to be successfully adopted, it needs to be done with a view to the long term. For example, an objective to enhance customer satisfaction may require that employees are retrained and that systems and quality control procedures are altered so as to improve product quality.

These changes will impact the financial performance measures negatively in the short term. If the organisation has a financial strategy objective to improve return on capital employed, this will only be achieved once the changes made have resulted in increased customer satisfaction which, in turn, results in increased customer loyalty, higher demand for the organisation's products, increased profitability, and an improved return on capital employed.

6 *The organisation's ability to offer current and accurate information to support the balanced scorecard may be undermined because it is currently capable of providing only a few of the outcomes and measures identified by the balanced scorecard analysis.* If the underlying systems and technology are incapable of providing the outcomes and measures required by the balanced scorecard, they must be reorganised and replaced if the balanced scorecard is to be implemented successfully.

7 *The performance measures selected are not aligned with the organisation's strategy.* One cause may be a desire to retain traditional measures because they have always been used rather than to abandon them. Developing a balanced scorecard requires that management reappraise the organisation and switch the emphasis from monitoring output and performance that fails to support the organisation's strategy in a meaningful way.

Change is crucial to the successful implementation of the balanced scorecard. The difference between a traditional financial-performance-related monitoring focus and the far broader and more focused balanced scorecard requires a major shift in perceptions and practices. Reluctance to change can seriously undermine the success of the balanced scorecard approach.

45.7 Strategic planning and budgeting

If you investigate when most organisations carry out these two activities, you will find that strategic planning and budgeting are typically done at different times of the year and led by different parts of the organisation.

Kaplan and Norton recommend that the budgeting process be integrated with the strategic planning process. To do so, the budgeting process should follow the strategic planning process. They also believe that the budget should represent year 1 of a three- or a five-year plan and that companies should be budgeting not only for financial measures but also for the measures in the other three perspectives as well.

They argue that by comparing the gap between where the organisation wants to be in 3–5 years and where it is today, the managers can assign new resources and strategic initiatives to close the gaps. This motivates additional spending in year 1. Discretionary spending, both operating and capital, is aimed at closing the forecast future gaps, rather than being devoted to the pursuit of short-term gains.

At the same time, if management specify how the initial spending and investment will start to improve measures in the customer, internal business processes and learning and growth perspectives, they will provide a ready-made yardstick by which to measure performance in pursuit of these changes.

The benefit of this approach is that costs rise in the short term but in a way that does not result in the perspectives being out-of-balance with each other. In the long term, all the perspectives benefit.

As a result, by integrating strategic planning and budgeting, managers can reach a consensus about the trade-offs between short-term financial performance and long-term benefit. There are potentially enormous benefits to be gained by organisations that adopt such an approach over those that stick with traditional financial-based performance measures.

45.8 Adoption of the balanced scorecard

It is not surprising that the balanced scorecard is becoming increasingly adopted as a means of offering a more focused approach to performance monitoring and measurement. It provides a far more focused approach than traditional financial-based performance measures and organisations that adopt it experience a greatly enhanced synergy between their mission, strategy and objectives and the means used to measure output and performance.

It is likely that adoption of the balanced scorecard will become ever more popular as organisations of all sizes and types become aware of its potential. However, it should not be overlooked that the traditional financial measures still have a significant role to play and that the balanced scorecard adds a new and complementary dimension to performance measurement rather than offering an outright alternative.

Learning outcomes

You should now have learnt:

1 The aims of the balanced scorecard.
2 The four perspectives of the balanced scorecard.
3 The two types of measures inherent in the balanced scorecard.
4 Some advantages of adopting the balanced scorecard.
5 Some of the problems that can arise when the balanced scorecard is adopted.
6 The difference between the balanced scorecard and a traditional financial-accounting-based performance appraisal system.

Answers to activities

45.1 It is very difficult to establish objectives if there is no overall organisational vision or strategy. Without a mission, vision and strategy the organisational objectives can be little more than guesses concerning whether or not they help the organisation pursue its strategy in a meaningful way. Establishing measures to achieve false objectives serves no meaningful purpose.

REVIEW QUESTIONS

45.1 What is the balanced scorecard?

45.2 Compare the balanced scorecard to traditional financial-accounting-based performance measurement?

45.3 Compare and contrast the two forms of measure applied by the balanced scorecard.

45.4 Compare and contrast the four perspectives of the balanced scorecard.

PART 10

The emerging business environment of accounting

Introduction

This part reviews increasingly popular recently developed approaches to managing the flow of information and data and enhancing the management of resources. It also looks at the emerging Internet-based business environment and the impact of e-commerce upon accounting.

CHAPTER 46

The supply chain and enterprise resource planning systems

Introduction

In this chapter you'll learn how organisations can improve their overall efficiency, reduce costs and increase revenues by adopting supply chain management. You'll also learn about the advantages of adopting enterprise resource planning and of the advantages of integrating an enterprise resource planning system with supply chain management. Finally, you'll learn why enterprise resource planning and supply chain management are important concepts for accounting and accountants.

46.1 Supply chain management

Manufacturing organisations purchase raw materials, convert them into finished goods, and then sell the finished goods. The term used to describe this sequence or chain of events is the **supply chain**. Everything within the two end-points of the chain is encompassed by the term. Thus, it includes, demand forecasting, scheduling of production, supplier identification, ordering, inventory management, carriage, warehousing at all stages, production, and customer service. **The more the supply chain can be made a seamless and seemingly continuous process (where each stage acts as the trigger for the stage that follows it and where all the links operate automatically when appropriate), the more successful a business will be.**

An example of a supply chain is shown in Exhibit 46.1. For simplicity, warehousing has been omitted and purchasing is shown as being triggered by customer orders. Obviously, ordering often anticipates demand rather than being led by it.

Exhibit 46.1

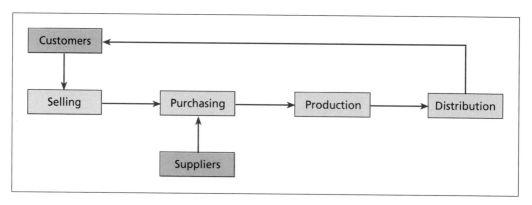

To achieve effective **supply chain management**, the organisation needs to have control over information and/or item flows both within and outwith the organisation. That is, all the external parties involved in the chain – suppliers, carriers, information systems providers, and customers – need to be linked through the supply chain management system into the supply chain at the appropriate points.

Supply chain management decisions fall into two broad categories: strategic and operational. Strategic decisions guide the design of the supply chain (by virtue of the supply chain needing to comply to and adhere with the strategic decisions of the organisation). The operational decisions relate to the flow through the supply chain and need to be compatible with the strategic decisions if the supply chain is to operate effectively and appropriately.

There are four stages at which these decisions need to be taken in supply chain management:

1 **Location.** The location of suppliers, warehouse facilities, and production facilities. Decisions need to be taken regarding physical location, size and number of such facilities. The location of each of these classes of facility determines the possible range of routes through the supply chain from supplier to customer and has a major impact on cost, time in the supply chain and level of service.

2 **Production.** At the strategic level, decisions must be made concerning what to produce and where, and which suppliers to use. The decisions made have a major impact upon costs. The strategic decisions include what products to produce, and which plants should produce them in, allocation of suppliers to plants, plants to distribution channels, and DCs to customer markets. They define the flow through the supply chain in yet greater detail than that defined by the location choices. Operational decisions at this stage are concerned with production scheduling, equipment maintenance scheduling, workload planning, and quality control. As with location, both categories of decision at this stage have a big impact on the costs, revenues, and the level of customer service.

3 **Inventory.** The key impact of the decisions at this stage is upon customer service. However, there is an obvious and clear impact upon production scheduling and upon costs that arise from whatever decisions are taken. The principal decisions to be taken concern the levels of inventory to hold. Whether any should be held at all at the start of the chain is a key strategic decision – should a just-in-time approach be taken whereby the supplier holds the stock of raw materials until ordered and orders are dispatched immediately by the supplier. The cost implications of such a decision are both obvious (there would be no need for raw material warehouse facilities) and less than obvious (there needs to be an excellent relationship with the supplier; access may well be needed to the supplier's inventory system, resulting in increased IT facility requirements and costs). Where a conventional inventory system is adopted, warehouse facilities will be required and an effective stockholding and ordering system must be established and maintained.

> **Activity 46.1**
>
> What operational decisions would need to be taken in order to establish and maintain an effective stockholding and ordering system?

4 **Distribution.** Decisions here are mainly strategic and relate to what form of distribution is to be used: lorry, van, train, plane, courier, etc. The decisions made need to consider distribution at all stages of the supply chain, i.e. receipts from suppliers, movements to storage facilities of finished and part-finished goods, and delivery to customers. While decisions at this stage often have less of an impact on cost to the business than some of the others that must be made, they are nonetheless crucial to the effective and efficient operation of the business and have both a direct and indirect impact upon customer service.

> **Activity 46.2**
>
> In what way can distribution decisions have both a direct and indirect impact upon customer service?

46.2 Advantages of effective supply chain management

A number of advantages have been identified as resulting from effective supply chain management:

- reduced costs
- reduced supply chain cycle times
- reduced lead times
- improved customer service
- improved inventory management
- improved distribution systems
- greater synergy between the objectives and actions of various elements of the organisation.

Note that product quality is *not* seen as being improved through supply chain management, but the level of customer service and the utilisation of resources are.

46.3 Difficulties in establishing supply chain management

The supply chain is a complex and dynamic network of facilities, departments and organisations with different, conflicting objectives. There are three principal difficulties encountered when a supply chain management system is being established:

1 **Bringing together all the conflicting objectives of the parties involved in the supply chain** so as to produce an effective, efficient and manageable process.
2 **Establishing effective relationships at all stages and between all elements of the supply chain.** Often this represents a significant change from the previous position. Suppliers, for example, may need to provide access to their inventory database or, at the very least, agree to prioritise orders and expedite deliveries. Stock control must be strengthened and the relationships between production and ordering and production and selling must become seamless where, previously, they may have been very informal and distant. Both the systems and the interpersonal relationships of those involved must be changed to accommodate the shift to supply chain management.

3 **IT systems need to be changed, frequently involving considerable initial and increased ongoing expense and changes in working practices.** There is certainly a requirement for many individuals to retrain in the new systems and software. Also, auditors have an enhanced and altered role in respect of the controls that are needed in such a system compared with a traditional purchasing/production/selling/distribution environment.

46.4 Accounting and supply chain management

Traditional approaches to accounting can identify some of the costs relating to supply chain management. However, because accounting focuses on transactions rather than business processes, it is only the directly visible costs and savings that arise from a supply chain management system that traditional accounting can record, monitor, and report.

Where an activity-based costing system has been adopted, there is an increased level of accounting-related information available (as it focuses upon the drivers of costs within business processes). As a result, many organisations that have adopted supply chain management have also adopted activity-based costing.

Nevertheless, there are considerable hidden costs and savings of introducing and operating a supply chain management system that even ABC cannot isolate and report. For example, it is difficult to put an accurate financial value on reductions in supply chain cycle times or on an increased synergy between the objectives of the various functions of an organisation involved in or affected by a supply chain. It is also hard to quantify the benefits of having stronger links with suppliers.

As accountants are generally involved in costing new projects, they are usually heavily involved in assessing the merits of proposals for new or amended supply chain management systems. Failure to capture the appropriate data and information means that the models and techniques of the accountant can be very inadequate in assessing the viability and worth of such proposals.

To play a meaningful role in supply chain management, accountants need to adopt a business process perspective and gather data relating to business events rather than individual transactions. Qualitative data needs to be gathered, processed, monitored and made available as well as quantitative data. At the same time, the range of quantitative data needs to be extended to include non-financial aspects of business events and processes, such as the names and other demographic information relating to customers, suppliers and employees.

This is seen as a sufficiently important area for accountants to become involved that, in 1999, the American Institute of Management Accountants published two reports, *Implementing Integrated Supply Chain Management for Competitive Advantage* (which includes a cost and performance measurement system to effectively control the activities of the supply chain) and *Tools and Techniques for Implementing Integrated Supply Chain Management*.

Software suppliers are developing and offer a range of supply chain management software. Some products include fully integrated accounting systems, others enable existing accounting systems to be linked into the supply chain management system. Either approach results in new challenges for accountants as they become more involved in looking beyond the numbers and in communicating effectively to managers on aspects of the organisation with which they were not previously involved.

46.5 Enterprise resource planning

The supply chain crosses outside the organisation at two points – to the customers and to the suppliers. As such, much of the philosophy of supply chain management entails involving these outside agents in working with the organisation in the pursuit of its objectives. This is not a simple task – only the largest organisations can put pressure on their suppliers

to the extent that they will agree to prioritise the organisation over all others. Similarly, most customers have a choice and may choose to avoid dealing with organisations that look for clearer indications of demand such as allowing them to access their inventory database and automatically provide new goods when the inventory reaches its reorder level.

Not surprisingly, supply chain management is a relatively recent development and the main beneficiaries have been the larger organisations who have embraced it. While small and medium sized organisations can and do also adopt supply chain management, they have far greater difficulty in achieving the commitment of the outside entities to their objectives.

Another integrating approach, but one that is internal to the organisation, is **enterprise resource planning (ERP)** system. ERP integrates the internal functions of the organisation and achieves savings through the efficiencies that result.

An ERP system is a suite of software modules. Each relates to a function of the organisation, such as order processing, production, creditor control, debtor control, payroll, marketing and human resources. The software modules are positioned on top of a centralised database, resulting in data being entered only once into the system but being accessible to all modules within it. Because the software modules all come from the same supplier, they are fully and seamlessly integrated from the start. There is no need to bolt together a range of software from different suppliers in order to achieve data integration.

There are two groups of applications within an ERP system:

1 **Core applications.** The applications that need to work or the organisation will be unable to function. They include, production, sales, distribution and planning. These are always fully integrated within the ERP system.
2 **Business analysis applications.** Examples include modelling, decision support, information retrieval, reporting, accounting, simulation and 'what if' analysis. Some ERP software includes these. Some provide links into the ERP system to third party software that performs tasks.

46.6 Difficulties of justifying ERP

Integrating all the functions of an organisation in this way is a non-trivial exercise. It is estimated that the average annual cost of an ERP system is £11 million. As with supply chain management, the benefits of such systems are hard to quantify in traditional accounting terms or through the use of traditional accounting data and techniques.

Instead, as with supply chain management, less quantifiable advantages must be considered and weighed up against the identifiable costs.

46.7 Advantages of ERP systems

The advantages of ERP systems compared to traditional information system architectures include:

- increased data consistency
- reduced data redundancy
- greatly enriched data, including access to qualitative data by functions that do not typically have access to it
- greatly increased depth and breadth of data analysis
- reduced response times to information requests
- reduced need for manual intervention in data access and analysis
- reduced risk of errors in data or in its analysis
- greatly enhanced exception reporting facility (due to the increase in the range of variables that can be flagged for monitoring)

- reduced time spent analysing exception reports (as the level of detail provided by the system is greatly enhanced)
- greatly reduced lead times in report generation
- greatly increased efficiency in materials ordering, requisition and deployment
- much closer ties between ordering, inventory control and production.

46.8 Organisational size

Since they first appeared, ERP systems have tended to be developed in the largest organisations. Software vendors have produced their products with this in mind. However, computing power has increased and its price has dropped to such an extent that medium-sized and even small organisations can now take advantage of the software and develop ERP systems. While ERP systems are costly, the benefits are generally seen as outweighing the costs, provided the installation of ERP systems is effective and appropriate.

It is likely that within a few years, ERP software will be as commonplace in organisations of all sizes as general accounting packages are at present and that, in some cases, it will provide all the functionality of those accounting packages along with everything else they currently provide as standard.

46.9 ERP systems and supply chain management

Those organisations that add supply chain management to their ERP systems achieve the greatest benefit. An efficient and effective ERP system enhances the ability to integrate all the internal functions of the supply chain while also integrating other support functions, such as human resources and accounting. **Supply chain management enhances the capability of the ERP system to record and monitor all aspect of the organisation's business and bring suppliers and customers within the co-ordinated control of the organisation.**

Many organisations are moving in this direction and their accountants are being seen as playing a vital role in the success of the emerging information systems. For their part, ERP software providers have recognised the pivotal role of the accountant and have for some years funded American universities to integrate their software into accounting courses. Whether this occurs elsewhere remains to be seen. However, there is no doubt that ERP and supply chain management are two subjects that accountants need to be aware of and prepared to be involved with.

Learning outcomes

You should now have learnt:

1 What is meant by the term 'supply chain'.
2 What is meant by the term 'supply chain management'.
3 About the advantages of supply chain management.
4 What is meant by the term 'enterprise resource planning'.
5 What the differences are between an enterprise planning system and a traditional information system.
6 Why organisations that integrate their ERP systems with supply chain management stand to benefit compared with those that do not.
7 Why supply chain management and ERP systems are both important concepts for accounting and accountants.

Answers to activities

46.1 Stockholding levels would need to be established for each item of raw materials: minimum level, safety stock level, reorder level (*see* Section 36.8).

46.2 Customer service is directly affected by the speed at which delivery is made and by the amount charged for the service. It is indirectly affected by the decisions made concerning shipping raw materials in from suppliers and, once again, it is the time factor that matters. A just-in-time system that allows suppliers a week to deliver raw material orders is going to result in a level of customer service that is somewhat less than one that requires delivery within 24 hours.

REVIEW QUESTIONS

46.1 What is the supply chain?

46.2 What is meant by the term, 'supply chain management'?

46.3 What are the advantages of effective supply chain management?

46.4 Why does supply chain management bring new challenges for accounting and accountants?

46.5 What is enterprise resource planning?

46.6 What are the advantages of an ERP system?

46.7 Why will those organisations that integrate their ERP systems with supply chain management benefit more than those that introduce only one or the other or these two concepts?

CHAPTER 47

E-commerce and accounting

Learning objectives

After you have studied this chapter, you should be able to:

- explain what is meant by 'e-commerce'
- explain what is meant by 'business-to-business' transactions
- explain what is meant by 'business-to-consumer' transactions
- describe a typical business-to-consumer transaction
- describe some of the benefits of e-commerce to sellers
- describe some of the benefits of e-commerce to buyers
- describe the impact of e-commerce upon the role of the financial accountant
- describe the impact of e-commerce upon the role of the management accountant
- describe the impact of e-commerce upon the role of the auditor, both internal and external
- explain why retail businesses cannot afford to stay out of e-commerce

Introduction

In this chapter you'll learn about e-commerce and its impact upon sellers, buyers and accountants.

47.1 Background

For many years, all business was undertaken face-to-face. Gradually, orders started to be placed by other means – letter, telegram, telex, fax, telephone, etc. However, when transactions were undertaken between businesses, paper was normally exchanged indicating an order was being placed and, subsequently, indicating how much the seller required to be paid for the goods ordered.

This is the business environment in which accounting developed. Accountants learnt to use the documents relating to the transaction in order to make entries in the accounting books. They ensured there was an audit trail running from the original paperwork right through to each entry in the ledger. Checking these entries was time consuming but always possible and, where original records did not exist, auditors would get very concerned as to the validity of transactions. Sometimes they accepted the word of the proprietor that transactions were valid. On other occasions, they did not and an investigation was launched in pursuit of evidence that things were recorded inaccurately.

Activity 47.1
What sorts of things were done in this investigation phase?

Other forms of business started to emerge. Ones where communication was electronic but, initially, all payment was by traditional means. Then payments too became increasingly electronic. Now, not only can communication and payment all be done electronically, but the seller may never physically possess the goods or services being sold and, in fact, the seller may not even be aware that a transaction has occurred (as the sale process is entirely automated). Also, products that were traditionally physical – books and CDs, for example – can now be sold as electronic files downloaded off the internet directly into the customer's PC.

This is **electronic commerce** and is the environment in which an increasing proportion of business is now conducted. It is expected that the total value of e-commerce transactions will rise by 400 per cent between 2001 and 2004 to around US$5,000 billion.

In a report issued in 2001, *The Global Online Retailing Study*, the accounting firm Ernst & Young stated that online retailing is no longer an option, but a *business requirement*. Retail businesses must move into e-commerce or watch their markets disappear into the hands of their competitors.

47.2 Electronic commerce

Electronic commerce can be defined as the use of electronic telecommunication technology to conduct business transactions over the Internet. It allows goods to be exchanged anytime, 24 hours a day, 7 days a week, anywhere the buyer has access to the Internet. It expands the market of every seller – in many cases, the market becomes global.

There are two principal e-commerce models:

1 **Business-to-business (B2B).** Businesses purchase from other businesses and/or sell their goods and services to other businesses; and,
2 **Business-to-consumer (B2C).** Businesses sell to consumers. For B2C to work:
   (*a*) the customer must have access to the internet
   (*b*) the customer must have a means of making payment electronically (normally, a credit or a debit card)
   (*c*) there must be a viable means of delivering the item(s) purchased to the consumer.

E-commerce involves the transmission of confidential, sensitive and valued information. To operate in this environment effectively, not only customers, but also business partners, must be convinced that a B2B or B2C business's systems are secure, reliable, available and properly controlled. While this is very much a necessity for effective supply chain management (Chapter 46), it is much more critical in an e-commerce environment and is the aspect of e-commerce that, more than any other, is impacting upon the role of the accountant and, in particular, the role of the auditor.

47.3 Business-to-business

B2B transactions are very similar to how transactions occur in a traditional business environment. Request for payment is often by traditional invoicing and payment follows at some date in the future.

The seller

B2B e-commerce offers the seller many advantages over a traditional business environment, including:

- cost savings by removing the need for a human salesperson to be involved in the transaction
- faster transaction times
- lower clerical costs as there is now a reduced level of paper records to be prepared and maintained
- richer analysis of sales due to greatly enhanced knowledge about the pattern of sale.

However, the major differences that e-commerce can bring to this form of e-commerce lie in the ability to integrate the B2B e-commerce system into the seller's accounting system. There is a growing range of integrated software available, including many of the ERP software packages referred to in Chapter 46.

Doing so has many advantages for the seller, including:

- better credit control at the time of sale
- better control over debtor balances
- potential to cut costs by automating the sale process, leaving it to be triggered by the level of inventory shown in the purchaser's inventory database.

The buyer

The buyer benefits from:

- faster transaction times
- greater confidence that orders will be filled in a timely manner
- (in many cases) a greatly increased market (geographically) in which to make a purchase
- cost savings arising from increased competition among sellers
- (often) visual confirmation that what is being ordered is what is required (as there is no longer a possibility that an ill-informed salesperson is dealing with the order/enquiry).

The accountant

There is less of a paper trail than under a traditional system. However, this has little effect on the day-to-day work of accountants working within the seller or buyer organisation. **Thus, accountants who work for the seller or buyer are relatively unaffected by the shift from a traditional environment.** Transaction data is entered automatically into the accounting records rather than manually by a clerk. Thereafter, the internal accountant handles the data in the normal way and can create and provide all the 'normal' accounting information that would be provided were this a traditional business environment.

Management accountants

There is the possibility of the management accountant providing more detailed and richer information to the decision maker, as B2B transactions are information rich compared with traditional ones. For example, far more qualitative and non-financial quantitative data is available or is available from a more reliable source.

Financial accountants

Financial accountants will not experience very much change in the nature of data from that experienced under a traditional computerised accounting environment. However, when the audit is being conducted, there will be a need to be able to explain to the auditor where the

data within the accounting system comes from and the controls that are in place to ensure that it is both accurate and reliable.

Auditors

In contrast to the two main groups of accountants, auditors (both internal and external) are greatly affected by the introduction of B2B e-commerce. As mentioned earlier, there is less of a paper trail than under a traditional system. In fact, there may be nothing on paper until a goods delivery note is prepared in order to ship the goods. Thus, they have an increased need to focus on the technology involved in each transaction. As a result, they need to focus on assurance. In particular, online assurance, i.e. whether the B2B system is working correctly and whether all the transaction details being recorded are accurate, reliable and complete.

This represents a major change in the nature of the audit, even where previously an organisation's accounting system was computerised. Often, in that case, auditors audited around the computer – that is, they checked that what came out was what they would have expected. In a B2B organisation, they need to audit through the computer – that is, they need to be assured that the computer is doing the correct things and that there are appropriate controls in place to ensure that errors are not made. This is particularly needed in the seller organisation because there is typically no human intervention in the transaction. In this case, the assurance should, preferably, be in real time. That is, the check on the controls on transactions should be done as transactions are being processed.

47.4 Business-to-consumer

This is the side of e-commerce that is most different from the traditional business environment. The seller is represented by a computer program which responds as appropriate to enquiries made by a consumer who can not only place an order but who will also provide a shipping address and make payment, all at the same time.

The consumer accesses the internet and navigates to the seller's website. At the website, the consumer checks the seller's catalogue for the item(s) required, often through a series of searches of the seller's inventory database. This in itself may be very different from a traditional high street purchase, for the seller may actually have little or no physical stock. Instead, the seller has built an inventory database of the items that can be shipped to a customer in a reasonable period of time. (You can see examples of this at sites such as www.amazon.co.uk)

When the decision is made to purchase something, the customer is directed to the seller's *online transaction server*, where all the customer's information, including personal details, the item(s) required, and credit or debit card details are entered. This information, particularly the credit card information, is usually encrypted as it is received. The information is then passed to the bank that issued the credit or debit card and to the seller's merchant bank (i.e. the bank that operates the receipt of funds in this form for the seller). If both banks accept the transaction, the seller is informed it has been accepted and provided with an order number for reference and an indication of when the item(s) will be shipped.

This B2C e-commerce system is presented in Exhibit 47.1.

Exhibit 47.1

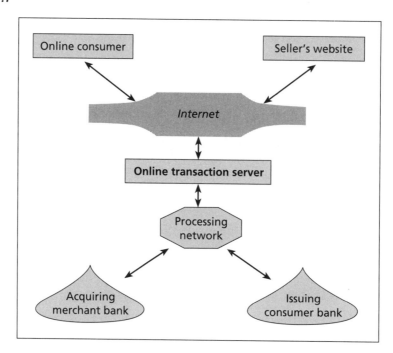

Activity 47.2

Compared with businesses operating in a traditional trading environment, what advantages concerning receipt of payment can you see for a business operating in a B2C environment?

47.5 Accountants and B2C e-commerce

B2C e-commerce has an impact upon the routine work of financial and management accountants similar to B2B. However, there are major issues with which accountants must be involved when the business first moves into a B2C environment:

1 The size of the transaction database. Is it going to be capable of handling a significant increase in transactions. In fact, what is that level of transactions likely to be?
2 The interface between the B2C systems and the accounting system.
3 The internal controls – the accountants need to emphasise the need for effective internal controls at the design stage, when it is easiest to incorporate them into the B2C system.

These are particularly difficult issues to deal with when the business is new and has no existing customer base, especially the question of size.

Auditors have similar issues to deal with as under B2B but, often, far more transactions to deal with. As individuals rather than other businesses are normally involved on the consumer side, there is a need to ensure that effective controls are in place in the system concerning credit card fraud and data security, for the liability of the system is breached may be far greater than if a B2B system is breached.

There is a further dimension for accountants to be concerned with concerning B2C transactions – globalisation.

47.6 Globalisation

Over 60 per cent of all B2C consumers resident outside the USA use B2C to purchase goods they wish to buy from sellers in other countries; over 50% do so because the goods they want are not available in their own country, and 30% do so because they have found goods cheaper to buy overseas.

For accountants, this adds problems concerning international tax and, for auditors especially, opens the possibility of international fraud.

47.7 E-commerce and accounting

E-commerce is changing and will continue to change the manner in which accountants carry out their role and, more importantly, it will change the nature of that role.

We already have a wide range of accounting software that eliminates the need to use traditional double entry to record transactions. Accountants have remained outside the system changes by continuing to do what they've always done and, instead, they have developed computer packages to check that the accounting software was working properly.

The accountants did not need to be retrained and, for many years, no attention was paid in the training of accountants to this shift in the environment of accounting. This was possible because business was still conducted in traditional ways. It was only the manner by which transactions were recorded that changed.

E-commerce changed this. An increasing proportion of transactions are now conducted electronically, both between businesses and between businesses and consumers. In many cases, there are no paper records and no written entries relating to these transactions. **Accountants can no longer check a transaction against the original invoice or order document. Neither can they check that someone with appropriate authority has approved an order by signing an authorisation.**

Take away the paper, take away the written signature, and take away the double entry and what have you left for an accountant to do? Even more to the point, what can an auditor do to check the validity and accuracy of the accounting records?

A knowledge of double entry is still important. No financial accountant will be able to function effectively all the time without it. Accountants need to understand the entries in the accounting records and need to be able to tell if they are appropriate and correct. They also need to know how to produce financial statements and how to make appropriate adjustments to the accounting figures when doing so. Thus, there is still a need for the traditional techniques, skills and understanding that have been covered in both volumes of *Business Accounting*.

However, they now need to add further techniques, skills and understanding to their role. They need to shift towards real time assurance – verifying that things are as they should be *in real time*. To do so, accountants need to become technologically competent. They need to know and understand the technological infrastructure of e-commerce in the same way as they have always needed to know the infrastructure of traditional business and the manner in which it is conducted and performed. They need to know how to recognise weaknesses and loopholes, and how to trap errors in an electronic business environment. They need to know how to distinguish between valid entries and those that are erroneous or falsified when the only evidence they have is electronic.

There are great changes coming in the role of the accountant. Some of the professional accounting bodies already have examinations which consider these issues, but those examinations are being sat by people who have already been working as accountants for a few years. Pre-work education always lags behind real life and it will be many years before it is normal to include these skills in accounting courses at schools, colleges and universities. Instead,

they will be learnt later, on the job, by attending training courses, or while studying for the examinations of the professional accountancy bodies.

As a student of accounting, you will be wise to become aware of this changing environment and to understand how it differs from the world as presented in the classroom and in your textbooks. Don't let it take you by surprise. Look at the Internet, learn how business is conducted upon it and consider how different it is from doing business face-to-face.

Learning outcomes

You should now have learnt:

1 What is meant by 'e-commerce'.
2 What is meant by 'business-to-business' transactions.
3 What is meant by 'business-to-consumer' transactions.
4 What occurs in a typical business-to-consumer transaction.
5 About some of the benefits of e-commerce to sellers and buyers.
6 About the impact of e-commerce upon the role of the financial accountant, management accountant, internal auditor, and external auditor.
7 Why retail businesses cannot afford to stay out of e-commerce.

Answers to activities

47.1 Contacting the customer or supplier and asking for confirmation; checking inventory to confirm that it had existed; checking the existence of fixed assets; etc.

47.2 No sales take place without prior payment which is guaranteed by the issuing consumer bank. There will, therefore, be no bad debts. Also, there is far greater control over cash flows as payment will always be received on time.

REVIEW QUESTIONS

47.1 What is e-commerce?

47.2 What happens in a typical business-to-consumer transaction?

47.3 What impact is e-commerce having upon the role of the accountant?

47.4 Why can retail businesses not afford to ignore e-commerce?

Interest tables

Table 1 Compound sum of £1

Year	1%	2%	3%	4%	5%	6%	7%	8%	9%	10%
1	1.010	1.020	1.030	1.040	1.050	1.060	1.070	1.080	1.090	1.100
2	1.020	1.040	1.061	1.082	1.103	1.124	1.145	1.166	1.188	1.210
3	1.030	1.061	1.093	1.125	1.158	1.191	1.225	1.260	1.295	1.331
4	1.041	1.082	1.126	1.170	1.216	1.262	1.311	1.360	1.412	1.464
5	1.051	1.104	1.159	1.217	1.276	1.338	1.403	1.469	1.539	1.611
6	1.062	1.126	1.194	1.265	1.340	1.419	1.501	1.587	1.677	1.772
7	1.072	1.149	1.230	1.316	1.407	1.504	1.606	1.714	1.828	1.949
8	1.083	1.172	1.267	1.369	1.477	1.594	1.718	1.851	1.993	2.144
9	1.094	1.195	1.305	1.423	1.551	1.689	1.838	1.999	2.172	2.358
10	1.105	1.219	1.344	1.480	1.629	1.791	1.967	2.159	2.367	2.594
11	1.116	1.243	1.384	1.539	1.710	1.898	2.105	2.332	2.580	2.853
12	1.127	1.268	1.426	1.601	1.796	2.012	2.252	2.518	2.813	3.138
13	1.138	1.294	1.469	1.665	1.886	2.133	2.410	2.720	3.066	3.452
14	1.149	1.319	1.513	1.732	1.980	2.261	2.579	2.937	3.342	3.797
15	1.161	1.346	1.558	1.801	2.079	2.397	2.759	3.172	3.642	4.177

Year	12%	14%	15%	16%	18%	20%	24%	28%	32%
1	1.120	1.140	1.150	1.160	1.180	1.200	1.240	1.280	1.320
2	1.254	1.300	1.323	1.346	1.392	1.440	1.538	1.638	1.742
3	1.405	1.482	1.521	1.561	1.643	1.728	1.907	2.097	2.300
4	1.574	1.689	1.749	1.811	1.939	2.074	2.364	2.684	3.036
5	1.762	1.925	2.011	2.100	2.288	2.488	2.932	3.436	4.007
6	1.974	2.195	2.313	2.436	2.700	2.986	3.635	4.398	5.290
7	2.211	2.502	2.660	2.826	3.185	3.583	4.508	5.629	6.983
8	2.476	2.853	3.059	3.278	3.759	4.300	5.590	7.206	9.217
9	2.773	3.252	3.518	3.803	4.435	5.160	6.931	9.223	12.166
10	3.106	3.707	4.046	4.411	5.234	6.192	8.594	11.806	16.060
11	3.479	4.226	4.652	5.117	6.176	7.430	10.657	15.112	21.199
12	3.896	4.818	5.350	5.936	7.288	8.916	13.215	19.343	27.983
13	4.363	5.492	6.153	6.886	8.599	10.699	16.386	24.759	36.937
14	4.887	6.261	7.076	7.988	10.147	12.839	20.319	31.691	48.757
15	5.474	7.138	8.137	9.266	11.974	15.407	25.196	40.565	64.359

Year	36%	40%	50%	60%	70%	80%	90%
1	1.360	1.400	1.500	1.600	1.700	1.800	1.900
2	1.850	1.960	2.250	2.560	2.890	3.240	3.610
3	2.515	2.744	3.375	4.096	4.913	5.832	6.859
4	3.421	3.842	5.062	6.544	8.352	10.498	13.032
5	4.653	5.378	7.594	10.486	14.199	18.896	24.761
6	6.328	7.530	11.391	16.777	24.138	34.012	47.046
7	8.605	10.541	17.086	26.844	41.034	61.222	89.387
8	11.703	14.758	25.629	42.950	69.758	110.200	169.836
9	15.917	20.661	38.443	68.720	118.588	198.359	322.688
10	21.647	28.925	57.665	109.951	201.599	357.047	613.107
11	29.439	40.496	86.498	175.922	342.719	642.684	1164.902
12	40.037	56.694	129.746	281.475	582.622	1156.831	2213.314
13	54.451	79.372	194.619	450.360	990.457	2082.295	4205.297
14	74.053	111.120	291.929	720.576	1683.777	3748.131	7990.065
15	100.712	155.568	437.894	1152.921	2862.421	6746.636	15181.122

Table 2 Present value of £1

Year	1%	2%	3%	4%	5%	6%	7%	8%	9%	10%	12%	14%	15%
1	0.990	0.980	0.971	0.961	0.952	0.943	0.935	0.926	0.917	0.909	0.893	0.877	0.870
2	0.980	0.961	0.943	0.925	0.907	0.890	0.873	0.857	0.842	0.826	0.797	0.769	0.756
3	0.971	0.942	0.915	0.889	0.864	0.840	0.816	0.794	0.772	0.751	0.712	0.675	0.658
4	0.961	0.924	0.889	0.855	0.823	0.792	0.763	0.735	0.708	0.683	0.636	0.592	0.572
5	0.951	0.906	0.863	0.822	0.784	0.747	0.713	0.681	0.650	0.621	0.567	0.519	0.497
6	0.942	0.888	0.838	0.790	0.746	0.705	0.666	0.630	0.596	0.564	0.507	0.456	0.432
7	0.933	0.871	0.813	0.760	0.711	0.665	0.623	0.583	0.547	0.513	0.452	0.400	0.376
8	0.923	0.853	0.789	0.731	0.677	0.627	0.582	0.540	0.502	0.467	0.404	0.351	0.327
9	0.914	0.837	0.766	0.703	0.645	0.592	0.544	0.500	0.460	0.424	0.361	0.308	0.284
10	0.905	0.820	0.744	0.676	0.614	0.558	0.508	0.463	0.422	0.386	0.322	0.270	0.247
11	0.896	0.804	0.722	0.650	0.585	0.527	0.475	0.429	0.388	0.350	0.287	0.237	0.215
12	0.887	0.788	0.701	0.625	0.557	0.497	0.444	0.397	0.356	0.319	0.257	0.208	0.187
13	0.879	0.773	0.681	0.601	0.530	0.469	0.415	0.368	0.326	0.290	0.229	0.182	0.163
14	0.870	0.758	0.661	0.577	0.505	0.442	0.388	0.340	0.299	0.263	0.205	0.160	0.141
15	0.861	0.743	0.642	0.555	0.481	0.417	0.362	0.315	0.275	0.239	0.183	0.140	0.123
16	0.853	0.728	0.623	0.534	0.458	0.394	0.339	0.292	0.252	0.218	0.163	0.123	0.107
17	0.844	0.714	0.605	0.513	0.436	0.371	0.317	0.270	0.231	0.198	0.146	0.108	0.093
18	0.836	0.700	0.587	0.494	0.416	0.350	0.296	0.250	0.212	0.180	0.130	0.095	0.081
19	0.828	0.686	0.570	0.475	0.396	0.331	0.276	0.232	0.194	0.164	0.116	0.083	0.070
20	0.820	0.673	0.554	0.456	0.377	0.319	0.258	0.215	0.178	0.149	0.104	0.073	0.061
25	0.780	0.610	0.478	0.375	0.295	0.233	0.184	0.146	0.116	0.092	0.059	0.038	0.030
30	0.742	0.552	0.412	0.308	0.231	0.174	0.131	0.099	0.075	0.057	0.033	0.020	0.015

Year	16%	18%	20%	24%	28%	32%	36%	40%	50%	60%	70%	80%	90%
1	0.862	0.847	0.833	0.806	0.781	0.758	0.735	0.714	0.667	0.625	0.588	0.556	0.526
2	0.743	0.718	0.694	0.650	0.610	0.574	0.541	0.510	0.444	0.391	0.346	0.309	0.277
3	0.641	0.609	0.579	0.524	0.477	0.435	0.398	0.364	0.296	0.244	0.204	0.171	0.146
4	0.552	0.516	0.482	0.423	0.373	0.329	0.292	0.260	0.198	0.153	0.120	0.095	0.077
5	0.476	0.437	0.402	0.341	0.291	0.250	0.215	0.186	0.132	0.095	0.070	0.053	0.040
6	0.410	0.370	0.335	0.275	0.227	0.189	0.158	0.133	0.088	0.060	0.041	0.029	0.021
7	0.354	0.314	0.279	0.222	0.178	0.143	0.116	0.095	0.059	0.037	0.024	0.016	0.011
8	0.305	0.266	0.233	0.179	0.139	0.108	0.085	0.068	0.039	0.023	0.014	0.009	0.006
9	0.263	0.226	0.194	0.144	0.108	0.082	0.063	0.048	0.026	0.015	0.008	0.005	0.003
10	0.227	0.191	0.162	0.116	0.085	0.062	0.046	0.035	0.017	0.009	0.005	0.003	0.002
11	0.195	0.162	0.135	0.094	0.066	0.047	0.034	0.025	0.012	0.006	0.003	0.002	0.001
12	0.168	0.137	0.112	0.076	0.052	0.036	0.025	0.018	0.008	0.004	0.002	0.001	0.001
13	0.145	0.116	0.093	0.061	0.040	0.027	0.018	0.013	0.005	0.002	0.001	0.001	0.000
14	0.125	0.099	0.078	0.049	0.032	0.021	0.014	0.009	0.003	0.001	0.001	0.000	0.000
15	0.108	0.084	0.065	0.040	0.025	0.016	0.010	0.006	0.002	0.001	0.000	0.000	0.000
16	0.093	0.071	0.054	0.032	0.019	0.012	0.007	0.005	0.002	0.001	0.000	0.000	
17	0.080	0.060	0.045	0.026	0.015	0.009	0.005	0.003	0.001	0.000	0.000		
18	0.069	0.051	0.038	0.021	0.012	0.007	0.004	0.002	0.001	0.000	0.000		
19	0.060	0.043	0.031	0.017	0.009	0.005	0.003	0.002	0.000	0.000			
20	0.051	0.037	0.026	0.014	0.007	0.004	0.002	0.001	0.000	0.000			
25	0.024	0.016	0.010	0.005	0.002	0.001	0.000	0.000					
30	0.012	0.007	0.004	0.002	0.001	0.000	0.000						

Table 3 Sum of an annuity of £1 for *n* years

Year	1%	2%	3%	4%	5%	6%	7%	8%
1	1.000	1.000	1.000	1.000	1.000	1.000	1.000	1.000
2	2.010	2.020	2.030	2.040	2.050	2.060	2.070	2.080
3	3.030	3.060	3.091	3.122	3.152	3.184	3.215	3.246
4	4.060	4.122	4.184	4.246	4.310	4.375	4.440	4.506
5	5.101	5.204	5.309	5.416	5.526	5.637	5.751	5.867
6	6.152	6.308	6.468	6.633	6.802	6.975	7.153	7.336
7	7.214	7.434	7.662	7.898	8.142	8.394	8.654	8.923
8	8.286	8.583	8.892	9.214	9.549	9.897	10.260	10.637
9	9.369	9.755	10.159	10.583	11.027	11.491	11.978	12.488
10	10.462	10.950	11.464	12.006	12.578	13.181	13.816	41.487
11	11.567	12.169	12.808	13.486	14.207	14.972	15.784	16.645
12	12.683	13.412	14.192	15.026	15.917	16.870	17.888	18.977
13	13.809	14.680	15.618	16.627	17.713	18.882	20.141	21.495
14	14.947	15.974	17.086	18.292	19.599	21.051	22.550	24.215
15	16.097	17.293	18.599	20.024	21.579	23.276	25.129	27.152
16	17.258	18.639	20.157	21.825	23.657	25.673	27.888	30.324
17	18.430	20.012	21.762	23.698	25.840	28.213	30.840	33.750
18	19.615	21.412	23.414	25.645	28.132	30.906	33.999	37.450
19	20.811	22.841	25.117	27.671	30.539	33.760	37.379	41.446
20	22.019	24.297	26.870	29.778	33.066	36.786	40.995	45.762
25	28.243	32.030	36.459	41.646	47.727	54.865	63.249	73.106
30	34.785	40.568	47.575	56.085	66.439	79.058	94.461	113.283

Year	9%	10%	12%	14%	16%	18%	20%	24%
1	1.000	1.000	1.000	1.000	1.000	1.000	1.000	1.000
2	2.090	2.100	2.120	2.140	2.160	2.180	2.200	2.240
3	3.278	3.310	3.374	3.440	3.506	3.572	3.640	3.778
4	4.573	4.641	4.779	4.921	5.066	5.215	5.368	5.684
5	5.985	6.105	6.353	6.610	6.877	7.154	7.442	8.048
6	7.523	7.716	8.115	8.536	8.977	9.442	9.930	10.980
7	9.200	9.487	10.089	10.730	11.414	12.142	12.916	14.615
8	11.028	11.436	12.300	13.233	14.240	15.327	16.499	19.123
9	13.021	13.579	14.776	16.085	17.518	19.086	20.799	24.712
10	15.193	15.937	17.549	19.337	21.321	23.521	25.959	31.643
11	17.560	18.531	20.655	23.044	25.738	28.755	32.150	40.238
12	20.141	21.384	24.133	27.271	30.350	34.931	39.580	50.895
13	22.953	24.523	28.029	32.089	36.766	42.219	48.497	64.110
14	26.019	27.975	32.393	37.581	43.672	50.818	59.196	80.496
15	29.361	31.722	37.280	43.842	51.659	60.965	72.035	100.815

Year	28%	32%	36%	40%	50%	60%	70%	80%
1	1.000	1.000	1.000	1.000	1.000	1.000	1.000	1.000
2	2.280	2.320	2.360	2.400	2.500	2.600	2.700	2.800
3	3.918	4.062	4.210	4.360	4.750	5.160	5.590	6.040
4	6.016	6.326	6.725	7.104	8.125	9.256	10.503	11.872
5	8.700	9.398	10.146	10.846	13.188	15.810	18.855	22.370
6	12.136	13.406	14.799	16.324	20.781	26.295	33.054	41.265
7	16.534	18.696	21.126	23.853	32.172	43.073	57.191	75.278
8	22.163	25.678	29.732	34.395	49.258	69.916	98.225	136.500
9	29.369	34.895	41.435	49.153	74.887	112.866	167.983	246.699
10	38.592	47.062	57.352	69.814	113.330	181.585	286.570	445.058
11	50.399	63.122	78.998	98.739	170.995	291.536	488.170	802.105
12	65.510	84.320	108.437	139.235	257.493	467.458	830.888	1444.788
13	84.853	112.303	148.475	195.929	387.239	748.933	1413.510	2601.619
14	109.612	149.240	202.926	275.300	581.859	1199.293	2403.968	4683.914
15	141.303	197.997	276.979	386.420	873.788	1919.869	4087.745	8432.045

Table 4 Present value of annuity of £1 per period

Year	1%	2%	3%	4%	5%	6%	7%	8%	9%	10%
1	0.990	0.980	0.971	0.962	0.952	0.943	0.935	0.926	0.917	0.909
2	1.970	1.942	1.913	1.886	1.859	1.833	1.808	1.783	1.759	1.736
3	2.941	2.884	2.829	2.775	2.723	2.673	2.624	2.577	2.531	2.487
4	3.902	3.808	3.717	3.630	3.546	3.465	3.387	3.312	3.240	3.170
5	4.853	4.713	4.580	4.452	4.329	4.212	4.100	3.993	3.890	3.791
6	5.795	5.601	5.417	5.424	5.076	4.917	4.766	4.623	4.486	4.355
7	6.728	6.472	6.230	6.002	5.786	5.582	5.389	5.206	5.033	4.868
8	7.652	7.325	7.020	6.733	6.463	6.210	5.971	5.747	5.535	5.335
9	8.566	8.162	7.786	7.435	7.108	6.802	6.515	6.247	5.985	5.759
10	9.471	8.983	8.530	8.111	7.722	7.360	7.024	6.710	6.418	6.145
11	10.368	9.787	9.253	8.760	8.306	7.887	7.499	7.139	6.805	6.495
12	11.255	10.575	9.954	9.385	8.863	8.384	7.943	7.536	7.161	6.814
13	12.134	11.348	10.635	9.986	9.394	8.853	8.358	7.904	7.487	7.103
14	13.004	12.106	11.296	10.563	8.899	9.295	8.745	8.244	7.786	7.367
15	13.865	12.849	11.938	11.118	10.380	9.712	9.108	8.559	8.060	7.606
16	14.718	13.578	12.561	11.652	10.838	10.106	9.447	8.851	8.312	7.824
17	15.562	14.292	13.166	12.166	11.274	10.477	9.763	9.122	8.544	8.022
18	16.398	14.992	13.754	12.659	11.690	10.828	10.059	9.372	8.756	8.201
19	17.226	15.678	14.324	13.134	12.085	11.158	10.336	9.604	8.950	8.365
20	18.046	16.351	14.877	13.590	12.462	11.470	10.594	9.818	9.128	8.514
25	22.023	19.523	17.413	15.622	14.094	12.783	11.654	10.675	9.823	9.077
30	25.808	22.397	19.600	17.292	15.373	13.765	12.409	11.258	10.274	9.427

Year	12%	14%	16%	18%	20%	24%	28%	32%	36%
1	0.893	0.877	0.862	0.847	0.833	0.806	0.781	0.758	0.735
2	1.690	1.647	1.605	1.566	1.528	1.457	1.392	1.332	1.276
3	2.402	2.322	2.246	2.174	2.106	1.981	1.868	1.766	1.674
4	3.037	2.914	2.798	2.690	2.589	2.404	2.241	2.096	1.966
5	3.605	3.433	3.274	3.127	2.991	2.745	2.532	2.345	2.181
6	4.111	3.889	3.685	3.498	3.326	3.020	2.759	2.534	2.339
7	4.564	4.288	4.089	3.812	3.605	3.242	2.937	2.678	2.455
8	4.968	4.639	4.344	4.078	3.837	3.421	3.076	2.786	2.540
9	5.328	4.946	4.607	4.303	4.031	3.566	3.184	2.868	2.603
10	5.650	5.216	4.833	4.494	4.193	3.682	3.269	2.930	2.650
11	5.988	5.453	5.029	4.656	4.327	3.776	3.335	2.978	2.683
12	6.194	5.660	5.197	4.793	4.439	3.851	3.387	3.013	2.708
13	6.424	5.842	5.342	4.910	4.533	3.912	3.427	3.040	2.727
14	6.628	6.002	5.468	5.008	4.611	3.962	3.459	3.061	2.740
15	6.811	6.142	5.575	5.092	4.675	4.001	3.483	3.076	2.750
16	6.974	6.265	5.669	5.162	4.730	4.033	3.503	3.088	2.758
17	7.120	5.373	5.749	4.222	4.775	4.059	3.518	3.097	2.763
18	7.250	6.467	5.818	5.273	4.812	4.080	3.529	3.104	2.767
19	7.366	6.550	5.877	5.316	4.844	4.097	3.539	3.109	2.770
20	7.469	6.623	5.929	5.353	4.870	4.110	3.546	3.113	2.772
25	7.843	6.873	6.907	5.467	4.948	4.147	3.564	3.122	2.776
30	8.055	7.003	6.177	5.517	4.979	4.160	3.569	3.124	2.778

Answers to review questions

Note: All the answers are the work of the authors. None has been supplied by an examining body. The examining bodies accept no responsibility whatsoever for the accuracy or method of working in the answers given.

Note: In order to save space, £ signs have been omitted from columns of figures, except where the figures refer to £000, or where the denomination needs to be specified.

1.1

Branch Stock (dates omitted)

	Memo			Memo	
Balance b/d	4,400	3,300	Branch debtors	21,000	21,000
Goods from head office	24,800	18,600	Cash sales	2,400	2,400
Gross profit		5,850	Returns to HO	1,000	750
			Goods stolen	600	450
			Profit and loss: Normal wastage	100	75
			Profit and loss: Excess wastage	152	114
			Balance c/d	3,948	2,961
	29,200	27,750		29,200	27,750

Branch Debtors

Balances b/d	3,946	Bad debts		148
Branch stock: Sales	21,000	Discounts allowed		428
		Bank		22,400
		Balance c/d		1,970
	24,946			24,946

1.2

(a) (dates omitted)

Branch Current Account

Balance b/d	20,160	Cash	30,000
Goods sent	23,160	Goods returned	400
Expenses paid	6,000		
Net profit	3,500	Balance c/d	22,420
	52,820		52,820

(b) Proof:

Branch assets	xxx
Less Branch liabilities	xxx
= Balance of branch current account	xxx

Indicates: Amount of money invested in branch

1.3

(a)(i)

Branch Stock (Selling Prices)

Goods from head office (82,400 + 10% 8,240 = 90,640 + 25%)	113,300	Cash sales	
		Sales: Branch debtors	89,940
		Goods to other branches	1,870
		Branch stock adjustment:	3,300
		Reductions	2,250
		Balance c/d	15,940
	113,300		113,300

(ii)

Branch Stock Adjustment *(profit margin)*

Goods to other branches	660	Branch stock	22,660
Branch stock: Reductions	2,250	(113,300 – 90,640)	
Profit and loss	16,562		
Balance c/d	3,188		
	22,660		22,660

*As cost to branch (original cost + 10%) is subject to further mark-up of 25%, therefore margin is 20%, and this is profit margin used in this account.

(b)

Book stock per branch stock account	15,940
Physical stock	14,850
	1,090

Four possible reasons for deficiency:

(i) thefts by customers;
(ii) thefts by staff;
(iii) wastages due to breakages, miscounting, etc.;
(iv) cash misappropriated.

(c) Figure to be taken for RST balance sheet:

Actual stock at selling price	14,850
Less 20% margin	2,970
Cost to branch	11,880
Less Head office loading (+10%=1/11th of adjusted figure) 1/11th	1,080
Actual cost to company	10,800

Therefore *(iii)* 10,800 is correct answer.

1.5

Packer & Stringer
Trading & Profit & Loss Account for the year ended 31 December 20X4

	Head Office		Branch	
Sales		39,000		26,000
Less Cost of goods sold				
Opening stock	13,000		4,400	
Add Purchases	37,000			
	50,000			
Goods to branch	17,200		17,200	
	32,800		21,600	
Less Closing stock	15,240	17,560	6,570	15,030
		21,440		10,970
Bad debt provision not required				20
				10,990
Salaries	4,500		3,200	
Administrative expenses	1,440		960	
Carriage	2,200		960	
General expenses	3,200		1,800	
Provision for bad debts	50			
Depreciation	150		110	
Manager's commission			360	
		11,540		7,390
Net profit		9,900		3,600

Packer: Commission		900
Interest on capital: Packer	840	
Stringer	240	
	1,080	
	1,980	
Balance of profits: Packer ³/₄	8,640	
Stringer ¹/₄	2,880	
	11,520	
		13,500

Balance Sheet as at 31 December 20X4

Fixed assets			
Furniture		2,600	
Less Depreciation		1,110	1,490
Current assets			
Stock		21,810	
Debtors	10,000		
Less Provision for bad debts	830	9,170	
Cash and bank		3,000	
		33,980	
Less Current liabilities			
Creditors	6,200		
Bank overdraft	1,350		
Manager's commission	120	7,670	
Working capital			26,310
			27,800

1.7

Nion
Trading and Profit and Loss Account for the year ended 31 October 20X1

	Head office		Branch	
	£000	£000		£000
Sales		850		437
Transfers to branch		380		
		1,230		
Less Cost of goods sold:				
Opening stock	8		20	
Add Purchases	914			
	922		375	
Add Goods from head office			395	
Less Closing stock	12		15	
		910		380
Gross profit		320		57
Less Expenses:				
Administrative	200		16.5	
Distribution	80.5		5	
Depreciation	35		10	
Changes in provision for bad debts	(6)	309.5	0.5	32
Net profit		10.5		25

Balance Sheet as at 31 October 20X1

	£000	£000
Fixed assets at cost		450
Less Depreciation to date		215
		235
Current assets		
Stocks (12 + 12 + 4*)	28	
Debtors	120	
Less Provision	6	
	114	
Cash and bank (15.5 + 13 + 50)	78.5	
	220.5	
Less Current liabilities		
Creditors	50	
		170.5
		405.5
Capital		
Balance at 1.11.20X0		410
Add Net profit		35.5
		445.5
Less Drawings		40
		405.5

$*5 \times {}^4/_5$

1.9

(a)

Conversion of Branch Trial Balance to Pounds Sterling

	Fl.	Fl.	Rate	£	£
Freehold buildings	63,000		7	9,000	
Debtors and creditors	36,000	1,560	8	4,460	195
Sales		432,000	9		48,000
Head office		504,260	Actual		60,100
Branch cost of sales	360,000		Below*	40,400	
Depreciation: Machinery		56,700			8,100
Administration costs	18,000		7	2,000	
Stock 30.6.20X8	11,520		8	1,440	
Machinery at cost	126,000		7	18,000	
Remittances	272,000		Actual	29,990	
Balances at bank	79,200		8	9,900	
Selling and distribution	28,800		9	3,200	
Profit on exchange			–		1,995
	994,520	994,520		118,390	118,390

*Cost of sales: Branch Fl. 360,000

Less Depreciation Fl. $\frac{12,600 \div 7 = £1,800}{347,400 \div 9 = £38,600}$

£40,400

(b)

Balance Sheet as at 30 June 20X8

Fixed assets

	£	£
Freehold buildings at cost		23,000
Machinery at cost	24,000	
Less Depreciation	9,600	14,400
		37,400
Current assets		
Stock	30,040	
Debtors	13,360	
Bank	14,500	
Cash in transit	1,990	
	59,890	
Less Current liabilities		
Creditors*	9,809	
Working capital		50,081
		87,481
Financed by:		
Share capital: Authorised and issued		40,000
Reserves		
Difference on exchange	1,995	
Profit and loss	45,486	47,481
		87,481

*Creditors HO 9,500 + Branch 195 + Manager 114 = 9,809.

(c)

(HO Books) *Branch Account*

	£	Fl		£	Fl
Balance b/d	25,136	189,260	Cash from debtors	36	320
Components	35,000	315,000	Remittances	28,000	256,000
Net profit	2,286	*24,000	Cash in transit	1,990	16,000
Difference on exchange	1,995	–	Balance c/d	34,391	255,940
	64,417	528,260		64,417	528,260

*This represents the profit per branch profit and loss account if it had been drawn up using florins.

EG Company Ltd

Trading and Profit and Loss Accounts for the year ended 30 June 20X8

	Head office £	Head office £	Branch £	Branch £
Sales		104,000		48,000
Less Cost of sales	58,400		38,600	
Depreciation	600		1,800	
	59,000		40,400	
Goods to branch	35,000			
		24,000		
Gross profit		80,000		7,600
Administration costs	15,200		2,000	
Selling and distribution	23,300		3,200	
Provison for unrealised profit on branch stock	300			
Manager's commission			114	
	38,800		5,314	
Net profit		41,200		2,286
				43,486
Add Balance from last year				2,000
Balance carried forward to next year				45,486

1.10

(a)

Trial Balance as at 31 December 20X0

	Crowns	Crowns	Rate	£	£
Bank	66,000		4	16,500	
Creditors		92,400	4		23,100
Debtors	158,400		4	39,600	
Fixed assets	145,200		5	29,040	
Head office		316,800	Actual		65,280
Profit and Loss		79,200	4.4		18,000
Stocks	118,800		4	29,700	
Difference on exchange			4		8,460
	488,400	488,400		114,840	114,840

(b) (Books of head office) Highland Branch

Balance b/d		65,280	Balance c/d	91,740
Difference on exchange		8,460		
Net profit		18,000		
		91,740		91,740

(c) Balance Sheet as at 31 December 20X0

Fixed assets		68,640
Current assets		
Stocks	56,100	
Debtors	58,080	
Bank	27,060	
	141,240	
Less Current liabilities		
Creditors	44,220	
Working capital		97,020
		165,660
Financed by:		
Issued share capital		86,400
Reserves		
Profit and loss	70,800	
Difference on exchange	8,460	
		79,260
		165,660

2.1

Machinery

20X3			
Jan 1	Vendor	6,000	

Vendor's Account

20X3				20X3		
				Jan 1	Machinery	6,000
Dec 31	Bank	846		Dec 31	HP interest	412
Dec 31	Bank	2,000				
Dec 31	Balance c/d	3,566				
		6,412				6,412
20X4				20X4		
Dec 31	Bank	2,000		Jan 1	Balance	3,566
Dec 31	Balance c/d	1,851		Dec 31	HP interest	285
		3,851				3,851
20X5				20X5		
Dec 31	Bank	2,000		Jan 1	Balance b/d	1,851
				Dec 31	HP interest	149
		2,000				2,000

Provision for Depreciation: Machinery

20X4				20X3		
Dec 31	Balance c/d	1,140		Dec 31	Profit and loss	600
				20X4		
				Dec 31	Profit and loss	540
		1,140				1,140
20X5				20X5		
Dec 31	Balance c/d	1,626		Jan 1	Balance b/d	1,140
				Dec 31	Profit and loss	486
		1,626				1,626

Balance Sheet as at 31 December 20X5

Machinery at cost		6,000
Less Depreciation		600
(included in Liabilities) Owing on HP	5,400	
	3,566	

2.3

(a) Bulwell's books

Motor Lorries

20X1	Granby Garages	54,000	

Hire Purchase Interest

20X1	Granby	11,250		20X1	Profit and loss	11,250
20X2	Granby	8,063		20X2	Profit and loss	8,063
20X3	Granby	4,078		20X3	Profit and loss	4,078

Bank

				20X1	Granby (Jan 1)	9,000
				20X1	Granby (Dec 31)	24,000
				20X2	Granby	24,000
				20X3	Granby	20,391

Granby Garages

20X1	Bank	9,000		20X1	Motor lorries	54,000
	Bank	24,000			HP interest	11,250
	Balance c/d	32,250				
		65,250				65,250
20X2	Bank	24,000		20X2	Balance b/d	32,250
	Balance c/d	16,313			HP interest	8,063
		40,313				40,313
20X3	Bank	20,391		20X3	Balance b/d	16,313
					Interest	4,078
		20,391				20,391

Depreciation

20X1	Balance c/d	12,500	20X1	Profit and loss	12,500
		12,500			12,500
20X2	Balance c/d	25,000	20X2	Balance b/d	12,500
				Profit and loss	12,500
		25,000			25,000
20X3	Balance c/d	37,500	20X3	Balance b/d	25,000
				Profit and loss	12,500
		37,500			37,500
20X4	Balance c/d	50,000	20X4	Balance b/d	37,500
				Profit and loss	12,500
		50,000			50,000

HP Interest

20X1	Bulwell	11,250	20X1	HP trading	11,250
20X2	Bulwell	8,063	20X2	HP trading	8,063
20X3	Bulwell	4,078	20X3	HP trading	4,078

Hire Purchase Trading

(20X1)

HP sales		54,000
HP interest		11,250
Cost of lorries		43,200
Provision for unrealised profit c/d		6,450
Gross profit		
	65,250	49,650 15,600

(20X2)

HP interest		8,063
Provision for unrealised profit b/d		6,450
Less Provision for unrealised profit c/d		3,263
Gross profit		3,187
		11,250

(20X3)

HP interest		4,078
Provision for unrealised profit b/d		3,263
Gross profit		7,341

Working: Unrealised profit

$$\text{Profit margin} = \frac{10,800}{54,000} \times \frac{100}{1} = 20\%$$

20% × £32,250 = £6,450
20% × £16,313 = £3,263

Balance Sheet as at 31 December

	20X1	20X2	20X3	20X4
Motor lorries cost	54,000	54,000	54,000	54,000
Less Depreciation to date	12,500	25,000	37,500	50,000
	41,500	29,000	16,500	4,000
Liabilities:				
HP debt outstanding	32,250	16,313	–	
Charge against profit:				
HP interest	11,250	8,063	4,078	
Depreciation	12,500	12,500	12,500	

NB: Calculation of interest
20X1 25% × £45,000 = £11,250
20X2 25% × £32,250 = £8,063
20X3 25% × £16,313 = £4,078

(b) Granby's books

Bulwell Aggregates

20X1	HP sales	54,000	20X1	Bank – deposit	9,000
	HP interest	11,250		– instalment	24,000
				Balance c/d	32,250
		65,250			65,250
20X2	Balance b/d	32,250	20X2	Bank – instalment	24,000
	HP interest	8,063		Balance c/d	16,313
		40,313			40,313
20X3	Balance b/d	16,313	20X3	Bank – instalment	20,391
	HP interest	4,078			
		20,391			20,391

Bank

20X1	Bulwell	9,000
	Bulwell	24,000
20X2	Bulwell	24,000
20X3	Bulwell	20,391

2.5

(a)(i)

Vehicles & Finance Co Ltd

20X7			20X7		
Dec 31	Cash	1,000	Dec 31	Motor lorry	3,081
Dec 31	Balance c/d	2,081			
		3,081			3,081
20X8			20X8		
Dec 31	Cash	1,199	Jan 1	Balance b/d	2,081
Dec 31	Balance c/d	1,090	Dec 31	HP interest 10% of 2,081	208
		2,289			2,289
20X9			20X9		
Dec 31	Cash	1,199	Jan 1	Balance b/d	1,090
			Dec 31	HP interest 10% of 1,090	109
		1,199			1,199

(ii)

Motor Lorry

20X7			
Dec 31	Vehicles and finance	3,081	

(iii)

Provision for Depreciation: Motor Lorry

20X7		
Dec 31	Profit and loss	770
20X8		
Dec 31	Profit and loss	578
20X9		
Dec 31	Profit and loss	433

(iv)

Hire Purchase Interest

20X8			20X8		
Dec 31	Vehicles and finance	208	Dec 31	Profit and loss	208
20X9			20X9		
Dec 31	Vehicles and finance	109	Dec 31	Profit and loss	109

(b)

Balance Sheet as at 30 September 20X8

Motor lorry at cost		3,081
Less Depreciation to date		1,348
		1,733
(Included in Liabilities) Owing on hire purchase		1,090

2.6   S Craven

Hire Purchase Trading Account for the year ended 30 September 20X6

Sales at hire purchase price (1,900 × 100)		190,000
Purchases	120,000	
Less Stock (100 × 60)	6,000	
	114,000	
Provision for unrealised profit and interest*	42,560	156,560
Gross profit		33,440
Less Rent	4,500	
Wages	8,600	
General expenses	10,270	23,370
Net profit		10,070

*Cash yet to be collected 190,000 − 83,600 = 106,400

Therefore provision $\dfrac{106,400}{190,000} \times 76,000 = 42,560$

Balance Sheet as at 30 September 20X6

Fixed assets			10,000
Current assets			
Stock		6,000	
HP debtors	106,400		
Less Provision: unrealised profit and interest	42,560	63,840	
Bank		10,630	
		80,470	
Less Current liabilities			
Creditors		8,400	
Working capital			72,070
			82,070
Financed by:			
Capital			
Balance at 1.10.20X5			76,000
Add Net profit			10,070
			86,070
Less Drawings			4,000
			82,070

2.7   RJ

Hire Purchase Trading and Profit and Loss Account for the year ended 31 December 20X8

Sales at hire purchase price (850 × 300)		255,000
Purchases	180,000	
Less Stock (50 × 200)	10,000	
Cost of goods sold	170,000	
Provision of unrealised profit	59,500	229,500
Gross profit		25,500
Less Wages and salaries	12,800	
General expenses	5,500	
Bank interest	400	18,700
Net profit		6,800

Balance Sheet as at 31 December 20X8

Fixed assets		10,000
Current assets		
Stock in warehouse	178,500	
Hire purchase debtors	119,000	
Less Provision for unrealised profit	59,500	119,000
		129,000
Less Current liabilities		
Creditors	16,600	
Bank overdraft	19,600	36,200
		92,800
		102,800
Financed by:		
Capital		100,000
Cash introduced		6,800
		106,800
Add Net profit		4,000
Less Drawings		102,800

2.11

(a)(i) *Machine Hire Purchase*

1.1.X8	Bank	2,000	1.1.X8	Machine	10,000
30.6.X8	Bank	3,056	1.1.X8	HP interest	7,280
31.12.X8	Bank	3,056			
31.12.X8	Balance c/d	9,168			
		17,280			17,280
30.6.X9	Bank	3,056	1.1.X9	Balance b/d	9,168
31.12.X9	Bank	3,056			
31.12.X9	Balance c/d	3,056			
		9,168			9,168
30.6.X0	Bank	3,056	1.1.X0	Balance b/d	3,056

(ii) *Machine Hire Purchase (see workings)*

1.1.X8	Machine HP	7,280	31.12.X8	Profit and loss	4,368
			31.12.X8	Balance c/d	2,912
		7,280			7,280
1.1.X9	Balance b/d	2,912	31.12.X9	Profit and loss	2,427
			31.12.X9	Balance c/d	485
		2,912			2,912
1.1.X0	Balance b/d	485	31.12.X0	Profit and loss	485

(b) *(Extracts) Balance Sheets as at 31 December*

	20X8	20X9	20X0
Fixed assets			
Machinery at cost	10,000	10,000	10,000
Less Depreciation to date	1,800	3,600	5,400
	8,200	6,400	4,600
Creditors			
Falling due within 1 year			
Hire purchase	3,685	2,571	
Falling due after 1 year			
Hire purchase	2,571		

(20X8 3,056 + 3,056 − 2,427)
(20X9 3,056 − 485)

Workings: Interest (sum of digits is 15)
To 31.12.20X8 (5/15 × 7,280) 2,427 + (4/15 × 7,280) = 4,368
To 31.12.20X9 (3/15 × 7,280) 1,456 + (2/15 × 7,280) 971 = 2,427
To 31.12.20X0 1/15 × 7,280 = 485
Depreciation (10,000 − 1,000) ÷ 5 = 1,800 p.a.

4.1

Bank

Application	20,000			
Allotment (30,000 less excess applications 5,000)	25,000			
First call (119,200 × 0.25)	29,800			
Second call (119,200 × 0.375)	44,700			
D Regan (800 × 0.9)	720	Balance c/d		120,220
	120,220			120,220

D Regan

Bank	800	Bank		720
		Forfeited shares		80
	800			800

Application and Allotment

Ordinary share capital	45,000	Bank		20,000
		Bank		25,000
	45,000			45,000

Ordinary Share Capital

Forfeited shares	800	Application and allotment		45,000
		First call		30,000
Balance c/d	120,000	Second call		45,000
		D Regan		800
	120,800			120,800

First Call

Ordinary share capital	30,000	Bank		29,800
		Forfeited shares		200
	30,000			30,000

4.1

Second Call

Dr	£	Cr	£
Ordinary share capital	45,000	Bank	44,700
		Forfeited shares	300
	45,000		45,000

Forfeited Shares

Dr	£	Cr	£
First call		Ordinary share capital	800
Second call			
D Regan			
Transfer to share premium			
	800		800

Forfeited Shares

Dr	£	Cr	£
First call	200	Ordinary share capital	600
Second call	120		
B Mills	120		
Transfer to share premium	160		
	600		600

B. Mills

Dr	£	Cr	£
Ordinary share capital	600	Bank	480
		Forfeited shares	120
	600		600

Balance Sheet

	£
Ordinary share capital	120,000
Share premium	220
	120,220

Ordinary share capital

Dr	£	Cr	£
	120,220		120,220

4.2

Bank

Dr	£	Cr	£
Application (32,600 × 0.50)	16,300	Application and allotment:	
Allotment (20,000 × 1.50 less excess application monies 5,000)	25,000	Refund of application monies	1,300
First call (19,900 × 2)	39,800	Balance c/d	100,160
Second call (19,880 × 1)	19,880		
B Mills (120 × 4)	480		
	101,460		101,460

Application and Allotment

Dr	£	Cr	£
Bank: Refunds	1,300	Bank	16,300
Ordinary share capital	40,000	Bank	25,000
	41,300		41,300

First Call Account

Dr	£	Cr	£
Ordinary share capital	40,000	Bank	39,800
		Forfeited shares	200
	40,000		40,000

Second Call Account

Dr	£	Cr	£
Ordinary share capital	20,000	Bank	19,880
		Forfeited shares	120
	20,000		20,000

Ordinary Share Capital

Dr	£	Cr	£
Forfeited shares	600	Application and allotment	40,000
Balance c/d	100,000	First call	40,000
		Second call	20,000
		B Mills	600
	100,600		100,600

4.3

(a)

Cosy Fires Ltd

Application and allotment

Dr	£	Cr	£
Cash: Return of unsuccessful applications 5,000 × 0.60	3,000	Cash application for 65,000 × 0.60	39,000
Share capital: Due on application and allotment: 40,000 × 0.70	28,000	Cash: Balance due on allotment (see workings)*	1,975
Share premium: 40,000 × 0.25	10,000	Balance c/d: Due from allottee in respect of 500 shares: 500 × 0.35 = 175; Less o/paid on application 250 × 0.60 = 150	25
	41,000		41,000
Balance b/d	25		

Share Capital

Dr	£	Cr	£
Forfeited shares: Amount called on shares forfeited: 500 × 0.70	350	Balance b/d	75,000
Balance c/d	115,000	Application and allotment	28,000
		Call	11,850
		Forfeited shares	500
	115,350		115,350

Share Premium

Dr	£	Cr	£
Balance c/d	10,375	Application and allotment	10,000
		Forfeited shares	375
	10,375		10,375

Forfeited Shares

Dr	£	Cr	£
Application and allotment	25	Share capital	350
Share capital	500	Cash: 500 × 1.10 per share	550
Share premium	375		
	900		900

Call

Dr	£	Cr	£
Share capital 39,500 × 0.30	11,850	Cash	11,850

(b)

Balance Sheet as at 31 May 20X7

Share capital			
Authorised: 160,000 ordinary shares of 1 each			160,000
Issued and fully paid: 115,000 ordinary shares of 1 each			115,000
Capital reserve:			
Share premium			10,375

*Workings:

Due on application 0.60 × 40,000	24,000		
Due on allotment 0.35 × 40,000	14,000		
	39,000		
Received on application: 0.60 × 65,000		38,000	
Less Refunded 5,000 × 0.60		3,000	36,000
Balance due on allotment			2,000
Less			
Amount due on application and			
allotment 500 × 0.95	475		
Received on application 750 × 0.60	450	25	
			1,975

First and Final Call

	250,000	Cash	247,500
		Forfeited shares	2,500
	250,000		250,000

Forfeited Shares

	2,500	Share capital	5,000
	5,000	Cash	4,500
	2,000		
	9,500		9,500

Share capital 250,000

Given Format 1 of the Companies Act 1985, there are two places where uncalled capital can be shown. These are either place A or C II (5).

If C II (5) is chosen it becomes:

Current assets

II Debtors

(5) Called-up share capital not paid		2,500
Issued share capital		
1,000,000 ordinary shares of £1 each		1,000,000
Reserves		
Share premium		302,000

The authorised share capital should be shown also as a note only.
The increase in share premium would also be shown as a note in the statement showing changes in reserves.

4.5

M Ltd

Ledger Accounts (dates omitted)

Cash

Application and allotment (750,000 × 85p)	637,500	Application and allotment (Refund 125,000 × 85p)	106,250
Application and allotment (500,000 × 25p – overpaid 125,000 × 85p)	18,750		
First and final call (495,000 × 50p)	247,500		
Forfeited shares (5,000 × 90p)	4,500		

Application and Allotment

Share capital	250,000	Cash	637,500
Share premium	300,000	Cash	18,750
Cash	106,250		
	656,250		656,250

Share Premium

Balance c/d	302,000	Application and allotment	300,000
		Forfeited shares	2,000
	302,000		302,000

Share Capital

Forfeited shares	5,000	Balance b/d	500,000
Balance c/d	1,000,000	Application and allotment	250,000
		First and final call	250,000
		Forfeited shares	5,000
	1,005,000		1,005,000

5.1

(a)

		Dr	Cr
(A1)	Bank	5,000	
	(A2) Ordinary share applicants		5,000
	Cash received from applicants.		
(B1)	Ordinary share applicants	5,000	
	(B2) Ordinary share capital		5,000
	Ordinary shares allotted.		
(C1)	Preference share capital	5,000	
	(C2) Preference share redemption		5,000
	Shares to be redeemed.		
(D1)	Preference share redemption	5,000	
	(D2) Bank		5,000
	Payment made to redeem shares.		

(a)

	Balances before	Effect Dr	Effect Cr	Balances after
Net assets (except bank)	20,000			20,000
Bank	13,000	(A1) 5,000	(D2) 5,000	13,000
	33,000			33,000
Preference share capital	5,000	(C1) 5,000		–
Preference share redemption	–	(D1) 5,000	(C2) 5,000	–
Ordinary share capital	15,000		(B2) 5,000	20,000
Ordinary share applicants	–	(B1) 5,000	(A2) 5,000	–
Share premium	2,000			2,000
	22,000			22,000
Profit and loss	11,000			11,000
	33,000			33,000

(b)

	Balances before	Effect Dr	Effect Cr	Balances after
Net assets (except bank)	20,000			20,000
Bank	13,000		(B2) 5,000	8,000
	33,000			28,000
Preference share capital	5,000	(A1) 5,000		–
Preference share redemption	–	(B1) 5,000	(A2) 5,000	–
Ordinary share capital	15,000			15,000
Capital redemption reserve	–		(C2) 5,000	5,000
Share premium	2,000			2,000
	22,000			22,000
Profit and loss	11,000	(C1) 5,000		6,000
	33,000			28,000

(A1) Preference share capital
    (A2) Preference share redemption
Shares to be redeemed.

(B1) Preference share redemption
    (B2) Bank
Cash paid on redemption.

(C1) Profit and loss appropriation
    (C2) Capital redemption reserve
Transfer per Companies Act.

(c)

	Balances before	Effect Dr	Effect Cr	Balances after
Net assets (except bank)	20,000			20,000
Bank	13,000	(A1) 1,500	(E2) 5,000	9,500
	33,000			29,500
Preference share capital	5,000	(D1) 5,000		–
Preference share redemption	–	(E1) 5,000	(D2) 5,000	–
Ordinary share capital	15,000		(B2) 1,500	16,500
Ordinary share applicants	–	(B1) 1,500	(A2) 1,500	–
Capital redemption reserve	–		(C2) 3,500	3,500
Share premium	2,000			2,000
	22,000			22,000
Profit and loss	11,000	(C1) 3,500		7,500
	33,000			29,500

(A1) Bank
    (A2) Ordinary share applicants
Cash received from applicants.

(B1) Ordinary share applicants
    (B2) Ordinary share capital
Ordinary shares allotted.

(C1) Profit and loss appropriation
    (C2) Capital redemption reserve
Part of redemption not covered by new issue, to comply with Companies Act.

(D1) Preference share capital
    (D2) Preference share redemption
Shares to be redeemed.

(E1) Preference share redemption
    (E2) Bank
Payment made for redemption.

(d)

	Effect Dr	Effect Cr
Preference share capital	(A1) 5,000	
Preference share redemption	(D1) 6,250	(A2) 5,000
		(B2) 1,250
Bank		(D2) 6,250
Capital redemption reserve		(C2) 5,000
Profit and loss	(B1) 1,250	
	(C1) 5,000	

(A1) Preference share capital
    (A2) Preference share redemption
Shares to be redeemed.

(B1) Profit and loss appropriation
    (B2) Preference share redemption
Premium on redemption of shares *not* previously issued at premium.

(C1) Profit and loss appropriation
    (C2) Capital redemption reserve
Transfer because shares redeemed out of distributable profits.

(D1) Preference share redemption
    (D2) Bank
Payment on redemption.

	Balances before	Effect Dr	Cr	Balances after
Net assets (except bank)	20,000			20,000
Bank	13,000		(D2) 6,250	6,750
	33,000			26,750
Preference share capital	5,000	(A1) 5,000		–
Preference share redemption	–	(D1) 6,250	(A2) 5,000 (B2) 1,250	–
Ordinary share capital	15,000			15,000
Capital redemption reserve	–		(C2) 5,000	5,000
Share premium	2,000			2,000
	22,000			22,000
Profit and loss	11,000	(C1) 5,000 (B1) 1,250		4,750
	33,000			26,750

(e)

	Dr	Cr
(A1) Bank	7,000	
(A2) Ordinary share applicants		7,000

Cash received from applicants.

	Dr	Cr
(B1) Ordinary share applicants	7,000	
(B2) Ordinary share capital		7,000

Ordinary shares allotted.

	Dr	Cr
(C1) Preference share capital	5,000	
(C2) Preference share redemption		5,000

Shares being redeemed.

	Dr	Cr
(D1) Share premium account	1,500	
(D2) Preference share redemption		1,500

Amount of share premium account used for redemption.

	Dr	Cr
(E1) Profit and loss appropriation	500	
(E2) Preference share redemption		500

Excess of premium payable over amount of share premium account usable for the purpose.

	Dr	Cr
(F1) Preference share redemption	7,000	
(F2) Bank		7,000

Amount payable on redemption.

	Balances before	Effect Dr	Cr	Balances after
Net assets (except bank)	20,000			20,000
Bank	13,000	(A1) 7,000	(F2) 7,000	13,000
	33,000			33,000
Preference share capital	5,000	(C1) 5,000		–
Preference share redemption	–	(F1) 7,000	(C2) 5,000 (D2) 1,500 (E2) 500	–
Ordinary share capital	15,000		(B2) 7,000	22,000
Ordinary share applicants	–	(B1) 7,000	(A2) 7,000	–
Share premium account	2,000	(D1) 1,500		500
	22,000			22,500
Profit and loss	11,000	(E1) 500		10,500
	33,000			33,000

5.3

(a)

	Dr	Cr
(A1) Ordinary share capital	6,000	
(A2) Ordinary share purchase		6,000

Shares to be purchased.

	Dr	Cr
(B1) Ordinary share purchase	6,000	
(B2) Bank		6,000

Payment for shares purchased.

	Dr	Cr
(C1) Profit and loss	4,500	
(C2) Capital redemption reserve		4,500

Transfer of deficiency of permissible capital payment to comply with Companies Act.

	Balances before	Effect Dr	Cr	Balances after
Net assets (except bank)	12,500			12,500
Bank	13,000		(B2) 6,000	7,000
	25,500			19,500
Preference share capital	5,000			5,000
Ordinary share capital	10,000	(A1) 6,000		4,000
Ordinary share purchase	–	(B1) 6,000	(A2) 6,000	–
Non-distributable reserves	6,000			6,000
Capital redemption reserve	–		(C2) 4,500	4,500
	21,000			19,500
Profit and loss	4,500	(C1) 4,500		–
	25,500			19,500

(b)

	Dr	Cr
(A1) Ordinary share capital	6,000	
(A2) Ordinary share purchase		6,000
Shares to be purchased.		
(B1a) Profit and loss	4,500	
(B1b) Non-distributable reserves	1,500	
(B2) Ordinary share capital		6,000
Transfers of profit and loss and non-distributable reserves per Companies Act.		
(C1) Ordinary share purchase	12,000	
(C2) Bank		12,000
Payment to shareholders.		

	Balances before	Effect Dr	Effect Cr	Balances after
Net assets (except bank)	12,500			12,500
Bank	13,000		(C2) 12,000	1,000
	25,500			13,500

	Balances before	Effect Dr	Effect Cr	Balances after
Preference share capital	5,000			5,000
Ordinary share capital	10,000	(A1) 6,000 / (C1) 12,000	(A2) 6,000 / (B2) 6,000	4,000
Ordinary share purchase	–			–
Non-distributable reserves	6,000	(B1b) 1,500		4,500
Profit and loss	21,000	(B1a) 4,500		13,500
	25,500			13,500

5.5

Workings: Opening balance 10% debentures (a/c below)

Originally issued	375,000
Less Redeemed previously	150,000
	225,000

10% Debentures

30/9 Debenture redemption	225,000	1/7 Balance b/d	225,000

Workings: Sinking fund investments (A/c below)

Appropriations to date	334,485
Interest invested (39,480 – 2,475)	37,005
	371,490
Less Sold – at cost	144,915
	226,575

Sinking Fund Investments

1/7 Balance b/d	226,575	2/8 Bank No. 2 Sale	73,215
2/8 Sinking fund: Profit (73,215 – 69,322)	3,893	25/9 Bank No. 2 Sale	160,238
25/9 Sinking fund: Profit (Cost 226,575 – 69,322 = 157,253. Sold for 160,238)	2,985		
	233,453		233,453

Workings: Sinking fund (A/c below)

Previous contributions	334,485
Interest on investments	39,480
Profit: Previous sales of investments (147,243 – 144,915)	2,328
Profit: Previous purchase debentures (150,000 – 147,243)	2,757
	379,050
Less Transfer to general reserve sum equal to debentures redeemed	150,000
	229,050

Sinking Fund A/c

30/9 Debentures redemption (Premium 1%)	2,250	1/7 Balance b/d	229,050
30/9 General reserve	236,889	7/7 No 2 Bank: Interest	1,756
		2/8 SF Investments: Profit	3,893
		13/9 No 2 Bank: Interest	1,455
		25/9 SF Investments: Profit	2,985
	239,139		239,139

No. 2 Bank A/c

1/7 Balance b/d	2,475	30/9 W Bank plc (deposit)	15,150
7/7 Sinking fund: Interest	1,756	30/9 Debentures redemption	212,100
2/8 SF investments: Sale	73,215	30/9 No. 1 Bank transfer of balance	11,889
13/9 Sinking fund: Interest	1,455		
25/9 SF investments: Sale	160,238		
	239,139		239,139

Debenture Redemption A/c

30/9 No. 2 Bank (225,000 Debentures – 15,000 B Ltd = 210,000 at 1% premium)	212,100	30/9 10% Debentures	225,000
30/9 Balance c/d (15,000 outstanding at premium 1%)	15,150	30/9 Sinking fund (premium)	2,250
	227,250		227,250

W Bank plc

30/9 No. 2 Bank	15,150		

5.7

(Dates omitted – all figures shown in £000)

Application and Allotment

	£		£
Ordinary shares	80	Bank	60
Share premium	20	Bank	40
	100		100

Call Account

	£		£
Ordinary shares	20	Bank	18
		Investments	2
	20		20

Investments (own shares)

	£		£
Call	2	Bank	11
Share premium	9		
	11		11

5.9

(Note: Some abbreviations are used)

(a) 10% Debentures

	£		£
31.12.X8 Debenture redemption	12,000	1.4.X8 Balance b/d	100,000
31.12.X8 Balance c/d	88,000		
	100,000		100,000

(b) Debenture Redemption Fund

	£		£
31.12.X8 Reserve (equal to debentures redeemed)	12,000	1.4.X8 Balance b/d	20,000
		31.12.X8 DRFI (profit on redemption)	1,400
		31.12.X8 DR (profit on purchase)	900
		31.12.X8 Bank	1,600
31.3.X9 Balance c/d	13,900	31.3.X9 Profit and loss (annual appropriation)	2,000
	25,900		25,900

(c) Debenture Redemption Fund Investment

	£		£
1.4.X8 Balance b/d	20,000	31.12.X8 Bank (sale)	11,400
31.12.X8 DR Fund (profit on sale)	1,400		
31.3.X9 Bank (2,000 + 300 + 1,600)	3,900	31.3.X9 Balance c/d	13,900
	25,300		25,300

(d) Debenture Redemption

	£		£
31.12.X8 Bank (purchase)	11,400	31.12.X8 10% Debentures	12,000
31.12.X8 DR Fund (profit on redemption)	900	31.12.X8 Debenture interest accrued	300
	12,300		12,300

(e) Debenture Interest

	£		£
30.9.X8 Bank ($100{,}000 \times 10\% \div 2$)	5,000		
31.12.X8 Debenture redemption (interest included in price $12{,}000 \times 10\% \times \tfrac{1}{4}$)	300		
31.3.X9 Bank ($88{,}000 \times 10\% \div 2$)	4,400	31.3.X9 Profit and loss	9,700
	9,700		9,700

6.1

Checkers Ltd

(a) Profit and Loss Account for the year ended 31 December 20X5

	Total	Basis of allocation	Pre-incorporation	Post-incorporation
Gross profit	28,000	Turnover	8,000	20,000
Less				
Salaries of vendors	1,695	Actual	1,695	
Wages	8,640	Time	2,160	6,480
Rent	860	Time	215	645
Distribution	1,680	Turnover	480	1,200
Commission	700	Turnover	200	500
Bad debts	314	Actual	104	210
Interest	1,650	Time	990	660
Directors' remuneration	4,000	Actual		4,000
Directors' expenses	515	Actual		515
Depreciation*				
Motors	1,900	Actual	400	1,500
Machinery	575	Actual	125	450
Bank interest	168	Actual		168
	22,697		6,369	16,328
Net profit	5,303		1,631	3,672
	28,000		8,000	20,000

*Depreciation:

Motors to 31 March 20X5 $20\% \times 3 \text{ months} \times 7{,}000 + 20\% \times 1 \text{ month} \times 3{,}000 = 400$

After $20\% \times 9 \text{ months} \times 7{,}000 + 20\% \times 9 \text{ months} \times 3{,}000 = 1{,}500$

(b) Transfer to capital reserve.

(c) Charge to a goodwill account.

6.2

Adjusted Profits

Profit per accounts		16,400		23,920		19,650
Add Motor expenses saved	620		660		700	
Depreciation overcharged	1,500		700		60	
Wrapping expenses saved	420		480		510	
Bank interest	180		590		740	
Preliminary expenses			690			
		2,720		3,120		2,010
		19,120		27,040		21,660
Less Extra management						
remuneration	1,500		1,500		1,500	
Investment income	290		340		480	
Rents received	940		420			
Opening stock			1,900			
Profit on property			4,800			
		2,730		8,960		1,980
Profits as adjusted		16,390		18,080		19,680

Average profit
16,390
18,080
19,680
54,150 ÷ 3 = 18,050

If 18,050 is a return of 25% on investment, then

$$\frac{18,050}{25} \times 100 = 72,200 \text{ purchase price.}$$

6.3

(a)

CK

Realisation

Freehold premises	8,000	CK Ltd: Value at which	
Plant	4,000	assets taken over	27,200
Stock	2,000	Discount on creditors	150
Debtors	5,000		
Profit on realisation	8,350		
	27,350		27,350

Capital

CK Ltd: Shares	24,150	Balance b/d	16,000
Cash	200	Profit on realisation	8,350
	24,350		24,350

CK Ltd (not asked for in question)

Realisation	27,200	Creditors	3,050
		Shares	24,150
	27,200		27,200

RP Ltd

Realisation

Freehold premises	4,500	CK Ltd: Value at which assets	
Plant	2,000	taken over	13,000
Stock	1,600		
Debtors	3,400		
Profit on realisation	1,500		
	13,000		13,000

Sundry Shareholders

		Share capital	4,000
CK Ltd	5,000	Profit on realisation	1,500
Cash	3,000	Revenue surplus	2,500
Shares	8,000		8,000

CK Ltd (not asked for in question)

Realisation	13,000	Bank overdraft	3,500
		Creditors	1,500
		Sundry shareholders: Cash	5,000
		Shares	3,000
	13,000		13,000

Journal of CJK Ltd

(b) (Narratives omitted)

Cash	5,000	
Share premium		3,000
Ordinary shares		2,000
Cash	7,840	
Discount on issue	160	
7 per cent debentures		8,000
Goodwill	7,000	
Freehold premises	10,000	
Plant	3,500	
Stock	2,000	
Debtors	5,000	
Provision for discounts receivable		150
Creditors		3,200
Provision for bad debts		300
Ordinary shares		24,150
Goodwill	500	
Freehold premises	5,500	
Plant	2,000	
Stock	1,600	
Debtors	3,400	
Creditors		1,500
Bank overdraft		3,500
Cash		5,000
Ordinary share capital		3,000
Formation expenses	1,200	
Cash		1,200

(c)

CJK Ltd
Balance Sheet as at 1 January 20X0

Fixed assets: at cost			
Freehold premises			15,500
Plant			5,500
Goodwill			7,500
			28,500
Current assets			
Stock			3,600
Debtors		8,400	
Less Provision for bad debts		300	8,100
Cash at bank			3,140
			14,840
Less Current liabilities			
Creditors		4,700	
Less Provision		150	4,550
Working capital			10,290
			38,790

7.1

(a)

Debenture Interest

20X3			20X3		
Dec 31	Bank	9,600	Dec 31	Profit and loss	12,800
Dec 31	Income tax	3,200			
		12,800			12,800

Income Tax

20X3			20X3		
Dec 31	Balance c/d	3,200	Dec 31	Debenture interest	3,200

Ordinary Dividends

20X3			20X3		
Jul 1	Bank	20,000	Dec 31	Profit and loss	50,000
Dec 31	Accrued c/d	30,000			
		50,000			50,000

Deferred Taxation

20X3			20X3		
Dec 31	Balance c/d	14,000	Dec 31	Profit and loss*	14,000

*35% of (£90,000 − £50,000) = £14,000

Corporation Tax

20X3			20X3		
Dec 31	Balance c/d	90,000	Dec 31	Profit and loss	90,000

(b)

Profit and Loss Account (extracts) year to 31 December 20X3

Net trading profit			220,000
Less Debenture interest			12,800
Profit on ordinary activities before taxation			207,200
Corporation tax		90,000	
Deferred tax		14,000	104,000
Profit on ordinary activities after taxation			103,200
Less Ordinary dividends: Interim		20,000	
Final proposed		30,000	50,000

Balance Sheet (extracts) as at 31 December 20X3

Creditors: Amounts falling due within one year		
Proposed ordinary dividend		30,000
Corporation tax		90,000
Deferred tax		14,000
Income tax		3,200

7.3

Workings:

(W1) Tax deducted from fixed interest income is $\frac{1}{3} \times £24,000 = £8,000$
(W2) Changes in deferred taxation account.
Timing difference:

Capital allowances allowable for tax (D)		90,000
Depreciation actually charged (D)		50,000
		40,000

Transferred to deferred tax account £40,000 × 35% = £14,000

Deferred Tax

20X2			20X2			
Dec 31	Balance c/d	81,000	Jan 1	Balance b/d	(J)	67,000
			Dec 31	Tax on profit on ordinary activities (W2)		14,000
		81,000				81,000

Income Tax

20X2				20X2			
Oct 31	Interest receivable	(C1)	8,000	Nov 30	Debenture interest	(B)	20,000
Dec 15	Bank		12,000				
			20,000				20,000

Interest Receivable

20X2				20X2		
Dec 31	Profit and loss		32,000	Oct 31	Bank (C1)	24,000
				Oct 31	Income tax (C1)	8,000
			32,000			32,000

Barnet Ltd
Profit and Loss (extracts) for the year ended 31 December 20X2

Net trading profit	(A)		560,000
Add Fixed rate interest (C1) (gross)		32,000	
Investment income (C2) (gross)		900	
			32,900
			592,900
Less Debenture interest (B) (gross)			80,000
Profit on ordinary activities before taxation			512,900
Tax on profit on ordinary activities*			165,000
Profit on ordinary activities after taxation			347,900
Less Dividends:			
Preference dividend		18,000	
Ordinary: Interim		75,000	
Final		120,000	
			213,000

*Notes attached to accounts giving make-up of this figure.

Balance Sheet (extracts) as at 31 December 20X2

Creditors: amounts falling due within one year		
Proposed ordinary dividend	120,000	
Corporation tax	154,000	
Deferred tax	81,000	

A final point concerns the difference in treatment of tax on investment income as compared with tax on other income, such as interest. It is only the tax on investment income which is treated as part of the final tax costs, while the tax on interest is simply deducted from charges paid by the company. You would have to study taxation in detail to understand why this happens.

7.5

BG Ltd
Profit and Loss Account for the year ended 31 December 20X7

Trading profit		50,000
Income from shares in related companies	3,000	
Other interest receivable and similar income	1,100	
		4,100
		54,100
Interest payable and similar charges		3,600
Profit on ordinary activities before taxation		50,500
Tax on profit on ordinary activities		24,000
Profit on ordinary activities after taxation		26,500
Undistributed profits from last year		9,870
		36,370
Transfers to reserves	5,000	
Dividends proposed	21,000	
		26,000
Undistributed profits carried to next year		10,370

Debenture Interest

20X2				20X2		
Nov 30	Bank	(B)	60,000	Dec 31	Profit and loss	80,000
Nov 30	Income tax	(B)	20,000			
			80,000			80,000

Investment Income

20X2				20X2		
Dec 31	Profit and loss	(C2)	900	Sept 1	Bank	900
			900			900

Corporation Tax

20X2				20X2			
Sept 30	Bank*		112,000	Jan 1	Balance b/d	(K)	115,000
Sept 30	Tax on profit on ordinary activities†	(K)	3,000	Dec 31	Tax on profit on ordinary activities	(L)	154,000
Dec 31	Balance c/d	(L)	154,000				
			269,000				269,000

*£115,000 owing – £3,000 reduction (K) = £112,000.
†Adjustment for amendment in tax bill.

Tax on Profit on Ordinary Activities

20X2				20X2		
Dec 31	Corporation tax		154,000	Sept 30	Corporation tax (K)	3,000
Dec 31	Deferred tax	(W2)	14,000	Dec 31	Profit and loss	165,000
			168,000			168,000

Preference Dividends

20X2				20X2		
Jun 30	Bank	(F)	18,000	Dec 31	Profit and loss	18,000

Ordinary Dividends

20X2				20X2			
Mar 31	Bank	(I)	90,000	Jan 1	Accrued b/d	(I)	90,000
Jul 15	Bank	(G)	75,000	Dec 31	Profit and loss		195,000
Dec 31	Accrued c/d		120,000				
			285,000				285,000

7.6
(All in £million)

(i)

Ordinary Dividends

31.8.X8	Bank (X7 final)	28	1.4.X8 Balance b/d	28
31.12.X8	Bank (X8 interim)	12	31.3.X9 Profit and loss	48
31.3.X9	Balance c/d	36		
		76		76

(ii)

Deferred Taxation

31.3.X9	Balance c/d	8	1.4.X8 Balance b/d	3
			31.3.X9 Profit and loss	5
		8		8

8.1
(a)

Either Ltd

		£000
Profit per draft accounts		157
(i) Stock: reduce to net realisable value	+	–
(ii) Directors' remuneration		35
(iii) Bad debt		43
(iv) Corporation tax saved on (i) + (ii) + (iii) × 50%		30
(v) Depreciation adjustment (W1)	54	30
(vi) Revaluation reserve (realised on sale)	125	
(vii) General reserve	80	
(viii) Loss brought forward (W2)	144	
	259	282
		net (23)

Maximum possible dividend		(23)
Preference dividend 6%	£9,000	134
Ordinary dividend	£125,000	

Research and development expenditure: assumed to have been carried forward in accordance with SSAP 13 and can be justified. Failing this it would have to be a realised loss.

(b) For a plc no changes required, except that the payment should not reduce net assets below called-up share capital and undistributable reserves = 400 + 150 + 100 = 650. A further bad debt might change this position.

(W1) *Reducing balance*

Cost 1.12.20X1	100,000
Depreciation 20X2	25,000
	75,000
Cost 1.6.20X3	25,000
	100,000
Depreciation 20X3	25,000
	75,000
Cost 29.2.X4	28,000
31.5.X4	45,000
	148,000
Depreciation 20X4	37,000
	111,000
Cost 1.12.20X4	50,000
	161,000
Depreciation 20X5	40,250
	120,750

Total 25,000 + 25,000 + 37,000 + 40,250 = 127,250

Straight line

		20X2	20X3	20X4	20X5
Cost 1.12.20X2	100,000	25,000	25,000	25,000	25,000
1.6.20X3	25,000		3,125	6,250	6,250
29.2.20X4	28,000			5,250	7,000
31.5.20X4	45,000			5,625	11,250
1.12.20X4	50,000				12,500
		25,000	28,125	42,125	62,000

Total 157,250

Extra depreciation 157,250 – 127,250 = 30,000

(W2) As profits after tax were £157,000 but were shown in the balance sheet as £13,000, this means that a deficit of £144,000 had been brought forward from last year.

9.1

(a)

Merton Manufacturing Co Ltd
Balance Sheet as at . . .

Fixed tangible assets

Freehold land and buildings at cost		95,000
Plant and equipment at written-down value (W1)		104,350
		199,350

Current assets

Stocks	25,000	
Debtors	50,000	
Bank (W2)	14,150	
	89,150	

Creditors: amounts falling due within one year		
Creditors	63,500	
Net current assets		25,650
Total assets *less* current liabilities		225,000
Long-term loans: 8 per cent debentures (W3)		150,000
		75,000

Capital and reserves		
Called-up share capital		
150,000 50p ordinary shares (W4)		75,000

Workings:

(W1)

Ordinary shares 50p (new)		90,000
(1 for 6 = 15,000 × 50p)	7,500	
6% preference shares (old)		150,000
Ordinary shares 50p (new)		100,000
(1 for 3 – preference –		
50,000 × 50p)	25,000	
11½% Debentures (old)		25,000
Share premium written off		
8% debentures		
(1 for 3 preference)	50,000	
8% debentures		
(exchange for 11½%)	100,000	
Ordinary shares 50p		
(1 for every £4		
old debenture)	12,500	
Goodwill written off	50,000	
Profit and loss written off	38,850	
Plant and equipment*	81,150	
	365,000	365,000

*Per (*vii*) of question – amount needed to balance.

(W2) Shares issued 60,000 shares × 50p = 30,000
Cash 30,000 – overdraft 15,850 = balance 14,150

(W3) See capital reduction – debit side (W1) new debentures 50,000 + 100,000 = 150,000

(W4) See (W1) 7,500 + 25,000 + 12,500 + new shares issued for cash 30,000 = 75,000

(b) (Main points)

		Old shareholdings	New shareholdings
Expected profit		22,500	22,500
Less Interest 11½%		11,500	
8%			12,000
Taxable profits		11,000	10,500
Less Corporation tax 33⅓%		3,667	3,500
Profits before dividends		7,333	7,000
Preference dividends – if profits sufficient		9,000	–

Before reconstruction
(Old) Preference shareholders
Before reconstruction it would have taken over 5 years at this rate before preference dividends payable, as probably deficit of 38,850 on the profit and loss account would have to be cleared off first.
(Old) Ordinary shares
Even forgetting the profit and loss account deficit, the preference dividends were bigger than available profits. This would leave nothing for the ordinary shareholder.

After reconstruction
The EPS is £7,000 ÷ 150,000 = 4.67p
If all profits are distributed the following benefits will be gained:
By old preference shareholders

50,000 shares × 4.67p	2,335
£50,000 8% debentures	4,000
	6,335

Plus any benefits from tax credits.
By old ordinary shareholders

15,000 shares × 4.67p	700

Plus any benefits from tax credits.

(c) Preference shareholders – points to be considered:
(i) What were prospects for income?

Based on projected earnings would have been no income for over 5 years, then earnings of 7,333 per annum if all profits distributed.

(ii) What are new prospects for income?

Total income of 6,333 per annum immediately.

(iii) Is it worth exchanging (i) for (ii)?

Obviously depends on whether forecasts are accurate or not. If the above are accurate would seem worthwhile.

(iv) What have preference shareholders given up?

Some of exchange consists of ordinary shares which are more risky than preference shares, both in terms of dividends and of payments on liquidation.

(v) What have they gained?

Debenture interest payable whether profits made or not.

9.2

(a) (Narratives omitted)

	Dr	Cr
Preference share capital	37,500	
Ordinary share capital	175,000	
Capital reduction		212,500

Preference shares reduced 25p each (0.25 × 150,000) and Ordinary shares reduced by 0.875 (200,000 × 0.875).

	Dr	Cr
Capital reduction	3,375	
Ordinary share capital		3,375

Ordinary shares issued re. preference dividend arrears, 27,000 × 0.125.

	Dr	Cr
Share premium	40,000	
Capital reduction		40,000

Share premium balance utilised.

	Dr	Cr
Provision for depreciation	62,500	
Capital reduction	72,500	
Plant and machinery		135,000

Plant and machinery written down to 75,000.

	Dr	Cr
Capital reduction	176,625	
Profit and loss		114,375
Preliminary expenses		7,250
Goodwill		55,000

Profit and loss account and intangible assets written off.

	Dr	Cr
Cash	62,500	
Ordinary share applicants		62,500

Applications for shares 500,000 × 0.125.

	Dr	Cr
Ordinary share applicants	62,500	
Ordinary share capital		62,500

500,000 ordinary shares issued.

(b) Balance Sheet as at 31 December 20X5

Fixed assets			
Leasehold property at cost		80,000	
Less Provision for depreciation		30,000	
			50,000
Plant and machinery at valuation			75,000
			125,000
Current assets			
Stock		79,175	
Debtors		31,200	
Bank		11,500	
		121,875	
Less Current liabilities			
Creditors		43,500	
Working capital			78,375
			203,375
Financed by:			
Share capital:			
Preference shares			
150,000 shares £0.75			112,500
Ordinary shares			
727,000 ordinary shares £0.125			90,875
			203,375

9.3

The Journal (narratives omitted)

	Dr	Cr
(a) Preference share capital	37,500	
Capital reduction		37,500
(b) Ordinary share capital	360,000	
Capital reduction		360,000
(c) Capital reserve	48,000	
Capital reduction		48,000
(d) Preference share capital	112,500	
Ordinary share capital	240,000	
New ordinary share capital		352,500
(e) (i) Debenture holders	150,000	
Debentures		150,000
(ii) Cash	150,000	
Debenture holders		150,000
(f) Capital reduction	445,500	
Goodwill etc.		210,000
Plant		45,000
Furniture		6,600
Profit and loss		183,900

Finer Textiles Ltd
Balance Sheet as at 31 March 20X6

Fixed assets		
Intangible: Goodwill		15,000
Tangible: Plant		169,800
Furniture		6,000
		190,800
Current assets		
Stock	170,850	
Debtors	65,100	
Bank	107,400	
Cash	150	
	343,500	
Creditors: amounts falling due within 1 year		
Creditors	31,800	
Net current assets		311,700
Total assets less current liabilities		502,500
Creditors: amounts falling due after more than 1 year		
Debentures		150,000
		352,500
Capital and reserves		
Called-up share capital		352,500

10.1
(a) Following is a brief answer:
(i) Such closure costs should be treated as an exceptional item, because:
- it is (probably) a material item;
- these are costs not likely to recur regularly or frequently.

(ii) This should be adjusted in tax charge for 20X7. Because it is not material (probably) it does not need to be disclosed separately.

(iii) The excess should be credited to a reserve account, and a note attached to the balance sheet. Depreciation to be based on revalued amount and on new estimate of remaining life of the asset, to be disclosed in a note to the accounts.

(iv) Treat as bad debt and write off to profit and loss. Because it is a material item it should be disclosed as an exceptional item in the profit and loss account.

(v) This is a prior period adjustment. The retained profit brought forward should be amended to allow for the change in accounting policy in the current year. The reasons: (1) it is material, (2) relates to a previous year, (3) as a result of change in accounting policy. The adjustment should be disclosed in a note to the financial statements.

(b) See Sections 10.25 and 10.39.

10.2
(i) The replacement cost is irrelevant. The stock should be shown at the cost of £26,500. This assumes historic cost accounts.

(ii) *Paramite:* Stock to be valued at direct costs £72,600 plus fixed factory overhead £15,300 = £87,900. Under no circumstances should selling expenses be included.
Paraton: As net realisable value is lower than the costs involved, this figure of £9,520 should be used (SSAP 9).

(iii) In this case there is a change of accounting policy. Accordingly a prior period adjustment will be made. On a straight line basis, net book value would have been:

Cost 160,000 less 12½% × 2 years =	120,000
Value shown	90,000
Therefore prior period adjustment of	30,000
to be added to retained profit at 1 November 20X4.	

For 20X5 and each of the following 5 years depreciation will be charged at the rate of £20,000 per annum (FRS 3).

(iv) The cost subject to depreciation is £250,000 less land £50,000 = £200,000. With a life of 40 years this is £5,000 per annum.
This also will result in a prior period adjustment, in this case 10 × £5,000 = £50,000. This will be debited to retained profits at 1 November 20X4. For 20X5 and each of the following 29 years the yearly charge of depreciation will be £5,000 (FRS 3).

(v) Write off £17,500 to profit and loss (SSAP 13).

(vi) As this development expenditure is almost definitely going to be recovered over the next 4 years it can be written off over that period (SSAP 13).

(vii) As this is unlikely to happen often it is an exceptional item. Charge to profit and loss on ordinary activities under the appropriate statutory heading (FRS 3).

(viii) As this is over 20 per cent, it is material and appears to be long-term. This means that Lilleshall Ltd is an associated company and accounts should be prepared accordingly. The post-acquisition profits to be brought in are 30% × £40,000 = £12,000.

10.5
The fact that this is a partnership does not mean that accounting standards are not applicable; they are just as applicable to a partnership as they are to a limited company.

(a) (i) These should be included as sales £60,000 in the accounts for the year to 31 May 20X7. This is because the matching concept requires that revenue, and the costs used up in achieving it, should be matched up. Profits: increase of £60,000.

(ii) Stock values are normally based on the lower of cost or net realisable value. In this case it depends how certain it is that the stock can be sold for £40,000. If a firm order can definitely be anticipated, then the figure of £40,000 can be used as this then represents the lower figure of net realisable value. Profit: an increase of £15,000. However, should the sale not be expected, then the concept of prudence dictates that the scrap value of £1,000 be used. Profit: a reduction of £24,000.

Tree diagram (item (d))

£15,000 (0.2)	£10,000 (0.1)	= £25,000	0.02	
	£20,000 (0.5)	= £35,000	0.10	
	£30,000 (0.4)	= £45,000	0.08	
£30,000 (0.5)	£10,000 (0.1)	= £40,000	0.05	
	£20,000 (0.5)	= £50,000	0.25	0.75
	£30,000 (0.4)	= £60,000	0.20	
£40,000 (0.3)	£10,000 (0.1)	= £50,000	0.03	
	£20,000 (0.5)	= £60,000	0.15	
	£30,000 (0.4)	= £70,000	0.12	
			1.00	

(b) It is important to establish the probability of the payment of the debt of £80,000. If it is as certain as it possibly can be that payment will be made, even though it may be delayed then no provision is needed. Profit change: nil.

However, the effect on future profits can be substantial. A note to the accounts detailing the possibilities of such changes should be given.

(c) The concepts which are applicable here are (i) going concern, (ii) consistency, (iii) accruals, (iv) prudence.

Following on the revelations in (b) and the effect on sales so far of the advertising campaign, is the partnership still able to see itself as a going concern? This would obviously affect the treatment of valuations of all assets.

Given that it can be treated as a going concern, the next point to be considered is that of consistency. The treatment of the expense item should be treated consistently.

The accruals concept is concerned with matching up revenues and costs, and will affect the decision as to how much of the costs should be carried forward. Some revenue in future periods needs to be expected with a high degree of certainty before any of this expenditure should be carried forward. It does not seem highly likely that large revenues can be expected in future in this case. In any case 75 per cent is a very large proportion of such expenditure to be carried forward. There is no easy test of the validity of the partners' estimates. Granted that under SSAP 13 for development expenditure some of it, under very stringent conditions, can be carried forward. If the partners' estimates can be accepted under this, then profits would be increased by 75% × (50,000 + 60,000) = £82,500.

(d) The expected profit/loss is as follows:

	Project A	Project B	Project C
Direct costs to date	30,000	25,000	6,000
Overheads to date	4,000	2,000	500
Future expected direct costs	10,000	25,000	40,000
Future expected overheads	2,000	2,000	3,000
Total of expected costs	46,000	54,000	49,500
Sale price of project	55,000	50,000	57,500
Expected total profit/loss	9,000	(4,000)	8,000
% Complete	75%	50%	15%

When a project is sufficiently near completion then a proportion of the profits can be taken as being realised.

Project A is 75 per cent complete and this indicates profit being taken. Whether or not 75 per cent can be taken, i.e. £6,750, will depend on the facts of the case. If completion at the above figures can be taken for granted then it might be reasonable to do so. Prudence dictates that a lesser figure be taken.

With project B there is an expected loss. Following the prudence concept losses should always be accounted for in full as soon as they become known.

In project C it is too early in the project, 15 per cent completed, to be certain about the outcome. No profit should therefore be brought into account.

Profit, dependent on comments about project A, will therefore be increased by £6,750 − £4,000 = £2,750.

(e) This is a case where the examiner has dipped into topics from other subjects. What is needed here is a tree diagram to show the probabilities.

There is a probability of 0.75 of achieving £50,000 sales. As this is greater than the specified figure of 0.70 then the stocks should not be written down. Effect on profits: nil.

(f) The opening stock should be shown as the revised figure. If error had not been found this year's profit would have been £7,000 greater.

The adjustment should be shown as a prior period adjustment in the current accounts.

Address
Date

10.6

(a)

The Chief Accountant
Uncertain Ltd

Dear Sir/Mr . . . ,

Report on Draft Profit and Loss Account for the year ended 30 September 20X6

Further to your letter/our meeting of . . . I would like to offer my suggestions for the appropriate accounting treatment of items (i) to (v).

(b)

Uncertain Ltd

Draft profit and loss account for the year ended 30 September 20X6

Sales		5,450,490
Manufacturing cost of sales (W1)		2,834,500
		2,615,990
Administration expenses	785,420	
Selling expenses (W2)	1,013,600	1,799,020
Operating profit		816,970
Continuing operations – redundancy payments	100,000	
Discontinued operations – factory closure costs	575,000	675,000
Profit before tax		141,970
Corporation tax (50%) (W3)		70,985
		70,985
Proposed dividend on ordinary shares		125,000
Reduction in retained profits		(54,015)

(W1) £3,284,500 – £100,000 (i) – £350,000 (iv) = £2,834,500
(W2) £629,800 + £258,800 (iii) + £125,000 (v) = £1,013,600
(W3) 50% of profits before tax

10.7

(a) (i) Post-balance sheet events consists of those events, whether favourable or unfavourable, which take place between the date of the balance sheet and the date on which the financial accounts and notes are approved by the directors.

(ii) Adjusting events are post-balance sheet events which give extra evidence of what was happening at the balance sheet date. The events included may be included because they are either of a statutory nature or taken into account by convention.

(iii) Non-adjusting events are balance sheet events concerned with matters which did not exist at the balance sheet date.

(iv) A contingent asset/liability is concerned with something which seems to be apparent at the balance sheet date but can only be verified by future events which are uncertain.

(b) Adjusting events: (i) debtor's inability to pay; (ii) subsequent discovery of frauds rendering accounts incorrect; (iii) when net realisable value is used for stock valuation and later shown to be wrong when stock sold; (iv) subsequent discovery of errors rendering accounts incorrect.
Non-adjusting events: (i) change in foreign exchange rates; (ii) strikes; (iii) nationalisation; (iv) share issues.

(c) (i) A material contingent liability should be accrued where some future event will give evidence of the loss, subject to the fact that it should be able to be determined with reasonable accuracy when the accounts are agreed by the directors.

(ii) Material contingent assets should be disclosed in the financial statements if it is very probable that they will be realised.

(i) Redundancy payments: £100,000
The reorganisation satisfies the requirements of FRS 3, that it had a material effect on the reporting entity's operations. As a result, the costs should be shown separately on the face of the profit and loss account after operating profit and before interest, and included under the heading of continuing operations. Relevant information regarding its effect on the taxation charge should be shown in a note to the profit and loss account. If there are other exceptional items in the financial period, and the tax effect differs between them, further information should be given, where practicable, to assist users in assessing the impact of the different items on the net profit or loss attributable to shareholders.

(ii) Closure costs of a factory
FRS 3 requires that material profits or losses on the termination of an operation should be treated as exceptional and shown separately on the face of the profit and loss account after operating profit and before interest, and included under the appropriate heading of continuing or discontinued operations. In calculating the profit or loss in respect of the termination, consideration should only be given to revenue and costs directly related to it. Clearly, the costs have been identified and are known and there is a loss on the termination. It should not have been deducted from reserves; it must go through the profit and loss account.

(iii) Change of basis of depreciation: £258,000
There should only be a change in the basis of depreciation if it brings about a fairer presentation of the accounting results and financial position of the company – see SSAP 12. This SSAP also requires that the depreciation should be shown as normal expenses, rather than as a prior period adjustment.
Because the item is a material one, and makes comparison difficult, a note as to the details should be appended to the accounts.

(iv) Additional expenses covered by fire: £350,000
These expenses are covered by SSAP 17 as post-balance sheet non-adjusting events. The fire happened after the balance sheet date, and therefore did not affect conditions as at that date. The figures in this year's accounts should not therefore be altered.
If the event was such as to call into question the continuation of the business, then there should be a note to the accounts on the going-concern basis. In this particular instance this does not seem to be the case, but good practice, although not necessary, would be to give details of the event in notes to the accounts.

(v) Bad debt: £125,000
The accounts have not yet been approved by the directors, and it does affect the valuation of assets at the year end. SSAP 17 would treat it as a post-balance sheet adjusting event. It should therefore be written off as a bad debt.
Where it is considered to be a material and unusual event, there should also be a note attached to the accounts.

Should you like to have further discussions concerning any of the points raised, will you please contact me. I hope that you will find my comments to be of use.

Yours faithfully,

CACA

11.1

(i) (For internal use)

Rogers plc
Trading and Profit and Loss Account for the year ended 31 December 20X2

	£	£
Sales		288,000
Less Returns inwards		11,500
		276,500
Less Cost of sales:		
Stock 1 January 20X2		57,500
Add Purchases	164,000	
Less Returns outwards	2,000	162,000
Carriage inwards		1,300
		220,800
Less Stock 31 December 20X2		64,000
		156,800
Gross profit		119,700

Distribution costs:	£	£
Salaries and wages	2,800	
Rent and rates	3,750	
General distribution expenses	4,860	
Motor expenses	3,600	
Depreciation: Motors	6,500	
Equipment	700	22,210
Administrative expenses:		
Salaries and wages	5,600	
Rent and rates	2,500	
General administrative expenses	3,320	
Motor expenses	3,600	
Auditors' remuneration	500	
Discounts allowed	3,940	
Bad debts	570	
Depreciation: Motors	3,500	
Equipment	1,100	24,630

	£	£
		46,840
		72,860
Other operating income: Royalties receivable		1,800
		74,660
Income from shares in undertakings in which the company has a participating interest	660	
Interest on bank deposit	770	1,430
		76,090
Interest payable: Debenture interest		2,400
Profit on ordinary activities before taxation		73,690
Tax on profit on ordinary activities		30,700
Profit on ordinary activities after taxation		42,990
Retained profits from last year		15,300
		58,290
Transfer to general reserve	8,000	
Proposed ordinary dividend	30,000	38,000
Retained profits carried forward to next year		20,290

(ii) (Published accounts)

Rogers plc
Profit and Loss Account for the year ended 31 December 20X2

	£	£
Turnover		276,500
Cost of sales		156,800
Gross profit		119,700
Distribution costs	22,210	
Administrative expenses	24,630	46,840
		72,860
Other operating income		1,800
		74,660
Income from shares in undertakings in which the company has a participating interest	660	
Other interest receivable	770	1,430
		76,090
Interest payable		2,400
Profit on ordinary activities before taxation		73,690
Tax on profit on ordinary activities		30,700
Profit for the year on ordinary activities after taxation		42,990
Transfer to general reserve	8,000	
Proposed ordinary dividend	30,000	38,000
Retained profits for the year		4,990

Notes to accounts on debenture interest.

11.2

(i) (For internal use)

Federal plc
Trading and Profit and Loss Account for the year ended 31 December 20X4

	£	£
Sales		849,000
Less Returns inwards		5,800
		843,200
Less Cost of sales:		
Stock 1 January 20X4		64,500
Add Purchases	510,600	
Less Returns outwards	3,300	507,300
Carriage inwards		4,900
		576,700
Less Stock 31 December 20X4		82,800
Cost of goods sold		493,900
Wages		11,350
Depreciation of plant and machinery		1,500
		506,750
Gross profit		336,450

Distribution costs	£	£
Salaries and wages	29,110	
Rent and rates	20,000	
Motor expenses	10,400	
General distribution expenses	8,220	
Haulage costs	2,070	
Depreciation: Motors	15,000	
Plant and machinery	8,000	92,800

11.3

(a)

Rufford plc
Profit and Loss Account for the year ended 31 March 20X6

	Notes	£000	£000
	(1)		
Turnover			642
Cost of sales (60 + 401 – 71)			390
Gross profit			252
Distribution costs (33 + 19)		52	
Administrative expenses (97 + 8)		105	
			157
Operating profit – continuing operations			95
Loss on disposal of discontinued operations	(2)		12
	(3)		83
Income from other fixed asset investments	(4)	14	
Other interest receivable		25	
			39
			122
Interest payable	(5)		6
Profit on ordinary activities before taxation			116
Tax on profit on ordinary activities	(6)		44
Profit for the year on ordinary activities after taxation			72
Dividends (21 + 42)	(7)		63
Retained profits for the period			9

Notes to the accounts:

1 Turnover is net of VAT.

2 Operating profit is shown after charging the following:

	£000	£000
Depreciation: distribution costs	19	
administrative expenses	8	
		27
Auditor's remuneration		20
Directors' emoluments		45
Hire of plant		12

3 Factory closure expenses.

4 Income from fixed asset investment is in respect of a listed company.

5 Interest payable is on a bank overdraft, repayable within 5 years.

6 Tax on profit on ordinary activities:

	£000	£000
Corporation tax at 50% on profits	38	
Transfer to deferred taxation	9	
Overprovision in 20X5	(3)	
		44

7 Dividends:

	£000
Interim 5p per share	21
Final: proposed 10p per share	42
	63

8 Earnings per share:
EPS of 17.1p per share based on earnings of £72,000 and on average 420,000 shares on issue throughout the year (see FRS 3 amendment).

(i) Federal plc (workings)

Administrative expenses

	£	£
Salaries and wages	20,920	
Rent and rates	5,000	
Motor expenses	5,200	
General administrative expenses	2,190	
Bad debts	840	
Discounts allowed	5,780	
Auditors' remuneration	2,000	
Directors' remuneration	5,000	
Depreciation: Motors	7,000	
Plant and machinery	5,000	
	58,930	
Less Discounts received	6,800	
		52,130

	£	£
Distribution costs and administrative expenses		144,930
		191,520
Income from shares in undertakings in which the company has a participating interest	3,500	
Interest from government securities	1,600	
		5,100
		196,620
Amount written off investment in related companies	14,000	
Debenture interest	3,800	
		17,800
Profit on ordinary activities before taxation		178,820
Tax on profit on ordinary activities		74,000
Profit on ordinary activities after taxation		104,820
Retained profits from last year		37,470
		142,290
Transfer to debenture redemption reserve	20,000	
Proposed ordinary dividend	50,000	
		70,000
Retained profits for the year		72,290

(ii) (Published accounts) Federal plc
Profit and Loss Account for the year ended 31 December 20X4

	£	£
Turnover		843,200
Cost of sales		506,750
Gross profit		336,450
Distribution costs	92,800	
Administrative expenses	52,130	
		144,930
		191,520
Income from shares in undertakings in which the company has a participating interest	3,500	
Other interest receivable	1,600	
		5,100
		196,620
Amounts written off investments	14,000	
Interest payable	3,800	
		17,800
Profit on ordinary activities before taxation		178,820
Tax on profit on ordinary activities		74,000
Profit on ordinary activities after taxation		104,820
Transfer to reserves	20,000	
Proposed ordinary dividend	50,000	
		70,000
Retained profits for the year		34,820

(b)

Balance Sheet extracts as at 31 March 20X6

	£000	£000
Creditors: amounts falling due within one year		
Other creditors including taxation and social security (W1)		77
Provisions for liabilities and charges		
Taxation, including deferred taxation (W2)		33

Workings:

	£000
(W1) Corporation tax for year to 31 March 20X6	35
Proposed dividend	42
	77
(W2) Deferred tax as given	24
Transferred from profit and loss	9
	33

Capital and reserves		
Called-up share capital		75,000
Share premium account		20,000
Other reserves:		
Capital redemption reserve	5,000	
General reserve	4,000	9,000
Profit and loss account		8,400
		112,400

Notes:

(i) Called-up share capital consists of:

50,000 £1 ordinary shares	50,000
50,000 preference shares of 50p each	25,000
	75,000

(ii) Land and buildings:

Cost		48,000
Depreciation to 31 December 20X0	12,000	
Depreciation for year to 31 December 20X1	4,000	16,000
		32,000

(iii) Plant and machinery:

Cost		12,500
Depreciation to 31 December 20X0	3,600	
Depreciation for year to 31 December 20X1	1,800	5,400
		7,100

12.1

Owen Ltd

Balance Sheet as at 31 December 20X1

	£000	£000
Called-up share capital net paid		150
Fixed assets		
Intangible assets		
Development costs	3,070	
Goodwill	21,000	24,070
Tangible assets		
Land and buildings	32,000	
Plant and machinery	7,100	39,100
Investments		
Shares in undertakings in which the company has a participating interest		35,750
		98,920
Current assets		
Stock		
Raw materials and consumables	3,470	
Finished goods and goods for resale	18,590	22,060
Debtors		
Trade debtors	17,400	
Amounts owed by undertakings in which the company has a participating interest	3,000	
Prepayments	1,250	21,650
		43,710
Creditors: amounts falling due within one year		
Debentures	6,000	
Bank overdrafts	4,370	
Trade creditors	12,410	
Bills of exchange payable	1,600	24,380
Net current assets		19,330
Total assets less current liabilities		118,400
Creditors: amounts falling due after one year		
Debentures	4,000	
Bills of exchange payable	2,000	6,000
		112,400

12.2

Belle Works plc

Balance Sheet as at 30 September 20X4

	£000	£000
Fixed assets		
Intangible assets		
Concessions, patents, licences, trade marks and similar rights and assets	1,500	
Goodwill	17,500	19,000
Tangible assets		
Land and buildings	72,500	
Plant and machinery	19,400	91,900
		110,900
Current assets		
Stock		
Raw materials and consumables	14,320	
Work in progress	5,640	
Finished goods and goods for resale	13,290	33,250
Debtors		
Trade debtors	11,260	
Other debtors	1,050	
Prepayments and accrued income	505	12,815
		46,065

Creditors: amounts falling due within one year

	£000	£000
Debenture loans	6,000	
Bank loans and overdrafts	3,893	
Trade creditors	11,340	
Bills of exchange payable	4,000	
Other creditors including taxation and social security	14,675	
		39,908
Net current assets		6,157
Total assets less current liabilities		117,057

Creditors: amounts falling due after more than one year

	£000	£000	£000
Debenture loans		12,000	
Trade creditors		1,260	13,260
Provisions for liabilities and charges			
Pensions and similar obligations		1,860	
Taxation, including deferred taxation		640	2,500
			15,760
			101,297

Capital and reserves

	£000	£000
Called-up share capital		70,000
Share premium account		5,000
Revaluation reserve		10,500
Other reserves		
General reserve	6,000	
Foreign exchange reserve	3,500	9,500
Profit and loss account		6,297
		101,297

Notes appended to the accounts on the details of tangible assets and depreciation, also exact details of items lumped under group descriptions.

12.3 Baganza plc

Profit and Loss Account for the year ended 30 September 20X7 (£000)

	£000	£000
Turnover		19,500
Cost of sales (W1)		14,700
Gross profit		4,800
Distribution costs	600	
Administrative expenses (W2)	1,390	1,990
		2,810
Other operating income (W3)		249
Profit on ordinary activities before taxation		3,059
Tax on profit on ordinary activities (W4)		870
Profit on ordinary activities after taxation		2,189
Extraordinary item		1,500
Profit for the financial year		3,689
Dividends (W5)		756
Retained profits for the year		2,933
Earnings per share (W6)		182.4p

Workings (in £000):

(W1) Opening stock 2,300 + Purchases 16,000 − Closing stock 3,600 = 14,700
(W2) Per trial balance 400 + Research 75 + Depreciation: Property (5% × 2,700) 135 + Plant (15% × 5,200) 780 = 1,390
(W3) Dividends received 249
(W4) Corporation tax 850 + Deferred tax 40 − Overpayment last year 20 = 870
(W5) Dividends: Interim 36 + Final 720 = 756
(W6) EPS = Profit 3,689,000 ÷ Shares 1,200,000 = 307.4p

Baganza plc

Balance Sheet as at 30 September 20X7

	£000	£000	£000
Fixed assets			
Tangible assets			
Land and buildings	2,305		
Plant and machinery	820	3,125	
Investments		2,000	5,125
Current assets			
Stocks		3,600	
Debtors		2,700	
Cash at bank		60	6,360
Creditors: amounts falling due within one year			
Trade creditors		2,900	
Corporation tax (850 + 360)		1,210	
Proposed dividend		720	4,830
Net current assets			1,530
Total assets less current liabilities			6,655
Taxation, including deferred taxation (460 + 40)			500
			6,155
Capital and reserves			
Called-up share capital			1,200
Profit and loss account (2,022 + 2,933)			4,955
			6,155

13.1

X Limited
Balance Sheet at 31 March 20X7

	Notes	£000	£000	£000
Fixed assets				
Intangible assets				
Development costs	(1)	35		
Tangible assets	(2)			
Freehold properties		1,040		
Plant and machinery		850		
Vehicles		285		
		2,175		
				2,410
Investments				
Investments in listed shares	(3)	200		
Current assets				
Stock	(4)	500		
Debtors and prepayments (see workings)		654		
Cash at bank		439	1,593	
Creditors: amounts falling due within 1 year				
Trade creditors and accrual		878		
Other creditors (see workings)		550	1,428	
Net current assets				165
Total assets less current liabilities				2,575
Creditors: amounts falling due after more than 1 year				
12% debentures 20X6			500	
Provisions for liabilities and charges				
Deferred taxation	(5)		128	628
				1,947
Capital and reserves				
Called-up share capital	(6)			1,000
Share premium				150
Revaluation reserve				612
Profit and loss account (see workings)	(7)			185
				1,947

Workings:

	£000
Profit and loss	356
Less Bad debt (225,000 × 76%)	171
	185
Debtors	825
Less Bad debt (225,000 × 76%)	171
	654
Other creditors: Proposed dividend	280
Corporation tax	270
	550

Notes to the balance sheet

1 Research and development
Research costs are written off immediately. Development costs are carried forward when there is a reasonable certainty of profitable outcome of the project and amortised over the useful life of the project.

2 Tangible assets

	Freehold property £000	Plant and machinery £000	Vehicles £000
Cost on 1 April 20X6*	800	1,500	220
Disposal at cost	(320)		
Addition			200
Revaluation adjustment	612		
On 31 March 20X7	1,092	1,500	420
Depreciation at 1 April 20X6*	80	500	55
Depreciation on disposals	(40)		
Provision in year	12	150	80
	52	650	135
Net book values	1,040	850	285

Exam note only: Found by working backwards, leaving these figures as difference.

Note: Freehold property was valued by Messrs V & Co, Chartered Surveyors, at a market value of £1,040,000 as compared with net book value of £428,000. The valuation figure has been included in balance sheet, and £612,000 has been credited to a revaluation reserve. Depreciation for 20X7 has been based on the revalued figure.

3 Investments
These had a market value of £180,000 on 31 March 20X7, but as this is not considered by the directors to be a permanent fall in value, the cost figure has been retained.

4 Stock

	£000
Finished goods	250
Raw materials	200
Work in progress	50
	500

The current replacement cost of goods is £342,000.

5 Deferred taxation

	£000
Provision as at 1 April 20X6	78
Add Provision during year	50
	128
Less ACT recoverable	70
	58

6 Share capital
1,000,000 ordinary shares of £1 each is the authorised capital, which has been fully issued and called up.

7 Reserves

	Profit and loss account	Share premium	Revaluation reserve
Balance at 1 April 20X6	?	150	–
Change during the year			612
	215	150	612

13.2

Billinge plc
Profit and Loss Account for the year to 30 June 20X6

	Notes	£000	£000
Turnover – continuing operations			1,500
Cost of sales (W1)			825
Gross profit			675
Distribution costs		55	
Administrative expenses (W2)	(2)	320	375
			300
Loss on disposal of discontinued operations	(3)		30
			270
Tax on profit on ordinary activities	(4)		130
Profit from ordinary activities after taxation			140
Dividends paid and proposed	(5)		100
Retained profits for the year			40
Earnings per share	(6)		28.0p

Billinge plc
Balance Sheet as at 30 June 20X6

	Notes	£000	£000
Fixed assets			
Tangible assets	(7)		187
Current assets			
Stocks: Finished goods and goods for resale		100	
Debtors		500	
Cash at bank		157	
		757	
Creditors: amounts falling due within one year			
Trade creditors		64	
Other creditors, taxation and social security (W4)		100	
Proposed dividend		100	
		264	
Net current assets			493
Total assets less current liabilities			680
Provisions for liabilities and charges			
Taxation including deferred taxation	(8)		100
			580
Capital and reserves			
Called-up share capital	(9)		500
Profit and loss account (40 + 40)			80
			580

Workings:

(W1)			
Opening stock		70	
Purchases		855	
		925	
Less Closing stock		100	
			825

(W2)			
Depreciation		340	
Less disposals		20	
		320	
Additions		60	
			380

	£000	£000
20% × 380		76
Loss on disposals	20	
Less Depreciation	(15)	
Less Cash	(3)	2
		78
Administrative expenses		242
		320

(W3)		£000	£000
C/T for year		100	
Deferred taxation		40	140
Less Previous overprovision			10
			130

(W4)		£000
Other creditors, taxation and social security:		
Corporation tax		100

Notes to the accounts:

1 Accounting policies
(a) The financial statements have been drawn up using the historical cost convention.
(b) Turnover consists of sales to external customers less VAT.
(c) Stocks are valued at lower of cost or net realisable value.
(d) Depreciation of fixed assets is based on cost, using the straight-line method over 5 years, salvage values being ignored.
(e) Deferred taxation is at the anticipated rate, taking into account the differing periods and the probability that a liability will occur.

2 Administrative expenses include depreciation £78,000.

3 Exceptional charges have arisen of £30,000 on the closure of a factory.

4 Taxation

	£000	£000
Corporation tax at 35% on profit for the period	100	
Deferred taxation	40	140
Less Adjustment re last year's corporation tax		10
		130

5 Proposed ordinary dividend of 20p per share.

6 EPS calculated by dividing profit after taxation by number of ordinary shares on issue during the period.

7 Tangible fixed assets:

	£000	£000	£000
Fixtures etc. at 1.7.20X5		340	
Additions		60	
		400	
Less Disposals		20	
		380	
Depreciation at 1.7.20X5	132		
For the period	76		
	208		
Less Disposals	15	193	
		187	

8

	£000
Deferred taxation at 1.7.20X5	60
Profit and loss charge	40
	100

9 Authorised, issued × fully paid ordinary £1 shares — 500

13.6

Scampion plc
Profit and Loss Account for the year ended 31 May 20X2

	£000	£000
Turnover (3,489 – VAT 259)		3,232
Cost of sales (1,929 + 330 + 51)		2,310
Gross profit		922
Administrative expenses (595 + 25 + 45)		665
Operating profit		257
Income from shares in related companies	5	
Other interest receivable (Note 2)	10	15
		272
Interest payable (Note 3)	18	
Written off investments (Note 7)	4	22
Profit on ordinary activities before taxation		250
Tax on profit on ordinary activities (Note 4)		100
Profit on ordinary activities after taxation		150
Proposed ordinary dividend		66
Retained profits for the year		84
Earnings per share (Note 5)		22.73p

Scampion plc
Balance Sheet as at 31 May 20X2

	£000	£000	£000
Fixed assets			
Tangible assets (Note 6)		1,372	
Investments (Note 7)		60	
			1,432
Current assets			
Stock	230		
Debtors (67 – 45)	22		
Investments (market value £115,000)	103		
Cash at bank and in hand	84		
	439		
Creditors: amounts falling due within one year (Note 8)	553		
Net current liabilities		(114)	
		1,318	
Total assets *less* current liabilities		1,318	
Creditors: amounts falling due after more than one year (Note 9)		50	
		1,268	
Capital and reserves			
Called-up share capital		660	
Share premium account		225	
Profit and loss account (Note 10)		383	
		1,268	

Notes:

1 Accounting policies
The historical cost convention has been used.
Provisions for depreciation are to write off the cost or valuation over the expected useful lives of the assets, by equal instalments, as follows:

Freehold buildings	40 years
Fixtures, fittings or equipment	10 years
Motor vehicles	5 years

Depreciation provisions have not been made on freehold land. The basis of the valuation of stock is the lower of cost or net realisable value.

2 Other interest receivable
This is income from government securities £10,000.

3 Interest payable

Interest on loans repayable within 1 year	12,000
Interest on loans repayable in more than 5 years' time	6,000
	£18,000

4 Taxation
(It has been assumed that 'tax charge based on the accounts for the year' means that the profit shown of £250 is same as the taxable profits.)
Corporation tax at the rate of 40 per cent on profits has been provided for.

5 Earnings per share $= \dfrac{150}{660} = 22.73\text{p}$

6 Tangible assets (£000)

	Valuation or cost at 31.5.X6	Additions at cost	Less disposals	Depreciation to: 31.5.X6	31.5.X7	Net
Freehold land and buildings	1,562	50	400	29	5	1,178
Fittings, fixtures and equipment	141	40		38	18	125
Motor vehicles	117	20		40	28	69
	1,820	110	400	107	51	1,372

7 Investments

Valuation by directors of shares in related companies	64,000
Less Written off during the year	4,000
	60,000

8 Creditors

Trade creditors (487,000 – Tax 120,000)	367,000
Corporation tax	100,000
Proposed dividend	66,000
Bank loan	20,000
	553,000

9 Creditors – amounts falling due after more than one year £50,000 12% debentures repayable in X years' time.

10 Reserves

	Revaluation	Profit and loss
Balance 31.5.20X6	150	149
Transfer to profit and loss	(150)	150
Retained profits for year to 31.5.X7	–	84
	=	383

14.1
See text of Chapter 14, Section 14.2.

14.3 Cash Flow Statement (using the direct method) for Lee Ltd for the year ended 31 December 20X4

Operating activities
Cash received from customers 6,550
Cash paid to suppliers (2,875)
Cash paid to employees (2,025)
Other cash payments (600)
Net cash inflow from operating activities 1,050
Dividends from joint ventures and associates –
Returns on investment and servicing of finance
Interest paid (100)
Taxation –
Capital expenditure and financial investment
Payments to acquire tangible assets (700)
Acquisitions and disposals –
Equity dividend paid (50)
Management of liquid resources –
Financing
Repurchase of debentures (100)
Increase in cash in the period 100

Notes to the cash flow statement:
1 Reconciliation of operating profit to net cash inflow from operating activities:
Operating profit 400
Depreciation charges 500
Decrease in stocks 100
Decrease in debtors 50
Net cash inflow from operating activities 1,050

Working:
Operating profit = profit for the year (300) + interest (100) = 400

14.5
See text of Chapter 14, Section 14.2.

14.6 Nimmo Limited
Cash Flow Statement (using the indirect method) for the year ended 31 December 20X9 (£000)

Net cash inflow from operating activities 2,150
Dividends from joint ventures and associates –
Returns on investments and servicing of finance
Taxation (3,200)
Capital expenditure and financial investment
Purchase of fixed assets (11,800)
Sale of fixed assets 1,000
Net cash outflow for capital expenditure (10,800)
Acquisitions and disposals –
Equity dividend paid (5,100)
Management of liquid resources –
Financing
Issue of debenture stock 150
Decrease in cash in the period (16,800)

Note to the cash flow statement:
1 Reconciliation of operating profit to net cash inflow from operating activities:
Operating profit 20,400
Depreciation charges 5,050
Loss on sale of fixed assets 700
Increase in stocks (10,000)
Increase in trade debtors (18,100)
Increase in prepayments (100)
Increase in trade creditors 4,000
Increase in accruals 200
Net cash inflow from operating activities 2,150

Working:
Loss on sale of fixed assets = 1,000 − (5,500 − 3,800) = (700)

14.7

Track Limited
Cash Flow Statement (using the indirect method) for the year ended 30 June 20X1 (£000)

	£000
Net cash outflow from operating activities	(75)
Dividends from joint ventures and associates	–
Returns on investments and servicing of finance	–
Taxation	(230)
Capital expenditure and financial investment	
Purchase of fixed assets	(175)
Sale of investments	150
Sale of fixed assets	20
Net cash outflow for capital expenditure	(5)
Acquisitions and disposals	–
Equity dividend paid	(150)
Management of liquid resources	–
Financing	
Issue of share capital	300
Net cash outflow for period	(160)

Note to the cash flow statement:
1 Reconciliation of operating profit to net cash inflow from operating activities:

	£000
Operating profit	180
Depreciation charges	110
Profit on sale of fixed assets	(5)
Increase in stocks	(300)
Increase in trade debtors	(200)
Increase in trade creditors	140
Net cash inflow from operating activities	(75)

Workings:
Profit before tax: 670 – 530 = retained loss of 140 + tax (190) + dividends (130) = 180
Profit on sale of fixed assets = 20 – (25 – 10) = (5)

14.10

Baker Limited

(a) *Forecast net cash position for the three quarters ended 30 Sept 20X7*

	31 March 20X7 £000	Quarter to 30 June 20X7 £000	30 Sept 20X7 £000
Receipts			
Trade debtors (W1)	235	290	345
Tangible fixed assets	12	–	–
Investments	10	–	–
Debentures	–	–	50
	257	290	395
Payments			
Trade creditors (W2)	150	230	285
Administration, selling and distribution expenses	37	40	42
Tangible fixed assets	–	240	5
Investments	–	–	–
Taxation	8	–	–
Dividend	15	–	–
	210	510	332
Forecast net cash flow	47	(220)	63
Add Opening cash	80	127	(93)
Forecast closing cash	127	(93)	(30)

(b)

Baker Limited
Forecast cash flow statement (using the direct method) for the nine months ended 30 September 20X7 (£000)

	£000
Operating activities	
Cash received from customers (W1)	870
Cash paid to creditors (W2)	(665)
Other cash payments (admin, selling and distrib.)	(119)
Net cash outflow from operating activities	86
Dividends from joint ventures and associates	–
Returns on investments and servicing of finance	–
Taxation	(8)
Capital expenditure and financial investment	
Purchase of fixed assets	(240)
Sale of fixed assets	12
Net cash outflow for capital expenditure	(228)
Acquisitions and disposals	–
Equity dividend paid	(15)
Management of liquid resources	
Addition to 90 day deposit	(5)
Realisation of 90 day deposit	10
Net cash inflow from management of liquid resources	5
Financing	
Issue of debentures	50
Net cash outflow for period	(110)

Note to the cash flow statement:
1 Reconciliation of operating profit to net cash inflow from operating activities:

	£000
Operating profit	34
Depreciation charges	27
Increase in stocks	(15)
Increase in trade debtors	(30)
Increase in trade creditors	70
Net cash outflow from operating activities	86

Workings:

W1 Trade debtors: forecast cash receivable:

	31 March 20X7 £000	30 June 20X7 £000	30 Sept 20X7 £000
Sales	250	300	350
Less Closing trade debtors	65	75	80
	185	225	270
Add Opening trade debtors	50	65	75
Forecast cash receipts from trade debtors	235	290	345

W2 Trade creditors: forecast cash payable

	31 March 20X7 £000	30 June 20X7 £000	30 Sept 20X7 £000
Opening stock	40	30	40
Purchases (by deduction)	190	250	295
	230	280	335
Less Closing stock	30	40	55
Cost of sales	200	240	280
Purchases (as above)	190	250	295
Less Closing trade creditors	120	140	150
	70	110	145
Add Opening trade creditors	80	120	140
Forecast cash payments to trade creditors	150	230	285

15.1

Contract

Year 1:
Plant	16,250	Work certified	58,000
Materials	25,490	Plant c/d	10,250
Wages	28,384	Stock and work in progress c/d	12,200
Direct expenses	2,126		
Gross profit to profit and loss	8,200		
	80,450		80,450

Year 2:
Plant b/d	10,250	Work certified	116,000
Stock and w-in-p b/d	12,200	Sale of plant	4,100
Materials	33,226		
Wages	45,432		
Direct expenses	2,902		
Penalty	700		
Gross profit to profit and loss	15,390		
	120,100		120,100

Workings:

Computation profit of Year 1:

Contract price		174,000
Less Actual expenditure		
25,490 + 28,384 + 2,126		
Estimated cost of plant (16,250 − 4,250)	56,000	
Estimated expenses Year 2	12,000	
		81,400
Estimated total contract profit: estimate made		
at end of year 1		24,600

Using formula given by question:

$$\frac{\text{Work certified}}{\text{Total contract price}} \times \text{Total estimated profit} = \text{Profit for Year 1}$$

$$= \frac{52,200 + 5,800}{174,000} \times 24,600 = 8,200$$

15.2

Stannard and Sykes Ltd
Pier Contract Account
Contract for Seafront Development Corporation valued at £300,000

Materials: direct	58,966	Materials on site c/d	11,660
from store	10,180	69,146	Work in progress c/d	151,167
Wages		41,260		
Hire of plant		21,030		
Direct expenditure		3,065		
Overheads		8,330		
Wages accrued c/d		2,826		
		145,657		
Profit and loss account				
(proportion of profit				
to date)		17,170		
		162,827		162,827
Materials on site b/d		11,660	Wages accrued b/d	2,826
Work in progress b/d		151,167		

A suggested method for prudently estimating the amount of profit to be taken to
November 30 is:

$$\frac{2}{3} \times \frac{\text{Cash received}}{\text{Value of work certified}} \times \frac{\text{Estimated profit (Value of work certified less cost}}{\text{of work certified)}}$$

Total expenditure to date		145,657
Less Materials on site at November 30 20X8	11,660	
Cost of work not yet certified	12,613	24,273
Cost of work certified (*a*)		121,384
Value of work certified (*b*)		150,000
Total profit to date (*b*) − (*a*)		28,616

16.1
See text Section 16.6.

16.2
See text Section 16.8.

16.3
See text Section 16.4.

16.4
See text Section 16.9.

17.1

P & S Consolidated Balance Sheet

Goodwill	10
Stock	140
Bank	50
	200
Share capital	200
	200

17.2

P & S Consolidated Balance Sheet

Fixed assets	3,800
Goodwill: negative goodwill	(300)
Stock	1,500
Debtors	700
Bank	300
	6,000
Share capital	6,000
	6,000

17.3

P & S Consolidated Balance Sheet

Fixed assets	62,000
Stock	27,000
Debtors	8,000
Bank	3,000
	100,000
Share capital	100,000
	100,000

17.6

P & S Consolidated Balance Sheet

Goodwill	300
Fixed assets	2,000
Stock	1,300
Debtors	900
Bank	300
	4,800
Share capital	4,000
Minority interest	800
	4,800

17.7

P & S Consolidated Balance Sheet

Goodwill: negative goodwill	(375)
Fixed assets	3,325
Stock	3,000
Debtors	2,000
Bank	200
	8,150
Share capital	8,000
Minority interest	150
	8,150

17.10

P, S1 & S2 Consolidated Balance Sheet

Goodwill		300
Negative goodwill		(900)
		(600)
Fixed assets		12,600
Current assets		5,900
		17,900
Share capital		10,000
Profit and loss		6,500
Minority interest		1,400
		17,900

17.11

P, S1 & S2 Consolidated Balance Sheet

Goodwill		600
Negative goodwill		(250)
		350
Fixed assets		9,450
Current assets		6,000
		15,800
Share capital		10,000
Profit and loss		2,000
General reserve		1,400
Minority interest		2,400
		15,800

18.1 *P & S Consolidated Balance Sheet as at 31 December 20X6*

Goodwill		950
Fixed assets		10,950
Current assets		3,900
		15,800
Share capital		10,000
Profit and loss (P 4,000 + S 1,800)		5,800
		15,800

18.2 *P & S Consolidated Balance Sheet as at 31 December 20X9*

Goodwill: negative goodwill		(1,790)
Fixed assets		47,400
Current assets		27,100
		72,710
Share capital		50,000
Profit and loss [14,000 – (70% of 400 = 280)]		13,720
General reserve		5,000
Minority interest (3,000 + 600 + 390)		3,990
		72,710

18.4 *P, S1 & S2 Consolidated Balance Sheet as at 31 December 20X5*

Goodwill		1,390
Fixed assets		36,900
Current assets		20,900
		59,190
Share capital		40,000
Profit and loss		8,270
General reserve		5,000
Minority interest		5,920
		59,190

Minority interest 40% of (10,000 + 2,800 + 2,000) = 5,920.

Goodwill S1 cost 8,150 – 60% of 10,000 + 1,100 + 2,000 = 290, S2 cost 11,400 – (8,000 + 500 + 1,800) = 1,100.

Profit and loss P 7,550 + S1 1,020 – S2 300 = 8,270.

19.1 *P & S Consolidated Balance Sheet as at 31 December 20X9*

Goodwill		850
Fixed assets		2,300
Current assets		
Stock (1,200 + 900 – 90)	2,010	
Debtors (2,100 + 1,400 – 220)	3,280	
Bank	500	
	5,790	
Less Current liabilities		
Creditors (900 + 700 – 220)	1,380	
Net current assets		4,410
		7,560

Financed by:

Share capital		2,000
Profit and loss		4,760
(P 3,700 – 90 + S 1,150)		
General reserve		800
		7,560

19.2 *P & S Consolidated Balance Sheet as at 31 December 20X4*

Goodwill		1,600
Fixed assets		14,200
Current assets		
Stock (3,100 + 7,200 – 50)	10,250	
Debtors (4,900 – 600 + 3,800)	8,100	
Bank	2,500	
	20,850	
Less Current liabilities		
Creditors (3,800 + 2,100 – 600)	5,300	
Net current assets		15,550
		31,350

Financed by:

Share capital		20,000
Profit and loss (P 4,000 – 50 + S 60% of 2,000)		5,150
Minority interest (40% of 10,000 + 5,500)		6,200
		31,350

19.3 *P, S1 & S2 Consolidated Balance Sheet as at 31 December 20X8*

Goodwill		3,000
Negative Goodwill		(3,000)
Fixed assets		65,000
Current assets		
Stock (£46,000 – £640)	45,360	
Debtors (£28,000 – £1,400)	26,600	
Bank	9,000	
	80,960	
Less Current liabilities		
Creditors (21,000 – 1,400)	19,600	
Net current assets		61,360
		126,360

Financed by:

Share capital		100,000
Profit and loss account:		
(£23,000 – £400 – £240 – S1 £5,000 + S2 $\frac{5}{6}$ of £1,800)		18,860
General reserve		2,000
Minority interest ($\frac{1}{6}$ of (£30,000 + £3,000))		5,500
		126,360

S1 Negative goodwill: Cost £39,000 – £30,000 – £8,000 – £4,000 = (£3,000).
S2 Goodwill: Cost £29,000 – $\frac{5}{6}$ of (£30,000 + £1,200) = £3,000.
Net goodwill = £3,000 – £3,000 = Nil.

19.6

Pagg Group of Companies
Consolidated Balance Sheet as at 31 March 20X0

			£000
Fixed assets			
Intangible assets (Note 1)			1,898
Tangible assets			3,500
			5,398
Current assets			
Stocks (1,300 + 350 + 100 – 10)		1,740	
Debtors (3,000 + 300 + 200 – 200 – 35)		3,265	
Cash at bank and in hand		270	
		5,275	
Creditors falling due within 1 year			
(270 + 400 + 4,000 – 200 – 35)		4,435	
Net current assets			840
Total assets *less* current liabilities			6,238
Minority interests (Note 2)			500
			5,738
Capital and reserves			
Called-up share capital			5,500
Profit and loss			238
			5,738

Notes:

1 Cost of control

		Ragg		Tagg
Consideration		3,000		1,000
Less Shares	(80%)	800	(60%)	300
Profit and loss	(80% × 600)	480	(60% × 100)	60
Goodwill		1,280		360
		1,720		640
Total amount written off				
to 31.3.20X0	(5 years)	430	(1 year)	32
Amount not yet written off		1,290		608
				1,898

2 Minority interests

	Ragg		Tagg	
Share capital called up	1,000		500	
Profit and loss	200		150	
	1,200		650	
	(20%)	240	(40%)	260
				500

3 Profit and loss:

Pagg	1,000
Ragg 80% of (200 – 600)	(320)
Tagg 60% of (150 – 100)	30
Goodwill (Note 1) 430 + 32	(462)
Intercompany profit on stock ($\frac{1}{6}$ of 60)	(10)
	238

20.1

60% Share capital and reserves 31.12.20X6			56,400
Shares bought 31.12.20X4	10,000	23,500	
Shares bought 31.12.20X6	14,000	31,000	
	24,000		
Negative goodwill		54,500	1,900

20.3

Shares bought		50,000
Profit and loss balance 31.12.20X7	36,000	
Add Proportion 20X8 profits before acquisition		
8/12 × 42,000	28,000	
	64,000	

Proportion of pre-acquisition profit:

$$\frac{50,000}{80,000} \times 64,000 = 40,000$$

	90,000

Paid-for shares 158,000
Therefore goodwill is 158,000 – 90,000 = 68,000.

21.1

P & S Consolidated Balance Sheet as at 31 December 20X7

Goodwill	1,000
Fixed assets	57,000
Current assets	15,000
	73,000
Share capital	50,000
Profit and loss account (H 19,000 + S 4,000)	23,000
	73,000

Workings: Goodwill: Cost 29,000 – 20,000 – 3,000 – Dividend 5,000 = 1,000.

21.3

P & S Consolidated Balance Sheet as at 31 December 20X9

Goodwill	14,000
Fixed assets	80,000
Current assets	33,000
Less Current liabilities	
Proposed dividend	1,500
Net current assets	31,500
	125,500
Share capital	80,000
Profit and loss account: (P 23,000 + S $\frac{3}{4}$ of 6,000 + $\frac{3}{4}$ of 7,000)	32,750
Minority interest ($\frac{1}{4}$ of (40,000 + 11,000))	12,750
	125,500

Workings: Goodwill: Cost 47,000 – $\frac{3}{4}$ of (40,000 + 4,000) = 14,000.

21.5 *Consolidated Balance Sheet of P Ltd & S Ltd as at 31 December 20X6*

Fixed assets

Intangible assets		
Goodwill (*see* Workings)		55,000
Tangible assets (Note 1)		680,000
Current assets		
Stocks	160,000	
Debtors	140,000	
Bank	40,000	
	340,000	
Creditors: amounts falling due within 1 year		
Trade creditors	212,000	
Preference dividend proposed	8,000	
		220,000
Net current assets		120,000
Total assets *less* current liabilities		855,000
Capital and reserves		
Called-up share capital: ordinary shares		
£1 fully paid		500,000
Reserves		185,000
Minority interest		170,000
		855,000

Note 1 Tangible fixed assets

	Cost	Depreciation to date	Net
Buildings	420,000	110,000	310,000
Plant and machinery	320,000	70,000	250,000
Motor vehicles	210,000	90,000	120,000
	950,000	270,000	680,000

Workings:

(*a*) *Goodwill*

Cost of investment		250,000
Less Ordinary shares (75%)	150,000	
Reserves (75%)	37,500	
		187,500
		62,500
Less Dividend from pre-acquisition profits		7,500
		55,000

(*b*) *Minority interest*

Preference shares		100,000
Reserves 25% × 80,000		20,000
Ordinary shares 25%		50,000
		170,000

The proposed preference dividend could be shown as part of the minority interest.

(*c*) *Reserves*

P Ltd		170,000
S Ltd 75% of extra reserves since		
acquisition 80,000 − 50,000 = 30,000		22,500
		192,500
Less Dividends received by P Ltd which		
were from pre-acquisition profits		7,500
		185,000

21.6

Reconciliation of current accounts

	X		Y	
Balance b/d		19	Balance b/d	14
			In transit	
Balance c/d		19	Bank (1)	2
			Stock (2)	3
		19		19

Reserves

X	220
20X6 retained profits	20
Proposed dividend Y 80%	8
80% Y profits for 20X6 × 18	14.4
	262.4
– Profit in goods in transit	0.4
– Profit in Y's stock	2	2.4
	260

Consolidated Balance Sheet for X plc & subsidiary Y plc as at 31 December 20X6

	Cost £000	Depreciation to date £000	Net £000
Goodwill			108
Tangible fixed assets			
Freehold property	280	18	262
Plant and machinery	245	52	193
	525	70	455
Current assets			
Stock (*see* Workings)	212	150.6	
Debtors	44	250	
Bank	20	24	
		424.6	
Less Current liabilities			
Trade creditors (130 + 80 + 2)	212		
Taxation	44		
Proposed dividends	20	276	148.8
			711.6

23.1 P, S1 & S2 Consolidated Balance Sheet as at 31 December 20X7

Goodwill		9,320
Fixed assets		127,000
Current assets		33,000
		169,320
Share capital		100,000
Profit and loss account		
(P 37,000 + S1 90% of 16,000 + S2 63% of 3,000)		53,290
General reserve		10,000
Minority interest		6,030
		169,320

Minority interest

Shares in S1	1,000	
Shares in S2 37% of 5,000	1,850	2,850
Profit and loss S1 10% of 23,000	2,300	
S2 37% of 4,000	1,480	3,780
		6,630
Less Cost of shares in S2 for minority interest		
of S1 10% of 6,000		600
		6,030

Goodwill: Cost of shares to group in S1

in S2 90% of 6,000	23,000	
	5,400	28,400
Less Shares: In S1	9,000	
In S2 63% of 5,000	3,150	
Profit and loss S1 90% of 7,000	6,300	
S2 63% of 1,000	630	19,080
		9,320

23.3 Sales Ltd & subsidiaries
Balance sheet as at 31 October 20X5

Negative goodwill (W8)			(9,000)

Fixed assets	Cost	Depreciation	Net
Buildings	184,000	–	184,000
Plant (W1)	260,000	92,400	167,600
	362,900	203,700	159,200
	806,900	296,100	

Current assets		
Stock (W2)		247,400
Debtors (W3)		275,200
Bank		50,600
		573,200
		510,800

Called-up share capital		
400,000 ordinary shares £1		400
Reserves (see Workings)		260
		660
Minority interest (see Workings)		51.6
		711.6

Workings:

Cost of control (remember to calculate it as on 1.1.X6) £000

Cost of investment		300
Less Nominal value shares bought 80%	120	
Reserves 80% × 90	72	192
		108

Minority interest

20% of reserves at 1.1.X6 × 90	18	
20% of 20X6 retained profit × 18	3.6	
20% of shares × 150	30	51.6
Stock		
X	80	
Y	70	
	3	
In transit	2	153
Less Profit element in Y's stock	0.4	
Profit element in Y's goods in transit		2.4
Bank		
X 10 + Y 12 + in transit 2		24

22.1 P & S Consolidated Balance Sheet as at 31 December 20X8

Goodwill		100,000
Fixed assets	500,000	
Less Depreciation	138,000	362,000
Current assets		205,000
		667,000
Share capital		500,000
Profit and loss account:		
(P 143,000 – 10,000 + S 32,000 + 2,000)		167,000
		667,000

22.3 P & S Consolidated Balance Sheet as at 31 December 20X7

Goodwill		19,000
Fixed assets	185,000	
Less Depreciation	33,500	151,500
Current assets		68,000
		238,500
Share capital		150,000
Profit and loss (P 77,000 + S 14,000 – 2,500)		88,500
		238,500

Less Current liabilities

Creditors (W4)	297,400	
Bank overdraft (W5)	26,100	
Corporation tax	129,100	
Proposed dividends	80,000	
Proposed dividends relating to minority interests (W6)	16,000	(548,600)
Net current assets		24,600
		526,400
Ordinary share capital		200,000
Revenue reserves (W7)		189,390
		389,390
Minority interest (W9)		137,010
		526,400

Workings:

Note: S Ltd owns 75% of M Ltd & 75% × 80% = 60% of C Ltd

Plant 102,900 + 170,000 + 92,000 =

(W1) *Less* (Note (g)) intercompany profit	364,900	
	2,000	
	362,900	
Depreciation 69,900 + 86,000 + 48,200 =	204,100	
Less 2 years on intercompany profit element 10% × 2,000 × 2	400	
	203,700	

(W2) Stock 108,500 + 75,500 + 68,400	252,400	
– Unrealised profit (Note (f)) 20% × 25,000	5,000	
	247,400	

(W3) Debtors 196,700 + 124,800 + 83,500			405,000
– Inter-indebtedness (Note (b))		56,900	
(Note (b))		28,900	
– Dividends: 80% of 10,000		8,000	
75% of 48,000		36,000	129,800
			275,200

(W4) Creditors 160,000 + 152,700 + 59,200		371,900
– Inter-indebtedness (Note (b))	28,900	
	45,600	74,500
		297,400

(W5) Overdraft	37,400	
– cheque in transit (Note (i))	11,300	
	26,100	

(W6) Minority interests: Shares of proposed dividends		
Components Ltd: Ordinary 20% × 10,000		2,000
Preference		2,000
Machinery Ltd: Ordinary 25% × 48,000		12,000
		16,000

(W7) Reserves S Ltd	154,000		
M Ltd	85,000		
C Ltd	74,000	313,000	
Add Reduction in depreciation of components 2,000 × 10% × 2 years = 400 × 60% ownership of components		240	
		313,240	
Less Profit on machinery	2,000		
Unrealised profit on stock	5,000		
Cost of control of C Ltd on 1.4.X3 60% × 60,000	36,000		
Minority interest in C Ltd 40% × 74,000	29,600		
Cost of control of M Ltd on 1.4.X3 75% × 40,000	30,000		
Minority interest in M Ltd 25% × 85,000	21,250	123,850	
		189,390	

(W8) Cost of control

C Ltd at date of purchase. Capital:		
Ordinary shares	100,000	
Reserves	60,000	
	160,000	
M Ltd had owned 80% =		
Then had paid	128,000	
Bringing about negative goodwill	96,000	
Of this 25% is owned by minority interest of M Ltd	32,000	
M Ltd at date of purchase: Capital	8,000	24,000
Reserve	120,000	
	40,000	
	160,000	
S Ltd owns 75%	120,000	
S Ltd paid	135,000	
Cost of control	15,000	
Net figure for negative goodwill	9,000	

(W9) Minority interest

		£000
Ordinary shares: 25% M Ltd	30,000	
40% C Ltd	40,000	40,000
Preference shares		
Increase in profit because of depreciation change 40% × 400		160
25% revenue reserves M Ltd × 85,000		21,250
40% revenue reserves C Ltd × 74,000		29,600
		161,010
Less 25% payment made by M Ltd for investment in C Ltd × 96,000		24,000
		137,010

24.1 Brodick plc & subsidiaries

Consolidated Profit and Loss Account for the year ended 30 April 20X7

	£000
Turnover (1,100 + 500 + 130)	1,730
Cost of sales (630 + 300 + 70)	1,000
Gross profit	730
Administrative expenses (105 + 150 + 20)	275
Profit on ordinary activities before taxation	455
Tax on profit on ordinary activities (65 + 10 + 20)	95
Profit on ordinary activities after taxation	360
Minority interests (20% × 40 + 40% × 20)	16
Profit for the financial year	344
Retained profits from last year (W1)	506
	850
Dividends paid and proposed	200
Retained profits carried to next year (Note 1)	650

Note 1

Retained profits carried to next year comprise:

	£000
Brodick plc (see W1)	590
Subsidiaries (see W1)	60
	650

Workings:

(W1) Retained profits b/d

Brodick			
Lamlash		460	
	106		
Less Minority (20%)	(21.2)		
Less Pre-acquisition (80% × 56)	(44.8)		
	30		
Corrie			
Less Minority (40%)	12		
Less Pre-acquisition (60% × 20)	12	24	6
			506
Retained profits for year (344 – 200)			144
			650

24.2 Norbreck plc & its subsidiary Bispham Ltd

Consolidated Profit and Loss Account for the year ended 30 September 20X7

	£000
Turnover	2,150
Cost of sales	995
Gross profit	1,155
Administrative expenses	475
Profit on ordinary activities before taxation	680
Tax on profit on ordinary activities	50
Profit on ordinary activities after taxation	630
Minority interest (20% × 180)	36
Profit for the financial year	594
Retained profits from last year	196
	790
Dividends	360
Retained profits carried to next year	430
Earnings per share (594/900)	66p

Norbreck plc & its subsidiary Bispham Ltd

Consolidated Balance Sheet as at 30 September 20X7

	£000	£000	£000
Goodwill			48
Fixed assets			
Tangible assets			1,720
Current assets			
Stocks	550		
Debtors (280 + 150 – 80 dividend)	350		
Cash and Bank	50		
		950	
Creditors: amounts falling due within one year			
Trade creditors	240		
Other creditors, taxation and social security	230		
Proposed dividends (270 + 20% × 100)	290		
		760	
Net current assets			190
Total assets less current liabilities			1,958
Provisions for liabilities and charges			
Taxation, including deferred taxation			480
			1,478
Capital and reserves			
Called-up share capital			900
Profit and loss account			478
			1,378
Minority interest (20% × £500)			100
			1,478

Workings:

Goodwill

	£000	£000
Investment		400
Nominal value of shares (80% of 400)	320	
Profit and loss (80% of 40)	32	
		352
Goodwill on acquisition		48

Retained profits b/d		£000
Norbreck		220
Bispham	70	
– Pre-acquisition	40	
	30	
	6	
– Minority interest (20%)		24
Retained profits of Group b/d		244
For the year (per consolidated P/L 594 – 360)		234
		478

25.1

(a)

Large Ltd & its subsidiary Small Ltd

Consolidated Profit and Loss Account for the year ended 30 September 20X6

	£000	£000
Turnover (10,830 + 2,000 – 108)		12,722
Cost of sales and production (3,570 + 1,100 – (²⁄₃ of 108))		4,598
		8,124
Administrative and marketing expenses	2,772	
Unpurchased goodwill written off (per Companies Act 1985)	50	
Research costs written off (*see* SSAP 13)	50	
		2,872
Profit on ordinary activities before taxation		5,252
Tax on profit on ordinary activities		2,504
Profit on ordinary activities after taxation		2,748
Minority interests		121
		2,627
Retained profits from last year		1,290
		3,917
Dividend		2,400
Retained profits carried to next year		1,517

(b)

Large Ltd & its subsidiary Small Ltd

Consolidated Balance Sheet as at 30 September 20X6

	£000	£000	£000	£000
Fixed assets				
Intangible assets				
Development costs		180		
Goodwill		48		
Negative goodwill (W1)		(129)		
			99	
Tangible assets				
At cost less depreciation			4,648	
				4,747
Current assets				
Stock (594 + 231 – 27)		798		
Debtors		2,620		
Bank		123		
		3,541		
Creditors: amounts falling due within one year				
Trade creditors		453		
Net current assets			3,088	
				7,835
Capital and reserves				
Called-up share capital				6,000
Profit and loss account				1,517
Minority interest (W2)				318
				7,835

Workings:

(W1) Investment in Small cost		525
Less Share capital	600	
75% Retained earnings of 72	54	
	654	
Negative goodwill on acquisition		129

(W2) Share capital	200
25% Retained earnings of 472	118
	318

(c) In this case merger accounting is not permitted. It can only be used when 90 per cent of the consideration is given as equity share capital, and here Large obtained 75 per cent for cash.

If merger treatment had been used the profits made before the merger could be distributed as dividends.

26.1

If Q plc is unable to exercise significant influence over N Ltd, the group comprises the parent undertaking (Q) and two subsidiaries (L and M). N Ltd should be excluded from consolidation (the grounds would be 'severe long-term restrictions') and treated as a fixed asset investment at cost. However, if Q plc is able to exercise significant influence over N Ltd, it should treat it as an associated undertaking using the equity method.

26.2

(a) There are two acquisition points. Any dividends received from the pre-acquisition (of the first investment) profits should be applied to reduce the initial investment of £80,000. Similar treatment should be applied to the £110,000 investment. The investment should be shown in the P's company balance sheet at cost of £190,000 less any such dividends received (or it could be shown at valuation). Dividends received and receivable should be shown in the profit and loss account after adjustment for any pre-acquisition element.

(b) At the time the investment became 21 per cent, the net assets of the clothing company were £840,000. The company's share of this is £176,400. The premium paid on acquisition, subject to adjustment for pre-acquisition reserves distributed, is £13,600 (£80,000 + £110,000 − £176,400) and, after any such adjustment required, it should either be written off to the reserves, or capitalised and amortised. Disclosure in the company's own financial statements is as for trade investments. The group profit and loss should show the company's share of the publishing company's pre-tax profits/losses and its attributable share of the associated undertaking's tax charge on those profits/losses. The group balance sheet carrying value in respect of this investment will comprise the cost of the investment plus the company's share of post-acquisition retained profits, less any amounts written-off either of these.

27.1

Solvency, profitability, efficiency, capital structure and shareholder.

27.3

Solvency	– see text, Section 27.3
Profitability	– see text, Section 27.2
Efficiency	– see text, Section 27.4
Capital structure	– see text, Section 27.6
Shareholder	– see text, Section 27.5

27.5

See text, Section:

(a) 27.4
(b) 27.6
(c) 27.2
(d) 27.3
(e) 27.5

27.7

(i) (b) and (d).
(ii) (b) and (d).
(iii) (d).
(iv) If current liabilities greater than current assets, (b) and (d); if current assets greater than current liabilities, (a) and (c).
(v) (b) and (d) but only after a customer takes up the offer.

27.9

(a) (i) Gross profit as % of sales: $\dfrac{20,000}{80,000} \times \dfrac{100}{1} = 25\%$ $\dfrac{24,000}{120,000} \times \dfrac{100}{1} = 20\%$

(ii) Net profit as % of sales: $\dfrac{10,000}{80,000} \times \dfrac{100}{1} = 12.5\%$ $\dfrac{15,000}{120,000} \times \dfrac{100}{1} = 12.5\%$

(iii) Expenses as % of sales: $\dfrac{10,000}{80,000} \times \dfrac{100}{1} = 12.5\%$ $\dfrac{9,000}{120,000} \times \dfrac{100}{1} = 7.5\%$

(iv) Stockturn: $\dfrac{60,000}{(25,000 + 15,000) \div 2}$ $\dfrac{96,000}{(22,500 + 17,500) \div 2}$
= 3 times   = 4.8 times

(v) Rate of return: $\dfrac{10,000}{(38,000 + 42,000) \div 2} \times \dfrac{100}{1}$ $\dfrac{15,000}{(36,000 + 44,000) \div 2} \times \dfrac{100}{1}$
= 25   = 37.5%

(vi) Current ratio: $\dfrac{45,000}{5,000} = 9$ $\dfrac{40,000}{10,000} = 4$

(vii) Acid test ratio: $\dfrac{30,000}{5,000} = 6$ $\dfrac{22,500}{10,000} = 2.25$

(viii) Debtor : sales ratio: $\dfrac{25,000}{80,000} \times 12$ $\dfrac{20,000}{120,000} \times 12$
= 3.75 months   = 2 months

(ix) Creditor : purchases ratio: $\dfrac{5,000}{50,000} \times 12$ $\dfrac{10,000}{91,000} \times 12$
= 1.2 months   = 1.3 months

(b) Business B is the most profitable: both in terms of actual net profits £15,000 compared with £10,000, but also, in terms of capital employed, B has managed to achieve a return of £37.50 for every £100 invested, i.e. 37.5 per cent. A has managed a lower return of 25 per cent. Reasons as follows – possibly – as not until you know more about the business could you give a definite answer.

(i) Possibly managed to sell far more merchandise because of lower prices, i.e. took only 20 per cent margin as compared with A's 25 per cent margin.

(ii) Maybe more efficient use of mechanised means in the business. Note that B has more equipment, and perhaps as a consequence kept other expenses down to £6,000 as compared with A's £9,000.

(iii) Did not have as much stock lying idle. Turned over stock 4.8 times in the year as compared with 3 for A.

(iv) A's current ratio of 9 far greater than normally needed. B kept it down to 4. A therefore had too much money lying idle and not doing anything.

(v) Following on from (iv) the acid test ratio for A also higher than necessary.

(b) Current debtor collection period (i.e. debtor days) $= \dfrac{583}{2,800} \times 365 = 76$ days.

If the collection period were 45 days, the new debtors amount would be:

$$\frac{45}{76} \times 583,000 = 345,200$$

The amount released if a 45-day debtors collection period could be imposed would be £237,800.

28.1

(a) *Trading and Profit and Loss Accounts for the year ended 31 December 20X9*

	X		Y	
Sales		480,000		762,500*
Less Cost of goods sold		400,000	(+10,000)	610,000
Gross profit		80,000		152,500
Less Admin. expenses (−10,000)	40,000			
Selling expenses	15,000	55,000	(−2,500)	57,500
				35,000 92,500
Net profit		25,000		60,000

* Assumed 25 per cent mark-up despite wrong stock valuation.

(b) Profitability:

	X	Y
Gross profit %	20%	25%

Net profit % $\dfrac{25}{480} \times \dfrac{100}{1} = 5.2\%$ $\dfrac{60}{762.5} \times \dfrac{100}{1} = 7.87\%$

Stockturn $\dfrac{400,000}{40,000} = 10$ times $\dfrac{610,000}{45,000^*} = 13.6$ times

* Adjusted to take into account inaccurate valuation.

Return on capital employed (ROCE) (previous owners)

X $\dfrac{25,000}{200,000} \times \dfrac{100}{1} = 12.5\%$ Y $\dfrac{60,000}{350,000} \times \dfrac{100}{1} = 17.14\%$

Based on purchase price of business the ROCE for Adrian Frampton would be:

X $\dfrac{25,000}{190,000} \times \dfrac{100}{1} = 13.15\%$ Y $\dfrac{60,000}{400,000} \times \dfrac{100}{1} = 15\%$

All ratios are favourable for Y. If gross profit ratios remained the same in future together with other expenses then Y business is best value.

However:
(i) Can gross profit ratios of X be improved as compared with those of Y?
(ii) Can stockturn be improved?
If so, then X could be cheapest business to buy as it gives a better ROCE.

(vi) Part of the reason for (iv) and (v) is that A waited (on average) 3.75 months to be paid by customers. B managed to collect in 2 months on average. Money represented by debts is money lying idle.

(vii) A also paid creditors more quickly than did B, but not by much.

Put all these factors together, and it is obvious that business B is run far more efficiently, and is more profitable as a consequence.

27.11

(a) The ratios reveal that L Ltd's relative profitability has fallen between the two years. The gross and net profit margins have both fallen, but this may be due to the new sales manager's price-cutting policy, rather than because of any change in costs.

The fall in return on capital employed is not what was hoped for from the new sales price policy. A drop from 31 per cent to 18 per cent is significant and suggests that the change in sales price policy and the investment in new machinery, although with the related increased borrowings, have led to short-term depressed returns. If the increased market resulting from the new sales policy can be retained, it would be worthwhile considering an increase in sales price to a point where a higher rate of return would be achieved.

The company appears solvent – there is no shortage of liquid assets. However, it has taken on considerably more long-term debt in order to fund the market expansion. This will have to be serviced and the level of profit should be monitored to ensure that margins do not fall further, raising the current level of risk to unacceptable levels. As 38.2 per cent (£192,000) of net profits before interest (£502,000) is already being used to meet debt interest payments, compared with only 3.8 per cent in 20X2, it would not take very large changes in costs or selling price to cause this to become a major problem. The current level of gearing will also inhibit the company's ability to raise additional loan funding in future.

Profitability	20X2	20X3
Gross profit : sales	$\dfrac{540}{900} \times 100 = 60\%$	$\dfrac{1,120}{2,800} \times 100 = 40\%$
Net profit : sales	$\dfrac{302}{900} \times 100 = 34\%$	$\dfrac{310}{2,800} \times 100 = 11\%$
ROCE	$\dfrac{302+12}{929+100} = 31\%$	$\dfrac{310+192}{1,267+1,600} = 18\%$

Solvency		
Current ratio	$\dfrac{125}{36} = 3.47 : 1$	$\dfrac{821}{186} = 4.41 : 1$
Acid test ratio	$\dfrac{125-30}{36} = 2.63 : 1$	$\dfrac{821-238}{186} = 3.13 : 1$

Capital structure		
Capital gearing	$\dfrac{100}{100+929} = 10\%$	$\dfrac{1,600}{1,600+1,267} = 56\%$

(c) (i) Need to know current assets and current liabilities in detail.
(ii) Are these similar businesses?
Type of business
Areas in which situated
Competition
Prefer several years' accounts to gauge trends
Quality of staff and whether they would continue.

28.2

(a) 20X4

	A £000	B £000	C £000
Return on capital of 20% = Profit*	120.0	120.0	120.0
Interest less tax		24.0	66.0
		13.2	36.3
		10.8	29.7
Profit for ordinary shares	120.0	109.2	90.3
Ordinary share capital	600	400	50
Profit return (%)	20	27.3	180.6

20X5

	A £000	B £000	C £000
Return on capital of 10% = Profit	60.0	60.0	60.0
Interest less tax		24.0	66.0
		13.2	36.3
		10.8	29.7
Profit for ordinary shares	60.0	49.2	30.3
Ordinary share capital	600	400	50
Profit return (%)	10	12.3	60.6

*Profit is assumed to be after tax but before interest.

(b) High gearing accentuates the rate of return to the ordinary shareholder. In the zero-geared position of Company A the return to the shareholder supply reflects the change in profits earned on trading. In the high-geared position of Company C the return to the shareholder decreases from 180.6 per cent to 60.6 per cent, i.e. to a reduction of 66.5 per cent as profits reduce by only 50 per cent. Company B reflects an intermediate position with a relatively moderate level of gearing.

High gearing increases risk to shareholders for two reasons. First if the profits earned are not sufficiently high to meet interest charges then the company may find itself failing since the lenders may seek a winding up order. Second the risk is increased simply because of exaggerated fluctuations in the returns which are accentuated in the high-geared situation.

However, it can be seen that if profits earned are higher than the interest rate, this will produce a significantly higher return to the shareholder in a high-geared company. The fact that interest is allowed as a deduction for tax purposes indicates that gearing may give an overall advantage. The market's assessment of the risk position will counter this, and will be based on the nature of the business and management.

28.4

(a) Refer to the text.

(b)

	Company A £000	%	Company B £000	%
Ordinary shares	300		800	
Revenue: Share premium	300		400	
Retained profit	400		200	
	1,000	62.5	1,400	87.5
8% preference shares	200		–	
10% loan – debentures			200	
12% loan – debentures	400			
	600	37.5	200	12.5
Total share capital and loan	1,600	100.0	1,600	100.0

Company A Debt : Equity = $\dfrac{37.5}{62.5}$ = 60%

B Debt : Equity = $\dfrac{12.5}{87.5}$ = 14.3%

(c) Company A is more highly geared than B since it is committed to paying a higher proportion of fixed dividend and interest payments for its profits. A higher level of gearing increases risk. (Note the answer in 28.2 (b) is appropriate.)

(d)

	A	B
Trading profit before interest	200,000	200,000
Less Interest charges	48,000	20,000
Net profit after interest charge	152,000	180,000
Preference dividend	16,000	
Ordinary dividend	45,000	120,000
	61,000	120,000
Retained profit	91,000	60,000

28.6

(a)

	20X4	20X5
Equity shares	100,000	150,000
Reserves	150,000	220,000
Total equity capital	250,000	370,000
Loans	40,000	40,000
Total capital employed	290,000	410,000
Profits (net after tax)	60,000	70,000
Return on total equity	24%	18.9%

(b) To Mr C. Black

The reduction in profits from 24 per cent to 18.9 per cent of total equity needs to be analysed into its causal factors. During the year the net profits have increased but not as fast as the equity capital which has gone up by £120,000 over the year. If the increase reflected an investment late in 20X5 it would reduce returns because a full year's profit could not be earned.

It is therefore essential to examine the nature of the investment and the future. Before shares are bought it is essential to examine future prospects. If these are good the historic analysis may not be important. However, if the new funds were used – clearly prospects may not be good and shares should not be bought.

(c) Reserves are profits retained within the business. The profits may be from revenue, i.e. from profits which could be distributed as dividends to shareholders or capital – for example where fixed amounts are revalued upwards to reflect current market value.

The creation of reserves reflects an increase in capital in the organisation which would normally be to reflect an increasing scale of operation. In this sense reserves reflect an alternative to issuing new shares. In the case of capital reserves from revaluation – these are simply 'paper adjustments' to value which do not in themselves indicate more resources in the organisation.

Revenue reserves may in fact be distributed as dividends whereas capital reserves would not normally be available for this purpose and are more akin to share capital.

28.8

(a) Profit and Loss Accounts for the year to 31 March 20X8

	Chan plc £000	Ling plc £000	Wong plc £000
Operating profit	300	300	300
Interest payable	–	–	(10)
	300	300	290
Taxation (30%)	(90)	(90)	(87)
Profit on ordinary activities after tax	210	210	203
Dividends: Preference	–	(20)	(30)
Ordinary	(100)	(60)	(40)
	(100)	(80)	(70)
Retained profit for the year	£110	£130	£133

(b) (i) Earnings per share

$$\frac{\text{Net profit after tax and preference dividend}}{\text{Number of ordinary shares in issue}} =$$

	Chan plc	Ling plc	Wong plc
	$\frac{210}{500}$	$\frac{210-20}{300}$	$\frac{203-30}{200}$
=	42p	63.3p	86.5p

(ii) Price/earnings ratio

$$\frac{\text{Market price of ordinary shares}}{\text{Earnings per share}} =$$

	Chan plc	Ling plc	Wong plc
	$\frac{840}{42}$	$\frac{950}{63.3}$	$\frac{1038}{86.5}$
=	20	15	12

(iii) Gearing ratio

$$\frac{\text{Loan capital} + \text{preference shares} \times 100}{\text{Shareholders' funds}}$$

Chan plc = Nil

Ling plc = $\frac{200}{300+100+130} \times 100 = 37.7\%$

Wong plc = $\frac{300+100}{200+100+133} \times 100 = 92.4\%$

(c) A gearing ratio expresses the relationship that exists between total borrowings (that is, preference share capital and long-term loans), and the total amount of ordinary shareholders' funds. It should be noted that other definitions of gearing are possible and are sometimes used.

Any company with a gearing ratio of, say, 70 per cent would be considered to be high geared, while a company with a gearing ratio of, say, 20 per cent would be low geared.

Gearing is an important matter to consider when investing in ordinary shares in a particular company. A *high-geared* company means that a high proportion of the company's earnings are committed to paying either interest on any debenture stock and/or dividends on any preference share capital *before* an ordinary dividend can be declared. If a company is low geared, then a high proportion of the company's earnings can be paid out as ordinary dividends.

Chan plc has not issued any long-term loans or any preference share capital. Gearing does not, therefore apply to this company, and all of the earnings may be paid out to the ordinary shareholders.

Ling plc is a relatively low-geared company. It has no debenture stock, and only a small proportion of its earnings are committed to paying its preference shareholders. The balance may then all be declared as an ordinary dividend.

Wong plc is an extremely high-geared company. A high proportion of borrowings (in this case consisting of both debenture stock and preference share capital) means that a high proportion of its earnings has to be set aside for both its debenture holders and its preference shareholders before any ordinary dividend can be declared. As a result, if the profits of the company are low, no ordinary dividend may be payable.

If profits are rising, a high-geared company may not be a particularly risky company in which to purchase some ordinary shares, but the reverse may apply if profits are falling.

For the year to 31 March 20X8, Chan, Ling and Wong's operating profit is identical. Wong is committed to paying interest on its debenture stock (which is allowable against tax), and both Ling and Wong have to pay a preference dividend (which is *not* allowable against tax).

In deciding whether to invest in any of the three companies, there are a great many other factors to be considered, including future prospects of all three companies. However, when profits are fluctuating an ordinary shareholder is more likely to receive a higher return by investing in Chan than by investing in either Ling or Wong. Similarly, an ordinary shareholder can expect a higher return by investing in Wong.

Based on the limited amount of information given in the question, therefore, an investor considering purchasing ordinary shares in only one of these three companies would be recommended to buy shares in Chan plc.

It should be noted that if profits were *increasing*, an investor would be recommended to buy shares first in Wong, then in Ling and finally in Chan. The earnings per share in both Ling and Wong are far higher than in Chan, so there is a much greater chance of an increase in the ordinary dividend, but this is not necessarily the case if profits are falling or fluctuating.

28.10

(a) (i)

Forecast Profit and Loss Appropriation Accounts

	20X6 £000	20X7 £000	20X8 £000
Forecast profits	1,800	500	2,200
Less Corporation tax (30%)	540	150	660
	1,260	350	1,540
Less Dividends proposed	1,260	350	1,540

Balance sheet extracts

Shareholders' equity

	20X6 £000	20X7 £000	20X8 £000
Issued ordinary shares of £1 each fully paid	6,000	6,000	6,000
Share premium account	1,000	1,000	1,000
Retained profits	1,650	1,650	1,650
	8,650	8,650	8,650

Current liabilities

Dividends proposed	1,260	350	1,540

(ii)

Forecast Profit and Loss Appropriation Accounts

	20X6 £000	20X7 £000	20X8 £000
Forecast profits	1,800	500	2,200
Less interest (12% × £2m)	240	240	240
	1,560	260	1,960
Less Corporation tax (30%)	468	78	588
	1,092	182	1,372
Less Dividends proposed	1,092	182	1,372

Balance Sheet extracts

Shareholders' equity

	20X6 £000	20X7 £000	20X8 £000
Issued ordinary shares of £1, each fully paid	5,000	5,000	5,000
Retained profits	1,650	1,650	1,650
	6,650	6,650	6,650

Deferred liabilities

12% debentures	2,000	2,000	2,000

Current liabilities

Dividend proposed	1,092	182	1,372

(b) (i) If planned expansion is financed by share issue, the forecast return on shareholders' equity for the next three years will be:

20X6 1,260/8,650 × 100 = 14.6%
20X7   350/8,650 × 100 = 4.0%
20X8 1,540/8,650 × 100 = 17.8%

(ii) If planned expansion is financed by debenture issue, the forecast return on shareholders' equity for the next three years will be:

20X6 1,092/6,650 × 100 = 16.4%
20X7   182/6,650 × 100 = 2.7%
20X8 1,372/6,650 × 100 = 20.6%

Note: All the above figures are, of course, net of tax and should be grossed by a factor of 100/70 if comparison with gross interest rates is to be made (on the assumption of 30 per cent tax rate).

(c) The return on shareholders' equity for the year ended 30 September 20X5 was 600/6,620 × 100 = 9.1 per cent, and it could have been 9.5 per cent if full distribution of the year's profit had been made. To have the return fluctuate between 2.7 per cent and 20.6 per cent, as it will do if the planned expansion is financed by the debenture issue, will surely unnerve all but the most sturdy shareholders. Such a violent swing from year to year will confuse, confound and alarm anyone looking at the shares as an investment.

To finance the planned expansion by a share issue does not improve matters greatly, as it will be seen that the return will still fluctuate between 4.0 per cent and 17.8 per cent. But since we are told that the industry is 'subject to marked variations in consumer demand' it does seem more appropriate to use share capital (by definition risk-bearing) rather than a debenture. The poor profits forecast for 20X7 suggest that it would not take much of a variation from the expected results to show no profit at all, and were this to occur, is there not a possibility that the debenture holders could not be paid their due interest? Failure to pay debenture interest on time would bring in a receiver (assuming the debentures were secured): his function would then be to collect not only the unpaid interest but the capital as well, as failure to pay interest would be a breach of the conditions under which the debenture was issued.

If shareholders are to miss a year's dividends as a result of there being no profits for distribution, the directors can expect a stormy annual general meeting, but that is far less dangerous than the entry of a receiver.

In practice, of course, it is unusual for a company to pay out all profits as dividends, and since shareholders will pay more attention usually to the level of dividends paid than to profits earned, it would make better financial sense if the 20X6 dividend were maintained at or slightly above the 20X5 level, enabling an addition to be made to retained profits. This in turn would enable a fund to be built up to supplement current profits for dividends and/or to redeem the debentures.

The all-shares or all-debentures choice is also an unrealistic one. Although there is much to be said for a broad share base to support what is obviously a risky business, it could make better sense to raise part of the required £2,000,000 by shares and part by debentures. A restrained dividend policy coupled with the use of the (probably enlarged) depreciation charge arising after the expansion had taken place could enable a debenture redemption programme to be established over the course of the next few years.

28.12

(a) (i) *Shareholders*

	20X6	20X7
Earnings per share (EPS)	$\frac{9,520}{39,680} = 24p$	$\frac{11,660}{39,680} = 29.4p$

Dividend cover
(= EPS ÷ dividend per share)

20X6 $\frac{24p}{(2,240 \div 39,680)}$
$= \frac{24p}{5.6p} = 4.3$ times

20X7 $\frac{29.4p}{(2,400 \div 39,680)}$
$= \frac{29.4p}{6p} = 4.9$ times

	20X6	20X7
(*ii*) *Trade creditors*		
Current ratio	$\frac{92,447}{36,862} = 2.5$	$\frac{99,615}{42,475} = 2.3$
Acid test	$\frac{40,210 + 12,092}{36,862} = 1.4 : 1$	$\frac{43,370 + 5,790}{42,475} = 1.2 : 1$
(*iii*) *Internal management* Debtor ratio/Sales*		
*Assumed credit sales	$\frac{40,210}{486,300} \times 52 = 4.3$ weeks	$\frac{43,370}{583,900} \times 52 = 3.9$
Return on capital employed (before tax)	$\frac{15,254}{40,740} = 37.4\%$	$\frac{18,686}{50,000} = 37.4\%$

(*b*) *Shareholders*

EPS. An increase of 5.4p per share has occurred. This was due to an increase in profit without any increase in share capital.

Dividend cover. Increased by 0.6 times because increase in profit not fully reflected in dividends.

Trade creditors

Current ratio. This has fallen but only marginally and it still appears to be quite sound.

Acid test. This has also fallen, but still seems to be quite reasonable.

Internal management

Debtor ratio. There appears to have been an increase in the efficiency of our credit control.

Return on capital employed. This has stayed the same for each of the two years. The increase in capital employed has seen a proportional increase in profits.

28.14

To the Board of G plc

From AN Other, Accountant

Subject: *Potential acquisition of either of companies A Ltd and B Ltd as subsidiaries in the machine tool manufacturing sector. Financial performances assessed.*

As instructed by you I have investigated the financial performances of these two companies to assist in the evaluation of them as potential acquisitions.

It should be borne in mind that financial ratio analysis is only partial information. There are many other factors which will need to be borne in mind before a decision can be taken.

The calculations of the various ratios are given as an appendix.

Profitability

While the main interest to the board is what G plc could obtain in profitability from A Ltd and B Ltd, all I can comment on at present is the current profitability enjoyed by these two companies.

Here the most important ratio is that of ROCE (return on capital employed). A's ROCE is 27.2 per cent as compared with B's 15.6 per cent.

The great difference in ROCE can be explained by reference to the secondary ratios of profit and asset utilisation. Both ratios are in A's favour. The profit ratios are A 34 per cent: B 20 per cent. The asset utilisation ratios are A 0.9 per cent: B 0.6, showing that A is utilising its assets 50 per cent better than B. It is the effect of these two ratios that give the ROCE for each company.

The very low working capital employed by A Ltd very much affects the asset utilisation ratio. How far such a low working capital is representative of that throughout the whole year is impossible to say.

Liquidity

It would not be sensible to draw a final conclusion as to the liquidity positions of the two companies based on the balance sheet figures. As a balance sheet is based at one point in time it can sometimes be misleading, as a reading of figures over a period would be more appropriate.

A Ltd does appear to have a short-term liquidity problem, as the current assets only just cover current liabilities. The 'quick' or 'acid test ratio' on the face of it appears to be very inadequate at 0.6.

By contrast, B Ltd with a current ratio of 1.4 and a 'quick ratio' of 1.0 would appear to be reasonably liquid.

However, much more light is shed on the position of the companies when the debtor collection period is examined. A collects its debts with a credit period of 9 weeks. In the case of B Ltd this rises to an astonishing 36.7 weeks. Why is this so? It could be due simply to very poor credit control by B Ltd. Such a long credit period casts considerable doubt on the real worth of the debtors. There is a high probability that many of the debts may prove difficult to collect. It might be that B Ltd, in order to maintain sales, has lowered its requirements as to the creditworthiness of its customers. If the credit period were reduced to a normal one for the industry it might be found that many of the customers might go elsewhere.

The problem with debtors in the case of B Ltd is also carried on to stock. In the case of A Ltd the stock turnover is 4.3 falling to 2.8 in B Ltd. There could be a danger that B Ltd has stock increasing simply because it is finding it difficult to sell its products.

Capital gearing

A Ltd is far more highly geared than B Ltd: 93.6 per cent as compared with 14.1 per cent. A comparison with this particular industry by means of interfirm comparison should be undertaken.

Limitations of ratio analysis

You should bear in mind the following limitations of the analysis undertaken:

(*i*) One year's accounts are insufficient for proper analysis to be undertaken. The analysis of trends, taken from, say, five years' accounts would give a better insight.

(*ii*) Differences in accounting policies between A Ltd and B Ltd will affect comparisons.

(*iii*) The use of historical costs brings about many distortions.

(*iv*) The use of industry interfirm comparisons would make the ratios more capable of being interpreted.

(*v*) The plans of the companies for the future expressed in their budgets would be of more interest than past figures.

Conclusions

Depending on the price which would have to be paid for acquisition, I would suggest that A Ltd is the company most suitable for takeover.

A N Other
Accountant

Appendix

		A Ltd	B Ltd
(i) *Return on capital employed*			
	$\dfrac{\text{Profits before interest and tax}}{\text{Capital employed}}$	$\dfrac{211}{775} \times 100 = 27.2\%$	$\dfrac{88}{565} \times 100 = 15.6\%$
(ii) *Assets utilisation ratios*			
Total assets turnover:	$\dfrac{\text{Turnover}}{\text{Total assets}}$	$\dfrac{985}{1,140} = 0.9$	$\dfrac{560}{990} = 0.6$
Fixed assets turnover:	$\dfrac{\text{Turnover}}{\text{Fixed assets}}$	$\dfrac{985}{765} = 1.3$	$\dfrac{560}{410} = 1.4$
Working capital turnover:	$\dfrac{\text{Turnover}}{\text{Working capital}}$	$\dfrac{985}{10} = 98.5$	$\dfrac{560}{150} = 3.6$
(iii) *Profitability ratios*			
Gross profit % Turnover	$\dfrac{\text{Gross profit}}{\text{Turnover}}$	$\dfrac{335}{985} \times 100 = 34\%$	$\dfrac{163}{560} \times 100 = 29\%$
Profit before taxation and interest as % turnover		$\dfrac{211}{985} \times 100 = 21\%$	$\dfrac{88}{560} \times 100 = 16\%$
(iv) *Liquidity ratios*			
Current ratio:	$\dfrac{\text{Current assets}}{\text{Current liabilities}}$	$\dfrac{375}{365} = 1.0$	$\dfrac{580}{425} = 1.4$
Acid test or Quick ratio:	$\dfrac{\text{Current assets} - \text{Stock}}{\text{Current liabilities}}$	$\dfrac{220}{365} = 0.6$	$\dfrac{440}{425} = 1.0$
Debtor ratio:	$\dfrac{\text{Trade debtors} \times 52}{\text{Credit sales}}$	$\dfrac{170}{985} \times 52 = 9$ weeks	$\dfrac{395}{560} \times 52 = 36.7$ weeks
(v) *Capital structure*			
Gearing ratio:	$\dfrac{\text{Long-term borrowing}}{\text{Shareholders' funds}}$	$\dfrac{220}{555} \times 100 = 39.6\%$	$\dfrac{70}{495} \times 100 = 14\%$
Proprietary ratio:	$\dfrac{\text{Shareholders' funds}}{\text{Tangible assets}}$	$\dfrac{555}{1,140} = 0.5$	$\dfrac{495}{990} = 0.5$

30.1

(a) T   (b) F   (c) T   (d) F   (e) T

30.4

£40,000

30.6

At 31 December 20X5, accumulated depreciation is:

$30\% \times 30,000 \times \dfrac{160}{90} = 16,000$

At 31 December 20X4, accumulated depreciation is:

$20\% \times 30,000 \times \dfrac{120}{90} = 8,000$

Depreciation charge for the year ended 31 December 20X5 is:

$10\% \times 30,000 \times \dfrac{160}{90} = 5,333$

Hence, depreciation provision at 31 December 20X5 is:

$8,000 + 5,333 = 13,333$

Backlog depreciation is $16,000 - 13,333 = 2,667$

30.8

Opening stock at average prices	$= 50,000 \times \dfrac{100}{80}$	$= 62,500$
Purchases		$= 450,000$
Closing stock at average prices	$= 70,000 \times \dfrac{100}{120}$	$= 58,333$
Current cost of sales		$= 454,167$
Historic cost of sales		$= 430,000$
Cost of sales adjustment		$= 24,167$

30.10

Opening working capital		$= 7,000$
Closing working capital		$= 10,000$
Change in the year		$= 3,000$

At average values:

Opening working capital	$= 7,000 \times \dfrac{240}{200}$	$= 8,400$
Closing working capital	$= 10,000 \times \dfrac{240}{280}$	$= 8,571$
Change in the year		$= 171$

The monetary working capital adjustment is $£3,000 - £171 = £2,829$

3 Gains and losses on net monetary assets are undisclosed.
Net monetary assets include both long- and short-term loans made to and by the entity, for example, debentures, and trade debtors and trade creditors. During a period of inflation, an entity gains on both long- and short-term borrowings. The gain arises because although the amount originally borrowed will eventually be repaid at its face value, its purchasing power will have been reduced; for example, £5,000 borrowed in 20X1 will not purchase the same quantity of goods in 20X5 as it did in 20X1. In 20X5 the borrower may have to pay (say) £8,000 to purchase the same quantity of goods as he might have done in 20X1. Hence the entity will have, in effect, gained £3,000 by borrowing during an inflationary period, because it is effectively having to pay back less in purchasing power (or in real terms, as it is known) than it borrowed.

By contrast, if the entity has *loaned* money during a similar period (perhaps by allowing its customers to buy goods on credit), it loses money because the purchasing power of the respective debts (which are fixed in monetary terms) will purchase fewer goods when they are eventually settled than they would have done when they were first incurred.

In financial reports prepared under the historical cost system, neither the gross nor the net effect of these types of transactions is disclosed.

4 Balance sheet values are unrealistic.
Fixed assets are normally recorded in the balance sheet at their original cost, that is, at their historical cost. During a period of inflation, the historical cost of the assets may be far less than their *current* cost, that is, at the value the entity places on them at the time that the financial reports are prepared. Hence the financial reports give a misleading impression of the entity's net worth as at the time that they are prepared.

5 Meaningful periodic comparisons are difficult to make.
A meaningful comparison of financial reports prepared under the historical cost convention over several accounting periods may be misleading since such accounts will normally have been prepared using, say, pounds sterling in one period and pounds sterling in all subsequent periods.

Financial reports prepared in such a way are not, however, strictly comparable. For example, £100 in 20X1 is not the same as £100 in 20X5, because £100 would not purchase the same amount of goods in 20X5 as it did in 20X1. In fact the comparison is just as meaningless as comparing financial reports prepared, say, in dollars with, say, reports prepared in euros. It is obvious to most users of such reports that 100 dollars are not the same as 100 euros, but it is less obvious that £20X1 are not the same as £20X5.

In order to be able to make a meaningful comparison between financial reports prepared in different time periods, therefore, it is desirable to translate them into the same currency, that is, to use the same price base. The argument behind this point is similar in principle to that used in translating dollars into euros or euros into dollars.

31.1
See text, Section 31.6.

30.12

	20X3	20X2
	£000	£000
Loan stock	200	200
Cash	145	50
Net borrowings	55	150

$$\text{Average net borrowings} = \frac{55,000 + 150,000}{2} = 102,500$$

	20X3	20X2
	£000	£000
Ordinary shares	250	250
Reserves	370	340
Current cost reserve	35	30
Shareholder interest	655	620

$$\text{Average shareholder interest} = \frac{655,000 + 620,000}{2} = 637,500$$

$$\text{Gearing adjustment percentage is:} \quad \frac{102,500}{102,500 + 637,500} = 13.85\%$$

30.14

Many accountants believe that during a period of inflation financial reports prepared under the historical cost convention are subject to a number of severe limitations. The question lists five such limitations, and a brief explanation of each one is as follows.

1 Stocks are undervalued.
Stock values are normally based on historical costs. This means that the historical closing stock will usually have cost less than its current economic value. Hence the cost of sales will tend to be higher than it would be if the closing stock was revalued at its current cost. As a result, the gross profit will be higher, and the entity may then pay out a higher level of net profit.

If the entity pays out a high level of profit and at the same time it has to pay more for its stocks (because prices are rising), it may be left with insufficient funds for it to be able to replace its stocks with the same *quantity* of goods that it had sold during the previous period. Hence it will not be able to operate at the same level of activity as it had previously experienced.

2 Depreciation is understated.
Depreciation is usually based on the historical cost of fixed assets. Such assets will normally increase in price during a period of inflation. The annual depreciation charge, therefore, may not reflect the amount needed to be able to replace the assets at their increased cost. Consequently, the accounting profit tends to be overstated, and this may mean that too much profit is withdrawn from the business. The cash resources may then prove insufficient to replace the assets at the end of their useful life. Like the stock valuation problem, therefore, the business may not be able to operate at the same level of activity that it has previously experienced.

31.2
See text, Section 31.6. Difficulties lie in trying to give these measures a value in money that would get universal acceptance. How can you place a money value on living conditions, for example?

31.3
See text, Section 31.7.

31.4
Basically, there are many things that could be done to improve the various parts of 'social well-being'. However, (a) benefits cost a lot of money in the short term, and (b) beneficial effects are felt only in the long term. Examples are better education and better housing.

31.5
See text, Section 31.10, social programme measurement.

31.7
The accountant's model of income measurement, with its reliance upon data that can be expressed in financial terms, can be said to be too narrow and fails to consider wider social and environmental issues. The air we breathe does not have a 'price' in financial terms. Yet, what businesses do may cause costs to be incurred by others as a result of their abuse of the air in their environment. Similarly, the true cost of a natural resource may never be accounted for – the rainforests being a very well known example: they are being removed upon payment of a financially stated price, but the price only satisfies the seller, it does little to replace the environment being destroyed. Thus the price being added into the cost of manufacturing paper from the trees in the rainforests does not include the social and environmental cost of their destruction.

Thus, in the income model, it could be argued only in a narrow sense of the term that 'capital' is being maintained. In reality, the destruction of natural resources that are not or cannot be replaced means that the 'capital' is being consumed and future consumption impaired as a result.

It is for reasons of this type that it can be argued that accountants ought to be involved in disclosing the effects of a company's business activities upon its environment, for only by doing so will a true view of a company's activities be revealed.

32.1
See text, Sections 32.1 and 32.2.

32.2
See text, Sections 32.1 and 32.2.

32.3
See text, Section 32.2.

32.4
See text, Section 32.3.

32.5
See text, Section 32.4.

32.6
See text, Section 32.7.

33.1
(i) f, h.   (ii) m.   (iii) a, c, e, g, j; $^4/_5$ of n.t.v.   (iv) b, d, i; $^1/_5$ of n, p, q, part of $^1/_4$ of w.   (v) l, r, s, z, part of $^1/_4$ of w.   (vi) o, k, v, y.

33.3

Raw materials consumed (120,000 + 400,000 – 160,000)	360,000
Haulage costs	4,000
Direct labour 70% × 220,000	154,000
Royalties	1,600
(a) Prime cost	519,600

Factory overhead

Factory indirect labour	66,000	
Other factory indirect expenses	58,000	
Travelling expenses	100	
Depreciation: Factory machinery	38,000	
Firm's canteen expenses	4,000	166,100
(b) Production cost		685,700

Administration expenses

Salaries	72,000	
Travelling expenses	200	
Firm's canteen expenses	2,000	
Depreciation: Acctg. and office machinery	2,000	
Cars of admin. staff	1,600	
Other administrative expenses	42,000	119,800

Selling and distribution expenses

Salaries	8,000	
Commission	1,400	
Travelling expenses	2,900	
Depreciation: Equipment	300	
Sales staff cars	3,800	
Other selling expenses	65,000	
Carriage costs on sales	7,800	89,200

Finance costs

Interest on loans and overdrafts		3,800
(c) Total cost		898,500

34.1
(a) Answers to be drafted by students in proper memo form.
Introduction:
Marginal cost is:

Direct labour	3.00
Direct materials	3.50
Variable expenses	2.25
	8.75

As selling price £9.00 exceeds marginal cost £8.75 we should accept (but see below)*

Proof

	Without new order	With new order
Direct labour	6,000	6,300
Direct materials	7,000	7,350
Indirect manufacturing costs		
Variable	4,500	4,725
Fixed	500	500
Administration expenses	1,200	1,200
Selling and distribution expenses	600	600
Finance expenses	200	200
	20,000	20,875
Sales	22,000	
Sales 22,000 + 900		22,900
Profit	2,000	2,025

*Depends on how other things affected besides simple accounting calculation.

(b) For extra order:

Marginal costs per unit (see (a))	8.75
Depreciation £300 p.a. ÷ 150	2.00
Running costs £600 p.a. ÷ 150	4.00
Marginal costs per unit	14.75

As £14.75 is greater than selling price £10 do NOT accept.

34.3
Year 1

(A) Magellan Ltd (Marginal)

Sales £29 × 900		26,100
Less Variable costs		
Direct labour £3 × 1,200	3,600	
Direct materials £5 × 1,200	6,000	
Variable overheads £2 × 1,200	2,400	
Total variable cost	12,000	
Less in (A) Valuation closing stock		
$\frac{300}{1,200}$ × £12,000	3,000	9,000
Fixed overhead		9,000
Total costs		18,000
Gross profit		8,100

(B) Frobisher Ltd (Absorption)

Sales £29 × 900		26,100
Less Variable costs		
Direct labour £3 × 1,200	3,600	
Direct materials £5 × 1,200	6,000	
Variable overheads £2 × 1,200	2,400	
Total variable cost	12,000	
Less in (B) Valuation closing stock		
$\frac{300}{1,200}$ × £12,000	5,250	6,750
Fixed overhead		9,000
Total costs		15,750
Gross profit		10,350

Year 2

	(A)		(B)	
Sales £29 × 1,200	34,800		34,800	
Less Variable costs				
Direct labour £3 × 1,300	3,900		3,900	
Direct materials £5 × 1,300	6,500		6,500	
Variable overheads £2 × 1,300	2,600		2,600	
Total variable cost	13,000		13,000	
Add in (A) Opening stock b/d	3,000			
Add in (B) Opening stock b/d			5,250	
	16,000		18,250	
Less in (A) Valuation closing stock				
$\frac{400}{1,300}$ × 13,000		4,000		
Less in (B) Valuation of closing stock				
$\frac{400}{1,300}$ × £22,000				6,769
	12,000		11,481	
Fixed overhead	9,000		9,000	
Total costs	21,000		20,481	
Gross profit	13,800		14,319	

Year 3

	(A)		(B)	
Sales £29 × 1,100	31,900		31,900	
Less Variable costs				
Direct labour £3 × 1,250	3,750		3,750	
Direct materials £5 × 1,250	6,250		6,250	
Var. overheads £2 × 1,250	2,500		2,500	
Total variable cost	12,500		12,500	
Add in (A) Op. stock b/d	4,000			
Add in (B) Op. stock b/d			6,769	
	16,500		19,269	
Less in (A) Valuation of closing stock				
$\frac{550}{1,250}$ × £12,500		5,500		
Less in (B) Valuation of closing stock				
$\frac{550}{1,250}$ × £21,500				9,460
	11,000		9,809	
Fixed overhead	9,000		9,000	
Total costs	20,000		18,809	
Gross profit	11,900		13,091	

34.5

(a) Subject to points raised in (c) the extra production should be taken on, as this results in greater profits amounting to £1,562,000. Proof is as follows:

Extra revenue 60,000 × £150		9,000,000
Less Extra costs		
Direct materials (W1)	3,141,600	
Direct labour 60,000 × 18.70 × 120% =	1,346,400	
Variable overhead 60,000 × 7.50	450,000	
Fixed costs	2,500,000	
		7,438,000
Extra profit		1,562,000

(W1) 60,000 × 74.80		4,488,000
Less saving 10% on extra materials		
saving 10% on materials		
used on day shift	448,800	
10% × 120,000 × 74.80	897,600	
		897,600
		3,141,600

(b) Break-even point to justify night shift

Sale price per unit	150.00
Less Costs per unit	
Material	74.80
Direct labour 18.70 + 20%	22.44
Variable overhead	7.50
	104.74
Contribution per unit	45.26

Total fixed costs $\dfrac{2,500,000}{45.26} = $ Break-even at 55,236 units = Break-even at 55,236 units

Note: No 10% reduction on materials because demand less than extra 60,000 units.

(c) (i) Would firm be able to maintain selling price of £187 on first 120,000 units per year?
(ii) Would it have been more profitable to subcontract extra units needed?
(iii) Could we diversify into a more profitable alternative product?
(iv) Could extra day facilities have been more profitable?

34.7

(a)

Arncliffe Ltd
Revenue Statement for the year ended . . .

	Crowns	Kings	Total
Sales	60,000	25,000	85,000
Direct costs:			
Raw mats	8,000	2,000	10,000
Labour	20,000	10,000	30,000
M/c running costs	12,000	3,000	15,000
	40,000	15,000	55,000
Contribution	20,000	10,000	30,000
Rate of contribution to sales	33.3%	40%	35.3%

(b) Best product mix for next year:

Crowns manufactured per hour = 20,000/8,000 = 2.5 per hour
Kings manufactured per hour = 10,000/2,000 = 5 per hour
Kings gives best contribution rate, so produce Kings up to maximum requirements.

	Crowns Units	Crowns Hours	Kings Units	Kings Hours
Minimum required	6,000 ÷ 2.5	2,400	6,000 ÷ 5	1,200
Produce up to maximum of 36,000 Kings			30,000 ÷ 5	6,000
		2,400		7,200

Still (10,000 – 7,200 – 2,400) = 400 hours left, so now produce Crown 1,000 ÷ 2.5 = 400 → 2,800

Best mix is therefore: Crowns (6,000 + 1,000) = 7,000
Kings (6,000 + 30,000) = 36,000

	Crowns		Kings
Sales therefore 7,000 × £3	21,000	36,000	×£2.5 = 90,000
Contributions: Crowns (33.3%)		7,000	
Kings (40%)		36,000	43,000
Floor space costs			15,000
Insurances			600
			15,600
Profit			27,400

(c) Product mix with extra machine
As maximum requirements for Kings have already been met in (b), all new output will be of Crowns.

	Crowns	Kings
Sales (as before) in £	21,000	90,000
Extra (10,000 hours × 2.5) = 25,000 × £3 =	75,000	
	96,000	90,000
Contributions: Crowns (33.3%)	32,000	
Kings (40%)	36,000	68,000
Hire of extra machine		20,000
Floor space costs		15,000
Insurance		600
		35,600
		32,400

(d) Briefly:
(i) Market demand maintained.
(ii) Flexibility of return of extra machine if demand falls.
(iii) To see if wholesaler will guarantee minimum orders.
(iv) Are there outlets possible other than wholesaler?
(v) Selling price to wholesaler?

34.9

(a)

Paul Wagtail
*Manufacturing Trading and Profit and Loss Account
for the year ended 30 April 20X9*

	Marginal method		Absorption method	
Purchases of raw mats (125,000 − 2,100)		122,900		122,900
Carriage of raw materials		1,500		1,500
		124,400		124,400
Less Stock raw materials		8,900		8,900
Cost of raw materials consumed		115,500		115,500
Production wages		105,270		105,270
Prime cost		220,770		220,770
Factory overhead expenses:				
Factory power	12,430		12,430	
Factory supervisors' wages	29,600		29,600	
Factory repairs	19,360		19,360	
Factory insurance (40%)	1,920		1,920	
Factory heating & light (40%)	1,440		1,440	
Depreciation of plant	17,600	82,350	17,600	82,350
		303,120		303,120
Less Work in progress (W1)		11,038		15,156
Production cost of goods completed c/d		292,082		287,964
Sales		464,360		464,360
Production cost b/d	292,082		287,964	
Less Stock finished goods (W2)	18,447	273,635	18,187	269,777
Gross profit		190,725		194,583
Less Expenses:				
Administration expenses	46,700		46,700	
Distribution expenses	25,400		25,400	
Selling expenses	23,800		23,800	
Insurance (60%)	2,880		2,880	
Heating and lighting (60%)	2,160		2,160	
Depn: delivery vehicles	35,200	136,140	35,200	136,140
Net profit		54,585		58,443

Workings:

(W1) $625 \times 80\% = 500$ equivalent making total $9,500 + 500 = 10,000$

Valuations: Marginal $\dfrac{500}{10,000} \times 220,770 = 11,038$

Absorption $\dfrac{500}{10,000} \times 303,120 = 15,156$

(W2) Marginal $\dfrac{600}{9,500} \times 292,082 = 18,447$

Absorption $\dfrac{600}{9,500} \times 287,964 = 18,187$

(b) *See text.*

34.13

(a)

	Q	R	S	T
Direct labour and materials	14	28	60	32
Variable overheads	4	8	13	12
Fixed overhead	2	4	7	6
Total cost per unit	20	40	80	50
Add Profit 10 per cent	2	4	8	5
Selling price	22	44	88	55

(b) Discontinue S. All other items are above marginal cost.

(c)

	(i) Followed our advice	(ii) Produced all items
Sales Q 100 × £33	3,300	3,300
R 100 × £39	3,900	3,900
S 100 × £7	–	7,000
T 100 × £49	4,900	4,900
	12,100	19,100
Less Costs		
Direct labour and materials		
(i) 14 + 28 + 32 × 100	7,400	
(ii) 14 + 28 + 60 + 32 × 100		13,400
Variable overhead		
(i) 4 + 8 + 12 × 100	2,400	
(ii) 4 + 8 + 13 + 12 × 100		3,700
Fixed overhead	1,900	1,900
	11,700	19,000
Net profit	400	100

Note: The net profit or loss could have been worked out using contributions per items
e.g. (i) Contributions per unit (i.e. Selling price *less* Marginal cost).

Q 33 – (14 + 4) = 15
R 39 – (28 + 8) = 3
S 49 – (32 + 12) = 5

23 × 100 of each = 2,300
Less Fixed costs 1,900
Net profit (same as using method shown) 400

In (ii) the contribution from S would be a negative one.

(d) Discontinue Q and T. All other items are above marginal cost.

(e)

	(i) Followed our advice	(ii) Produced all items
Sales Q 100 × £17	–	1,700
R 100 × £48	4,800	4,800
S 100 × £140	14,000	14,000
T 100 × £39	–	3,900
	18,800	24,400
Less Costs		
Direct labour and materials		
(i) 28 + 60 × 100	8,800	
(ii) 14 + 28 + 60 + 32 × 100		13,400
Variable costs		
(i) 8 + 13 × 100	2,100	
(ii) 4 + 8 + 13 + 12 × 100		3,700
Fixed overhead	1,900	1,900
	12,800	19,000
Net profit	6,000	5,400

35.1

	Production departments				*Service departments*		
	A	B	C	D	K	L	M
Indirect lab.	4,000	6,000	8,000	2,000	1,500	3,000	4,100
Other exp.	2,700	3,100	3,600	1,500	4,500	2,000	2,000
	6,700	9,100	11,600	3,500	6,000	5,000	6,100
Apportionment of costs:							
Dept K	1,500	1,800	1,200	600	(6,000)		900
Dept L	3,000		1,500	500		(5,000)	
							7,000
Dept M		2,100	3,500	1,400			(7,000)
	11,200	13,000	17,800	6,000	–	–	–

(a) Overhead rates per direct labour hour

Department A $\dfrac{£11,200}{2,000} = £5.6$

Department C $\dfrac{£17,800}{4,450} = £4.0$

(b) Overhead rates per machine hour

Department B $\dfrac{£13,000}{2,600} = £5.0$

Department D $\dfrac{£6,000}{2,400} = £2.5$

35.2

Job Cost Sheet Job 351 Dept. A

Direct materials		190
Direct labour	56 × £2.1	117.6
Factory overhead	56 × £5.6	313.6
		621.2

Job Cost Sheet Job 352 Dept. B

Direct materials		1,199
Direct labour	178 × £1.7	302.6
Factory overhead	176 × £5.0	880
		2,381.6

Job Cost Sheet Job 353 Dept. C

Direct materials		500
Direct labour	130 × £2.4	312
Factory overhead	130 × £4.0	520
		1,332

Job Cost Sheet Job 354 Dept. D

Direct materials		666
Direct labour	90 × £2.3	207
Direct overhead	64 × £2.5	160
		1,033

Job Cost Sheet Job 355 Depts. C and B

Dept C	Direct materials		560
	Direct labour	160 × £2.4	384
	Factory overhead	160 × £4.0	640
Dept B	Direct materials		68
	Direct labour	30 × £1.7	51
	Factory overhead	20 × £5.0	100
			1,803

35.5

(a) *See text, Section 35.5*

(b) (i)

	Materials	Labour	Overhead
Finished items	4,000 (90%)	4,000 (75%)	4,000 (55%)
W-I-P (600)	540	450	330
Total units	4,540	4,450	4,330

(ii) Cost per complete unit

Material	£8,172 ÷ 4,540 =	1.80
Labour	£7,120 ÷ 4,450 =	1.60
Overhead	£5,196 ÷ 4,330 =	1.20
		£4.60

(iii) Value of work in progress

Material	540 × 1.80 =	972
Labour	450 × 1.60 =	720
Overhead	330 × 1.20 =	396
		£2,088

35.7

(a) Allotment: where overheads traced directly to units.
Apportionment: where overheads not directly traceable and have to be apportioned between units.
Absorption rates: the total amount of overheads calculated as being charged to each unit.

(b) Because the figures belong to the future and therefore cannot be known precisely.

(c) (i) and (ii). Note that parts (i) and (ii) illustrate two different methods in use. The method in (iii) is not in the text.

Continuous apportionment (repeated distribution) method:

	Production departments			Service departments	
Line	A	B	C	X	Y
1 Allocation per analysis	14,000	12,000	8,000	4,000	3,000
2 Allocation of X	(35%) 1,400	(30%) 1,200	(20%) 800	(4,000)	(15%) 600
3 Allocation of Y	(30%) 1,080	(40%) 1,440	(25%) 900	(5%) 180	(3,600)
4 Allocation of X	(35%) 63	(30%) 54	(20%) 36	(180)	(15%) 27
5 Allocation of Y	(30%) 8	(40%) 12*	(25%) 7	(5%) 0	(27)
	16,551	14,706	9,743		(= total 41,000)

*Rounded off

Explanation:
Steps:
(1) Allocate X overheads to others by % shown.
(2) Allocate Y overheads to others by % shown.
Keep repeating (1) and (2) until the figures left under X and Y are insignificant.

(iii) Elimination method:

	Production departments			Service departments	
Line	A	B	C	X	Y
1 Allocation per analysis	14,000	12,000	8,000	4,000	3,000
2 Allocate service dept X	(35%) 1,400	(30%) 1,200	(20%) 800	(4,000)	(15%) 600
3 Allocate service dept Y	(30/95) 1,137	(40/95) 1,516	(25/95) 947	—	(3,600)
	16,537	14,716	9,747		(total 41,000)

Explanation:
Steps:
(1) Allocate service department overheads which does largest proportion of work for other departments, i.e. department X.
(2) Allocate next service department per (1), in this case is only Y.
(3) When doing (2) nothing is charged to service departments already allocated, i.e. in this case X.
(4) Note that since (3) happens the ratios in the next allocation change. As X 5% of Y is not returned then A gets 30/95 of Y, not 30% and so on.

(iv) The answer will depend on whichever approach is adopted. No one can categorically state which method is the most accurate; there is no 'ideal' method.

35.9

(a) and (b) *See text.*

(c) (i)

Batch No. 23

Raw materials 300 × 1.60	480
Direct labour 4.20 × 20 hours	84
Setting up of machine	21
Overheads 3.60 × 20 hours	72
Total cost	657

Cost per unit 657 ÷ 300 = £2.19

(ii)

Batch No. 23

Raw materials 300 × 1.60		480.00
Less Received for scrap 20 × 0.86		17.20
		462.80
Direct labour:		
Normal 20 × 4.20	84.00	
Rectification 9 × 4.20	37.80	121.80
Setting up:		
Normal	21.00	
Rectification	18.00	39.00
Overheads: Running time 3.60 × 20	72.00	
Rectification 3.60 × 9	32.40	104.40
		728.00

Per usable unit £728 ÷ 280 = 2.60

(iii) Loss because of extra costs 728 – 657 = 71.00
Loss because of faulty products 657 × 20/300 = 43.80
114.80

36.1

	Jan	Feb	Mar	Apr	May	June
Opening stock	740	690	780	1,100	1,400	1,160
Add Production	750	1,010	1,410	1,620	1,240	800
	1,490	1,700	2,190	2,720	2,640	1,960
Less Sales	800	920	1,090	1,320	1,480	1,020
Closing stock	690	780	1,100	1,400	1,160	940

36.2

(a)

Opening stock		140
Add Production	?	(C)
		(B)
Less Sales total – see question		1,550
Closing stock		150

Missing figure (B) must be 1,700
Missing figure (C) must then be 1,560
Equal production per month 1,560 ÷ 12 = 130 units.

(b) Given figures per (a)

	(J)	(F)	(M)	(A)	(M)	(J)	(J)	(A)	(S)	(O)	(N)	(D)
	140	160	70	130	50	60	90	150	250	210	230	210
Opening stock	130	130	130	200	180	190	130	130	130	130	130	130
Add Production	270	290	240	200	130	220	280	380	340	360	150	150
Less Sales	110	180	170	150	120	100	70	110	170	130	110	190
Closing stock	160	110	70	50	60	90	150	250	210	230	210	150

Lowest closing figure is April 50 units.
If stock is not to fall below 80 units an extra 80 − 50 = 30 units will have to be produced in January making production for that month of 160 units.

37.1

(a)

Ukridge: Cash Budget

	May	Jun	Jul	Aug	Sept	Oct
Balance b/d		5,305	4,305	1,305		
Overdraft b/d					6,695	9,695
Receipts from debtors	400	4,000	8,000	12,000	9,000	5,000
Capital	5,005					
	5,405	9,305	12,305	13,305	2,305	(4,695)
Payments	100	5,000	11,000	20,000	12,000	7,000
Balance c/d	5,305	4,305	1,305			
Overdraft c/d				6,695	9,695	(11,695)

(b) There are the possibilities of delaying payments to creditors, delaying purchases or somehow getting debtors to pay up more quickly. Apart from these it is possible that a credit factoring firm could help in 'buying' the amounts of debtors from Ukridge.

If none of these is possible only a really fantastic product could warrant interest at 100 per cent per annum. This would rarely be the case, although there are many people whose optimism about their products exceeds the true profitability.

37.2

N. Morris: Cash Budget

	Jul	Aug	Sept	Oct	Nov	Dec
Balance b/d	1,200		250			420
Overdraft b/d		260		160	540	
Receipts	4,000	6,400	5,800	8,000	6,000	9,500*
	5,200	6,140	6,050	7,840	5,460	9,080
Payments (see schedule)	5,460	5,890	6,210	8,380	5,880	5,410
Balance c/d		250				3,670
Overdraft c/d	260		160	540	420	

*Includes £2,500 legacy

Payments schedule

July

Raw materials	320 (Jul) × £4	1,280
	300 (Jun) × £1	300
Direct labour	320 × £8	2,560
Variable	300 × £1 + 320 × £1	620
Fixed expenses		400
Drawings		300
		5,460

Aug

Raw materials	350 (Aug) × £4	1,400
	320 (July) × £1	320
Direct labour	350 × £8	2,800
Variable	350 × £1 + 320 × £1	670
Fixed expenses		400
Drawings		300
		5,890

Sept

Raw materials	370 (Sept) × £4	1,480
	350 (Aug) × £1	350
Direct labour	370 × £8	2,960
Variable	370 × £1 + 350 × £1	720
Fixed expenses		400
Drawings		300
		6,210

Oct

Raw materials	380 (Oct) × £4	1,520
	370 (Sep) × £1	370
Direct labour	380 × £8	3,040
Variable	380 × £1 + 370 × £1	750
Fixed expenses		400
Drawings		300
Machinery		2,000
		8,380

Nov

Raw materials	340 (Nov) × £4	1,360
	380 (Oct) × £1	380
Direct labour	340 × £8	2,720
Variable	340 × £1 + 380 × £1	720
Fixed expenses		400
Drawings		300
		5,880

Dec

Raw materials	310 (Dec) × £4	1,240
	340 (Nov) × £1	340
Direct labour	310 × £8	2,480
Variable	310 × £1 + 340 × £1	650
Fixed expenses		400
Drawings		300
		5,410

37.3

(a)

Cash Budget

Receipts	July	Aug	Sept
Cash sales (W1)	9,600	4,800	7,200
Credit sales (W2)	17,640	14,112	7,056
	27,240	18,912	14,256
Payments			
Purchases	3,600	5,400	8,100
Direct labour	1,600	2,400	3,600
Direct production expenses	4,800	2,400	3,600
Variable selling expenses	4,000	3,200	1,600
Fixed expenses	1,820	1,820	1,820
	15,820	15,220	18,720
Balance start of month	3,900	15,320	19,012
Balance at end of month	15,320	19,012	14,548

(W1) July $\;\;\;800 \times 40\% \times £30 = 9,600$
August $\;600 \times 40\% \times £30 = 4,800$
September $600 \times 40\% \times £30 = 7,200$

(W2) July $\;\;\;1,000 \times 60\% \times £30 = 18,000 - 2\% = 17,640$
August $\;\;\;800 \times 60\% \times £30 = 14,400 - 2\% = 14,112$
September $400 \times 60\% \times £30 = 7,200 - 2\% = 7,056$

(b)
(i) Can forecast when and if money needs to be borrowed.
(ii) Can forecast when surplus funds are available so that they can be invested elsewhere.
(iii) To use as basis when dealing with supplier as to creditworthiness or bank for borrowing powers.

37.5

Receipts	July	Aug	Sept	Oct
Sales this month 20%		9,000	9,000	9,000
Sales last month 70%		32,000	31,500	31,500
Sales 2 months ago 10%			4,000	4,500
Other receipts from drs	40,000			
	40,000	41,000	44,500	45,000
Payments				
Wages	2,000	2,000	2,000	2,000
Bank loan and interest	242	242	242	242
Drawings	500	500	500	500
Purchases	34,000	38,250	38,250	45,750
PAYE tax	500	500	500	500
Rent	1,250			1,250
Rates				2,250
Value added tax		8,150		
Motor van	5,000			3,950
	43,492	49,642	41,492	56,442
Current account balances				
Start of month	5,000	1,508	(7,134)	(4,126)
End of month	1,508	(7,134)	(4,126)	(15,568)

37.6

(a) In brief:
Current ratio of 210,000 : 150,000 = 1.4 : 1
Acid test ratio not known. Very dangerous situation because if bank manager asks for repayment of overdraft it is unlikely it can be repaid in the short term.
Profits get ploughed back into the company in all sorts of ways, e.g. extra fixed assets, more stock. It has no direct connection with the balance at the bank. (Use cash flow statements as an illustration.)

(b)

Cash Budget

Receipts	Apr	May	June	July
Cash sales	40,000	40,000	40,000	40,000
Credit sales	65,000	70,000	70,000	70,000
	105,000	110,000	110,000	110,000
Payments				
Purchases	60,000	58,000	61,000	55,000
Selling and administration	5,700	6,600	6,600	6,600
Administration charges	10,000	10,000	10,000	13,500
Final dividend 20X9/X0		7,500		
Interim dividend 20X0/X1				4,000
	75,700	82,100	77,600	79,100
Balance overdraft start of month	(150,000)	(120,700)	(92,800)	(60,400)
Balance overdraft end of month	(120,700)	(92,800)	(60,400)	(29,500)

(c)
Would seem to be proceeding satisfactorily to eliminate overdraft.
Could be further reduced by:
(i) Issuing new shares
(ii) Getting debtors to pay more quickly
(iii) Delaying payment of creditors
(iv) Selling off fixed assets
(v) Issuing debentures.

38.1

(a) Stock Budget 20X7

	Aug	Sept	Oct	Nov	
Opening stock	5,000*	7,000	8,000	7,000	(A)
Add Purchases	20,000	23,500	21,500	31,000	(B)
	25,000	30,500	29,500	38,000	(C)
Less Cost of sales	18,000	22,500	22,500	27,000	(D)
Closing stock	7,000	8,000	7,000	11,000	(E)

* After special sale of £8,000 goods at cost.
To work out missing figures:
August (A) is known. (D) is 24,000 – 25%

(D) 18,000

Therefore, as stockturnover is 3, $\dfrac{(D)\,18,000}{[(A)\,5,000 + (E)\,\text{question}] \div 2} = 3$

Therefore bottom line is 6,000 so (E) must be 7,000.
Repeat following months.

(b) Cash Budget 20X7

Receipts:	Aug	Sept	Oct	Nov
Capital	10,000			
Soul's debtors	20,250			
Debtors			24,000	30,000
Special sale	8,000	–		
	38,250	–	24,000	30,000
Payments:				
Creditors	10,000	20,000	23,500	21,500
General expenses	700	700	700	700
	10,700	20,700	24,200	22,200
Bank: Opening	(20,000)	7,550	(13,150)	(13,350)
Closing	7,550	(13,150)	(13,350)	(5,550)

(b)

D. Smith
Forecast Trading and Profit and Loss Accounts for the six months ended 30 June 20X4

Sales		16,500
Less Cost of goods sold:		
Purchases	11,410	
Less Closing stock (130 × £7)	910	10,500
Gross profit		6,000
Add Rent received		300
		6,300
Less Expenses:		
Assistants' salaries	1,560	
Other expenses	900	
Depreciation: Shop fixtures	150	
Motor van	100	2,710
Net profit		3,590

Balance Sheet as at 30 June 20X4

	Cost	Dep'n	Net
Fixed assets			
Premises	20,000	–	20,000
Shop fixtures	3,000	150	2,850
Motor van	1,000	100	900
	24,000	250	23,750
Current assets			
Stock-in-trade		910	
Debtors		5,400	
		6,310	
Less Current liabilities			
Creditors	2,310		
Other expenses owing	150		
Bank overdraft	510	2,970	
Working capital			3,340
			27,090
Financed by:			
Capital			
Cash introduced			25,000
Add Net profit			3,590
			28,590
Less Drawings			1,500
			27,090

38.3

(a) Cash Budget

	Jan	Feb	Mar	Apr	May	June
Opening balance	25,000					
Opening overdraft		+890	–370	–600	–740	–600
Received (see schedule)	400	600	1,750	2,200	2,900	3,550
	25,400	1,490	1,380	1,600	2,160	2,950
Payments (see schedule)	24,510	1,860	1,980	2,340	2,760	3,460
Closing balance	+890					
Closing overdraft		–370	–600	–740	–600	–510

Cash Receipts Schedule

	Jan	Feb	Mar	Apr	May	June
Cash sales	400	600	800	1,000	1,300	1,400
Credit sales		–	800	1,200	1,600	2,000
Rent received			150			150
	400	600	1,750	2,200	2,900	3,550

Cash Payments Schedule

	Jan	Feb	Mar	Apr	May	June
Drawings	250	250	250	250	250	250
Premises	20,000					
Shop fixtures	3,000					
Motor van	1,000					
Salaries of assistants	260	260	260	260	260	260
Payments to creditors		1,200	1,320	1,680	2,100	2,800
Other expenses		150	150	150	150	150
	24,510	1,860	1,980	2,340	2,760	3,460

38.6

(a)

Issa Ltd
Trading and Profit and Loss Account for the year ended 31 December 20X1

	£000	£000
Sales		900.0
Less Cost of goods sold		
Opening stock	80.0	
Purchases (difference)	570.0	
	650.0	
Less Closing stock	65.0	
		585.0
Gross profit		315.0
Less Expenses		
Administration expenses	63.6	
Selling and distribution expenses (54 + 15)	69.0	
Financial charges	20.8	
Provision for doubtful debts	2.5	
Depreciation	60.0	
		215.9
Net profit		99.1
Profit on sale of land and buildings		150.0
Retained earnings from last year		350.0
		599.1
Less Appropriations		
Bonus share issue	50.0	
Preference share dividends	9.0	
Ordinary dividend	7.5	
		66.5
Retained earnings carried to next year		532.6

(b)

Balance Sheet as at 31 December 20X1

	£000	£000	£000
Fixed assets at cost (750 – 50)		700.0	
Less Depreciation to date		204.0	
			496.0
Investment in Yates Ltd at cost			100.0
Current assets			
Stock		65.0	
Trade debtors	100.0		
Less Provision	7.5		
		92.5	
Bank		350.1	
		507.6	
Less Current liabilities			
Trade creditors	56.0		
Expense creditors	15.0		
		71.0	
			436.6
			1,032.6
Financed by:			
Ordinary share capital (200 + 100)			300.0
Share premium (150 – 50)			100.0
9% Preference shares			100.0
Retained earnings			532.6
			1,032.6

(c) Advantages:

(i) Business can establish desired profit in advance. It can then take necessary action to try to achieve it.
Desired ROCE can be set as target.
Also helps in forecasting dividends/planning for taxation purposes/organising necessary finance/for use with financial backers.

(ii) Manage working capital to ensure its sufficiency when needed.
Managing cash balances to seek overdrafts/loans from bank when needed.
Ensure creditors paid on time to gain discounts. Invest surpluses as and when they may occur.

38.7

Cash Payments Schedule

	Jul	Aug	Sept	Oct	Nov	Dec
Direct materials	240	140	160	220	200	160
Direct labour	450	450	450	450	450	450
Variable overhead	210	270	270	270	270	270
Fixed overhead	90	90	90	90	90	90
Machine	500					
Motor vehicle			2,000			
	1,490	950	2,970	1,030	1,010	970

Cash Receipts Schedule

	Jul	Aug	Sept	Oct	Nov	Dec
Debenture					5,000	
Receipts from debtors	990	900	1,080	1,440	1,800	1,850
	990	900	1,080	1,440	6,800	1,850

(a) *Cash Budget (£)*

	Jul	Aug	Sept	Oct	Nov	Dec
Opening balance	7,100	6,600	6,550	4,660	5,070	10,860
Add Receipts	990	900	1,080	1,440	6,800	1,850
	8,090	7,500	7,630	6,100	11,870	12,710
Less Payments	1,490	950	2,970	1,030	1,010	970
	6,600	6,550	4,660	5,070	10,860	11,740

(b) *Debtors Budget (£)*

	Jul	Aug	Sept	Oct	Nov	Dec
Opening balance	1,890	1,980	2,520	3,240	3,650	3,515
Add Sales	1,080	1,440	1,800	1,850	1,665	1,295
	2,970	3,420	4,320	5,090	5,315	4,810
Less Receipts	990	900	1,080	1,440	1,800	1,850
Closing balance	1,980	2,520	3,240	3,650	3,515	2,960

(c) *Creditors Budget (£)*

	Jul	Aug	Sept	Oct	Nov	Dec
Opening balance	540	520	580	580	500	440
Add Purchases	220	200	160	140	140	180
	760	720	740	720	640	620
Less Payments	240	140	160	220	200	160
Closing balance	520	580	580	500	440	460

(d) Raw Materials Budget (£)

	July	Aug	Sept	Oct	Nov	Dec
Opening stock	300	340	360	340	300	260
Add Purchases	220	200	160	140	140	180
	520	540	520	480	440	440
Less Used in production	180	180	180	180	180	180
Closing stock	340	360	340	300	260	260

(e) Gregg Ltd
Forecast Operating Statement for the six months ended 31 December 20X6

Sales		9,130
Less Cost of goods sold		
Operating stock finished goods	1,800	
Add Cost of goods completed (£10 × 540)	5,400	
	7,200	
Less Closing stock finished goods (220 × £10)	2,200	5,000
Gross profit		4,130
Less Expenses:		
Fixed overhead		540
Depreciation: Machinery	700	
Motor vehicles	600	
Office fixtures	30	1,330
Net profit		2,260

(f) *Forecast Balance Sheet as at 31 December 20X6*

	Cost	Depreciation to date	Net
Fixed assets			
Tangible assets			
Land and buildings	40,000	–	40,000
Plant and machinery	10,500	6,700	3,800
Motor vehicles	8,000	3,400	4,600
Office fixtures	500	250	250
	59,000	10,350	48,650
Current assets			
Stocks: Finished goods	2,200		
Raw materials	260		
Debtors	2,960		
Cash and bank	11,740		
	17,160		
Creditors: amounts falling due within 1 year			
Creditors for raw materials	460		
Creditors for variable overhead	270	730	
Net current assets			16,430
Total assets less current liabilities			65,080
Creditors: amounts falling due after more than 1 year			
Debentures			5,000
			60,080
Capital and reserves			
Called-up share capital			50,000
Profit and loss account (7,820 + 2,260)			10,080
			60,080

38.8
A (a) *Debtor budget*

	July	Aug	Sept	Oct
Balances from last month	52,250	52,250	49,500	51,750
Add Credit sales	24,750	24,750	27,000	33,000
	77,000	77,000	76,500	84,750
Less Paid by debtors	24,750	27,500	24,750	24,750
Balances at end of month	52,250	49,500	51,750	60,000

Note: sales are July 900, Aug 900, Sept 900, Oct 1,100. October is taken to be June figure + 10%.

(b) *Raw material budget* (in kg)

	July	Aug	Sept	Oct
Stock from last month	1,800	1,800	1,800	2,200
Add purchases	1,800	1,800	2,200	2,200
	3,600	3,600	4,000	4,400
Less Used	1,800	1,800	1,800	2,200
Stock at end of month	1,800	1,800	2,200	2,200

B *See text, Section 36.8*

$$EOQ = \sqrt{\frac{2 \times 12,000 \times £10}{£6}} = 200 \text{ units}$$

(i) Based on estimates which obviously can vary a lot from actual.
(ii) Consumption may be uneven at times; EOQ assumes even usage.
(iii) Such things as strikes, catastrophes, etc. can render it useless.

38.9
A *Workings:*
1 Raw materials 294,400 ÷ 64,000 = 4.6 per unit
2 Direct labour 236,800 ÷ 64,000 = 3.7 per unit
3 Power 38,400 ÷ 64,000 = 0.60 per unit
4 Repairs are 51,200 − 25% × (12,800) = 38,400 fixed. Variable 12,800 ÷ 64,000 = 0.20
5 Indirect wages 64,000 − 15% × (9,600) = 54,400 fixed. Variable 9,600 ÷ 64,000 = 0.15.

Bedford Ltd

Flexible Budget at Varying Levels of Production

	Level of Production						
	60%	70%	75%	90%	85%	Actual	Variance +(–)
Units	48,000	56,000	60,000	72,000	68,000	68,000	
Variable costs (£)							
Raw materials	220,800	257,600	276,000	331,200	312,800	310,750	2,050
Direct labour	177,600	207,200	222,000	266,400	251,600	249,100	2,500
Power	28,800	33,600	36,000	43,200	40,800	39,800	1,000
Repairs and Maintenance	9,600	11,200	12,000	14,400	13,600	14,650	(1,050)
Indirect wages	7,200	8,400	9,000	10,800	10,200	10,850	(650)
	444,000	518,000	555,000	666,000	629,000	625,150	3,850
Fixed costs							
Repairs and Maintenance	38,400	38,400	38,400	38,400	38,400	38,400	–
Insurance	1,300	1,300	1,300	1,300	1,300	1,350	(50)
Heating/lighting	1,250	1,250	1,250	1,250	1,250	1,200	50
Indirect wages	54,400	54,400	54,400	54,400	54,400	54,400	–
	95,350	95,350	95,350	95,350	95,350	95,350	–
Total costs	539,350	613,350	650,350	761,350	724,350	720,500	3,850

Briefly: generally efficient as most variances are favourable. Comment in detail on each variance.

B See text.

39.1

(a) *Standard cost per unit*

	X	Y	Z
Material 1	0.6	1.8	2.4
Material 2	3.0	2.1	1.5
Material 3		2.5	0.9
Material 4	0.4		
	4.0	6.4	4.8
Labour: Dept A	4.0	4.2	4.8
Dept B	3.0		3.6
	7.0		8.4
Production cost	11.0	10.6	13.2
Overheads			
Production (1.8 per hour)	9.0	5.4	10.8
	20.0	16.0	24.0
Administration (50%)	10.0	8.0	12.0
Selling	5.0	4.0	6.0
Standard cost	35.0	28.0	42.0
Profit (1/7 of standard cost)	5.0	4.0	6.0
Standard selling price	40.0	32.0	48.0

(b) *Sales budget in units*

	X	Y	Z
Budgeted at std price	800,000	1,280,000	2,400,000
Unit selling price	40.0	32.0	48.0
Sales budget in units	20,000	40,000	50,000

(c) *Production budget in units*

	X	Y	Z
Needed for sales	20,000	40,000	50,000
For stock purposes	5,000	10,000	10,000
To produce	25,000	50,000	60,000

(d) *Direct materials purchases budget*

	X	Y	Z
Materials	1	3	4
Product X	2		
Product Y (kg)	–		
Product Z	100,000	300,000	480,000
	700,000	500,000	1,080,000
	900,000	360,000	1,560,000
	1,440,000	1,160,000	
	2,340,000		
Cost (£)	234,000	290,000	78,000

40.1

(i) Net variance:

	£
Actual cost per unit 37 × £18	666
Standard cost per unit 34 × £20	680
Net variance (favourable)	14

Made up of:

Favourable price variance £2 × 34	68
Adverse usage variance 3 × £18	54
Net variance (favourable)	14

(ii) Net variance:

Actual cost per unit 46 × £19	874
Standard cost per unit 50 × £17	850
Net variance (adverse)	24

Made up of:

Favourable usage variance 4 × £17	68
Adverse price variance 46 × £2	92
Net variance (adverse)	24

(iii) Total variance:

Actual cost per unit 18 × £14	252
Standard cost per unit 15 × £12	180
Variance (adverse)	72

Made up of:

Adverse price variance 15 × £2 (+ £6 common)	36
Adverse usage variance 3 × £12	36
Total variance (adverse)	72

(iv) Total variance:

Actual cost per unit 27 × £37	999
Standard cost per unit 29 × £40	1,160
Total variance (favourable)	161

Made up of:

Favourable price variance 27 × £3	81
Favourable usage var. 2 × £37 (+ £6 common)	80
	161

40.5

(a) See text.

(b) Standard hours produced in March

	£
Dishwashers 150 × 10	1,500
Washing machines 100 × 12	1,200
Refrigerators 90 × 14	1,260
Total standard hours	3,960

(c) (i) Standard hours × Standard hourly rate

	£
3,960 × £4	15,840
Actual wages	18,450
Total direct labour variance	2,610 (Adverse)

(ii)

	£
Standard pay 4,100 × £4	16,400
Actual pay	18,450
Direct labour rate variance	2,050 (Adverse)

(iii) Direct labour efficiency variance

Standard hours − Actual hours × Standard rate

$3{,}960 - 4{,}100 \times £4 = 560$ (Adverse)

(d) Labour rate variance:
1 Higher grade labour used than necessary.
2 Job running behind time so extra people brought in to help.

Direct labour efficiency variance:
1 Using unsuitable machinery.
2 Workers slowing up work so as to get overtime rates paid.

40.7

(a)

Profit Statement for the month of July 20X1

	Budgeted		Actual	
Sales		1,000,000		1,071,200
Less Manufacturing costs				
Direct materials	200,000		201,285	
Direct labour	313,625		337,500	
Variable overheads	141,400		143,000	
Fixed overheads	75,000		71,000	
		730,025		752,785
Gross profit		269,975		318,415
Less Variable sales o/h	64,400		69,500	
Admin. costs	150,000		148,650	
		214,400		218,150
		55,575		100,265

(v) Total variance:

		£
Actual cost per unit 154 × £8		1,232
Standard cost per unit 145 × £7		1,015
Total variance (adverse)		217

Made up of:

	£
Adverse price var. 145 × £1 (+ £9 common)	154
Adverse usage variance 9 × £7	63
	217

(vi) Total variance:

	£
Actual cost per unit 9,850 × £22	216,700
Standard cost per unit 10,000 × £25	250,000
Total variance (favourable)	33,000

Made up of:

	£
Favourable price variance £3 × 9,850	29,550
Favourable usage variance 150 × £22 (+ £450 common)	3,750
	33,300

40.3

(i)

		£
Actual cost per unit	218 × £2.1	457.8
Standard cost per unit	220 × £2.1	462
Favourable labour efficiency variance		4.2

(ii)

Actual cost per unit	115 × £1.9	218.5
Standard cost per unit	115 × £1.7	195.5
Adverse wage rate variance		23.0

(iii)

Actual cost per unit	240 × £1.8	432
Standard cost per unit	200 × £1.8	360
Adverse labour efficiency variance		72

(iv)

Actual cost per unit	104 × £2.0	208
Standard cost per unit	120 × £2.0	240
Favourable labour efficiency variance		32

(v)

Actual cost per unit	68 × £1.5	102
Standard cost per unit	68 × £1.8	122.4
Favourable wage rate variance		20.4

(vi)

Actual cost per unit	34 × £1.7	57.8
Standard cost per unit	30 × £1.7	51
Adverse labour efficiency variance		6.8

(vii)

Actual cost per unit	77 × £1.6	123.2
Standard cost per unit	70 × £1.6	112
Adverse labour efficiency variance		11.2

(viii)

Actual cost per unit	100 × £2.0	200
Standard cost per unit	100 × £1.9	190
Adverse wage rate variance		10

(b) (i) Materials price variance
= (Standard price – Actual price per unit) × Quantity purchased
= 10.00 – 10.65 = 0.65 × 18,900 = 12,285 Adverse

Material usage = (Standard quantity – Actual quantity used) × Standard price
= (20,000 – 18,900) × 10 = 11,000 Favourable

Summary:	Materials price variance	12,285	(A)
	Materials usage variance	11,000	(F)
	Materials cost variance	1,285	(A)

(ii) Labour rate variance
= (Standard rate per hour – Actual wage rate) × Actual hours worked
= (6.50 – 6.75) × 50,000 = 12,500 (A)

Labour efficiency variance
= (Standard labour hours – Actual hours) × Standard rate per hour
= (48,250 – 50,000) × 6.50 = 11,375 (A)

Summary:	Labour rate variance	12,500	(A)
	Labour efficiency variance	11,375	(A)
	Labour cost variance	23,875	(A)

(c) In each case find out why the variance has occurred. Then it must be established whether the variances were outside the control of anyone in the firm or whether they were caused by the actions, or lack of action, by people in our organisation. Any necessary corrective action can then be taken.

41.1

(a)
Actual overhead	5,840
Overhead applied to production × £6	6,000
Favourable variable overhead expenditure variance	160

(b)
Actual overhead	21,230
Overhead applied to production 5,000 × £4	20,000
Adverse variable overhead expenditure variance	1,230

(c)
Actual fixed overhead	11,770
Budgeted fixed overhead	12,000
Favourable fixed overhead expenditure variance	230

(d)
Actual fixed overhead	41,390
Budgeted fixed overhead	40,000
Adverse fixed overhead expenditure variance	1,390

(e)
Actual hours × Standard rate (7,940 × £3)	23,820
Budgeted hours × Standard rate (8,000 × £3)	24,000
Favourable variable overhead efficiency variance	180

(f)
Actual hours × Standard rate (15,000 × £4)	60,000
Budgeted hours (4,860 × 3) × Standard rate (14,580 × £4)	58,320
Adverse variable overhead efficiency variance	1,680

41.3
The standard variable overhead rate is:

$\frac{£400,000}{80,000} = £5$ per direct labour hour and £10 per unit

The standard fixed overhead rate is:

$\frac{£160,000}{80,000} = £2$ per direct labour hour and £4 per unit

The variances are:

Variable overhead

(i) *Expenditure variance*
Actual overhead	403,600
Overhead applied to production 78,500 × £5	392,500
Adverse expenditure variance	11,100

(ii) *Efficiency variance*
Actual hours × standard rate 78,500 × £5	392,500
Budgeted hours × standard rate (42,000 units which should be produced in 42,000 × 2 hours = 84,000 hours × £5	420,000
Favourable efficiency variance	27,500

Fixed overhead

(i) *Efficiency variance*
Actual units produced × Std rate 42,000 × 2 hrs per unit × £2	168,000
Actual Labour hours × Standard rate 78,500 × £2	157,000
Favourable fixed overhead efficiency variance	11,000

(ii) *Expenditure variance*
Actual overhead	157,200
Budgeted overhead	160,000
Favourable fixed overhead expenditure variance	2,800

(iii) *Capacity variance*
Actual hours × Standard rate 78,500 × £2	157,000
Budgeted hours × Standard rate 80,000 × £2	160,000
Adverse fixed overhead capacity variance	3,000
	10,800

The variances can be explained further:

Variable overhead
Actual overhead	403,600
Budgeted overhead for actual production 42,000 units × £10	420,000
Net favourable variance (made up of favourable efficiency variance £27,500 *less* adverse expenditure variance 11,100)	16,400

Fixed overhead
Actual overhead	157,200
Overhead based on units of production 42,000 × £4	168,000
Net favourable variance (made up of favourable efficiency variance £11,000 *plus* favourable expenditure variance £2,800 *less* adverse capacity variance £3,000)	10,800

41.5

		£
Actual units sold 150,000 × Budget price	£2.50 =	375,000
150,000 × Actual price	£2.375 =	356,250
Adverse price variance	£0.125	18,750

		£
Actual units sold 150,000 × Budget gross profit £1.00 =		150,000
Budgets units sold 125,000 × Budget gross profit £1.00 =		125,000
Favourable volume variance		25,000

41.7

	Actual units sold £	Budget price £	Actual price	Unit price variance	Total price variance
M	840	5	5.10	+0.10	+84
N	1,680	8	7.90	−0.10	−168
P	280	7	7.30	+0.30	+84
	2,800			Total price variance	0

	Actual units sold	Actual units in budget (%)	Budget sales	Variance in units	Budget gross profit per unit £	Total variance £
M	840	700	800	−100	1.00	−100
N	1,680	1,400	1,600	−200	1.50	−300
P	280	700	800	−100	1.20	−120
	2,800	2,800	3,200	−400		−520

	Actual units in budget (%)	Actual units sold	Variance in units	Budget gross profit per unit £	Total variance £
M	700	840	+140	1.00	+140
N	1,400	1,680	+280	1.50	+420
P	700	280	−420	1.20	−504
	2,800	2,800	−		+56

Summary of sales variance

Price variance	0
Volume variance adverse	520
Mix variance favourable	56
Net adverse variance	464

41.9

(a) See text, Section 40.1.

(b)

(i)

Singleton Ltd
Manufacturing Account for the year ended 31 August 20X9

	Actual £	Budget £	Variance £
Raw material consumed	90,000	80,000	(10,000)
Direct labour wages	115,600	120,000	4,400
Direct expenses	6,000	5,800	(200)
Prime cost	211,600	205,800	(5,800)
Factory overhead expenses:			
Factory rent	10,000	10,000	–
Factory maintenance	6,100	6,700	600
Heating and lighting	3,900	2,900	(1,000)
Depreciation	10,500	8,900	(1,600)
Wages, maintenance labour	24,000	18,000	(6,000)
Other factory overhead	10,000	12,700	2,700
Production cost of goods completed	276,100	265,000	(11,100)

(ii)   *Trading Account for the year ended 31 August 20X9*

		£	
Sales			405,000
Stock of finished goods 1 Sep X8		28,900	
Production cost		276,100	
		305,000	
Less Stock of fin. goods 31 Aug X9		35,000	
Cost of sales			270,000
Gross profit			135,000

(c) See text.

Note to exercises on break-even analysis:
The general idea of the questions is to get you to draw up the schedules of costs and revenues and then to draw them carefully on graph paper. It will be a waste of time if you do not use graph paper. It illustrates that accounting data can be represented in diagram form for some users in a more effective way than just using figures. It also puts over the idea that businesses exist to make a profit, and that until sufficient volume is achieved then the business will incur losses. The impact of fixed costs on firms can be revealed quite sharply by this sort of analysis.

42.1
(i)

No. of units	Fixed cost	Variable cost	Total cost	Revenue	Profit	Loss
0	8,000	–	8,000	–	–	8,000
1,000	8,000	4,000	12,000	6,000		6,000
2,000	8,000	8,000	16,000	12,000		4,000
3,000	8,000	12,000	20,000	18,000		2,000
4,000	8,000	16,000	24,000	24,000	nil	nil
5,000	8,000	20,000	28,000	30,000	2,000	
6,000	8,000	24,000	32,000	36,000	4,000	
7,000	8,000	28,000	36,000	42,000	6,000	
8,000	8,000	32,000	40,000	48,000	8,000	
9,000	8,000	36,000	44,000	54,000	10,000	
10,000	8,000	40,000	48,000	60,000	12,000	

(ii) Similar in style to Exhibit 42.2 in the chapter.

42.2
(a) (i) £24,000 (ii) £36,000 (iii) £44,000 (iv) £30,000
(b) (i) £18,000 (ii) £48,000 (iii) £33,000.

42.4
(i) Loss £2,000 (ii) Profit £12,000 (iii) Nil (iv) Profit £6,000 (v) Profit £9,000.

42.6
(a)

(i) $\text{Break-even point} = \dfrac{\text{Total fixed costs}}{\text{Selling price per unit} - \text{Variable cost per unit}}$

For 20X1 = $\dfrac{250,000}{130-110}$ = 12,500 units

= sales of 12,500 units × £130 = £1,625,000 sales

For 20X2 = $\dfrac{275,000}{129-118.5}$ = sales of 26,190 units × £129

= £3,378,510 sales

For 20X3 = $\dfrac{275,000}{128.5-122}$ = sales of 42,308 units × £128.5 = £5,436,578 sales

(ii)

Polemic Ltd

Actual & Forecast Profit & Loss Accounts for years to 30 September (£000)

	Actual 20X1	Forecast 20X2	Forecast 20X3
Sales	6,500	6,708	6,810.5
Direct materials	2,500	2,860	2,915
Direct labour	1,500	1,638	1,749
Variable production	500	572	636
Direct expenses	250	260	318
Variable sales overhead	750	832	848
	5,500	6,162	6,466
Contribution	1,000	546	344.5
Fixed costs			
Production	50	55	55
Overhead	200	220	220
	250	275	275
	750	271	69.5

(b) Should best be on graph paper. General idea follows:

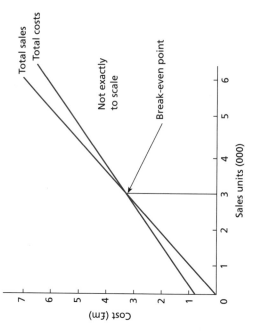

(c) The management of Polemic should be explaining to the union that their demand is unreasonable. As it is, profits have fallen dramatically and the break-even point in 20X3 will be over three times higher than in 20X1.

It is therefore almost impossible for the company to raise prices still further and maintain their level of sales. To try to do so would almost certainly mean a fall in demand and a shedding of a large part of the workforce.

(d) See text.

42.8

A

Hampshire plc

Profit Statement for first and second quarters

	First quarter		Second quarter	
Sales		126,000		143,640
Materials	32,850		39,420	
Labour	18,900		22,680	
Variable factory o/h	12,600		15,120	
Variable selling costs	7,650	72,000	9,180	86,400
Contribution		54,000		57,240
Fixed costs:				
Factory overhead	21,375		21,375	
Selling and admin.	16,125	37,500	16,125	37,500
Net profit		16,500		19,740

$$\text{Contribution per unit} = \frac{54,000}{9,000} = 6.00 \qquad \frac{57,240}{10,800} = 5.30$$

B Draw on graph paper. Break-even points are at:

$$\text{First quarter} = \frac{37,500}{14.00 - 8.00} = 6,250 \text{ units}$$

$$\text{Second quarter} = \frac{37,500}{13.30 - 8.00} = 7,075 \text{ units}$$

Margins of safety above these points.

C Profit statements incorporating suggestions:

	(i)	(ii)	(iii)	(iv)	(v)
No. of units sold	11,880	11,556	12,960	10,800	10,800
Sales (W1)	158,004	158,317	155,131	143,640	143,640
Materials	46,926	43,913	47,304	39,420	see (W2)
Labour	24,948	27,734	27,216	22,680	
Variable factory o/h	16,632	16,178	18,144	15,120	
Variable selling o/h	10,098	9,823	11,016	11,340	
Total variable costs	98,604	97,648	103,680	88,560	87,900
Contribution	59,400	60,669	51,451	55,080	55,740
Fixed costs					
Factory	21,375	21,375	21,375	21,375	see (W3)
Selling, etc.	16,125	16,125	16,125	12,025	35,000
	37,500	37,500	37,500	33,400	35,000
Net profit	21,900	23,169	13,951	21,680	20,740
Redundancy					12,000

Workings:

(W1) Selling price per unit (i) 13.30 (ii) 13.70 (iii) 11.97 (iv) 13.30 (v) 13.30.

(W2) Per accounts of second quarter in A 86,400 + extra costs 5p per component, $30,000 \times 0.5p = 1,500$. Total 87,900.

(W3) Fixed costs 37,500 − saving 2,500 = 35,000. Assumed that the 20 per cent of the firm's fixed costs would still continue as they would have to be paid anyway. Question not too clear on this point.

D Briefly:

(i) Would increase profit by 21,900 − 19,740 = 2,160. Seems to be a sensible opportunity which should be considered.

(ii) Apparently increases profit by 23,169 − 19,740 = 3,429. No mention as to what the cost of maintaining the guarantee is likely to be. Until this is known it is impossible to come to a conclusion.

(iii) Fall in profit of 19,740 − 13,951 = 5,789. Should not be considered.

(iv) Increases profit by 21,680 − 19,740 = 1,940. Have to renegotiate terms of employment with sales staff. Worth considering.

(v) Firm

(a) If we stop making components how can we be certain that suppliers will not later raise prices?

(b) Would we have to keep larger stocks of components in case of breakdown of supply?

(c) Possible that newly established firm has got its prices wrong and will be unable to maintain at this price for long.

(d) Effect on morale of other employees. Local community: write generally about effects of unemployment and knock-on effects.

E *See* text Section 27.4.

42.10

(a)

Magwitch Ltd

Summarised Profit and Loss Account for the year to 31 May 20X1

Sales volume: units		20,000
		£
Sales £1.50 + 10% = 1.65 per unit		33,000
Variable costs (20 − 10) × 0.50 + 10% = 55p per unit		11,000
Contribution		22,000
Fixed costs 0.50 + 10% = 55p per unit		11,000
Profit		11,000

(b)

Compeyson plc

Balance sheet as at 31 May 20X1

Fixed assets (40 + 160)		200
Current assets (65 + 340 − 24 *see* W2)	381	
Short-term liabilities (26 + 110)	136	245
		445
Share capital (200 + 60 *see* W2)		260
Share premium (60 × 0.80)		48
Reserves (190 − 53)		137
		445

Workings:

(W1) Purchase price 12 × 11 =   132

     Net assets taken over   71

     + revalued property   8

                                     79

     Goodwill written off to reserves   53

(W2) Method of payment of purchase price

     Shares 40 × 3/2 = 60 × 1.80   108

     Cash (balance)   24

                                   132

(c) Shares 6,000 × 3/2 = 9,000 shares

    Cash 6,000/40,000 × 24,000 = £3,600

43.1

(a) $12,000 \times 0.09 \times \dfrac{56}{365} = 165.70$

(b) $6,000 \times 0.15 \times \dfrac{80}{365} = 197.26$ Discount

therefore amount paid = £5,802.74

43.3

The amount borrowed is:

3,000 × 1/4 =	750.00
2,250 × 1/4 =	562.50
1,500 × 1/4 =	375.00
750 × 1/4 =	187.50
Equivalent loan for 1 year	1,875.00

$r = \dfrac{1,000}{1,875} = 0.533$ or 53.3%

43.4

£1,000 will accumulate to $£1,000 \times (1 + 0.12)^5 = £1,762$

Interest is £1,762 – £1,000 = £762

43.7

The present value of an annuity of £4,000 p.a. for four years at 10% = £4,000 × 3.170 = £12,680 or:

$$\text{Present value} = £4,000 \times \left[\dfrac{1 - \dfrac{1}{(1 + 0.1)^4}}{0.1} \right] = £12,680$$

As it exceeds the present value of the rent, you should accept the offer of £15,000.

43.9

$$\text{Paid in per year} = \dfrac{\text{Value} \times (r)}{(1 + r)^n - 1}$$

$$= \dfrac{£20,000 \times 0.08}{(1.08)^{10} - 1}$$

$$= £1,380 \text{ per year}$$

43.11

£20,000 × present value factor of an annuity = £64,800. Therefore the present value factor = 64,800/20,000 = 3.24, which is 9% according to the tables.

43.12

Factor present value of an annuity of £1 for six years at 16% = 3.685

£4,000 × 3.685 = £14,740 capital value of the lease.

44.1

	20X2	20X3
Equipment purchased	40,000	
Sale of old equipment		(10,000)
Installation of equipment completed and paid	12,000	
Costs incurred in commissioning equipment	18,000	10,000
Rent on premises up to completion date (6 months)	6,000	
Training costs		3,000
Working capital		4,000
		14,000
Net cash outlay	76,000	21,000

44.2

Capital cost 20X2	76,000		
20X2 25% WDA	19,000		@ 40% tax £7,600 received 20X3
balance c/d	57,000		
New expenditure	17,000		excluding scrap value and additional working capital
	74,000		
20X3 25% WDA	18,500		@ 40% tax £7,400 received 20X4
balance c/d	55,500		
20X4 25% WDA	13,875		@ 40% tax £5,550 received 20X5
balance c/d	41,625		
20X5 25% WDA	10,406		@ 40% tax £4,162 received 20X6
balance c/d	31,219		

This will continue over the life of the equipment. In 20X4 the cash received from the sale of old equipment will be taxed at 40 per cent, resulting in a tax outflow of £4,000.

	20X2	20X3	20X4	20X5	
Capital cash flow	(76,000)				etc.
Tax relief		7,600	7,400	5,550	
Tax on sale		(7,000)	(4,000)		etc.
Net cash flow	(76,000)	600	3,400	5,550	

44.3

	Net cash flow	Discount factor 10%	Present value
20X2	(76,000)	0.909	(69,084)
20X3	600	0.826	496
20X4	3,400	0.751	2,553
20X5	5,550	0.683	3,791
		NPV at start	(62,244)

44.7

Period	Amount	Balance
0	(10,000)	(10,000)
1	8,000	(2,000)
2	4,000	–
3	2,000	–
4	1,000	–

payback at 1 plus 2,000/4,000 years = 1.5 years

44.8

Period	Amount	Discount factor 12%	Present value
0	(10,000)	1.000	(10,000)
1	8,000	0.893	7,144
2	4,000	0.797	3,188
3	2,000	0.712	1,424
4	1,000	0.636	636
Overall net present value of cash flows			2,392

44.9

Period	Amount	Discount factor (28%)	Present value	Discount factor (32%)	Present value
0	(10,000)	1.000	(10,000)	1.000	(10,000)
1	8,000	0.781	6,248	0.758	6,064
2	4,000	0.610	2,440	0.574	2,296
3	2,000	0.477	954	0.435	870
4	1,000	0.373	373	0.329	329
			15		(441)

28% discount rate gives NPV of   15
32% discount rate gives negative NPV of   441
456

The IRR is $\dfrac{15}{456} \times 4\% = 0.13\% + 28\% = 28.13\%$

44.10

The present value of an annuity of £1 for four years at 12% is 3.037. The NPV according to 44.8 is £2,392, therefore the annualised amount = 2,392/3.037 = 787.62

44.17

Net present value (10%)
Machine A project   4,522
Machine B project   11,566

The Machine B project should be selected.

44.18

Internal rate of return
Machine A project   22.4%
Machine B project   20.2%

The Machine A project would be preferred. However, comparing the NPV and IRR results, and remembering the rule of thumb that NPV should be followed when the two methods disagree, the Machine B project should be selected.

44.21

The present value of an annuity of £1 for five years at 10% is 3.791. Therefore the annualised amount = 3,100/3.791 = 817.73

44.23

Cost of machine £60,000 × (1 − 0.4) = 36,000
Cost of leasing £14,633 × (1 − 0.4) = 8,780

Present value for five years $= \dfrac{36,000}{8,780} = 4.1$

which is 7% according to the tables.

44.24

(a)(t)
BN
Roadhog

	0	1	2	3	4	5
Cash inflow		12,500	15,000	20,000	20,000	20,000
Cash outflow						
fixed		2,000	2,000	2,200	2,400	2,400
variable		3,000	3,600	4,800	4,800	4,800
Operating cash flow		7,500	9,400	13,000	12,800	12,800
Capital	40,000					8,000
	40,000	7,500	9,400	13,000	12,800	20,800
	1.00	0.909	0.826	0.751	0.683	0.621
	40,000	6,817	7,764	9,763	8,742	12,916

NPV = 6,002 positive

FX Sprinter

	0	1	2	3	4	5
Cash inflow		12,500	15,000	20,000	20,000	20,000
Cash outflow						
fixed		1,800	1,800	1,800	2,000	2,200
variable		4,000	4,800	6,400	6,400	6,400
Operating cash flow		6,700	8,400	11,800	11,600	11,400
Capital	45,000					9,000
	45,000	6,700	8,400	11,800	11,600	20,400
	1.00	0.909	0.826	0.751	0.683	0.621
	45,000	6,090	6,938	8,862	7,923	12,668

NPV = 2,519 negative

VR Rocket

	0	1	2	3	4	5
Cash inflow		12,500	15,000	20,000	20,000	20,000
Cash outflow						
fixed		1,500	1,500	1,400	1,400	1,400
variable		3,500	4,200	5,600	5,600	5,600
Operating cash flow		7,500	9,300	13,000	13,000	13,000
Capital	50,000					14,000
	50,000	7,500	9,300	13,000	13,000	27,000
	1.00	0.909	0.826	0.751	0.683	0.621
	50,000	6,817	7,682	9,763	8,879	16,767

NPV = 92 negative

(ii) To the Directors of Road Wheelers Ltd
The NPV anticipated for the three vehicles is as follows:

BN Roadhog	£6,002	Positive
FX Sprinter	£2,519	Negative
VR Rocket	£ 92	Negative

On the basis of NPV assessment using a discount rate of 10 per cent the BN Roadhog appears to be the best option.

The payback position on the three vehicles is as follows:

BN Roadhog	3 years	9.3 months
FX Sprinter	4 years	3.8 months
VR Rocket	4 years	3.2 months

This indicates that the BX Roadhog recovers the cash outlay faster than the other two options which is in its favour.

Since the capital outlay on the BX Roadhog is also significantly lower than the other options this indicates a lower risk and will enhance the ROC on the balance sheet figures.

The BN Roadhog appears to be the best choice.

(b) The problems in evaluating capital projects are essentially related to the estimates involved in forecasting the revenues and costs associated with the project. In this evaluation the relative performance of the three alternatives may be more reliable than overall estimates of the environment. In some situations important factors in the decision may not be readily quantified especially in areas of new technology where many factors are unknown.

The techniques of evaluating the cash flow data are well understood but care must be taken that an appropriate 'cost of capital' is chosen and that risk is taken into account.

44.26

(a) Revised Operating Budget

Ship A

	20X5	20X6	20X7	20X8	20X9
Estimated revenue receipts	5	7	9	11	13
Extra revenue 10%	0.5	0.7	0.9	1.1	1.3
	5.5	7.7	9.9	12.1	14.3
Operating payments	4.0	5.0	6.5	7.5	9.0
Net cash flow Ship A	1.5	2.7	3.4	4.6	5.3

Ship B

	20X5	20X6	20X7	20X8	20X9
Estimated revenue receipts:					
Private	2.5	3.5	5.0	6.5	7.5
Commercial	3.45	4.6	5.85	6.5	7.8
	5.95	8.1	10.85	13.0	15.3
Operating payments	4.8	6.0	7.9	9.0	10.8
Net cash flow Ship B	1.15	2.1	2.95	4.0	4.5

(b)

Cash flows	Ship A	Factor 15%		Ship B	Factor 15%	
0	(10.0)	1.0	(10.0)	(14.1)	1.0	(14.0)
20X6	1.5	0.870	1.3	1.15	0.87	1.0
20X7	2.7	0.756	2.0	2.1	0.756	1.6
20X8	3.4	0.658	2.2	2.95	0.658	1.9
20X9	4.6	0.572	2.6	4.0	0.572	2.3
20X0	5.3	0.497	2.6	4.5	0.497	2.2
NPV			0.7			(5.0)
Assumed value of ship on market $^{15}/_{20}$ × cost	7.5	0.497	3.7	10.5	0.497	5.2
			4.4			0.2

Note: The calculation has been done with a zero assumption about cash value of ships at the end of year 5 and then with an assumed value equal to the unexplained cost value based on a 20-year life.

(c) The evaluation assumes an interest rate of 15 per cent and evaluates cash flows over the first five years' life of the ships. If the assumption is that at the end of five years the ships will have no value then ship A has a positive NPV of £0.7m while B has a negative NPV of £5.0m. However, it is unlikely that the ships would be valueless at the end of year 5 and if an assumption is made to take 15/20 of the cost as the realisable value then both NPVs become positive at £4.4m and £0.2m respectively.

From this evaluation ship A looks to give a better return. It is worth noting, however, that ship B does have much higher capacity. If operating revenues were to expand more than forecast over the five years and thereafter, this ship might provide much higher returns. This operating forecast and the likely market values of the two vessels should therefore be closely examined.

45.1 *See* text.
45.2 *See* text.
45.3 *See* text.
45.4 *See* text.

46.1 *See* text.
46.2 *See* text.
46.3 *See* text.
46.4 *See* text.
46.5 *See* text.
46.6 *See* text.
46.7 *See* text.

47.1 *See* text.
47.2 *See* text.
47.3 *See* text.
47.4 *See* text.

APPENDIX 3

Glossary

Abnormal loss (Chapter 35): A loss arising in the production process that should have been avoided.

Absorption costing (Chapter 34): The method of allocating all indirect manufacturing costs to products. (All fixed costs are allocated to cost units.)

Activity-based costing (Chapter 34): The process of using cost drivers as the basis for overhead absorption.

Adverse variance (Chapter 40): A difference arising that is apparently 'bad' from the perspective of the organisation. For example, when the total actual materials cost exceeds the total standard cost due to more materials having been used than anticipated. Whether it is indeed 'bad' will be revealed only when the cause of the variance is identified. It may, for example, have arisen as a result of an unexpected rise in demand for the product being produced.

Annuity (Chapter 43): An income-generating investment whereby, in return for the payment of a single lump sum, the annuitant receives regular amounts of income over a predefined period.

Articles of Association (Chapter 3): The document that arranges the internal relationships, for example, between members of the company, and the duties of directors. The Companies Act 1985 gives a model known as Table A.

Associated undertaking (Chapter 26): A company which is not a subsidiary of the investing group or company but in which the investing group or company has a long-term interest and over which it exercises significant influence.

Attainable standard (Chapter 39): A standard that can be achieved in normal conditions. It takes into account normal losses, and normal levels of downtime and waste.

Balanced scorecard (Chapter 45): A technique that assesses performance across a balanced set of four perspectives – customers, internal processes, organisational learning and growth, and financial.

Bonus shares (Chapter 9): Shares issued to existing shareholders free of charge. (Also known as scrip issues.)

Break-even point (Chapter 42): The level of activity at which total revenues equal total costs.

Budget (Chapter 36): A plan quantified in monetary terms in advance of a defined time period and usually showing planned income and expenditure and the capital employed to achieve a given objective.

Business-to-business (B2B) (Chapter 47): Businesses purchase from other businesses and/or sell their goods and services to other businesses.

Business-to-consumer (B2C) (Chapter 47): Businesses sell to consumers.

By-product (Chapter 35): Products of minor sales value that result from the production of a main product.

Capital redemption reserve (Chapter 5): A 'non-distributable' reserve created when shares are redeemed or purchased other than from the proceeds of a fresh issue of shares.

Capital reserve (Chapter 8): A reserve which is a balance of profit retained that can never be used for the payment of cash dividends. These are normally created specifically under the provisions of the Companies Acts 1985 and 1989. Examples include a capital redemption reserve and a share premium account.

Consolidation accounting (Chapter 16): This term means bringing together into a single balance sheet and profit and loss account the separate financial statements of a group of companies. Hence they are known as group financial statements.

Contribution (Chapter 34): The difference between sales income and marginal cost. (It can also be defined as sales income minus variable cost, which would virtually always produce the same answer.)

Corporation tax (Chapter 7): A form of direct taxation levied on the profits of companies. The rate is determined each year in the Finance Act.

Cost centre (Chapter 33): A production or service location, function, activity, or item of equipment whose costs may be attributed to cost units.

Cost of control (Chapter 17): An alternative expression to goodwill.

Cost unit (Chapter 33): A unit of product or service in relation to which costs are ascertained.

Debenture (Chapter 4): A bond or document acknowledging a loan to a company, normally under the company's seal and carrying a fixed rate of interest.

Deferred taxation (Chapter 7): Timing differences arise between the accounting treatment of events and their taxation results. Deferred taxation accounting adjusts the differences so that the accounts are not misleading.

Economic order quantity (EOQ) (Chapter 36): A mathematical method of calculating the amount of stock that should be ordered at a time and how frequently to order it, so that the overall total of the costs of holding the stock and the costs of ordering the stock can be minimised.

Electronic commerce (e-commerce) (Chapter 47): The use of electronic telecommunication technology to conduct business transactions over the internet.

Enterprise resource planning (ERP) system (Chapter 46): A suite of software modules, each of which relates to a function of the organisation, such as order processing, production, creditor control, debtor control, payroll, marketing, and human resources.

Equity accounting (Chapter 26): A method of accounting for associated undertakings that brings into the consolidated profit and loss account the investor's share of the associated undertaking's results and that records the investment in the consolidated balance sheet at the investor's share of the associated undertaking's net assets including any goodwill arising to the extent that it has not previously been written off.

Favourable variance (Chapter 40): A difference arising that is apparently 'good' from the perspective of the organisation. For example, when the total actual labour cost is less than the total standard cost because fewer hours were worked than expected. Whether it is indeed 'good' will be revealed only when the cause of the variance is identified – it may be that fewer hours were worked because demand for the product fell unexpectedly.

Finance lease (Chapter 2): This is an agreement whereby the lessee enjoys substantially all the risks and rewards associated with ownership of an asset other than legal title.

Flexible budget (Chapter 38): A budget which, by recognising the difference in behaviour between fixed and variable costs in relation to fluctuations in output, turnover or other factors, is designed to change appropriately with such fluctuations.

Gross equity accounting (Chapter 26): A form of equity accounting applicable to joint ventures under which the investor's share of the aggregate gross assets and liabilities of

the joint venture is shown on the face of the balance sheet and the investor's share of the joint venture's turnover is noted in the profit and loss account.

Hire purchase agreements (Chapter 2): These are legal agreements by which an organisation can obtain the use of an asset in exchange for payment by instalment.

Holding company (Chapter 16): The outdated term for what is now known as 'parent undertaking'.

Ideal standard (Chapter 39): A standard that is based upon the premise that everything operates at the maximum level of efficiency. It takes no account of normal losses, or of normal levels of downtime and waste.

Irrelevant costs (Chapter 44): Those costs of the future that will not be affected by a decision.

Job costing (Chapter 35): A costing system that is applied when goods or services are produced in discrete jobs, either one item at a time, or in batches.

Joint product (Chapter 35): Two or more products, each of which has significant sales value, created in the same production process.

Joint venture (Chapter 26): An entity in which the reporting entity holds an interest on a long-term basis and which is jointly controlled by the reporting entity and one or more other venturers under a contractual arrangement

Limited company (Chapter 3): A form of organisation established under the Companies Acts as a separate legal entity, and required to comply with the provisions of the Acts. The members of the company, known as shareholders, are liable only to pay the full price of the shares, not for any further amount, i.e. their liability is limited.

Limiting factor (Chapter 34): Anything that limits activity. Typically, this would be the shortage of supply of something required in production, for example, machine hours, labour hours, raw materials, etc. However, it could also be something that prevents production occurring, for example a lack of storage for finished goods, or a lack of a market for the products.

Margin of safety (Chapter 42): The gap between the level of activity at the break-even point and the actual level of activity.

Marginal costing (Chapter 34): An approach to costing that takes account of the variable cost of products rather than the full production cost. It is particularly useful when considering utilisation of spare capacity.

Master budget (Chapter 38): The overall summary budget encompassing all the individual budgets.

Memorandum of Association (Chapter 3): The document that discloses the conditions governing a company's relationship with the outside world.

Minority interests (Chapter 17): Shareholders in subsidiary undertakings other than the holding undertaking who are not therefore part of the group.

Net present value (NPV) (Chapter 43): The sum of the present values of a series of cash flows.

Operating lease (Chapter 2): An agreement whereby the lessor retains the risks and rewards associated with ownership and normally assumes responsibility for repairs, maintenance and insurance.

Parent undertaking (Chapter 16): Although FRS 2 should be studied for a full and proper definition, the one that will suffice for the time being is 'an undertaking which controls or has a dominating influence over the affairs of another undertaking'.

Pre-incorporation profits or losses (Chapter 6): Profits or losses which arise immediately before a limited company is legally incorporated. Any such profits will be treated as capital

profits not for distribution while, for sake of prudence, any such losses will be set against post-incorporation profits.

Present value (Chapter 43): The amount that a future cash flow is worth in terms of today's money.

Process costing (Chapter 35): A costing system that is applied when goods or services are produced in a continuous flow.

Provision (Chapter 8): An amount written off or retained by way of providing for depreciation, renewals or diminution in value of assets, or retained by way of providing for any known liability of which the amount cannot be determined with 'substantial accuracy'.

Relevant costs (Chapter 44): Those costs of the future that will be affected by a decision.

Revenue reserves (Chapter 8): A balance of profits retained available to pay cash dividends including an amount voluntarily transferred from the profit and loss appropriation account by debiting it, reducing the amount of profits left for cash dividend purposes, and crediting a named reserve account, such as a general reserve.

Rights issue (Chapter 4): An issue of shares to existing shareholders.

Share discount (Chapter 4): Where a share was issued at a price below its par, or nominal value, the shortfall was known as a discount. However, it is no longer legal under the Companies Acts to issue shares at a discount.

Share premium (Chapter 4): Where a share is issued at a price above its par, or nominal value, the excess is known as a premium.

Shares at no par value (Chapter 4): Shares which do not have a fixed par, or nominal value.

Sinking fund (Chapter 5): An external fund set up to meet some future liability such as the redemption of debentures. Cash is paid into the fund at regular intervals to accumulate with compound interest to the required future sum.

Standard cost (Chapter 39): An estimate of what costs should be.

Standard costing (Chapter 39): A control technique that compares standard costs and standard revenues with actual costs and actual revenues in order to determine differences (variances) that may then be investigated.

Subsidiary company (Chapter 16): The outdated term for what is now known as a 'subsidiary undertaking'.

Subsidiary undertaking (Chapter 16): An undertaking which is controlled by another undertaking or where that other undertaking exercises a dominating influence over it.

Sunk costs (Chapter 44): A cost which has already occurred and cannot, therefore, be avoided whatever decision is taken. It should be ignored when taking a decision.

Supply chain (Chapter 46): Everything within the two end-points of the continuous sequence running from demand forecasting through to receipt of payment from customers.

Supply chain management (Chapter 46): The system of control over the information and/or item flows both within and outwith the organisation that comprise the supply chain.

Variance (Chapter 39): The difference between budget and actual.

Variance analysis (Chapter 40): A means of assessing the difference between a predetermined cost/income and the actual cost/income.

Work certified (Chapter 15): The value of work in progress on a contract as certified by, for example, an architect or an engineer.

Index

Note: This index does not include references to the glossary, but may be used in conjunction with it.